FREUD'S WORLD

FREUD'S WORLD

AN ENCYCLOPEDIA OF HIS LIFE AND TIMES

Luis A. Cordón

 GREENWOOD

AN IMPRINT OF ABC-CLIO, LLC
Santa Barbara, California • Denver, Colorado • Oxford, England

Library of Congress Cataloging-in-Publication Data

Cordón, Luis A.
  Freud's world : an encyclopedia of his life and times / Luis A. Cordón.
      p. cm.
  Includes bibliographical references and index.
  ISBN 978-0-313-33905-9 (hbk. : alk. paper) — ISBN 978-0-313-08441-6
(ebook)   1. Freud, Sigmund, 1856–1939.   2. Psychoanalysis—History—
19th century—Encyclopedias.   3. Psychoanalysis—History—20th century—
Encyclopedias.   I. Title.
  BF109.F74C665   2012
  150.19'52092—dc23   2011048755

ISBN: 978-0-313-33905-9
EISBN: 978-0-313-08441-6

16   15   14   13   12   1   2   3   4   5

This book is also available on the World Wide Web as an eBook.
Visit www.abc-clio.com for details.

Greenwood
An Imprint of ABC-CLIO, LLC

ABC-CLIO, LLC
130 Cremona Drive, P.O. Box 1911
Santa Barbara, California 93116-1911

This book is printed on acid-free paper ∞

Manufactured in the United States of America

For Joanne, Anna, and Tomás. Thank you for
your support. I promise not to write
anything else for a few months.

CONTENTS

PREFACE

Sigmund (née Sigismund) Freud is almost certainly the most controversial figure in the history of psychology, and has arguably had a greater impact on the larger society beyond the psychological and medical communities than anyone else before or since. He has been alternately praised and condemned in approximately equal measure, and has frequently aroused otherwise cautious scholars to remarkable rhetorical heights. In 1959, for example, sociologist Philip Rieff, a prominent Freud scholar who wrote several authoritative books about the man and his legacy, proclaimed Freud's written works to be "perhaps the most important body of thought committed to paper in the twentieth century." From the opposing perspective, Sir Peter Medawar, the English biologist who received the 1960 Nobel Prize in medicine, famously called psychoanalytic theory "the most stupendous intellectual confidence trick of the century."

As I write this preface in the year that marks the 155th anniversary of Freud's birth, he has gone from being among the most influential psychologists in the world to little more than a historical footnote, at least among psychological researchers. As the field became more and more scientifically rigorous, it became more and more clear that Freud's ideas were neither based in nor supported by anything resembling a careful and reproducible program of research, and his theories have consequently become steadily less and less important in the education of a psychologist. In other areas of scholarship, however, Freud, along with such intellectual heirs as Carl Jung and Jacques Lacan, remains an important influence to be reckoned with. Although current psychological journals are largely devoid of psychoanalytic content, journals in the humanities continue to publish Freudian and psychoanalytic criticism of art and literature at a steady pace.

It is this controversy that first drew me to write this volume. As a psychologist educated in child cognitive development in the 1980s and 1990s, I encountered very little of Freud's work; his name was not even among those on the reading list for my comprehensive doctoral examinations. If he appeared at all in my course work, it was as one of psychology's also-rans, whose developmental stages had long been supplanted by those of Jean Piaget and others. As the husband of an English scholar, however, I was also aware that the Modern Language Association has long featured Freud-related panels at its annual conferences, and a search of the MLA's online database of scholarly publications turns up nearly 4,000 articles at present. My exposure to Freud as a student was quite limited and usually provided by professors who were extremely dismissive of his ideas. This triggered a long-standing fascination with Freud, but from the point of view of an intrigued outsider rather than a follower or an adherent.

It is this perspective that I propose to provide in the present volume: A portrait of Sigmund Freud, his influences, and those whom he influenced, written by someone whose interest in the subject is driven purely by curiosity, accompanied by a certain degree of skepticism. It is not my goal to turn anyone against Freud and psychoanalysis, no more so than it is my goal to help turn out a fresh generation of shiny new psychodynamic theorists. I wish instead to simply explore the work of this fascinating maverick, along with the world in which that work occurred. Since Freud gained such popularity in the 20th century, to such a degree that his name is known almost universally among the educated, even those who have never read a word that he wrote, it is all too easy to forget how truly radical his ideas were when he first began to publish them. *The Interpretation of Dreams,* first published in 1899, for example, remains in print today and is easily Freud's most widely read work, with millions of copies in print. The first print run of 600 copies, however, took nearly a decade to sell out, and Freud despaired of its failure in numerous letters to friends and colleagues. How Freud went from a struggling Vienna neurologist, whose revolutionary ideas about human nature either caused great offense or were ignored entirely, to a name known to all, whether they be supporters or detractors, is a fascinating story, told here in a series of 60 encyclopedia entries averaging more than 3,000 words per entry. Including boldfaced cross-references and bibliographies of additional information resources, the entries are devoted to Freud's books, ideas, influences, followers, detractors, and the world events and political and intellectual movements that shaped his ideas as well as those of later generations of psychoanalysts. In short, welcome to Freud's world.

ACKNOWLEDGMENTS

Thank you to all who put up with me and the slow progress of this manuscript, especially my immediate family and the editors at Greenwood and ABC-CLIO. Thanks also to Dream Theater, Devin Townsend, Opeth, and Jake Shimabukuro. Without the ability to listen to *a lot* of music, I would never have gotten this done.

Abraham, Karl (1877–1925)

Karl Abraham was an early member of Freud's inner circle and has been credited with substantial contributions to the early development of psychoanalysis. His friendship and professional relationship with Freud, unlike those of many other early stars of the psychoanalytic firmament, remained cordial from their first acquaintance in 1907 until Abraham's death in 1925. This was at least in part because Abraham never wavered in either his personal fealty to Freud or his adherence to the classical principles of psychoanalysis. In addition to their personal loyalty to each other, Freud also valued the fact that unlike the rest of the members of the inner circle, at least after Jung left, Abraham was trained as a psychiatrist and was thus able to command somewhat more respect within the psychiatric establishment than the rest of them, accustomed as they were to being treated as pariahs by the mental-health community.

Karl Abraham was born in Bremen, Germany, into a well-established and successful Jewish family. His father, Nathan Abraham, was a former Hebrew scholar and religion teacher who had given up his educational career in favor of becoming a businessman instead, which he apparently did for economic rather than spiritual or intellectual reasons. Despite the reasons, the switch clearly had an effect on his son: Karl Abraham abandoned his Jewish faith fairly early, and his writings reflect no interest in religious issues, either from a positive perspective like those of Otto **Rank** or from Freud's atheistic and antireligious perspective.

In his teens, Karl developed a keen interest in philology and linguistics, eventually becoming fluent in at least five languages. This would serve him well in later life, when he would exert a large influence on the field of psychoanalysis simply by being the analyst who first worked with a number of people who would go on to become prominent psychoanalysts themselves, including several who he was able to treat in English. Later, at the University of Freiburg, he performed brilliantly in his medical studies; as a result, he was able to gain a position at the Burghölzli mental hospital in Zurich, Switzerland, working under Eugen **Bleuler**. While working at the Burghölzli, Abraham became the first assistant physician to Carl Jung, at a time when Jung was first experimenting with psychoanalysis and writing to Freud.

Freud welcomed the attention, as he saw an alliance with this major psychiatric clinic as crucial; he believed that the support and endorsement of such a prestigious institution would do wonders to broaden the appeal of psychoanalysis beyond its early audience of Jewish intellectuals in Vienna. Without such broader support, Freud frequently worried that psychoanalysis would come to be regarded as "a Jewish national affair," only of interest to Austrian Jews rather than providing a useful approach for the broader range of humanity. Abraham proved to be an important part of this apparent Swiss support, despite his Jewishness, publishing his first scholarly paper from the Burghölzli in 1907, before Jung's published work began explicitly supporting Freud. The essay was unequivocal in its support of Freud, actually opening with the phrase, "According to Freud."

Jung and Abraham had difficulty getting along from the very beginning, however. Abraham was put off by Jung's personality and by his apparent efforts, right from the beginning, to alter some of the basic principles of psychoanalysis, which Abraham saw as a clear threat to the scientific status of psychoanalysis. In a 1908 letter to Abraham, however, Freud proposes another possible explanation for their failure to get along—Jung's anti-Semitism:

> I nurse a suspicion that the suppressed anti-Semitism of the Swiss that spares me is deflected in reinforced form upon you. But I think we as Jews, if we wish to join in anywhere, must develop a bit of masochism, be ready to suffer some wrong. Otherwise there is no hitting it off. (July 23, 1908, from Falzeder, 2002)

Karl Abraham, founder of the Berlin Psychoanalytic Institute, about 1935. (Imagno/Getty Images)

This part of the letter is remarkable as the earliest sign in print that Freud recognized a streak of anti-Semitism in Jung, and Freud essentially advises Abraham to accept it as something he will simply have to learn to accept in order to be successful in his chosen field. For his part, Jung wrote to Freud of his own dislike of Abraham, with Jewishness conspicuously absent from the reasons. Jung complained that Abraham was unpopular with his patients and lacked the necessary empathy to be an effective psychoanalyst. Jung also described Abraham as sly and dishonest: "He pricks up his ears whenever Bleuler and I talk about what we are investigating, etc. He then comes up with a publication" (August 19, 1907).

The Vienna Psychoanalytical Society officially came into being in 1908, and in April of that same year its first international conference, the first Psycho-analytical Congress, was held in Salzburg. Thanks to the conflict and animosity between Jung and Abraham, the first psychoanalytical conference was also the occasion of the first serious rift between the society's members. Some conflict was even present at the naming of the conference, however: Although it is usually referred to in books as the International Psychoanalytical Congress, which is the name Ernest Jones favored for the meeting, thanks to Jung it was actually called the First Congress for Freudian Psychology, a more appropriate name simply because the International Psychoanalytical Association did not yet exist (although it was to be formed as a result of the meeting).

At the congress, numerous presentations were made that were important to the subsequent development of psychoanalysis, including Freud's first presentation of the case of the **Rat Man,** but it was the separate presentations on the origins of schizophrenia that would lead to Abraham's departure from Zurich. In a conflict that has had reverberations to the present day in the field of psychiatry, Abraham and Jung presented conflicting views on the origins of this serious mental illness. Abraham presented the purely psychoanalytical idea that masturbation, along with narcissism, lay at the root of schizophrenia, whereas Jung presented the possibility that in addition to psychological reasons involving the inward rather than outward direction of sexual energy, there was also a purely physiological element in the development of schizophrenia. This conflict was important for several reasons, not least of which was that it represented Jung's first public expression of ideas that clearly differed from those of Freud, although his approach was very careful and nonconfrontational. Somewhat ironically, given the different points of view that they were presenting, Jung's anger at Abraham was actually centered on an accusation against Abraham of plagiarism. Jung accused Abraham of presenting his and Bleuler's ideas and work without attribution, focusing on the parts that agree with Freud and leaving out the rest. Since Abraham learned about psychoanalysis from Jung and Bleuler, who were after all his mentors, it may have been true that he found out about that approach to schizophrenia from them, and so he was not so much plagiarizing as failing to accept the parts of their presentation that went beyond Freud. What is clear from Freud's published correspondence with both men, however, is that Freud was actually to some degree orchestrating and encouraging the conflict.

While continuing his friendly correspondence with Jung in which they discussed some of what Jung intended to say, Freud was also encouraging Abraham to present his ideas at the same conference. When the conflict became public, Freud stepped back and chastised both men for their inability to get along. In this instance, Abraham may have been a victim of Freud's political machinations to keep Jung in the position of his apparent successor, as it was not the first time Freud had essentially played the two against each other in his correspondence. In several 1907 letters, for example, Freud assures Abraham that he finds him much easier to communicate with than Jung: he starts each letter with the salutation "Dear Colleague." During the same period, however, his letters to Jung begin with "My dear friend and heir" and reminisce affectionately about time they have just spent together.

Following the 1908 congress, Abraham moved to Berlin, where he set up a private practice and founded the Berlin Psychoanalytical Society. His practice grew into the Berlin Institute of Psychoanalysis, a major center for psychoanalytic practice, research, and training. A number of major second-generation psychoanalysts received analysis and training there under Abraham, including Karen **Horney,** Sandor Rado, and Helene Deutsch. In addition to his direct influence on the next generation of psychoanalysts, Abraham also produced 4 books and 49 papers, introducing a number of new ideas into psychoanalysis. Where so many others had failed to do so, Abraham was able to make original contributions to the field without alienating Freud, perhaps because he always remained within an orthodox Freudian framework while doing so. By working within Freud's theory rather than against it, Abraham was able to contribute new insights while retaining Freud's support. Some of Abraham's ideas had an influence on Freud, and some were even eventually incorporated into his work.

Abraham's early writings on manic-depressive illness, which we now know as bipolar disorder, for example, led directly to Freud's own 1917 paper "Mourning and Melancholia." In 1911, most psychoanalytic writing (and therapy) was focused on neuroses and hysteria rather than on the more debilitating psychotic and depressive disorders, and so Abraham was a bit of a pioneer in boldly stepping forth and addressing depression directly, which he recognized in the opening sentences of "Notes on the Psycho-Analytical Investigation and Treatment of Manic-Depressive Insanity and Allied Conditions":

Whereas states of morbid anxiety have been dealt with in detail in the literature of psycho-analysis, depressive states have hitherto received less attention. Nevertheless the affect of depression is as widely spread among all forms of neuroses and psychoses as that of anxiety. The two affects are often present together or successively in one individual; so that a patient suffering from an anxiety-neurosis will be subject to states of mental depression, and a melancholic will complain of having anxiety. (1966, p. 15)

Given his reverence for Freud's ideas, Abraham then goes on to, rather unsurprisingly, state that depression is a result of repression of both sexual feelings and negative emotions such as hatred and violent urges. The source of the manic phase of the disorder must therefore lie in the same unconscious conflict:

The onset of the mania occurs when repression is no longer able to resist the assaults of the repressed instincts. The patient, especially in cases of severe maniacal excitation, is as if swept off his feet by them. It is especially important to notice that positive and negative libido (love and hate, erotic desires and aggressive hostility) surge up into consciousness with equal force. (1966, p. 28)

The manic phase represents, according to Abraham, a return to a state the patient has not known since childhood in which the libido is very near the surface, and the id seeks free expression in the absence of ego and superego constraints that have not yet developed. Abraham's description of the concepts of positive and negative energies as equal forces is important here, as Freud would not present his idea of both love and death instincts for many years yet. In this and other papers, it is Abraham who introduces this notion as a centerpiece of psychoanalysis.

Abraham also included this positive-negative libido dichotomy in his contributions to Freud's stages of psychosexual development. In the 1924 essay "The Influence of Oral Eroticism on Character Formation," Abraham added a crucial element to the oral stage: biting. Where Freud focused on the oral activity of sucking, especially focusing on the recognition that this activity is pleasurable not just because of the ingestion of food but also because of the mouth's function as an erogenous zone, Abraham simply added a second activity:

First of all there is the process of the irruption [sic] of teeth, which, as is well known, causes a considerable part of the pleasure in sucking to be replaced by pleasure in biting. We need only call to mind how during this stage of development the child puts every object it can into its mouth and tries with all its strength to bite it to pieces. In the same period of development the child begins to have ambivalent relations to external objects. It is to be noted that the friendly as well as the hostile aspect of its attitude is connected with pleasure. (1966, p. 154)

In the ensuing discussion, Abraham proposes that infants relate to objects in two different ways, *incorporation* (via sucking) and *destruction* (through biting), representing the positive and the negative side of the libidinal impulses. This provides infants with their first experience of conflict and is thus directly influential on the subsequent development of the ego.

One other area in which Abraham expanded on Freud's ideas but somehow failed to alienate his mentor is quite surprising, given Freud's hostility toward such ideas from others. Whereas Freud himself turned away from the **seduction theory** in favor of the view that people who remember childhood sexual abuse are actually remembering fantasies, Abraham acknowledged that sexual predators who seek out children exist and even argued that childhood sexual abuse was common among neurotic and psychotic patients. In 1907, in other words, years after Freud had disavowed the seduction theory, Abraham essentially brought it back. As one of the first psychoanalysts with experience treating psychotic patients, Abraham expanded on Freud's original idea, which focused on the role of childhood sexual trauma in the genesis of hysteria, by proposing child sexual abuse as a primary cause of *dementia praecox,* or schizophrenia.

Abraham's version of the seduction theory went beyond Freud's in another way, however, which has made Abraham's name a source of controversy among those who study the effects of incest up to the present day. Central to Abraham's approach to the problem is the idea that there are certain psychological characteristics developed in early childhood that make certain children far more likely to be sexually abused than others. These children, therefore, become victims of abuse because of their own traits rather than an adult's pathological sexuality, a theory that has been frequently characterized as a way of blaming the victim. This idea, which eventually crept into the mainstream of psychoanalytic thought and remained there for decades, may have been quite damaging to the therapeutic prospects of incest survivors, along with another idea that also originated with Abraham's 1907 paper: in "The Experiencing of Sexual Traumas as a Form of Sexual Activity," Abraham writes that what leads to later psychological disorders is not the experience of the sexual encounter itself but the guilt that arises from having done something seen as wrong by our society. Combining Freud's old idea (the seduction theory) with his newer approach (infantile sexuality), Abraham produced a theory that acknowledges that some children desire sexual contact with adults and suggests that any resulting psychological trauma is a product of socially induced guilt rather than a result of the actual sexual abuse. This may have led, directly or indirectly, to the heavily psychoanalytic psychiatric community of the mid-20th century regarding the social problem of incest as a problem of young girls rather than something to be treated in adult men.

In public, Freud was consistently supportive of Abraham throughout their acquaintance, and he never repudiated Abraham's approach to incest in any open forum, but in their private correspondence, Freud was harshly critical of Abraham's papers on the subject. Abraham dropped the subject shortly thereafter, publishing nothing further on the issue and discouraging any further dialogue on the persistent questions raised by his work. As a result, psychoanalytic investigation of, and indeed interest in, the subject of child sexual abuse appears to have entirely stopped until Sándor **Ferenczi** brought it up again briefly in the early 1930s, emerging again only rarely for the next 50 years.

Karl Abraham died in Berlin on December 25, 1925, at the relatively young age of 48. The extent of his influence on the field of psychoanalysis, both good and bad, has only come to be appreciated many years after his death, but he was clearly a major influence on Freud's thinking and on many who came after, not least because of his role at the Berlin Institute, where he was the first analyst seen by many prominent members of the next generation of psychoanalysts.

Further Reading

Abraham, K. (1966). *On Character and Libido Development: Six Essays* (Bertram Levin, ed.). New York: Norton.

Falzeder, E., ed. (2002). *The Complete Correspondence of Sigmund Freud and Karl Abraham.* London: Karnac.

Good, M. (1995). Karl Abraham, Sigmund Freud, and the Fate of the Seduction Theory. *Journal of the American Psychoanalytical Association,* 43(4), 1137–1167.

Adler, Alfred (1870–1937)

Alfred Adler was a key member of Freud's inner circle in the early days of psychoanalysis and later became the first prominent defector from the movement, disagreeing in some important and fundamental ways with Freud and departing to start his own influential movement. In the beginning, however, Adler was one of the founding members of the **Vienna Psychoanalytical Society,** in its first 1902 incarnation as the Wednesday Psychological Society, invited by postcard to the first Wednesday evening discussions in Freud's home. When the Vienna Psychoanalytical Society was formed in 1908, replacing the Wednesday society, Adler served as its first president.

The invitation by postcard would later prove important to Adler personally, as he kept the original invitation and was able to use it to demonstrate the erroneous nature of the popular perception of him as a pupil of Freud who had later turned against his teacher. Adler was in fact an original thinker who had been invited by Freud to join his discussions as a colleague, *not* as a student. When they later had a falling-out, and Freud and his circle were very dismissive of Adler's credentials, he produced the postcard during at least one interview with a reporter to refute the notion that he had been anything other than a professional colleague to Freud.

Like most of the members of Freud's early inner circle, Alfred Adler was trained as a physician, though his arrival at that particular career choice is itself interesting from a psychodynamic point of view and was indeed seen by Adler himself as a major influence on his later theory. Adler, the second of seven children born in a Vienna suburb to a Hungarian-born Jewish grain merchant and his wife, developed rickets in early childhood. Rickets, now known to be caused by a vitamin D deficiency, has now been all but eliminated by the simple addition of vitamin D to most milk that is sold for drinking but was in Adler's time a fairly common illness of childhood. The primary symptoms of rickets include slow or abnormal bone growth, as well as unusually fragile bones, muscle weakness, and skeletal abnormalities and malformations. Adler's case was fairly typical: he first walked at the age of four, and he nearly died of pneumonia at the age of five. Following the pneumonia, he resolved to pursue an education as a physician so he could help other children avoid the sort of experiences he had lived through.

Adler received his medical degree from the University of Vienna in 1895, and his college years were also a time of political activism, which would come to

Alfred Adler, creator of individual psychology and the founding president of the Vienna Psychoanalytical Society. (Library of Congress)

influence his eventual theories, particularly his emphasis on the social injustices that he felt Freud ignored, just as much as his medical and scientific education. He became involved with a group of socialist students, eventually marrying one of them, a Russian student and social activist named Raissa Tomofeyevna Epstein.

At the start of his professional career, Adler worked as an ophthalmologist, but he promptly switched to a general practice and set up a clinic in a poor area of Vienna, directly across from the Prater, an amusement park and circus. The Prater is still in operation today and is now a major Vienna landmark featuring a giant Ferris wheel and Austria's largest disco. In Adler's time, however, it was a struggling enterprise in a questionable part of town, and the sorts of patients he saw from the circus, with their unusual strengths and weaknesses and highly developed but unusual talents, are often assumed to have influenced Adler's later insights into inferiority, superiority, and compensation.

Adler's Theory

Adler's idiosyncratic transition from medicine to psychiatry began with the 1907 *Study of Organ Inferiority and Its Physical Compensation,* which was initially well received by the psychoanalysts in Vienna, despite its presentation of a very different approach to neurosis than what Freud was expounding at the time. Contrary to the simplistic perspective often presented in psychological histories that Adler theorized for a time well within the boundaries of psychoanalysis and only later began to deviate from the Freudian path, an examination of the ideas laid out in 1907 demonstrates that his ideas were incompatible with Freud's right from the beginning.

The theory of organ inferiority began as a general perspective on medical pathology: Adler speculates that illnesses and physical handicaps and disabilities are all the result of inferior organs or body structures. As a medical theory, this has not been very influential, but its psychological implications have wielded an enormous influence on subsequent therapeutic approaches, as well as in the English language. The crucial part of Adler's theory for psychology lies, somewhat subtly, in his *definition* of organ inferiority: the inferior organ is unable to perform its function to a sufficient degree "to satisfy a standard of required effectiveness" (1917, p. 10). The particular standard against which inferiority is judged, in other words, is not a medical criterion, objective and intrinsic, but rather an externally imposed standard forced on the organ. An inferior organ, in other words, is determined to be inferior by its inability to meet the demands of the culture. He is not arguing, of course, that an organ cannot be inferior by heredity, but he is introducing the idea that actual illness requires a convergence between the weak organ and environmental demands that it cannot meet. Organ inferiority had a third component as well, which surely formed part of the idea's appeal to the early psychoanalysts: an organ's failure to meet cultural demands was not a function merely of the organ's weakness and the strength of the cultural demands placed on it but also of the relative drive strength associated with the particular organ. A weaker organ may have a stronger drive strength—the weaker eye has a greater drive to see, the inferior sexual organ the stronger sex drive, the weaker leg the stronger drive to run, and so on.

In the book, Adler was concerned not as much with actual disabilities or limitations as with how individuals coped with them, the *compensation* part of the book's title. While a physical defect may be beyond an individual's control, as are the environmental pressures that interact with the defect, the individual can choose the attitude he or she takes toward the defect. Depending on the attitude, compensations for disabilities or limitations will be either satisfactory and effective or unsatisfactory and ineffective. Adler gave examples of people whose compensations were effective, including the ancient Greek orator Demosthenes, who overcame an early speech impediment to become a great speaker, and the famous runner Nurmi, who overcame a limp. These people compensated by finding ways to excel, whereas others with similar problems sometimes used their defect as an excuse to preserve the fantasy that they *would have* gained success and prestige if only they had not had the defect.

From this understanding of organ inferiority and the ways that a person might psychologically compensate for it, Adler began to see feelings of inferiority as a standard part of human existence and a key determinant of adult personality. Like Freud, Adler saw the child's early response to physiological pressures as important in determining later psychological development, but where Freud focused on underlying drive states, Adler's focus came to be centered far more on the social environment and the child's feelings about his or her place in it. According to Adler,

> To be a human being *means* to feel oneself inferior. The child comes into the world as a helpless little creature surrounded by powerful adults. A child is motivated by his feelings of inferiority to strive for greater things. When he

has reached one level of development, he begins to feel inferior once more and the striving for something better begins again, which is the great driving force of mankind. (1964, p. 131)

In this view, inferiority feelings are a human universal: every person experiences them, whether they will or can admit it or not. As in psychoanalysis, a child will emerge at each stage having either resolved the conflict at that stage or having failed to do so, which may then exert a large influence on later psychopathology. At each developmental stage in Adler's approach, however, the healthy outcome is for the child to emerge with feelings of self-efficacy rather than inferiority (or superiority—too *much* self-efficacy can be bad as well). In this view, neuroses arise when the individual's efforts to compensate for his or her own feelings of inferiority are either too weak, and thus ineffective as defenses, or excessive, resulting in over-compensation, attempting to wield power aggressively.

Adler says that cultural forces teach us to regard the feeling of inferiority as a sign of weakness or as something to be ashamed of, thus leading to a strong natural tendency to conceal it. People vary greatly in their attitude toward this feeling, however, which causes large individual differences in the amount of effort expended in attempting to conceal it. In some cases, the individual may put so much energy into concealing the feeling as to cease to be aware of it, having become entirely preoccupied instead with the consequences of the feelings of inferiority and how to conceal them instead. It is possible for an individual to so thoroughly focus his or her entire mental life on avoiding the feelings of inferiority that he or she becomes occupied instead with feelings of superiority.

Negative responses to these feelings of inferiority then manifest themselves as either the inferiority complex *or* the superiority complex. Although they appear to be opposites, they are actually just different sides of the same psychopathological coin, as both reflect deep-seated feelings of inferiority. The inferiority complex characterizes those who feel inferior and act that way as well, lacking confidence in their ability to succeed at tasks or form relationships. People with superiority complexes also feel inferior, but out of denial present themselves instead as powerful and superior, trying to dominate others. Although both complexes result from a poor self-image, express theirs by pursuing selfish goals, refusing to cooperate with others, and attempting to take without giving. Feelings of inferiority are universal, but development of inferiority or superiority complexes is not. Psychologically healthier people are driven by feelings of inferiority to strive to solve their problems successfully, whereas the inferiority and superiority complex actively prevent them from doing so.

The developmental impetus resulting from the universal feelings of inferiority is the *striving for superiority,* an innate force that carries individuals from one stage to the next. A fundamental difference between Freud and Adler is that Adler viewed the striving for superiority as far more important than sexuality as a motivating force in human action. In his early writings, Adler referred to the striving for superiority as an *aggressive* drive—the later name reflects his understanding that much more than aggression is involved in seeking success, including altruism and self-improvement. Many early readers of Adler, especially followers of Nietzsche, also equated the striving for superiority with Nietzsche's *will to power*. Adler actually saw the striving for power as a major source of neurosis and crime and saw the lust for power in and of itself as a mental disease reflecting a superiority complex.

Tensions between Freud and Adler appear to have existed from fairly early on in their relationship, and these tensions only grew stronger as Adler continued not only to recognize the ways in which his theory had different implications for human development than Freud's but also to express openly where those differences lay. Probably the largest incompatibility between the two perspectives lay in Freud's emphasis on sexuality as the ultimate source of everything, whereas Adler saw this as far too narrow a view of humanity and regarded feelings of inferiority, along with the striving for superiority, as the real underlying motivational force for humanity. Adler was not shy about exploring the ramifications of this fundamental difference for some of Freud's more precious concepts and publicly expressing his opinions on the subject.

The notion of penis envy, for example, was for Adler a clear-cut example of Freud's tendency to apply a sexual interpretation to a phenomenon that was clearly more readily explained in terms of (nonbiological) feelings of inferiority, informed in part by the socialist politics of Adler's youth. He agreed with Freud that girls grow up with feelings of envy toward boys but couldn't fathom why Freud chose to interpret that dynamic in terms of the presence or absence of a penis. To Adler, it was obvious that in early 20th-century Vienna, men had many privileges and rights, as well as differing educational opportunities beginning in childhood, that were not available to women. That this situation would result in particular inferiority feelings in girls, which boys would not experience, seemed equally obvious. Of course, girls were envious of boys, but it seemed to Adler that a model that recognized the social and political sources of the resulting feelings of inferiority fits the circumstances better than Freud's focus on unconscious sexuality.

Although Freud harbored resentment against Adler, he actually appears to have remained quite popular among the other members of the Vienna Psychoanalytical Society, and so it was actually something of a surprise to many of them when, in 1911, Freud announced that he was returning to chair the society in the wake of the resignation of its president, Adler. In the minutes of society meetings, there is little evidence of open animosity prior to that time, and none of the division of the society into pro-Adler and pro-Freud camps. Freud appears to have kept much of his antipathy toward Adler to himself in public, though he expressed his feelings quite openly in his correspondence of the time.

On February 26, 1911, four days after Adler resigned the presidency of the Vienna Psychoanalytical Society, Freud wrote to Oskar **Pfister** as follows:

> Adler's theories were departing too far from the right path, and it was time to make a stand against them. He forgets the saying of the apostle Paul the exact words of which you know better than I: "and I know that ye have not love in you." He has created for himself a world system without love, and I am in the process of carrying out on him the revenge of the offended goddess Libido. I have always made it my principle to be tolerant and not to exercise authority, but in practice it does not always work. (1963, p.103)

As the recipient of the letter is a Christian minister, Freud's reference to Paul is not surprising, but it is intriguing that the stridently antireligious Freud chooses to characterize the core of his theoretical system, Libido, as an offended deity, and himself as her vengeful prophet. Perhaps his audience influenced his choice of metaphor—his communication with Karl Abraham a few days earlier, regarding the same situation, was far more direct:

> Adler's behavior was no longer reconcilable with our psychoanalytical interests, he denies the importance of the libido, and traces everything back to aggression. The damaging effects of his publications will not take long to make themselves felt. (1965, p. 43)

In this letter, Freud repeats the idiosyncratic criticism of Adler's ideas that he also expressed in his correspondence with Jung, as well as in his 1914 *History of the Psycho-Analytic Movement*: that Adler's system traces everything back to a particularly masculine "aggressive instinct," leaving no place for the role of sexual energy, or libido, at all. In his more poetic moments, as in his correspondence with Pfister, he views Adler's individual psychology as a psychology without love, based purely on the drive for superiority. While caricaturing Adler's psychological system, Freud also went out of his way to caricature Adler's own personal psychology, presenting him as paranoid and power-hungry, a characterization that was taken up and built on by other psychoanalysts and Freud biographers such as Ernest Jones.

Freud's motive for the particular vehemence with which he went after both Adler's ideas and his character is, in context, understandable, if not entirely justifiable. He was troubled not just by Adler's deviance from his own theories but more so by Adler's, and later Jung's, stubborn insistence on continuing to use the term "psychoanalysis" for what was clearly a divergent approach to psychology. In the *History* (1914/1957), Freud writes the following regarding both Adler and Jung:

> I am not concerned with the truth that may be contained in the theories which I am rejecting, *nor shall I attempt to refute them* [italics mine]. . . . I wish merely to show that these theories controvert the fundamental principles of analysis . . . and that for this reason they should not be known by the name of analysis. (pp. 49–50)

While Freud's personal animosity toward Adler was quite evident to all involved, his professional animosity had as a particular goal the preservation of the term "psychoanalysis" for work that properly reflected the truth about humanity as Freud saw it. Personal resentment aside (and a powerful resentment it was—most biographers use the same word for Freud's and Adler's mutual feelings for the rest of their lives: *hate*), both Adler and Jung would fairly soon begin to use different names for their approaches. Adler began to refer to his work as a completely new movement, *individual psychology,* whereas Jung stayed a bit closer to the source with *analytic psychology.*

Individual Psychology

Once he had left the inner circle of Viennese psychoanalysis, Adler's chosen label for his theory underwent an evolutionary process that accompanied the continuing development of the theory. Early on, he used the term that so offended Freud, calling his own work *free psychoanalysis* as a way of distinguishing it from the rigid traditional psychoanalysis still practiced by Freud and his followers. As his own thinking moved further away from Freud's, he actually chose the label of "individual psychology" as a way of setting his own work apart from a completely different Germanic tradition: Wilhelm Wundt's *Volkerpsychologie.* The term translates as people's psychology, and refers to the approach of looking at the behavior of people in groups that eventually became modern social psychology.

Adler saw his own psychology as focused on the individual rather than on groups but distinct from psychoanalysis in its holistic approach to the individual—rather than focusing on the role of underlying drives and instincts and viewing the personality in terms of individual parts such as id, ego, and superego, Adler preferred to consider the person as a unitary whole.

Where Freud viewed internal forces of sexuality and libido as central to human motivation, Adler shifted the focus of his psychology to environmental factors and the individual's response to those factors. He gave special prominence to social factors, arguing that developmental tasks involve either combating or confronting three sets of forces: love (meaning filial love, friendship, and love of humanity in general), work, and sexual love. He later saw his rejection of Freud's focus on the unconscious as his primary contribution to psychology and central to the establishment of individual psychology. He wrote in 1937:

> Individual Psychology was the first school of psychology to break with the assumption of inner forces, such as instincts, drives, unconsciousness, etc., as irrational material. When it comes to the understanding and appraisal of an individual or a group, this break has proved most helpful. (Adler, 1959, p. 3)

In calling his own approach the first school of psychology to accomplish that separation, he appears to be claiming credit over other prominent movements of the time, such as behaviorism, which also rejected the unconscious.

Individual psychology is built around several assumptions, chief among them being that the primary determinants of behavior are the individual's opinion of himself or herself and his or her interpretation of the environment he or she has to cope with in any given situation. Every individual is unique, and the proper subject matter of psychology is the manner in which individuals behave in response to the changing problems presented by life. Although his emphasis is superficially on the role of the environment, Adler's environmental psychology is very different from behaviorism, in which the individual's behavior is entirely determined by the environmental consequences of his or her actions. In Adler's psychology, the focus is firmly on the individual and on the individual's cognitive interpretation of the environment.

Another assumption that is central to individual psychology is that the *striving for success* is at the core of the very structure of life, and so always influences the choices an individual makes. Even the striving for success will look different for each individual, as the individual determines what constitutes success, and every person may define it differently.

Another key concept in Adler's individual psychology is *social interest,* which he saw as a natural drive in all of humanity, much as Freud saw the libido as central to everyone's functioning. Social interest, *gemeinshaftsgefühl* in Adler's original conception, refers to a goal of contributing to the general welfare of the community to which we belong and further involves placing the needs of the community ahead of our own more selfish needs. Adler defined social interest as so central a human trait that

> the individual is faced exclusively with such problems as can be solved only with sufficient social interest. He may have had this from childhood, or may have acquired it later. . . . One finds a degree of social interest, although this is usually inadequate, in all men . . . and even in animals. We therefore feel justified in assuming that this social interest which is demonstrated throughout life is rooted in the germ cell. But it is rooted as a potentiality, not as an actual ability. (Adler, 1959, p. 4)

Adler is here arguing that social interest is genetic and innate, and therefore an important driving force for human activity, but also must be developed to a higher degree, and so social interest is both an instinctive drive and a skill that must be developed in each individual. Failure to adequately develop a sense of self-efficacy, as in a person with feelings of inferiority, will of course interfere with the development of social interest, as will a superiority complex, which tends to focus on self-interest. This focus on the pursuit of the general welfare over selfish goals makes it very difficult to recognize this as the theory of the same man who Freud accused of producing a psychology without love, based solely on aggression.

The development of social interest is dependent on the development of the individual's style of life, or lifestyle, a word that has become quite firmly established, if not abused, in modern pop psychology. To Adler, the lifestyle is simply the individual's own striving toward significance and belonging, which can be observed as a clear pattern that manifests itself early in life and is consistent over time, forming a sort of theme that permeates all aspects of an individual's life. The lifestyle is the sum of the passions, values, knowledge, deeds, and even eccentricities that characterize each individual—if you understand a person's lifestyle, that person's behavior will make sense. As a clinician, Adler saw four distinct lifestyles. The first type, which is the healthiest, and the ultimate goal for a clinician to achieve with his clients, is well adjusted and seeks to solve problems in ways that are useful to others as well as to himself or herself, without striving for personal superiority or dominance. This type is clearly motivated primarily by social interest. The second type, by contrast, wishes to prove his or her personal superiority by dominating and ruling over others. Adler saw this type as clearly pathological. The third type, also pathological, tries to meet all his or her needs through others without expending any personal effort or struggle. The fourth type copes by simply avoiding making any decisions at all.

A crucial distinction between Adler and the determinism of both Freud and the behaviorists is Adler's commitment to the role of free will in clinical psychology. The lifestyle emerges as a result of the individual's *creative self*: the individual, through how he or she has defined success and how he or she chooses to perceive and interpret the world, is responsible for his or her own lifestyle. Another relevant Adlerian concept here is *private intelligence*: we justify our actions logically, in ways that make sense to us. When a person's actions are morally wrong or self-destructive, what is necessary is to examine the reasoning behind the actions. In the absence of sufficient social interest, an individual may be able to justify antisocial acts via reasoning that makes sense to himself or herself, even though it is based on faulty premises. Understanding this private intelligence allows the therapist to make an effort to change it.

The goal of Adlerian therapy is to help the individual to uncover the values and assumptions underlying that person's behavior, and the therapist's job is to correct those assumptions when they are mistaken and help to guide the person to a more positive and even useful way of living. Adler believed that simply coming to honestly adopt new goals could produce a radical change in character and behavior, as perceiving and reacting to life differently will produce a major change in lifestyle. The Adlerian construct of lifestyle is similar to other theorists' definition of personality, as an underlying set of traits that characterize an individual consistently across situations and over time, and so Adler is arguing that actual, permanent change of personality is a realistic goal for therapy. In a therapeutic situation, this is a very upbeat view of human potential when compared to Freud, which led Adler to declare individual psychology "a gay and optimistic science" (1959, p. 5).

In his later years, Adler came to see permanent positive change as a goal for individual psychology not just in the therapeutic situation, but also for the human condition as a whole, titling one influential essay "The Progress of Mankind." In that essay, Adler adopts an existentialist point of view quite similar to that of *Viktor* **Frankl** in which he adapts Jean-Paul Sartre's notion that when an individual makes a choice about how to live his or her life, he or she is making that choice not just for himself or herself, but for all humanity. Adler makes his point in a roundabout way, starting with an anecdote about a self-made multimillionaire who grew up in poverty:

> He consulted a lawyer and told him the size of his fortune, as well as that he wanted to protect his descendants to approximately the tenth generation. The lawyer took his pen and began to figure. When he was finished he turned to his client and said: "Your fortune is . . . completely sufficient to provide for your descendants adequately up to the tenth generation. But do you know that if you do this, you are protecting children, each of whom is related to over 1000 persons of your generation as closely as he is related to you?"
>
> It follows from this consideration, if we widen our view to include 100 and more generations, that everything that people have contributed, even if only in the apparent interest of their own families, is irrevocably for the benefit of the whole of mankind. (1959, p. 6)

Following this logic, Adler argues that each of us is born into a world in which we find all the previous useful contributions of our ancestors, and via our own compensatory striving for success, we each continue to build upon these earlier contributions. The life of humanity is thus a process of steady advancement, improvement, and change, pushed along by our innate drive for social interest.

Where Freud was moved by the events of his lifetime to propose an innate drive for destruction that was as strong an instinctive force as the libido (see ***Civilization and Its Discontents*** for more), Adler instead saw our fundamental drives as forces that would continue to improve the human condition steadily. This did not result from failing to acknowledge the negative parts of humanity; in "The Progress of Mankind," as a Jewish scholar writing during the period of Nazi expansion throughout Europe, he describes social interest as "not strong enough at present to solve human difficulties for the benefit of the entire human family." He nonetheless believed that humanity could and *would* be made better by an increased focus, in and out of therapeutic situations, on social interest as an innate driving force of human motivation, and one that could be increased by experience.

Further Reading

Adler, A. (1917). *Study of Organ Inferiority and Its Psychical Compensation.* New York: Nervous and Mental Disease Publishing Company.

Adler, A. (1959). The Progress of Mankind. In K. Adler and D. Deutsch, eds. *Essays in Individual Psychology.* New York: Grove, pp. 3–8.

Adler, A. (1964). *Social Interest: A Challenge to Mankind.* New York: Capricorn Books.

Freud, S. (1914/1957). *On the History of the Psycho-Analytic Movement. Standard Edition, 14.* London: Hogarth Press, pp. 7–66.

Freud, S. (1963). *Psychoanalysis and Faith: The Letters of Sigmund Freud and Oskar Pfister* (Translated by E. Mosbacher). London: Hogarth Press.

Freud, S. (1965). *A Psycho-Analytic Dialogue: The Letters of Sigmund Freud and Karl Abraham* (Translated by B. Marsh and H. Abraham). New York: Basic Books.

Anna O. (Bertha Pappenheim) (1859–1936)

When speaking of the origins of psychoanalysis to an audience at Clark University on his first (and only) visit to the United States, Sigmund Freud famously gave the credit to Josef Breuer instead of himself.

> Granted that it is a merit to have created psychoanalysis, it is not my merit. I was a student, busy with the passing of my last examinations, when another physician of Vienna, Dr. Josef Breuer, made the first application of this method to the case of an hysterical girl.

The girl Freud mentioned was given the pseudonym "Anna O." when Breuer and Freud published her case in the 1895 *Studies on Hysteria* and was thenceforth frequently described as the first patient successfully treated via the talking cure of psychoanalysis.

According to Freud, Anna O. was a highly intelligent 21-year-old who had been ill for at least 2 years when she sought help from Breuer, presenting with a remarkable variety of symptoms. The symptoms first occurred when she spent long hours at the bedside of her father, who was sick with the illness (pleurisy) that eventually killed him. She had developed a paralysis and loss of feeling in both right limbs, which occasionally also affected her left extremities. Her eye movements were erratic, resulting in a significant vision impairment. She regularly became nauseous when attempting to eat and at one point was extremely thirsty but unable to drink for several weeks. She also suffered from facial pain so severe that surgery on one of her facial nerves was briefly considered as a treatment. In addition, she experienced frequent olfactory hallucinations. Along with all of this, she had a nervous cough and a loss of neck muscle strength, such that she had difficulty holding up her head. She also suffered from aphasia, sometimes having difficulty either speaking or understanding German. The most striking symptom was what Freud called *states of absence,* in which she experienced extreme confusion and her whole personality seemed to change. This was a much larger and more complex array of symptoms than was typically presented by a hysterical patient, and many modern writers have speculated on what diagnosis she might receive today, with a majority of opinions leaning toward temporal lobe epilepsy, with some supporters for schizophrenia as well.

Medical and neurological examinations did not reveal any underlying organic cause for these bizarre symptoms, however, and so Breuer was presented with a mystery, as there was no standard treatment at the time for such an odd case. The inspiration for what would eventually become the psychoanalytic approach began with Breuer's observation that during the absences, Anna would mumble certain words or phrases over and over again. Assuming these words reflected the information with which her mind was occupied during the absence, Breuer began to repeat the words back to her (sometimes employing hypnosis first). She would reply by relating what she was thinking about at the time, which frequently consisted of elaborate daydreams and fantasies that usually began with a girl beside her father's sickbed. After relating several of these daydreams, she would be freed from the absence for at least a few hours, though she would return for more of the same the next day. According to Freud, the patient was actually the one who coined the phrase "talking cure," though she also favored the term "chimney sweeping." Both of these designations were originally made in English, oddly enough, as that was the only language she could speak and understand during this phase of her treatment.

An 1882 image of Anna O. (Bertha Pappenheim), the first patient to be subjected to Freud and Breuer's "talking cure." (Imagno/ Getty Images)

It quickly became clear to Breuer that it might be possible to accomplish more than just a temporary reprieve from her symptoms through this new technique of free association. He discovered that if he could get Anna to remember, under hypnosis, the actual circumstances under which a symptom first appeared, and to openly express the emotions she felt at the time, the symptom could be made to disappear permanently. Freud wrote, for example, about how the extreme thirst, coupled with an inability to drink, was dispatched. Anna recalled a time when, on a hot day, she had been extremely thirsty and had seen her English governess's small dog (which she hated—she wasn't especially fond of the governess either) take a drink from the governess's glass of water. Following social convention of the time, she held her tongue and didn't say anything about it. Under hypnosis, she expressed her utter disgust quite openly, and then took a large drink of water. According to Breuer and Freud, the symptom was gone permanently.

Breuer then proceeded to attempt to discover the underlying causes of other hysterical symptoms, now basing his treatment on a new understanding of neurosis that would be the core of psychoanalysis. This was the origin of the belief that symptoms originated in specific traumas and were determined by the patients' specific memories of those experiences. As hysterical or neurotic symptoms had up to that point been regarded as fairly arbitrary signs of the illness, this more deterministic approach was revolutionary because it represented a new and very different understanding of the underlying cause of **hysteria,** which after all derives its name from the belief that the etiology has to do with possession of a uterus. Freud expressed this new understanding clearly and concisely in his second lecture at Clark University: "Our hysterical patients suffer from reminiscences." In the case of Anna O., Freud's account in that same lecture ends with the successful treatment of the paralysis of her right arm, at which point "the paralysis . . . was cured, and the treatment ended." Other accounts of the case, however, do not end quite so tidily.

Possibly the best-known element of the end of her treatment, not mentioned by Freud in his 1910 account, comes from Ernest Jones's biography of Freud. According to Jones, Breuer had become excessively preoccupied with Anna O., and she with him, to the point that Breuer's wife was jealous and unhappy (knowledge of this relationship surely influenced Freud's discovery of transference), and so Breuer, seeing that Anna O. was much improved, ended her treatment. On that day, however, Breuer was called back to see the patient, who he found experiencing the apparent labor pains of a hysterical pregnancy, announcing that she was giving birth to his child. Not only was this a rather more dramatic end to the treatment than what is found in either Freud's or Breuer's published accounts, but the suggestion in Freud's account that she was successfully cured seems to be rather off the mark as well. Far from being cured, she instead spent time in multiple institutions over the next several years and spent her adulthood fighting further episodes, while nevertheless becoming quite successful.

Much of what is known about her later life comes from the revelation by later writers, and via the publication of many of Freud's letters, of her true identity. Anna O. was actually Bertha Pappenheim, a highly successful author, translator, poet, philanthropist, and feminist leader, who at the time of treatment was a friend of Martha Bernays (Freud's fiancée at the time, and later Mrs. Freud). Pappenheim was a remarkably influential woman whose impact was such that in 1954, Germany issued a postage stamp bearing her image (as part of a Benefactors of Mankind series).

In 1888, at the age of 29, her physical and mental health was much improved, and she moved with her mother from Vienna to Frankfurt, where the family became involved in various philanthropic efforts, and where Bertha began to publish works both literary and political, often under the pseudonym P. Berthold. These works include several books of stories and novellas for children, as well as a play that directly confronted the experience of German anti-Semitism and pogroms. She also produced the first German translations of several important Yiddish works. She also went to work in an orphanage for Jewish girls, and by 1896 she had become its director. She spent the next 12 years changing the focus of the girls' education from preparation for eventual marriage to true vocational independence. In 1895, the year that Breuer and Freud published her case study, Pappenheim participated in the first Frankfurt meeting of the Allgemeiner Deutscher Frauenverein (ADF; General German Women's Association), and subsequently began to author a series of articles on the subject of women's rights. She also produced a German translation of Mary Wollstonecraft's seminal "A Vindication of the Rights of Woman." Her groundbreaking work as a feminist continued with a trip to Spain's Galicia region to investigate human trafficking to Germany, which she reported on in 1904, the same year that she was elected the first president of the Jüdischer Frauenbund (JFB; League of Jewish Women), a position she held for 20 years. Despite the controversy that she stirred up, the JFB grew rapidly, with 32,000 members in 1907.

In her work on behalf of Jewish women, she was controversial and fearless. In the fight against those trafficking in Jewish women, she focused her attention not just on the plight of the Jewish women but also on the complicity of Jewish men. These women became her life's work, and in 1907 she opened the Neu Isenburg home for endangered girls and unwed mothers, providing security and shelter for women who had been involved in prostitution or otherwise victimized by trafficking, along with their children. From a start of just 10 residents in 1908, the facility had 152 residents by 1928. After Pappenheim's death in 1936, following the rise of the Nazis, the remaining residents were taken away to concentration camps and the home shut down. In 1997, however, the 50th anniversary of Pappenheim's death was marked by the dedication of a conference facility and memorial to Bertha Pappenheim on the former Neu Isenberg site. In the home, this remarkable woman was able to arrange for thorough medical and psychiatric care for the residents, but Pappenheim did not allow the use of psychoanalysis.

Further Reading

Freud, S. (1910). The Origin and Development of Psychoanalysis. *American Journal of Psychology* 21: 181–218.

Jones, E. (1953). *The Life and Work of Sigmund Freud.* New York: Basic Books.

Attachment

One of the most successful exports of psychoanalytic ideas to the world of developmental psychology beyond the psychoanalytic community is surely John Bowlby's attachment theory. *Attachment* is an emotional bond, usually between child and parent, characterized by the child's tendency to seek and maintain proximity to the parent, especially under stressful conditions. John Bowlby, a British psychoanalyst, developed attachment theory in the 1950s and 1960s as a way of explaining certain elements of personality and of psychopathology that were not already accounted for by other psychoanalytic theorists. Specifically, the genesis of the theory comes from Bowlby's work with juvenile delinquents in pre–World War II England. He was impressed by how often the early experiences of young criminals included severe disruptions in their relationships with their mothers. At the time, most psychoanalytic theory concerning childhood experiences was based on retrospective interviews with adults, and so Bowlby's plan to study children via direct observation was nearly revolutionary. The result was an interesting, and rather surprising, blend of traditional Freudian psychoanalysis and evolutionary theory.

The evolutionary elements came from Austrian zoologist Konrad Lorenz's studies of imprinting. Lorenz was the originator of the science of ethology, or the study of genetic sources of group and individual behavior patterns, for which he won a Nobel Prize in Physiology. Lorenz discovered that ducklings come into the world with an instinctive drive to follow the first thing that passes by. When a large object or creature appears before them, it triggers this instinctive response, known as imprinting. Immediately after hatching, if baby ducklings see a large object move past them, they will follow the object as though it were their mother, regardless of what the object actually is. It could be a duck, a cardboard box pulled by a string, or even, in the most famous case, ethologist Konrad Lorenz (1903–1989).

Imprinting is a special case of a more general category of instinctive responses that he discovered, called innate release mechanisms. In his studies of fish and birds, he found that organisms are often genetically predisposed to be *especially* responsive to certain stimuli. The duck's tendency to follow any large moving object that happens by at the right moment is just one well-documented example of this behavior. Another is the behavior of the male stickleback, a small fighting fish. A male stickleback will attack any other male stickleback that approaches his nest in a manner identical to the way every stickleback attacks. Furthermore, it will attack anything that resembles another male stickleback, even a paper model, as long as it displays the distinctive red spot that all male sticklebacks bear. In the case of both the ducks and the sticklebacks, the advantage of this mechanism to the animal is fairly clear: a complex behavior pattern occurs without any learning.

Influenced by Lorenz's ethological studies of imprinting among animals, Bowlby believed that humans might also be biologically predisposed to form a powerful, long-lasting bond to a specific individual. Such a bond would certainly serve a survival function, especially given the extreme helplessness of human infants, and so the idea fit right in with an evolutionary perspective. Bowlby was also influenced by Harry Harlow's work with rhesus monkeys. In a classic experiment, Harlow presented infant monkeys with a choice of two surrogate mothers, both made of chicken wire. One was made of bare wire but was equipped with a nipple that dispensed milk. The other provided no food, but had a soft covering and was warm. Harlow found that contact comfort (access to the warm, cloth-covered mother) was more important to infants than the food. This discovery upset the then-dominant view that the physiological need for food assured attachment.

Combined with the psychoanalytic belief in the power of early experiences to either produce lifelong psychological adjustment or lifelong psychological problems, the result of Bowlby's evolutionary thinking was a theory in which failure to form a healthy mother-child attachment could serve as an explanatory mechanism for many developmental problems later in life. (As with so much of psychoanalytic thinking, mothers are central to the theory, whereas fathers barely rate a mention at all.) According to Bowlby, the mother-child bond is formed during a sensitive period in childhood and is carried forward through the rest of the life span in the unconscious mind.

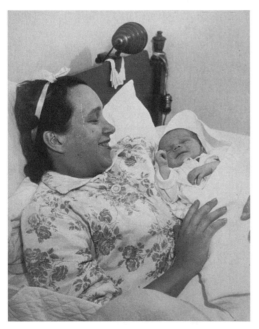

Mother and child: In attachment theory, the most important relationship one will ever have. (National Library of Medicine)

Unlike most other theories rooted in psychoanalysis, however, attachment theory has proven fairly popular among more scientifically oriented developmental psychologists (although they tend to discard the notion of the unconscious influence on all other psychological development), largely because of its roots in actual observational research on children. The primary laboratory technique used to measure the attachment relationship is the Strange

Situation, developed by Mary Ainsworth, which has now been used in thousands of studies. In the Strange Situation, a mother and a child (or, in some recent research, father and child) are brought into a laboratory space, typically containing two chairs and a pile of toys in the middle of the floor. The room is usually equipped with a two-way mirror to allow for unobtrusive observation and/or videotaping. The only other participant is a stranger, usually a woman, for whom the primary selection criterion is that she must be completely unfamiliar to the baby. The Strange Situation typically consists of the following seven phases, though some variations have been occasionally used:

- Parent and infant are introduced to the experimental room. Parent and infant are alone. Parent places infant on the floor near the toys and sits in a chair. Parent does not participate while infant explores.
- Stranger enters, sits in chair, converses with parent. Stranger then approaches infant and engages in play with infant. Parent then leaves inconspicuously.
- First separation episode: Stranger's behavior is responsive to that of infant—if infant is comfortable with the stranger, play continues. If infant is distressed, the stranger attempts to soothe the infant. The timing of this episode is quite variable—if the baby is highly distressed, the next phase begins immediately.
- First reunion episode: Parent greets and comforts the infant. Stranger leaves. Once infant is calm, parent leaves again.
- Second separation episode: Infant is alone.
- Continuation of second separation episode: Stranger enters and gears behavior to that of the infant. As with the first separation episode, the second separation episode may be brought to an end prematurely if the infant is highly distressed—the goal is to make accurate observations of the parent and the child, not to traumatize the baby.
- Second reunion episode: Parent enters, greets infant, and picks up infant; stranger leaves inconspicuously.

The child's behavior during the reunion episodes is the primary basis for classifying the infant's attachment. The Strange Situation is usually used with children who are one year of age or older, for several reasons: First, mobility is necessary, and most children are at least crawling by that age, if not actually attempting to walk. Second, there are crucial developmental milestones, usually reached by that age, which are necessary for the attachment relationship to be evaluated.

For at least their first half-year, many infants appear fairly undiscriminating in their affections, showing equal levels of comfort with most adults, whether friend or stranger. By the first birthday, however, most have started showing signs of stranger anxiety (also called stranger distress), as well as separation distress (crying and general emotional upset in response to the departure of the mother or other primary caregiver). Both of these are among the signs sought as evidence of the quality of attachment in the Strange Situation, along with such things as proximity-seeking behavior, and body language and eye contact upon reunion.

Based on infant behaviors in the Strange Situation, Ainsworth has identified three distinct patterns of attachment responses, resulting in three attachment classifications: secure, anxious/avoidant, and anxious/resistant. Secure infants explore freely while the mother is in the room, making frequent eye contact and returning to the mother's side from time to time—this behavior is frequently described as using the mother as a home base for exploration. These infants show some distress when left with the stranger, but they reunite with the mother enthusiastically and calm down very quickly. Anxious/avoidant infants sometimes show little distress when the mother leaves, and they actively avoid the mother when reunited. Anxious/resistant infants are distressed throughout the procedure.

Attachment classifications appear to result from the interaction of several variables, including both maternal responsiveness and infant temperament. Mothers who are sensitive to infant needs and adjust their behavior to that of their child have securely attached infants. Secure attachment has been found to impact positively other characteristics of the infant's life as he or she grows up. Among other things, securely attached infants, unlike other infants, may grow up to be more curious and more comfortable with exploration of new situations, as well as better problem solvers. They also tend to be more socially competent and less likely to experience emotional problems.

Attachment has become a popular outcome variable in child development research, as the positive or negative impact of various childhood experiences on development is often assessed through attachment classifications. One of the more controversial uses of such data has been in the study of the impact of day care on child development. As more families switch from a single income to dual income, requiring more and more nonparental child care, developmental psychologists have become concerned over the impact this might have on the children's social and emotional development. A large-scale review of research by Jay Belsky and David Eggebeen created a tempest when it came out in 1991, due to its conclusion that children who were placed in full-time day care during the first six months of life were less likely to be securely attached to their mothers (though the article argued persuasively that the relative quality of care was a major confounding factor). The primary criticism of the use of attachment data in research on day care, and to a lesser extent in research on children of divorce, is that the American family, and the behavior society expects of it, has changed dramatically since Bowlby first identified the importance of the attachment bond. Specifically, the behaviors sought as evidence of a secure attachment (moderate distress upon mother's departure, stranger anxiety) may not be appropriate to expect in a child whose mother drops him off, sometimes to a stranger, on a daily basis. That child may appear insecure to some observers simply because he doesn't react with distress.

Attachment has also been shown to vary according to different national and cultural contexts. Compared to American children, more German children are insecure/avoidant, more Japanese children are insecure/resistant, and Israeli children raised on a kibbutz (a communal, collective farming community in which children are not reared by their own parents) are more insecure/resistant. Within the United States, attachment classifications vary widely according to ethnicity. African American infants, who often have multiple caregivers, are less reactive than white children to the Strange Situation. Hispanic mothers intervene more with their children to maintain suitable public behaviors. Similarly to the international samples, this can lead to large numbers of children being classified as, respectively, insecure/avoidant or insecure/resistant. As with children in day care, these differences may reflect secure attachment consistent with cultural norms rather than suggesting unhealthy developmental outcomes.

Some researchers have attempted to extend research on parent-child attachment to adult populations, following psychoanalytic tradition by retrospectively evaluating childhood conditions with a questionnaire called the Adult Attachment Interview. It classifies adults' childhood attachments into four categories (labeled differently than the established infant-attachment categories): autonomous, dismissing, preoccupied, and unresolved. This has allowed researchers to classify mothers' childhood attachments and explore the relationship between their bond with their own parents and the caregiving style they adopt with their children. This research has provided rare empirical verification of a classic psychoanalytic idea: that mothers' memories of and feelings about their own parents have an impact (either positive or negative) on the mothers' own behaviors and beliefs as parents.

Attachment theory has unfortunately also had a very negative influence, as the inspiration behind a particularly dangerous example of therapeutic pseudoscience: *rebirthing* as a treatment for reactive attachment disorder. Reactive attachment disorder is a controversial diagnosis with two distinct subtypes, in which teens who either have difficulty relating to others socially (the inhibited subtype) *or* show excessive familiarity with strangers (disinhibited) are said to have developed the disorder as a result of failing to form a normal attachment to a primary caregiver in early childhood. The disorder is most frequently identified in children who have suffered a severe disruption in early patterns of care, as with death of parents followed by extensive time in orphanages or foster care. Mainstream approaches to helping these children tend to focus on improving the responsiveness of primary caregivers or switching caregivers entirely.

Advocates of *rebirthing,* however, have tended to identify reactive attachment disorder in adopted adolescents who show behavior problems, and have in the past suggested that the child and the adoptive mother have failed to bond because they did not share the birth experience. They therefore recommend re-creating the birth experience for the child, to provide a fresh start. This reexperiencing of birth has often involved rolling the child up inside blankets, rugs, and so forth, and applying pressure while the child crawls out of the tunnel thus created. Curiously, most current information published by rebirthing advocates entirely omits any mention of reexperiencing birth, focusing instead on a definition of rebirthing as a series of deep-breathing techniques intended to reduce stress, increase energy, and bring ease and pleasure to one's life and relationships.

This may be due to the sentencing of two rebirthing therapists in Colorado, on June 18, 2001, to 16 years of prison on charges of reckless child abuse resulting in death, along with lesser charges of criminal impersonation and unlawful practice of psychotherapy. The deceased patient, only 10 years old, was allegedly being helped to bond with her adoptive mother, who was present at the time of the fatal therapy. The therapists felt that if she reexperienced the birth process, she and her adoptive mother could have a fresh start together, and her behavior problems would be left behind. This resulted in the girl being wrapped in a flannel blanket and covered with pillows, and then being sat upon by several adults, who did everything they could to prevent her from emerging. Their activities included shouting, "Go ahead and die!" in response to her anguished cries that she could not breathe. One result of her death was the passage of Colorado House Bill 1238, which prohibits reenactment of the birth process when accompanied by any sort of restraint. Clearly, rebirthing therapists have good reason to de-emphasize that part of the technique and focus instead on the breathing method.

The scientific ground under the breathing method of rebirthing, however, is nearly as shaky. Due to developmental changes in both brain physiology and strategy use, most adults remember little or nothing prior to about the age of four, and certainly nothing before two years, a phenomenon known as *infantile amnesia*. The idea, therefore, that they can resolve all adult problems by reexperiencing a memory that they don't have to begin with, seems absurd. There is no evidence for either of the two central tenets of rebirthing: that an adult has a memory of his or her birth or that reliving the experience will somehow help to repair psychological damage that has occurred in the interim.

Further Reading

Ainsworth, M. D. S., Blehar, M. C., Waters, E., and Wall, S. (1978). *Patterns of Attachment: A Psychological Study of the Strange Situation.* Hillsdale, NJ: Erlbaum.

Belsky, J., and Eggebeen, D. (1991). Scientific Criticism and the Study of Early and Extensive Maternal Employment. *Journal of Marriage & the Family* 53(4): 1107–1110.

Bowlby, J. (1988). *A Secure Base: Parent-Child Attachment and Healthy Human Development.* London: Routledge.

Lorenz, K. (1981). *The Foundations of Ethology.* New York: Springer-Verlag.

Ray, S., and Orr, L. (1983). *Rebirthing in the New Age.* Berkeley, CA: Celestial Arts.

Sarner, L. (2001). "Rebirthers" Who Killed Child Receive 16-Year Prison Terms. Available at www.quackwatch.org/04ConsumerEducation/News/rebirthing.html.

Bauer, Ida. *See* Dora

Bibliotherapy

Little known and sometimes regarded as a fringe therapy, outside the mainstream of general practice, bibliotherapy is generally endorsed by its advocates as an adjunct approach rather than as a replacement for better-established treatments. Unusually among therapeutic models, bibliotherapy has over the last century received far more attention from the publications of librarians than from psychological journals. This is perhaps to be expected, given the nature of bibliotherapy, defined succinctly by Mayo Clinic hospital librarian Ruth Tews as "the use of reading in the treatment of the sick . . . often used to denote the use of books in the treatment of the mentally ill" (1962, p. 98).

The term *bibliotherapy* has been used to refer to a wide range of approaches, rather than to a single, philosophically unitary style of treatment, but all have in common the idea that the written word, and the arts generally, can directly benefit the emotional and psychological health of the creator, observer, or reader. The idea itself was not new in the early 20th century; indeed, it has been extant since Aristotle described the phenomenon of emotional catharsis, if not earlier. Advocates of the notion of treatment of mental illness through assignment of the right works of literature often cite Freud as a major influence, however, thanks to several pithy statements he made on the subject. On his 70th birthday, for example, he repeated his oft-voiced sentiment that he owed an enormous intellectual debt to the many creative artists who had, long before his own work, first discovered the unconscious mind and its importance in determining human behavior. Another Freudian source of inspiration to bibliotherapists came in the form of Freud's observation that "storytellers are valuable allies [in the therapeutic process] and their testimony is to be rated high, for they usually know many things between heaven and earth that are not yet dreamt of in our philosophy" (1956, p. 27).

In this statement, Freud endorses the notion that the great works of literature may possess unique insights regarding human nature that exceed what is understood scientifically at present, while also appearing to implicitly endorse Shakespeare's *Hamlet* as an example of the same, clearly alluding to Hamlet's exchange with Horatio in act 1, scene 5:

There are more things in heaven and earth, Horatio,
Than are dreamt of in your philosophy. But come;

Here, as before, never, so help you mercy,
How strange or odd soe'er I bear myself,
As I perchance hereafter shall think meet
To put an antic disposition on,
That you, at such times seeing me, never shall,
With arms encumber'd thus, or this headshake,
Or by pronouncing of some doubtful phrase . . .
to note That you know aught of me . . . Swear.

Freud's particular choice of allusion here is intriguing in that in this particular speech, Hamlet is informing his friend that he intends to feign mental illness as part of his scheme to exact vengeance for his father's death. Freud has chosen to make his point about the psychological insights of great literature by alluding to a passage regarding the difficulty of determining whether another's symptoms are genuine or not.

Although its advocates have often cited Freud as a key influence, bibliotherapy was not his term. It may have first been used in print to refer to the use of assigned reading as a form of therapy by Samuel McChord Crothers in 1916, in an *Atlantic Monthly* article describing a series of case studies gathered by a doctor of his acquaintance, who established what he called a *bibliopathic institute*. In Crothers's words,

The other day, on going by my friend Bagster's church, I saw a new sign over the vestry:—"Bibliopathic Institute. Book Treatment by Competent Specialists. Dr. Bagster meets patients by appointment. Free Clinic 2–4 P.M. Out-patients looked after in their homes by members of the Social Service Department. . . . Tired Business Men in classes. Tired Business Men's tired wives given individual treatment. Tired mothers who are reading for health may leave their children in the Day Nursery." (p. 291)

Bagster's, and by extension Crothers's, basic argument in favor of the unique usefulness of books in therapy is quite simple: Sometimes talking to a human therapist is difficult, and there are times when the best attitude for the therapist is to be quiet and let the patient think about the new thoughts that have arisen as a result of their conversation. According to Bagster, by way of Crothers, a book "can't follow you about. It can't button-hole you and say, 'one word more.' When you shut up a book, it stays shut" (p. 292). Bagster was also very aware of the limitations of his approach, and its lack of replicable scientific support, acknowledging that bibliotherapy was such a new idea that no consensus existed regarding the actual effect that any particular book could be expected to have.

The wide circulation of the *Atlantic Monthly* ensured that Bagster's words would be widely read, and bibliotherapy began spreading rapidly through the mental hospitals of the United States, most of which already maintained libraries for their patients. These libraries existed due to the already widely held belief that the right books could contribute significantly to recovery. In the same year as Crothers's account of Bagster's clinic, Elizabeth Green and Sidney Schwab, a librarian and a clinical neurology professor, respectively, published an article titled "The Therapeutic Use of a Hospital Library" in a hospital social service journal. In the article, they advocate the general idea that a properly maintained hospital library is vital to the well-being of its patients and that carefully prescribed reading can be an effective part of a treatment plan.

In the years following World War I, the approach and philosophy described by Green and Schwab become quite popular in American mental hospitals, where the general model was to regard bibliotherapy as simply another weapon in the arsenal of the psychiatric physician, rather than as a stand-alone treatment modality. In this point of view, the physician/bibliotherapist prescribes specific reading material just as he would prescribe particular medications, and the hospital librarian acts as the pharmacist, filling those prescriptions for the patients. Into the relative vagueness of this model, some researchers attempted to bring some scientific rigor to the proceedings. In 1937, for example, Dr. William Menninger, of the very influential Menninger Clinic, published a report on a five-year experimental study of bibliotherapy. In this article, he laid out a very specific outline of the respective responsibilities of the psychiatrist and the librarian in his clinic, which quickly became the standard model for the relationship between physician/bibliotherapist and librarian:

> In the development of our program we have evolved a plan by which certain responsibilities are delegated to the physician and certain other responsibilities to the librarian. It is the established attitude that reading is a treatment method and, as such, must be directed *by the physician* [italics mine]. The librarian is the tool who carries out the mechanics and reports observations. (Quoted in Hannigan, 1962, p. 187)

Librarians were somewhat predictably less fond of this description of the distribution of labor, in which they are mere *tools* of the doctor, than were the physicians. Menninger went on to describe their respective duties:

> The physician is responsible for at least six functions with regard to the program. First, he is responsible for the contents of the library and must approve books before they are purchased. It is expected that the librarian will make herself familiar with new literature available, and prepare the current reading assignments to the patients as submitted by the librarian. Third, he prescribes the first reading assignment given to a patient after having interviewed the patient; this is not only to insure a wise choice but also to enlist the patient's

interest in it. Fourth, he holds weekly conferences with the librarian regarding problems that have arisen and the results that have been obtained. Fifth, it is his responsibility to communicate the historical data and the psychological status of each new patient, along with that patient's particular reading habits and interests, to the librarian for her aid and guidance. Last, he must express a personal interest in and carry on frequent discussions with the patient regarding his therapeutic reading.

The librarian's responsibilities include, first, the mechanics of purchasing and distributing the books. Second, she must have a personal acquaintance with the books she lends to the patients. Third, she interviews each patient as to the impressions and satisfaction gained from each assigned or chosen reading. Last, she is responsible for making a written report of the patients' comments and reactions to their reading for the physician's information. (Quoted in Hannigan, 1962, p. 187)

Menninger's approach to bibliotherapy makes great demands on librarians, while reserving credit and ultimate authority and responsibility to the physician, and as such was an approach that hospital librarians were not fond of. As it turns out, physicians were not especially anxious to implement such a plan either, given the number of extra duties it added to their already busy lives, to say nothing of the requirement that they be extremely well-read and up-to-date on the latest available books. As a consequence, while the idea and practice of bibliotherapy spread widely through American hospitals, its primary practitioners were librarians rather than physicians or psychotherapists. As a further consequence, most of the scholarly work on bibliotherapy over the next three decades was published in library journals rather than in psychological, psychiatric, or medical periodicals and presented at gatherings of librarians rather than at medical conferences.

The apex of this underground (in the sense that much of the psychological community was unaware of its existence) literature came with the publication of an entire issue of *Library Trends,* a mainstream library journal not generally involved in medical or psychological concerns, devoted to nothing *but* the subject of bibliotherapy. The *Library Trends* special issue, revealing to the outer world the popularity of bibliotherapy in hospital libraries, marked a turning point for bibliotherapy, as the subject began to be examined more closely by scholars outside the world of librarians. In 1978, a review of the bibliotherapy literature by Rubin revealed that, while 35 percent of published articles on the subject still appeared in library journals, 65 percent of the available research had been published in the journals of other fields, including nursing, education, occupational therapy, and even psychology. Academic respect was slow in coming: In 1980, some 64 years after the *Atlantic Monthly* told the world of Dr. Bagster's Bibliopathic Institute, Villanova University offered the first graduate course in bibliotherapy. Maintaining tradition, however, the course was offered through the School of Library Science. Furthermore, although the course was being offered, at that time there were still no formal training programs in bibliotherapy and no certification in the subject.

A lot has changed during the last 30 years: The literature on bibliotherapy has now explored its usefulness for a wide range of problems, and its use by a far broader range of practitioners than hospital librarians, though as often happens in the early history of a treatment, the published research varies wildly in terms of scientific rigor. Research since 1990 has examined the use of bibliotherapy by social workers, mental health nurses, school counselors, teachers, cognitive-behavioral therapists, sex therapists, and of course librarians. Problems researchers have set out to address with bibliotherapy include behavior problems in adopted children, coping with death and dying, divorce, aggression, obsessive-compulsive disorder, child abuse and neglect, depression, homelessness, self-injurious behavior, sexual performance anxiety, and sleep disorders. Reported benefits of bibliotherapy include greater empathy, increased self-awareness and self-esteem, improved coping and problem-solving skills, improved development of ethnic identity, increased emotional maturity, and improved appreciation of differences in culture and viewpoint. Additionally, researchers widely report reductions in stress and anxiety.

As a wide range of practitioners have begun to use bibliotherapy, a wide range of ideas regarding how it might work has also emerged, though they can be broadly identified as split between a cognitive-behavioral approach and, in recognition of Freud's importance as an inspiration to the movement, a more psychodynamic approach. The modern form of the psychodynamic approach dates back to a pioneering 1950 article by Schrodes in which she explained the role of literature in therapeutic work almost entirely in terminology borrowed from Freud and his followers, focusing especially on processes of identification, catharsis, and transference as crucial steps along the way to therapeutic benefit. In keeping with Freud's fondness for Shakespeare, this is the model typically seen when the prescribed literature is imaginative, such as fiction, drama, or poetry.

When the tools involved are taken from the nonfiction, self-help genre, however, results are usually interpreted in a far more straightforward cognitive-behavioral way. These researchers begin with the assumption that to change the person's state of health, what needs to change is the person's behavior, which may require something as simple as how the person thinks about or interprets stimuli, both internal and environmental. A book's role in this approach is to help the reader to better understand his or her own motives and behaviors, as well as to instruct the reader explicitly in some ways to change how he or she thinks about things. To a psychodynamic bibliotherapist such as Schrodes (1950), however, "didactic literature . . . is more apt to contribute to man's intellectual awareness whereas imaginative literature is more likely to afford the reader an emotional experience without which effective therapy is impossible" (p. 33).

Here, captured in the small nutshell that is the debate over bibliotherapy, is the essential conflict between psychoanalysis and the more scientific forms of psychotherapy. The psychoanalyst focuses on the emotional experience of reading the story and the meaning, unique to the individual, which the patient may take away from it, as the basis for meaningful therapeutic effects. To the cognitive-behavioral therapist, on the other hand, the treatment will work, if it works at all, in exactly the same quantifiable way for everyone who reads the same book, as they will have learned the same skills and strategies.

Given the philosophical gulf that divides the different groups of bibliotherapists, and the fact that writers in both camps usually take pains to point out that the use of literature is a complementary procedure, not a substitute, for the therapeutic process, it is to be expected that determining whether bibliotherapy actually *works* is a complicated matter. Though several meta-analyses of the literature have been attempted, they have all run into a few basic problems. Probably the biggest obstacle is this: Despite a bounty of case studies and anecdotal reports, only a very limited number of empirical studies exist. There are so few empirical studies, indeed, that at least one major meta-analysis (Marrs, 1995) did not include them at all. In the studies that do exist, sample sizes have often been very small, and the samples themselves so unrepresentative of the population at large that comparisons across studies would be meaningless. Furthermore, there is no standardized approach to using literature in therapy, and many published studies give so little information about their own procedure as to render replication impossible. This especially becomes a problem when considering that bibliotherapy has generally been included as an adjunct to other treatment, with no means by which to judge the unique contribution of bibliotherapy above and beyond that of whatever other therapy was involved. Marrs's (1995) meta-analysis, like most, is led therefore to the unsatisfactory conclusion that the research provides only "some limited evidence for the effectiveness of bibliotherapy" (p. 865).

At the time of the Marrs meta-analysis, however, a new trend was emerging in bibliotherapy research: well-designed research, using a standardized treatment procedure and a large sample, on the use of bibliotherapy to treat a single, clearly defined psychological problem. A growing body of research has indicated that *cognitive* bibliotherapy is an effective treatment for depression in adults (Jamison and Scogin, 1995; Smith et al., 1997). In these studies, cognitive bibliotherapy is defined as reading a self-help book for depression that is based on principles of cognitive therapy, in most studies *Feeling Good* by David Burns (1980).

In the series of studies by Jamison and Scogin and their colleagues, the effects of bibliotherapy have been compared both to the effects of regular cognitive therapy and to a placebo, and bibliotherapy has been found to be effective on its own, and just as effective as antidepressant medication in at least one study. After nearly a century, it appears that Dr. Bagster may have been on the right track after all.

Further Reading

Burns, D. (1980). *Feeling Good: The New Mood Therapy*. New York: Morrow.

Crothers, S. McC. (1916). A Literary Clinic. *Atlantic Monthly* 118: 291–301.

Freud, S. (1956). *Delusion and Dream and Other Essays* (Philip Rieff, ed.). Boston: The Beacon Press.

Green, E., and S. I. Schwab. (1919). The Therapeutic Use of a Hospital Library. *The Hospital Social Service Quarterly* 1: 147–157.

Hannigan, M. (1962). The Librarian in Bibliotherapy: Pharmacist or Bibliotherapist? *Bibliotherapy* (Ruth M. Tews, issue editor). *Library Trends* 11(2): 184–198.

Jamison, C., and F. Scogin (1995). The Outcome of Cognitive Bibliotherapy with Depressed Adults. *Journal of Consulting and Clinical Psychology* 63 (4): 644–650.

Marrs, R. W. (1995). A Meta-Analysis of Bibliotherapy Studies. *American Journal of Community Psychology* 23(6): 843–870.

Schrodes, C. (1950). *Bibliotherapy: A Theoretical and Clinical-Experimental Study*. Unpublished doctoral dissertation, University of California at Berkeley.

Smith, N. M., M. R. Floyd, F. Scogin, and C. S. Jamison. (1997). Three-Year Follow Up of Bibliotherapy for Depression. *Journal of Consulting and Clinical Psychology* 65(2): 324–327.

Tews, R. M. (1962). Introduction. *Bibliotherapy* (Ruth M. Tews, issue editor). *Library Trends* 11(2): 97–105.

Bleuler, Eugen (1857–1939)

Eugen Bleuler was a Swiss psychiatrist who played a crucial role in the spread of Freud's ideas in the international psychiatric community. He and Freud first came to each other's attention through Carl Jung, who was an employee of Bleuler's—Bleuler was the director of the Burghölzli sanatorium when Jung joined it in 1900. Burghölzli was the psychiatric clinic for the University of Zurich, and under Bleuler it became a world center of research on mental illness. Its influence was great enough that physicians from many other countries traveled to Switzerland simply to observe Bleuler and his staff in action. Bleuler also regularly sent his staff members abroad to stay abreast of developments in treatment in other countries. The crucial difference between Bleuler's clinic and others was in its director's commitment to science: where most psychiatrists, including Freud, based their ideas on their own interpretations of their own limited clinical experience, Bleuler considered himself a scientific researcher as much as a clinician, and accordingly believed in putting all ideas to the test with a range of patients.

Bleuler's influence on the world of psychiatry was great, both through his training of others at the Burghölzli and through his own contributions to the science of mental illness. His most enduring contribution is certainly the creation of a new word on April 24, 1908—*schizophrenia.* At a meeting of the German Psychiatric Association in Berlin, he introduced this term as a replacement for the then-current term *dementia praecox,* coined by Emil Kraepelin. The term literally translates as "precocious (or youthful) loss of mental faculties"—Bleuler's argument against it centered on the simple observation that neither precocity nor dementia was an essential feature of the illness. While it does manifest at a young age compared to some other syndromes (like dementia), this is not a necessary part of the definition, and to describe it as a kind of dementia is to misrepresent the symptoms while simply ignoring a large part of what occurs in the illness.

Whereas Kraepelin based his description and naming of the disorder on the reading of patient records, looking for common symptoms, Bleuler based his description of the disorder on material collected directly from his own clinical work with 647 patients at the Burghölzli. In focusing on patients encountered in real space and time (rather than examining records), Bleuler recognized that the condition shouldn't be thought of as a single disease with a single set of symptoms, referring instead to a whole group of schizophrenias that shared some features

Carl Jung's mentor, Eugen Bleuler, best known today for giving schizophrenia its name. (National Institutes of Health/History of Medicine)

in common, but by no means all. The name he gave the disorder reflects his sense of what the various illnesses have in common: schizophrenia literally translates as split mind. Bleuler saw the splitting of different mental functions from each other, leading to a loss of unity in the personality, as the most important characteristic of schizophrenia. Whereas dementia generally is a condition reflecting the presence of organic brain damage, he saw schizophrenia as characterized primarily by the presence of contradictory tendencies coexisting in the same mind (delusions and hallucinations accompanied by a belief that one's perceptions of the world are accurate, for example).

Contrary to the conventional wisdom of the time, Bleuler's observation that the brain damage of dementia is not a necessary condition for schizophrenia also led him to conclude that schizophrenia is *not* invariably incurable. In his work on schizophrenia, Bleuler also introduced another term to the psychiatric lexicon that would have a large impact—*autism.* At the time of its introduction, autism referred to the schizophrenic's detachment from reality, with inner life becoming more important than social contact. Because of its use by Bleuler, the term was eventually applied by Leo Kanner in 1943 to children with a disorder primarily characterized by symptoms that looked a lot like what Bleuler described. The other primary symptoms of schizophrenia were the loosening of associations (the ordinary logical connections we make between ideas become far more bizarre), affective disturbances (emotional responses may be absent, muted, or wildly inappropriate for the context), and ambivalence (the state of holding two contradictory ideas, attitudes, or drives toward a person, idea, or object at the same time). In his emphasis on this last symptom, Bleuler was surely influenced by his contact with Freud.

Bleuler may have been an early catalyst for Jung's interest in Freud and psychoanalysis, when he assigned Jung to read *The Interpretation of Dreams* and report on it to the Burghölzli staff. In addition to sparking Jung's interest, this encounter with Freud's work also intrigued Bleuler, who later became an early member of the Vienna Psychoanalytical Society. After Jung became associated with Freud, he worked on assuaging some of Bleuler's initial doubts about Freud's ideas, writing to Freud in a 1906 letter that Bleuler was now "completely converted." This conversion was crucial to the international acceptance and development of psychoanalytic psychiatry, given Bleuler's transcontinental reputation as a premier scientific investigator and educator of other physicians. Bleuler was one of the first psychiatrists to apply psychoanalytic methods in a research setting, attempting to show that the same mechanisms that Freud identified in neurotic patients also operated in psychotic patients—demonstrating this would of course support his contention that psychoses, including schizophrenia, were the result of purely psychological causes rather than brain damage. Years later, Bleuler would publish *Textbook of Psychiatry* (1924), which immediately went into wide use throughout Europe, in which he credited Freud with numerous important ideas, such as describing anxiety as clearly connected with sexuality. By way of this text, Freud's ideas entered the mainstream of psychiatry to a far greater degree than they had previously.

Bleuler's association with Freud, while certainly profitable for both, did not always follow a smooth path. A high point, indicative perhaps of how highly each thought of the other, was the 1908 International Psychoanalytic Congress, which resulted in the formation of the first psychoanalytic periodical, *Jahrbuch für Psychoanalytische und Psychopathologische Forschungen* (Yearbook for Psychoanalytical and Psychopathological Research), listing Freud and Bleuler as directors and Jung as editor. Though they continued to admire each other's work, however, this close association did not last, largely as a result of theoretical and organizational differences of opinion. Bleuler, like many others, was impressed enough by Freud's ideas to center his research on them, and yet he doubted the necessity of the emphasis on sexuality as a primary explanatory mechanism. He was far more troubled, however, by Freud's emphasis on tight control over his disciples and their ideas, and in 1911, a mere three years after the Salzburg Congress, he resigned from the International Psychoanalytical Association. In doing so, he specifically denounced Freud's "who is not for us is against us" attitude as appropriate for religious communities and political parties, but certainly not for science, which must always be open to new ideas and interpretations of data. For his part, Freud continued to develop his professional relationship with Bleuler, but privately (in a letter to Sándor **Ferenczi,** for example) called him "insufferable."

Further Reading

Bleuler, E. (1934). *Textbook of Psychiatry* (A. A. Brill, translator). New York: MacMillan.

Fusar-Poli, P., and P. Politi (2008). Eugen Bleuler and the Birth of Schizophrenia. *American Journal of Psychiatry* 165(11): 1407.

Gay, P. (1988). *Freud: A Life for Our Time*. New York: W. W. Norton.

Bonaparte, Princess Marie (1882–1962)

Princess Marie Bonaparte was a French author, philanthropist, and psychoanalyst who remains better known for her lifelong close friendship with Freud and his family than for her substantial contributions to the psychoanalytic literature, perhaps because of her widely reported key role in Freud's escape to England from Nazi-occupied Vienna. At the dawn of a modern, democratic Europe, she came by the title of "princess" not only honestly but also from several directions at once: the great-granddaughter of Napoleon's brother Lucien, she was also the wife of Prince Georges of Greece (younger brother of Constantine I, king of the Hellenes), as well as the first cousin of King Christian X of Denmark. At the time of her birth, a separate, dynastic branch of the Bonaparte family continued to claim the French imperial throne from exile. Marie's great-grandfather Lucien, however, was one of Napoleon's disinherited brothers, and so her father had the royal lineage without any of its fortune. Her maternal grandfather, however, was the principal real-estate developer in Monte Carlo, and so the family was tremendously wealthy despite the disconnection from the royal family.

Marie Bonaparte was born on July 2, 1882, in Saint-Cloud, France. She was the only daughter of Prince Roland Bonaparte and Marie-Félix Blanc (who died a month after her birth). In 1907, she married Prince George, with whom she had two children, Eugénie and Pierre. She was thereafter officially also known as *Princess George of Greece and Denmark*. The relationship began promisingly enough, with Marie sure that she would be quite happy. At the time of their meeting, she described him in a diary in this way:

> But he is a handsome giant! A giant Scandinavian from the race of the Polar hero Nansen, but handsomer! Slim, blond with a long blond mustache like his father, a straight nose, sky-blue, smiling eyes. Only a little hair, he is bald. But so what? He is tall, beautiful, blond and especially he seems nice, so nice. (Bonaparte, 1952, pp. 956–957)

In this and other passages, she describes the strength of her love for her future husband in terms of Nordic heroes, both mythic and real—it is important to her that he is of the same race as Hamlet (like her fiancé, a Danish prince) and Nansen (the Norwegian polar explorer). In the same memoir, however, written many years later, after a long period of professional work as a psychoanalyst, she also acknowledges a deeper attraction based in her fixation on her own father. In addition to being some 12 years older than she was, the prince was also the man her father wished her to marry.

Wealthy and highly connected, Marie Bonaparte faced the conundrum of life as royalty without power in a democratic age. Possessing a sharp and intensely curious intellect, she wasn't interested in the primarily ceremonial existence among socialites that came to characterize the anachronistic European nobility in the 20th century, and she was apparently unsatisfied both intellectually and sexually by her husband, the prince. Multiple extramarital affairs with prominent men followed, including a relationship with Aristide Briand, a prominent French politician who served 11 separate terms as the prime minister of France, as well as a dalliance with Rudolph Loewenstein, a prominent psychoanalyst along with whom she would eventually founded the Psychoanalytic Society of Paris (Societé Psychanalytique de Paris).

Her first encounter with psychoanalysis and with Freud came in 1925, when René LaForgue, a French colleague (and former student) of Freud, recommended her to Freud for treatment, introducing her as a patient with an obsessional neurosis, but also with a powerful intellect and strength of character that kept the neurosis from compromising her ability to function. Her particular neurosis involved a sensation of impending catastrophe, which troubled her enough that she would at times wish for some sort of astronomical event to destroy the planet. Up to this point, her primary coping mechanism involved retreating to the shelter of her imagination, and by the time she met Freud she had already published works both creative and philosophical.

In 1924, for example, Bonaparte published a collection of stories, *Le Printemps sur mon jardin* (Spring in My Garden). She had also published an article, pseudonymously, reflecting some of her later psychoanalytic concerns. The article, titled "Consideration of the Anatomical Causes of Frigidity in Women," concerned the subject of clitoral surgery. She would also later publish a novel that symbolically treated the disappointments of her sexual and emotional life titled *Les glauques aventures de Flyda des Mers* (The Sad Adventures of Flyda des Mers). She had actually coped with life through writing for many years: she spent her childhood, raised by a nurse, filling notebooks with stories of imaginary characters. She rediscovered these notebooks, which she called *bêtises* (whimsies), near the time of her father's death in 1924, and they, along with another book that she found on her father's nightstand, Freud's *Introductory Lectures on Psychoanalysis,* may have inspired her to seek LaForgue's introduction to Freud.

Freud, however, was wary of committing to the treatment of a patient with her personal history and connections, and insisted that LaForgue vouch personally for her personal worth and seriousness of commitment to treatment. Freud also required that she speak English or German, as he no longer trusted his French—this was a commitment the expensively educated princess had no difficulty agreeing to. Even after LaForgue agreed to all conditions, Freud engaged in some additional foot-dragging, only agreeing to finally see the princess after she wrote to him directly. In her diary entry dated September 30, 1925, she recorded that she had just returned from their first session.

Freud was wary of her commitment to treatment in part because of the intensity of treatment she desired: she saw him for only two months, for a full two hours a day, five days a week, and then returned to Paris where she helped to organize the French psychoanalytic movement. This brief period of analysis, however, became the basis for a new professional identity for the princess, as well as for a lifelong friendship and professional relationship with Freud.

Throughout the remainder of Freud's life, Bonaparte corresponded with him regularly, visited him when she could, and even bailed out his publishing house when needed. She confided in him to a degree she trusted nobody else, even handing over her *bêtises* to him for him to determine whether she should use them as source material for analysis. For his part, Freud repaid her confidence with confidences, seeking her counsel about his recurring dreams and even giving her a nickname: in his correspondence, he called her his "energy devil."

Their correspondence has served as a rich source of information and minutiae for later researchers, because the level of detail is that seen in communications between close friends or family members rather than just professional colleagues. Freud's biographers know when he added the famous couch to his office suite, for example, thanks to her careful notes in which she indicates not just when he obtained it but also from whom: according to Bonaparte, the couch was a gift from a "grateful patient, Madame Benvenisti, around 1890."

Upon her return to Paris in 1925, Bonaparte immediately became more closely involved with the French psychoanalytic community and was one of the eight founding members (along with Loewenstein and LaForgue) of the Psychoanalytic Society of Paris (Societé Psychanalytique de Paris). Bonaparte's role in the Societé was largely to act as Freud's advocate against the French psychoanalysts, especially those of Saint-Anne's Hospital, who were attempting to create a more French variety of psychoanalysis free of overtly German influence.

Among her first professional efforts in the psychoanalytic field were translations of several of Freud's works, including *Leonardo da Vinci and a Memory of His Childhood* (1910), *An Autobiographical Study* (1925), *Jokes and Their Relation to the Unconscious* (1905), *The Future of an Illusion* (1927), and some of his papers on *metapsychology*. *Metapsychology* refers to work on areas of psychology that lend themselves poorly to study by empirical science, and one of Bonaparte's own best-known areas of interest, the human recognition of the passage of time, is often classified in this category by psychoanalysts.

Metapsychology

In 1940, the princess published a paper titled "Time and the Unconscious" in the *International Journal of Psychoanalysis*. In this paper, she argues that one of the central psychological conflicts that arises in child development, and which is a contributing factor to many of the other conflicts, has to do with differences between how children perceive time and how adults perceive it. According to Bonaparte, the child lives in a timeless world in which the child is not constrained by the linear, objective, irreversible limits of Newtonian time. Adults are constantly aware of these limits, however, and attempt to impose them on a child who cannot perceive or understand them. Although the child lives without a clear sense of past or future, however, the child's subjective experience is not of infinity stretching out in either direction. It is rather the experience of a present moment of limitless duration. Attempts made by adults to impose time limits are experienced as intrusions from a strange and hostile world.

The here-and-now, everlasting present is, according to Bonaparte, highly charged with a mostly positive emotional tone, most of the time. The bliss is of course interrupted by brief periods of disappointment, sadness, pain, hostility, or frustration, but the happy periods occupy most of the child's time. In adulthood, we seek the misplaced paradise of our childhood in states of altered consciousness like dreams—whereas the child experiences the sense of eternity all the time, adults can only grasp at a bit of it when unconscious or in an altered state.

Bonaparte describes five different situations under which adults can briefly regain the bliss of eternity, allowing the pleasure principle (which was, after all, only dominant in early childhood) to again prevail:

1. *Dreams.* In dreams, which we know generally only last a few short minutes, we can experience the passage of enormous stretches of time, but we also have dreams in which the subjective time elapsed occupies mere seconds.

2. *Daydreams.* In daydreams, we often experience a feeling of omnipotence and freedom from everyday constraints.

3. *The intoxication of love.* People in love can sometimes experience, in the company of a lover, the subjective dilation or distortion of time.

4. *Drugs.* Bonaparte suggests that the actual source of the high experienced by users of marijuana and opium derives from the sense of release from time's constraints.

5. *Mystic ecstasy.* In states of ecstasy achieved during sex or as a result of various mystical practices, eternity is given an objective existence.

The underlying theme of Bonaparte's paper is a simple one: one of the primary forces motivating adults is the desire to achieve timelessness and taste eternity. This happens for two different reasons. We are motivated by the desire to once again experience the bliss of timelessness that we experienced as children, but we are also, as Freud pointed out, motivated by the fear of death. The knowledge of our own impending mortality is uniquely human and is a major force driving neuroses. To remove the sense of time is to remove that awareness. Drugs, by getting rid of the time sense, also remove the fear of death, and thus the high is, in a sense, actually the feeling of eternal life.

Several other threads in psychoanalytic thought can be seen in new ways through this metapsychological lens. The well-known phenomenon of infantile amnesia, for example, looks very different from Bonaparte's point of view. Perhaps the reason that people do not remember experiences from early childhood has nothing to do with repression or underdeveloped memory mechanisms, but is instead due to the fact that at the time the child did not experience the passage of time in a way that makes any sense to adults. High-risk behavior in adolescence also looks rather different from this perspective: the adolescent becomes aware, as a result of further cognitive development, that time is limited and that death is inevitable, while still experiencing that sense of immortality. Thus, an adolescent can be aware on a rational level that an activity is extremely dangerous and can cause death but still be feeling subjectively that time has no limits.

Female Sexuality

Beyond her work on metapsychology, Bonaparte also wrote on a range of other subjects, including a two-volume psychoanalytic study of the life of Edgar Allan Poe, published in 1933. She also published research on applied psychology, war, criminality, and female sexuality in the *Revue française de psychanalyse* (French Review of Psychoanalysis), a journal that she founded along with René LaForgue and others. Her talks at the Institut de psychanalyse de Paris (Paris Institute for Psychoanalysis), along with her articles from the *Revue française de psychanalyse,* were collected after the war into several volumes, including *Psychanalyse et biologie* (Psychoanalysis and Biology, 1952), *Introduction à la théorie des instincts* (Introduction to the Theory of Instincts, 1951), and *Psychanalyse et anthropologie* (Psychoanalysis and Anthropology, 1952).

She also returned to the whimsies of childhood, publishing the diaries along with psychoanalytic commentary. In addition to their longtime friendship, she also collaborated creatively with the Freuds: Anna and Sigmund Freud translated her book *Topsy: The Story of a Golden-Haired Chow* into German.

Although her range of interests was broad, the work for which Bonaparte would ultimately be best known, indeed infamous, would be her work on female sexuality, the most notorious of which predates her friendship with Freud. Despite her many lovers, Bonaparte complained of sexual frigidity, a term which in her time was used

Friends in high places: Marie de Bonaparte arrives in Paris with Sigmund Freud, shortly after personally escorting him and his family out of Nazi-occupied Vienna, 1938. (AFP/ Getty Images)

to refer to an inability to achieve complete sexual satisfaction, rather than the lack of sexual interest that the term often denotes today. Despite a strong interest in sexual contact, she also felt a distinct lack of passion in relationships. Both of these concerns arose in her analysis with Freud, but she had already attempted to correct the problem via purely biological means prior to making his acquaintance.

Troubled by her difficulties, Marie had engaged in research on the female sexual response, heavily influenced by Freud's position that fully developed female sexuality required vaginal orgasm, whereas clitorally induced orgasm represented incomplete femininity. In 1924, she presented her results, under the pseudonym A. E. Narjani, in the Belgian medical journal *Bruxelles-Médical*. In this paper, she presented a theory of frigidity based on the actual physical distance between the clitoris and the vagina. She claimed to have measured this distance in 243 women, from whom she also obtained information regarding their sexual history. Based on those measurements and her analysis of their histories, she concluded that the ability to achieve orgasm was entirely dependent on the distance between these two organs. Based on her data, she divided women into three distinct groups. Women with a short distance, the "paraclitoridiennes," reached orgasm quite easily during intercourse. Women whose measurement was more than two-and-a-half centimeters, the "téleclitoridiennes," had difficulties achieving orgasm. A third group, the "mesoclitoridiennes," were in between these two groups.

Having identified these categories, Marie felt she had found the explanation for her own troubles, as she considered herself a "téleclitoridienne." As she understood the cause to be physiological, the cure must clearly be physiological as well, and she took what can only be described as fairly drastic action, especially for her time. As the cause is too long a distance between the clitoris and the vagina, she proposed a simple surgical procedure in which the ligaments supporting the clitoris in place are severed to allow it to be stitched into place further down, nearer to the vagina. She viewed the procedure as so simple that she enlisted the surgeon Josef

Halban to perform the first procedure and offered herself as the surgery's subject. Having undergone the procedure, she published an account in which she dubbed it the Halban-Narjani operation. Bonaparte reports on the results of the surgery in five other women, in whom the results were decidedly mixed. No follow-up was possible in two cases, the surgery was definitely unsuccessful in another, and two showed favorable but inconclusive results. Although the procedure, which she had done in 1927 (over Freud's objections), appears to have done nothing to improve her own prospects, in 1930 she took Halban up on his offer to try again but was once again disappointed. This did not stop her from having a third surgery in 1931, which again proved unsuccessful in facilitating the sought-after outcome for Marie. As Mary Roach points out in her recent history of sex and science, *Bonk* (2008), Marie's own writing on the subject indicates how unnecessary such a procedure was—she recommends, in the very same paper that describes the surgery, that téleclitoridiennes can achieve relief by simply changing their sexual position so that the clitoris receives more stimulation. It is unclear why she felt so strongly as to attempt multiple surgeries instead.

It should perhaps be noted here that one of Freud's most widely quoted observations was originally addressed to Marie Bonaparte, in a letter, as follows:

> Die grosse Frage, die nie beantwortet worden ist und die ich trotz dreißig Jahre langem Forschen in der weiblichen Seele nie habe beantworten können, ist die: Was will das Weib? [The great question that has never been answered and which I have not yet been able to answer, despite my 30 years of research into the feminine soul, is "What does a woman want?"] (Quoted in Jones, 1953)

The princess's initial visits with Freud concerned, at least in part, her sexual struggles, and she spent a fair amount of her subsequent professional career attempting to answer Freud's question more thoroughly.

Marie Bonaparte's writings have been largely forgotten or ignored over the last several decades, but as they become increasingly difficult to find in academic libraries, one remains widely and readily available: her 1953 book, *Female Sexuality*. In the essays collected therein, she attempts to give a thorough accounting of the causes of, in her own words, "woman's frequent maladaptation to the erotic function." Her description of women's sexuality is based firmly on core Freudian principles, but deviates from basic psychoanalytic ideas in that her explanation is almost entirely biological rather than psychological—she focuses much of her argument on basic physiological differences between men and women.

She begins with an idea that underlies all the rest: all women start life with an innate, inherent bisexuality. In early childhood, they have urges that can be seen as both masculine and feminine, and subsequent development depends, in true psychoanalytic fashion, on how they resolve the conflicts of early childhood. According to Bonaparte, girls grow up to become three different kinds of women, depending on how they handle the stresses of the Oedipal period. The three groups are distinguished as children by how they cope with *penis envy,* and as adults by whether they are able to achieve orgasm vaginally or primarily via the clitoris. Members of the first group, the *acceptives,* replace the desire for a penis with the desire for a child, and become true women—normal, vaginally orgasmic, and maternal. Those in the second group, the *renouncers,* abandon all competition with men, along with all hope of obtaining an external love object—all sexual drive is sublimated into other things. Bonaparte likens these women, unflatteringly, to worker ants and bees, as they are highly productive and hard workers, but completely asexual beings. The *claimers,* the third group, deny reality and never accept their role as women, which Bonaparte viewed as essentially passive. Instead, they cling desperately to the psychic and organic male elements that are innate in all women, including masculinity and the clitoris. Bonaparte treats the somewhat penislike clitoris as a biological vestige of masculinity rather than as a biologically female organ, suggesting that the vagina is the proper locus of purely feminine pleasure. This is a perspective that her own surgery seems incompatible with—she clearly recognized, at least in her personal life, that the two are related in production of the female sexual response. Perhaps because of this history, she seems most intrigued by, and focuses most of her discussion on, the claimers.

Acknowledging that she is following in Freud's footsteps and merely expanding on his ideas, Bonaparte argues that achieving full feminine development requires that a woman change both her dominant infantile erotogenic zone (from the clitoris to the vagina) and her original love object (from mother to father). Here she distinguishes herself from Freud by arguing that in the Oedipal conflict, both boys and girls have the same first love object, the mother. Although the daughter will later form a similar bond to the father, both sexes must first deal with their attachment to their mother. The reader may note that in this version of the Oedipal conflict, *both* boy and girl resolve it by bonding to the father and separating from the mother.

Bonaparte argues further that there are two distinct kinds of claimer, who grow up to become two very different kinds of women. When a girl gives up neither the erotogenic zone nor the love object, the result is homosexuality. In this view, a lesbian is a woman who has failed to become fully female, both via failing to transfer her erotic feelings from clitoris to vagina and by failing to see her father as a potential love object. Other women make the love object transition but fail to make the transition from clitoris to vagina, and the resulting woman is heterosexual but has an unusually, possibly pathologically strong sex drive. This theory of course dates to a time when an unusually strong sex drive in women was regarded as a disorder (nymphomania) in need of treatment.

In this theory, proper female development involves passage from primarily clitoral sexual satisfaction to essentially vaginal sexual satisfaction. Bonaparte distinguishes between *partial frigidity* and *total frigidity.* In partial frigidity, which she described as frigidity that is limited to vaginal anesthesia, the woman is still able to achieve climax through clitoral stimulation, whereas the woman with total frigidity is unable to achieve sexual fulfillment at all. Oddly, partial frigidity has a poorer prognosis than total frigidity, because the woman with total frigidity does not need to first be broken of the (remarkably persistent) habit of clitoral stimulation. In both cases, treatment of course involves psychoanalysis of the mother fixation. In the woman with partial frigidity, the focus on clitoral stimulation is seen as a manifestation of unresolved penis envy, as stimulation of the clitoris represents stimulation of the absent penis. Bonaparte observes that this form of frigidity is the most resistant to treatment, and also far more frequently observed than total frigidity.

According to Bonaparte, the girls' reactions to infantile events that lead to adult sexuality have to be seen in terms of basic, biological bisexuality. A big influence on this point of view, acknowledged by Bonaparte, is a 1930 book by Gregorio Marañon, *The Evolution of Sex and Intersexual Conditions.* The central thesis of the book is that every human being is endowed at birth with characteristics of both sexes— under hormonal influences, one sex predominates, without completely suppressing the characteristics of the other. Echoing a lot of psychoanalytic writers, he suggests that biological evidence supports the idea that the male is naturally *progressive,* while the female is *regressive*—only the male can attain the full somatic development possible. Woman's sexual development stops at puberty, due to the hormonal influences of the maturation of the reproductive system needed to have babies.

Males are not stopped in their development at the same early point, and so the male passes through what Bonaparte calls the *intersexual crisis* before full puberty is reached, thus the male's sexual identity is fully determined and developed by adulthood. The female, on the other hand, does not complete this process until after menopause, when the ovaries stop being an influence. The orgasm is a function of the libido, which is fully developed in males by adulthood, but as full development of the libido is sidetracked by childbearing, orgasm is often debilitated and belated in women. Bonaparte argues that the clitoris reaches full development rather late, in the 40s or older, unlike the penis, which is why many women become more orgasmic as they get older.

Bonaparte enlists the evolutionary process to explain how such a disparity would fail to die out over time. The reason women's adaptation to their erotic function has barely improved throughout human history is because men's erotic and reproductive functions are thoroughly intertwined. A man's achievement of sexual satisfaction coincides with reproductive function—he cannot do one without the other, whereas the female anatomy allows orgasm without reproductive effect. Bonaparte sees some predictable sex differences in temperament resulting from this anatomical destiny:

Woman has a far greater hunger than man to be loved, cherished, and petted, like some grown-up child. The male, bearer of the phallus, is far more self-sufficient . . . woman, for her part, subsists and depends far more and much more exclusively on love; love of the male, love of husband and child. (1953, p. 68)

Bonaparte's embrace of evolution also leads to a far stranger idea: *vitellinism* (from *vitellus*—Latin for yolk). She begins with the recognition that differentiation of function of cells begins early on in embryonic development of most species, with specialization of function leading some cells to develop into particular body parts, while others become the structure that passively feeds them. Bonaparte treats this as a metaphor for the differentiation between male and female, which also occurs early in embryonic development, transforming an embryo that initially shows no visible sign of belonging to one sex or another. Human eggs lack a yolk, as the placenta develops to feed the baby. Bonaparte points out that after birth, the baby seeks the breast, and thus the mother is serving the function of feeding. The mother will also prepare food for the family, and thus, in the nourishing aspect of woman, we encounter the vitellinism of the bird's egg, extended to the total function of the woman's existence. This is seen in sexual dimorphism as well, as women tend to store fat to a greater degree than men, accompanied by a weaker muscular structure, which Bonaparte describes as less adapted to motor activity.

In this description, the passivity of the egg yolk or placenta is seen as essential to woman's very being, a passivity Bonaparte refers to as *dynamic inertia*. When this *dynamic inertia* extends to the libido, it hampers sexual fulfillment, as dynamic *expression* is necessary for orgasm.

Bonaparte then puts a mildly feminist spin on this grim view of female sexual satisfaction. Other psychoanalytic writers had concluded that the biological division of woman's sexual life into separate spheres of sexual expression and maternity means that their libido is less concentrated, less active, and in the princess's memorable phrase, "less explosive in the sexual act." Bonaparte views this perspective as a profound mistake, writing that it is in the psychical acceptance of maternity that a woman becomes able to truly, totally embrace her vaginal eroticism. Complete sexual fulfillment requires an acceptance of biology.

Ultimately, women's frigidity is, according to Bonaparte, caused by three interacting forces within a woman: her femininity, her masculine nature, and her culture.

1. *Femininity.* Because she is female, a woman naturally possesses a lower libidinal energy than men. With less libido comes less ability to achieve sexual satisfaction.

2. *Masculinity.* All people have both a masculine and a feminine complex within them. As a woman is a naturally bisexual being, she tolerates her masculinity complex far better than man tolerates his femininity. Her greater acceptance

of this part of herself aggravates matters, by making it harder for the libido to adapt to woman's passive, vaginal role.

3. *Morality and culture.* Betraying a more feminist perspective than some other parts of her argument, Bonaparte argues that patriarchal civilization imposes a clear double standard in which man imposes sexual inhibitions on woman while reserving a greater latitude for himself. From childhood on, women therefore encounter a much stronger repression of their sexuality than do men, and theirs is already biologically weaker and less clearly heterosexual.

An important function of psychoanalysis with women is therefore to help them to overcome the three great obstacles they face on the way to conquest of their full erotic function: their *femininity,* their *masculinity,* and their *morality.*

Later in the book, unlike most other psychoanalytic writers on the subject, she directly addresses the issue of genital mutilation and what it says about a culture that practices it. In her view, the practice of *clitoridectomy*—surgical removal of the clitoris—represents an attempt to further *feminize* the women, by removing a last vestigial bit of manhood from them. Recalling that Bonaparte also views passivity as an essential feature of femininity, the goal of such a practice is not simply aesthetic, but rather it also functions to emphasize passivity. She connects it with the traditional Chinese practice of foot-binding, which would appear superficially to have very different goals. As with genital mutilation, however, the purpose is both to further reduce the masculinity of appearance (as men do generally have larger feet than women) and, explicitly in this case, to increase the passivity of the woman. An intriguing part of her analysis lies in her clear recognition of these practices as being driven by the need of patriarchal societies to repress female sexuality and activity, despite which she is able to tie it into a theory that presents female passivity and reduced libido as biologically driven, without noting any sexism in the theoretical approach.

Freud's Departure from Vienna

Marie Bonaparte's friendship and financial assistance were both invaluable to the Freud family innumerable times, but never more so than in 1938, when the Nazis arrived in Vienna. At first Freud, advanced in age and in poor health, was reluctant to recognize what was happening to Jews all around him, as well as loath to leave his home, despite encouragement and offers of assistance from his many friends abroad. In those last days in Vienna, Ludwig Binswager offered asylum in Switzerland, and Ernest Jones encouraged him to come to London, but Freud at first expected his status as an internationally renowned scholar to protect him.

This hope evaporated on March 15, a day after Hitler's arrival in Vienna, when both Freud's apartment and his psychoanalytic publishing house were invaded by

Nazi troops. His son Martin was prevented from leaving the publishing office all day, but the Nazis failed to find the documentation of Freud's financial resources outside the country (he had prepared somewhat for this day). Meanwhile, Anna opened the safe in the apartment and encouraged the Nazis to take whatever they wanted. Despite her cooperation, however, Anna was then summoned to Gestapo headquarters for questioning, unsure whether she would ever return.

While all of this was going on, powerful forces were working behind the scenes both for and against Freud's departure. Himmler, for example, wanted to imprison Freud and the other remaining psychoanalysts, but Goring, not wishing to alienate the Americans, who had already requested that Freud be allowed to leave, prevented it. How the Freud family viewed the situation, and Bonaparte's role in it, is captured well in a recent memoir by Sophie Freud, Sigmund's granddaughter:

> Events followed each other rapidly. The American Ambassador, Mr. Messerschmidt, following a direct request from President Roosevelt intervened with the Nazi authorities who had no wish to alienate the United States. Martin did not sleep at home, but in his pied-à-terre; over the weekend he went with his girlfriend to Baden. Anna had to go to the Gestapo headquarters to be interrogated, but was released with flying colors. Dr. Ernest Jones from England and Marie Bonaparte from France arrived to act as guardian angels for the Freud family and soon procedures for emigration were initiated. (2007, p. 137)

The exact role of these guardian angels was quite remarkable. Once Freud had become convinced to leave, several obstacles, both diplomatic and financial, remained to be overcome. Ernest Jones had strong ties with the British cabinet, and he appears to have been instrumental in getting the U.S. ambassador to France, William Bullitt, involved in advocating for the Freuds with the Nazi authorities. A bigger sticking point in the negotiations involved money—once the Nazis had agreed in principle to let Freud emigrate, the question arose of who would pay for his family's travel. The government was willing to transport a small party, but Freud wanted all of his family who wished to go to be allowed to leave with him. This resulted in a party of 16 people, far larger than the Nazis were willing to allow out. Marie Bonaparte contributed her considerable financial resources to the cause, thus ensuring that Freud could leave. In addition to providing substantial financial assistance for Freud and his family to travel out of the country, however, Bonaparte truly earned the family nickname of "guardian angel": her assistance included putting herself in potential danger by accompanying Anna Freud to the Gestapo headquarters for interrogation, where she remained until Anna was freed. She may also have been involved in the behind-the-scenes machinations that led the Gestapo to give up their questioning rather quickly and let her go.

Eventually, passage to Paris was arranged for the Freuds. When Freud finally arrived in Paris, on the way to his eventual new home in London, he was greeted at the train station by Bonaparte, who took him immediately to her house for a pleasant, relaxing day before his nighttime boat crossing to England. Once the Freuds were settled in London, the princess kept a close watch on them. As Freud's mouth cancer continued to worsen in his London exile, Marie Bonaparte remained in near-constant contact with him, consulting French doctors on his behalf and making tentative plans for Freud to travel to Paris for radium treatment. Freud's personal physician in the last decade of his life, Max Schur, came into Freud's life on her recommendation and was allowed to accompany Freud to London. On the occasion of Freud's 83rd birthday, in his last months, Bonaparte paid him a final visit, staying in his London home for several days. She also remained in close touch with the rest of the Freud family, including those in America. In her memoir, Sophie Freud reports that "the Princess Bonaparte" visited her in America and brought along as a gift a pearl necklace, which had belonged to Sophie's aunt Minna.

During the later Nazi occupation of France, Bonaparte lived in Cape Town, South Africa, where she wrote multiple articles presenting a psychoanalytic perspective on warfare and the myths surrounding it. Following the war, she continued to work as a psychoanalyst until her death of leukemia in Saint-Tropez, in 1962. Though her own contributions to the psychoanalytic literature have been largely overlooked, the importance of her support to both the movement and its founder was widely recognized in the international psychoanalytic community. In 1953, for example, her former lover Rudolph von Loewenstein edited the book *Drives, Affects, Behavior,* a collection of 23 essays written in the princess's honor by a wide spectrum of psychoanalytic authors. A contemporary review describes it in this way: "The contributions are sufficiently varied—both in content and in viewpoint—to ensure any reader's being stimulated by some and irritated by others" (anon., 1954, p. 152).

Princess Marie Bonaparte's ultimate impact on the world is difficult to gauge, given the small but crucial ways in which she may have affected history. A major source of insight into Freud's process and thought, for example, has been the collected correspondence between Freud and Wilhelm **Fliess**—it was Bonaparte who preserved Freud's side of the correspondence despite Freud's wish that the letters be destroyed. Another instance of her subtle influence may have occurred at the coronation of Queen Elizabeth II of the United Kingdom. On that occasion, Marie and her husband, Prince Georges, attended as the representatives of their nephew, King Paul of Greece. Bored with the pomp of the long ceremony, Marie struck up a conversation about psychoanalysis with the man sitting next to her. She proceeded to provide psychoanalysis for him for the remainder of the ceremony, and he seemed deeply affected by the conversation. The fellow who received her clinical services at the coronation was François Mitterrand, the future president of France.

Further Reading

Anon. (1954). Review of *Drives, Affects, Behavior*. *Journal of Consulting Psychology* 18(2): 152.

Bonaparte, M. (1940). Time and the Unconscious. *International Journal of Psycho-Analysis* 21: 427–468.

Bonaparte, M. (1952). *À la Mémoire des Disparus* [To the Memory of the Departed]. 2 Vols. Vol. 1: *Derrière les Vitres Closes: les souvenirs d'enfance* [Behind Closed Windows: Childhood Memories]. Vol. 2: *L'Appel des Sèves: les souvenirs de jeunesse* [The Quickening: Memories of Youth]. London: Imago.

Bonaparte, M. (1953). *Female Sexuality*. New York: Grove.

Freud, S. (2007). *Living in the Shadow of the Freud Family*. Westport, CT: Praeger.

Jones, E. (1953). *The Life and Work of Sigmund Freud*. New York: Basic Books.

Roach, M. (2008). *Bonk: The Curious Coupling of Science and Sex*. New York: W. W. Norton.

Bowlby, John (1907–1990)

Among psychoanalytic theorists, perhaps the most influential among child researchers who do *not* follow a psychoanalytic orientation has been John Bowlby, whose **attachment** theory has become a standard part of the education of all developmental psychologists who study children. According to attachment theory, which contains a rather unique blending of evolutionary biology and psychoanalysis, infants are primed by evolution to form close emotional bonds with their caregivers. Like all unconscious drive states in psychoanalysis, it is the way the need is met by caregivers, rather than the need itself, which will influence and shape personality development, interpersonal relationships, and the development of neuroses and other psychological problems in later life. Lack of a healthy attachment relationship has been blamed for everything from a predisposition to depression to eating disorders, conduct disorders, obsessive-compulsive disorders, and poor academic achievement.

According to attachment theory, an infant will either develop a secure or an insecure attachment to his or her primary caregiver—for cultural reasons, Bowlby primarily focused on mothers, but an attachment relationship can be formed with whoever the primary caregiver may be. Secure attachment results from caregivers who are consistently supportive and responsive to the infants' needs. These children learn to see themselves and other people in a positive way, and thus develop trust in their relationships. Children whose caregivers are unsupportive, inconsistent, and unresponsive to their expressed needs, on the other hand, develop insecure attachments, which may result in excessive self-criticism and dependence, feelings of unworthiness, and fear of abandonment. In Bowlby's view, these children were at far greater risk for developing depression in response to a loss or stress.

Bowlby was born in London in 1907, the fourth of six children. His father, Sir Anthony Bowlby (a baronet in addition to being a surgeon), was appointed surgeon to the king's household and John Bowlby therefore followed the usual pattern in those days for the children of wealth: raised primarily by a nanny, he ordinarily only saw his mother for one hour of the day after teatime, though they spent more time together in the summer. It was common among women of Mrs. Bowlby's station at the time to consider parental attention and affection dangerous habits that would lead to spoiling children. When Bowlby was only four years old, his nanny, who was of course his primary caregiver, left her position, an event he would describe many years later as a tragedy equal to the loss of a mother. He left home for boarding school at the age of seven and spent little further time with his parents. Numerous writers have speculated that this upbringing exerted a powerful influence on his later interest in studying the parent-child bond, a speculation that is certainly supported by Bowlby's own writings on the matter. In his book *Separation: Anxiety and Anger,* he describes his first year at boarding school as a terrible time for him, later observing, "I wouldn't send a *dog* away to boarding school at age seven" (quoted in Schwartz, 1999, p. 225). Note, however, that his objection was not to boarding school as an institution but merely to the age at which he was sent there— he had no objection to boarding school for boys aged eight or older, observing that it may sometimes be a very good thing for them:

> If the child is maladjusted, it may be useful for him to be away for part of the year from the tensions which produced his difficulties, and if the home is bad in other ways the same is true. The boarding school has the advantage of preserving the child's all-important home ties, even if in slightly attenuated form. . . . Moreover, by relieving the parents of the children for part of the year, it will be possible for some of them to develop more favorable attitudes toward their children during the remainder. (Bowlby, 1973, p. 89)

This attitude toward his boarding school days reflects the general premise of attachment theory—that parental attitudes toward children have a great deal to do with how they turn out and that negative interactions may do more harm than separation.

As a young man, Bowlby earned a degree in genetic psychology—the old term for what is now known as developmental psychology—at Cambridge University, followed by a short-lived job in 1928 at a progressive school for maladjusted children. It was during his time at this school that he first became seriously interested in studying the effects of early parent-child relationships on personality development, and he became determined to become a child psychiatrist, entering medical school at University College Hospital in London. At about the same time, Bowlby also embarked on training in psychoanalysis at the British Psychoanalytic Institute, where in the late 1920s the dominant voice in child psychoanalysis was that of Melanie **Klein**. Klein dramatically expanded the role that unconscious fantasy played in Freud's theory, arguing that children's emotional problems were almost entirely the result of fantasies that grew out of internal conflicts, rather than being influenced by actual events in the outside world. Klein's great influence on Bowlby may have consisted primarily in motivating him to try to prove her wrong, as over the next several years Bowlby became less and less able to support this viewpoint. Bowlby was instead becoming increasingly convinced that family experiences were the primary cause of emotional disturbance in children.

After medical school, Bowlby entered into private practice, where his interest in the disruptive effects of early family experiences only deepened as he encountered a series of children with serious, even criminal behavior problems:

> Working as a child psychiatrist before the Second World War, I was struck by the high incidence of seriously disrupted mother-child relationships during the early years among delinquent and sociopathic children. This led me to make a study of the problem and to publish a monograph. (Bowlby, 1986, p. 18)

The resulting research report, "Forty-Four Juvenile Thieves: Their Characters and Home-Life," was published in the *International Journal of Psycho-Analysis* in two parts in 1944 and came out as a book in 1946, but follow-up work on the effects of early parental deprivation would have to wait, as the onset of World War II pushed Bowlby out of a clinical career and much deeper into research, eventually providing him with the opportunities and experience that would lead him to attachment theory. During the war, he was assigned to the Tavistock Clinic in London, to help in the development of better officer selection procedures. Where most psychiatrists, especially psychoanalysts, had a fairly low level of sophistication in the use of statistics, this job resulted in Bowlby emerging from the war with an unusually firm grasp of quantitative research methods. After the war, Bowlby was invited to remain at Tavistock as permanent head of the Children's Department, a position he occupied for the rest of his career. He made some changes right away, however, immediately rechristening his division the Department for Children and Parents, reflecting his conviction that studying and treating children's disorders required working with both groups. In 1949, he made this point explicitly, publishing what is widely considered the first scholarly paper on family therapy, in which he described breakthroughs that were only achieved by interviewing parents about their own childhood experiences while their troubled offspring listened.

Attachment theory is ultimately the result of the combination of a psychoanalytic approach with another more scientific point of view by which Bowlby became intrigued in the early 1950s: ethology. Presented most famously to the world in the works of Konrad Lorenz, ethology is the study of innate, instinctive, species-specific behavior in animals, usually conducted in their natural habitat. Almost certainly the most famous of Lorenz's examples is the pattern of duck behavior that he labeled *imprinting*. Immediately after hatching, if baby ducklings see a large object move past them, they will follow the object as though it were their mother, regardless of what the object actually is. This instinctive response serves a clear survival function, of course: newly hatched ducklings are quite helpless to take care of themselves, so following their mother is quite vital to survival. Unfortunately, this instinctive behavior can be triggered by *any* large object in motion, whether it be a duck, a cardboard box pulled by a string, or even, in his most famous example, Konrad Lorenz himself. The ducklings come into the world with an instinctive drive to follow the very first thing that passes by, so any large object or creature that appears in front of them can trigger this imprinting response.

Imprinting is just a special case of a more general category of instinctive responses that Lorenz discovered, which he called innate release mechanisms. In his studies of various animals, Lorenz discovered the more general principle that organisms are often genetically predisposed to be *especially* responsive to certain stimuli. The duckling's tendency to follow any large moving object that happens by at just the right moment is just one well-established example of this. Another of Lorenz's favorites was the behavior of the male stickleback, a small fighting fish. A male stickleback will attack any other male stickleback that approaches his nest in a manner identical to the way every stickleback attacks. As it turns out, however, the trigger for the attack is neither the particular motion nor the actual presence of another male stickleback, but rather the presence of a distinctive red spot that appears on all male sticklebacks. The fish will attack anything that resembles another male stickleback, even if that something is a piece of paper, so long as it displays that red spot. For survival purposes, the adaptive function of this response is just as clear as that of the imprinting behavior: a complex behavior pattern that helps to ensure the organism's safety occurs without any learning being necessary.

As a result of his psychoanalytic training, Bowlby saw instincts and drives as vitally important in human development, and so his subsequent work focused on the idea that attachment, like imprinting, is a useful adaptation from an evolutionary point of view. Bowlby argued that attachment behaviors, such as crying, smiling, clinging, and proximity-seeking, increase the odds of survival by keeping infants close to the people who protect and take care of them.

Lorenz's work had a big impact on Bowlby's first important publication on attachment, the result of a commission by the World Health Organization (WHO). In 1950, WHO asked Bowlby to produce a report on a subject he was already engaged in studying: the mental health of children who had been orphaned by World War II. This provided an opportunity to gather all available information on the topic and to consult with other experts, including the ethologists. In addition to the importance of evolved patterns of behavior, he was also influenced by the ethologists' notion of critical periods—periods of rapid early development during which a behavior pattern can develop, after which the capacity to develop it is lost. Among Lorenz's ducks, for example, ducklings deprived of the opportunity to imprint on the mother (or other large object) within the first 24 hours would simply fail to ever do so. In the report, Bowlby argues that the importance of the early attachment relationship is amplified by the requirement that it develop in early infancy, as the child who is deprived of early contact with a caregiver may become incapable of forming close bonds with anyone else.

The resulting report brought together expert information from the seemingly disparate fields of child development, psychoanalysis, and ethology to present the basics of attachment theory. The report was very carefully put together, with Bowlby personally traveling to various countries in Europe to consult with local refugee authorities and experts, as he knew that his conclusions would be met with skepticism:

> At that date, there was little recognition in psychiatric or psychological circles that disrupted emotional relationships during early childhood could have an adverse effect on mental health, and those dealing only with adults were deeply sceptical of any such idea. Nevertheless, there was already published evidence additional to my own . . . and the problem was well recognized by child psychiatric and child care agencies. (Bowlby, 1986, p. 18)

The report, ultimately published in 1951 as *Maternal Care and Mental Health,* was highly influential, selling 400,000 copies in its first edition and eventually translated into 14 languages. Given Bowlby's educational background, the report is largely written in heavily psychoanalytic terms, but the main conclusion marked the real start of attachment theory, in unambiguous language that is remarkably free of psychoanalytic jargon:

> What is believed to be essential for mental health is that the infant and young child should experience a warm, intimate, and continuous relationship with his mother (or permanent mother-substitute) in which both find satisfaction and enjoyment. (Bowlby, 1952, p. 11)

Although the report was quite widely read, and quickly became one of the most cited psychological papers of all time, Bowlby reflected many years later that he had been right to expect some resistance:

> Reception was mixed. Those with practical experience of the problem, notably social workers, psychologists, and psychiatrists dealing with children, were enthusiastic. Learning theorist psychologists were bitterly critical, pointing to the deficiencies of the data and the lack of theory to link alleged cause and effect. . . . To my surprise and disappointment, most of my psychoanalytic colleagues were also critical. Freud had long since turned his back on childhood trauma as a cause of neurosis, and emphasis was now insistently on fantasy. (Bowlby, 1986, p. 18)

In addition to bringing the world's attention to bear on the problem of early parental deprivation, the book served the perhaps more important purpose of bringing Bowlby's ideas to the attention of other researchers who would build on them and add scientific rigor to their supporting data. Bowlby's ability to collaborate with others from a wide array of professional disciplines was an important factor in producing such a generative theory. Despite his later work with people far outside of psychoanalysis, for example, Bowlby actually presented his first scholarly papers on attachment theory, in the late 1950s and early 1960s, to the British Psychoanalytical Society in London, despite that body's rejection of his conclusions in the WHO report. Those three papers have since become classics in the field, and they lay out the bare bones of attachment theory very clearly and once again in language that has been largely stripped of psychoanalytic jargon, a feature that is immediately evident in their titles: "The Nature of the Child's Tie to His Mother," "Separation Anxiety," and "Grief and Mourning in Infancy and Early Childhood."

Bowlby's work has had a widespread impact in part because of his collaborators—he was very good at mentoring people whose own ideas and research both informed and confirmed his own theories. The researcher whose name has been most closely associated with Bowlby's is certainly Mary D. Salter Ainsworth, an American psychologist who joined Bowlby's research team at Tavistock in 1950. She was not entirely new to the study of attachment—prior to meeting Bowlby, she had already written her dissertation on what she called *security* theory, which posits that infants need to develop a secure sense of dependence on their parents before they can comfortably explore unfamiliar situations. Although Bowlby started as Ainsworth's mentor, she quickly became a collaborator on his research on parent-child attachment, and even though she went back to the United States after four years, she continued to develop attachment theory and translate Bowlby's ideas into empirically testable hypotheses for the next several decades. Following the example of Bowlby's own work with European war refugees, Ainsworth traveled to Uganda to observe children's separations from and reunions with caregivers in a natural setting. This research led directly to her attempts to develop reliable ways to measure the attachment relationship, which would of course finally make empirical research on the relationship possible.

This work culminated in the 1970s with Ainsworth's development of the Strange Situation, which became the standard research protocol for the assessment of attachment in infants and toddlers. In the Strange Situation, a parent and child are placed in an unfamiliar setting, after which the parent leaves briefly. Following this, a stranger enters the room and attempts to engage the child in play. The child's response when the parent leaves, the stranger arrives, and the parent returns is used as a measure of the child's quality of attachment.

Research using the Strange Situation has revealed differences between infants with secure attachment and children with two different kinds of insecure attachment: anxious-avoidant and ambivalent-resistant. In the Strange Situation, securely attached children appear confident in the parent's presence, show mild distress when the parent leaves, and reestablish contact, with all distress gone, quite quickly upon the parent's return. Children with an insecure anxious-avoidant attachment appear to ignore the parent at the start of the interaction, seem untroubled upon the parent's departure, and often actively avoid contact when the parent returns. The pattern of insecure ambivalent-resistant attachment is less clear-cut, with the babies showing a confused blend of positive and negative responses to the parent. The Strange Situation, and the categories of attachment that it identifies, has become a standard piece of the training of most child development scientists today.

Another important American psychologist whose work shows Bowlby's heavy influence is Harry F. Harlow (1905–1981). Unlike Ainsworth, Harlow never collaborated directly with Bowlby, but through his own distinctive experiments, Harlow is probably the single person most responsible for establishing the idea of evolution-based attachment in American psychology. Starting in the late 1950s, the Madison, Wisconsin–based Harlow initiated a correspondence with the British psychoanalyst, and the two eventually met several times and struck up a productive collegial relationship, regularly citing each other's work. Like Bowlby, Harlow studied mother infant bonds, but he approached the question from the perspective of comparative psychology, a subfield of psychology that investigates animal behavior with the twin goals of understanding the behavior of nonhumans for its own sake as well as gaining useful insights into human behavior. Harlow's best-known research project is certainly his series of experiments on attachment behavior in rhesus monkeys.

In these classic experiments conducted between 1957 and 1963, Harlow removed suckling rhesus monkeys from their mothers and offered them a choice between two artificial surrogate mothers. One of the fake mothers was a wire frame with a plastic face, and the other was essentially the same, but covered in soft terry cloth. The studies were inspired by John Bowlby's *Maternal Care and Mental Health,* a 1950 report commissioned by WHO that reviewed research on the effects of institutionalization on child development. It was this report that first presented the bare bones of Bowlby's attachment theory, including the very specific claim that the mother's role in feeding is not the primary basis for the development of the attachment relationship, which is based instead on maternal responsiveness to the child's needs. Harlow provided much-needed empirical support for this argument by fitting only one of the two artificial monkey mothers with the means for feeding the baby: The wire mother had an attached baby bottle, containing milk. The terry cloth mother could provide no food. In another condition, both surrogates could provide food. In comparing the behavior of the baby monkeys across both conditions, Harlow found that the baby monkeys would cling to the terry cloth mother whether or not it provided them with food, whereas they would only cling to the wire mother when it was the only source of food, and even then they would return to the terry cloth mother when they had finished feeding. When a frightening stimulus, a mechanical spider, was introduced, the monkeys ran directly to the terry cloth mother for comfort and protection, regardless of which mother had provided food.

In other Harlow experiments, the young monkeys displayed patterns of behavior that Ainsworth would later see in human children in the Strange Situation. When the monkeys were left in an unfamiliar room with the cloth surrogate, they remained clinging to it until they felt secure enough to explore, but once they had begun to explore, they occasionally returned to the cloth mother for comfort. Left alone in the room without the cloth mother, the monkeys behaved very differently, crying, freezing in fear, sucking their thumbs, and crouching down. Some even ran around the room, from object to object, appearing to search for the cloth mother, while crying and screaming. Placed in the same situation but with the wire mother present, the infant monkeys behaved in the same way as the monkeys left completely alone.

Once the monkeys had been weaned onto solid food, they were separated from the cloth mothers for three days. When they were reunited with their cloth-covered mothers, the monkeys clung to them and did not explore the room. Harlow concluded from this that their need for contact comfort, provided by the cloth mother but not by the wire mother, was stronger than the need to explore.

Harlow also found that although monkeys raised with either a wire mother or a cloth mother gained weight at about the same rate, the monkeys with the wire mother experienced diarrhea more frequently. Harlow's interpretation of this was that a lack of contact comfort is psychologically stressful to the monkeys. In another series of studies, Harlow separated baby rhesus monkeys from their mothers for two to three weeks. At first, the babies reacted to the separation vocally and violently, with an abundance of screaming and crying, but they then descended into a depressive state of low activity, minimal play, and occasional crying. These responses closely matched Bowlby's earlier description of maternal separation in human children. In humans, the children's reactions began with a stage Bowlby called *protest,* followed by *despair.* From an evolutionary perspective, these reactions made adaptive sense. Protest is simply a way of signaling distress, along with current location, to the caregiver. The silence that follows in despair is also adaptive, as a way of conserving resources and avoiding predation when the caregiver fails to respond.

Harlow's findings were groundbreaking because they contradicted two major themes in popular psychological advice on childrearing, and because they laid the groundwork for wider acceptance of Bowlby's description of the attachment relationship in humans. In the 1950s, parents were frequently advised to limit or avoid physical contact with their children due to concern over the possibility of spoiling them, a notion that was supported by the then-dominant behaviorist approach to psychology: picking up or hugging an obviously distressed child was expected to reinforce the fussing, crying, or tantrum behavior that preceded the contact. Additionally, child-rearing advice from the behaviorist perspective suggested that emotions were a relatively unimportant part of the human experience and should be neglected in favor of more readily controlled responses.

In that context, feeding was believed to be the key factor in the formation of the mother-child bond. Harlow concluded something truly revolutionary instead: that the reason nursing strengthened the mother-child bond was primarily because of the body contact involved, rather than the food.

Harlow's work was particularly important to the further development of attachment theory because it showed quite plainly that the close mother-child bond was something physiologically based and evolutionarily determined and that it was based on the mother's responsiveness to the infant's emotional needs, rather than just the merely physiological ones. Bowlby had worked heavily with orphaned war refugees and young male delinquents who had poor or nonexistent relationships with their mothers, but for obvious ethical reasons had been unable to conduct actual experiments in removal of babies from their mothers; Harlow, working with monkeys, had been able to fill in those missing experimental results.

Though most of Bowlby's work, as well as that of his followers such as Ainsworth and Harlow, focused on parent-infant attachment and its consequences for later development, Bowlby's final book, *Loss, Sadness and Depression* (1980), addresses the potential long-term consequences of different attachment patterns in producing depression. Bowlby describes three different personalities that predispose individuals to depression, and the descriptions sound very closely related to the categories of parent infant attachment. People in insecure relationships characterized by anxious ambivalence and excessive dependence, for example, are especially vulnerable to depression following the loss of a loved one. Insecure relationships characterized by anxious avoidance and excessive independence, on the other hand, are more susceptible to depression following a personal failure and its accompanying loss of self-esteem. A third group of people identified by Bowlby as prone to depression are compulsive caregivers, who Bowlby identified among people who were taking care of ill parents. These individuals are both resentful about having to stay home from an early age to provide care, and simultaneously anxious about eventually leaving home. As a result of this internal tension, they become overwhelmed with guilt and preoccupied with caring for others the way they themselves would like to have been cared for.

While internecine conflict over ideas is hardly rare within the psychoanalytic community, Bowlby is almost unique in having gone from rejection within the psychoanalytic community to extremely widespread, mainstream acceptance throughout developmental psychology. Although quarrels continue regarding the actual effects of insecure attachment, along with debate over the correct ways to evaluate it (see **attachment**), two fundamental ideas that arose from Bowlby's theory are now nearly universally accepted among those who study children:

a. that immediate responsiveness to infants' needs, including picking them up when they are distressed and feeding them on demand, leads to positive outcomes rather than spoiling, and

b. that early close physical contact is for the bond between parent and child.

In the field of psychology, the level of consensus important that has been achieved on these two notions is remarkably rare, and all the more so for theories that began in psychoanalysis. Unsurprisingly, attachment theory is not entirely without its critics. Some critics have interpreted Bowlby's emphasis on parental behavior as a way of following in the perceived psychoanalytic tradition of blaming the parents for anything that later goes wrong in a child's life. Although this was probably not Bowlby's intention, the criticism is not entirely without merit, as he did see the early parent-child relationship as a powerful factor in the development of the later psyche. Rather than accepting the attachment relationship as the single crucial factor in later psychopathology, the prevailing view among developmental psychologists today is that the parent-child relationship is only one of many factors that interact with each other to create a vulnerability to depression or any other psychological problem.

Further Reading

Ainsworth, M.D.S., and J. Bowlby (1991). An Ethological Approach to Personality Development. *American Psychologist* 46: 333–341.

Bowlby, J. (1951). *Maternal Care and Mental Health*. Geneva: World Health Organization.

Bowlby, J. (1958). The Nature of the Child's Tie to His Mother. *International Journal of Psycho-Analysis* 39: 350–373.

Bowlby, J. (1960a). Grief and Mourning in Infancy and Early Childhood. *The Psychoanalytic Study of the Child* 15: 9–52.

Bowlby, J. (1960b). Separation Anxiety: A Critical Review of the Literature. *Journal of Child Psychology and Psychiatry* 1(4): 251–269.

Bowlby, J. (1966). *Attachment and Loss*. Vol. 1: *Attachment*. London: Hogarth.

Bowlby, J. (1973). *Attachment and Loss*. Vol. 2: *Separation, Anxiety and Anger*. London: Hogarth.

Bowlby, J. (1980). *Attachment and Loss*. Vol. 3: *Loss, Sadness and Depression*. London: Hogarth.

Bowlby, J. (1986). Citation Classics: Maternal Care and Mental Health. *Current Contents: Social and Behavioral Sciences* 50: 18.

Bowlby, J. (1988). *A Secure Base: Clinical Applications of Attachment Theory.* London: Routledge.

Seay, B., E. Hansen, and H. F. Harlow (1962). Mother-Infant Separation in Monkeys. *Journal of Child Psychology and Psychiatry* 3: 123–132.

Schwartz, J. (1999). *Cassandra's Daughter: A History of Psychoanalysis in Europe and America.* London: Penguin UK.

Breuer, Josef (1842–1925)

One of the most important influences on the early development of psychoanalytic theory, Josef Breuer was so crucial to the genesis of Freud's approach to therapy that when Freud detailed its origins for an American audience, he modestly gave Breuer full credit: "Granted that it is a merit to have created psychoanalysis, it is not my merit. . . . another physician of Vienna, Dr. Josef Breuer, made the first application of this method to the case of an hysterical girl" (Freud, 1910, p. 181). Indeed, it was Breuer, not Freud, who first proposed that neuroses could arise from unconscious processes and that those neurotic symptoms could be made to disappear when these underlying causes were made a part of the conscious mind.

Breuer shared Freud's interest in the treatment of patients suffering from **hysteria**, and the two men entered into a collaboration when Breuer shared his findings with Freud regarding the young woman who is now widely regarded as the very first psychoanalytic case study, **Anna O**. The patient suffered from a wide range of hysterical symptoms, described by Freud as follows:

> Dr. Breuer's patient was a girl of twenty-one, of a high degree of intelligence. She had developed in the course of her two years' illness a series of physical and mental disturbances which well deserved to be taken seriously. She had a severe paralysis of both right extremities, with anaesthesia, and at times the same affection of the members of the left side of the body; disturbance of eye-movements, and much impairment of vision; difficulty in maintaining the position of the head, an intense *Tussis nervosa* [nervous cough], nausea when she attempted to take nourishment, and at one time for several weeks a loss of the power to drink, in spite of tormenting thirst. Her power of speech was also diminished, and this progressed so far that she could neither speak nor understand her mother tongue; and, finally, she was subject to states of "absence," of confusion, delirium, alteration of her whole personality. . . . When one hears of such a case, one does not need to be a physician to incline to the opinion that we are concerned here with a serious injury, probably of the brain, of which there is little hope of cure. (Freud, 1910, pp. 181–182)

What was special about this case, of course, was Breuer's recognition that no serious brain injury was apparent, and so the cause of this wide range of serious symptoms

Joseph Breuer, the man to whom Freud gave credit for the founding of psychoanalysis. Drawing by Emil Fuchs, 1897. (Imagno/Getty Images)

must lie elsewhere, perhaps in purely mental rather than physical trauma. Breuer found that he could diminish the severity of Anna's symptoms by encouraging her to describe her fantasies and her occasional hallucinations, and he began to use hypnosis to make the process easier. He found that if he could get her to recall a series of memories, ending with the traumatic memory that was the source of a symptom, the symptom would then disappear. Her inability to drink water, for example, ended when Breuer helped her to recall a time that she had been disgusted by the sight of a governess's little dog sharing her glass of water. Having recalled this, she immediately took a long drink.

Soon, Breuer was hypnotizing Anna and helping her to dig through her memories twice a day, and eventually he reported that all of her symptoms were gone, a process from which he drew two key conclusions that would become central to psychoanalysis after he shared them with Freud: that her symptoms were the result of memories buried deep in her mind, away from conscious awareness, and that when these thoughts were shared out loud and joined the conscious mind, the symptoms disappeared. Anna O. herself referred to the process as "chimney sweeping," and also coined the more serious term that would become widely used among psychotherapists: the "talking cure." Her case became the centerpiece of the book that first made Freud's reputation, *Studien über Hysterie* (Studies of Hysteria), which originally listed Freud as the second author, with Breuer receiving primary credit.

After Anna O., Freud went on to develop Breuer's insights into a vast, complex theory, but Breuer never personally treated another hysterical patient. He claimed that the demands of a busy medical practice left him with no time to pursue psychotherapy, but Freud believed that he was upset by the strong attachment that Anna developed for Breuer toward the end of her treatment. Indeed, the treatment was actually terminated by Breuer when, during a treatment session, Anna complained of severe abdominal pains and then indicated to Breuer that she was pregnant and about to give birth to his child. It was this incident that led Breuer to refer her to Freud for further treatment, and which inspired Freud to begin considering the importance of *transference* in the therapeutic relationship.

Following the publication of *Studien über Hysterie,* both the professional col-laboration and the friendship between Breuer and Freud came to a fairly abrupt end, apparently over two distinct issues. Breuer was primarily interested in medicine and physiology and was ambivalent regarding the value of his work with Freud, whereas Freud (clearly) intended to devote his life to the treatment of neuroses. A larger point of contention between the two men concerned the question of child-hood memories of sexual seduction. At the time of their collaboration, Freud took these memories as evidence that his patients had actually been sexually abused as children (see **seduction theory**), whereas Breuer, once again arriving at an insight that would later prove central to Freud's theory, speculated that these were memo-ries of childhood fantasies, buried in the unconscious mind.

Josef Breuer's work with Freud, coming at the start of Freud's career, actually occurred rather late in an already illustrious career for Breuer. Breuer was born in Vienna, Austria, in 1842, finished medical school in 1867, and had published his first important scientific work by the age of 26 (in 1868, nearly 30 years before *Studien über Hysterie*). In collaboration with Ewald Hering, a physiology profes-sor at the Vienna military medical school in Vienna, the young physician demon-strated that breathing occurs as a reflex, a phenomenon still known today as the Hering-Breuer reflex. Their experiments changed the way that scientists viewed the relationship between the lungs and the autonomic nervous system, and also greatly advanced their understanding of the function of the vagus nerve.

Breuer's subsequent research was conducted from his home, while he worked as a private physician, without benefit of a university's facilities or support. Study-ing the physiology of the ear, he discovered how the semicircular canals actually work, providing the basis for the modern understanding of the vestibular sense (how the body detects position, balance, and acceleration). The semicircular canals were already known to be associated with balance, but the underlying process by which this happened was still unknown until 1870, when Breuer discovered another process that still bears his name. The Mach-Breuer theory of endolymph shift, a widely accepted explanation for how the semicircular canals actually work to send sensory information to the brain, was actually discovered independently by Breuer and by Ernst Mach. In an excellent illustration of the degree to which 19th-century scholars generally failed to confine their investigations to a single academic field, Ernst Mach is also the man whose work in physics led to his name being used to designate multiples of the speed of sound (e.g., Mach 1, Mach 2, Mach 3, etc.).

Although he is probably best known to readers today as a collaborator of Sigmund Freud, Breuer was in fact one of the best-known and most influential scientists and physicians in 19th-century Vienna. In addition to his scientific work, he was so trusted by the medical establishment that he was the personal physician of many of Vienna's professors of medicine, along with the prime minister of Hungary. An unusual way in which his influence on the intellectual world may be gauged further concerns the frequency with which he has appeared as a character in fictional treatments of 19th-century Austria. Irvin Yalom's 1992 international bestseller *When Nietzsche Wept,* for example, centers on a series of fictional meetings between Breuer and the philosopher Friedrich Nietzsche, thoroughly exploring both men's thought in the process. Breuer also appears as a minor character in Joseph Skibell's 2010 novel, *A Curable Romantic,* and is a central character in an unproduced film script by Jean-Paul Sartre, *The Freud Scenario,* commissioned by John Huston but never filmed. Playwright Jerome Coopersmith fictionalized the relationship between Breuer and his most famous patient in 1992's *The Mystery of Anna O.* Far more than a mere collaborator of Freud, Breuer was a very influential scientist in his own right and has even cast a long shadow into 21st-century fiction and drama.

Further Reading

Freud, S. (1910). The Origin and Development of Psychoanalysis. *American Journal of Psychology* 21: 181–218.

Jones, E. (1953). *The Life and Work of Sigmund Freud.* New York: Basic Books.

Charcot, Jean. *See* Hypnosis

Civilization and Its Discontents (1930)

First published in German in 1930 as *Das Unbehagen in der Kultur* (The Uneasiness of Culture), the book most widely known by its English title of *Civilization and Its Discontents* remains one of Sigmund Freud's most widely read works. The book continues Freud's project, begun in **Totem and Taboo** and **The Future of an Illusion,** along with *Beyond the Pleasure Principle,* of taking his description of the development of the individual, including such elements as the Oedipal conflict and the development of the superego, and applying it to the development of human society as well. The book has become notorious for its dark, pessimistic tone and grim view of human nature, which many commentators have attributed to the context in which Freud was writing it. He began writing the book in a land devastated by the destruction and massive casualties of World War I, and completed it as the various fascistic and anti-Semitic elements that would become the **National Socialist German Workers' Party (Nazis)** began to win regional political battles in and around Germany. Indeed, the destruction wrought by Hitler led many to see the book as somewhat prophetic.

The central idea of *Civilization and Its Discontents* is a simple one, which had been knocking around in psychoanalytic circles, notably in the work of Helene Deutsch, for at least a decade: the concept of libido needed to be expanded beyond erotic drives to embrace negative, destructive drives as well. Whereas positive drives, including both sexual and creative instincts, had long been central to psychoanalytic theory, Freud had come to feel that aggressive, destructive drives were just as important in the human psyche, calling these two opposing forces "eros" and "thanatos," or life instincts and death instincts. Since our natural impulses included aggressive, destructive tendencies, we have developed civilization to counteract these impulses that threaten the well-being of the human community.

Since the desire to kill and the insatiable desire for sexual gratification are both primitive instincts that we carry within us, civilization has to create laws that prohibit killing, rape, and adultery, and implements severe punishments for those who violate these prohibitions. Because these prohibitions require the repression of instincts, however, civilization by its very existence creates resentment, discontent, and mental pathology in its members. According to Freud, this generates an unavoidable paradox: civilization is a human creation intended to protect us from unhappiness, but it is also our greatest *source* of unhappiness, because it can only exist as long as we willingly frustrate our own instinctive drives.

In describing how society has arrived at its present dysfunctional state, Freud draws on his own model of child psychosexual development. Just as the child represses anal eroticism in favor of a need for order and cleanliness, so society achieves its structure by sublimating our natural instincts into useful activity, which is accomplished only through a repressive renunciation of the very instincts that make us human. Although the positive impulses of eros help us to band together and work for the common good, the aggressive tendencies of thanatos lurk just beneath the surface and must be either further repressed or directed against another culture. In the context of pre–World War II Germany and Austria, with the rise of virulent anti-Semitism developing in parallel with strong nationalistic fervor, this analysis seems prophetic indeed.

Freud also found a place for the Oedipal conflict in the development of human culture, repeating his argument from *Totem and Taboo* that both civilization and religion have their origin in an ancient Oedipal scenario of brothers banding together to kill their father, and then beginning civilization by instituting the incest taboo, to be followed in short order by many additional restrictions on behavior, which would eventually become laws. As a result of this resolution, the instinctive love we feel toward a particular sexual object becomes diffused and directed toward all of our culture, and humanity in general. In contrast to standard religious teaching, especially in Christianity, Freud refuses to see this nonjudgmental affection for everyone as the ultimate goal and purpose of human love, however, instead positioning it as the result of so many laws and taboos and restrictions that the fundamental ill will that must be repressed in order to achieve it will inevitably reassert itself in some other way. Just as the Oedipal conflict is resolved by identification with and submission to the authority of a father figure, Freud saw its resolution by human culture as resulting in submission to a strong authority figure, whether it be God or government, against which resentment will always linger just beneath the loving, civilized surface.

Just as Freud saw a certain amount of guilt and neurotic repression of instinct as necessary for people to live in families, *Civilization and Its Discontents* argues that those same elements make civilization possible as well, and their excessive application leads to pathology on a cultural level just as certainly as can occur on an individual level. The book has remained in print and has been widely read since its publication, in part because the events of the rest of the 20th century, including the Nazi atrocities, Stalinist and Khmer Rouge genocides, the use of atomic weapons against Japan, the conflicts in Rwanda and Sudan, and many other similarly grim examples, appear to confirm its prescient, prophetic view of humanity as fundamentally driven toward murder and destruction.

Further Reading

Freud, S. (1930/1989). *Civilization and Its Discontents.* New York: W. W. Norton.

Cocaine

In addition to his many contributions to the intellectual discourse of the 20th century, Sigmund Freud may have also directly contributed to the popularity of cocaine, one of the century's great scourges. In the late 19th century, cocaine was a rather little-known drug that was seen as possessing some promise as a versatile panacea, based primarily on explorers' dispatches regarding its use in South America. Freud became interested in its properties and potential uses following reports that a German army doctor had experimented with using cocaine to improve his men's stamina.

Freud's interest in cocaine may have been intensified by curiosity about whether it might help a friend. Dr. Ernst von Fleischl-Marxow was a physiological researcher who, like Freud, had studied the nervous system in Ernst Brücke's laboratory. Earlier in his career, however, while apprenticed to a pathologist, Fleischl-Marxow lost a finger to amputation following an accident during an autopsy. Despite near-constant pain as a result of peripheral nerve damage during the amputation, Fleischl-Marxow had a remarkable career and made a series of important discoveries about the brain. For example, he demonstrated the occurrence of electrical impulses on the surface of the cerebral cortex in response to sensory stimulation (these weak charges had previously been undetectable) and also demonstrated the feasibility of the electronencephalogram (EEG) through animal studies. He also developed several different medical tools and instruments that were widely adopted.

Throughout his career, however, Fleischl-Marxow had also been battling severe pain and had, as a result, become addicted to morphine, as well as to its synthetic sister, heroin. Freud obtained a sample of cocaine from the Merck company and quickly set about experimenting with it, primarily by ingesting small doses of it himself and documenting the sensations it caused. As a result of these experiments, he noticed that cocaine caused a numbing of the lips and tongue when ingested orally (in a 5 percent solution, which Freud recommended to a friend as a cure for intestinal pains). Freud felt that this numbing might be a useful property, which he happened to mention to his ophthalmologist friend, Carl Koller, before leaving Vienna for a visit to Martha Bernays, his fiancée. Upon Freud's return to Vienna, he found that Koller had experimented on animals and himself and found that cocaine effectively rendered the eyes impervious to pain. In 1884, Koller presented his discovery to the world—the first effective local anesthetic, which revolutionized

Carl Koller, the ophthalmologist who first used cocaine anesthesia in eye surgery, after being given the idea by Sigmund Freud. (National Library of Medicine)

surgical practice and greatly increased the number of medical researchers experimenting with cocaine.

Given the effectiveness of cocaine in numbing pain, it struck Freud that it might be useful in alleviating Fleischl-Marxow's pain and helping to break his addiction to opiates, and he enthusiastically recommended it to his friend. He also wrote a journal article, "Über Coca" (On Cocaine) in which he reported on his own experiences while also excitedly and uncritically advocating its use for a wide range of applications. This must be seen in its proper context. Unlike today, the drug was legal and poorly understood at the time, so his downplaying of any risks involved in its use must be seen in part as a sign of the times in which he wrote the article. Nevertheless, several of his observations bear mentioning here. In addition to describing cocaine as far less harmful than alcohol, he also characterizes it in the article as "not detrimental to the body." He therefore recommends cocaine as a treatment of choice both for stomach trouble due to overindulgence and for nervous disorders of the digestive system and also recommends long-term use of cocaine for anemia and degenerative tissue ailments. He additionally cites the use of cocaine as an aphrodisiac in South America, suggesting that direct application to the male genitals is a sure cure for impotence. Indeed, Freud recounts the case of a young writer who was helped to resume his work after an illness via the consumption of cocaine, yet had to stop taking it because he was overcome by sexual excitement as a side effect.

Where Freud's friend Fleischl-Marxow was concerned, the most important section of "Über Coca," however, is the recommendation of cocaine as a way of eliminating withdrawal symptoms from morphine, or at least making them tolerable. Freud further suggests, in a passage that would have a wide influence, that cocaine will not replace one addiction with another, as one can simply stop taking cocaine once the addiction to morphine has been beaten. Freud's article was widely read, thus helping to form many other researchers' initial impressions of cocaine, but within two years of its publication, he had stopped taking cocaine regularly himself (though some sources suggest he continued to occasionally indulge into the mid-1890s) and had entirely stopped advocating its use. This was at least in part due to Fleischl-Marxow's experience with the drug. Rather than beating his addiction to opiates, he developed a worse addiction to cocaine and died at the age of 45 without defeating either his pain or his addiction. Some of this may be due to Freud's addition of a potentially even worse idea to the notion of defeating morphine addiction with cocaine; he recommended delivery via injection. Prior to this, cocaine was primarily ingested orally in a weak water solution, which appears to have been far less addictive than injection or the other later development, snorting.

Further Reading

Freud, S. (1984). Über Coca. *Journal of Substance Abuse Treatment* 1(3): 206–217. (Originally published in 1884.)

Gay, P. (1988). *Freud: A Life for Our Time.* New York: W. W. Norton.

Defense Mechanisms

In its challenging task of mediating conflict between the *id,* the *superego,* and reality, the ego will inevitably fail with some frequency, resulting in anxiety. Freud classified anxiety into three categories—*reality anxiety, neurotic anxiety,* and *moral anxiety.* Reality anxiety is produced by fears of real or possible events, such as fear of a neighbor's vicious dog. This anxiety can generally be resolved by simply removing oneself from the situation (walking away from where the dog is, for example). The other two forms of anxiety are somewhat more challenging. *Neurotic* anxiety stems from the unconscious fear that the impulses of the **id** will take over, leading to trouble and eventual punishment. Moral anxiety results from the fear of violating the **superego**'s moral code and produces feelings of shame and guilt.

When anxiety occurs, the mind first responds with attempts at problem-solving, seeking a rational escape from the anxiety-provoking situation. Such a clear-cut escape is not always available, however. In psychoanalytic theory, failure to resolve inner conflicts effectively is the source of psychological problems in general, so it is important that the ego has some tools available to prevent anxiety from getting out of hand. Freud proposed a set of such tools, a group of mental strategies known as ego-defense mechanisms, or simply defense mechanisms. Use of defense mechanisms is a normal part of human functioning, but when used to excess, they are a major source of neuroses as well. These mechanisms all have two essential features: they usually operate unconsciously, and they all reduce anxiety by distorting reality to some degree.

Repression: This term is sometimes referred to by Freud as "deliberate forgetting." In repression, thoughts and feelings that arouse anxiety are banished from consciousness. In one of his lectures at Clark University, Freud described repression, and its eventual consequences, by drawing an analogy to a disruptive audience member in the otherwise very polite crowd listening to him. Such a person would make it impossible to continue the lecture, and would therefore be forcibly removed from the lecture hall, and the door locked behind him. He is therefore repressed, and the audience members may block the door with furniture (resistance), but he may make an even greater fuss once he's outside, yelling and banging on the door. Freud's point is that anxiety-provoking thoughts and memories are never completely repressed, and they can only be made to stop disrupting the ego by being allowed back in during psychoanalysis, thus stripping them of their disruptive power. Repression is a basic mechanism underlying the other defense mechanisms, as they *all* serve the purpose of protecting the mind from unwelcome thoughts and impulses. The idea of repression has had a great, and often negative, influence in more recent times as the source of Western society's widespread belief in buried memories of trauma.

Regression: A person handles conflict by retreating to an earlier, more infantile state of development, as when a child reverts to thumb-sucking during the first few days of school. Freud explained regression as a flight from unsatisfying reality into an earlier phase of sexual development in which satisfaction was more easily obtained, along with a retreat to more primitive forms of self-expression as well. This second part can be seen clearly when an adult reacts to overwhelming stress by throwing a childlike tantrum.

Reaction formation: The ego unconsciously makes unacceptable impulses look like their opposites. This is often seen on school playgrounds, where information that one is liked by another child is often greeted by exaggerated revulsion. More formally, since instincts and drives can be arranged as pairs of opposing tendencies (life/death, dominance/submission, love/hate, etc.), the ego may handle anxiety-arousing emotions and impulses by facilitating the expression of their opposites. Reaction formation is in danger of becoming a sort of all-purpose explanatory mechanism, which has been used to explain everything from homophobia (a reaction to internal, hidden homosexual tendencies) to Stockholm syndrome (fear of captors is so overwhelming that hostages come to love them instead). The danger of relying too heavily on reaction formation as an explanation of behavior, of course, is that any behavior at all can be represented as actually revealing its opposite—a pacifist is actually hiding sadistic tendencies, the charitable worker is actually a misanthrope, and so forth.

Projection: Threatening, anxiety-provoking impulses are disguised by being attributed to others. The individual sees his or her fault very clearly—in someone else. The married man may deal with his own adulterous impulses by becoming convinced that his wife is cheating, for example. Projection especially appears to be a key mechanism in racism, in which impulses or wishes the individual finds completely unacceptable, shameful, or dangerous are attributed to members of another group to which he or she does not belong, where they can then be identified and condemned. Freud saw this as central to anti-Semitism and a central reason why racists so often see criminality and sexual immorality in the other. Carl Jung refined the idea of projection further, suggesting that every act of projection inevitably results in a *counterprojection*—in other words, when you imagine your dark impulses in someone else, he will come to see them clearly in you as well.

Rationalization: Whether it is being discussed by a philosopher as a common logical fallacy or by a psychoanalyst as a defense mechanism, the essential definition of *rationalization* is the same: self-justifying explanations for decisions, actions, or beliefs are generated to replace and conceal the actual path by which the person arrived there. Like all defense mechanisms, this process occurs unconsciously to protect the ego from the real reasons for its actions, as when the habitual heavy drinker says that he or she drinks just to be sociable. Rationalization is also regularly employed as a companion to *denial,* allowing a person to ignore evidence that a particular impulse or habit is harmful by focusing on other information instead. I once heard a daily cigar-smoker (whose wife had developed emphysema after smoking cigarettes for many years) insist that cigars are healthy, because George Burns smoked them daily and lived to the age of 100.

Denial: When a person is faced with information that is too shameful, uncomfortable, or unpleasant to accept, one way of handling the tension is to simply reject it outright, sometimes despite overwhelming evidence. Denial has had a long life beyond Sigmund Freud's original writings, starting with his daughter, Anna **Freud,** who saw denial as an immature defense mechanism that interferes with the crucial developmental process of learning from experience. Denial is probably the most frequently mentioned defense mechanism in American pop culture, partly because of its ubiquity in discussions of addiction—12 step programs typically begin with the step of recognizing the existence of a problem. Elisabeth Kübler-Ross made denial the first of her five steps in the confrontation of impending death by dying patients, which spread the idea further. As seen with reaction formation, there is a real danger that overuse of denial as an explanatory mechanism will simply lead to unfalsifiable (and therefore useless) hypotheses—anything the subject of the hypothesis says or does that seems to disprove the hypothesis can be interpreted as the subject being *in denial* rather than the hypothesis being wrong.

Displacement: Sexual or aggressive impulses toward a person who is an unacceptable target for those feelings are diverted onto a safer target. A man who is humiliated by his boss cannot express his rage directly, as it would get him fired, so he goes home and yells at his wife instead. The wronged spouse may then yell at a child (and may perhaps, via rationalization, believe she is legitimately punishing the child).

Sublimation: Sublimation is a process by which a socially forbidden, shameful, or otherwise unacceptable impulse finds a useful, socially acceptable means of expression without stigma, rather than continuing to be repressed. Freud saw this as primarily involving artistic expression, where sexual instinct was concerned—his most forthright statement of the role of sublimation comes in a paper he wrote in which he believed he had achieved a partial explanation of the genius of Leonardo da Vinci. Sublimation also helps people with powerful aggressive drives, however, who may find expression for their drives in competitive sports such as boxing and football.

Further Reading

Freud, A. (1937). *The Ego and the Mechanisms of Defence.* London: Hogarth Press and Institute of Psycho-Analysis.

Vaillant, G.E. (1992). *Ego Mechanisms of Defense: A Guide for Clinicians and Researchers.* Arlington, VA: American Psychiatric Publishing.

Dora (Ida Bauer) (1882–1945)

In 1905, five years after the publication of *The Interpretation of Dreams,* Freud published a brief case study of his unsuccessful treatment of a patient he called Dora, under the title "Fragment of an Analysis of a Case of Hysteria." This case was very important to Freud, as it appeared to him to provide confirmation of some of his ideas about dream analysis, at a time when *Interpretation* had not been well received and had sold poorly, as well as confirmation of the Oedipal dynamic that he viewed as central to human development. Additionally, the case appears to have been crucial to the development of the idea of transference and counter-transference, which he had not yet fully conceived. The case has been just as important to Freud's detractors over the years, however, as it seems just as clear to them that it provides evidence of Freud's tendency to overlook obvious, parsimonious explanations in favor of far more unlikely scenarios that supported his theory, as well as his ability to ignore social forces restricting women's roles, along with a wholehearted acceptance of Victorian social stereotypes regarding women.

Freud's exploration of Dora's difficulties began in 1900, when Dora's father brought the 18-year-old to Dr. Freud for consultation. Her father was well-known to Freud, who had treated him six years earlier for syphilis, which he had contracted many years earlier, prior to marrying Dora's mother. In the time since the treatment for syphilis, Freud had become well-acquainted with the man's family and had even met Dora two years earlier. Dora had for several years shown signs of what we would today call depression, and her father's decision to seek Freud's assistance followed his finding of an apparent suicide note, along with witnessing her sudden loss of consciousness following an argument a few days later.

These were not the first manifestations of her illness, however, as she actually had a long history of what appeared to be hysterical symptoms, beginning at around the age of six or seven. At that age she began to wet her bed, which went on for about a year. In later years, she had a chronic vaginal discharge—both symptoms were later determined by Freud to be caused by masturbation. When she was eight years old, she also developed a problem with shortness of breath, which today would probably be seen as asthma and/or an allergic problem. At the time, however, a family doctor diagnosed it as a nervous disorder, and Freud's later reconstruction of her history suggested that it began shortly after Dora gave up masturbation. Around age 12, Dora began to have migraine headaches and a nervous cough.

The migraines eventually cleared up, by around age 16, but the *tussis nervosa* continued periodically. It would begin with a complete loss of voice and last from three to five weeks, and no effective treatment for it had been found. At age 17, Dora experienced severe abdominal pain, which due to its location was diagnosed as appendicitis, but the next day a menstrual period began, accompanied by more severe pains—Freud would later call this a hysterical childbirth.

Before examining Freud's interpretations of the sources of Dora's problems, it may be helpful to examine her actual family circumstances, as they bear a powerful resemblance to the plot of a particularly lurid television soap opera. First, note again the aforementioned syphilis, which her father brought with him into the marriage, and which may have been passed along to his children—this alone would explain some of Dora's symptoms, but Freud appears to have ignored it as a possible factor. Second, note that the family was very close to another family, simply called K____ in Freud's writings, who figure quite prominently in Dora's problems. When Dora's father was sick with tuberculosis (when Dora was about six years old), the family moved to a small town in southern Austria, identified by Freud as B____, where they stayed for 11 years. There they met the K family. Frau K worked as a nurse with Dora's father, and meanwhile Herr K was kind and generous with Dora, taking her on frequent outings and buying her presents—in short, giving her the sort of attention that her father was incapable of providing. As Dora got older, she regularly took care of the K children, and became very close to Frau K.

When Dora was 16, she and her father traveled to the Alps to visit the vacationing K family. According to Dora, Herr K made sexual advances toward her after taking her alone to a lake. She was very offended and told her mother about the incident, after which her father confronted Herr K about the incident. Herr K of course denied everything, and suggested that Dora had been reading inappropriate books that had caused her to become obsessed with sex, which led her to imagine his proposition. This proposition was not the first—Dora told Freud that Herr K had also made advances on her at the age of 14, at which time he arranged to be alone with her and suddenly kissed her on the lips. For some time after that, she was careful to never be alone with him.

Meanwhile, it appears that both marriages were unhappy, and that Dora's father was having an affair with Frau K. As for Dora's mother, Freud appears to have heard only negative things about her from both her husband and her daughter, and describes her as an uncultivated and foolish woman who focused all her attention on domestic matters. He goes so far as to diagnose her with housewife's psychosis, and describes her as so concerned with keeping her home spotlessly clean that the family was unable to use or enjoy any of its furnishings. This is a remarkably negative and judgmental portrayal of a woman Freud does not appear to have ever met.

When Dora was brought to Freud for treatment, her father's goals in bringing her for psychoanalysis were clearly different from hers, and recovering her health was clearly not foremost in his mind. Her father blamed her depression, irritability, and suicidal tendencies on the incident with Herr K at the lake, as Dora had been begging him ever since to break off the affair with Frau K. Rather than acknowledging her feelings, he told Freud that breaking off the affair was out of the question, and asked him to help her to become reasonable. While Dora felt that she was being treated unjustly by the adults in her life, and wanted them to acknowledge both the affair and the incident at the lake, Freud agreed that her characterization of her father was accurate, writing "She had been handed over to Herr K as the price of his tolerating the relations between her father and his wife" (Fragment, p. 34). Nevertheless, Freud aligned himself with neither set of goals, hoping only to rid her of her various hysterical symptoms by helping her to acknowledge her unconscious fantasies and desires concerning her father and Frau and Herr K. Rather than seeing in her case the straightforward outrage and depression of a young woman who had been propositioned by her father's friend and ignored so that her father could continue an extramarital affair, Freud saw a perfect illustration of an unresolved Oedipal conflict. Since her recent symptoms and behaviors seemed to be oriented toward breaking up the affair, Freud suggests it would actually interfere with her therapy if he persuaded her father to break it off. Though he agrees that this would help Dora recover, Freud says it would be bad for her in the long run, as she would then have learned to use this powerful weapon in the future (her tendency toward poor health, that is) to get her way.

Given her initial resistance to psychoanalytic treatment, which she only attempted under pressure from her father, the short duration of Dora's time with Freud is unsurprising—after 11 weeks, she had endured his ignoring of the basic, superficial outlines of her problems for long enough. Rather than considering that a normal 14-year-old girl might genuinely be disgusted by a sexual advance by a man for whom she worked as a babysitter, Freud describes the kiss as follows:

> This was surely just the situation to call up a distinct feeling of sexual excitement in a girl of 14 who had never before been approached. In this scene, the behaviour of this child of 14 was already entirely and completely hysterical. Instead of the genital sensation would certainly have been felt by a healthy girl in such circumstances, Dora was overcome by disgust. (Fragment, pp. 28–29)

He goes on to describe the real source of the disgust as the displacement of her feelings of excitement at feeling his erect penis against her as they embraced.

Rather than confirming that the incident at the lake occurred, Freud goes on to suggest that what she described there is a fantasy as well, revealing complex passionate feelings for Herr K, her own father, and Frau K; what Peter Gay describes as feelings of "puppy love, incest and lesbian desires . . . competing for pre-eminence in her adolescent mind" (1988, p. 249). Further support for the idea that some of Dora's problems stem from unresolved Oedipal feelings comes from the dynamics of the rest of the family: where Dora was hostile toward her mother and took her father's side in the ongoing conflict between them, her brother Otto was hostile toward his father and always sided with his mother. Clearly neither sibling has resolved his or her sexual feelings toward the opposite-sex parent by identifying more closely with the same-sex parent, and this has resulted in neuroses—Freud felt that he had found an excellent illustration of that portion of his theory in this family.

Freud's interpretations of Dora's feelings have their basis largely in his interpretations of two of her dreams, which he saw as excellent examples of the utility of dream analysis. In the first dream, Dora is awakened at night by her father, because the house is on fire. Her mother wishes to save a small jewelry box, over the objections of her father, who is trying to save the children instead. In Freudian dream interpretation, of course, the surface, *manifest* content of the dream is less important than the symbolic *latent* content, and the jewelry box became an important symbol to Freud. When he asked Dora about associations she might make with a jewelry box, she revealed that Herr K once gave her a fairly expensive jewelry box. To Freud, the jewelry box, or *schmuckkästchen,* represents the female genitalia. Her father, the man entering her room to take the jewelry box, actually represents Herr K, and she is prepared to give up her jewelry box to him, giving him what his wife refuses. Also, in the dream the fire was put out—Freud described this as a reference to masturbation and Dora's attempts to repress it, due to its association with her bed-wetting as a child. Many of the elements of the dream represent their opposites (her father as Herr K, his coming in to get the box rather than her offering it freely) because the impulse is deeply repressed. She is reawakening her old love for her father to protect her from the real impulse. Freud suggests that Dora is more afraid of this truth (her desire to be sexually involved with Herr K) than she is of his actual advances, thus making her hysteria a reaction to her repression of her own sexual desires, rather than her actual disgust at his actions and intentions. Freud was not surprised that Dora resisted this interpretation of her dream, which he took as confirmation that he was correct.

Dora's resistance to Freud's interpretations intensified with his interpretation of a second dream, following which she terminated treatment. In the dream, Dora is in a strange town when she receives a letter from her mother informing her that her father has died. She has difficulty reaching the train station, as a consequence of which she is late to the cemetery for her father's funeral. In Freud's remarkably complex interpretation of this dream, the railway station and the cemetery both become additional symbolic representations of the female genitalia, and he concludes that the dream is a fantasy of the loss of virginity via forced seduction. Once again, the dream is interpreted in terms of Dora's unconscious love for Herr K. At the very next session following Freud's presentation of this interpretation, Dora announced that she would not be returning.

Freud eventually learned a lot from Dora's departure, which would lead to some important refinements in psychoanalytic practice. Freud had not yet perfected the concept of *transference,* for example, but its genesis in Dora's case is clear—Freud interpreted her refusal to return to him for further treatment as an act of revenge, handling her hostility toward him by denying him the opportunity to cure her. This attitude was echoed by some of his followers, most notably Ernest Jones, who described her as "a disagreeable creature who consistently put revenge before love; it was the same motive that led her to break off treatment prematurely" (Jones, 1955, p. 256). It was only later understood by Freud as an expression of her hostility toward her father, which was transferred onto her therapist. He also failed until later to recognize his own *countertransference,* the result of which was that his own reactions to Dora's hostility and her interpretations of her own motivations prevented him from seeing clearly all the relevant factors in her hysteria. Both ideas, transference and countertransference, were still poorly understood by Freud at the time of Dora's treatment and became far more central to psychoanalytic thought as a result of this case. Another important thing that Freud learned from this case, which he wrote about quite plainly, was that his interpretations needed to be presented to patients slowly and carefully—perhaps Dora would not have been so resistant to Freud's analysis if he hadn't been so insistent about ideas that, by his own admission, were so unacceptable to her that she had deeply repressed them. The remaining major insight Freud took away from this case, which he only wrote about explicitly much later, in a 1937 paper, was that psychoanalysts must carefully avoid putting their patients in the no-win situation of always being wrong. In that 1937 paper, he wrote, "If the patient agrees with us, then [we are] right, but if he contradicts us, then that is only a sign of his resistance, which again puts us in the right." In that paper, he acknowledges that this is a stereotypical portrayal of psychoanalysis (he even quotes the English saying "Heads I win, tails you lose" in making the point) and warns that this approach is an abuse of authority—without openly acknowledging the extent to which that was his approach with early cases like Dora, however.

On April 1, 1902, Dora visited with Freud one more time, apparently to seek help once again. This time, she was experiencing facial neuralgia, but Freud was unconvinced of her sincerity (oddly, given her symptoms, he was moved to this decision by her facial expression) and declined to resume treatment. In this same visit, she reported that she had been feeling much better, in part because she had confronted both Frau and Herr K and had received satisfactory confessions from both of them. This knowledge did not affect Freud's interpretations of Dora's accounts as representative of her fantasies, however, and Freud describes this encounter as important primarily because it allowed him to forgive Dora for depriving him of the opportunity to cure her.

Although it is a record of a case in which he failed to effect a cure, the Dora case study was important enough to Freud to publish, as he viewed his analysis of this young woman as providing support for important elements of his theory. Much of the criticism of this case study in the intervening century has focused, consequently, on his emphasis on research in this case at the expense of actually providing therapy—he may have been so caught up in confirming the ideas in his recent, poorly received *Interpretation of Dreams* that he was insufficiently sensitive to the needs of the young woman in front of him. This criticism was most cogently made by Erik **Erikson,** though he wrote it in 1964, with the benefit of six decades of hindsight. According to Erikson, the primary developmental crisis of adolescence is the establishment of one's own identity as an individual distinct from one's parents, a development that requires supportive and loving adults who can serve as role models and examples, as well as targets of rebellion. As an 18-year-old, Dora was working out her relationship to the adult world and her place in it. According to Erikson, adolescents are typified by their concern for the truth, as they are developing the capacity to pledge loyalty and fidelity to people or causes. The adults in Dora's life betrayed her and then lied about the betrayal. By so clearly siding with the adults who made Dora feel threatened and insecure, and interpreting the entire situation in terms of her own fragile sexual development, Erikson says that Freud overlooked this central need, and was thus incapable of providing the help that Dora needed.

As for Dora herself, she became aware of the article when it was published in 1905, and according to some sources, was pleased to have appeared in the psychoanalytic literature as a famous patient. Far from protecting her identity, she would brag about her status from time to time.

Further Reading

Decker, H. (1981). Freud and Dora: Constraints on Medical Progress. *Journal of Social History* 14(3): 445–464.

Erikson, E. (1994/1964). *Insight and Responsibility*. New York: W. W. Norton.

Freud, S. (1937/1989). Constructions in Analysis. *The Standard Edition of the Complete Psychological Works of Sigmund Freud, Volume XXIII (1937-1939)*. New York: W. W. Norton.

Freud, S. (1963/1905). *An Analysis of a Case of Hysteria*. New York: Collier Books.

Gay, P. (1988). *Freud: A Life for Our Time*. New York: W. W. Norton.

Jones, E. (1955). *The Life and Work of Sigmund Freud*. Vol. 2. New York: Basic Books.

Ego. *See* Id, Ego, and Superego

Erikson, Erik (1902–1994)

Erik Erikson, one of the most influential psychoanalysts other than Sigmund Freud himself, is often described as the father of life span developmental psychology, as he was the first psychologist to propose a theory that followed development throughout life, rather than treating everything beyond adolescence as a single stage (as did Freud and Jean Piaget). As Erikson was a Freudian ego psychologist, implying that he accepted Sigmund Freud's ideas as essentially correct, the first few stages of his developmental model map quite neatly onto Freud's *stages of psychosexual development.* Rather than focus on the instincts and unconscious conflicts over sexuality, however, Erikson was much more interested in the relationships between the individual and society and culture, and how these relationships influence the development of identity.

Like many prominent psychoanalytic thinkers, Erikson became interested in pursuing psychoanalysis as a profession after undergoing psychoanalysis himself. While teaching the arts at a Vienna private school, he made the acquaintance of Anna **Freud,** and went on to be trained by her after experiencing psychoanalysis firsthand. Early on in his practice, Erikson realized that Freud's description of child development was flawed, in that it failed to recognize the continuation of ego development throughout adulthood—Freud proposed that development of the self occurs in a series of stages, but the final stage begins in adolescence. Erikson refined and expanded on all previous stage theories by recognizing that psychological development does not stop at age 12 or 13. Erikson instead proposed eight separate stages, extending from birth to old age. According to Erikson, everyone proceeds through the stages in a universal and invariant sequence; the timing may vary, but everyone goes through them in the same order.

At each stage, a developmental crisis must be resolved, and success or failure in that resolution will influence what occurs in the later stages—this is of course very similar to Freud's description of the psychosexual stages. Erikson's stage descriptions abandon Freud's focus on sensual experience, to emphasize instead what must be achieved. Each stage is named by indicating both what must be learned in that stage and what the result of not learning it will be. If a stage is managed properly, in other words, a certain virtue or psychological strength will be carried away from it, which will help in later stages. Failure to resolve the crisis in a particular stage, on the other hand, will lead to a weakness or maladaptation that will endanger

Erik Erikson, pioneer of life span developmental psychology, photographed in his study in 1975. (Ted Streshinsky/Time Life Pictures/Getty Images)

a person's progress in all later stages (essentially the same idea as a *fixation* in Freud's model). The infant's task, for example, is known as *trust versus mistrust*: in this stage the child will either learn to mostly trust people and circumstances or instead become untrusting.

The various stages are as follows (age ranges, especially in adulthood, are just approximations and can vary dramatically):

1. **Age 0–1 (infancy). Trust versus Mistrust:** The task is to develop trust without completely losing the capacity for mistrust; to be completely trusting could be maladaptive and lead to being taken advantage of by others. It is up to the parents to help the infant to develop the feeling that the world is a safe place to be, and that people are reliable. If the parents are unreliable or neglectful, or if they reject or harm the child, then the result will be mistrust: the infant will become anxious and suspicious of people. The resulting social withdrawal could eventually result in depression or even psychosis. Note, however, that Erikson also believed that parents who were overprotective could also cause harm, by producing an overly trusting, gullible child. This stage corresponds to Freud's *oral* stage, with its focus on children trusting parents to fill their food needs.

2. **Age 2–3 (toddler). Autonomy versus Shame and Doubt:** If parents and caregivers permit the toddler to explore and act on his or her environment, the child will develop a sense of autonomy and independence. If the parents are discouraging of the child's attempts to explore, however, the child may feel incapable of acting on his or her own, or will feel ashamed of having tried to do so. Giving children either too much help rather than letting them learn to do it themselves or unrestricted freedom to try things for themselves can result in their thinking too little of their own capabilities or believing themselves capable of anything, and developing no shame and doubt at all. This

stage corresponds to Freud's *anal* stage, with its focus on the child developing a sense of autonomy or control over defecation.

3. **Age 3–6 (preschool). Initiative versus Guilt:** Initiative is simply feeling purposeful and able to try out new skills and responsibilities. Parents should encourage children to try out their ideas and use their imaginations. At this stage, the children are also able to begin imagining the consequences of their actions, however, and so the capacity for guilt also appears. As with other stages, the goal is to develop a proper amount of guilt rather than either an excess or too little. Since Erikson is a Freudian, and this stage corresponds to the *phallic* stage in Freud's model, he also considers the role of the Oedipal conflict in this stage. In Erikson's view, the Oedipal crisis involves the child's reluctance to give up his or her closeness to the opposite-sex parent. The parent's responsibility is to encourage the child to become more mature but not too harshly because if it is done improperly, the child learns to feel guilty about those feelings. Too much initiative and too little guilt produces ruthlessness—the person has the initiative to pursue goals, but doesn't care about the consequences for anyone else. Left unchecked, this tendency can eventually develop into sociopathic behavior. Too much guilt and too little initiative results in a person so inhibited that he or she will not try new things. On the sexual front, due to the Oedipal conflict, the child who emerges from this stage with excessive guilt may grow up to be incapable of achieving sexual satisfaction.

4. **Age 7–12 (school age). Industry versus Inferiority:** Here the key players include teachers and peers, not just parents. Depending on the encouragement and acceptance provided by each key player, the child will either learn to enjoy the feeling of success, and thus become more industrious, or will instead develop feelings of inferiority or incompetence. Erikson consistently sees too much of a good thing as bad, and industry is no exception. Children with too much industry develop a maladaptive tendency called narrow virtuosity. These are children who have been pushed hard into a single area of competence, without being allowed to develop other interests or even to just be a kid. According to Erikson, this is frequently seen in prodigies. This stage is Freud's *latency* stage, in which the emphasis on sensual pleasure disappears for a few years while the child concentrates on scholastic pursuits.

5. **Age 12–18 (adolescence). Ego-Identity versus Role Confusion:** This is probably the best known of Erikson's stages, as the phrase "identity crisis" has since passed into common usage. The adolescent's task is to achieve ego-identity, which is nothing less than deciding who or what kind of person he or she really is and how he or she will fit into the rest of society. The adults' role

is to provide a society and role models worthy of respect. Erikson especially emphasized the importance of rites of passage in providing a clear demarcation line between childhood and adulthood. In a society that does not clearly provide these, the result may be uncertainty about one's place in the world, which Erikson saw as related to the high rate of suicide among teens. Some adolescents deal with the identity crisis by taking a *psychosocial moratorium,* a break from growing up. This could be taking a year off to work before going to college, for example, or traveling for a summer before getting a job or going to school. Erikson thought this was healthy, since too many young people in modern society become obsessed with achieving success before they have adequately identified what would actually constitute success. As with other virtues, however, there is such a thing as too much identity. Some people become so involved with a particular role or a particular subculture that they become very intolerant of everyone else. This is fanaticism. Worse is the lack of identity, however: some adolescents repudiate their need for identity and their membership in the world of adults, taking refuge in a group that will provide the identity for them, such as gangs, religious cults, hate groups, and so forth. Note that Erikson sees a lot more going on in the adolescent's development than Freud proposed in his clearly labeled *genital* stage. Where Freud focused on the importance of childhood experiences, going no further in his description of development, Erikson's stages keep going.

6. **Late teens–about 30 (young adulthood). Intimacy versus Isolation:** The task here is to find intimacy with another person to spend the rest of life with, rather than remaining in isolation. The ability to do this is heavily influenced by the results of the prior stage: if someone has no clear sense of who they are, it is difficult to achieve intimacy with someone else. Too much intimacy— becoming intimate too freely and easily—results in promiscuity, in which relationships with others remain very shallow. Too little intimacy results in exclusion, which can result in developing hatefulness as a way of dealing with loneliness. Successful negotiation of this stage will of course result in love, here defined as "mutuality of devotion," by which Erikson refers not just to marital love but also to friendship and good relationships with coworkers.

7. **Late 20s–early 50s (middle adulthood). Generativity versus Self-Absorption:** This is the period during which people are actively raising children as well as pursuing careers. Generativity refers to the extension of love into the future by the things done today. This can be achieved by raising children well; or via teaching, art, social activism, music, or anything that may contribute to the welfare of future generations. Insufficient generativity leads to extreme self-absorption or stagnation. The stagnant person is no longer a productive member of society. It is at this stage that a midlife crisis may arise,

in which the person looks around at his or her life and wonders about the purpose of it all. If he or she has not accomplished enough in life, there may be a misguided attempt to recapture one's youth. The person who is sufficiently generative, however, can usually weather such a crisis. Too much generativity causes a person to become overextended by trying too hard to be generative, leaving no time for rest and relaxation.

8. **50s and beyond (older adulthood). Integrity versus Despair:** The last stage begins around the age of retirement, after the children have moved away to pursue their own adult lives. The task is to develop ego integrity without an excess of despair. At this age, people may come to feel less useful and more detached from society, accompanied by an increasing sense of biological obsolescence, as the body is no longer capable of all the things that it used to do. With the coming of menopause, this can be an especially trying time for women. There are also fears of things that were not so frightening at younger ages: simply falling down can now be especially dangerous, for example. In addition to greater fear of illness (concerns about diabetes, heart disease, and various cancers are inevitably greater than they used to be), death becomes more familiar as others of the same generation begin to die. A certain amount of despair is to be expected, but too much can lead to paranoia, depression, hypochondriasis, and a preoccupation with regrets of the past. Being able to look back and come to terms with the life lived and the choices made, and thus become less fearful of death, is to achieve ego integrity; and Erikson defines wisdom as the ability to face death without fear.

Erikson in many ways embodied the crises about which he wrote. Take the matter of his identity, for example: Born in Germany to a Danish mother in1902, his name growing up was Erik Homburger. He never knew his biological father, who left before Erik was born. His mother subsequently married Dr. Homburger, who had treated her during her pregnancy. Erikson was part Jewish, but his appearance, blonde hair, blue eyes, was very Nordic, and so he had a difficult time fitting into either subculture in the Germany of the early 20th century. After training in psychoanalysis with Anna Freud, he emigrated to the United States, where he took the opportunity to rename himself. The message buried in that new name is difficult to interpret, but Erikson translates as "son of Erik," suggesting he considered himself solely responsible for his identity, having overcome the influence of his parents.

His emigration to the United States was partly a result of larger historical forces: the **Nazis** had just come to power in Germany as Erikson graduated from the Vienna Psychoanalytical Institute in Vienna, in 1933. Erikson and his wife fled first to Denmark, and then to the United States, where they settled first in Boston. As Boston's very first child psychoanalyst, Erikson established himself as an in-demand clinician through his work at the Judge Baker Guidance Center. Named for Judge Harvey Humphrey Baker, a juvenile court judge who oversaw a shift in juvenile justice away from simple punishment and toward treatment and rehabilitation, the center is still in operation today as the Judge Baker Children's Center. Erikson was very busy during this period, also working in positions at Harvard Medical School and Massachusetts General Hospital.

In 1936, he left Boston for New Haven, working at Yale's Institute of Human Relations and teaching in the School of Medicine. This was followed by a year observing children on a Sioux reservation in South Dakota, after which he took a position at the University of California at Berkeley. Erikson temporarily left the academic world behind in 1950, at the height of the Congressional persecution of suspected communists, when he refused to sign a loyalty oath. In the 1960s, when that particular political fashion had faded, he returned to Harvard as a professor of human development and remained there until his retirement in 1970, at which time he appears to have experienced the rest of his life, as his own theory would have it, with a sense of integrity rather than despair.

Further Reading

Erikson, E. H. (1994). *Identity and the Life Cycle.* New York: W. W. Norton.

Eugenics

To modern readers, there is little in the history of American ideas that is quite as shocking as the huge popularity of eugenics among the educated classes during the first half of the 20th century. The term *eugenics* was introduced in 1883, along with the idea it represents, by the British naturalist and mathematician Francis Galton, and defined as "the study of the agencies under social control that may improve or impair the racial qualities of future generations, either physically or mentally" (Galton, 1883, p. 17). This lofty definition was toned down by Charles B. Davenport, one of the leading American advocates of eugenics, who defined it more bluntly as "the science of the improvement of the human race by better breeding" (1911, p. 1). The idea of improving the human species through selective breeding, much like breeders of race horses increase the speed of their animals by selecting only the fastest animals for stud duty, failed to catch on in Galton's homeland, but found a ready reception in America.

Francis Galton (1822–1911)

It is unfortunate that Galton is most notorious today for his creation of eugenics, for his influence on modern psychology, and on scientific inquiry in general, is difficult to estimate, given the sheer scope of his intellectual pursuits and innovations. Galton was fascinated by modern science in general, but especially in the possibilities afforded by the human ability to find a way to measure almost anything. His research, discoveries, and inventions include the entire field of modern meteorology, for example, as he discovered, and indeed invented the very idea of, high- and low-pressure systems and cold and warm fronts, along with inventing the weather map to depict their movements. He is also credited with the idea of using fingerprints to identify perpetrators of crimes, along with a variety of statistical ideas and techniques, including correlation analysis and the normal distribution (also known as the bell curve). He also conducted the earliest survey research, invented the word association technique, conducted the first twin studies to examine the interaction of heredity and environment, and introduced the use of the terms "nature" and "nurture" to distinguish between their influences. Probably his biggest influence on the modern world, however, was the invention of the idea of mental testing. Like many scientists in 19th-century Europe, Galton was fascinated by the advances that had been made in the physical sciences, especially regarding new means of objectively and precisely measuring natural phenomena, and he set out to find ways to measure human traits just as precisely as other natural phenomena were being measured. He was influenced in this regard by an idea that was quite widespread among 19th-century scientists confronted by their growing awareness of non-European, non-Christian, and occasionally nonwhite people: that surely these people were inferior to white European men, and there must be ways of demonstrating this scientifically.

Galton set out to collect as much information as he could on human variability, taking advantage of a large international fair in London to collect data on a scale that had not previously been attempted. At the 1884 International Health Exposition in London, visitors to Galton's Anthropometric Laboratory paid three pence each to be tested and measured for 13 separate characteristics: reaction time, keenness of sight and hearing, height, weight, color discrimination, ability to judge length of a line segment, strength of pull and of hand squeeze, strength of blow, arm span, breathing power, and breathing capacity. More than 9,000 visitors were tested, and the exhibit proved so popular that it was installed in the South Kensington museum for an additional six years, eventually generating raw data on more than 17,000 people. This enormous data set allowed the calculations that led to the aforementioned statistical discoveries, including the normal distribution, one of the most important concepts in modern intelligence testing. Examining his data, Galton discovered that with a large enough number of scores (and 17,000 is a *much* larger sample than is usually gathered for any scientific study), no matter what was being measured, the data would form a roughly symmetrical, bell-shaped distribution, with most scores clustered around the mean and fewer and fewer scores appearing toward either end. This observation became a fact of vital importance in statistical analysis and in the design and scoring of psychological tests of all types, but especially intelligence tests.

A 1903 portrait of Sir Francis Galton, painted by Charles Wellington Furse. (Library of Congress)

Indeed, though Galton's subjects were unaware of it, they had participated in a trial of the very first intelligence test battery. While a modern observer would not recognize the list of tasks given previously as measures of intelligence, they reflect Galton's understanding of intelligence quite well. He believed that people of higher intelligence had faster reactions, keener senses, greater strength, and better health, and that it ought to be possible to measure intelligence indirectly by measuring these physical traits. He also believed that intelligence was entirely inherited, as he argued in the book *Hereditary Genius.*

His method was to examine the genealogy of 286 English judges. He found that about one in nine was the father, son, or brother of another judge, and that the judges were also related to many other eminent men than were members of the general population. Galton also rather egotistically found evidence to support this idea within his own family, as Charles Darwin was his cousin, and clearly both Darwin and himself qualified as geniuses. Failing to consider any environmental explanations or even such simple factors as nepotism, inherited wealth, and the rigidity of the English class system, Galton concluded that he had proven his thesis that men's abilities are derived entirely from heredity. From this research, he generated the idea of eugenics, inspired by his cousin.

Charles Darwin's ideas about natural selection and survival of the fittest fascinated Galton. He became convinced that many of humanity's social problems were the result of the irresponsible activities of the least intelligent, and that it might be possible to improve the human species through selective breeding, in much the same way that animal breeders had selectively bred dogs to favor certain desirable traits. Galton argued that if the most fit, that is to say, intelligent, members of the species reproduce together, the general level of human intelligence will be raised, thus eventually eliminating the many social problems (crime, poverty, feeblemindedness, alcoholism, rebelliousness, general immorality, etc.) brought about by those of low intelligence.

Eugenics in America—Henry Goddard

Galton's idea took hold in the United States in a big way, where others took the concept considerably further than Galton ever intended. Where Goddard advocated a somewhat utopian approach that emphasized encouraging the most fit to produce more children, he never explicitly advocated the active *prevention* of reproduction among the unfit, though that was clearly the logical next step if he was correct, and it was a step some of his American apostles were willing and eager to take.

One of the first to publicly advocate eugenic ideas in the United States was Henry H. Goddard, director of research at the Vineland Training School for Feebleminded Girls and Boys in New Jersey. In working with the feebleminded, who would today be classified as people with mental retardation, he became convinced that the real danger to our society came not from the institutionalized population with which he worked, but rather from the higher-functioning individuals who had not yet been identified and separated from the rest of us, and were therefore free to wreak havoc in the outside world. The institutionalized population was mostly divided into two categories, idiots and imbeciles, which were readily identifiable by professionals because of the severity of their affliction. Far more threatening were the high-grade defectives who could function in society and were far more difficult to identify. Goddard coined a new term for these people, a word that would eventually join "idiot" and "imbecile" among the now-discarded technical terms that eventually became colloquial insults: he called them "morons," from a Greek word meaning "foolish."

Goddard saw the morons as a very real menace, because of his broad acceptance of Galton's notion that low intelligence underlies all societal troubles. Around 1900, Mendel's genetic experiments with pea plants were rediscovered by the scientific community and became widely known, and provided Goddard and others like him with a plausible, though very simplistic, scientific mechanism with which to underpin their prejudices: intelligence is determined by a single gene with dominant and recessive variants, just like the smoothness of the outer membrane of a pea! In 1920, Goddard expressed his central idea in this way:

> Stated in its boldest form, our thesis is that the chief determiner of human conduct is a unitary mental process which we call intelligence: that this process is conditioned by a nervous mechanism which is inborn; that the degree of efficiency to be attained by that nervous mechanism and the consequent grade of intellectual or mental level for each individual is determined by the kind of chromosomes that come together with the union of the germ cells: that it is but little affected by any later influences except such serious accident as may destroy part of the mechanism. (Cited in Gould, 1996, p. 190)

Here Goddard indicates that intelligence is a single unitary ability that underlies all other human activity, along with the idea that, as a genetically based trait, it is largely immune to any environmental influence. Both of these would become central ideas in the American eugenics movement, helped along by Goddard's contagious conviction that he had found a way to easily and objectively measure this simple genetic trait, using the newly developed intelligence tests.

When Alfred Binet published the first modern intelligence test, in 1905, he had developed the test with a very specific goal in mind: helping school authorities to identify students who might require, and benefit from, special assistance in the classroom. Binet did not call it an intelligence test, and he did not intend for any purpose except to identify people in order to better help them. Goddard was immediately enthusiastic about the test, however, which he regarded as a useful way to measure the single, innate entity (intelligence), which he saw as the underlying cause of the deterioration of American society. Goddard was the first translator into

English of the Binet test, as well as the first to apply it to institutionalized populations and agitate for its general use with the American public in order to identify the morons. The purpose of such testing was made very clear by Goddard, as the implications of a single-gene explanation of intelligence were obvious to him:

> If both parents are feeble-minded, all the children will be feeble-minded. It is obvious that such matings should not be allowed. It is perfectly clear that no feeble-minded person should ever be allowed to marry or to become a parent. It is obvious that if this rule is to be carried out the intelligent part of society must enforce it. (Goddard, 1914, p. 561)

This passage is one of the earliest to appear in print explicitly advocating what would become known as negative eugenics, to distinguish it from Galton's positive eugenics. In advocating the active prevention of breeding among the morons, Goddard made clear that simply preventing marriages was not sufficient:

> They are not only lacking in control but they are lacking often in the perception of moral qualities; if they are not allowed to marry they are nevertheless not hindered from becoming parents. So that if we are absolutely to prevent a feeble minded person from becoming a parent, something must be done other than merely prohibiting the marrying. To this end there are two proposals: the first is colonization, the second is sterilization. (1914, p. 566)

Though he did not object to the idea of sterilization, Goddard viewed it as an impractical solution because the rest of society was not yet sufficiently enlightened and rational to embrace such action, and might be horrified by it. Instead, he favored concentrating the feebleminded in institutional settings like his own school at Vineland, where they could be given work appropriate to their intellectual abilities and live happy lives, deprived only of the opportunity to exercise their biological urges. Building the number of colonies that would be necessary to implement this solution would of course be hugely expensive, but Goddard justified the expense by arguing that the money saved in annual losses of property and life, since the criminal element would all be locked up, would be more than enough to offset the cost.

Having identified the cause of feeblemindedness as a single gene, however, Goddard saw a second step as necessary to save the American gene pool from itself: in addition to preventing the native morons from reproducing, it was important to keep new feebleminded immigrants from entering the country in the first place. In the wake of the Industrial Revolution, immigrants had flowed into the American cities in large numbers, bringing with them the problems that always appear in overcrowded cities, including increased crime. To men like Goddard, the trouble in the cities was a result not of overcrowding but of the influx of many new feebleminded people. In order to help with the problem, Goddard and his associates traveled to Ellis Island, where most new immigrants from Europe were processed, and proceeded to administer the Binet test to a select sample of immigrants. Through interpreters, Goddard's idiosyncratic English version of a test originally written in French was translated on the fly, by people with no experience at all with the test, into the native languages of immigrants from various non-English-speaking countries. This created obvious problems that Goddard appears to have gone out of his way to ignore, as in his description of the very first test subject:

> We picked out one young man whom we suspected was defective, and, through the interpreter, proceeded to give him the test. The boy tested 8 [mental age] by the Binet scale. The interpreter said, "I could not have done that when I came to this country," and seemed to think the test unfair. *We convinced him* [my italics] that the boy was defective. (1913, p. 105)

Note that the boy was selected for testing because Goddard and his associates believed that he *looked* feebleminded—Goddard was convinced that people with experience in the field could easily spot the morons from a distance, even when there were no signs that were apparent to anyone else.

Eventually Goddard and his female associates (for he believed that women were better at spotting the feebleminded than men) tested 35 Jews (of unspecified nationality), 22 Hungarians, 50 Italians, and 45 Russians. In selecting them, Goddard indicates that they "passed by the obviously normal. That left us the great mass of 'average immigrants'" (1917, p. 244). According to the test, which Goddard continued to view as valid even when given in real-time translation to people from very different cultures, who had just emerged from a long and arduous ocean voyage, 83 percent of the Jews, 80 percent of the Hungarians, 79 percent of the Italians, and 87 percent of the Russians were feebleminded. This means that these immigrants, all of them adults, scored at a mental age of 12 or lower on the Binet scale. Rather than recognizing that the test was clearly not valid when given under such circumstances, however, Goddard refused to acknowledge any possibility of environmental influences having affected the outcome, instead arguing that the current crop of immigrants were of surprisingly low intelligence. The high proportion of morons simply indicated that, whereas previous waves of immigration had been more representative of the overall population distribution of intelligence, by the time he began testing America had begun receiving only the lowest-quality immigrants instead. He did briefly note a fact that should have influenced his conclusions, however: he only tested third-class passengers, who were mostly poor and illiterate, whereas the upper-deck passengers were never examined. Based largely on Goddard's success in convincing others of the validity of his test, deportations for mental deficiency increased by 350 percent in 1913 and 570 percent in 1914 as compared to the average of the previous five years.

Goddard's translation of the Binet test was not his only tool in convincing Americans of the reality of the menace of the feebleminded, however. Prior to his work on Ellis Island, he had already provided what was widely regarded as scientific proof of the heritability of both high and low intelligence with his study of the Kallikak family. Beginning with a young woman who was institutionalized at Vineland, Goddard decided to trace her family lineage back a number of generations in order to demonstrate the source of her feeblemindedness. What his research allegedly uncovered was an apparently unbroken line of poor, illiterate, "defective" individuals, "all the worst sorts of humanity," which could be traced back to the illicit union of a revolutionary war soldier and an allegedly feebleminded tavern waitress. The same man later married a "worthy Quakeress" and started another family lineage made up entirely of upstanding citizens—in Goddard's book about the family, these lineages are illustrated with pedigree charts similar to the ones that usually accompany the purchase of a purebred dog. Since the ancestor had sired both a good and a bad line, Goddard combined the Greek words for those two characteristics, *kallos* and *kakos,* and gave the ancestor the pseudonym Martin Kallikak.

The most interesting question raised by the Kallikak study is probably this: How was Goddard able to demonstrate feeblemindedness in the relatives, living and dead, of his pseudonymous charge Deborah Kallikak? The answer is as simple as it is revealing of the flaws in his methods: he wasn't. Even with the living relatives, no Binet tests were administered. Instead, his method consisted of dispatching women trained to recognize the feebleminded on sight, to the New Jersey Pine Barrens to observe the patient's relatives. Several of them were identified on the sole basis of possessing

> the unmistakable look of the feeble-minded. The whole family was a living demonstration of the futility of trying to make desirable citizens from defective stock through making and enforcing compulsory education laws. . . . The father himself, though strong and vigorous, showed by his face that he had only a child's mentality. . . . In this house of abject poverty, only one sure prospect was ahead, that it would produce more feeble-minded children with which to clog the wheels of human progress. (Goddard, 1913, pp. 77–78)

Keeping in mind that Goddard traced the Kallikak history back more than a century, the methods used to evaluate the intelligence of the sometimes long deceased are even less rigorous than those used to evaluate the living. Goddard's conclusions were based on second- or third-hand descriptions of family members, often by people who were not even born yet when the person being described passed away, and inferring the necessary information in that way. Some town records were consulted, as were family records, including family Bibles. While it is true that many family Bibles include pages on which to record marriages, baptisms, and other religious milestones, however, such books do not generally include a record of substance abuse problems, criminal convictions, and other evidence of either poor moral character or low intelligence. Goddard's early work was quite influential despite its clear methodological weaknesses, however, and laid the groundwork for a far more organized effort among American advocates of eugenics.

Eugenics in America: The Eugenics Record Office

At about the same time that Goddard was misusing intelligence tests and family records, other eugenically minded scientists had found a more scientific tool to use, with the rediscovery of Mendel's laws of heredity in 1900. Gregor Mendel (1822–1884) was an Augustinian monk and science teacher, whose experiments on the inheritance of skin texture in peas are now a standard part of every high school biology program. At the time that he conducted the experiments, however, they remained largely unknown, despite their potential for providing support for Darwin's 1865 breakthrough in evolutionary biology. It was only after his work was independently replicated at the turn of the century that he received posthumous recognition for his accomplishments. What Mendel had discovered was that certain simple traits, such as whether the skin of a pea is wrinkled or smooth, are passed along by genetic material from both parents, with each parent contributing either a dominant or a recessive version of the gene. If either parent contributes the dominant version, the dominant version of the trait will be expressed; for the recessive version of the trait to be present, both parents must contribute the recessive form of the gene.

By 1910, most biologists in America recognized that Mendel's theory could be applied to all organisms that reproduce sexually, including human beings, and the scientific community pursued simple Mendelian models of heredity with great enthusiasm, attempting to demonstrate dominant/recessive patterns in the distribution of as many different simple traits as possible. Between 1900 and 1910, geneticists were able to demonstrate that several human traits follow the strict Mendelian model of inheritance, including red-green color blindness, blood type, polydactyly (presence of extra fingers and toes), as well as several hereditary metabolic disorders. The sudden availability of what appeared to be a predictive and experimentally testable concept of heredity was very exciting to the American eugenicists, as it appeared to arm them with a powerful analytical tool by which to verify their prejudices. Using pedigree analyses like those Goddard had gathered on the Kallikak clan, eugenicists in the United States began to study a wide range of physical, mental, and moral traits in humans, with the goal of demonstrating that these more complex phenomena could be explained according to a similar mechanism to that governing eye color.

In order for eugenics to become a dominant perspective, however, the eugenicists needed to mount a far more coordinated effort than they had managed thus far. That coordination arrived in earnest with the 1910 establishment of the Eugenics Record Office at Cold Spring Harbor on Long Island, under the direction of Charles B. Davenport. The Eugenics Record Office (henceforth ERO) was founded as a subdivision of the already established, and more scientific-sounding, Station for the Experimental Study of Evolution (SEE). The ERO and SEE provided the eugenics movement with two crucial things: the appearance of genuine scientific credentials and an institutional base for the coordination of eugenic efforts both in the United States and abroad. The ERO quickly became a clearinghouse for eugenics information and propaganda, a storage facility for eugenics records, a meeting place for the international community of eugenicists, and the home of several eugenic publications. The ERO was not the only important eugenics advocacy group in the country—an important role in the movement's growth and public acceptance was also played by the American Breeders' Association, whose Eugenics and Immigration committees were actually the first explicitly eugenical organizations in the nation. Also worthy of mention are the American Eugenics Society, the Eugenics Research Association, the Galton Society, the Institute of Family Relations, and the Race Betterment Foundation. As the only major eugenics organization with its own buildings, institutional research facilities, and a paid staff, however, the ERO came to be the best-funded and most influential body of eugenicists.

The American Breeders' Association played a special role in laying the groundwork for the ERO, as the first organization intended to bring together academic biologists with an interest in heredity with practical breeders of animals, as both groups saw Mendel's laws of heredity as the most important guide yet developed for the study of plant and animal heredity. Upon the organization's founding in 1903, their objective was to provide an easy way to bring the records gathered by the breeders together with the theoretical work of the academic biologists, so that the two enterprises could work together and assist each other. Their concerns soon became broader, however, with the establishment of the Eugenics Committee in 1906. The committee was formed with two explicit objectives: "to investigate and report on heredity in the human race" and "to emphasize the value of superior blood and the menace to society of inferior blood" (Kimmelman, 1983, p. 163). This was the first formally organized eugenics advocacy group in the United States, and their explicit goal right from the start was to demonstrate the superiority of some groups over others, and to find ways of fighting the menace of the inferior. This was no fringe group; the chairman was David Starr Jordan, president of Stanford University (and a respected ichthyologist). Other prominent names on the committee include leading entomologist Vernon Kellogg, plant breeding expert Luther Burbank, and even inventor Alexander Graham Bell.

Before starting the ERO, Charles Davenport was active in the American Breeders' Association. Although he was at first involved in poultry genetics and the breeding of racehorses, by 1908 his attention had shifted primarily to eugenics, and he was instrumental in the eventual transformation of the association into the American Eugenics Association in 1913. He started by playing a leading role in expanding the work of the Eugenics Committee and dividing it into 10 subcommittees, which were each concerned with a particular kind of hereditary problem, including feeblemindedness, epilepsy, deaf-mutism, hereditary insanity, and criminality. An additional subcommittee focused on sterilization. Davenport also successfully argued for the inclusion of eugenics articles in the group's official publication, the *Report of the American Breeders' Association.* Once the group was renamed in 1913, the journal was renamed the *Journal of Heredity* and became the top periodical for the popular treatment of eugenics in readable, nontechnical articles.

Although the American Breeders' Association had been quite helpful in gaining wider acceptance for eugenic ideas, Davenport became convinced that to properly develop a national eugenics movement, an organization was needed which was better-funded and which had an institutional base on which to build its reputation. Davenport found the necessary funding, along with the physical location of the ERO, thanks to an extremely wealthy widow in search of a cause worthy of her philanthropy. Mary Williamson Harriman was the widow of railroad tycoon Edward Henry Harriman, whose estate at the time of his death in 1909 was worth an estimated $70 million. Davenport was able to enlist her support for his cause, in part because he had taught her daughter in the summer of 1906 at the Biological Laboratory School of the Brooklyn Institute, which that same year became the home of the SEE. The result of a series of meetings with Mrs. Harriman was the purchase and donation of a 75-acre site next to the SEE, including an immense mansion that had been the summer home of a wealthy New Yorker, along with an agreement to fund the office's complete operating expenses for five years. Mrs. Harriman's commitment also included building a fireproof vault for storage of field records, along with a separate office-laboratory complex. Construction costs exceeded $121,000 (in 1910 dollars). Between 1910 and 1918, Mrs. Harriman spent nearly half a million dollars on the ERO.

Davenport's skills in soliciting the top philanthropists of the day came in handy as Mrs. Harriman's commitment wound down, and in 1917 the Carnegie Institution of Washington took over the annual operating expenses and future expansion of the ERO. In transferring the entire operation to the Carnegie Institution, Mrs. Harriman also gave the ERO an additional endowment of $300,000, ensuring its continued operation for the foreseeable future. Once he had secured adequate funding and property, Davenport took on the task of finding the right person to run the ERO, and settled on Harry Laughlin as the new supervisor of the facility. A biology teacher in the department of agriculture at Kirksville Normal School in Missouri, Laughlin was enthralled by eugenics and readily agreed to join Davenport in his new enterprise.

In his first official report, in 1913, Laughlin laid out a very clear mission for the ERO, breaking it down into a set of specific functions that the office would perform. As its foremost function, the ERO was to "serve eugenical interests as a repository and clearinghouse." It was to function as a data bank for information that would be gathered around the country on the inheritance patterns of a wide range of traits. People who had participated in the studies, and their relatives, would be able to consult the office for information about their own family histories. In a related func-

Harry Hamilton Laughlin, the most influential of the American eugenicists. (Courtesy of Harry H. Laughlin Collection; Pickler Library; Truman State University; Kirksville, MO 63501)

tion, the office was to "build up an analytical index of traits in American families." Davenport had devised a complex classification system he called *The Trait Book,* which classified every imaginable human physical, physiological, and mental trait imaginable according to a numbering scheme not unlike the Dewey Decimal System. Information on chess-playing ability, for example, would be filed under the number 4598: 4 indicates a mental trait, 5 indicates general mental ability, 9 indicates a specific game-playing ability, and 8 pinpoints the specific game, chess. The information was placed in folders that were filed either by family name or by the name of the caseworker who had gathered the information, and an index was maintained on 3 × 5 cards, which were cross-referenced by family name, trait number, and geographic location.

The actual traits being tracked in this system include the expected physical deformities and mental deficiencies, but also some that are remarkable both for their specificity and for the questions they raise regarding how the trait was measured. The system included codes, for example, indicating rowdyism, moral imbecility, and *train-wrecking,* in addition to the aforementioned ability to play chess. Information was organized into five main categories of traits: physical (including height, weight, eye color, deformities), physiological (color blindness, diabetes), mental (intelligence, feeblemindedness, insanity, depression), personality (easily the oddest category, as traits included rebelliousness, irritability, conservatism, along with such things as lack of foresight, nomadism, and missile throwing), and social traits (things like criminality, alcoholism, patriotism, and prostitution). Because so many traits were being monitored, the office had gathered more than half a million cards by the start of 1918 and would collect double that number before finally closing in 1939.

The third purpose in Laughlin's 1913 report is "to study the forces controlling and hereditary consequences of marriage-matings, differential fecundity, and survival migration." Of the various kinds of demographic information listed here, eugenicists were from the beginning particularly concerned with the differential fertility issue, convinced as they were that the less fit were reproducing at a significantly higher rate than the superior members of society. The fourth goal was "to investigate the manner of inheritance of specific human traits." Based on pedigree charts built from raw data collected from families, Laughlin hoped to be able to determine whether a particular trait was inherited, whether it was dominant or recessive, whether it was sex-linked, and to what degree its expression was influenced by environmental factors.

With all this information in hand, the ERO also intended "to advise concerning the eugenical fitness of proposed marriages." Laughlin encouraged potential marriage partners to visit or write to the ERO for help in determining whether they should get married, based on their family histories coupled with the ERO's growing expertise regarding whether various traits were hereditary. This was a primitive form of what would today be called genetic counseling, and in the 1913 report Laughlin noted that the ERO had already received 77 requests for such consultations. Laughlin's success in pushing eugenics into the mainstream may be gauged by the fact that by 1916, it was possible for young couples attending state and county fairs around the country to pay a small fee for similar counseling out of a carnival booth, complete with blue ribbons indicating that theirs is a good marriage. During the same period, eugenic-themed Better Babies contests also became popular at fairs, in which babies were entered into competition to see who best exemplified a white, Aryan ideal.

To gather the necessary data to carry out their mission, the ERO also listed as an official function the need "to train fieldworkers to gather data of eugenical import." To fulfill this function, the ERO ran a short training program for eugenics field workers each summer, featuring lectures by Laughlin and Davenport, along with guest appearances by experts in such areas as evolutionary theory, Mendelian genetics, and the writing of eugenic legislation. Students studied the various intelligence tests and learned how to administer them, and also memorized various classification schemes for insanity, epilepsy, criminality, as well as the basics of how to physically measure brain size via the indirect assessment of cranial capacity. In order to make sure that the eugenics field workers would know what they were looking for, the program also included a series of field trips to nearby hospitals and mental institutions, as well as to Ellis Island, that they might learn to spot mental defectives attempting to enter the country. To complete training, each student was required to conduct and complete a research project that involved the collection and analysis of eugenical data. By 1917, about 156 field workers had been trained, all but 25 of them women, and the ranks of the workers included 8 PhD s and 7 MDs.

Once they had been trained, most of the eugenic field workers took jobs in a variety of institutional settings, including state mental hospitals, insane asylums, and poorhouses, although some went to work for the ERO itself. In many cases, the salaries of the field workers in institutional settings were paid jointly by the institution and the ERO, since their primary purpose was to collect data for the ERO. Their work consisted of taking family histories of patients within the institution in order to ascertain the degree to which their conditions were hereditary. These linear studies, remarkably similar to Goddard's pedigree-chart work, despite being put together by workers with significant, allegedly scientific, training, were then filed at the ERO, where they could be used to study the heritability of a wide range of mental difficulties from mental deficiency to Huntington's chorea. The volume of data collected was quite impressive; in the first three years of the field research, 32 field workers collected 7,369 pages of family case histories and 800 pages of pedigree charts. The training program, like much of the ERO's work, is a testament to Davenport's remarkable ability to gain the support of the era's top philanthropists, as it was funded for the first seven years by personal bequests from John D. Rockefeller, Jr., and for the rest of its existence it was supported by the Carnegie Institution.

Laughlin's report included two other goals for the ERO: encouraging new centers for eugenics research and education, and publishing and disseminating the results of eugenics research. As for the first goal, Laughlin felt strongly that the ERO should both encourage the formation of new eugenics groups and convince existing organizations that eugenics should form a part of their already established programs. An early success in this regard was Laughlin's recruiting of the YMCA to participate, both by making available information on their members and engaging in propaganda efforts to promote eugenic ideals of physical fitness. Regarding the dissemination of eugenics research, Laughlin arranged for the ERO itself to publish a series of monographs on eugenic ideas by himself and by Davenport, as well as lengthy pieces by the likes of Henry Goddard, among others, as well as mounting a concerted effort to encourage the passage of eugenics-related legislation across the country.

Davenport in particular was, through his published work, instrumental in guaranteeing the spread of eugenic ideas across the land. In 1911, Henry Holt & Co., one of America's more prestigious publishing houses, brought forth Davenport's textbook, *Heredity in Relation to Eugenics.* The textbook presented the usual arguments against immigration and for a simple Mendelian explanation of the heredity of a wide range of undesirable traits, and strongly advocated for mass compulsory sterilization and incarceration of the unfit, along with more marriage restriction laws. The book was widely adopted for newly created eugenics courses at colleges across the country, including such prestigious institutions as Harvard, Princeton, Yale, Purdue, Northwestern, and the University of Chicago. By 1914, 44 major institutions offered eugenics courses, and by 1924 that number had grown to hundreds. High school textbooks soon followed, with eugenics-influenced biology textbooks teaching that inferior families are responsible for all of our society's ills and are quite different genetically from superior families.

Despite Davenport and Laughlin's emphasis in all of their writings on the rigorous scientific nature of eugenics research, however, writers who have actually examined the files collected by the ERO have found that the very subjective, impressionistic approach followed by Goddard in the study of the Kallikaks was apparently the norm in eugenics research. Although the ERO officially ceased operations in 1939, the files collected up to that point have been preserved intact and can now be found in the basement of the Dight Institute of Human Genetics at the University of Minnesota. As an example of the methods used in those files, Garland Allen reports on the study of the Dack family in western Pennsylvania: "[the field worker] did no mental testing, and the data consist solely of 'community reactions,' a euphemism for 'common gossip'" (Allen, 1986, p. 243). The field worker's account of William Dack, half a century after his death, reveals much about the research approach:

> William Dack (I2) was born in Ireland and came to the United States about 1815. . . . William died almost fifty years ago, but he is remembered by a few of the oldest settlers of the locality as a peculiar, silly old fellow who drank a good deal, stole sheep and household valuables from his neighbors, and did not seem to be very intelligent. . . . William's second wife was (I3) Mary Murphy. . . . An old resident of Bushville, now deceased, once stated to a woman who was interviewed by the writer that William and Mary were first cousins. (Reported in Allen, 1986, p. 243)

The information contained in this account is plainly unverifiable, and consists of gossip passed along second- or third-hand from people who weren't even alive to be interviewed, yet the researchers at the ERO used this account and others like it to create a pedigree chart, indicating that hereditary feeblemindedness ran in the family.

In many cases, interviews were not even conducted with families or with the people who knew them, and all data were obtained from questionnaires sent out to them. These data are of course subject to the problems that always attend self-report data, particularly the simple assumption that the person filling out the questionnaire is being honest. In addition to the possibility of lying, such a questionnaire also assumes that the person filling it out actually knows the information in the first place. This could have especially presented a problem with the ERO questionnaire, since it asked about a variety of physical traits, including height, for family members both living and deceased. Much of what was collected by the ERO therefore actually required a fair amount of guessing and estimation on the part of the person filling out the questionnaire.

As unscientific and imprecise as the data collection appears to have been, the actual application of the data also suffered from a range of serious methodological flaws. The primary analytic tool of choice for the eugenicists was the pedigree chart, which cannot actually provide the sort of evidence that the eugenicists appear to have assumed that it could, based on the experiences of animal breeders. Animal breeders work in a very controlled environment, in which all births are supervised and carefully documented, and they can often be certain that no direct lineal relatives have been left out of the analysis. It should be clear from the quotations in the preceding text regarding the Dack family, however, that the completeness of the pedigree charts produced by the ERO was far from assured. In an incomplete chart, a trait that appears frequently may appear to be a dominant trait, when in fact it may only seem to appear frequently because some family members are missing from the analysis. A far more critical problem with pedigree charts, however, lies in the assumption with which every ERO analysis appears to have started: that any traits that appear to be passed along from one generation to another must necessarily be determined genetically rather than environmentally. Rather than considering any environmental factors that might be involved in the appearance of a trait or behavior in multiple generations, the eugenicists assume that *everything* is genetically determined.

Allen (1986) provides an excellent analysis of how this sort of oversimplification sometimes led to nearly comical examinations of personality traits that are almost certainly *not* genetic: Davenport's 1919 study of the inheritance of what he called *thalassophilia,* or love of the sea. The book, published by the Carnegie Institution, was titled *Naval Officers: Their Heredity and Development* and purported to examine why naval careers seemed to run in families. As with such things as intelligence and morality, the eugenicist decided that the explanation lay in a simple, single-gene Mendelian mechanism. He begins by pointing out that nomadism is clearly hereditary, since particular racial groups such as Gypsies and Comanches were all nomadic—note that this explanation completely ignores the role of culture and social influence, which would suggest that a person born into an entirely nomadic culture is likely to be raised to be a nomad. In the family pedigrees collected by the ERO, there were numerous instances of nomadism, most of them male, including traveling salesmen, tramps, and truant boys. Because the trait seemed to appear mostly in men, but in a minority of them, Davenport concluded that it must be both sex-linked and recessive, passed by mothers to half of their sons. Since thalassophilia is a form of nomadism, it must behave the same way:

> Sometimes a father who shows no liking for the sea . . . may carry a determiner for sea-lust recessive. It is theoretically probable that some mothers are heterozygous for love of the sea, so that when married to a thalassophilic man half of their children will show sea-lust and half will not. (Quoted in Allen, 1986, p. 245)

Incredibly, Davenport then argues his case by drawing an analogy between thalassophilia and the inheritance of comb size in chickens: "It is possible . . . that the irresistible appeal of the sea is a trait that is a sort of secondary sex character in males in certain races, just as a rose comb is a male characteristic in some races of poultry" (Allen, 1986, p. 245). Rather than even considering environmental factors such as a naval father's encouragement of his sons to enter on a similar career, in other words, Davenport instead reduces such a choice to a secondary sexual characteristic, such as the development of facial and body hair.

Given Laughlin and Davenport's wholesale rejection of any role for environmental influences in human behavior, it is unsurprising, if a bit unsettling, that the ERO, calling on the support of what appeared to outsiders to be solid science, actively discouraged philanthropists from donating to charities. Such donations were a waste of resources, after all, since the social problems they sought to solve were all the result of bad genes rather than insufficient resources. This was Davenport's point of view before the ERO even came into existence: in 1909, he told the Committee on Eugenics of the American Breeders' Association that "Vastly more effective than the million dollars to 'charity' would be ten million to eugenics. He who, by such a gift, would redeem mankind from vice, imbecility and suffering would be the world's wisest philanthropist" (quoted in Allen, 1986, p. 245). Such a worldview assumes that the poor, without exception, are only in dire straits because of their own genetic inferiority, and therefore any effort expended in trying to improve their lot is wasted. In addition to wholeheartedly feeling that charitable work was a waste of time, Davenport believed that so were attempts at rehabilitation and treatment of the mentally ill, for much the same reason. Treatment, after all, assumes that changes in environmental factors, which here would mean anything but the patients' genes, might make a difference in their condition.

Eugenics Becomes the Law

To modern readers, more startling than the eugenicists' callousness toward the suffering of the poor and mentally ill is their great success in making these ideas part of the mainstream of American and European thinking in that era. Through political activism and publications, most notably *Eugenical News,* begun in 1916, Laughlin had a remarkable impact on American public policy, especially in the 1920s and 1930s. Laughlin was instrumental in raising public awareness of the menace posed by feebleminded immigrants, a problem long suspected by racist elements of America but first given scientific credibility by Goddard following his visits to Ellis Island. During World War I, the Army Alpha and Beta intelligence tests were given to more than a million military recruits, and the data showed alarmingly poor performance by recent immigrants, especially those from non-English-speaking countries, as well as by poor people, especially impoverished Southern Black soldiers. Along with Goddard's work, such data provided a strong case against immigration, especially in the hands of Laughlin, who refused to consider any sort of environmental explanation for such data. Laughlin's testimony before Congress, in which he presented large quantities of data demonstrating the inferiority of Southern, Central, and Eastern European immigrants, especially Jews, was widely publicized, and the hearings before which he testified resulted in the passage of the Immigration Restriction Act of 1924, also known as the Johnson Act. This law put into place a system of strict quotas regarding the number of immigrants to be allowed into the country from a variety of European destinations, with some of the strictest limitations placed on central and eastern European Jews. This particular eugenic success would eventually have far-reaching consequences in the wake of another application of eugenic principles: because of the Nazi persecution of Jews, many fled to the West in the late 1930s, only to be turned away by the United States, thanks to the immigration quotas put in place in 1924.

The second major political implementation to which Davenport and Laughlin lent their strong support in the 1920s was an idea to which Davenport had shown an allegiance right from the beginning of the ERO: the advocacy of laws allowing the involuntary, mandatory sterilization of those regarded as genetically inferior. In 1922, Laughlin presented Congress with the suggested wording for a proposed federal law, but the members of Congress were unwilling to take such a radical step. Laughlin had rather more success at the state level, however, where his lobbying eventually convinced a number of states to pass laws based, sometimes verbatim, on his "Model Eugenical Sterilization Law." The idea of such a law was not new; the first compulsory sterilization bill to be introduced in a state legislature was proposed in Michigan in 1897, but it was not passed. In 1905, a similar law was successfully passed by Pennsylvania's legislature, but it was vetoed by the governor. The first *successful* attempt at establishing an involuntary sterilization law occurred in Indiana in 1907 and was followed closely in 1909 by Washington and California. Such laws were eventually passed in 33 American States, and more than 65,000 individuals were sterilized.

A large portion of the public was opposed to mandatory sterilization laws, despite the best propaganda efforts of the ERO, and many state officials continued to harbor doubts regarding the legality and constitutionality of the statutes, and so sterilization rates across the country remained fairly low prior to 1927. In that year, the case of *Buck v. Bell* reached the Supreme Court. Originating in Virginia, the case involved a young woman (known to the court by the pseudonym "Carrie Buck") who, prior to the age of 17, had never been described or diagnosed as feebleminded or defective in any way. At the age of 17, she bore an illegitimate child, and on that basis was institutionalized and found to be morally and mentally defective. This made sense under the Virginia law, which was modeled directly on Laughlin's text, as its list of people who should be considered feebleminded and antisocial cut quite a wide swath through the population, including "unwed mothers, prostitutes, petty criminals and children with disciplinary problems" (cited in Gould, 1996, p. 365). Her mother, a prostitute, had been institutionalized under similar charges a few years earlier, and the claim was made that Carrie Buck's infant child was also feebleminded, thus providing evidence of the problem running in a family for at least three generations. Despite a complete lack of evidence for this last claim, the Supreme Court used the three-generations motif prominently in its ruling, authored by Oliver Wendell Holmes. After comparing surgical sterilization with mandatory vaccinations, as both help to contain the spread of disease, the decision compares giving up fertility to the sacrifice made by young men who join the military and go off to war:

> We have seen more than once that the public welfare may call upon the best citizens for their lives. It would be strange if it could not call upon those who already sap the strength of the state for these lesser sacrifices. . . . Three generations of imbeciles are enough. (Gould, 1996, p. 364)

In a final irony, school records show that Carrie Buck's daughter was an honors student in elementary school before she died prematurely.

With the Supreme Court endorsing the constitutionality of mandatory involuntary sterilization, the floodgates were opened and the number of sterilizations being performed in the United States increased dramatically. Although the primary targets of the sterilization campaign were the mentally ill and the feebleminded, many of the state laws targeted people with physical handicaps as well, including the deaf, the blind, epileptics, and people with physical deformities. As the Virginia law demonstrates, moral failures were often also grounds for sterilization, including promiscuity, vagrancy, prostitution, alcoholism, and even simple childhood misbehavior. There are also widespread reports of Native American and African American women being sterilized against their will and without their knowledge in many states, often while hospitalized for other procedures, particularly child-birth. Since criminality was one of the eugenic targets, some sterilizations took place in prisons, but these represented only a small proportion of the total.

The number of sterilizations performed in the United States rose steadily into the early 1940s, and provided inspiration for eugenics sympathizers who were watching overseas. From the start of the **Nazi** Party in 1920, their platform included the notion of eugenics in the form of racial purification, purging the German bloodline of all non-Nordic (and therefore inferior) influence. When the Nazis came to power in 1933, one of their first actions was to pass an involuntary sterilization law, targeting a wide range of physical and mental ills, and eventually expanding the pool of allowable sterilizations to include entire ethnicities as well. Eventually, the Nazis took eugenic principles one logical step further than anyone had dared to propose in America—if it is acceptable, and indeed a national priority, to prevent certain undesirable people from reproducing, then it may also make sense to actively remove those people from the country entirely, and to kill them as well. After World War II, when the full extent of the Nazi implementation of eugenic principles became known, most commentators neglected to point out the American influence on the Nazis, even though the original sterilization law appears to have taken Laughlin's model law as its starting point.

In the early days of the Nazi regime, the *Eugenical News* expressed high praise for the official Nazi governmental involvement in eugenics, with Laughlin specifically praising the Third Reich for passing the 1933 law. At this point, Laughlin had already published invited pieces in German publications on the spread of legalized sterilization in America and had also published pieces by Nazi writers in America. Laughlin's support for Nazi race-hygiene practices in the pages of *Eugenical News* became a source of alarm and consternation among American eugenicists and geneticists, to whom the ERO had clearly become the main propagandists in America for the Nazi cause. Carnegie Institution officials began to have some doubts about continuing to fund the organization, doubts that were made worse in 1936, when Laughlin was informed that he was to receive an honorary Doctor of Medicine degree from the University of Heidelberg at the celebration of its 550th anniversary. At this point, the Nazis had already taken control of all universities and expelled Jewish scholars, and so any recognition by such an institution was in fact official Nazi recognition, at a time when it was already becoming clear to the rest of the world that the Third Reich was a racist dictatorship bent on going to war. Laughlin's reply to the invitation was a public relations nightmare for the Carnegie Institution:

> I consider the conferring of this high degree upon me not only as a personal honor, but also as evidence of a common understanding of German and

American scientists of the nature of eugenics as research in the practical application of those fundamental biological and social principles which determine
the racial endowments and the racial health . . . of future generations. (Quoted
in Allen, 1986, p. 253)

Such eager acceptance of the degree, and such enthusiastic recognition of common scientific goals for Americans and the Nazis, made many of the people around
Laughlin, including those on whom his livelihood depended, fairly uncomfortable.
As a concession to those concerns, Laughlin did not travel to Germany to receive
the honor, but he did go as far as the German consulate in Manhattan, where
the degree was awarded. Though it was not the only factor, Laughlin's embrace
of the Nazis helped to seal the fate of the ERO, which closed its doors on December 31, 1939.

Once the horrors of the Holocaust became widely known after World War II,
public opinion regarding eugenics in general, and sterilization programs in particular, became far more negative. Although sterilizations did not stop immediately,
they slowed down dramatically, and over the next couple of decades most states
quietly stopped the practice. Many states were quite slow to repeal the laws, however. As of 1956, 27 of the 33 states that passed sterilization laws still had the statutes on the books, and several states had still not officially overturned the laws in
the early 1980s.

After World War II, the large numbers of eugenics advocates did not just disappear, but they did quietly change their organizations' names and stated goals, and it
soon became very difficult to find anyone willing to bear the label of "eugenicist."
Most who had borne that distinction switched to the "geneticist" label instead, and
over the next several decades the last remnants of open, official eugenics advocacy
slowly disappeared. Some scholars took longer to distance themselves from the
eugenic philosophy than others, as with the 1969 rechristening of *Eugenics Quarterly* as *Social Biology*.

Further Reading

Allen, G. E. (1986). The Eugenics Record Office at Cold Spring Harbor, 1910–1940: An
Essay in Institutional History. *Osiris* 2: 225–264.

Black, E. (2003). *War against the Weak: Eugenics and America's Campaign to Create
a Master Race.* New York: Four Walls Eight Windows.

Davenport, C. B. (1911). *Heredity in Relation to Eugenics.* New York: Henry Holt.

Galton, F. (1883). *Inquiries into Human Faculty and Its Development.* New York: Dutton.

Goddard, H. H. (1913). *The Kallikak Family: A Study in the Heredity of Feeble-
Mindedness.* New York: MacMillan.

Goddard, H. H. (1914). *Feeble-Mindedness: Its Causes and Consequences.* New York:
MacMillan.

Goddard, H. H. (1917). Mental Tests and the Immigrant. *Journal of Delinquency* 2: 243–277.

Gould, S. J. (1996). *The Mismeasure of Man.* New York: W. W. Norton.

Kimmelman, B. A. (1983). The American Breeders' Association: Genetics and Eugenics in an Agricultural Context 1903-1913. *Social Studies of Science* 13(2): 163–204.

Ferenczi, Sándor (1873–1933)

Sándor Ferenczi was born Sándor Fränkel in Miskole, Hungary, to Baruch Fränkel and Rosa Eibenschütz, both Polish Jews. To deal with the anti-Semitic climate in Hungary, which became quite oppressive in his adulthood, he changed his name to the more Magyar-sounding Ferenczi. Ferenczi was an early member of the Vienna Psychoanalytical Society and a close friend and confidant of Freud, even accompanying him, along with Carl Jung, on his sole visit to America (see **United States, Freud's Visit to**), which makes their later falling out all the more striking.

In Vienna, Ferenczi quickly developed a reputation as the man who was not afraid of difficult or even hopeless cases, which was actually quite unusual in that circle. Freud had a reputation for being very reluctant to take on seriously disturbed patients, and thus attracted artists, intellectuals, and his fellow psychiatrists. Ferenczi, on the other hand, quickly developed a reputation for helping to heal the cases that the other psychoanalysts shied away from.

His approach to therapy came to differ quite a bit from Freud's as well. Where the usual approach of the therapist in psychoanalysis is a fairly passive one, listening neutrally to the patient and basing treatment decisions on a physician's judgment of psychopathology, Ferenczi advocated a far more active role for the analyst. He viewed the analyst's empathic response to the patient as the core of treatment, with reciprocal self-disclosure by the therapist playing an important role. What was important, in other words, was centering the therapy on a back-and-forth, nonjudgmental interaction between doctor and patient. This approach has clearly cast a long shadow in the therapeutic world, both within and outside of psychoanalytic circles. The humanistic approach of Carl Rogers and his person-centered therapy, for example, clearly owes a great debt to Ferenczi, as does the interpersonal-relational movement within American psychoanalysis, the methods of which sound quite directly inspired by Ferenczi.

Despite this clear influence, his name rarely comes up in discussions of psychoanalysis, especially those involving Freud and the other early leading lights of psychoanalysis. As in numerous other instances, another of Freud's disciples has been largely erased from psychoanalytical history because he had the temerity to disagree on fundamentals with Freud. "Erased" may not be too strong a word: in Ernest Jones's biography of Freud, he describes Ferenczi as "mentally ill" at the end of his life, failing to mention that Ferenczi was in fact ill with pernicious anemia, which was incurable at the time, and furthermore that mere months before this allegedly mentally ill man died, he presented his most famous paper to the 12th International Psycho-Analytic Congress in Wiesbaden, Germany. The problem for Freud and his establishment was the content of that last paper.

Titled "The Confusion of Tongues," the paper revived an idea that Freud had famously proposed, and then dismissed, decades earlier (see **seduction theory**): serious psychological disorders develop in adults as a result of sexual exploitation in childhood. The confusion of tongues is what happens when the child and adult interpret the same action or expression very differently from each other. The child behaves affectionately but innocently, communicating in an infantile tongue, and the adult responds pathologically, interpreting the child's behavior using a passion tongue, which the child does not speak, touching the child inappropriately (or worse) while conveying to the child that somehow this is what he or she indicated a desire for. According to Ferenczi, the real damage results not from the inappropriate contact but rather from the adult's denial of the trauma, shift of responsibility for the trauma onto the child's shoulders, unprepared as they are for such a burden, or actual threats against the child if he or she reveals the event to others.

There is little in Ferenczi's description that is surprising or controversial to modern ears, but in proposing it he was denying a cornerstone of Freud's whole theoretical edifice: the idea that such accounts of adult seduction are actually fantasies created by the children, and a natural part of resolving the conflicts of early childhood. To the contrary, Ferenczi proposes quite clearly and openly that the assumption that children create such fantasies is a creation of the therapist, and that the therapist who makes that assumption is actually re-enacting the role of the abusive adult by again denying the reality of the trauma. As Freud regarded the Oedipal conflict and its resolution (or failure to be resolved) as the foundation of *all* neurosis, to suggest that patients who recalled such conflict were being truthful was absolutely incompatible with his theories, and as a consequence Ferenczi was no longer welcome in the inner circles of psychoanalysis.

Ferenczi's idea of mutual analysis (in which the analyst and patient would actually take turns free-associating on the couch) grew directly out of his treatment of patients who had been sexually abused—he wanted the therapeutic situation to be as welcoming as possible, so as not to play the role of the abuser, and such interactive, empathic methods are quite widespread both within and beyond psychoanalysis today, but they are rarely associated directly with Ferenczi. The title of a paper by Sharon Kahn describes his fate quite eloquently: "Ferenczi's Mutual Analysis: A Case Where the Messenger Was Killed and His Treasure Buried."

Further Reading

Ferenczi, S. (1949). Confusion of Tongues between the Adult and the Child. *The International Journal of Psychoanalysis* 30: 225–230.

Kahn, S.K. (1996). Ferenczi's Mutual Analysis: A Case Where the Messenger Was Killed and his Treasure Buried. Paper presented at the Annual Meeting of the Eastern Psychological Association, Philadelphia, March 30, 1996.

Kahn, S.K. (1997). Intolerance, Ambivalence, and Oedipus: The Reversal of Roles between Sigmund Freud and Sándor Ferenczi. *Psychoanalytic Inquiry* 17(4): 559–569.

Fliess, Wilhelm (1858–1928)

Wilhelm Fliess, a Berlin otorhinolaryngologist (ear, nose, and throat doctor), was a close friend of Sigmund Freud early in his career, and his correspondence with Freud has played an important part in the historical reconstruction of the beginnings of psychoanalysis. The two young doctors first met in 1887, introduced by Josef Breuer, after Fliess attended several conferences organized by Breuer. Freud wrote many letters to Fliess, who acted as both confidant and confessor to Freud, and even occasionally as inspiration; the prehistory of many of Freud's later ideas is clearly visible in their correspondence, with some influence clearly flowing to Freud from Fliess. It appears to have been Fliess, for example, who first drew Freud's attention to the psychological significance of jokes. Freud's letters to Fliess were first published in English in 1954, a posthumous publication that would not have pleased Freud, who had ordered that his letters to Fliess be destroyed (his letters had been bought at auction, and the buyer felt differently).

While the extent of his role as an early influence on Freud continues to be the source of some debate among Freud scholars, there is no doubt that Fliess made his own completely original (and frankly bizarre) contributions as well, ideas that have quite deservedly failed to have the impact of his friend's far better-known theory. Though he was an ear, nose, and throat man rather than a neurologist, he shared Freud's and Breuer's fascination with hysterical patients. Given his own medical specialty, it is almost inevitable that he would find the source of women's neuroses and hysterical complaints to be somehow associated with the nasal passages. Specifically, he proposed that there was a profound direct connection between women's nasal passages and the genitalia, resulting in varied and widespread symptoms that were actually manifestations of *nasal reflex neurosis.* Signs of nasal reflex neurosis included, among other things, frequent masturbation (due to the *nasogenital reflex*) and *vicarious nosebleeds,* in which a woman experiencing amenorrhea (absence of menstruation) bleeds from the nose instead of the uterus.

Fliess began to treat hysterical patients by applying cocaine to the nasal passages, a treatment that, perhaps unsurprisingly, resulted in immediate, if temporary, improvement in patients experiencing depression or excessive anxiety. For those patients who did not improve sufficiently under the influence of cocaine, Fliess decided that cauterizing the nasal passages would be an effective treatment for menstrual problems. Eventually, this too seemed an insufficient treatment, and Fliess came to believe that the best treatment for nasal reflex neurosis was the surgical removal of the turbinate bone from the nose.

In 1894, Fliess visited Freud in Vienna, and Freud introduced his friend to a patient, Emma Eckstein. In conversation with Freud, he discovered that the patient's difficulties included masturbation (which at the time was considered a serious health risk) and suggested that an operation on her nose would take care of the problem. With Freud's and Eckstein's consent, Fliess removed her turbinate bone, but he botched the procedure, accidentally leaving nearly half a meter of surgical gauze inside her face. A few days later she began to experience severe pain accompanied by bleeding, and another surgeon, called in by Freud, found a thread in her nose and pulled on it. The gauze came out, and Eckstein nearly bled to death. She remained disfigured for life. Remarkably, Freud protected his friend's reputation by arguing that Eckstein was a hysterical bleeder, and even that the bleeding was a manifestation of her repressed desire for Freud. Even more remarkably, Emma Eckstein not only accepted his explanation, but eventually became

Sigmund Freud (*left*) with Wilhelm Fliess, whose cure for hysteria involved nasal surgery, in the early 1890s. (Imagno/Getty Images)

a psychoanalyst herself. Some writers have suggested that the Eckstein case was central to Freud's rejection of the **seduction theory,** as he came to sincerely believe his explanation of Eckstein's bleeding. This required acknowledging that, if her bleeding was a result of internal rather than external factors, then maybe her recollections of childhood molestation were also fantasies.

Absurd though the nasogenital connection sounds, it is important to note here that in late 19th-century otorhinolaryngeal circles, the idea was taken quite seriously and was briefly popular. In the last two decades of the century, for example, articles published in major medical journals included "On the Etiology of Some Nasal Reflex Neuroses," "Reflex Nasal Neuroses," "Some Nervous and Mental Manifestations Occurring in Connection with Nasal Disease," and "The Physiological and Pathological Relations between the Nose and the Sexual Apparatus of Man," among many others. Within another decade, such references largely disappeared from the medical literature.

Fliess's other idea, biorhythms, never gained acceptance in the scientific community, but has had much greater staying power, at least within a niche of the general public. *Biorhythms* is the name that became popular when the idea became a fad in the 1970s; Fliess actually called it by the more unwieldy name of *vital periodicity.* The central idea of biorhythms is the notion that all vital physical and mental processes, both normal and pathological, occur in cycles that last either 23 or 28 days. Since he associated a 28-day cycle with menstruation, Fliess referred to that as a female cycle and the 23-day period as a male cycle. Knowing how far along a person is in a cycle allows calculation of recovery time after surgery, how long a person will be ill, or even the most likely date of that person's death. Fliess took this idea very seriously, even informing Freud that he could expect to die at age 51, a prediction that was of course off by several decades.

Fliess's discovery has far more in common with numerology than with science—it began with his discovery that he could figure out a way to express any whole number at all in terms of either 23, 28, or both, using the formula $23x + 28y$, where x and y are either positive or negative integers. He wrote a book that consists of almost nothing but page after page on which he shows how this formula matches up with measurements of various natural phenomena. This is not as amazing as it seemed to Fliess. Martin Gardner has pointed out that any two positive integers with no common divisor can be substituted for 23 and 28, and the formula will still be able to express any positive integer. The two numbers to which he attributed such power, in other words, are completely unnecessary to produce the phenomenon. Lack of evidence, usefulness, and truth rarely stop a popular fallacy from spreading, however. Within a few years, Professor Herman Swoboda at the University of Vienna claimed to have also independently discovered the 23- and 28-day cycles, and in the 1920s, a third, 33-day mind cycle was added by Alfred Telscher, also in Austria. The idea was popularized in the United States in the 1970s by multiple authors, with the three cycles now known as the physical, emotional, and intellectual cycles. The 28-day female period became the emotional cycle for both sexes, with no scientific evidence at all behind it—in fact, the one part of biorhythm theory that might be salvageable, the idea that due to hormonal differences women experience cycles that men do not, was eliminated from the popular version of the theory. After a period of popularity in the 1970s and 1980s, biorhythms have largely faded from public consciousness, but a quick Internet search reveals that the fad is alive and well online, where a startling number of websites are available to calculate your cycles (for a fee in some cases, naturally).

Further Reading

Freud, S. (1957). *The Origins of Psychoanalysis: Letters, Drafts and Notes to Wilhelm Fliess, 1887–1902* (Marie Bonaparte, Anna Freud, and Ernst Kris, eds.). Garden City, NY: Doubleday.

Gardner, M. (1957). *Fads and Fallacies in the Name of Science.* Mineola, NY: Dover.

Randi, J. (1982). *Flim-Flam.* Buffalo, NY: Prometheus.

Frankl, Viktor (1905–1997)

Viktor Frankl was, like Freud, a Jewish neurologist practicing in Vienna and shared Freud's interests in philosophy and the problem of man's inhumanity to man. In his early career, Frankl was heavily influenced in his thinking by the work of Freud and Adler, like many other European psychiatrists of the time. Like so many others, however, he also eventually diverged from Freud's influence, and did so somewhat more drastically than others. Where Freud's atheism and generally negative attitude toward religion was well-known, and only became stronger over time, Frankl's *logotherapy* emphasized the crucial importance of the spiritual dimension of life.

Frankl's eventual theoretical path was in many ways a product of a fundamental difference between Freud's life circumstances and his own. Where Freud, with the help of such influential friends as Princess Marie **Bonaparte,** was able to leave Vienna before the Nazis rounded up prominent Jewish scholars, and live out his remaining days in London, Frankl was deported to a concentration camp in September of 1942. Frankl remained in the camps until their liberation by American soldiers in 1945, and was his family's sole survivor, apart from a sister who had emigrated to Australia before the war.

Within a year of the liberation, Frankl had written the book that established the new field of *existential analysis,* published in English as *Man's Search for Meaning,* which, while a memorable title, is far less descriptive of the contents than the original German title, which may be translated as *Saying Yes to Life in Spite of Everything: A Psychiatrist Experiences the Concentration Camp.* The central insight of the book, and of all his work to follow, was the idea that the most important factor in psychological development, regardless of early experiences or present circumstances, was the ability to find some meaning or purpose in one's life. He initially based this on his observations of the wide range of ways in which people reacted to life in the concentration camps. In Frankl's view, it was the ability to see a purpose to their suffering that best distinguished those who were able to survive the horrific conditions in the concentration camps with their mental health largely intact.

In many ways, Frankl's work during and beyond his time in the camps was simply a logical extension of what he had been doing prior to the arrival of the Nazis. In medical school, he specialized in the study of depression and suicide, and early in his career he developed a special program for the counseling of teen students before

The wholly remarkable existential analyst Viktor Frankl, author of *Man's Search for Meaning,* at the University of Vienna in 1954. (Imagno/Getty Images)

and during the time when they were to receive their grades. At the time, suicides were fairly common among students who were not performing well. Frankl's program was quite successful, as during the time he ran the program, not a single suicide was reported among the students of Vienna. His remarkable success with such a usually intractable problem, and at such a young age (he established the suicide prevention program in 1924, when he was not yet 20 years old), brought him to the attention of some of the influential psychoanalysts of the day, garnering an invitation from Wilhelm **Reich** to lecture in Berlin, for example.

After finishing medical school, he continued his work on suicide prevention, heading a special ward, known as the Selbstmörderpavilion, or *suicide pavilion,* at a Viennese hospital. Between 1933 and 1937, his team treated more than 30,000 women at risk for suicide. With the arrival of the Nazis in Vienna, however, his Jewish identity became more important than his obvious skill as a therapist, and he was no longer allowed to treat Aryan patients. He went into private practice and was eventually hired to head the neurological department of the Rothschild Hospital, the only such establishment in Vienna that still admitted Jews as patients. At this point in his career, he was already doing what he could to quietly defy the Nazis—in the days before they began deporting Jews en masse to the camps, the Nazis first established euthanasia programs in which people who were not expected to continue to live productive lives, especially Jews and members of other undesirable groups, were put to death. Frankl used his position to save numerous patients from this fate via his expert medical opinions.

In 1942, Frankl was transported to the Theresienstadt concentration camp, along with his wife and his parents. Once inside the camp, Frankl made himself useful, as he was immediately put to work as a physician. Once it became known that he was a skillful and experienced psychotherapist as well, he was asked to set up a program to help new arrivals to deal with their feelings of shock and grief. This unit quickly evolved into a suicide watch program, returning him to his early area of study. All signs of suicidal thoughts were reported to him by other camp inmates, and he spent his time in the camp working hard to try to cure his fellow prisoners' depression and prevent suicides. He also managed to organize his fellow psychologists within the camp into a small professional society to whom he would occasionally deliver lectures on a wide range of topics. His ability to fight his own despondency by immersing himself so thoroughly in helping other people, and thus giving purpose and meaning to his own suffering, would eventually form the core of his therapeutic philosophy.

Frankl's own suffering at the hands of the Nazis, it should be noted, was significant. In his recollections about the conditions in the camps, for example, he notes that the apathy and resignation to which other psychologists have given a variety of psychodynamically based interpretations were actually just the logical effects of severe sleep deprivation. Concentrating so many humans in a small area invited intrusion by large numbers of rats and other vermin, and sleep was constantly interrupted by these creatures' search for food, which often involved walking across reclining bodies. Frankl spent a full two years under the appalling conditions at Theresienstadt, until he was sent on to Auschwitz for processing. After a few days in Auschwitz, he went on to Türkheim, part of the Dachau complex, for six months as slave labor. While this was going on, his wife was transferred to Bergen-Belsen, where she was killed, and his parents were both killed in Auschwitz. Upon the liberation of the camps in 1945, Frankl emerged with no family and no resources. Where most other surviving Jews left Europe, never to return, Viktor Frankl found solace in the existential philosophers and set about turning his experiences in the camps into a new kind of psychotherapy.

Existentialism

As it plays such a role in Frankl's ideas and those of later existential psychologists, a brief introduction to existentialism seems appropriate here. Freud's theories are quite deterministic, with our actions and choices often directed by forces, both internal and external, quite beyond our own influence or control. This same determinism is also at the core of the ideas of other major 20th-century psychological theorists, including those whose work at first glance seems philosophically to be quite far removed from Freud, such as behaviorists like B. F. Skinner. For this reason, existentialist psychology is sometimes referred to as a *third force* in psychology, representing something fundamentally different from the determinist approach of the other two major philosophical approaches to early 20th-century psychology.

Existentialism as a philosophy comes in many varieties, but all have in common two things: an indifferent and confusing universe that neither causes nor cares about human action and the supremacy of the individual human will over all other influences. In existential philosophy, any meaning derived from an individual's existence is self-generated, rather than being placed there by either God or nature. This places all responsibility for succeeding or failing in life, and making rational choices that benefit humanity, as well as the ability to make choices that do not, on the individual.

As a modern philosophical movement, existentialism is a 19th- and 20th-century phenomenon, but some writers find early evidence of existentialist content as far back as the writings of Socrates, and even the Bible. A favorite Biblical text of existentialists, for example, is the Book of Ecclesiastes. Unlike the rest of the Bible, it presents an essentially Godless universe—alone among the canonical texts, it contains not a single action by the deity, nor indeed of any of his representatives. Ecclesiastes further presents human activity in general as essentially pointless and vain:

> Vanity of vanities, all is vanity. What profit has man of all his labor wherein he labors under the sun? One generation goes, and another generation comes, but the earth abides forever. . . . That which has been is that which shall be, and that which has been done is that which shall be done, and there is no new thing under the sun. (Ecclesiastes 1:2–3, 1:9)

Although existentialism is today often represented and understood as a primarily atheistic movement, religion was an important part of the philosophy of several of its central early figures, and this text served equally as inspiration for both the theist and atheist figures in the movement. To the theologian, Ecclesiastes illustrates the pointlessness of life without the purpose provided by God, and yet to the atheist existentialist thinker, it illustrates exactly the same thing: our existence possesses no higher purpose in and of itself but instead bears only the meaning we give it.

Blaise Pascal, often regarded as one of the earliest figures in existentialist philosophy, presented human life as made up of a series of paradoxes and contradictions, which in turn presented each individual with the need to constantly make choices regarding how to confront and interpret those conundrums. Unlike many later existentialists, Pascal presents belief in God (or a god, at any rate) as important in providing ultimate meaning to our lives beyond the daily obstacles of life. He is perhaps best known today for his response to the apparent paradox of belief in a benevolent, omniscient deity in the face of what seemed to many of Pascal's contemporaries as overwhelming evidence of God's absence in the world. Acknowledging that, based on current evidence, God may or may not exist, he suggests that his reader consider the potential future consequences of both belief and nonbelief. If there is indeed nothing beyond this earthly life—no afterlife, no meeting God— then believer and nonbeliever will experience the same eternal nothingness. The believer will have been proven wrong, but will be no worse for wear than the nonbeliever. If, however, the theologians are correct about the afterlife, then the believer has salvation and eternal happiness to look forward to, whereas, depending on the brand of religion involved, the nonbeliever might well be consigned to eternal damnation, or at the least left out of paradise. Given the stakes involved, Pascal recommends belief as the more sensible choice, as the believer who has wagered that God exists has everything to gain if he is right, and nothing to lose if he is wrong—this is often referred to as *Pascal's wager.*

Frankl's brand of existentialism is closer to that of Søren Kierkegaard, widely regarded as the founder of modern existentialism. Kierkegaard argued that the human condition is fundamentally a state of uncertainty and irrationality, which only gains meaning through the individual's actions and choices, which ideally include a serious commitment to leading a moral and personally meaningful life. Like Pascal, Kierkegaard saw an important role for the spiritual side of life in this process. Following a creative, meaningful path in life often means confronting and opposing societal norms, which in turn entails risk and occasional failure. To Kierkegaard, avoiding despair required a commitment to God and a Christian approach to life.

Along with this relatively optimistic, spiritually oriented brand of existentialism, the movement also produced a far more pessimistic, even misanthropic approach to the human condition in the hands of atheists like Friedrich Nietzsche. The central, crucial element in Nietzsche's philosophy is the primacy of the individual human will in giving meaning to life. The most fully developed, enlightened human being, the Übermensch (or Superman), is that rare creature who rejects the concept of a higher power or higher purpose and commits fully to the passionate pursuit of entirely self-determined goals. Moral conformity is a kind of weakness when engaged in purely in the hope of achieving a good end in the afterlife; the superior human is the rare one who genuinely understands that human existence will eventually end in death and meaninglessness. The only true meaning in our lives is that which we, through sheer force of will, impose on them ourselves.

Martin Heidegger carried forth Nietzsche's central ideas without much variation. To Heidegger, the world we confront is confusing and indifferent to our needs. In that world, there is no caring, benevolent deity watching over us and providing us with meaning. Instead, each individual is responsible for determining how to give his or her life meaning, and then pursuing those self-chosen goals with passion and conviction, recognizing that death is the only certain outcome, and that no higher purpose guides life or rewards us after death.

The actual label of *existentialism* was first applied by a philosopher to his own work in the early 20th century, when the French writer Jean-Paul Sartre coined it to identify his own philosophical movement. Sartre took pessimistic, atheistic existentialism to more extreme positions than his predecessors. He saw uncertainty and confusion as man's natural state, calling it the *nausea* of existence. His play *Huis Clos,* a title usually translated as *No Exit,* sums up his view of the necessity of confronting the challenge of human life quite well in the title, and the play's famous final line captures a uniquely pessimistic view of how likely our fellow humans are to be helpful in this process. A character who has died spends the entire play trapped in a small room with a group of people who bicker and fight pettily throughout the play, never resolving anything, and finally comes to a realization about where he is: "L'enfer, c'est les autres!" (Hell is other people! To Sartre, our need to find a rational purpose for our existence is futile, as are our attempts to do so. All we have is our free will, and the real meaning in our lives derives from accepting the responsibility that goes along with that will and trying to make choices that benefit humanity. Sartre further believed that all choices, no matter how minor or unimportant they may seem, must be considered in light of their effects on all of humanity, not just in their impact on the individual. Everything about our existence is the product of individual free will, and so leading a productive life that benefits others is a choice, as is despair.

Clearly existentialism is a broad category that allows some fairly wide variations, particularly regarding the role of God in the universe, but there are several common themes across the various brands. One of these is moral *individualism,* along with the very closely related notion of moral *relativism.* If there are no universal, objective moral standards to guide human behavior, then each individual must discover for himself or herself how to determine right from wrong. Having arrived at a personal moral code, the person can then understand truth only by acting consistently on those beliefs and principles. Moral individualism is complicated further by moral relativism: If there are no objective, absolute standards for what is right and moral, then the individual must also sometimes recognize that moral standards may change across situations. What is right under one set of circumstances may not be the correct choice under others. All existentialists emphasize this subjectivity of moral choices.

Another standard feature of existentialism is what Sartre labeled rather vividly as the nausea of existence—the recognition that life is a source of constant anxiety, also sometimes called dread or anguish, depending on the particular existentialist. To live is to experience guilt, suffering, and the sense of an underlying nothingness, a vast emptiness or abyss beneath the surface of life. Existential dread is especially challenging because it is not related to any particular object, unlike fear, which is usually fear of something in particular. Existential dread is more like what modern psychiatrists would call *free-floating anxiety,* a general sense of unease without a particular cause. A person who fears a particular object, place, or situation, as in a phobia, can challenge that fear and learn to overcome it. Without a particular object or cause, however, dread cannot be confronted and defeated and thus remains a constant companion.

A further common existential theme is the futility or absurdity of existence. We exist on this earth for a very brief period of time, a virtual nanosecond compared to the vast period of cosmic evolution that preceded our arrival and the similarly immense stretch of time that will no doubt follow our departure. During this eyeblink of existence, we are responsible for discovering our own moral guidelines, behaving ethically, and giving meaning to our own lives. Looked at in this way, our engagement in these processes of life may seem futile and confusing or absurd and comical, and often both, depending on the particular existentialist.

Another ongoing theme in existentialism is the aforementioned void, or abyss, of nothingness, which inevitably follows the rejection of the idea of objective moral guidelines or ideologies. The advantage of preexisting guidelines, such as those provided by religion, is that they help to structure an orderly view of the world, and an understanding of our place within it. In the absence of such structures, a person may feel lost and without purpose or direction, with nothing to look forward to but the emptiness of death. In the more optimistic forms of existentialism, such as Frankl's, awareness of one's own mortality can be a strong motivator toward making decisions that give one's life greater purpose and meaning. Heidegger, for example, recognized that a key task in life is to recognize and acknowledge the inevitability of death. This acceptance reduces the anxiety caused by death, thus also reducing the anxiety produced by small matters, allowing the person to focus on the important tasks he or she faces in this life.

Existentialists also often focus on the extent to which the important tasks and goals in life are made more difficult by isolation from other people. Humans are fundamentally social animals, with an inborn, instinctive need to interact and make connections with other human beings. These social connections are integral to our development of meaning, as well as to the reduction of anxiety—the void is less frightening when we can share our dread with others. We will ultimately die alone, however, and thus the final responsibility for our choices in life remains our own.

Logotherapy

Viktor Frankl's experiences under the Nazis led him to a psychology that borrowed heavily from the existentialist philosophers. The central idea of his psychology is that we all possess free will, via which we can choose how we view or interpret a situation, thus creating our own meaning. In any situation, even under circumstances such as those experienced by concentration camp inmates, it is possible to find meaning in suffering, and thus reasons to go on living. When people suffer from neuroses and other psychological disorders, it is often at least partly because of a failure to recognize meaning in their lives, along with a failure to recognize their own responsibility for establishing that meaning. In his introduction to logotherapy, *The Doctor and the Soul* (1955), Frankl describes the fundamental reason for modern man's unhappiness with life in this way:

> I have said that *man should not ask what he may expect from life, but should rather understand that life expects something from him* [italics in original]. It may also be put this way: in the last resort, man should not ask "What is the

meaning of my life?" but should realize that he is himself being questioned. Life is putting its problems to him, and it is up to him to respond to these questions by being responsible; he can only answer to life by answering *for his life*. (1955/1986, p. xxi)

Frankl saw this absence of purpose as a fundamental problem in modern culture, and the primary source of the anxiety with which so many people are afflicted, which he referred to as "the disease of our time."

Frankl called this widespread anxiety, in a century in which humanity as a whole probably had far less reason for anxiety than in past eras, a *collective neurosis,* characterized by four symptoms. The first symptom, which Frankl saw as originating during World War II, is the *planless, day-to-day attitude toward life.* People learned to live from one day to the next while waiting for the end of the war, in a time in which further planning made no sense. By the 1950s, the source of anxiety had shifted to the atom bomb, with people widely taking on the attitude that none of their actions mattered, since we could all be wiped out by nuclear war at any time. Frankl astutely observes that "This anticipation of atomic warfare is as dangerous as any other anticipatory anxiety, since, like all fear, it tends to make its fears come true." This attitude leads naturally to Frankl's second symptom, the fatalist attitude toward life. Where the human living day-to-day considers planning ahead to be unnecessary or wasteful, the fatalist sees it as impossible. He or she feels helpless and unable to act, whether as the result of outer circumstances or inner conditions.

The third symptom is collective thinking, in which a person thinks of himself or herself as part of the mass of humanity rather than as an individual; Frankl notes that in doing so, the person abandons the idea of himself or herself as either free or responsible. Not everyone responds to modern fear and anxiety by ignoring his or her own ideas and personality, however. The fourth symptom, a sort of opposite to collectivism, is fanaticism:

While the collectivist ignores his own personality, the fanatic ignores that of the other man, the man who thinks differently. Only his own opinion is valid. In reality, his opinions are those of the group and he does not really have them; his opinions have *him.* (1955/1986, p. xxiii)

Frankl saw this collective neurosis, which was particularly widespread in nations with totalitarian regimes, as especially dangerous in a time of nuclear weapons and warlike posturing, because of the potential effect of one on the other:

Fanaticism crystallizes in the form of slogans which produce a chain reaction. This psychological chain reaction is even more dangerous than the physical one which takes place in the atom bomb. For the latter could never be employed were it not preceded by the psychological chain reactions of slogans. (1955/1985, p. xxiii)

He goes on to refer to the pathological spirit of his time as a mental epidemic and notes that epidemics of physical disease are frequent consequences of war, while mental epidemics are potential *causes* of war. Having described the symptoms, Frankl indicates the seriousness of the problem by referring to research he and his colleagues have carried out with ordinary, non-neurotic people, in which only one person was completely free of all four symptoms, but fully 50 percent displayed at least three of the four signs.

According to Frankl, all four symptoms are a result of man's fear of responsibility and escape from freedom, factors that were partly responsible for the rise of fascist and totalitarian regimes in Europe. The widespread abdication of these two facets of human existence is in part due to contemporary man's weariness with all spiritual things, as Frankl says that responsibility and freedom are primary components of the spiritual domain of man. Frankl's most fundamental break with Freud and other psychoanalysts focuses on this spiritual domain, and he states this quite explicitly:

It is true that Freud once declared in conversation: "humanity has always known that it possesses a spirit; it was my task to show that it has instincts as well." But I myself feel that humanity has demonstrated *ad nauseum* in recent years that it has instincts, drive. Today it appears more important to remind man that he has a spirit, that he is a spiritual being. Psychotherapy should remember this, particularly when dealing with collective neurosis. (1955/1986, p. xxiv)

A fundamental problem with the concept of man implicit in psychoanalysis and other forms of psychotherapy is its emphasis on deterministic views of heredity and environment, while leaving out the spiritual side of life entirely. According to Frankl, this is because the spiritual is now being treated as something that can be explained away in terms of heredity and environment, rather than as what Frankl calls a *thing-in-itself,* and this is a serious mistake. In Frankl's view, spirituality is irreducible and cannot be explained by something not spiritual. Although bodily functions affect the unfolding of the spiritual life, they neither cause nor produce it. Frankl was not using the term *spiritual* to refer to belief in any particular religion, or indeed to belief in a deity at all, but rather to the recognition of a sense of purpose and responsibility in every individual.

Frankl's focus on the primacy of free will and the spiritual over determinism and the instinctual was brought into focus very plainly by his experiences and observations in the concentration camps, where he became convinced that Freud was wrong about the supremacy of instincts. Freud famously proposed a thought experiment:

> Try and subject a number of very strongly differentiated human beings to the same amount of starvation. With the increase of the imperative need for food, all individual differences will be blotted out, and, in their place, we shall see the uniform expression of the one unsatisfied instinct. (Freud, quoted in Frankl, 1955/1986, p. xxv)

Frankl refutes this statement quite simply and elegantly, writing, "But in the concentration camps we witnessed the contrary; we saw how, faced with the identical situation, one man degenerated while another attained virtual saintliness" (1955/1986, p. xxv). Frankl interprets this as demonstrating that, contrary to most psychological thinking of the mid-20th century, people are not merely products of heredity and environment, as a third element is equally important: decision. Ultimately, responsibility for our own lives rests on our own ability to decide for ourselves how we will respond to environment and heredity, and any psychotherapy must incorporate an appeal to free will to be effective.

Frankl's objection to the determinism of psychoanalysis was not limited to its focus on the role of instincts, but also to its rejection of religion, which Freud and his followers sometimes treated as something emerging from the id, with God representing a projected father image. In this view, religion is simply a product of instinctual drives, akin to sexual desire. While Frankl admired Jung's willingness to delve far more deeply into spiritual realms than Freud, he saw Jung also committing a version of the same mistake by reducing religion to a function of the collective unconscious, and God to an archetype. The extent to which he viewed this as an error, and to which he rejected the atheism that was practically a job requirement in psychoanalysis, is captured well in the following:

> I was once asked after a lecture whether I did not admit that there were such things as religious archetypes. Was it not remarkable that all primitive peoples ultimately reached an identical concept of God—which would seem to point to a God-archetype? I asked my questioner whether there was such a thing as a Four-archetype. He did not understand immediately, and so I said: "Look here, all people discover independently that two and two make four. Perhaps we do not need an archetype for an explanation; perhaps two and two really do make four. And perhaps we do not need a divine archetype to explain human religion either. Perhaps God really does exist!" (1955/1986, p. xxvii)

In case his clear difference of opinion with Freud's view of the human psyche is not obvious to the reader, Frankl follows this anecdote with the observation that Freud's id-ego-superego model is "not a correct picture of man, but a caricature of man. The results sound like a tall story by Baron Munchhausen, with the ego pulling itself out of the bog of the id by its own super-ego bootstraps" (1955/1986, p. xxvii). Frankl then follows this statement by observing that presenting a concept of humanity in which man is an automaton, a product of instincts, heredity, drives, reactions, and environment, is simply feeding and encouraging the modern nihilism to which people are already prone.

The solution Frankl proposes to these various problems in 20th-century psychology and psychotherapy is *logotherapy,* from the Greek *logos,* a word with multiple possible connotations, including "word" and "meaning." In his own words, he coined the term to refer to "A psychotherapy which not only recognizes man's spirit, but actually starts from it. In this connection, *logos* is intended to signify 'the spiritual' and, beyond that, 'the meaning'" (1955/1986, p. xvii). Frankl is careful to point out in a footnote to this definition, however, that within the context of logotherapy the word "spiritual" does not refer to any particular religion, but rather to the general human dimension of spirituality.

In defining what distinguishes logotherapy from other contemporary approaches, Frankl tended to contrast its focus explicitly with that of psychoanalysis. In *Man's Search for Meaning,* for example, he relates an anecdote in which a man asks him to describe the difference between logotherapy and psychoanalysis:

> "Yes," I said, "but in the first place, can you tell me in one sentence what you think the essence of psychoanalysis is?" This was his answer: "During psychoanalysis, the patient must lie down on a couch and tell you things which sometimes are very disagreeable to tell." Whereupon I immediately retorted with the following improvisation: "Now, in logotherapy the patient may remain sitting erect but he must hear things which sometimes are very disagreeable to hear." (1959, pp. 97–98)

In this anecdote, Frankl is observing that whereas psychoanalysis is retrospective in its method, focusing on the past and its influence, logotherapy focuses far more on the future than on the past, emphasizing assignments to be fulfilled and meanings not yet achieved by the patient. Frankl points out that a major advantage of this method over that of psychoanalysis is that it takes the patient's attention away from himself and the mechanisms that have led to his neuroses. This breaks up the "typical self-centeredness of the neurotic" (1959, p. 98) instead of continuing to foster and reinforce it, which Frankl saw as an effect of psychoanalysis. According to Frankl, a typical sign of the truly neurotic individual is that he makes every effort to escape from full awareness of his life task, and so an effective therapy must confront him with the meaning and purpose of his life, rather than focusing on his past. Genuinely overcoming neurosis requires awakening to a fuller awareness of one's life task.

Where Freud talks of the pleasure principle, which Frankl renames the *will to pleasure,* and Adler and other individual psychologists write of the status drive, which is often also considered by Nietzsche's term *will to power,* Frankl wishes to focus more on what he suggests calling the *will to meaning.* Just as innate as the drives that Freud and Adler emphasize, Frankl proposes a deep-rooted, hardwired desire to give as much meaning as possible to one's life. This drive for meaning, unlike the drives emphasized by the psychoanalysts, is the most human of the drives, as no animal encounters existential dread about the meaning of its existence. Without recognizing the unique importance of this drive, many psychotherapists would see the will to meaning as a frailty, as a neurotic complex to be gotten rid of, thus ignoring and giving away one of their most valuable assets. Frankl specifically indicts the psychoanalysts in this regard, noting that "some authors . . . contend that meanings and values are 'nothing but defense mechanisms, reaction formations and sublimations' " (1959, p. 99). His rejoinder to this point of view is simple and straightforward: people do not find in their defense mechanisms a reason to live, nor are they willing to die to save their reaction formations, yet human history is littered with examples of people ready and willing to live and die in the service of their ideals and values.

One reason for Frankl's focus on the terminology of free will rather describing a *drive* to achieve meaning or purpose is to further distinguish his approach from that of psychoanalysts. Their focus is on drives, whereas his focus is on values and meaning, a crucial distinction in terms of how these forces act to motivate people. Whereas the libido and other forces emphasized by psychodynamic theorists drive, and therefore *push,* a person in a particular direction, values instead *pull* a person forward. Where drives exert a deterministic influence on people, the reference to being *pulled* by values implicitly suggests that there is freedom involved, freedom to choose whether or not to fulfill one's potential meaning or purpose. Following this same logic, Frankl asserts that a *moral* or *religious* drive cannot exist, at least not in the same sense that other drives represent basic instincts. Man cannot be driven to moral behavior; each instance of moral behavior instead requires a *decision* to behave morally. To be moral, behavior must be chosen freely, or it no longer fulfills any recognizable human definition of morality. Instead of occurring to fulfill a physical drive, Frankl argues that moral behavior occurs for the sake of a cause to which a person has committed himself, whether that cause be a political or social cause, love of another person or people, or obedience to a God. Taking the religious metaphor a bit further, Frankl argues that the saints were driven only by service of God and humanity rather than a drive to sainthood, because if they had actually been driven primarily by the goal of sainthood, the result would surely be that they would instead have become perfectionists, not saints.

Logotherapy, then, is an approach to therapy in which the focus is squarely on the discovery of meaningful goals in one's life. Unlike the proponents of the schools of therapy against which he compares his own approach, Frankl is actually quite cautious, even humble, regarding what he expects logotherapy to be able to accomplish, as well as who he expects will be helped by it. He notes explicitly that logotherapy is intended as a supplement to psychotherapy rather than a substitute for it. His primary goal is to get therapists to pay attention to the spiritual dimension rather than ignoring it, but he does not expect the setting of goals and discovery of meaning to be any sort of cure-all. He is also careful to note that logotherapy is by its very nature concerned with what he calls *noögenic* neuroses, in which the primary underlying problem is a lack of meaning.

Noögenic neurosis was a term coined by Frankl to distinguish between psychogenic neuroses, the kind generally referred to by psychotherapists, and neuroses resulting from existential frustration. Whereas psychogenic neuroses are said to emerge from conflicts between drives and instincts or between instincts and values, noögenic neuroses derive from conflicts between various values, resulting in what Frankl called moral conflicts or spiritual problems. What makes logotherapy the proper approach to these existential problems over psychoanalysis is simply that it is a therapy that takes the spiritual dimension of human life seriously. When confronted with spiritual issues such as a person's aspiration for a meaningful existence, and his or her frustration at failing to achieve it, Frankl points out that in the hands of the logotherapist, the problem will be "taken sincerely and earnestly instead of being traced back to unconscious roots and sources, thus being dealt with merely in *instinctual* terms" (1959, p. 102).

Frankl illustrates the dangers of failing to distinguish between the spiritual and instinctual dimensions rather vividly, with the story of a high-ranking American diplomat in Vienna who arrived at his office hoping to continue psychoanalytic treatment that he had already been undergoing for five years in New York. When Frankl asked him why he had been in analysis in the first place, he replied that he was unhappy in his job and was having trouble complying with American foreign policy. To Frankl it was self-evident that the man was simply unhappy in his work and should probably be doing something else, but the psychoanalyst had instead told him that the U.S. government and his superiors were father images, and his dissatisfaction with his job was an expression of his unconscious hatred of his father. What would cure him was reconciliation with his father, which he had been struggling with for five years. After a few meetings with Frankl, the man gave up his job, found a new line of work, and was happy. An important insight Frankl reported from this case was that the man had no neurotic condition, and did not require any psychotherapy, nor indeed did he require logotherapy. Where other forms of therapy focused on treating everyone as a patient, Frankl captures the core of logotherapy by observing,

> Not every conflict is necessarily neurotic; some amount of conflict is normal and healthy. In a similar sense suffering is not always a pathological phenomenon; rather than being a symptom of neurosis, suffering may well be a human achievement, especially if the suffering grows out of existential frustration. . . . A man's concern, even his despair, over the worthwhileness of life is a *spiritual distress* but by no means a *mental disease*. It may well be that interpreting the first in terms of the latter motivates a doctor to bury his patients' existential despair under a heap of tranquilizer drugs. (1959, 105)

Again, Frankl did not dismiss the existence of real mental disease, for which he did not view logotherapy as the appropriate treatment. Indeed, Frankl estimated, based on his own empirical work, that noögenic neurotics probably represented less than 20 percent of all neurotic patients.

Under extreme conditions, however, the number of people facing a serious existential crisis may be considerably higher. Drawing on both his concentration camp experiences and his history of successful suicide prevention programs, Frankl notes that a successful appeal to continue living, under even the worst conditions, can be made only when survival has a meaning, and that meaning must be specific and personal, as every person is unique. Although his time in the concentration camps was important to the development and confirmation of his ideas, however, Frankl was often frustrated by the popular narrative of how he developed logotherapy, writing in a new preface to the third edition of *The Doctor and the Soul:*

> Let me . . . say a few words regarding the story behind the book—a story that has often been obscured by the misconceptions of the mass media whose representatives never weary of proclaiming that Viktor Frankl came out of Auschwitz with a brand-new psychotherapeutic system he had developed in the concentration camp. The very opposite is true: I *entered* the camp with a full-length book manuscript (hidden under the lining of my overcoat) which was indeed an outline of the basic concepts of logotherapy. (1955/1986, p. ix)

The manuscript was taken away from him and burned almost immediately upon his imprisonment, however, an experience he likened to watching his children murdered before his eyes. His own experience confirmed one of his basic concepts, however: that the will to meaning has clear survival value. Inmates who were oriented toward the future, whether focused on a task to be completed or a reunion with loved ones, were more likely to survive the horrors of the camps than those who lacked a clear purpose. Since his book would no longer survive his time in the camps, it was imperative to Frankl that *he* survive, in order to rewrite the book and incorporate into it the fresh insights he was gaining daily. A few months prior to the liberation of the camps, for example, Frankl became ill with typhus, one of the diseases that spread unchecked through the camps and claimed many victims. As a physician, he knew that the principal fatal danger of the disease was dying of a vascular collapse in his sleep. Frankl reports that he managed to stay awake until the danger was past by writing out notes in shorthand with the stolen stub of a pencil, on the backs of stolen scraps of paper, which would later form the core of his reconstruction of the destroyed manuscript.

The Psychology of the Concentration Camp

The resulting books, especially the chapter of *The Doctor and the Soul* titled "On the Psychology of the Concentration Camp," have exerted a powerful influence on subsequent writers attempting to grapple with the horrors of the concentration camps and their impact on the human psyche. Frankl began by examining the factors that might make his own observations less reliable than he might wish, pointing out that human existence was so thoroughly deformed in the camp that there is some doubt that an observer who is himself an inmate could possibly be sufficiently objective to draw any useful conclusions. Such an observer would have endured psychological and ethical warping that might render him unable to evaluate either his own behavior or that of others. Meanwhile, an outsider would conversely be too far removed from the immediate experience of the camps to be capable of truly understanding what was going on or empathizing with the victims. Borrowing from Einstein, Frankl proposes that, as in relativity, any standard of measurement applied to the camp experience is itself distorted by the perspective of the observer, and so his analysis begins with the simple observation that we have no adequate description of what took place.

Despite this difficulty of perspective, however, Frankl notes that a few basic facts about the psychology of the concentration camp seem to be beyond serious dispute. The reactions of camp inmates fall into three distinct phases: reception into the camp, actual camp life, and the phase after discharge or liberation. In the first phase, the inmate undergoes *reception shock,* a reaction to the new, unaccustomed environment in which the inmate draws a clear line of demarcation between his old life and his new circumstances. All his possessions have been taken away, and he has nothing, not even his previous identity. Inmates respond with agitation and intense anger, but some deal with the constant threat of death by determining that they will take that power away from their captors by committing suicide, often by deliberately running into the electrified fences.

The second phase arrives after a few days or weeks and is characterized by a profound apathy, which emerges as a kind of psychic self-defense mechanism. It is as though the camp dweller has put on a sort of mental armor, which repels everything that used to either excite or anger him, arouse either indignation or despair, as well as anything he is forced to either watch or participate in. He has adjusted to his bizarre environment by reducing his level of emotional life, with events around him reaching consciousness in a blurred form. His conscious focus has narrowed and been concentrated on a single point: simply surviving another day. According to Frankl, inner life in the concentration camp becomes quite primitive, with even the contents of dreams reduced to such mundane items as bread, cigarettes, and a bath. Where gatherings of men often lead to conversation about sex, especially dirty jokes, Frankl reports that in the camps that subject was met with indifference. Because of chronic undernourishment, the members of work squads instead tended to focus their conversations on food, exchanging recipes and planning meals they will prepare for each other some day, after getting out of the camp.

During this second phase, many psychologists have also noted changes in character in some inmates, with many developing inferiority complexes, while some others, who were given some power over their fellow inmates, developing a sort of megalomania. A popular approach to writing about these developments in the postwar years was to present it as evidence for a fairly extreme environmental interpretation, in which individuals are ultimately slaves to their social surroundings. In the right environment, anyone's character can be profoundly changed. To psychoanalytic writers, these changes represent regression to a more primitive existence, driven by instinct. To this, Frankl gave a clear, dissenting response:

> Does not all this support the view that a character type is marked out by the environment? Does it not prove that man cannot escape the destiny of his social surroundings? Our answer is: It does not. . . . is [a man] still spiritually responsible for what is happening to him psychically, for what the concentration camp has "made" of him? Our answer is: He is. (1955/1986, pp. 96–97)

In Frankl's view, under all circumstances, even amid the horrors of the concentration camps, the individual still retains both the freedom and the responsibility to give shape to his own existence. Far from being all-powerful, the forces of the concentration camps were unable to warp the character of all inmates. Instead, there are many examples of people who behaved heroically on behalf of their fellow inmates, rather than simply submitting to the new rules of their existence.

Frankl goes on to observe that evidence suggests that the people who fit the standard picture of camp inmates, who succumbed to the negative roles provided by the social environment, were by and large people who had given up the spiritual struggle to lead a meaningful life *before* their arrival in the camps. The freedom to select the attitude with which they would face their new circumstances had not been taken away from them; they had instead given up that freedom willingly. From this, Frankl derives an observation that was both true of camp inmates and, outside the camps, was applicable to neurotic patients in general: that a neurotic symptom is never *just* a consequence of a physiological factor or the expression of something psychic, but also an expression of a spiritual factor, which Frankl calls a *mode of existence*. Ultimately, every individual possesses the freedom and responsibility to decide whether or not to be influenced by his surroundings. Those people who surrendered without a struggle to those influences were people who had lost their spiritual support. This is why Frankl felt that logotherapy, a therapeutic approach that emphasizes the importance of the spiritual and of meaning, was so important—other therapeutic approaches neglect that crucial support.

As an example of the importance of that spiritual support in allowing people to exercise their freedom to decide, Frankl gives the example of what he calls the "futurelessness" of life in the camps. At the time that most of the inmates were delivered to the camps, very little was known about what actually went on there, except that they were believed to be places from which nobody returned. Once imprisoned, an inmate's uncertainty about his fate was reduced, along with its concomitant anxiety, to at least a small degree—he no longer doubted that he would die. Instead, as the days stretched onward, with no sense at all of how long he would stay in the camp, the inmate came to feel more and more alienated from the outside world. The indefinite nature of his imprisonment, with no sentence, led the inmates to a sense of life imprisonment, with no thoughts at all about the future, as he felt certain he had none. According to Frankl, under normal circumstances our entire present existence is focused on a point in the future, and our objectives and the meaning we ascribe to our lives have to do with that future. The hopelessness and apathy experienced by the prisoners, with no sense of those future objectives, removed their sense of having any agency in their own lives. The inmates who were more likely to survive, and who retained their psychological health, were those who were able to devise ways to envision a future, either by setting goals or by simply finding ways to remind themselves of their existence outside the camps. Frankl himself, whose outside identity was defined by his work as a doctor and a scholar, was able to survive in part by delivering lectures on various medical and psychological topics, sometimes to his fellow inmates but also sometimes to no audience at all.

The third phase of the inmates' reaction to the camps, liberation, also provided valuable insights for logotherapy. Frankl notes that the liberated prisoner is still in need of psychological care, as the sudden throwing-off of the massive pressure of camp life is itself "a psychological hazard of prime magnitude" (1955/1986, p. 103). Upon release, the prisoner experiences everything at first like a dream, a dream he is hesitant to believe is real, as he has been deceived by such dreams before. Many times in the past he has dreamt of being back home among family and friends, only to be awakened into the harsh reality of camp life. Upon liberation, the camp inmate must still live with the constant sense of depersonalization, having to learn to live with freedom all over again. Frankl observes that those who were most successful at reaching the point where the past is a distant nightmare, and realize that they need fear nothing (a feeling that was often accompanied by a resurgent religious faith), were those who had a clear sense of responsibility and purpose while still in the camps.

Frankl's logotherapy, in its emphasis on personal responsibility and freedom of choice, runs counter to a number of 20th-century cultural trends, but perhaps nowhere so much as in his treatment of the meaning of suffering. Frankl addresses this countercultural approach quite directly, noting, "Those who worship the superficial cult of success obviously will not understand such conclusions" (1955/1986, p. 106). The conclusions to which he refers actually sound very much like a central tenet of both Christianity and traditional Judaism, reflecting again his greater sympathy with religion as compared to Freud:

> Attitudinal values . . . are actualized whenever the individual is faced with something unalterable, something imposed by destiny. From the manner in which a person takes these things upon himself, assimilates these difficulties into his own psyche, there flows an incalculable multitude of value-potentialities. This means that *human life can be fulfilled not only in creating and enjoying, but also in suffering!* [italics in original] (1955/1986, pp. 106–107)

This difference in emphasis from psychoanalysis follows logically from the fundamental difference between the two approaches in their very conception of humanity. In *Man's Search for Meaning,* Frankl describes this difference by pointing out that logotherapy

> considers man as a being whose main concern consists in fulfilling a meaning and in actualizing values, rather than in the mere gratification and satisfaction of drives and instincts, or in merely reconciling the conflicting claims of id, ego and superego, or in the mere adaptation and adjustment to society and environment. (1959, p. 105)

In emphasizing the role of human will, choice, and responsibility in how we respond to the influences of both heredity and environment, up to and including terrible suffering, Frankl's existential approach to psychology offers a third alternative to the major 20th-century movements out of Vienna, psychoanalysis and Adler's individual psychology. For this reason, the existential approach has often been referred to as "third force" of Viennese psychology, and more recently the much larger movement of existential/humanistic/phenomenological psychology has often been called third force psychology.

Controversy: The Waldheim Affair

Although a 1991 survey by the Library of Congress listed *Man's Search for Meaning* as one of the 10 most influential books in America, Frankl's actions, though apparently consistent with his existential approach to life, have occasionally stirred up controversy in the international Jewish community. As a survivor of the Nazi concentration camps, in which he lost most of his family, Frankl has taken a far more conciliatory approach toward Austria's history during the Nazi era than most Jewish writers on the Holocaust. This has of course always been the attitude called for by his philosophy, in which terrible experiences gain meaning based on how we choose to treat them and great suffering can serve a positive purpose. After the war, Frankl was one of the few Jewish intellectuals who chose to remain in Vienna, adopting the position that there are only two kinds of people, decent and indecent, and that these two types occur in all groups of people, even the Nazis. The Holocaust could thus have been perpetrated in any country, and the proper attitude in its aftermath was one of forgiveness and reconciliation.

Frankl's postwar arguments against the concept of collective guilt and in favor of forgiveness toward the Nazis were rather controversial, and did not sit well with some Jewish organizations. In 1978, for example, Frankl gave a lecture at the Institute of Adult Jewish Studies at Congregation B'nai Jeshrun in New York City. The audience booed him, and at least one audience member called him a Nazi pig. Some responses were less restrained and more outrageous, as when a swastika was smeared on his front door with feces. A Holocaust survivor organization spoke out against him and rejected him for membership when they discovered that immediately after the war, Frankl allowed a medical colleague and former Hitler Youth member to hide in his apartment from the police. Although his actions were all emblematic of the reconciliatory, forgiving attitude that Frankl felt was necessary in order to allow the world to move on, he has come to be seen by some survivors as helping Austria to avoid confronting and atoning for its role in the Holocaust.

Austria represents a bit of a special case among European countries overrun by the Nazis: Unlike what happened in many other nations, Austria was not taken by military force. To the contrary, many contemporary sources note that Hitler's arrival in Vienna was greeted by huge, celebratory crowds in the streets and squares of the city. This may have been because Hitler was himself Austrian, along with several other key Nazi officials, and was thus a national hero to many of those gathered in the capital, a city in which anti-Semitic feeling had run high long before the arrival of the Nazis. In the immediate postwar period, the strength of this feeling was reflected especially in one particular statistic: Austria had more than 600,000 registered Nazi Party members.

Despite all this, the government of Austria has spent much of the time since the war attempting to quietly distance itself from recognition of its official cooperation with the Nazis, preferring instead to be portrayed as the first *victim* nation of the *Wehrmacht.* For an internationally known and highly respected scholar like Viktor Frankl to propose forgiveness rather than dwelling on the guilt of the Austrian people for their complicity has therefore made him a fair number of enemies. International discomfort with the Austrian attitude toward their Nazi past reached a peak in 1986, with the election of Kurt Waldheim as president of Austria. Waldheim had actually already led a long international career as a diplomat and politician, having even served as secretary general of the United Nations from 1972 to 1981. While he was secretary general, a position to which his election required that he receive votes from the European nations that were still recovering from the wounds inflicted by the Nazi war effort, he became known for his humanitarian efforts, going out of his way to assist the victims of other genocidal endeavors. In 1979, for example, he helped Paul McCartney to organize the Concerts for the People of Kampuchea, a series of benefits to raise funds to help rebuild Cambodia in the wake of Pol Pot's Khmer Rouge regime.

Prior to Waldheim's election as president, however, evidence emerged that he had misrepresented the degree of his own involvement with the Nazi war effort. He had described himself as having merely served as a clerk and translator, and as having had no knowledge at all of the large-scale killing of Jews. In fact, he appears to have served in the Wehrmacht and the SS as an intelligence officer, in which capacity he served in several different countries, and one source reports that he personally reviewed and approved leaflets that were dropped to Russian soldiers on the Eastern Front, encouraging them to kill all the Jews and thus end the war quickly. Another investigator reported that for a time, Waldheim occupied an office only a few hundred yards from a location where locals were routinely rounded up and shot. In another account, famed Nazi-hunter Simon Wiesenthal reported that Waldheim spent some of his time stationed five miles from Salonika, in Greece, and was there when the entire Salonika Jewish community, a full third of the population, was rounded up and sent off to Auschwitz over a period of several weeks. Waldheim replied to the charge by denying any knowledge of this. Long before this controversy erupted, Waldheim had enraged the international Jewish community, among many others, with his response to the rescue mission in which Israeli commandos successfully retrieved hostages who had been held in Entebbe, Uganda, after the Israeli airplane on which they had been passengers was hijacked. While the rest of the world applauded the audacity and boldness of the raid (it was even the basis for a highly successful action movie), Waldheim opined, in his capacity as UN secretary general, that Israel had violated international law and failed to respect Ugandan sovereignty in rescuing its citizens.

In response to the international controversy stirred up by the charges that Waldheim had misrepresented his service to the Nazis, the Austrian government appointed an international committee of historians to examine Waldheim's record during the war. The committee reached two key conclusions, the first of which is especially important in light of Frankl's subsequent actions: There was no evidence that Waldheim had had any personal involvement in any war crimes. They also concluded, however, that his repeated claims that he was unaware of such crimes taking place were disingenuous, and that he must certainly have known about them. Wiesenthal replied to Waldheim's denial by citing the committee's report, writing that "I could only reply what the committee of historians made clear in its report: 'I cannot believe you'" (1999, p. 91). The general international reaction to the whole affair centered on the recognition that, as it was clear that Waldheim had lied about his war record, and had stood idly by while atrocities happened around him, he certainly shouldn't be president of a modern nation.

Viktor Frankl, however, had spent his time since the war urging forgiveness and a recognition that many of the people in German service at the time had been powerless to stop what was going on around them, and thus should not all be held accountable for the war's excesses. As has been seen, this had already made him many enemies, but he stirred up sentiment against himself even further by allowing himself to be photographed in 1988, accepting a medal from President Waldheim. The medal, the Grosse silberne Ehrenzeichen mit dem Stern (Great Silver Badge of Honor with the Star), was presented to him as a former "concentration camp prisoner . . . who in the Hell of National Socialism lost his entire family." This was seen by many in the international Jewish community as a betrayal—where they believed a camp survivor as recognized and respected as Frankl ought to refuse such an award and take the opportunity to instead speak out against the complicity of ordinary Austrians with the Germans, Frankl was instead providing instrumental support to the rehabilitation of Waldheim's reputation on the world stage.

Further Reading

Frankl, V.E. (1955/1986). *The Doctor and the Soul: From Psychotherapy to Logotherapy*. New York: Vintage.

Frankl, V.E. (1959). *Man's Search for Meaning: An Introduction to Logotherapy*. Boston: Beacon.

Pytell, T. (2000). The Missing Pieces of the Puzzle: A Reflection on the Odd Career of Viktor Frankl. *Journal of Contemporary History* 35(2): 281–306.

Wiesenthal, S. (1999). The Waldheim Case. In D. Lorenz, ed. *Contemporary Jewish Writing in Austria*. Omaha: University of Nebraska Press, pp. 81–95.

Freud, Anna (1895–1982)

The sixth child of Sigmund and Martha Freud, Anna was also the only one of their offspring who followed in her father's footsteps and became a psychoanalyst. Her childhood coincides almost perfectly with the period during which her father was developing his ideas and making his largest impact on the intellectual world, as she was born in the same year that also saw the publication of *Studien über Hysterie* (Studies of Hysteria), the first published account of what would become psychoanalysis. From earliest childhood, she was very close to her father, far closer than any of her siblings, and conversely had a very poor relationship with her mother. Of the lack of closeness with her mother, she would in later life say that she had written so little about mother-daughter relations because she had never experienced them.

In a career in which his handpicked successors such as Jung and Adler parted ways with him and pursued their own versions of analytic psychology, Freud was ultimately succeeded in the eyes of many of the world's psychoanalysts by his own daughter. This transition was not an obvious path during her childhood: although the elder Freud was full of praise for her intellectual gifts in adulthood, he did not support the teen Anna's hopes for a university education, sending her instead to the Cottage Lyceum, a teachers' college. On her own, however, she had already learned to fluently speak Hebrew, German, English, French, and Italian. She finished at the Lyceum at age 17, at which time she traveled alone to England with the specific goal of improving her English, though contacts she made there would serve her well in later years. With the outbreak of World War I in 1914, she was helped to return to Vienna by friends she had made in the diplomatic community. Once back home, she became a teacher trainee, and later a teacher, at her old school, where she remained until forced by tuberculosis to quit in 1920.

The loss of her teaching job was an important turning point for Anna, as she then began to work more closely with her father, becoming his secretary, assistant, and promoter. Though today many psychologists would see his actions as inappropriate and unethical, in 1918 Sigmund Freud began the psychoanalysis of his daughter, and she quickly became immersed in the psychoanalytic world. She attended her first meeting of the Vienna Psychoanalytical Society that same year and was soon translating papers, attending to the business of organizing meetings, and even analyzing patients herself. Lacking a medical degree, she was one of the

The apple remained close to the tree: Anna Freud in Berlin, 1928. (Imagno/Getty Images)

first lay analysts who met with her father's approval. Anna Freud presented her first paper to the Vienna Psychoanalytical Society in 1922 and was accepted as a member of the organization soon thereafter.

In 1923, the same year that her father was diagnosed with cancer, she established her own private practice, and from then on she was also the elder Freud's primary caretaker and intellectual sounding board, in addition to the work she already did for him as a secretary. Anna Freud's theoretical contributions to the field of psychoanalysis were fairly limited, as she largely accepted her father's ideas as they stood, but her influence on the practice of psychoanalysis as therapy has been profound, particularly in its application to children. Although her earliest patients were adults, her experience as a teacher soon led her to instead undertake the psychoanalytic study of the child, which would become her life's work. In 1925, Anna Freud and a group of other analysts established the first private psychoanalytically oriented preschool, along with what has been acknowledged to be the first modern day care center for underprivileged infants, which led to the city of Vienna appointing her in 1926 to train elementary and preschool teachers to apply psychoanalytic theory in education. In addition to these efforts, she also delivered an important series of lectures in 1926, which were later published as *An Introduction to the Technique of Child Analysis,* a book that served to establish child psychoanalysis as a legitimate subspecialty. In 1931, Anna Freud became editor of the *Journal of Psychoanalytical Education,* which would later evolve into *The Psychoanalytic Study of the Child.*

Her influential early work on the use of psychoanalysis with children was not the only important contribution by Anna Freud during the pre-*Anschluss* period in Austria, however. She is also widely considered the founder of what has become known as *ego psychology,* which is the label a majority of modern psychoanalysts would apply to their work. Although she made no fundamental changes in her father's theory, Anna Freud emphasized the role of the ego, as the active agent in resolving intrapersonal conflict, over her father's emphasis on the unconscious processes of the id and the superego. This emphasis led her to try to define the parameters of *normal* child development rather than following her father's emphasis on the development of pathology, an idea she first explored in depth in the very influential *The Ego and the Mechanisms of Defense* (1936). This book's impact was so great that ever since then, most discussion of **defense mechanisms** has, consciously or otherwise, referenced Anna Freud's description of them rather than Sigmund's. The book also explains why she thought that child analysis could teach us so much more about child development than adult analysis: Although it seems transparently obvious to a modern reader, she had to convince the psychoanalytic community of her time that speaking with children as they are actually going through the conflicts of childhood might provide a more accurate account of those conflicts than retrospective interviews with adults. Furthermore, she argues that children respond to both the pressures of the world and their own internal conflicts with a broader and more creative range of defense mechanisms than adults are capable of summoning up.

The explosive growth of child and ego psychoanalysis was interrupted, however, by the rise of the Nazis. As early as 1933, the Nazi Party in Germany had banned Sigmund Freud's work as Jewish science and ordered his books to be burned in Berlin. In 1938, when the Nazis arrived in Vienna, Sigmund Freud was very ill, and his psychoanalytic publishing enterprise, largely run and supervised by his son and by Anna, fell under Nazi scrutiny. With insufficient funds to buy the family's way out of the country, and the senior Freud's health too poor to travel easily, the Freuds were in very real danger. Anna Freud was arrested and taken for questioning by the Gestapo, facing the distinct possibility of never returning, but was quickly released thanks to the intervention of influential family friend Princess Marie **Bonaparte**. Along with other friends, including Ernest **Jones** in Great Britain and Ludwig Binswager in Switzerland, Bonaparte had been trying for some time to arrange the Freuds' departure from Vienna, but Sigmund Freud had refused to leave, believing that his international scholarly reputation and celebrity would protect him from the Nazis. Bonaparte had actually traveled *into* Nazi-occupied Austria to try to reason with him, and she accompanied Anna Freud when she was taken by the Gestapo, helping to secure her release. With Bonaparte's help, the Freuds traveled first to her home in Paris, and then to London, where Sigmund Freud would remain until his death, and where Anna Freud would make her greatest impact on the world.

Once safely arrived in England, Anna Freud immediately started seeing patients again, and she founded the Hampstead Wartime Nursery for Homeless Children, a refuge for children who had been separated from their parents by the war. In addition to providing treatment to the children, the nursery also served as a natural laboratory in which Freud could explore the impact of parental separation on child development, a research program that quickly resulted in two books: *Infants without Families* (1939) and *Reports from the Hampstead Nurseries* (1945). In these books, coauthored by her longtime friend and fellow analyst Dorothy Burlingham, the authors attempted to outline a program of service and research intended to prevent further harm to the children, while also proposing an ideal nursery model for the education of young children in peacetime. In her work at Hampstead, Anna Freud deviated from her father's essential concerns by trying not just to understand the etiology in childhood of psychopathology, but also to describe *normal* development in some detail.

Throughout her work at Hampstead, a fundamental concern came to the fore: the idea that separation from family could have a more deleterious effect on the children than the experience of war itself. Where her father had focused on the role of the parent-child relationship in the production of psychopathology, it became clear to Freud that the parental bond is just as supremely important in normal development. Possessing a famous, instantly recognizable surname was an advantage Anna Freud made good use of, and her work at Hampstead was quickly translated into government policy, which shifted from sending children away from their families for their own safety during the war, and institutionalization of mentally ill children after the war, to an emphasis on supporting at-risk children and keeping them with their families instead.

As had happened to her father before her, Anna Freud soon found herself at odds with others who were also exploring the use of psychoanalysis with children. For several years before Freud's arrival on British soil, another child psychoanalyst, Melanie **Klein,** had already made her name with the application of psychoanalysis to children. The two women had some very fundamental differences of opinion regarding the use and applicability of psychoanalysis, especially where very young children were concerned. Probably the most basic difference between the two concerned the possibility of using psychoanalytic techniques with toddlers. Freud regarded psychoanalytic treatment, like her father and Josef **Breuer** before her, as essentially a *talking* cure, which naturally ruled out analyzing children before they had mastered language. Whatever educational and therapeutic techniques were to be used with very small children must therefore take into account their unique developmental level and individual idiosyncrasies. Klein, however, believed that the same techniques could be applied to children and adults, whether they could speak or not. Klein introduced the notion of play therapy, expecting that children's behaviors with toys could be just as revealing of their psyches as the search for repressed memories with adults. Freud objected vehemently to what she saw as the over-interpretation of children's actions and expressions in play as signs of internal conflict, suggesting that Klein and her followers had too narrow a view of what could be considered normal in children's play. Freud also believed that child therapy required parental participation and support, which could be directly observed where Klein instead took an arguably more traditional approach by interpreting play behaviors as symbolic of the child's relationship with his or her parents. Another point of disagreement in which Freud opposed Klein's somewhat more traditionally psychoanalytic view concerned the universal usefulness of psychoanalysis: whereas Klein suggested that all children could benefit from analysis, Anna Freud openly doubted that everyone needs it.

Given their profound differences, it seems unavoidable that there would be open conflict between the two women's students and followers, and indeed the British Psychoanalytical Society quickly began to fracture into Freudians and Kleinians, though a third contingent of Independents took no side in the debate.

The British Psychoanalytical Society's response to this internal disarray was to formally try to work things out by staging a formal series of scholarly debates, the Controversial Discussions, over a period of several years in the 1940s. Lasting from 1941 to 1946, the discussions sought simply to determine whether the new views on child development and treatment advocated by Melanie Klein and her supporters were compatible with the more traditional approach taken by Anna Freud and her followers in Berlin and Vienna. If it was determined that the two sets of views were *not* compatible, the ultimate expectation was that Klein would be expelled from the international psychoanalytic community.

Although the discussions arose out of the disagreements between Klein and Freud, they really stood in for a broader conflict between the indigenous British approach to psychoanalysis, heavily but not exclusively influenced by Klein, and the more traditional Continental approach, often characterized by a slavish adherence to the works of Sigmund Freud. The debate might never have come to a head without the Nazi occupations on the continent, which led to the emigration to England and America of most of the largely Jewish leading figures of psychoanalysis. As a medical degree was required to practice psychoanalysis in America, Anna Freud, who like Klein had no university education, remained in England after escaping Vienna with her father, and so she and Klein had no choice but to share the same intellectual territory.

The Controversial Discussions were remarkable in their clear-cut organization. Each side gathered papers by its respective leading lights, and a committee was appointed to judge the scholarly papers to be presented by each side. The committee, comprised of leading U.K. psychoanalysts, was chaired by Ernest Jones. Four scholarly papers on the theory and practice of psychoanalysis were submitted by each side—all the papers were collected as a book that remains in print today (King and Steiner, 1991). Though all involved expected a winner to be named by the committee, the actual end result was a compromise, by which the divisions within the British Psychoanalytical Society were formalized. The Kleinians and the Freudians were of course defined by their loyalty to one side or the other, whereas the Independents were at first cynically defined as the analysts to whom neither Klein nor Freud was willing to refer cases.

After the Controversial Discussions, Anna Freud became less involved with the affairs of the British Psychoanalytical Society, concentrating her efforts instead on the Hampstead Clinic. After the war, the Wartime Nursery was supplanted by the Hampstead Child Therapy Course and Clinic, which became the largest child analytic treatment and training center in the world, and the model for many similar facilities in other countries. For the next four decades, Anna Freud trained, supervised, and consulted with analysts at the clinic while also speaking internationally and publishing numerous books. Her impact on the world's attitudes toward children and their relationships with their parents was not limited to her work in the 1930s and 1940s, however, as she would undertake another hugely influential project in the early 1960s, collaborating with the Yale Child Study Center in a series of seminars on family law and child custody conflicts. In the books resulting from her work at Yale, Freud articulated a principle for making decisions regarding child custody that continues to guide judges today: the idea that the "best interests of the child" should prevail over other concerns. Freud argued that the best interests of the child are best met by selecting the "least detrimental alternative" that allows the child to maintain stable parental relationships.

Based on a lifetime of working with children, and a career-long desire to focus the attention of psychoanalysis on normal development as well as psychopathology, Anna Freud produced one of her most influential works quite late in life. First published in 1966, *Normality and Pathology in Childhood: Assessments of Development* focuses on several important themes. Unlike many psychoanalysts, Anna Freud in this book supported the idea of creating assessment tools to determine children's level of development, as well as the establishment of developmental norms for behavior. She also departs rather dramatically from her father's emphasis on the Oedipal conflict as the root cause of all psychopathology by expressing the belief that neurosis can have many different origins, and furthermore that psychopathology may take different forms in childhood and adulthood, and that these may not even be causally related to each other. She advocated a future for psychoanalysis, in other words, in which her father's old model was far too simplistic to explain much of human behavior.

Further Reading

Freud, A. (1966). *Normality and Pathology in Childhood: Assessments of Development.* [*Writings of Anna Freud,* Vol. 6]. London: International Universities Press.

Freud, A. (1975). *An Introduction to the Technique of Child Analysis.* London: Ayer.

Freud, A. (1976). *Infants without Families/Reports from the Hampstead Nurseries.* [*Writings of Anna Freud,* Vol. 3]. London: International Universities Press.

Freud, A. (1977). *The Ego and the Mechanisms of Defense.* [*Writings of Anna Freud,* Vol. 2: *1936*]. London: International Universities Press.

King, P., and R. Steiner, eds. (1991). *The Freud-Klein Controversies 1941–1945.* London: Tavistock/Routledge.

Freudian Slip. *See Parapraxes*

Fromm, Erich (1900–1980)

Erich Fromm was born in the German city of Frankfurt-am-Rhein in 1900. After studying at the Universities of Heidelberg, Munich, Frankfurt, he trained as a psychoanalyst at the Institute of Psychoanalysis at Berlin. Prior to the psychoanalytic training, his education was fairly eclectic—he studied Jewish law and religion, and obtained a doctorate on the Jewish Diaspora from Heidelberg University. Following his time in Berlin, he became a part of the scholarly movement that became known as the Frankfurt School, at the Institute of Social Research at the University of Frankfurt am Main.

The Frankfurt school was an interdisciplinary group of social theorists, primarily dissident Marxists who had become disillusioned with the ways in which Karl Marx's ideas had come to be narrowly presented in both the academic and political spheres, put in service of the defense of various Communist parties. As a group, they were critical of both capitalism and the Soviet brand of socialism, feeling that Marxist theory alone could not sufficiently account for the rapid expansion and development of capitalist societies in the 20th century. While their affiliations with each other were fairly loose and disorganized, the scholars of the Frankfurt School had a common set of assumptions in mind, a common paradigm from which to draw the important questions. Essentially, they set out to handle the apparent omissions in traditional Marxism by seeking answers in the insights of other disciplinary approaches, including sociology, psychoanalysis, and existentialist philosophy, among others. As Marxists, their concern was largely with understanding the conditions under which real social change is possible, along with the establishment of rationally guided institutions.

When the rise of the Nazis made emigration prudent for prominent Jewish scholars, Fromm was among the first psychoanalysts to leave. As the Nazis viewed both psychoanalysis and Marxism as Jewish science, Fromm would have been in even greater danger than most, so he brought his intriguing blend of Marxism and psychoanalysis to America in 1934. In New York, Fromm lectured at Columbia University, while also setting himself up in a psychoanalytic practice. When the remnants of the Frankfurt Institute of Social Research reopened as the New School for Social Research in Manhattan, he taught there as well. Fromm became a U.S. citizen in 1940, following which he added further to his teaching résumé with stints at Bennington College and Yale University. Eventually, as the United States became less hospitable to openly Marxist scholars in the early 1950s, he accepted the directorship of Instituto Mexicano de Psicoanálisis at the National Autonomous University in Mexico City.

The Marxist influence is clear in Fromm's basic departures from Freud's theory. Despite agreeing with large portions of Freud's perspective, Fromm felt that Freud committed a basic error in presenting the libido's desires and passions as the basic motivational force in humans, and their frustrations as the primary cause of mental illness. It seemed to Fromm that, powerful though the sexual drive and its associated desires are, a more powerful force motivates human behavior, which Fromm called the "human situation." That situation is the problem of human self-awareness, which evolved from our earlier, animal state, resulting in problems that are unique to humans. Unlike animals, we find ourselves pondering our existence, the nature of truth, and the ultimate meaning and purpose of our lives. It is this constant endeavor to understand life that is the primary motivation behind all human behavior, including moral behavior:

> Man is the only animal who finds his own existence a problem which he has to solve and from which he cannot escape. . . . Indeed, the tremendous energy in the forces producing mental illness, as well as those behind art and religion, could never be understood as an outcome of substrated or sublimated physiological needs; they are attempts to solve the problem of being born human. All men are idealists . . . striving for the satisfaction of needs that transcend the physiological needs of the organism. The difference [between individuals] is only that one idealism is a good and adequate solution, the other a bad and destructive one. (Fromm, 1968b, pp. 308–312)

While reflecting the Marxist influence, this passage also echoes Freud's distinction between life instincts and death instincts, while suggesting that the striving to understand how those instincts are to be properly expressed is what drives us, rather than the instincts themselves.

Fromm's religious training played an important role in his formulation of the importance of choice over instinct, as seen in his discussion of the Hebrew noun *yetzer,* which has often posed a problem for translators of religious literature. The word is often used to refer to inclination or impulse, but derives from a root meaning "to form" or "to fashion." When used with reference to the mind, it is translated as "imagination," "purpose," or "drive." According to Fromm,

> The Hebrew word indicates the important fact that evil (or good) impulses are possible only on the basis of something that is specifically human: Imagination. For this very reason, only man—and not animals—can be evil or good. An animal can act in a manner which appears to us cruel (for instance a cat

playing with a mouse), but there is no evil in this play, since it is nothing but the manifestation of the animal's instinct. The problem of good and evil arises only where there is imagination. (1968, p.126)

Beyond their differences on the importance of instinct and drives, Fromm was also critical of what he saw as Freud's failure to acknowledge the role of larger social forces in the development of an individual's personality. One of the more striking differences, in fact, between the two men's theories, is the actual locus of the conflict that drives development, with Freud focusing primarily on internal conflict, while Fromm gives equal emphasis to conflict *outside* the individual. Given Fromm's thorough grounding in the ideas of Karl Marx, the focus on larger forces outside the individual is hardly surprising, echoing Lev **Vygotsky**'s emphasis on the social origins of all cognitive functions in his Marx-inspired take on child development.

Where Freud focused on the primacy of an individual's wants, needs, and desires in motivating his actions, and consequently his development, Fromm felt that Freud failed to acknowledge that every individual lives within a social setting, and so the individual is forced to accommodate the society's needs and wants in addition to his own. Whatever the individual does to accommodate his own drives must be interpreted against the backdrop of how his choices affect other people as well—personal adjustment has a social component that must be met as well. An individual who has successfully reduced internal conflict but has as a result increased conflict with his society, and thus reduced the extent to which he fits in with and contributes to that society, cannot be said to be psychologically well adjusted. Development involves a balancing act that Fromm felt that Freud had ignored, between sometimes meeting one's own internal demands and sometimes submitting to the conflicting demands of the society.

Erich Fromm, the man who blended psycho-analysis and Marxism, 1955. (Leonard Mccombe/Time Life Pictures/Getty Images)

Fromm also brought a Marxist perspective to bear in his quest for an explanation of the forces that had led him to flee Germany. Marx had predicted that the rise of capitalism would result in uprisings and political upheaval in Europe, resulting ultimately in more egalitarian societies all around. What happened instead was the rise of authoritarian regimes that oppressed their citizens even more harshly than their predecessors had, even in the ostensibly Marxist (in name, anyway) Union of Soviet Socialist Republics. That this had happened was a puzzle, the resolution of which inspired intellectuals throughout the world, but it was especially puzzling to Marxists like Fromm, who had expected a very different outcome. Fromm combined Marxism and psychoanalysis to produce an intriguing solution to the 20th century's great riddle. In *Escape from Freedom* (1941), he proposed that the rise of capitalism and the modern industrial age, by breaking up the tight-knit communities that had characterized human society throughout history, led inevitably to alienation, emptiness, and loneliness. Western capitalism produces a world in which people come to feel that their quality of life is entirely determined by forces outside themselves, and beyond their own interests and wishes. In such a world, the only apparent possibility of happiness lies in acceptance of those forces, and submission to them. Capitalism, in this model, leads inevitably to the common people's acceptance of fascism, much as Fromm had just seen happening in Germany.

According to Fromm, a primary goal of psychotherapy is to help people to respond in the healthiest way possible to these external forces. Psychological problems arise when people respond by alienating themselves and engaging in hostile, selfish, and aggressive forms of behavior. Overcoming these negatives requires both regulation and community. Fromm emphasized the human need to unite with others and feel a sense of what later humanistic psychologists referred to as *belongingness,* a need that can be met by family, small institutions such as churches, or even nations. Fromm warned that, like most needs, this one can be met in both healthy and unhealthy ways. Attempts to fulfill the need to belong can easily lead to *narcissism,* which he defined as "intense attachment to oneself, to one's own group, clan, religion, race, etc.—with consequent serious distortions of rational judgment" (Fromm, 1994, p. 101). Fromm also emphasized that, in achieving this sense of community, the setting of clear limits, through boundaries, rules, and laws, is a vital component.

American culture struck Fromm as an outstanding example of how these needs could be met in an insalubrious fashion. In *To Have or to Be* (1976), he critiqued the American model of the surplus society, in which everyone has too much of everything, as emphasizing *having* over *being.* Excessive consumption, along with the rise of mass-media pop culture and the dominance of work over private life, has led to modern humans losing touch with what is meaningful in their lives: we *have* everything, but we *are* nothing. To continue acquiring consumer goods that we don't actually need, people are forced to work long hours at dehumanizing jobs, with no time left for family and community. Work is an oppressive factor when it is allowed to dominate over other concerns, and neuroses and sadism can be directly traced to the modern tendency to define ourselves primarily in terms of what we *do* (and by extension, what we are able to possess as a result) rather than who or what we *are*. The epidemic levels of substance abuse in our culture are a direct result of our passive consumerism, providing a means of avoiding our existential fears of alienation from humanity, and attempting to fill the spiritual void in our lives. Fromm was not without hope, however—considering the future, he wrote,

> I believe in the possible realization of a world in which man can *be* much, even if he *has* little; a world in which the dominant motivation of existence is not consumption; . . . a world in which man can find the way of giving a purpose to his life as well as the strength to live free and without illusions. (1994, p. 104)

Fromm's proposed solution to our culture's ills was simple: in *Humanist Socialism* (1965), a volume of essays he coedited, the authors argued that such humanist values as tolerance, the right to an education, and the right to free thought were directly connected to the rise of Socialist thought of the time. The conclusion was that genuine humanism would follow from socialism, but not from capitalism. Fromm argued against the cultural norm of measuring progress purely in terms of economic growth alone, proposing that humanist values and unselfish love could counterbalance the influence of mechanization and increased reliance on technology, leading to a more humane society. In such books as *The Art of Loving* (1956) and *The Revolution of Hope* (1968b), Fromm emphasized the importance of relating to others in a loving, caring fashion, and he especially highlighted the importance of *altruistic* love, which he defined as an act of giving rather than receiving, with the ultimate goal of unselfish concern for the well-being of others. Driven by these goals, Fromm eventually became actively involved in the U.S. antiwar movement during the Vietnam conflict, as well as an advocate of nuclear disarmament.

Further Reading

Fromm, E. (1956). *The Art of Loving*. New York: Harper Collins.

Fromm, E. (1968a). *The Revolution of Hope: Toward a Humanized Technology*. New York: Bantam.

Fromm, E. (1968b). *Ye Shall Be as Gods: A Radical Interpretation of the Old Testament and Its Tradition*. New York: Holt Rinehart Winston.

Fromm, E. (1994). *On Being Human*. New York: Continuum.

Fromm, E., and R. Xirau, eds. (1968). *The Nature of Man*. New York: Macmillan.

The Future of an Illusion (1927)

Sigmund Freud's work on this, one of his most controversial published works, began in the spring of 1927, and was finished and published by the month of November of the same year. *The Future of an Illusion* marks the beginning of a new set of concerns and studies that would occupy him for the next and final decade of his life and marks a change from the subject matter that had absorbed his efforts up to that point. In 1935, Freud added a postscript to his *Autobiographical Study* in which he addressed this change of emphasis from matters of individual psychological development to the origins and development of human civilization:

> My interest, after making a long detour through the natural sciences, medicine, and psychotherapy, returned to the cultural problems which had fascinated me long before, when I was a youth scarcely old enough for thinking. (Quoted by Strachey, 1989, p. 4)

He had actually returned to those concerns previously, at the height of his studies of individual psychology, in **Totem and Taboo,** but it was *The Future of an Illusion* that began the remarkable series of books on the subject that would occupy him for the rest of his days, a series that would also include *Civilization and Its Discontents* and *Moses and Monotheism*.

On the very first page of the book, Freud makes a clear statement about his ultimate goal for the present work: whereas he has previously attempted to consider the origins of civilization, most notably in *Totem and Taboo,* he will now set out "to ask what further fate lies before it and what transformations it is destined to undergo" (Freud, 1989, p. 5). Having laid out such a grandiose objective, however, Freud quickly acknowledges the difficulties involved in the presentation of a single person's expectations and predictions of the future, given the impossibility of an individual having access to all relevant knowledge and information, and humbly backs away for a while:

> Thus anyone who gives way to the temptation to deliver an opinion on the probable future of our civilization will do well to remind himself of the difficulties I have just pointed out, as well as of the uncertainty that attaches quite generally to any prophecy. It follows from this, so far as I am concerned, that

I shall make a hasty retreat before a task that is too great, and shall promptly seek out the small tract of territory which has claimed my attention hitherto, as soon as I have determined its position in the general scheme of things. (Freud, 1989, p. 6)

Having determined to return to his own prior analysis of civilization, Freud starts with a very straightforward definition: civilization is "all those respects in which human life has raised itself above its animal status and differs from the life of beasts" (1989, p. 6). He follows this definition with a clarification intended to forestall any future arguments among translators regarding his intentions, pointing out that he makes no distinction between *culture* and *civilization.*

Freud divides the characteristics of human civilization into two categories. First, he observes that we have acquired and developed the knowledge and capacity necessary to control and extract the wealth of the world and society to accomplish the satisfaction of human needs. Along with this, we have also acquired all the regulations needed for the adjustment of the relationships between people and the distribution of wealth among them—this last clause is one of the numerous subtle digs at Marxism that appear in the book. This description of the accomplishments of civilization is followed immediately by a quick series of observations regarding the implications of those accomplishments, observations that form the basis of the arguments presented throughout the rest of the book. First, and crucially, the two trends in civilization, means and regulations, are not independent of each other, but rather require each other, because

the mutual relations of men are profoundly influenced by the amount of instinctual satisfaction which the existing wealth makes possible; secondly, because an individual man can himself come to function as wealth in relation to another one, in so far as the other person makes us of his capacity for work, or chooses him as a sexual object, and thirdly, moreover, because every individual is virtually an enemy of civilization, though civilization is supposed to be an object of universal human interest. (Freud, 1989, pp. 6–7)

As wealth becomes greater, allowing humans more freedom in how they pursue satisfaction of their instincts, in other words, the need for regulations also becomes greater, because of the greater potential for mutual abuse and exploitation. Furthermore, that abuse and exploitation is what we are naturally driven to do, thus making every man an enemy of civilization, as the use of civilization's rules to ensure the greater good interferes with the ability of individuals to do what they really want to do. Civilization must actively defend itself against the individual, and its institutions and rules are actually made for, and directed toward, this task. This is an altogether darker and more pessimistic Freud than is discernible in his earlier writings, based as it is on the destructive, antisocial and anticultural forces he has come to believe are as basic and universal a part of human nature as the instincts that focus on survival and pleasure, and these determine the behavior of many people.

Given the tension that exists between individual drives and the goals of culture, Freud concludes that every civilization must therefore be built on coercion and the renunciation or repression of instincts. Like many thinkers of his time, Freud was certainly influenced in his thinking by the requirement that any comprehensive theory or philosophy concerning human behavior must somehow account for the massive loss of life, helped along by new technological innovations such as machine guns and chemical warfare, seen across Europe during World War I. He points out the need for human regulations to "protect everything that contributes to the conquest of nature and the production of wealth against men's hostile impulses. Human creations are easily destroyed, and science and technology, which have built them up, can also be used for their annihilation" (Freud, 1989, p. 7). In the wake of World War I, such statements recognizing that science and technology, which have made modern civilization and its conveniences possible, might also hold the seeds of human extinction became a standard part of many philosophical approaches to the problems of humanity, as the issue had been brought into sharp relief by recent events.

The coercive regulations that make civilization possible are imposed on the majority by a ruling minority, a state of affairs that Freud describes as absolutely necessary, and impossible to do without, for the simple reason that the masses of humanity are lazy and unintelligent. According to Freud, this need for coercion from above is due to two widely distributed human characteristics: that people are "not spontaneously fond of work" (1989, p. 9), and that "arguments are of no avail against their passions" (1989, p. 9). We require forceful leadership for the simple reason that, left to ourselves, we will not undertake the labor necessary to maintain our civilization—and furthermore, nobody will be able to convince us to go against our own internal wishes in order to do so. Because of this, we require leaders to set an example for the rest of us, and these leaders are only effective if the masses recognize their leadership, because only then can the people be induced to perform the necessary work, and undergo the renunciations of their own individual desires and drives, on which the very existence of civilization depends. Once again looking for causes of the early 20th century's enormous political upheavals, Freud added the following:

All is well if these leaders are persons who possess superior insight into the necessities of life and who have risen to the height of mastering their own instinctual wishes. But there is a danger that in order not to lose their influence they may give way to the mass more than it gives way to them, and it therefore seems necessary that they shall be independent of the mass by having means to power at their disposal. (1989, p. 9)

This and similar passages have been read by Freud's critics as antidemocratic, and even as an endorsement of the rise of authoritarian or totalitarian leaders, as such leaders do not require the approval of the masses, who after all are too apathetic and unintelligent to contribute usefully in any case. Anticipating such criticism, and keeping in mind that the Soviet Union's wholesale abuse of its own people still lay in the future, Freud takes pains to point out that he is not addressing or endorsing any political system, especially "the great experiment in civilization that is now in progress in the vast country that stretches between Europe and Asia" (1989, pp. 10–11).

To the contrary, Freud is highly critical of the utopian ideologies then becoming current in Europe, including socialism, especially over the objection he anticipated to his characterization of the mass of humanity as lazy and unintelligent:

It will be said that the characteristic of human masses depicted here . . . is itself only the result of defects in the cultural regulations, owing to which men have become embittered, revengeful, and inaccessible. New generations, who have been brought up in kindness and taught to have a high opinion of reason, and who have experienced the benefits of civilization at an early age, will have a different attitude to it. (1989, p. 9)

Here Freud expresses skepticism over the idea that a brand new political system, employing a whole new set of coercive or educational tools, can produce a society of individuals who are far more willing to make the necessary sacrifices in order to preserve the culture, without the need for coercive rules and regulations. Freud asks why no culture has yet produced human masses of such a high quality, and suggests that maybe the problem is simply that nobody has thought of the right regulations that would be capable of influencing people in this way. He undercuts this argument immediately, however, noting that it may simply not be possible to set up this kind of social regulations. Furthermore, assuming that such regulations are devised, Freud pointed out the following:

It may be asked where the number of superior, unswerving and disinterested leaders are to come from who are to act as educators of the future generations, and it may be alarming to think of the enormous amount of coercion that will inevitably be required before these intentions can be carried out. (1989, p. 10)

Freud here anticipates the massive reigns of terror that ultimately occurred in the various nations that attempted to impose new, communist or socialist social orders on their citizens, and he offers an explanation for why such sweeping change is unlikely to work: Because a different cultural environment will not eliminate the two characteristics of human masses that make the direction of human affairs so difficult to begin with. Any attempt at creating a new civilization will have to contend with people's own reluctance to work harder as well as the futility of intellectual arguments in getting them to deny their own instincts and drives.

Freud's overall opinion of society is fairly clear here: he thinks that the baser nature of the human masses is ultimately a more powerful force than all our achievements as a civilization. Part of this is to be expected from psychoanalytic theory in general, given Freud's emphasis from the start on the Darwin-influenced notion that we are inherently biological creatures and are therefore, like the rest of the animal kingdom, in the end helpless prisoners of our instinctual drives and desires. That new biological emphasis, always a key to Freud's thinking, combined with the horrors of World War I to shatter the idealism of the Enlightenment in many thinkers' eyes, with Freud among the first to philosophically incorporate this new pessimism into a coherent view of humanity. Many of Freud's successors would become far more pessimistic, embracing Freud as an early avatar of this new point of view, after witnessing the far greater excesses of the nominally socialist regime of Hitler. Freud was of course writing before the rise of the Nazis, and witnessed only the early years of their policies before his death, and so he had no way of knowing how bad things would eventually get.

Having established his pessimistic view of idealistic plans to alter human civilization, Freud begins the second part of the essay with a fairly direct attack on Marxist solutions to the problems of humanity, pointing out that economics are not the source of the problems, and therefore economic answers that consist primarily of altering the means of acquiring and distributing wealth cannot be the solution. Instead, civilization rests on a compulsion to work and a renunciation of instinct, which provokes resistance from those affected by those demands. Rather than focusing on economic systems, there are psychologically based means by which civilization can be defended, which Freud refers to as the *mental assets* of civilization. Describing these assets requires some new terminology: Freud proposes calling the fact that an instinct cannot be satisfied a "frustration," the regulation that establishes the frustration a "prohibition," and the condition resulting from the prohibition a "privation."

There are two kinds of privations: those that affect everyone and those that only affect groups, classes, or even single individuals. The earliest privations are the first group, those that affect everyone, and they represent the start of the process by which human beings began to detach from their primordial, animal condition. Freud is here summarizing, and assuming the reader's familiarity with, his analysis in *Totem and Taboo,* in which he argued that the start of civilization occurred with the establishment of the incest taboo. According to Freud, the earliest privations in human history are still operative today and still form the kernel of hostility toward civilization, because in every child the instincts opposed by these privations are born anew. These primitive instinctual wishes include incest, cannibalism, and the desire to kill. According to Freud, one way of thinking of neurotics is as a category of people in whom the frustration of these wishes produces asocial behavior.

As in *Totem and Taboo,* Freud here draws a parallel between the development of civilization and the development of the individual psyche. A common argument in Freud's time regarding the role of evolution in psychology, which remains popular today in the evolutionary psychology journals, is that the human mind developed in response to very different environmental pressures, and so a lot of the stress-related mental illness we say today is a result of that primitive mind, which has remained unchanged since our primitive beginnings, being overwhelmed by the pressures of modern life. Freud has a clear rebuttal to that point of view:

> It is not true that the human mind has undergone no development since the earliest times and that, in contrast to the advances of science and technology, it is the same today as it was at the beginning of history. We can point out one of these mental advances at once. It is in keeping with the course of human development that external coercion gradually becomes internalized; for a special mental agency, man's super-ego, takes it over and includes it among its commandments. (Freud, 1989, pp. 13–14)

The development of the superego is a process that occurs universally, in every child, and according to Freud it is only by means of that development that the child becomes a moral and social being. According to Freud, people in whom this development has occurred turn from being civilization's opponents to being its vehicles, and the security of a culture depends on the numbers of its members in whom the superego has developed. The superego is therefore a development that has occurred since humanity's primitive past, and it made civilization possible.

Freud notes that in most people, in most places, the internalization of the most primitive prohibitions has been fairly complete: cannibalism, incest, and unrestrained killing are not usually widespread problems in civilized nations, though obviously the neurotics are always with us. Freud notes, however, that internalization of privation is far less universal and complete when we consider other instinctual claims, especially those concerning the moral demands of civilization:

> Most of one's experiences of man's moral untrustworthiness fall into this category. There are countless civilized people who would shrink from murder or incest but who do not deny themselves the satisfaction of their avarice, their aggressive urges or their sexual lusts, and who do not hesitate to injure other people by lies, fraud, and calumny, so long as they can remain unpunished

for it; and this, no doubt, has always been so through many ages of civilization. (1989, p. 14)

There are, in other words, numerous cultural prohibitions that the majority of people obey only because of external coercion, and even then only when the coercion is effective and has made itself feared. In an analysis that is more than a little reminiscent of Marx, Freud then suggests that the problem is especially pronounced regarding the restrictions that only apply to certain social classes. We should expect that the underprivileged will envy the luxuries of the more privileged classes and will do all they can to reduce their own burden of privation. Since this is not usually possible, a certain amount of discontent will persist within the culture, which can lead to dangerous revolts:

> If, however, a culture has not got beyond a point at which the satisfaction of one portion of its participants depends upon the suppression of another, and perhaps larger, portion—and this is the case in all present-day cultures—it is understandable that the suppressed people should develop an intense hostility towards a culture whose existence they make possible by their work, but in whose wealth they have too small a share. (Freud, 1989, p. 15)

This is an argument very similar to Marx's notion of the inevitable class warfare between the *proletariat* (the oppressed working class) and the *bourgeoisie* (the wealthy ruling class), due to the inherent unfairness of the capitalist economic system. The primary difference between Freud and Marx on this subject simply lies in the underlying mechanisms of the impending revolt, which Freud explains in entirely psychoanalytic terms. The prohibitions inherent in the cultural arrangements that have imposed different restrictions on different classes of people are simply not internalized by the lower classes to the same degree that they become a part of the superego for the more privileged groups. Rather than being prepared to acknowledge the prohibitions, they are to some degree intent on actually destroying the culture instead. Freud then makes a remarkably bold statement, which again echoes some of Marx's arguments about the inevitability of class warfare: "It goes without saying that a civilization which leaves so large a number of its participants unsatisfied and drives them into revolt neither has nor deserves the prospect of a lasting existence" (1989, p. 15). Unlike Marx, however, Freud's argument does not end there, with the unfair and uneven application of cultural rules leading inevitably to class warfare.

Although the coercions and other means used to bring about the renunciations of instincts are an important part of civilization, Freud sees an additional category of mental assets in human civilization: the means developed to recompense people for their sacrifices. Since civilized life involves prohibitions and privations, which deprive people of the satisfaction of their instincts, civilization also must be built on recompensation, which according to Freud often can be found in the form of a culture's ideals and artistic creations, and the satisfaction that can be derived from those sources. Ideals are a culture's estimates of what achievements are the highest and therefore the most to be pursued. Rather than determining the achievements of a cultural unit, however, Freud argues that ideals are based on a culture's early achievements, which are then held up as something to be striven toward and carried further. The satisfaction provided to a culture by its ideals is thus somewhat *narcissistic,* resting on the people's pride in what has already been achieved. This pride is strengthened by comparing a culture's achievements to those of other cultures, which have of course aimed at different achievements and developed ideals. This allows every culture to feel superior and look down on every other nation, and allows cultural ideals to become a source of discord and enmity between different cultures, thus reducing the pressure that would otherwise be directed toward destroying one's own culture. The advantage of national pride is that it can be shared by both the favored classes and the suppressed people, whose ability to despise people outside their culture compensates them for the wrongs they continue to suffer within their own nation. In this way, the suppressed class actually comes to identify with the ruling class that exploits them. They may actually come to admire the privileged classes, seeing the cultural ideals in them and therefore becoming emotionally attached to them; Freud says that without such relations, it would be impossible to understand "how a number of civilizations have survived so long in spite of the justifiable hostility of large human masses" (1989, p. 17).

Art is also a crucial part of a civilization's mental assets, serving as a substitute source of satisfaction for deeply felt instinctual renunciations, including the most primitive, and therefore the most deeply felt. Artistic creation, according to Freud, serves better than anything else does to reconcile people to the sacrifices they have made on behalf of civilization. Freud takes a rather elitist view of art, however, commenting that it is largely inaccessible to the masses of humanity, who, in addition to being engaged in exhausting work, are largely uneducated. The use of art to compensate for the frustration of primitive instinctual urges is therefore largely reserved to the privileged classes, but art serves a different purpose to the larger body of a civilization. To the ordinary, overworked citizen, art serves the important purpose of heightening his or her feelings of identification, because artistic creations often picture the achievements of the artist's culture or bring to mind its ideals, which once again caters to the narcissistic satisfaction associated with the promotion of those ideals.

Freud describes a third set of mental assets on which a culture depends, and which he calls "the most important item in the psychical inventory of a civilization" (1989, p. 17): its religious ideas, which he also refers to as its illusions. To Freud, the particular value of religion is to assist civilization in one of its most basic purposes, its actual raison d'être, which is to defend us against nature. Freud asks the reader to consider the consequences we would face if the prohibitions of civilization were suddenly lifted:

> If, then, one may take any woman one pleases as a sexual object, if one may without hesitation kill one's rival for her love or anyone else who stands in one's way, if, too, one can carry off any of the other man's belongings without asking leave—how splendid, what a string of satisfactions one's life would be. True, one soon comes across the first difficulty: everyone else has exactly the same wishes as I have and will treat me with no more consideration than I treat him. (1989, p. 18)

The rules and prohibitions of civilization, in other words, are all that stands between us and the state of nature, in which we would be destroyed quite coldly, cruelly, and relentlessly, and possibly by exactly those drives that civilization prohibits us from fulfilling. It is precisely because of the dangers of nature that we developed civilization in the first place. Civilization performs its appointed task, defending us against nature, reasonably well, but we have certainly not vanquished all the threats posed by nature, nor is anyone under the illusion that we will ever do so. Natural disasters, such as earthquakes, storms, and floods, are quite beyond our ability to control, we are constantly under siege by microorganisms bent on making us sick, and we are all helpless against our eventual and inevitable surrender to death. With these frightening powers, nature brings us face-to-face with our weakness and helplessness, from which civilization has not provided an escape.

Our civilization imposes privation on us, and the actions of our fellow human beings bring us additional suffering, and the injuries inflicted by nature are piled onto this. Freud has argued that we respond to the privation and the injuries caused by other humans by developing a hostility and resistance toward the rules of civilization. As far as defending ourselves against the attacks of nature, however, civilization has relieved us of that responsibility through religion. The first step toward robbing the universe of its terrors is achieved via the *humanization* of nature:

> Impersonal forces and destinies cannot be approached; they remain eternally remote. But if the elements have passions that rage as they do in our own souls, if death itself is not something spontaneous but the violent act of an evil Will, if everywhere in nature there are Beings around us of a kind that we know in our own society, then we can breathe freely, can feel at home in the uncanny and can deal by psychical means with our senseless anxiety. (Freud, 1989, p. 20)

If we conceive of the forces of nature as being somehow like ourselves, we may still be defenseless against them, but the feeling of absolute powerlessness goes away. We may not even feel defenseless any more, since we can try to employ the same methods with these supernatural superbeings that we employ within our own society; perhaps we can bribe them, appease them, flatter them, or in some way influence them, thus taking away some of their power.

Once again drawing on the argument he made in *Totem and Taboo,* Freud argues that the humanization of nature in the form of gods has a prototype in the development of a small child. In early childhood, we have ambivalent feelings toward our parents, especially our fathers: we fear him, and what he might do if he found out about our desires and thoughts, but we also look to him for protection from other known dangers, and trust that he will provide that protection. According to Freud, in the same way, we do not simply make the forces of nature into other people that we can associate with as equals, but rather we give them the character of a father. In *Totem and Taboo,* Freud made the argument that religion began when humans began in shame to revere the father whom they had killed, placing prohibitions on their actions, including the incest taboo, in order to never repeat their shameful action. Here Freud refers back to that argument, asserting that in making the forces of nature into a father figure, we are following "not only an infant prototype but a phylogenetic one" (1989, p. 21). Because of the early history of primitive man, in other words, along with the natural path of individual development, the creation of father-figure deities is a natural and inevitable outcome of being human.

According to Freud, the gods have the following three responsibilities:

1. They must exorcise the terrors of nature.
2. They must reconcile humanity to the cruelty of fate, particularly as it is shown in death.
3. They must compensate humanity for the sufferings and privations imposed by living a civilized life.

Over time, the relative emphasis placed on these three responsibilities changed, particularly as empirical observation improved humanity's understanding of the actual workings of nature. As we came to grasp the extent to which natural phenomena occur regularly and in conformity with discoverable natural laws and rhythms, the first of the three became less important, with a corresponding increase in the importance of the other two. Apart from the occasional report of miracles, as if to remind us that they have not relinquished any of their original power, the deities came to be seen as having simply arranged the world to be as it is and then left it to itself. The role of the gods and goddesses evolved to where they and nature are regarded as largely autonomous and independent of one another. Furthermore, it became clear over time that the helplessness of humanity in fighting destiny has not gone away, and indeed the area of Fate is the one in which the gods are most likely to fail. In many old pantheistic religions, such as the Greek system, Fate actually stands above the gods, who have destinies of their own, and are thus largely power-less to affect ours. Over time, therefore, morality became the primary domain of the deities, along with the responsibility "to even out the defects and evils of civiliza-tion, to attend to the suffering which men inflict on one another in their life together and to watch over the fulfillment of the precepts of civilization, which men obey so imperfectly" (Freud, 1989, p. 22). Those precepts were themselves given di-vine origin, elevated beyond their creation by human societies and extended to all of nature and the universe. Thus a set of rules for governing human society, and inci-dentally preventing the expression of some primitive instinctual drives, becomes a set of unviolable commandments handed directly to Moses by his God, for example.

The extension of the origin of society's rules to the mind of God or gods serves, according to Freud, to protect humanity in two ways. First, it defends us against the dangers of both nature and Fate; second, it protects us against the injuries that threaten us from human society itself. With the assumption of Divine involvement in the creation of our culture, several further assumptions naturally follow:

1. Life serves a higher purpose of some sort, which we cannot guess at.
2. That purpose involves perfecting human nature in some way, and it probably involves the soul, which is separate from the body.
3. Everything that happens is an expression of a superior intelligence which orders all things for the best and which is benevolent and watching over us.

It further follows that death itself is not an end, a return to lifelessness and noth-ingness, but rather the beginning of some new sort of existence along a path of de-velopment to something higher. Furthermore, the laws and precepts that we follow are given to us by that higher intelligence and govern the entire universe beyond our society, and so they are maintained by some sort of celestial court with greater consistency than we are able to maintain here on earth. Because of this, we can be confident that in the end all good is rewarded and all evil punished, even when that seems quite far from the truth in our present life. This superior wisdom, infinite goodness, and justice have all been accepted as attributes of the divine beings that created us and the world as a whole, "or rather, of the one divine being into which, in our civilization, all the gods of antiquity have been condensed" (1989, p. 24). The development of monotheism, which Freud attributes to the Egyptians and to Moses elsewhere (***Moses and Monotheism***), was a vital part of the development of civilization, because it revealed what had been behind the development of every divine figure in human history: the father figure. Since God was now a single per-son, it was possible for man's relation to him to be as intense and intimate as the child's relationship with his or her father. To Freud, this relationship to the divine is treated by humanity as the most precious possession that civilization can give to its members, treasured more highly than medicine, science, or the means of acquiring wealth, because people feel that life would be intolerable without their valued religious ideas.

Nearly halfway into the essay, Freud gives a quick definition of religious beliefs, which he defines as "teachings and assertions about facts and conditions of external (or internal) reality which tell one something one has not discovered for oneself and which lay claim to one's beliefs" (1989, p. 31). To clarify what makes a religious belief unique, Freud gives the example of a child in a geography class, who will learn about the locations of various towns, monuments, and natural marvels around the world, of which he or she has no personal experience. These sorts of teachings demand belief in their contents, but they produce grounds for their claim—they are the result of a longer process of thought based on observation and inferences, and the individual can also go back through that process himself or herself, in order to verify the claim. A child reading about the Grand Canyon, for example, may one day travel there and verify that it is where the books said it would be, and is much as described in them. It is of course impractical to verify every fact in our schoolbooks in this way, and so we are generally satisfied with trusting in what we learn in school, but the path to personally acquiring the knowledge in a more direct way always remains open.

According to Freud, applying the same test to a religious teaching is a distinctly unsatisfactory process. An inquiry into the basis for a religious claim is met with three answers, which are not necessarily compatible with each other:

> Firstly, those teachings deserve to be believed because they were already believed by our primal ancestors; secondly, we possess proofs which have been handed down to us from those same primaeval times; and thirdly, it is forbidden to raise the question of their authentication at all. In former days anything so presumptuous was visited with the severest penalties, and even today society looks askance at any attempt to raise the question again. (Freud, 1989, p. 33)

According to Freud, the third point is the one that should make us the most suspicious, since the only reason for such a prohibition must be that the claim is a very insecure one, and society is well aware of this. The first point, that we should believe because our ancestors did, requires that we take a good hard look at our ancestors and notice that they were far more ignorant of how the universe operates than we are today, and consequently believed a fair number of things that we would not take seriously today. Freud notes that it is conceivable that religious doctrines belong to this last category. As to the notion that ancient proofs support belief, Freud notes that those proofs often ultimately rely on the assertion that the doctrines were written as a result of divine revelation. Since divine revelation is itself one of the precepts for which proof is being sought, it can hardly serve as proof of itself. Freud points out that it is precisely the information that seems to be of the greatest importance to humanity, which is tasked with solving the riddles of the universe and reconciling us to the suffering we must all endure, for which we have the least evidence, which is surprising given the standard of evidence we have for much of the rest of human knowledge. He points out, for example, that nobody would believe that whales give birth to live young rather than by laying eggs, if the process had not actually been witnessed by researchers.

According to Freud, there are two historically important attempts to evade the question of evidence for religious views. The first of these, which Freud refers to as having "a violent nature," is a doctrine dating back to the early Church Fathers of Christianity, known as the *credo quia absurdum.* According to this argument, the church's religious doctrines are above reason and not subject to its limitations. Their truth is something that must be felt inwardly, and they need not be fully comprehended in order to be believed. Freud expresses his own feelings about the difficulties with this position by simply reminding the reader, in a footnote, that the phrase *credo quia absurdum,* attributed to the early theologian Tertullian, translates from Latin as "I believe because it is absurd." According to this position, the truth requires something above and beyond reason and is only accessible to the select few who experience that inward feeling that it is true. Those who have not had such an experience can therefore have no access to universal truths. Adopting this position, Freud argues, frees humanity of any obligation to employ reason at all, as it will lead us no closer to truth.

The second attempt to evade questions of evidence comes from what Freud calls the philosophy of "as if." This is the position that states that our mental activity is filled with a great number of hypotheses whose groundlessness and even absurdity we fully recognize, yet we behave, for a variety of reasons, as if we believe them. This is also the case for religious doctrines, because of their incomparable importance in preserving our human society. Our society is too dependent on the idea of God for its moral foundations and laws, and we could cause those institutions to crumble by questioning religious teachings, so we should avoid doing so and behave as if they are true whether we believe them or not. Freud dismisses this position quite simply, by pointing out that it is a doctrine that only a philosopher would be capable of putting forward. In an ordinary person's mind, unpolluted by the mechanisms of philosophy, the discussion would be over the moment it is admitted that an idea is absurd or contrary to reason.

In describing the lack of purely rational or empirical grounds for the acceptance of religious doctrines, Freud arrives at what he considers the most interesting question associated with religion, the question that gives his essay purpose: "We must ask where the inner force of those doctrines lies and to what it is that they owe their efficacy, independent as it is of recognition by reason" (1989, p. 37). As a psychoanalyst, Freud finds the power of religious doctrines not in reason or in evidence, but rather in the psychical origin of such ideas. Religious ideas, according to Freud, are not based in experience, nor are they the end result of rational thinking. They are instead illusions, whose power derives from their function: to fulfill the oldest, strongest, and most urgent wishes of mankind. The strength of religious ideas lies in the strength of those wishes. The feeling of helplessness, and consequent desire for protection by a strong father, which characterizes childhood in all of us, turns out in adulthood to be a feeling that lasts throughout life, making it necessary for us to cling to the existence of a more powerful Father.

Religious beliefs serve a clear function in preserving human civilization: as we have often been so poor at fulfilling the demands of justice, belief in the establishment of a moral world order beyond our laws reassures us that good will eventually triumph and evil will be punished, even if it fails to happen here on earth. Belief in a benevolent divinity ruling all and watching over all helps to allay our fear of the many dangers of life, and the belief in the continuation of life beyond our earthly existence provides the temporal and geographical location in which these wish fulfillments can take place. Answers to the great questions that puzzle humanity, such as how the universe began or what the relation is between body and mind, are then developed in conformity with the underlying assumptions of this system, as are the questions themselves. These two questions, for example, assume both that body and mind are separate and that the universe had a definite beginning, both of which are assumptions made by virtually every body of religious doctrine. According to Freud, this takes some of the burden off the individual psyche because some of the childhood conflicts arising from the Oedipus complex, conflicts that the individual psyche never completely overcomes, are removed from it and given a universal solution.

Freud clearly recognizes that he will cause offense to many readers by this analysis, and so he takes great pains to clearly define his use of the word *illusion,* beginning by making a fundamental distinction between illusion and error:

> An illusion is not the same thing as an error, nor is it necessarily an error. Aristotle's belief that vermin are developed out of dung (a belief to which ignorant people still cling) was an error; so was the belief of a former generation of doctors that *tabes dorsalis* [a difficulty in motor control now known to be a side effect of syphilitic infection of the spinal cord] is the result of sexual excess. It would be incorrect to call these errors illusions. (1989, p. 39)

These errors are presented by Freud as the result of mistakes in interpreting data, whereas an illusion is an error in which wishes play a fundamental part. As an example of an illusion, Freud presents Columbus's belief that he had discovered a new sea route to the Indies. Although he made an error in interpreting the evidence before him, the role played by his wish is quite clear. Another example, surely a vivid one for a Jewish scholar in an anti-Semitic society, is "the assertion made by certain nationalists that the Indo-Germanic race is the only one capable of civilization" (1989, p. 39). What is most characteristic of illusions, according to Freud, is that they are derived from human wishes. People who believe themselves superior to all others, for example, will approach the world from a point of view that readily interprets all evidence as supporting their own superiority.

Anticipating a criticism from his fellow psychoanalysts, Freud points out that in being derived from wishes, illusions resemble psychiatric delusions. Apart from the more complicated structure of delusions, however, illusions and delusions are distinguished by their relationship to fantasy and reality. An essential feature of a delusion is that it contradicts reality in some way. An illusion, on the other hand, is not necessarily false or in opposition to reality. As a quick example of this, Freud gives the example of a middle-class girl who believes that a prince will someday come and take her away as his bride. While this is highly unlikely and improbable, it has been known to happen in a few instances. Although hoping for such a thing to happen, in the absence of any good reason to expect it, will almost always be futile, it does not contradict reality in the way that a psychotic's belief that the government is listening to his thoughts over a radio does.

Having drawn this distinction between illusion and delusion, Freud follows up the prince analogy with a more controversial example to illustrate his point:

> That the Messiah will come and found a golden age is much less likely [than the prince's arrival and betrothal]. Whether one classifies this belief as an illusion or as something analogous to a delusion will depend on one's personal attitude. . . . Thus we call a belief an illusion when a wish-fulfillment is a prominent factor in its motivation, and in doing so we disregard its relations to reality, just as the illusion itself sets no store by verification. (1989, p. 39)

Based on this definition, Freud concludes that religious doctrines are illusions, a conclusion that does not rely on the truth or falsity of the ideas, but rather just on their relationship to wish fulfillment. They can neither be proved nor refuted, and so adherence to them relies on wishes rather than on evidence:

> Some of them are so improbable, so incompatible with everything we have laboriously discovered about the reality of the world, that we may compare them—if we pay proper regard to the psychological differences—to delusions. We still know too little to make a critical approach to them. (1989, p. 40)

Because of the implausibility and untestability of many religious doctrines, Freud notes that just as one cannot be compelled to believe in them by evidence or reason, those same factors can also not compel anyone to stop believing in them.

Recognizing that his argument will have aroused the ire of some religious readers, Freud anticipates the standard objection: if religious tenets cannot be refuted by reason, why shouldn't one believe in them? They have tradition and widespread human belief on their side, and they provide such consolation. To this, Freud provides a strongly worded rebuttal:

> If ever there was a case of a lame excuse we have it here. Ignorance is ignorance; no right to believe anything can be derived from it. In other matters so sensible person will behave so irresponsibly or rest content with such feeble grounds for his opinions and for the line he takes. It is only in the highest and most sacred things that he allows himself to do so. (1989, p. 41)

Freud goes on to suggest that many modern people's religious faith is itself often an act of intellectual dishonesty, in order to remain in line with what seems to be important to functioning as part of a human society. Rather than attending a particular church or adhering to the practices of a particular community, "they give the name of 'God' to some vague abstraction which they have created for themselves; having done so they can pose before all the world as deists, as believers in God, and they can even boast that they have recognized a higher, purer concept of God, notwithstanding that their God is now nothing more than an insubstantial shadow and no longer the mighty personality of religious doctrines" (Freud, 1989, p. 41).

Clearly, religious doctrines serve an important function in human affairs, especially if people who have clearly begun to recognize them as illusions go to such lengths to keep their own thought compatible with those beliefs. Considering the question of why we cling to them so firmly, Freud notes that it would certainly be a good thing for us if there actually were a benevolent, providential, creator who lent a moral order to the universe, both during our lives and in an afterlife. He also notes, however, that it is a "very striking fact" that all this is exactly as we are bound by our circumstances to wish it to be, and so these are exactly the beliefs we would expect our primitive ancestors to have come up with.

Having presented his idea that religion is based on illusions that, like dreams, serve the function of wish fulfillment and alleviation of primeval anxieties, Freud anticipates some of the criticisms to which he expects to be subjected, chief among them the objection that, since religious doctrines form such an important foundation for human civilization, it is dangerous to discuss and criticize religion in the same way we criticize other human institutions. Freud notes that it has often been argued that the maintenance of human civilization itself is based on a majority of humans believing in religious doctrines:

> If men are taught that there is no almighty and all-just God, no divine world-order and no future life, they will feel exempt from all obligation to obey the precepts of civilization. Everyone will, without inhibition or fear, follow his asocial, egoistic instincts and seek to exercise his power; Chaos, which we have banished through many thousands of years of the work of civilization, will come again. (1989, p. 45)

The only thing keeping us from reverting to a primitive, uncivilized state of nature, in other words, is maintenance of religious illusions. Furthermore, the writer who convincingly makes the argument that religion is just an illusion is committing an act of great and purposeless cruelty, since many millions of people live very hard lives, which they can only bear through the consolation of religious doctrines, the only consolation they have. To make the argument is to take from them the only support they have, without offering anything to replace it.

Before presenting his rebuttals to those objections, Freud first engages in a tactic he often employs in work such as this: soliciting sympathy from the reader for the hostile reception that his ideas are sure to receive, not because of their content, but because they are his. Indeed, Freud was often met with harsh criticism, which he generally regarded as evidence that the critic had misunderstood him, and he suggests that he is no longer as susceptible to injury from such criticism as he was in his younger days:

> The one person this publication may injure is myself. I shall have to listen to the most disagreeable reproaches for my shallowness, narrow-mindedness and lack of idealism or understanding for the highest interests of mankind. But on the one hand, such remonstrances are not new to me; and on the other, if a man has already learnt in his youth to rise superior to the disapproval of his contemporaries, what can it matter to him in his old age when he is certain soon to be beyond the reach of all favour or disfavour? (1989, pp. 45–46)

He anticipates that the worst that can happen is that the book will be banned in some countries, particularly in countries that are convinced of having set high standards for their intellectual culture, but again notes that this sort of thing is not new to him. The only real harm he professes to worrying about is the harm that might be done to the field of psychoanalysis itself, as it has already met with much mistrust and ill will. As its creator, Freud recognizes that any pronouncements he makes on the subject might lead to the general impression that psychoanalysis leads to the denial of both God and an objective moral ideal, just as many of his critics have long suspected. He notes, however, that many of his fellow psychoanalysts do not share his views on religion, and that psychoanalysis should therefore be able to weather this storm. Indeed, he notes that psychoanalysis is simply a tool, "a method of research, an impartial instrument" (1989, p. 47), which he compares to the calculus used by physicists. If a physicist were to discover, with the help of mathematical calculations, something about when the earth will be destroyed, a certain amount of distress might ensue, but it is unlikely that anyone would call for a ban on calculus itself, because of its destructive tendencies. Freud views psychoanalysis as the same sort of research tool as mathematics, in that the instrument is not responsible for the data that result from its use.

To the charge that to reveal religion as an illusion would destroy civilization, Freud suggests that its influence as a force for good has been overstated. Religion has contributed in a big way to the taming of our antisocial and asocial instincts, and has been a vital part of human civilization. According to Freud, however, it has not done enough. Human society has been essentially ruled by religion for many millennia, which has surely been long enough for it to have shown what it can achieve:

> If it had succeeded in making the majority of mankind happy, in comforting them, in reconciling them to life and in making them into vehicles of civilization, no one would dream of attempting to alter the existing conditions. But what do we see instead? We see that an appallingly large number of people are dissatisfied with civilization and unhappy in it, and feel it as a yoke which must be shaken off. (Freud, 1989, p. 47)

If religion is truly the basis of civilization, in other words, it is time to admit that it has failed at its task. Freud recognizes that a common objection to that perspective is that this current state of affairs is not the result of religion, but rather is due to religion's loss of influence over the human masses in the face of the advancement of science. Freud's response to this last objection is a deceptively simple one: there is no reason to believe that people were generally happier in more unrestrictedly religious times, and they certainly were not any more moral.

Freud goes on to argue that, contrary to the idea that religion leads to increased morality, the social contract inherent in religion, especially Christianity, actually guarantees the continuation of immorality, very much as it was without the influence of religion. In ensuring people's ability to obey the rules, it was important that priests emphasize God's kindness and forgiveness in addition to his judgment. In typical religious practice, one commits a sin, then makes a sacrifice or does a penance, and is then free to sin again. Freud points out that some Russian theologians have gone so far as to conclude that sin is indispensable for the enjoyment of divine blessings, and so it can be argued that sin is actually pleasing to God. Freud argues that these concessions to man's instinctual nature such as these were an indispensable part of the rise of religion, for without them nobody would have submitted to religious practices. Freud sums the situation up in this way: "In every age immorality has found no less support in religion than morality" (1989, p. 48).

Given the continuing rise of the scientific point of view in the civilized world, Freud goes on to argue that civilization may actually run a greater risk from maintaining the current, unquestioning attitude toward religion than it does from giving up religion entirely. Certainly, religion, especially European Christianity, no longer has the same influence on people that it once did. The reason for this loss of influence, furthermore, is not because the promises of religion have grown less, but simply because people find them less credible, primarily because of "the increase of the scientific spirit in the higher strata of human society" (1989, p. 49). People no longer view religious texts as the inerrant word of God (or gods), recognizing both that they contain many errors and that the teachings of the major religions strongly resemble the totemistic ideas of the world's most primitive peoples. As education becomes accessible to more and more people, the falling away from religious belief becomes more widespread as well. Contrary to the usual arguments in favor of religion, Freud points out the following:

> Civilization has little to fear from educated people. . . . In them the replacement of religious motives for civilized behaviour by other, secular motives would proceed unobtrusively; moreover, such people are to a large extent themselves vehicles of civilization. (1989, p. 49)

The educated people, who have moved beyond the use of religious justification for all aspects of civilization, will not be the source of any problems that arise in the decline of religion. The problems will arise with the majority of humanity, the uneducated and oppressed, about whom Freud has repeatedly made the point that they are motivated by their circumstances to be the enemies of civilization.

Freud suggests that the conciliatory approach to religion, in which the educated classes make a pretense of continuing to adhere to religion despite no longer believing in it, will only help to maintain civilization so long as the oppressed masses do not find out that some of the people no longer believe in God. This situation is unsustainable, as they *will* inevitably find out, Freud says, even if his own book goes unpublished. The masses are already the enemies of civilization; upon discovering this weak spot in its structures, they will throw themselves against it and try to bring it down. If the only reason preventing you from killing your neighbor is because God has commanded you not to do so, accompanied by the threat of severe punishment in either this or the next life, then the news that there is no God and you need not fear his punishment will surely result in your killing your neighbor without hesitation. According to Freud, this leaves only two options for human civilization: either become far more oppressive, keeping the masses away from any possibility of intellectual awakening, or fundamentally alter the relationship between civilization and religion. Of the two, Freud favors the second proposal as the obvious solution to the problem.

Freud suggests that the only thing preventing human society from having already carried out this proposal, removing religious justifications for the underlying principles of civilization, is fear that we will somehow expose civilization to a greater danger. The precepts of civilization, according to Freud, did not originally carry religious justifications along with them, as they already serve the clear function of making communal life possible. Without a rule against killing your neighbor, for example, our social existence would not be practicable. One who kills another would draw down the vengeance of the victim's family, and would thus ultimately not benefit from his or her own act at all. Without any rules in place, this would start an endless chain of killings, and the ultimate outcome would be that humans would exterminate one another. The very insecurity of life led the earliest societies to establish rules to prevent this from happening. Long before the currently widespread religious doctrines, such rules already existed, as communities would not be possible without them.

By proclaiming many generations later that God is the source of the prohibition, we invest the rule with a special solemnity and importance, but we also run the risk of making observation of the rule dependent on belief in God. Freud's proposal for the future development of civilization is that we should retrace that step, and no longer attribute to God rules that genuinely reflect our own will, based on logically defensible reasons. By doing this, we avoid all the risks attached to making our morality dependent on belief in forces that will only become more and more difficult for the majority of humanity to believe in. Furthermore, one of the difficulties inherent in placing God at the core of our society's rules, and one of the forces driving down religious belief, is the often internally contradictory nature of our moral code. This is to be expected; of course our human rules show signs of human inadequacy. Freud proposes removing God's authority from these prohibitions and honestly recognizing their human origin:

> Since it is an awkward task to separate what God Himself has demanded from what can be traced to the authority of an all-powerful parliament or a high judiciary, it would be an undoubted advantage if we were to leave God out altogether and honestly admit the purely human origin of all the regulations and precepts of civilization. (1989, p. 53)

In addition to removing their pretense at sanctity, Freud suggests that the rules would also lose their excessive rigidity and resistance to change: A law passed by humans may be far more readily amended than a commandment handed down by the all-powerful Creator of the universe. People would then arrive at the recognition that our rules and laws exist to serve us, rather than the reverse, and with a friendlier attitude toward the basic rules of civilization, it might become easier to improve the rules further. To Freud, this would represent a major step in the development of civilization; regarding the title of the book, his view of the ideal future of this illusion is clear: he would prefer to strip it of a future entirely.

As a psychoanalyst, however, Freud has particular reasons for favoring the end of religion that extend well beyond the historical and philosophical arguments already presented. Continuing the argument he first presented in *Totem and Taboo,* Freud states again that the relationship we as individuals have to our own fathers is paralleled by the relationship between the species and the primal Father. God and religious doctrine, therefore, represent a real, historical truth, albeit a heavily disguised one. As in *Totem and Taboo,* Freud treats the killing of the primal Father, and the resulting guilt and institution of the earliest taboos, as a real historical event. This assumption allows him to make the odd argument that, since that primal Father was eventually reshaped by subsequent generations into God, then God was himself actually involved in the genesis of the prohibitions against killing and incest. The religious doctrine of the commandments is therefore literally true in one sense.

He then draws a simple, clear parallel between the anxiety and conflicts of early childhood development and the development of religion by our species. Because of the many instinctual demands that conflict with the child's rational intellect, and the resulting necessity of a series of acts of suppression, "a human child cannot successfully complete its development to the civilized stage without passing through a phase of neurosis" (1989, p. 54). The anxiety produced by internal unconscious conflict is dealt with by repression and other defense mechanisms, and most of these infantile neuroses, which resemble obsessional neuroses, are overcome spontaneously, without requiring treatment.

Freud suggests that a similar process was experienced by the human species as a whole, and for similar reasons. In a time in which humanity was ignorant and intellectually weak, much like a small child, renunciation of our instinctual drives was necessary to make communal existence possible. Religion arose under these circumstances in the same way as the temporary neuroses of childhood, as the

> universal obsessional neurosis of humanity; like the obsessional neurosis of children, it arose out of the Oedipus complex, out of the relation to the father. If this view is right, it is to be supposed that a turning-away from religion is bound to occur with the fatal inevitability of a process of growth, and that we find ourselves at this very juncture in the middle of that phase of development. (Freud, 1989, p. 55)

According to this analysis, religion is simply a developmental phase that humanity has been going through, and like the Oedipus complex in each individual's development, successful maturation demands that it be outgrown and cast aside. The future of this illusion, in Freud's view, should be its removal from human affairs, as a developmental challenge that we have successfully moved beyond. Although it is one of his shortest works, *The Future of an Illusion* has been one of Freud's most controversial essays since its publication, for reasons that should be clear to the reader.

Further Reading

Freud, S. (1989 edition). *The Standard Edition of the Complete Psychological Works of Sigmund Freud.* Vol. 21: *The Future of an Illusion* (1927) (Translated by James Strachey). New York: W. W. Norton.

Gestalt

One of the most influential movements in psychological history, the Gestalt school of psychology, was born when a group of German researchers described the principles that govern human perception of familiar stimuli. At the time, psychologists such as Wilhelm **Wundt** were focusing on attempts to break down human cognitive and perceptual experiences into their component parts. Following the lead of chemistry and physiology, many psychologists approached the study of the human mind from a bottom-up perspective in which the goal is to break down all phenomena into their simplest components. The major insight of the Gestalt psychologists was to recognize that this sort of analysis is not appropriate in situations in which the simple components only gain meaning from their position as part of a larger construct. The Gestalt psychologists argued, for example, that people perceive sights and sounds as organized patterns rather than as discrete components, and the perception of that whole pattern becomes more than the mere sum of its parts. Consequently, they advocated a bottom-down approach instead, in which the psychological experience is studied as a unitary whole rather than in pieces. To study the individual components of the experience rather than examining it as a coherent whole would be to lose the phenomenon that is being studied in the first place.

The German word *gestalt* can be roughly translated as "whole object" or "whole pattern," thus these researchers became known as Gestalt psychologists. The best known among them were Max Wertheimer, Kurt Koffka, and Wolfgang Köhler. The movement began with Max Wertheimer's attempt to understand the working of a simple child's toy. In 1910, Wertheimer was on a train, on his way to a family vacation in the Rhineland, when he began pondering how a common optical illusion, motion parallax, which had certainly been noticed by innumerable people previously, actually worked. Motion parallax is the technical term for the apparent movement of stationary objects past a moving vehicle, with nearer objects appearing to go by faster, while more distant objects pass by at a more stately pace. Looking out the window of his train compartment, Wertheimer realized that, despite his recently acquired doctorate in psychology, he had not the slightest idea how the brain turned its sensory input into apparent motion. Pondering further, Wertheimer began to think more broadly about illusions of apparent motion, especially in the context of a popular toy of the time, the stroboscope.

Max Wertheimer, the original Gestalt psychologist, 1938. (Bettmann/Corbis)

The word *stroboscope* now refers to a fairly sophisticated piece of laboratory equipment, but in 1910 it was the name of a primitive motion picture device. Like the recently invented technology used in movie theaters, it relied on rapid exposure to the eyes of a series of images that changed very slightly from frame to frame. The stroboscope was hand-cranked and relied on the child's skill at turning the handle at exactly the right speed to make the pictures appear to move. The illusion had been made quite popular by the Lumiére brothers and Thomas Edison, along with other movie pioneers, but they were content to exploit it without actually understanding how or why it worked to fool the brain. Wertheimer was far more curious, however, and he became so intrigued by the connection he had just made between the two different kinds of apparent motion that he got off the train in Frankfurt (not his intended destination) in order to consult a former mentor, perception expert Professor Friedrich Schumann, who had recently accepted a position at the University of Frankfurt. Upon departing the train station, Wertheimer went straight to a toy store, where he purchased a stroboscope, which he then spent the evening tinkering with in a hotel room. The stroboscope came preloaded with pictures of a boy and a horse who would appear respectively to trot and to walk when the handle was turned at the correct speed. Struck by an idea, Wertheimer removed those pictures and replaced them with lines he drew on blank paper, parallel to each other. He discovered that if he operated the device at just the right speed, the resulting impression was of a single line moving smoothly from one location to the other.

The next morning, Wertheimer visited Schumann at the university and explained what he had observed, along with his tentative explanation of it—clearly, the motion was not contained in the stimuli themselves, thus the brain was somehow filling in the gaps. Schumann offered the use of his laboratory, along with his new tachistoscope, a precision instrument that allowed much greater control over the speed with which stimuli were presented, as well as the duration for which they were seen. Since he needed experimental subjects to whom he could present stimuli,

Schumann introduced Wertheimer to his lab assistants, Wolfgang Köhler and Kurt Koffka. The three men hit it off at once, beginning a lifelong collaboration and a new psychological movement.

In the lab, Wertheimer simply adapted what he had been doing with the toy to the more advanced equipment. In the most basic experiment, two three-centimeter horizontal lines were alternately presented, parallel and about two centimeters apart. Different phenomena appeared at different speeds: When they were presented slowly, subjects saw first one and then the other; at a high rate of speed, the set of parallel lines was seen together; at an intermediate rate, a single line appeared to smoothly glide from one position into the other. In the crucial insight to arise from this early research, Köhler, Koffka, and Koffka's wife were all unable to *not* see the motion, even while fully aware that the lines were stationary. This indicated clearly that this perceptual illusion occurred at the level of perception rather than sensation, as the motion was not a part of the original stimuli. Wertheimer called the apparent motion the *phi* (or) phenomenon, using the Greek letter to represent something that intervenes between *a* and *b* (the letters designated different areas of the retina sending information to the brain). Somehow, what Wertheimer called a *psychological short- circuit* occurred in the brain between the two cortical areas receiving information from *a* and *b*. While this description does not stand up well anatomically, the basic insight revealed here forms the core of Gestalt psychology: incoming pieces of sensory information are perceived as a single unitary experience, with properties beyond those possessed by discrete pieces of the sensory experience. That set of sensations, perceived as a unitary whole, was a *Gestalt*. Wertheimer's insight (that the mind adds meaning and structure that are not present in the original, discrete sensations) was important in overthrowing the anti-mentalist approach to laboratory psychology which had dominated German research since before Wundt's lab was established, and which had also become a major force in America. Freud, James, and the psychologists emerging from Würzburg (where both Wertheimer and Koffka had studied) were all interested in phenomena that called for explanation in terms of higher mental processing, and the Gestalt psychologists pointed the way toward successfully studying such phenomena in the scientific laboratory. Many years later, Köhler (1942) summed up the excitement of those early days as follows:

> Those were years of cheerful revolt in German psychology. We all had great respect for the exact methods by which certain sensory data and facts of memory were being investigated, but we also felt quite strongly that work of so little scope could never give us an adequate psychology of real human beings. . . . [We] suspected that at the very bottom of the new science there were some premises which tended to make its work sterile. (p. 97)

Gestalt Research on Perception

Although Wertheimer's ultimate goal was to propose a whole new mentalist psychology, most of the research carried out by the Gestalt psychologists focused more narrowly on perception and its relationship to sensation. Based on this research, they discovered numerous basic principles that describe how the perceptual system makes sense of raw sensory information, which they frequently tested and demonstrated through the use of optical illusions. Over time, Wertheimer and his colleagues and students discovered many such principles, which are still foundational to the study of perception. A few of these *Laws of Gestalten* are illustrated here:

Proximity: Objects or events that are close to each other are perceived as belonging together. For example, the following pattern is usually described as three pairs of Xs, rather than as six Xs (although that would also describe it accurately): XX XX XX.

Similarity: Similar elements are automatically perceived as belonging to a group. The following pattern is usually described in terms of columns of Xs and Os, rather than as mixed rows. The Xs seem to belong together, as do the Os.

X O X O
X O X O
X O X O
X O X O

Continuity: Sensations that appear to create a continuous shape are perceived as doing so.

Closure: We mentally fill in the missing parts of incomplete objects—we may mentally fill in gaps that appear in a picture.

Common Fate: Stimuli that move together in the same direction, at the same speed, are perceived together. This is why doing the wave in stadiums is so popular; to observers across the field, it is seen as a single smooth motion by a large object, the crowd, rather than a large number of people moving individually. This is also an example of Wertheimer's *phi* phenomenon, in which apparent motion is created by the appearance of a series of separate stimuli in sequence.

Gestalt Research on Learning and Problem Solving

Although the Gestalt psychologists' largest influence has been on the study of perception, Wertheimer's dreams of creating a new mentalist psychology were brought to at least partial fruition by the work Köhler did with chimpanzees in the Canary Islands. Köhler's research provides a rare example in which the chaos of war led to a unique research opportunity. In 1913, having continued working in Frankfurt for an additional three years following the initial experiments with Wertheimer, Wolfgang Köhler took over the post of director of the Prussian Academy of Sciences' ape research station on the island of Tenerife, a Spanish territory off the northwest coast of Africa. Once he arrived, he would be unable to leave for more than six years, trapped first by the outbreak of World War I and later by the chaos of postwar Germany. He was watched closely during the war, as several British intelligence agents were convinced that he was a German spy—scholars continue to debate whether or not there was any truth in their suspicions.

Stuck for years in a research facility with chimpanzees, Köhler found ways to keep himself occupied. In the research station, he had access to a large outdoor pen and a total of nine chimpanzees, of various ages. Köhler described the pen as a playground, and it was equipped with a range of objects that the chimpanzees liked to play with, including boxes, poles, and sticks. Köhler used these facilities to continue to investigate mental phenomena, using the problem-solving abilities of apes to illustrate a new theory of learning. He created a wide range of problems for the chimpanzees to solve, most involving making their favorite food, bananas, difficult to reach. Solutions to Köhler's problems often required use of tools, and always required use of a novel strategy with which the ape lacked prior experience. In the simplest experiment, food was put on the far side of a section of fence. In prior experiments, dogs and cats had repeatedly failed this test, as the sort of goal-oriented behavior that would ordinarily work (and thus receive reinforcement) for those animals could not work here. The apes, however, would immediately turn away from the goal and follow a circuitous route to the food. In another simple problem, which Köhler captured on film, bananas were hung just out of reach, and a wooden box was left nearby. Typically, the chimpanzee will first attempt to jump and retrieve the bananas. Following a series of unsuccessful attempts, the chimpanzee looks angry or disgusted and walks away from the bananas. This is followed by a period during which the chimpanzee looks at the food, then at the various objects in the pen, then back at the bananas, then at his surroundings again. The chimpanzee will then use the objects in the enclosure in further attempts at retrieving the food. The most straightforward solution to this simplest puzzle is to slide the box over and stand on it, but the chimpanzees also tried other, equally creative solutions that were less successful, including an attempt at quickly climbing up a carefully placed pole before it could fall over.

Köhler found big individual differences in performance on these tasks—some of the chimpanzees were far more effective problem-solvers than others. When he raised the bananas to a greater height, some of the chimpanzees never really got the hang of stacking boxes on top of one another, while at least one succeeded in using a tower of four boxes to retrieve food. Köhler's star pupil, a big male named Sultan, solved more complex problems than the others. In one experiment, the bananas were placed outside the pen, along with a long stick, outside a *different* area of the pen—both were out of reach to Sultan, even extending a hand as far as he could between the bars. Inside the enclosure, Sultan had only a short stick. At first, Sultan extended the short stick between the bars, trying to get the bananas and failing. He then looked around the pen, seeming reflective. After a long pause, he suddenly scrambled across the pen to where the long stick was, and quickly used to short stick to pull it toward him. He then went back to the bananas, armed with the larger stick, and secured the food. Sultan also solved an even more complicated problem, in which the bananas were placed outside the enclosure, well out of reach of both available sticks. One stick was smaller and thinner than the other, however, and could be pushed into a depression in the base of the larger stick to make a longer stick. After trying and failing to get the bananas for about an hour, Sultan gave up and sat on a box idly handling the sticks. At one point while doing this, Sultan happened to hold the sticks in such a way that they lined up correctly. He immediately stuck them together and ran for the bananas, which he was able to reach with the longer stick.

Köhler's crucial insight as a result of these ape experiments was the observation that the chimpanzees appeared to be solving the problems by way of a kind of cognitive trial and error, as though they were mentally trying out possible solutions before actually selecting a tool and trying out a solution. Each solution was characterized by a long pause in which the ape carefully looked at his surroundings before appearing to suddenly see the solution and quickly implementing it. Köhler called this *insight* learning, and noted that it clearly involved a different mechanism than the kinds of learning already being described by the early behaviorists, as the problem solution, at least the first time, was a new behavior that the chimpanzee had not engaged in before, and so it could not represent either a prior pairing of stimulus and response *or* the results of reinforcement. Köhler also noted that once the animals had achieved an insight, they could generalize and apply that solution to other, similar problems.

Köhler shared his findings with the world in the 1921 book *The Mentality of Apes,* paving the way for Gestaltist studies of *human* problem solving using essentially the same techniques. Karl Duncker, who had studied with both Wertheimer and Köhler at Berlin, conducted an experiment with humans that was almost identical to what Köhler did with Sultan: He had eight very young children, ranging from 8 to 13 months of age, sit at a table on which a toy was placed out of reach, and also gave each child a stick. Two of the children solved the problem immediately, and another five played with the stick until it ended up near the toy, at which point they had the insight that they could use it to retrieve the toy. Only the youngest child failed to figure it out.

Encouraged, Duncker carried out a series of classic studies with adults between 1926 and 1935. Rather than placing food or toys out of reach, however, he instead would seat them at a table covered with an assortment of objects, and then ask them to perform a task for which none of the materials seemed appropriate. The goal was to determine the conditions under which the subjects would consider new uses for the objects. In one version of the task, the subject was asked to mount three small candles on the wall and light them, and was provided with three small cardboard boxes: one was full of matches, one was full of tacks, and one held small candles. A correct solution requires the insight that a box, once emptied, can be attached to the wall with tacks, thus providing a platform on which to mount the candles. As Köhler had seen with the apes, the correct solution was often preceded by frustration and a reflective pause, followed by rapid solution. Duncker was just as intrigued by the subjects who failed to solve the problem, however, which in the case of this problem means more than half of them. A far larger proportion solved the problem when the boxes were empty at the start of the session, with the other objects simply spread on the table near them. This suggested to Duncker that once the subjects had seen the boxes used *as boxes,* they had a harder time seeing them in the unboxlike way necessary to solve the problem. Duncker called this inability to see an object in a role different from its usual one *functional fixedness,* and suggested that it is a common and serious impediment to problem solving, explaining why the most knowledgeable experts on a particular subject are often incapable of solving a new problem that arises in their field. It appears that, although a novel solution can be generalized to new problem-solving situations, that same solution can also be an impediment in future situations if the expert has come to rely on a solution that cannot solve the new problem. In the time in which behaviorism, with its focus on conditioned responses and its disdain of mentalistic explanations, was becoming dominant in America, the Gestalt psychologists made it clear that some types of learning can only be explained with the use of mental concepts.

Popularizing Gestalt psychology with American audiences became a major goal for the Gestalt psychologists by the early 1930s, as all the principals had immigrated to America as a result of political forces in Germany. Prior to the rise of the Nazis, anti-Semitism was already a powerful force in both political and academic circles. Of the three original Gestalt psychologists, Wolfgang Köhler was the only non-Jew, and consequently was also the only member of the group who rose to a tenured position as director of an institute. Following his directorship of the Tenerife Research Station, Köhler directed the Psychological Institute at the University of Berlin. Wertheimer was also there until 1929, at which time he went to Frankfurt, and Karl Duncker was part of the final wave of researchers to work there under Köhler. The institute was a thriving research facility, and served as the de facto world headquarters for Gestalt psychology. When the Nazis gained power in the early 1930s, one of their first actions at German universities was the dismissal of Jewish professors, along with other scholars considered hostile to the new regime. This, of course, meant that Wertheimer and Koffka, as well as Duncker, had to find ways to leave the country as soon as possible, and all eventually found their way to America. Köhler briefly resisted the Nazi incursions into academe, marveling at the cowardice of his fellow scholars who stood by silently while their colleagues were dismissed. In April 1933, Köhler published what appears to be the last anti-Nazi article openly published in Germany under the new regime, in which he says of the scholars who did not join the Nazis, "Never have I seen finer patriotism than theirs." Surprisingly, Köhler was not arrested, and he continued to resist the Nazi takeover of his institute in a variety of ways, including doing whatever he could to help his displaced colleagues and lab assistants to reach safety and employment. In 1935, with the Nazi takeover of the university complete, Köhler resigned his post and joined his colleagues in the United States.

Gestalt Therapy

The name *Gestalt* has also been applied to a type of therapy, which has little in common with the perception and cognition research of the same name. Gestalt therapy is an amalgam of ideas from psychoanalysis, humanistic psychology, and the work of Gestalt psychologists. Its focus is on the idea that people create their own internal reality, and psychological growth requires perceiving, remaining aware of, and acting on true feelings.

Symptoms of mental disorder are said to be the result of people not being aware of all aspects of themselves, and so Gestalt therapy is designed around creating conditions that allow clients to become more self-aware and self-accepting, thus able to grow again. This often requires confrontation, with the therapist pushing the clients to acknowledge uncomfortable feelings or pointing out inconsistencies in what they say, with an emphasis on the importance of body language in revealing feelings that the client hasn't acknowledged.

Further Reading

Henle, M. (1978). One Man against the Nazis—Wolfgang Köhler. *American Psychologist* 33(10): 939–944.

Köhler, W. (1942). Kurt Koffka 1886–1941 (obituary). *Psychological Review, 49*: 97.

Köhler, W. (1944). Max Wertheimer 1880–1943 (obituary). *Psychological Review* 51(3): 143–146.

Köhler, W. (1976/1925). *The Mentality of Apes.* New York: Liveright.

Köhler, W. (1992). *Gestalt Psychology: An Introduction to New Topics in Modern Psychology.* New York: Liveright.

Perls, F. S., and Wysong, J. (1992). *Gestalt Therapy Verbatim.* Highland, NY: Gestalt Journal Press.

Graf, Herbert. *See* "Little Hans"

Homosexuality

To the modern Western reader, it may appear puzzling that Freud and his contemporaries devoted as much attention as they did to attempted explanations of homosexuality, which is now generally regarded, both by the psychiatric profession and the larger culture, as a normal variation in sexual development. This contemporary attitude, however, is of rather recent vintage, and only became standard within psychiatry and clinical psychology in 1973, in a revised printing of the *DSM-II* (*Diagnostic and Statistical Manual of the American Psychiatric Association*—the standard reference for psychological disorders). In the 1968 edition, homosexuality was still listed as a disorder. In Freud's time, therefore, homosexuality was a mental illness in need of explanation, and variations on the psychoanalytic or psychodynamic explanation dominated for most of the 20th century, both in the DSM and in the world beyond.

The psychoanalytic theory of homosexuality began, of course, with Freud, who presented the essential outline in his *Three Essays on the Theory of Sexuality,* but then continually revised and refined it for the next 20 years. It is perhaps important to note from the outset that Freud was actually far less judgmental in his writings on homosexuality than most of his contemporaries—this is actually one of the elements that made his form of psychology so controversial. At the core of his view of homosexuality is the distinction he drew between the sexual drive itself (the libido) and the object of that drive, the person (or thing) toward which that drive is directed. Freud's great insight was that one libidinal object could be substituted for another without changing the essential nature of the libido itself. Libido in a heterosexual does not fundamentally differ from the libido of a homosexual; what distinguishes the two is merely the person toward whom that energy is addressed. Much of Freud's career was consumed by the examination of how these substitutions occurred, what psychic forces required them to be made, and what effect they had on psychological functioning in general. It is important to note here that Freud was not driven particularly by the need to explain what had gone wrong in homosexuality, but merely to explain the unconscious processes, whether involving anxiety, psychic defense mechanisms, or internal conflict, which led to that orientation rather than another. Freud did not privilege heterosexuality in this regard: he saw *all* forms of adult sexuality as the end products of complex processes involving inhibitions and transformations of libidinal energy, and all therefore shaped and determined by unconscious processes. Although Freud clearly defined homosexuality as a neurotic result of these processes, he saw heterosexuality in exactly the same way, and he saw it as a phenomenon that was just as much in need of explanation as was homosexuality.

Although he did develop a theory to account for homosexuality, it must be seen as just a part of a more comprehensive description and explanation of the psychic mechanisms that determined all other variations in adult sexual behavior as well. In Freud's developmental model, sexuality is present in very young infants, who have no particular sexual orientation, be it homosexual or heterosexual. These infants can be stimulated and excited by a wide range of experiences, most of which are not at all sexual from an adult perspective. He referred to this initial state of wide-ranging excitability as **polymorphous perversity**.

Polymorphous perversity simply refers to the ability of young children to derive sexual pleasure from any part of the body, with no consideration for the rules that determine what is considered perverse in adulthood. Freud here applies "perversion" as a nonjudgmental term, referring to any behavior that falls outside socially acceptable norms.

Polymorphously perverse sexuality continues from birth to around age five or six, progressing through the first three stages of **psychosexual development**. An infant's *libido* is unfocused, able to derive sexual pleasure from any part of the body, and driven by instinct to do so. In each stage, the child's attention is primarily focused on a particular area of the body, such as the child's attention to the mouth during the *oral* stage. This drive is also directed at any *object* that might provide pleasure. During the oral stage, for example, the child forms an important early bond to mother by deriving pleasure from sucking the breast. This pleasure is quickly generalized to other stimuli, however, and the child comes to derive satisfaction from putting virtually anything in his or her mouth. The *anal* and *phallic* stages proceed similarly, with the libido's focus shifting to other parts of the body. In the phallic stage, which begins at around four years of age, the libido concentrates on the genitals—the penis for boys and the clitoris for girls—as sensual pleasure becomes unmistakably sexual for the first time.

Central to this developmental scheme is the recognition that sexual development, at least in these early stages, operates as a biological process of maturation, with a universal sequence of shifts in locus of pleasure from mouth to anus to genitals, with anxiety and inhibition playing no significant role. As that shift from one body region to another occurs, certain libidinal objects are preferred over others, but this preference is based purely on their ability to stimulate and give pleasure, and certainly not due to any inherent male or female quality they possess. In the first few years of childhood, therefore, children are neither heterosexual nor homosexual—what matters to them is simply the experience of pleasure acting on their sensory apparatus.

The developmental sequence only becomes psychological, with the possibility of neurosis, with the start of the phallic stage, as new factors interfere with the biological maturational processes. The most important new influence is that the child, having developed a separate identity and become more aware of the world, can now recognize sex differences. To the four-year-old boy, who has come to recognize how great a source of pleasure is provided by his penis, the world comes to be divided into two clear-cut groups: those with penises and those without them. Furthermore, according to Freud, girls are not simply people born without penises. They are, rather, something far darker and more anxiety-provoking: people who once had penises, but who have mysteriously lost them.

As the boy arrives at these realizations, he actively seeks to spend more time with the adult who has been the source of so much of his sensual excitement, especially during the oral stage: his mother. While he has no clear idea of what is involved in adult sexuality, his penis is now the source of his greatest pleasures, and so he also hopes to act on her in some mysterious way with it. He is of course faced with competition in his bid to possess his mother, which leads him to wish to eliminate his rival, perhaps by killing, or at least castrating, his father. At the same time, however, the Oedipal conflict also involves another set of drives or fantasies to compete with these, in which the boy also yearns for his father. Although his desire to receive pleasure and attention from his father is expressed more passively than his desire to possess his mother, he nonetheless also experiences an intense rivalry with the mother for sole possession of the father. Central to the Oedipus complex is the fact that both sets of wishes occur simultaneously.

As Freud regarded the Oedipal conflict as the nuclear complex underlying *all* neurosis, it is unsurprising that it lies at the base of sexual development as well. What makes the resolution of the Oedipus complex so vital to the boy's sexual development is that his sexual wish to possess one or both parents, however strong, is balanced by a similarly strong fear of retribution from the rival parent. Keeping in mind the boy's newfound recognition of basic anatomical sex differences, and the current focus of pleasure on the penis, the fear that balances out the possessive sexual fantasy is naturally the fear of losing that same organ. Incestuous wishes for one parent are counterbalanced by the equally strong fear of castration by the other parent. In Freud's model of child development, this is the central psychic conflict of childhood, and how the boy resolves it will determine the subsequent developmental path to his adult sexual identity.

The resolution that leads to heterosexuality, and therefore in the minds of many psychoanalysts the preferred, correct, normal developmental path, is to decide the conflict between desire and fear on the side of fear. The mother is without a penis, and therefore castrated: this shows the boy that such a fate is possible, and may be the inevitable result of the father's anger, should he discover that a rival for his wife's affection lives under his roof. In response to this *castration anxiety,* the boy gives up his claim on his mother, who as a result of this conflict is now partly hated, and sets out to make things right with the father by deferring to his authority and identifying with him. This he does by internalizing the image of the father and striving to become more like him, thus establishing the foundation for his superego.

In Freud's view, the boy has undergone a transformation from a natural, purely pleasure-seeking animal into a neurotic human being whose impulses are now internally controlled by his superego. In achieving this metamorphosis, the boy psychologically abandons sexual rivalry and enters into the *latency stage* of psychosexual development, defined primarily by the absence of sexual impulses or development that characterizes it. A sort of amnesia over the Oedipal conflict settles in, and the boy devotes himself to nonsexual, academic, or vocational goals as he learns how to function in the social world, at least until adolescence.

Sexual impulses reappear with the onset of puberty, when the boy now focuses his libidinal energy on others. He will now unconsciously seek a libidinal object that bears a superficial resemblance to his mother, the now-forgotten object of his earlier desires. It is important, however, that the new object of his affections differ enough from her that his castration anxiety will not be engaged once again. According to Freud, that anxiety will never entirely leave him, however, and may reemerge anytime his deeper sexual or aggressive nature is awakened. Following this pattern, in which the adult sexual object is of the opposite gender, became the standard for male resolution of the Oedipus complex, and in the hands of Freud's successors in the psychoanalytic profession came to be regarded as the only natural, and therefore normal, way for things to work out. Again, this was not how Freud regarded it: Although this was certainly the most common outcome, it was hardly the only one, and Freud saw heterosexuality as a neurotic development, just as homosexuality was one. *Both* involve the deferral of natural drives, in response to anxiety and the imposition of social rules from without, and both result in a lifetime of anxiety and guilt.

Freud saw the resolution of the Oedipus complex that resulted in heterosexuality as fairly universal, but he recognized four different forms of homosexuality, resulting from four different responses to Oedipal anxiety.

One characteristic is common to all four developmental paths: whereas the heterosexual surrendered his libidinal object in response to castration anxiety, all four homosexual resolutions involve an attempt to maintain the erotic connection to the Oedipal object while minimizing the experience of castration anxiety.

In the first and simplest version, the boy tries unconsciously to maintain the libidinal connection to his mother, but doing so requires somehow reducing the intensity of his castration fear. The greatest reassurance that castration is not a possibility would come from finding that his libidinal object has not been deprived of a penis after all, and therefore his father's horrible revenge is less likely.

In seeking this reassurance, he searches for a libidinal object that brings together some characteristics of the mother and the possession of a penis: he finds
it in a young, effeminate boy, who to his unconscious mind stands in for a woman
with a penis. Homosexual men who resolved the Oedipus complex in this way will
look for partners only among young men and boys. Their ability to form stable,
long-term relationships is hampered by lingering fear of castration, which becomes
a fear of commitment. According to Freud, these men also tend to conceal powerful feelings of hatred for women. Freud's description of these men and the etiology of their adult sexuality is actually quite similar to his account of the origin of
fetishes, which he also described as anchored in the search for unconscious reassurance that women actually have penises after all.

The second variety of homosexuality originates in the same basic wish to maintain the Oedipal bond with the mother, although by different means. Instead of
trying to preserve the mother as unconscious libidinal object, these boys tried to
unconsciously retain their *relationship* to their mothers. Instead of identifying with
their fathers, as the heterosexual boys do, they identify with their mothers, wanting to be more like them. As partners they therefore seek men who resemble their
own idealized image of themselves, and try to love them either as they imagine
they were once loved themselves, or at least as they *wish* they had been loved by
their mothers. Since they identify strongly with their mothers, these men tend to
be effeminate and maternal in both behavior and personality. Since they seek a libidinal object resembling an idealized version of themselves, these men look for
ideally handsome men, as near to perfect in appearance as they can find.

Whereas the first two types result from attempting to maintain the mother as
the primary Oedipal object, the third variation is quite different, resulting instead
from the boy's longing to be the passive libidinal object of his father. In Freud's
view, all boys experience these wishes, and they remain in the unconscious mind
of all adult men. These wishes vary greatly in intensity, however, and in most men
erotic feelings toward the father are weaker than those for the mother. In some
boys, however, the father is the object of the stronger libidinal feelings. Boys can
become fixated at this inverted piece of the Oedipus complex, and thus as adults
desire libidinal objects that most strongly resemble their fathers. This type of homosexuality can also occur in boys who desired the mother more strongly than the
father, if their Oedipus complex causes so much anxiety that they seek refuge in
the less anxious relationship with the father. These men attach themselves to older
men, who serve as father figures and teachers to them. They may harbor fantasies
of bearing these older men's children, or of incorporating some of their masculinity through sexual submission, thus possibly becoming more like these idealized
men themselves.

The fourth variety of homosexuality differs from the others in that it results not
from erotic wishes but rather from aggressive ones. As in the first two types, the

boy refuses to give up the erotic attachment to the mother, but the boy's unconscious focus is on his rivalry with erotic competitors, rather than on maintaining the bond with his mother. The primary erotic competitor is of course the boy's father, but older brothers can also play a role. The boy's feelings of rivalry may become intense and murderous, leading to fantasies of violent, bloody attacks, resulting in fantasies of equally violent retribution directed at himself by his rivals.

The boy eventually masters these feelings via one of Freud's most basic **defense mechanisms**: *reaction formation.* In reaction formation, unacceptable impulses, wishes, and feelings are converted into their more socially acceptable opposites. In this case, this means that the hostile feelings toward the father (or other rivals) remain, but the boy's feelings of hatred and rivalry toward virile men become feelings of love and erotic attraction. Unlike other homosexual men, Freud describes these men as typically quite masculine in appearance, and usually possessing strong feelings of esteem and admiration for other men.

Although Freud only outlined these four etiological processes in detail, he recognized that these were almost certainly not the only ones, with many more yet to be discovered and described. Several ideas which are implicit in these descriptions, and which Freud and his immediate circle took very seriously, were largely ignored, when not explicitly denied, by the later psychoanalysts. The first of these is perhaps the most important: Homosexuality as described by Freud is not a single, unitary thing. Indeed, apart from their attachment to libidinal objects of the same sex as themselves, members of the four groups have no more in common with each other than they do with heterosexual men, and it would be more accurate to describe multiple homosexualities than to treat the term as though it always meant the same thing.

Second, these four varieties, along with any other forms of homosexuality that may exist, represent a wide range of psychological adaptation, very much like the wide spectrum from pathology to normality that exists among heterosexuals. Because of this, Freud did not advocate the view that a homosexual orientation is necessarily a form of psychopathology, nor is there anything in Freud's theory to suggest or support such a view. Indeed, the underlying mechanisms, whether instincts, drives, fantasies, or defenses, that are implicated in the development of homosexuality are part of the universal lot of humanity, rather than anything specific to homosexuality.

Given the absence of any clear pathology to distinguish homosexual from heterosexual development, Freud saw attempts to cure the condition as pointless, as from a psychoanalytic point of view, there is nothing more (and nothing less) to cure here than in heterosexuality. Furthermore, in addition to such a cure being pointless, in Freud's view it is also almost certainly impossible in any case. A homosexual's orientation is determined by the most basic developmental processes, and the same ones that result in a heterosexual orientation. Freud stated this quite explicitly, writing that "to undertake to convert a fully developed homosexual into a heterosexual is not much more promising than to do the reverse" (Freud, 1920, p. 151). As should be clear from the foregoing, homosexuality is not in Freud's view a learned response, either the result of modeling or of seduction, but rather it is the result of a complicated set of unconscious mechanisms, and the process is complete by the time a boy is about six years old.

In the early days of psychoanalysis, unsurprisingly given Freud's view of its origins, the usual attitude toward homosexuality tended to be neutral or positive. Freud and his followers certainly encountered some troubled or unhappy homosexuals, but they were not seen as typical, since most people seeking psychiatric treatment tend to be troubled or unhappy in some way. Freud also wrote about homosexual patients who were happy and well-adjusted and wrote on multiple occasions about the apparent relationship between homosexuality and creative achievement. A belief in the essential bisexuality of all humans was an important element of Freud's theory, and among the early Freudians was an important explanatory mechanism for both good and bad outcomes in heterosexuals.

Given all of this, Freud would not have recognized the view of homosexuality that would come to dominate the psychoanalytic community during much of the ensuing century, as his successors came to take a more and more negative approach to homosexuality, eventually coming to regard it almost universally as a pathological condition, a view that came to dominate psychiatry as a whole. The origin of this shift in the psychoanalytic view of homosexuality may be in the increased emphasis that later psychoanalysts placed on the first two stages of psychosexual development. Where Freud traced the origin of sexual orientation, along with most neurosis, in the phallic stage and the resolution of the Oedipal conflict, some of those who came later, such as Melanie **Klein**, viewed that emphasis as misplaced, instead looking to earlier developmental crises for the origins of both healthy and pathological development. In Klein's (1932) view, making it to the phallic stage in order to negotiate the Oedipus complex was a sign that a child had already successfully navigated earlier, more basic conflicts.

Eventually the idea of the centrality of pre-Oedipal crises, especially those occurring during the oral stage, became a major school of thought within psychoanalysis, popularized especially by such female psychoanalysts as Klein and Margaret **Mahler**, who sought to create a psychoanalysis based in more than just sexual conflict and giving the mother a central role beyond that of libidinal object.

Oral theories of psychosexual development differ from the traditional approach in some very basic ways, but especially in the emphasis on a simple dyadic relationship between mother and child rather than the more complex, triangular dynamic of the Oedipal conflict. Whereas in the phallic stage, the primary crisis involves the tension between desire for the Oedipal object and the fear of the father's retaliation, the oral stage is focused on what Mahler calls *separation-individuation*: the baby's psychic differentiation of the self from the mother. The baby starts without a sense of existing as a separate individual from his mother, and the successful achievement of that sense of self is a primary achievement of the oral stage. As the baby cannot stay attached to the breast at all times, but possesses only an id, which cannot delay gratification, the drive to be mastered in this stage is aggression and rage, rather than the libido that dominates the phallic stage.

The basic oral theory of the development of homosexuality is fairly straight-forward: An infant who grows up to be homosexual has not completed the process of separation-individuation from his mother. Having failed to achieve a clear boundary between himself and his mother's breast, he becomes fixated at the oral stage, and never even embarks on the Oedipal conflict. Instead, he remains identified with his mother in a primitive way, as he hasn't clearly separated his identity from hers, and is thus prevented from establishing a secure, stable male identity. His identification with his mother remains unstable, as he simultaneously wishes to recapture his lost bond with his mother, while simultaneously wishing to flee that same union, with its consequent complete loss of identity.

In this view, the homosexual is caught up in mutually contradictory quests for both union and independence, which inevitably affects the pattern of his later erotic relationships. In these later relationships, he seeks his mother's breast in his partner's penis, while simultaneously filled with rage at his own failure to achieve a clearly differentiated self. Given their seriously divided ego, these men are seen as prone to substance abuse, emotional instability, compulsive sexual behaviors, and ultimately an inability to experience intimacy, unsure as they are of their own identity. Given the oral fixation, their development was arrested before they could experience the Oedipus complex, crucial though it is to the development of the superego. In the absence of a stable superego, these men have great difficulty controlling their impulses and following basic social conventions.

Clearly this view of homosexuality is very much at odds with Freud's views on the subject. Where Freud presents homosexuality as resulting from the same basic mechanisms as heterosexuality, and entailing neither better nor worse psychological adjustment than does a heterosexual orientation, the oral theory presents homosexuality as fundamentally pathological. Furthermore, the suggestion that homosexuals lack a fully developed superego implies that they may naturally be prone to more immorality.

Beyond the oral theorists, the mainstream of psychoanalysis also came to view homosexuality as unnatural or disturbed. As early as 1940, only two years after Freud's death, major psychoanalytic publications began to part ways with Freud's insistence on the universality of bisexuality. Rado (1940), for example, wrote in an influential paper that homosexual or bisexual tendencies were *not* a part of a healthy constitution, and that sexual desire by a man for another man was in itself a sign of psychopathology, which was interfering with more natural heterosexual inclinations. This sort of portrayal of the typical homosexual as mentally ill and abnormal was characteristic of a substantial proportion of psychoanalytic writing on homosexuality all the way up to the 1970s.

One influential theory regarding the origins of homosexuality was promulgated by Ovesey (1969), who drew a distinction between *true* homosexuality and *pseudohomosexuality*. True homosexuals experienced an actual disturbance of normal sexuality, but pseudohomosexuals, who made up the majority of homosexuals and were the population of real interest to Ovesey, became the way they were because of feelings of inferiority. Pseudohomosexuals were men who felt profoundly incompetent in the social world, which led to feelings of failure, which led them to act in response to a set of unconscious equations: "I am a failure = I am castrated = I am not a man = I am a woman = I am a homosexual" (Ovesey, 1954, p. 247). In Ovesey's view, many or even most cases of overt homosexuality resulted from despair over competence, which caused normal heterosexual function to be displaced onto the safer arena of homosexual behavior. Since these men were not truly homosexual, it was possible to treat and cure them of their apparent homosexuality by uncovering and analyzing their fear of competence and helping to strengthen their weakened sense of masculinity. In this perspective, a homosexual man is simply a man who does not feel secure enough in his masculinity.

A different approach to the issue, which proved quite popular in the 1960s, was published by Bieber and his colleagues in 1962. They surveyed a sample of more than 100 homosexual men in psychoanalytic treatment, and proposed a model for the development of homosexuality based on the results obtained from this sample of admittedly disturbed individuals. The model focused on the men's family histories, with a special emphasis on their mothers. According to the researchers, most of the men in their sample had what they called "close-binding-intimate mothers," who behaved seductively toward their sons and interfered with their relationships with their fathers and peers, thus preventing them from developing masculine personalities. Bieber et al. (1962) further reported that not a single participant in the study recalled having a warm and supportive relationship with his father. The men instead recalled fathers who were detached, hostile, or rejecting. According to the resulting theoretical perspective, homosexuality is a pathological condition reflecting damage for which a particular type of faulty parent, especially the mother, was culpable. While this approach at least acknowledges that a cure is unlikely, it nonetheless suggests that homosexuality might be preventable through parent education.

In the early days of psychoanalysis, Freud made it plain that he believed homosexuality to be a naturally occurring orientation, produced partly as a result of unconscious intrapsychic processes which operate within all of humanity, and which have done their work by the time children attend first grade. Furthermore, homosexuality was no more pathological an outcome to those processes than was heterosexuality. Following Freud's death, however, the psychoanalytic community changed direction dramatically, and until the early 1970s homosexuality became widely regarded as a psychiatric disturbance in need of treatment (though with wildly different causal explanations competing for dominance). This would not change in an official way until the 1973 revision of the DSM-II, and then as a result of a new consensus being reached outside the psychoanalytic community, among more scientifically minded psychiatrists and psychologists. The consensus that has now taken root, however, reflects Freud's writings from 100 years ago far more than it does the psychoanalytic thought of the intervening decades: that homosexuality is one of several naturally occurring sexual orientations, which is in itself neither particularly unhealthy or healthy psychologically, taken on its own.

Incidentally, the astute reader will have noticed that most of the theorizing on homosexuality has focused exclusively on *male* homosexuality, while largely ignoring female homosexuality. Several psychoanalytic theorists offered explanations of female homosexuality as well, but they tended to stay far closer to Freud's ideas and focus largely on naturally occurring bisexuality, and thus have stirred up far less controversy. (For an example of such a theory, see Princess Marie **Bonaparte**.)

Further Reading

Bayer, R. (1981). *Homosexuality and American Psychiatry.* New York: Basic Books.

Bergler, E. (1956). *Homosexuality: Disease or Way of Life?* New York: Hill and Wang.

Bieber, I., H. J. Dain, P. R. Dince, M. G. Drellich, and H. G. Grand (1962). *Homosexuality: A Psychoanalytic Study of Male Homosexuals.* New York: Basic Books.

Freud, S. (1905). Three Essays on the Theory of Sexuality. In *The Standard Edition of the Complete Psychological Works of Sigmund Freud* (Ed. James Strachey). Vol. 7. London: Hogarth Press, pp. 125–245.

Freud, S. (1910). Leonardo da Vinci and a Memory of His Childhood. In *The Standard Edition of the Complete Psychological Works of Sigmund Freud* (Ed. James Strachey). Vol. 11. London: Hogarth Press, pp. 59–137.

Freud, S. (1920). The Psychogenesis of a Case of Female Homosexuality. In *The Standard Edition of the Complete Psychological Works of Sigmund Freud.* Vol. 18. London: Hogarth Press, pp. 147–172.

Klein, M. (1932). *The Psychoanalysis of Children.* London: Hogarth Press.

Ovesey, L. (1969). *Homosexuality and Pseudohomosexuality.* New York: Science House.

Rado, S. (1940). A Critical Examination of the Concept of Bisexuality. *Psychosomatic Medicine,* 2: 459–467.

Horney, Karen (1885–1952)

Karen Horney is widely revered among feminist scholars for having introduced a clearly, resolutely feminine perspective into the male-dominated world of psychoanalysis. Perhaps more revolutionary than her attempts to create a psychoanalysis based on the experiences and impulses of both genders, however, was her insistence on overcoming the other major weakness she perceived in Freudian psychology: the generalizing of the experiences and impulses of neurotic patients to the rest of the population. Indeed, although her emphasis on giving equal weight to feminine drives and experiences receives far more attention, it is important to note that throughout her most comprehensive revisionary work, *New Ways in Psychoanalysis* (1939), Horney is very careful to acknowledge that Freud's ideas are legitimate extrapolations from the experiences of the people he studied—the problem is that he didn't find out what was going on in the minds of normal people. For this she is both admired and derided among psychoanalysts in general, depending on their degree of Freudian orthodoxy.

She was born Karen Clementine Theodore Danielsen, daughter of Berndt Henrik Wackels Danielsen and Clotilde Marie van Ronselen, outside of Hamburg on September 15, 1885. Her father, a naturalized German citizen of Norwegian background, was a 50-year-old widower on his second marriage, who already had four teenage children when he met Clotilde. The German-Dutch Clotilde was 18 years his junior, and Karen was their second child together. Her brother Berndt was four years older, and biographical sources suggest that he was his parents' clear favorite.

If a person's childhood can be said to have clearly molded the direction of her thought in adulthood, as of course any self-respecting psychoanalyst would agree, then Karen Danielsen may provide an excellent illustration of this. In *New Ways in Psychoanalysis,* one of her fundamental disagreements with Freud concerns the Oedipal conflict—rather than assuming that changes in attachment to parents originate universally in incestuous feelings, she proposed that a child's attachment to the opposite-sex parent may be more readily based in feelings of anxiety and insufficient security. Her own relationship with her father, who has been described as demanding, stern, emotionally distant, may provide some insight here. As a seafaring man, he was away for long periods during her childhood, adding physical distance to the emotional, and Horney recalls the anxiety remaining when he was

Karen Horney, the first genuinely feminist psychoanalyst. (Bettmann/Corbis)

gone—when present, he was intimidating and frequently made negative observations regarding her appearance and her intelligence. Despite this, Horney reports having had great respect and admiration for him in his professional capacity and fondly remembered being allowed to accompany him occasionally on his oceanic travels.

Early on, she rejected her father's derision toward her intellectual gifts, taking her schooling very seriously and impressing her mother with her accomplishments. At the same time, however, she took his other insults to heart, famously saying of herself, "If I couldn't be beautiful, I decided I would be smart." Furthermore, her success in school was itself an act of rebellion—like many men of his time, Berndt Danielsen disapproved of education for women. Her decision that she would eventually pursue a medical education was made by around age 12, at a time when this was not a realistic hope for a woman in Germany. Fortunately, by the time she was old enough, both the necessary college preparatory education and university admission had become available to women. Her father's cooperation had not, however—he continued to disapprove of her choices. His cooperation in providing both her tuition and his permission (still required for girls in those days) to attend the preparatory school was obtained only by Karen's promise that if he gave it, she would never ask him for anything else.

By the time Karen graduated and began medical school at the University of Freiburg, in 1906, the age difference and various other tensions had taken their toll, and Clotilde had left her husband and moved to Freiburg to be close to her daughter. As one of the few women in medical school, over the objections of some of the faculty who believed that women had no place there, Karen was grateful for the support, and she continued to excel in a hostile environment in which very few women were allowed to succeed. In 1906, she met economics student Oskar Horney, and in 1909 they married. In the next two years, she lost both parents and had her first daughter, and over the next four years after that she had two more daughters and earned her medical degree from the University of Berlin, writing her dissertation on the causes of psychosis while also caring for her infants. Her development of difficulties with chronic fatigue and depression, which would plague her throughout her life, is less than surprising under these circumstances and, combined with her professional interest in neurology and mental illness, may have rendered her eventual contact with psychoanalysis inevitable.

While working at the Lankwitz-Kuranstalt neuropsychiatric hospital in Berlin, she met Karl Abraham, then president of the Berlin Psychoanalytic Society. She joined the society and also entered into analysis with Abraham, who saw her as an analysand over the next two years, and praised her in correspondence with Freud. Right from the start of her association with the institute, however, she found herself at loggerheads with some of Freud's basic notions—her first formal presentation before the institute, in 1917, was a paper devoted to the potential for lifelong development and growth, a perspective that was seen as a challenge to Freud's childhood determinism. She accepted most of Freud's basic premises, however, and embarked on private practice as a psychoanalyst in 1919.

She also wielded influence on the next generation of psychoanalysts, teaching at the Berlin Psychoanalytic Institute until 1932, leaving only when she immigrated to the United States. Her departure from Germany, at age 47, was occasioned by an invitation to work with Franz Alexander at the Chicago Institute of Psychoanalysis. After two years there, she moved on to New York City, where she taught at the New School for Social Research and the New York Psychoanalytic Institute. It was her experiences with American clients during the Great Depression that led to one of the ideas that most informed her writing, and most alienated her fellow psychoanalysts: the people who came to her for therapy often needed help with real problems arising out of their present circumstances, rather than an examination of (for example) their memories of infantile sexuality. She further alienated some of her fellow practitioners by charging clients on a sliding scale based on ability to pay, believing that people should not be deprived of treatment due to economic circumstances.

Horney's major contributions to psychoanalysis can be described as falling into two broad categories: First and foremost, the reinterpretation of basic psychoanalytic concepts into a *Feminine Psychology* (the title of her most widely read collection of essays) that recognizes that the female experience is fundamentally different from the male and cannot simply be interpreted in terms of masculine drives and needs. The other innovation, in many ways just as important as the first, was to follow in the footsteps of Alfred Adler and others in arguing that Freud's emphasis on innate sexual drives as the primary guiding force in personality development excludes other factors that may be far more important in determining personality in most normal, non-neurotic people. Indeed, a core idea of her new psychoanalysis is that Freud's theory is flawed primarily because he based it exclusively on psychiatric patients who aren't representative of the rest of the population. This is also a common criticism of Freud from the wider psychological world beyond the psychoanalytic community, which may account to some degree for her ongoing lack of acceptance by substantial portions of that community.

Her first significant foray into feminine psychology was the paper she presented in 1922 at the Seventh International Psychoanalytical Congress, titled "On the Genesis of the Castration Complex in Women." The paper is noteworthy for several reasons, not least of which is that it was the first paper on the psychology of women to ever be presented at an international meeting *by a woman*. It was also the first salvo fired in Horney's long war against what she saw as Freud's conception of female development as having meaning only in terms of feelings of inferiority as compared to men, particularly the idea of penis envy. This is especially intriguing given that the chair of the session in which she presented the paper was Sigmund Freud. She was respectful in this presentation, even explicitly accepting the basic idea of penis envy, but arguing that it should be seen as an expression of femininity rather than as its formative experience. In the same presentation, however, she also objected to the male narcissism that led the psychoanalysts, almost all male, to so readily accept the notion that half of the human race is dissatisfied with its gender.

With this first paper (later published in 1924), Horney was off and running. In 1926, she responded in print to Freud's further writings on the consequences of anatomical differences with the observation that a man created psychoanalysis, and the people who have refined his ideas have mostly been men, so the fact that they had developed a masculine psychology could hardly surprise anyone. Horney's ultimate goal in her early psychoanalytic writings was fairly straightforward: in a community that continued to define women primarily in terms of the ways in which they weren't men, she simply wanted to establish plainly that femininity is not a result of, or a reaction to, masculinity, but rather an essential attribute of women. She largely stood alone in this fight, at least at first, as other female psychoanalysts largely went along with Freud. Jeanne Lampl-de Groot, for example, described the girl in early childhood thus: "In her love aim and object choice she is actually a little man." Support came from an unexpected source among the old guard of Vienna, as Ernest Jones published a series of papers in which he demurred from Freud's view of women, and in 1935 explicitly defended Karen Horney in a paper delivered to the Vienna Psychoanalytical Society, arguing that the essential question is "whether a woman is born or made."

By 1939, Horney's critiques of basic Freudian notions came to full flower with the publication of *New Ways in Psychoanalysis,* in which center stage is taken by her dual themes of (1) excessive reliance on sexuality as an explanatory mechanism and (2) describing women strictly in terms of pathological responses to not being men. Her focus is less on tearing down Freud than it is on constructing a more solid empirical base for psychoanalysis, as her criticism often focuses on what Freud's analysis is missing rather than on outright rejection of his ideas. Her take on the Oedipus complex provides a good illustration of this constructive criticism.

Horney approaches the Oedipal conflict from three different directions: she doubts its universality, objects to the idea that it is always based on incestuous feelings, and rejects Freud's assertion that it is the central conflict underlying all later neuroses. Regarding its genesis, a central part of her own view of child development is the notion that children with troubled relationships with their parents can have these difficulties for a large variety of reasons, including anxiety, conflicting feelings of dependency and hostility, parental coldness and distance, and feelings of insecurity, which have nothing whatsoever to do with incestuous desires, or indeed sexual feelings of any sort. She did not doubt that some adult patients actually do recall incestuous feelings, but she acknowledged Ferenczi's view that what they are remembering is actual inappropriate sexual contact from trusted adults. Like Ferenczi, she also regarded these situations as relatively uncommon. Furthermore, she questioned the wisdom of generalizing to all of humanity a set of feelings or behaviors that were observed in clinical patients, pondering whether these feelings arise at all under normal conditions.

Horney was suspicious of Freud's placement of the Oedipus complex at the core of development, and of all subsequent psychological problems, because of the resulting holes in psychoanalytic theory, in which "too many factors extremely relevant to a child's growth are regarded as comparatively superficial, and hence are not given the weight that they deserve" (1939/1966, p. 86). She goes on to list these neglected factors, including parental attitudes of interest and respect, warmth, reliability, and sincerity. In Horney's view, the sort of anxiety produced by parents who are hostile, excessively demanding and critical, unjust, and dominating, and who explain to the child that these attitudes are all expressions of love, may produce a neurotic need for affection that

> may look exactly like what Freud describes as the Oedipus complex: passionate clinging to one parent and jealousy toward the other or toward anyone interfering with the claim of exclusive possession. In my experience the vast majority of infantile attachments to parents, as they are retrospectively revealed in the analysis of adult neurotics, belongs to this group. (1939/1966, p. 83)

Freud regarded later attitudes toward others as so heavily influenced by the Oedipus complex that they are, in Horney's view, largely repetitions of the person's relationships with parents. While discarding that notion, Horney advocated keeping the important, but broader, central idea embedded therein—that early relationships *in their totality* influence later character to an enormous degree, and merit special attention.

Horney reserved her harshest criticism of Freud, and also of the female psychoanalysts who followed him unquestioningly, for the concept of *penis envy*. She objected on a fundamental level to the idea that feminine psychology can be largely explained as a function of the lack of a penis. Indeed, Freud wrote in the *Introductory Lectures on Psychoanalysis* that "the discovery of her castration is the turning point in the life of the girl." Rather than positing heterosexual attraction as basic to both genders, Freud suggests further that, just like boys, girls feel their first sexual attraction toward the mother, only switching their affections to their fathers as a result of fearing the mother (who after all castrated them) and hoping to obtain a penis from the father. Horney expresses a particular disdain for what she saw as Freud's interpretation of adult women's most significant desires and drives as driven by their wish for a penis.

As girls grow up, the desire to have a penis is transferred to a desire to have a child—and Freud saw the desire to have a male child as the strongest wish of all women, as this would represent "a sort of wish-fulfillment in the sense of penis-possession" (Horney, 1939/1966, p. 103). Women who are happy during pregnancy are showing symbolic gratification in the possession of a penis (the baby), and a delayed birth reveals a reluctance to let go of the penis/child. Horney was further appalled at the notion that women who *reject* motherhood also do so as a result of penis envy, as motherhood is a powerful reminder of femininity (and therefore of lost masculinity). By the same token, depression, irritability, and cramps during menstruation occur because the menstrual period is also a reminder of femininity, and cramps are also interpreted as the result of fantasies in which the father's penis is swallowed. Any kind of striving for independence or attempts to surpass men's achievements can also be interpreted as a result of penis envy, which causes the woman to reject men's help or to be hostile to them. In Horney's words, "there is scarcely any character trait in woman which is not assumed to have an essential root in penis-envy" (1939/1966, p. 104), including physical modesty (an attempt to conceal inferior genitals), ambition (compensating for the lack of a penis), feelings of inferiority (hatred toward femininity because they lack a penis), and even the desire to be beautiful or to marry a prominent, successful man.

Horney's criticism of the concept takes several forms, beginning with simple agreement with Alfred **Adler** that while it is clear that many girls grow up envious of boys, what they envy is the privileges and superior social position granted to boys, rather than their anatomy. In a time and place in which Horney was herself among the first women to earn a medical degree, such envy is hardly surprising. She further points out that, although girls are sometimes known to emulate the behavior of boys, this has become rarer during her own lifetime as girls have been granted more freedom. In addition, while acknowledging that adult women do sometimes explicitly acknowledge a desire to be a man or experience dreams in which they clearly have a penis, these sorts of symptoms do not present in the clinic nearly as frequently as some psychoanalysts might suggest, and furthermore only appear in neurotic women. Horney indicates that such clear signs of penis envy are in fact extremely rare, if not actually nonexistent, in non-neurotic women.

Horney's explanation for the vehemence with which Freud and other psychoanalysts find overwhelming evidence *for* penis envy concerns cultural prejudices, which are then reflected in theoretical assumptions. In a profession primarily populated by men, unwelcome behaviors presented by women, such as independence, disobedience, ambition, self-sufficiency, and the tendency to berate men or boss them around, are readily accepted as pathological and in need of explanation. Horney accuses Freud and his associates of a certain degree of hypocrisy, in that the same symptoms (excessive ambition, insecurity, dominating others) are also seen in male neurotics, but never attributed to any discomfort with their own biology. Furthermore, the behaviors in question are directed by women against children and other women as well, not just against men, thus explaining them purely as a reaction to masculinity makes no sense. The same sort of hypocrisy is visible in dream interpretation, in which anything that sounds like a wish for masculinity or a penis is taken at face value, in clear violation of the usual psychoanalytical attitude toward manifest and latent dream content—Horney sees this as clear evidence of theoretical preconceptions driving the analyst's approach. Furthermore, she saw the concept of penis envy as self-sustaining, since women who sought psychoanalysis were already familiar with the concept, and would easily learn to see signs of penis envy throughout their own behaviors, feelings, and dreams, saving their analysts the trouble of doing it for them. This, in Horney's view, actually prevents treatment from being effective, as "interpretations in terms of penis-envy bar the way to an understanding of fundamental difficulties, such as ambition, and of the whole personality structure linked up with them" (1939/1966, pp. 109–110).

In later writings, based on her experiences with patients, Horney took her critique of penis envy further, while agreeing with the basic notion that members of one gender envied the biology of the other. She disagreed regarding which gender envied which, however, proposing that men are instead jealous of women's ability to conceive and carry new life within them. Rather than penis envy, she proposed that some of her neurotic patients suffered from *womb envy.*

Another Freudian idea that Horney attacked with some vehemence, closely related to the notion of penis envy and feminine self-hatred, was that femininity has a special relationship to masochism. Helene Deutsch, one of her fellow female psychoanalysts, went so far as to call masochism the elemental power in feminine mental life. Deutsch argued that what women seek in sexual relationships is rape and violation, while also desiring humiliation in mental life. Menstruation is meaningful to women because it feeds masochistic fantasies, and women want to have children in part because of the greatest masochistic experience of all, childbirth. Beyond the birth, motherhood entails a lot of sacrifice and self-denial, thus constituting an extremely long and drawn-out masochistic experience. According to Deutsch, the woman who doesn't feel raped or humiliated in intercourse will be incapable of achieving satisfaction.

Horney responds to the idea of feminine masochism by once again reminding the reader that the data on which Deutsch's conclusions are based concern only neurotic women. Horney acknowledges that masochistic fantasies are certainly seen sometimes in clinical cases, and it may even be true that neurotic women are more likely than neurotic men to present with masochism as a symptom. Where Deutsch's explanation is that the higher rate of masochism among women is a clear sign of penis envy, Horney instead argues, against the flow of psychoanalytic thought at the time, that masochism isn't primarily a sexual phenomenon, but rather a result of certain types of conflict in interpersonal relationships. To the extent that masochism appears more frequently in women, it is as a result of cultural factors—in our culture, she argues, the fear of losing love is basic even to the healthy women, because the culture favors men's needs and desires so heavily. Again, she argues, if women in our culture feel inferior because they are women, it has nothing to do with biology and everything to do with living in a culture that considers them inferior. Clinicians who implicitly accept the idea that feelings of inferiority are due to biology will of course find signs of those feelings, and they will fail to consider alternative explanations for them.

Although her critiques of Freud continue today to be her best-known work, Karen Horney's contributions go well beyond that, to her own original theoretical contributions. She believed neuroses resulted not from old unconscious conflicts, but rather from anxiety caused by conflict in interpersonal relationships. This anxiety results in particular needs that the neurotic attempts to fulfill. Horney identified 10 neurotic needs, grouped into three categories: needs that move the person *toward* others, needs that move the person away from others, and needs that move the person *against* others. Needs in the first category lead the person to appear excessively needy and clingy and insecure; needs in the second category result in being perceived as hostile, cold, indifferent, and aloof. The third category consists of the needs that are central to people who are hostile and wish to control others. The 10 neurotic needs are as follows:

1. Affection and approval—people with this need are hypersensitive to rejection and criticism, and fearful of others.

2. A partner who will take over one's life—people with this need fear abandonment and may believe that being in a relationship will fix all problems.

3. Need to restrict life within narrow borders—some people are undemanding, content with little, and prefer to be inconspicuous. They may make their own needs secondary to others', and undervalue their own potential.

4. Power—people with this need seek power, despise weakness, and will exploit or dominate others. They fear situations that they cannot control.

5. The need to exploit others—People with this need consider others in terms of what can be gained from them, and take pride in their own skills as manipulators and exploiters.

6. Prestige—These people value themselves in terms of personal acclaim and public recognition. They evaluate personal possessions and relationships in terms of prestige and value, and fear embarrassment and public humiliation.

7. Personal admiration—This need results in narcissism and inflated self-image.

8. Personal achievement—People driven by this need are essentially insecure, and so push themselves to achieve great things and then to top them.

9. Self-sufficiency and independence—People driven by this need distance themselves from other people and avoid being dependent on anyone but themselves.

10. Perfection and unassailability—People driven by this need constantly search for personal flaws in order to repair or hide them, as their primary goal is complete perfection. By setting up impossible standards for themselves, they are dooming themselves to failure.

The book in which Horney presented this view of neurosis, *Self-Analysis* (1942), was among the first psychological self-help books, and also helped to further alienate some of the psychoanalytic establishment, via its implicit suggestion that readers could carry out the task of the psychoanalyst all by themselves.

Having left an indelible mark on the world of psychotherapy, Karen Horney died of cancer on December 4, 1952, knowing that her friends and former patients were planning to open a clinic in her name. The Karen Horney clinic, in New York City, opened its doors in 1955, operating both as a research and training center and as the fulfillment of Horney's desire to provide a low-cost mental health center for people who could not afford to go to most traditional psychoanalysts.

Further Reading

Freud, S. (1989). *Introductory Lectures on Psychoanalysis.* New York: Liveright.

Horney, K. (1939/1966). *New Ways in Psychoanalysis.* New York: W. W. Norton.

Paris, B. (1994). *Karen Horney: A Psychoanalyst's Search for Self-Understanding.* New Haven, CT: Yale University Press.

Rubins, J. (1978). *Karen Horney: Gentle Rebel of Psychoanalysis.* New York: Dial.

Hypnosis

Sigmund Freud was probably the single largest influence on the continuing use of hypnosis by therapists, and the use of hypnosis is a key element of the popular media image of Freudian psychoanalysis. The extent to which he inspired many others to follow in his footsteps and incorporate hypnosis as a technique to recover repressed memories is rather ironic, given that Freud actually set aside hypnosis quite early in his career, having decided that it was not an effective technique. He came to this decision, however, only after making extensive use of hypnosis in his early work with Josef **Breuer** with hysterical patients.

Hypnotism was first discovered and used for medical treatment by Franz Anton Mesmer (1734–1815), though he was unaware that he was making use of a psychological phenomenon, having instead created an elaborate and completely wrong explanation of it that relied on magnetism. Mesmer believed that everything in the universe was surrounded by a magnetic force, which he described as flowing through the human body as an invisible magnetic fluid. Illness, both physical and mental, was therefore caused by either insufficient magnetism or interruptions of the flow of this fluid, problems that could be corrected via the application of magnets directly to the affected areas of the body, thus restoring normal magnetic flow. He found that when he passed magnets over his clients' bodies, they indeed often felt better immediately, and over time his procedures became more and more elaborate—at one point, his salon in France included a tub filled with iron filings that he would stir with long magnetic rods. Eventually, Mesmer discovered that he could produce the same effects without using magnets at all, by simply waving his hands in front of the client's body. Mesmer came to believe that this was because his own personal magnetic force, which he called his "animal magnetism," was so powerful that he was able to influence the magnetic flow in other people using only his own body.

Though such a magnetic flow does not actually exist, Mesmer had inadvertently discovered the tremendous power of suggestion in willing subjects who are in a relaxed state. For hypnosis to become a subject worthy of scientific study, it needed to be stripped of Mesmer's pseudo-physics, a task that fell on a distinguished panel of scientists. By 1784, Mesmer's salon in Paris had become quite popular and had developed a reputation among the keener intellects as the work of charlatans. Concerned that many of his nation's prominent citizens might be falling

LE MAGNÉTISME ANIMAL
Importante Découverte par M.ʳ Mesmer, Docteur en Medecine, de la Faculté de Vienne en Autriche.

This cartoon, published around 1780, gives a clear sense of the wealthy social class to which Mesmer provided his services. The original caption reads: "Animal Magnetism: the important discovery by Mr. Mesmer, doctor in medicine, faculty of Vienna in Austria." (National Library of Medicine)

prey to a con artist, King Louis XVI appointed a board of inquiry to investigate whether or not animal magnetism actually existed. Three of the panel's members would later become household names as a result of their scientific and political contributions. The panelists included Antoine de Lavoisier, one of the founding fathers of modern chemistry, Benjamin Franklin, at the time serving as the U.S. ambassador to France, and Joseph-Ignace Guillotin, a pain expert whose efforts to make capital punishment more humane resulted in the infamous device that bears his name, and which in an ironic twist would eventually be used on Lavoisier in the wake of the French Revolution.

The panel conducted a series of ingenious tests of Mesmer and one of his students, Charles d'Eslon, which demonstrated two facts quite plainly: (1) people were genuinely affected by mesmerism and (2) whatever mesmerism was, it had nothing to do with magnetism, animal, or otherwise, but rather appeared to be a result of the clients' suggestibility. In one experiment, d'Eslon claimed that he could transfer his personal magnetism to inanimate objects, such as trees, so the panel had him go into an orchard and magnetize a tree, after which a group of his clients entered the orchard with a simple assignment: find the magnetized tree. Since his animal magnetism routinely caused patients to have a sort of fainting spell/seizure, which Mesmer called the "healing crisis," this was also expected to occur if a client approached the tree to which this power had been transferred. The scientists were startled when such a crisis did occur; they were rather less impressed when it became clear that it kept happening in front of the wrong tree.

In another experiment, patients were concealed behind a series of doors. On the other side of the doors, d'Eslon would pick one and transfer his magnetism through the door and into the person on the far side. Again, a healing crisis was seen, but it usually was seen in a person other than the one who had just been treated. The committee's final report was very clear: although mesmerism had clear effects, they were plainly due to imagination and belief rather than the result of any sort of invisible energy being transferred from one body to another. Writing for the majority, Franklin proclaimed mesmerism a fraud.

No longer welcome in Paris, Mesmer retreated to Vienna, where he continued to practice mesmerism. Meanwhile, with the magnetic nonsense removed, the phenomenon began to be studied scientifically by a group of physicians in Scotland who approached mesmerism as something that needed to be examined from a psychological and physiological point of view. Dugald Stewart, for example, made the keen observation that the physical effects produced by Mesmer were actually far more intriguing from a medical point of view in the absence of the magnetic fluid than they would have been if Mesmer's explanation had proven correct. One of Stewart's students, the physician James Braid, gave the phenomenon a new name and a new sense of scientific respectability, calling it "neuro-hypnology" and studying its usefulness in a medical setting, including its applicability as anesthesia. Almost immediately, Scottish physicians began to report remarkable successes, claiming to have used hypnosis as an effective anesthetic in a variety of operations, including amputation of limbs and removal of a cancerous woman's breasts. While these were isolated cases, Esdaile, another Scot working in India, used hypnotic anesthesia on more than 300 people with tumors, many of them cancer of the scrotum. Under his care, the mortality rate from scrotal tumors dropped from 50 percent to under 5 percent, quite an impressive change. As chemical anesthetics began to be discovered in the 1840s, however, hypnotic anesthesia became unnecessary, and the study of hypnosis focused on other applications instead.

Braid's explanation of hypnosis focused on the then newly discovered ideomotor response. First described by Braid's colleague William Benjamin Carpenter, the ideomotor response is simply an involuntary muscle movement influenced by expectation and imagination. A classic example of an ideomotor occurs with divination via pendulums, a technique still popular for allegedly determining whether a pregnant woman is carrying a boy or a girl. The pregnant woman, or a helper, simply suspends a pendulum over the woman's abdomen and tries to hold it still. The suggestion is then made that if the pendulum begins to swing back and forth, the baby is a boy, but if it swings in a circle, the baby is a girl (or vice versa—the specifics don't matter, as long as the person holding the pendulum hears the suggestion). Inevitably, the pendulum will begin to move, but not because of any supernatural force. The person holding the pendulum may be unaware of causing the movement, but tiny involuntary muscle movements are inevitable, and the person's own hopes and expectations regarding the child's gender will influence the outcome. Another well-known example of the ideomotor effect in action is the Ouija board—although all participants will insist that the pointer moved on its own, electromyelograph electrodes attached to their forearms will show that they were in fact pushing it, and so the answers provided by the board will tell us nothing of the desires of the spirit world, but may reveal quite a bit about the hopes of the people using the board.

In Braid's formulation, hypnotic effects are just a special case of the ideomotor principle, and the effect of focusing attention in hypnotic induction is simply to enhance the ideomotor reflex response. Braid's careful attempt to put hypnosis on more objective, scientific footing was largely forgotten in the late 19th century, however, as the work of Jean-Martin Charcot in France gained prominence. Charcot was influenced far more by the mesmerists than by Braid, and he operated

The man who taught Freud to use hypnosis: Jean-Martin Charcot, 1880. (National Library of Medicine)

a clinic at the Salpêtriere hospital in Paris in which he trained clinicians from across Europe in the use of hypnosis. Far from Braid's description of hypnosis as a manifestation of a normal phenomenon that affects everyone, involuntary muscle movements, Charcot instead argued that the hypnotic state was an abnormal state of the nervous system which only occurred in hysterical women, and which manifested in a series of physical reactions (hysterical symptoms).

Because of his view of the relationship between **hysteria** and hypnosis, it was natural that a young neurologist interested in the treatment of hysteria would seek training with him and attempt to incorporate hypnosis into his own practice, and so Sigmund Freud traveled to Paris and spent a few months studying hypnosis under

Charcot. Early on, Freud took a more expansive view of the utility of hypnosis than Charcot, as Charcot regarded it only as a tool for developing a greater understanding of hysteria but not as a part of treatment. This was in part because Charcot regarded hysteria as incurable, and so attempting to treat it using hypnosis would be pointless. Despite Charcot's influence, however, Freud returned to Vienna as an enthusiastic proponent of hypnotherapy, and his early pre-psychoanalytic work with Josef Breuer is replete with examples of the use of hypnosis in the treatment of hysteria. While the book with Breuer, *Studies in Hysteria,* became an important founding text for the therapists who continue today to use hypnosis in an attempt to help people recover repressed memories, Freud himself abandoned the technique shortly thereafter. His abandonment of hypnosis did not occur for any particular philosophical or scientific reason, but rather for a purely practical one: he found other techniques that worked better and more consistently. Some people were much more difficult to hypnotize than others, and Freud found that he could get just as much information out of his clients through the technique of free association, which involves simply getting them to talk about whatever is on their minds.

Within the field of psychology, the 19th-century debate over whether hypnosis represents a simple physiologically based phenomenon in need of no deeper explanation, or an altered state of consciousness that may be representative of certain types of mental illness, remains unresolved to some degree. The standard description of hypnosis, often encountered in introductory psychology textbooks, states that under hypnosis, the subject will experience a loss of volition and become very willing to follow suggestions, along with becoming highly susceptible to hallucinations and delusions. While in the hypnotic state, a person may be able to remember things that were not remembered prior to hypnosis. Memory of what went on during the session may be gone afterward as well, along with memories and physical urges that the subject wished to be rid of. After the hypnotic session, if the person has been given a post-hypnotic suggestion, he or she may still respond to the suggestion of the hypnotist.

This view of hypnosis is still widely accepted by the general public, but the academic and clinical psychological communities have distanced themselves from it over the last several decades. Although some psychologists still refer to hypnosis as an altered state of consciousness, others now view the hypnotic state as nothing more than the enactment of a prescribed social role—this is sometimes referred to as the state/nonstate debate. The most popular state theory, which insists that hypnosis involves an alteration of conscious awareness, is Ernest Hilgard's *neodissociation* theory. According to Hilgard, the mind contains multiple parts that are not all conscious at the same time, and which are ordinarily under the influence of a centralized control structure. Under hypnosis, a dissociation, or split in consciousness, occurs in which subjects surrender to the hypnotist some of their usual control over voluntary actions, while gaining some control over typically involuntary processes, such as sensitivity to pain.

Control over pain has of course been a major concern of research on hypnosis since James Braid's time, and Hilgard conducted a classic study intended to explain it in terms of dissociation. Hilgard had hypnotized subjects immerse one hand in ice water following a hypnotic suggestion that they would feel no pain, a technique now known as the *cold pressor test*. Subjects were asked to press a key with the other, nonimmersed hand, if they felt any pain. Verbally, subjects typically reported almost no pain, but the key pressing indicated a substantial amount of pain. Hilgard explains that a hidden observer was reporting on the pain, while no pain was experienced by the part of the mind that had conscious awareness. Whether a hidden observer is actually present or not, research from Braid's time up to the present day has repeatedly shown that hypnosis can sometimes be useful in reducing pain.

Hilgard's explanation, however, has recently been widely eclipsed by a nonstate view variously called role theory, the cognitive-behavioral view, or the sociocognitive view. According to nonstate advocates, the view of hypnosis as a dissociative state is simply unnecessary and potentially misleading. Role theory maintains that hypnotic phenomena can be explained in terms of compliance with social demands and acting in accordance with a special social role. The hypnotized person does behave differently from nonhypnotized people, but this is because he or she has agreed to act out an established role, with certain expectations and rules. The hypnotized person does feel less in control and becomes far more suggestible, but it happens voluntarily, as part of a social ritual. Furthermore, there is no evidence of any changes in neurophysiological responses during hypnosis, unlike what is seen in actual altered states of consciousness, such as sleep or the effects of psychedelic drugs. Indeed, in studies in which some people are hypnotized and given suggestions while other, nonhypnotized people are asked to do the same things, a typical finding is that motivated but unhypnotized volunteers can duplicate most classic hypnotic effects, including such impressive outcomes as limb rigidity and pain insensitivity. Nonstate theorists maintain that hypnotic behaviors and experiences represent no change in cognitive processes but rather reflect the action of normal cognitive processes under special social circumstances.

Within psychology, the myth about hypnosis most in need of debunking is one that originated with Freud, though he abandoned it early on: the idea that hypnosis is uniquely helpful in recovering lost or repressed memories. Sometimes, for example, age regression is used to help people recover lost memories by having the hypnotized subject return to a childhood mentality and think and behave like a child. Such age regression can be quite dramatic, with the adult subject adopting a childlike voice and demeanor and producing childlike drawings. On closer examination, however, the drawings typically resemble what adults expect children's drawings to look like, while bearing little resemblance to drawings by actual children, just as the childlike voice is used to say things following adult syntax rather than actually sounding like a child's speech.

As for the memories produced under hypnosis, research has demonstrated that they are less accurate than memories produced by the same subjects without hypnosis. A key element of hypnosis, after all, is an increased susceptibility to suggestion and fantasy, thus making it an inappropriate tool for attempting to recover accurate memories. Furthermore, people who have recalled an incident under hypnosis tend to be more confident about the accuracy of that memory than they are about their own real memories. This combination of factors has led to a huge scandal in the clinical world, involving a large number of criminal cases in which people have been accused and put on trial for committing child sexual abuse, murder, and other serious crimes despite a lack of any forensic evidence, based solely on the hypnotically recovered memories of the alleged victims, who did not have any recollection of the crime until after multiple hypnotic regression sessions.

Further Reading

Braid, J.S. (1843). *Neurypnology; or, The Rationale of Nervous Sleep Considered in Relation with Animal Magnetism.* London: John Churchill.

Wagstaff, G.F. (1999). Hypnosis. In S. Della Sala, ed. *Mind Myths: Exploring Popular Assumptions About the Brain and the Mind.* New York: Wiley.

Hysteria

The origins of psychoanalysis, both as theory and therapy, concern female patients suffering from physical symptoms with no obvious physiological cause. In the era in which Sigmund Freud was trained, hysteria was widely viewed as an illness that primarily struck women, which is clearly indicated by the name of the disorder. Hysteria derives from the Greek *hysterikos,* a term coined by Hippocrates to refer to madness that would arise in women as a result of underuse of the uterus, which would consequently wander out of position in the chest cavity and compress other internal organs. In Freud's time, the wandering uterus hypothesis was being supplanted by the idea that hysteria represented a dysfunction of the nervous system, but many doctors still accepted the idea that it was a strictly female disorder.

While popular with Victorian-era physicians, and known to the ancient Greeks, the diagnosis of hysteria predates all of them. Indeed, it may well be the most ancient of all medical diagnoses. The earliest sources of recorded medical knowledge are Egyptian and Mesopotamian; the earliest known Egyptian medical papyrus, the *Kahun Papyrus,* is also the oldest known document concerning hysteria. Dating from about 1900 BC, the papyrus describes the cases of several women experiencing mysterious physical symptoms with no clear physical cause, as in the case of a woman experiencing pain in all four limbs, accompanied by pain in the eye sockets. In all instances, the women's symptoms are attributed to a dislocation or starvation of the uterus, and so the ancient Egyptian physician's recommendations for treatment involve either providing nourishment to the organ or returning it to its proper position in the abdominal cavity. Given the assumption that the womb had somehow wandered out of its usual place, treatments included attempts to lure the offending organ back into position by applying sweet perfumes to the external genitalia, or conversely by eating or inhaling substances that tasted or smelled unpleasant, to drive the uterus away from its unaccustomed location in the upper torso and back to where it belonged.

In Freud's time, theories about the origins of hysterical symptoms had begun to gain in sophistication (and anatomical realism), as the idea gained popularity that hysteria was actually neurological in origin and had nothing to do with the uterus. The main source for the spread of this ideology was Jean-Martin Charcot, with whom Freud studied for a year (1885–1886) at the Salpêtrière in Paris. The two important ideas that Charcot taught, which were then to become highly influential in the hands of his students, were that hysteria results from a traumatic shock to the nervous system and that it is also a product of a hereditary disposition. By placing hysteria firmly in the category of neurosis—at the time a term that simply indicated that symptoms were based in nervous system dysfunction—Charcot recognized, and opened up to others, the possibility that hysteria should be seen in both women and men and could be treated medically.

This fundamental change in how the etiology of hysteria was conceptualized was long overdue. Although the diagnosis and treatment of hysterical symptoms had become somewhat more anatomically sophisticated than it had been in ancient Egypt, there remained little agreement on either its underlying physiological mechanisms or its proper treatment, with the exception of one remarkably common approach that remained quite widespread across the centuries: pelvic massage. In this last treatment, the physician would massage the genitalia until the woman experienced a paroxysm or epileptic seizure, indicating a release of tension and immediate relief of symptoms, which would last until treatment became necessary again. This treatment fits in well with Galen's diagnostic criteria, as he and other physicians into the middle ages described the disorder in a much more straightforward manner as the result of sexual deprivation in passionate women, and it was thus especially common in nuns, virgins, and widows. In the late 19th century, a mechanical vibrating device was first marketed to assist in the treatment of hysteria, and by the turn of the century electrical devices were available for the same purpose. A similar device powered by water had been a part of the offerings at spas since around 1800. Many sources concerning Freud mention that when he first began treating hysterical patients, possible treatment options included electrotherapy and hydrotherapy, but they rarely point out that this is what those terms sometimes refer to.

The great mystery of hysteria is the near-total disappearance of the diagnosis in the early 20th century. By the time of the publication of the first edition of the American Psychiatric Association's *Diagnostic and Statistical Manual of Mental Disorders* in 1952, the diagnosis did not even make an appearance in the standard reference. This is remarkable given how widespread the diagnosis was at the time Charcot took over as the Salpêtrière's head physician in 1862. The Salpêtrière was a hospital originally built 200 years earlier to imprison prostitutes and adulterers (only the female ones, however), but which had since become an asylum in which Charcot's major task was to distinguish between hysterics and several major categories of patients, particularly epileptics, neurasthenics, nymphomaniacs, and women suffering from general nervousness and insanity. The hospital was vast, housing between 5,000 and 8,000 women, by some estimates. In 1883, two years prior to Freud's arrival, an estimated 17.8 percent of those women suffered from

Jean-Martin Charcot demonstrates hypnosis on a hysterical patient at the Salpêtrière. Photoprint based on an oil painting by Pierre-André Brouillet, 1887. (National Library of Medicine)

hysteria. This is the figure for just one institution in one European city, yet less than 70 years later, the diagnosis was no longer in use.

Several different explanations may account for the disappearance of the diagnosis of hysteria. First, it may be that at least some forms of the diagnosis did not disappear at all, but were rather simply renamed: every edition of the DSM up to the current one (DSM-IV-TR) has included the categories of somatization disorders and conversion disorders. In these categories, the primary symptoms involve physical symptoms that lack a clear physiological etiology. In conversion disorders, these symptoms are explicitly described as being caused by anxiety that has become converted into the physical signs. It may be that a form of hysteria is still with us, but is no longer conceptualized as a female disorder or as one that necessarily results from either sexual frustration or the wandering uterus. However, as Ernest Jones notes in his biography of Freud, the disappearance of the widespread cases of female hysteria throughout Europe predates the DSM-I by several decades, and seems to have coincided with the end of World War I in 1918. Numerous historians have speculated that the diagnosis (and its implicit sexism) became untenable as the hospitals filled with shell-shocked veterans, who today would receive the diagnosis of post-traumatic stress disorder, displaying psychological and physical symptoms much like those previously attributed to hysterical women—and all being displayed by patients who, to a man, clearly lacked a uterus.

It may also be that women's suffrage, and the feminist movement more generally, played a part in killing hysteria. Hysteria was after all a disorder that had always been defined by male physicians, with a vague definition that could make virtually any behavior displayed by a woman appear to be a symptom of disease. In 1880, for example, the physician George Beard published a 75-page listing of possible symptoms, and indicated that his list was incomplete. Some idea of the ease with which a woman could be diagnosed can perhaps be gleaned from the presence in his catalog of symptoms of both excessive drinking and thirstlessness. Symptom lists from that era also frequently include some variation on tendency to cause trouble.

In a world in which women were rapidly gaining political power and greater freedom of expression, as well as finally expecting that sexual gratification was something that belonged to them as much as to men, a diagnosis that some feminist scholars suggest existed as much to medicalize ordinary rebellion as to actually treat illness was understandably doomed. Beard may have seen the change coming; by the mid-1890s his papers are devoted to many of the same symptoms, but they have become symptoms of *neurasthenia* and *nervous exhaustion,* with nary a mention of hysteria in sight.

Further Reading

Appignanesi, L., and J. Forrester (1992). *Freud's Women.* London: Basic Books.

Beard, G. (1880). *A Practical Treatise on Nervous Exhaustion.* New York: William Wood and Company.

Briggs, L. (2000). The Race of Hysteria: "Overcivilization" and the "Savage" Woman in Late Nineteenth-Century Obstetrics and Gynecology. *American Quarterly* 52(2): 246–273.

Veith, I. (1965). *Hysteria: The History of a Disease.* Chicago: University of Chicago Press.

Id, Ego, and Superego

In Sigmund Freud's model of the human personality, there are three essential components that determine, via their interactions with each other, how people think and behave: *id, ego,* and *superego.* The id and the superego belong entirely to the realm of the unconscious mind, whereas the ego represents the conscious part of the psyche, of which we are aware and which we show others. The three components do not appear simultaneously in the course of a child's development—only the id is already present at birth. The ego begins to develop during infancy and early childhood, and the superego appears some time later. The importance to Freud of the unconscious portions in determining behavior is well-illustrated by his use of the metaphor of an iceberg to describe the structure of the human mind: when an iceberg is floating in the sea, only about 10 percent of it is visible above the water's surface, with the remaining 90 percent unseen beneath the surface. So it is with the psyche—the vast majority of it is hidden from view, even to its possessor.

The Id

As the only inborn component, the id is the psychic agent representing the natural instincts and drives. In Freud's own words, the id "contains everything that is inherited, that is present at birth, that is laid down in the constitution—above all, the instincts" (Freud, 1938/1973, p. 2). The infant, without reason or restraint, is filled with inborn, instinctive needs demanding fulfillment. These unfulfilled needs cause libidinal energy within the id to build up, creating a pressure that demands release, a release that is experienced by the infant as pleasure. Conversely, the postponement or prevention of release is experienced as pain. The infant, possessing no ability to delay release, demands immediate gratification. The id is therefore said to operate according to the *pleasure principle*: it is driven solely by the goal of experiencing as much enjoyment and avoiding as much pain as possible. The psychoanalytic view of the newborn is of a creature entirely governed by the id, constantly demanding immediate gratification of its needs for food, for drink, for eliminating bodily wastes, and for affection. The id is quite irrational, knowing nothing of rules or social conventions, demanding that its needs be met regardless of present circumstances. Anyone who has ever handled a hungry infant but been unable to feed him or her right away can certainly see the truth in this. There is no reasoning with the newborn, no making of excuses. Any attempt to do so is met only with increased anger and agitation. Furthermore, the newborn's view of the world is quite vague and undefined, with no clear distinctions between the self and the environment. The baby's awareness is, at first, limited to two things: discomfort, created by unfulfilled needs that demand attention, and pleasure and relief when those needs are satisfied.

Over time, the infant's increasing interaction with its environment inevitably begins to create an increasing consciousness of its surroundings, making possible what Freud called the personality's *primary process*—the baby's act of creating in its mind the image of an object that will fulfill a need. Every time an infant feels hungry and is not fed immediately, he or she will cry until somebody feeds the infant, thus reducing the tension of hunger and producing the feeling of pleasure. This cycle will be repeated many times, so that eventually the baby's memory will store a representation of both the food and the feeder, via their taste, smell, sight, sound, and feel. This process would of course be described differently by behaviorists and cognitive psychologists, but all would recognize the result: the baby can now bring to mind the objects that will provide a particular kind of satisfaction (in the present case, food), in response to a particular way of releasing libidinal energy (in the present case, crying).

The id is not only irrational but completely amoral. With no internalized notion of social conventions regarding right and wrong (this will develop later), the id is purely hedonistic. What brings pain and discomfort is always wrong, and what gives pleasure is unequivocally right. Clearly, a person would not get far in life if the psyche did not develop beyond the id. The adult (or older child) who always demands immediate gratification of all urges, be they related to food, drink, elimination, or physical pleasure, would soon discover how intolerant of such a self-indulgent life our customs and laws are. Fortunately, another component will soon develop that functions, at least in part, to keep us alive and out of jail. What is required is a component that, unlike the id, recognizes the limits and requirements of the environment, while also being aware of the demands of the id, and can therefore find morally acceptable ways of relieving the pressure of *libido,* or instinctual energy. This second component, the *ego,* develops directly from the raw material of the id.

The Ego

Of the three major components of the personality, it is the ego that actually interacts consciously with the world and has the job of ensuring that the release of libidinal energy in the world occurs in an acceptable fashion. A major part of its function, in other words, is to help the id to delay gratification until its needs can be met in ways that do not violate the rules of which the id remains unaware. The ego, according to Freud, develops directly out of the id and is actually a part of the id that has been modified by external influences, thanks to its conscious awareness of that outside world. The id, meanwhile, remains unconscious and unaware, and as irrational and hedonistic as ever.

One way of conceiving of the ego's function is as a referee, or mediator, constantly negotiating the conflicts that inevitably arise between the id's (often unreasonable) demands and the reality of the requirements of the social and physical environments. The id's needs demand satisfaction, but that satisfaction must conform to the limitations agreed on by the society in which the child is growing up. This is difficult for an entity that exists entirely below the threshold of consciousness and lacks any awareness of the real world. Unlike the id, however, the ego is conscious and quite aware of the restrictions of the environment. The ego is therefore responsible for providing the child with an initial recognition of the rules and customs of his or her society, as well as an understanding of the penalties that may accompany violations of those regulations. Although Freud equates the ego with the conscious self, going to sleep at night, thus allowing hidden conflicts to be expressed in dreams, he also allows that the ego continues to function as a mediator even in sleep, censoring the content of those same dreams.

Whereas the id, which knows only the pursuit of pleasure and the avoidance of pain, operates according to the pleasure principle, the ego, with its awareness of the real social and physical environments, operates according to the *reality principle*. The ego is able to recognize what the id does not—that simply expending the libidinal energy of the drives, especially the sexual and aggressive drives, in ways that are socially inappropriate, is ultimately detrimental to one's chances of survival, whereas observing society's rules and releasing that energy in more acceptable ways will ultimately result in greater satisfaction and less pain. In similar fashion, whereas the id operates according to the primary process (forming mental representations of objects that will fulfill needs), it is the ego's task to translate these images into actions that can actually be implemented, in accordance with the rules. Freud called this function of the ego the *secondary process*. In order for the ego to choose actions that follow those rules, however, those rules must first be internalized in some way. This is the job of the *superego*.

The Superego

In contrast to the position taken by many philosophers and theologians throughout the history of those disciplines, in Freudian theory, there are no innate, inborn moral principles—morality is entirely socially constructed, in other words. Upon their arrival in this world, as previously noted, infants are amoral hedonists, with no sense of right or wrong at all. Though without moral values, however, newborns do come into the world armed with the capacity to gradually internalize the values they are exposed to, and which are imposed on them, by their environment and by the people in it. These values are initially presented by parents or other caregivers, but as the child grows older, these values begin to also come from all the others that the child interacts with, including other children, teachers, religious leaders, electronic and print media, and others. Along with the ability to make these values a part of themselves, children also come into the world with emotional reactions that can be evoked by violating the rules as well as by following them. When we act in a way consistent with our values, we feel pride and contentment, whereas acting in opposition to our values results in guilt, shame, and fear of punishment. These internalized values become the *superego,* which Freud saw as emerging from the ego just as the ego develops out of the id.

The superego's job is to bring aboard the monitoring functions that have previously been performed by people in the external world: it observes the ego, gives it orders, judges it, and threatens it with punishments, exactly like the parents and others whose place it has taken. Popular treatments of Freudian theory often equate the superego with the conscience, which is not entirely correct: it is at the very least an oversimplification. The ego is made up of two components: the *conscience* is one of them and the other is the *ego ideal.* The *conscience* represents an internal listing of the prohibitions of the child's society, the should nots, the actions that will result in punishment. The *ego ideal* represents positive moral values, the shoulds. Very young children, operating as puppets of the id, must be consistently punished for violations and rewarded for good behavior, whereas older children and adolescents often do not require outside consequences, either positive or negative. As they have now internalized values and accepted them as their own, both punishment and approval now emerge from within as well. When they break the rules, they experience remorse and shame, courtesy of the conscience. When they adhere to their values, doing what they know is right and good, the ego ideal provides praise, pride, and general good feelings.

With the superego added to the id and ego, the psychoanalytic structure of personality is now complete, and the ego's job has just become harder. In older children, adolescents, and adults, the choice of how to behave now requires the ego to negotiate among *three* conflicting sets of demands. The id, irrational as ever, demands immediate gratification, with no regard for propriety, morality, or present circumstances. Meanwhile, the ego must also contend with present circumstances in the environment, which often determines the conditions under which wishes can actually be satisfied, and which is usually beyond the individual's control to at least some degree. While dealing with those demands, the ego must also satisfy the superego, which demands that the individual live up to a particular set of moral values, and which is frankly just as irrational in its demands as the id. Just as the id demands gratification with no regard for practical or moral considerations, so the superego demands adherence to the rules, with no allowances made for present circumstances or the strength of the id's requirements. Assume, for example, a situation in which a person is on the verge of starvation, and the only possible source of food requires stealing it. The id is of course very straightforward in its desires, insisting, with no regard for the law, that the food be taken immediately! The superego, with just as little regard for practical considerations, vehemently insists that stealing is always wrong, without exceptions! The ego's job is then to take both sets of demands into consideration, along with the real circumstances, and choose a course of action. Clearly, there is no course of action that will serve to satisfy both the id and the superego, and so whatever action is taken, the result will inevitably include some internal conflict, much of which, like the id and superego themselves, will remain unconscious.

Not all conflict resulting from our chosen actions is unconscious, however. As children grow up, they encounter an ever-expanding range of social and environmental encounters. Living in a social world, they learn to try to satisfy their physical and psychological needs without generating conflict with others, and they witness the example of others, both in their immediate environment and in books, movies, and television programs, resolving conflicts and moral dilemmas. Based on this, they learn a variety of ways to handle such situations, as well as ways that are more or less effective at meeting conflicting demands. As the ego matures, it becomes more and more capable of meeting conflicting demands directly and resolving dilemmas honestly and rationally, in ways that acknowledge both the instinctive demands and the social rules.

It is inevitable, however, that circumstances will arise in which resolving the inner conflict in ways that produce no guilt, shame, or other inner trouble will simply not be possible, resulting in anxiety. For these situations, the ego has a specialized set of tools intended to minimize the anxiety resulting from internal conflict. Freud called these techniques *ego defense mechanisms,* often shortened simply to **defense mechanisms**. These are simply strategies taken to reduce anxiety when more rational approaches to resolving a problem have failed. What all defense mechanisms have in common is that they occur automatically and unconsciously, and when not used to excess, their implementation is normal and even psychologically healthy. Anxiety and failure to address inner conflict are after all the primary sources, in Freud's theory, of mental illness and maladjustment, and defense mechanisms have protection from these things as their primary purpose.

Further Reading

Freud, S. (1938/1973). *An Outline of Psychoanalysis.* London: Hogarth.

The Interpretation of Dreams (1899)

First printed in 1899, though the date printed on the title page of the first edition is actually 1900, *The Interpretation of Dreams* is widely regarded as Sigmund Freud's most important work, and it remains his most widely read book today. On first publication, however, *Die Traumdeutung* (a more literal translation would be simply *Dream Interpretation*) was a failure by any usual standard. The first print run, consisting of some 600 copies, took eight years to sell out. In the first year and a half of its existence, the book went without reviews in any scientific or medical journal, and it was largely ignored by the psychological publications, apart from those that printed devastatingly negative reviews. By 1910, however, Freud had become rather well known, and so a second edition was put into circulation. The book was translated into both English and Russian in 1913, with six more languages following by 1938. Within Freud's lifetime, there would be a total of eight editions, each issued with a new preface by the author explaining what had changed since the last. From edition to edition, most changes were fairly minor, though the portion of the book devoted specifically to dream symbols, originally only a few pages long, changed quite a bit across the lifetime of the book.

The book's initial reception disappointed Freud, but he remained confident in the originality and importance of the ideas it contained, and reflected on its impact in the preface to the eighth edition (the third English edition):

> This book, with the new contribution to psychology which surprised the world when it was published (1900), remains essentially unaltered. It contains, even according to my present-day judgement, the most valuable of all the discoveries it has been my good fortune to make. Insight such as this falls to one's lot but once in a lifetime. (Freud, 1953, p. xxxii)

This passage makes clear that Freud, well into the establishment of an international network of psychoanalysts, continued to regard the ideas in *The Interpretation of Dreams* as among his most important contributions. For a time, he also acknowledged the important contributions of the ideas of others to the book, particularly those of Otto **Rank**. Rank entered into Freud's inner circle by reading the book's first edition and sending Freud his own 1905 *The Artist,* an exploration of the importance of symbolism in art that was inspired by Freud's work. Freud was so

DIE

TRAUMDEUTUNG

VON

Dᴿ SIGM. FREUD.

›FLECTERE SI NEQUEO SUPEROS, ACHERONTA MOVEBO.‹

LEIPZIG UND WIEN.
FRANZ DEUTICKE.
1900.

The first edition of the book that remains the most widely read of all Freud's works: *The Interpretation of Dreams* (*Die Traumdeutung*), 1900. (Sigmund Freud, *Die Traumdeutung*, Berlin: International Psychoanalytic University, 1900)

impressed that Rank immediately became an important part of his organization, as well as a key collaborator.

The preface to the third edition of *The Interpretation of Dreams* includes the following acknowledgment:

Herr Otto Rank has afforded me invaluable assistance in the selection of supplementary examples, and has revised the proofs of this edition. I have to thank him and many other colleagues for their contributions and corrections. (Freud, 1953, p. xxvii)

In addition to this acknowledgement in the preface, Freud cites Rank as a source of both examples and ideas throughout the book, in passages such as this one, crediting Rank with the idea that dreams involving a need to urinate are actually sexual in nature:

O. Rank, whose conclusions . . . I have here followed, argues very plausibly that a large number of "dreams due to urethral stimulus" are really caused by sexual stimuli, which at first seek to gratify themselves by way of regression to the infantile form of urethral erotism. (p. 252)

With the fourth edition of *The Interpretation of Dreams,* Rank's substantial contribution was acknowledged far more directly, as his contribution of entire chapters on poetry and myth led to the appearance of his name below Freud's on the title page, where it would remain through the seventh edition. Subsequent editions, which appeared after Freud had ended his friendship and professional ties with Rank, reverted to listing Freud as the sole author.

The book originally arose out of Freud's self-analysis, inspired by his observation that dreams often played an important role in his analysis of hysterical patients. Their free association often led them to their dreams, which would in turn lead to other associations and help to illuminate important connections in their past experience that they would not have otherwise brought up at all. Combining this with his observation that hallucinations in psychotic patients were very dreamlike, Freud began to believe that, like daydreams, sleeping dreams served the function of wish fulfillment. Since Freud had always been a very active dreamer, his self-analysis focused heavily on dreams, and before long he decided to write a book about the role of dreams in resolving unconscious conflicts.

The central argument of the book is that the motivation of all dreams is wish fulfillment, and that the instigating source of the dream can often be located in the events of the day preceding the dream, which he called the "day-residue." This can be seen quite readily in very young children, according to Freud, because they have very straightforward dreams of the fulfillment of wishes that they were thinking about the previous day. In adults, however, the process of tracking down the source of a dream is rather more complicated, since their dreams, unlike those of the children, have become distorted. In Freud's model, every dream has two kinds of content, or two levels of functioning, just as the mind itself has both a conscious and an unconscious component. The surface content, which he called *manifest* content, is a heavily disguised version of unconscious wishes and desires, which he called the *latent* content. Correct interpretation of the symbolic meaning of a dream's content can therefore provide a direct link, what Freud called "the royal road," to the unconscious.

In Freud's view, many of our unconscious motivations are so unacceptable to us that the only way to release the tension created by the intrapsychic conflict between the ego and the unconscious parts of the mind is to allow the forbidden content to surface in dreams. The controversial content, however, must be disguised to cause as little anxiety as possible, because even in dreams, the individual's resistance to these unacceptable impulses remains too strong to acknowledge them directly. As a result of this, the dream's real significance is completely concealed from the dreamer, and dreamers are no more able to grasp the actual meaning of their dreams without the help of an analyst than hysterical patients are able to understand the origin and function of their neurotic symptoms. In the first edition, Freud described the latent dream content as having been transformed by a mental force he called the "censor," though as his terminology developed in later edition, this became the work of the ego's defenses, at the mercy of the superego. To Freud, every dream is a compromise, allowing the disguised fulfillment of repressed wishes, serving the purpose of preventing sleep from being interrupted by an impulse so disturbing that it might wake the dreamer.

In the book, the very first dream that Freud subjects to the technique of dream interpretation is one of his own dreams, which came to be referred to as "Irma's injection," and which has inevitably been reanalyzed by many later writers. Freud describes the dream, featuring one of his patients, who he calls "Irma," as follows:

A large hall—numerous guests, whom we were receiving.—Among them was Irma. I at once took her on one side, as though to answer her letter and to reproach her for not having accepted my "solution" yet. I said to her: "If you still get pains, it's really only your fault." She replies: "If you only knew what pains I've got now in my throat and stomach and abdomen—it's choking me."—I was alarmed and looked at her. She looked pale and puffy. I thought to myself that after all I must be missing some organic trouble. I took her to the window and looked down her throat, and she showed signs of recalcitrance, like women with artificial dentures. I thought to myself that there was really no need for her to do that.—She then opened her mouth properly and on the right I found a big white patch; at another place I saw extensive whitish grey scabs upon some remarkable curly structures which were evidently modelled on the turbinal bones of the nose.—I at once called in Dr M, and he repeated the examination and confirmed it . . . Dr M looked quite different from usual; he was very pale, he walked with a limp and his chin was clean-shaven . . . My friend Otto was now standing beside her as well, and my friend Leopold was percussing her through her bodice and saying: "She has a dull area low down on the left." He also indicated that a portion of the skin on her left shoulder was infiltrated. (I noticed this, just as he did, in spite of her dress.) . . . M said: "There's no doubt it's an infection, but no matter; dysentery will supervene and the toxin will be eliminated. . . . We were directly aware, too, of the origin of the infection. Not long before, when she was feeling unwell, my friend Otto had given her an injection of a preparation of propyl, propyls . . . propionic acid . . . trimethylamin (and I saw before me the formula for this printed in heavy type). . . . Injections of this sort ought not to be given so thoughtlessly. . . . And probably the syringe had not been clean. (Freud, 1953, p. 107)

Later in the book, Freud uses this dream to illustrate some of his ideas regarding the significance and sources of various elements of a dream. Day residues, for example, explain much of the manifest content, including the presence both of his colleagues, with whom he has interacted earlier in the day, and of Irma's symptoms as well. The dream is a fulfillment of a wish, in this case to be able to absolve himself of what happened to an actual patient. The key element here is the presence of the turbinate nasal bones in Irma's throat—these were the bones that Freud's friend and college, ear-nose-and-throat doctor Wilhelm **Fliess,** proposed to remove surgically as part of his cure for hysteria. Fliess's treatment of one of Freud's patients, Emma Eckstein (described in detail in the entry on Wilhelm **Fliess**), went terribly wrong when Fliess left a large amount of gauze inside her nasal cavity, resulting in infection and hemorrhaging. As Freud was involved in that case, and felt guilt over it along with his conviction that Fliess was the one at fault, a dream in which one of Freud's patients is ailing and the source of the infection is clearly and entirely the fault of one of his colleagues would serve the purpose of fulfilling the wish to deflect all responsibility onto someone else. Notably absent from this first dream presented in the first edition are the sexual symbols that would come to form such a large part of later dream interpretation; those would become far more important in later editions of the book, thanks in part to the contributions of Otto Rank.

In the book, Freud describes the particular distorting processes that are applied to repressed wishes in producing the manifest content, resulting in a dream that is quite different from the latent dream thought that can be reached through analysis. Psychoanalytic retrieval of the latent content depends on reversing these processes. The distorting operations include the following:

1. *Condensation:* Via this process, one manifest dream object can stand in symbolically for several different associations and ideas, which results in manifest content that is brief and concise compared to the wide range and depth of the latent content, so much so that Freud remarked that it is impossible to ever tell if one has interpreted a dream completely. In the case of Irma, for example, Freud himself suggested that she represented anxieties over multiple patients beyond the obvious example of Emma Eckstein.

2. *Displacement:* A dream element's emotional significance is separated from its real object or content and attached to an entirely different one, as this makes it less likely to arouse the censor's suspicions.

   Thus, Freud's real anxiety over a medical error involving gauze becomes attached in the dream to a completely different error, a contaminated needle, which has nothing to do with the real-life source of the conflict.

3. *Representation:* A thought, even an abstract one, is translated in the dream into visual images. An unacceptable urge such as an inappropriate sexual desire will appear as a visual symbol. In one of Freud's examples, a woman's unwanted lesbian sexual impulses are represented in a dream in which she is traveling alone in a train, but has two purses by her feet.

4. *Symbolism:* Representation rarely involves literal translation of an idea into an image, instead taking the form of symbols that require elaboration in order to uncover the idea to which they refer, as in the foregoing example.

These are the processes by which the unconscious mind allows the expression of unconscious wishes and desires, and Freud recognized that these processes work better sometimes than at other times. Not all dreams succeed in the goal of wish fulfillment, and the result of failures in this dream work was the appearance of anxiety dreams and nightmares. Far from contradicting his model, these dreams demonstrate how the ego responds to awareness of repressed wishes that are very powerful and that have been insufficiently disguised.

Based on his analysis of his own dreams and those of others, Freud came to believe that certain elements in the manifest content of dreams tend to correspond consistently with certain latent content, much of it concerning repressed sexual wishes. Phalluses, for example, are symbolically replaced in manifest content by a wide range of objects that are similar to them in their form, including most long or tall things that jut out in some way, thus a penis can be suggested by mountains, trees, poles, sticks, umbrellas, spires, monoliths, and so forth. Phallic symbols also include objects that have the purpose of penetrating the body and doing harm, including most weapons, such as swords, lances, spears, and guns of all sorts. The list of phallic representations also includes objects from which water runs or sprays, such as pipes, fountains, geysers, crashing waves, garden hoses, and watering cans. Objects that can change their shape by lengthening can also represent the phallus, including balloons, antennas, springs, and even snakes. The number three is also symbolic of the male genitalia, as well as any dream thoughts that consist of three parts, thus even the appearance of the Trinity in a Christian's dreams may represent the phallus.

Female genitalia may be represented by any hollow objects that can contain other objects, including bottles, dishes, boxes, bottles, mineshafts, caves, tunnels, pockets, tins, closets, churches, houses, forts, purses, and even landscapes. Among animals, snails, mussels, clams, scallops, oysters, and the like also represent female genitalia, whereas fruits such as apples, peaches, pears, and coconuts generally symbolize breasts. Dreams in which playing occurs, whether it be the playing of outdoor games or the playing of musical instruments, are symbolic of masturbation, along with any sliding, slipping, or breaking of branches. Meanwhile, a dream that includes the extraction of teeth is symbolic of *punishment* for masturbation. A wide range of other activities and elements represent sexual intercourse itself, including climbing or descending ladders or stairs, traveling on a train, dancing, riding horses, raising a weapon, or running into a house.

The Interpretation of Dreams is Freud's most influential work not just because of its impact on how humanity thinks about dreaming, but also because it truly is the first book to introduce the psychoanalytic method to the world. His previous work, including the case studies published with Josef Breuer, was pre-psychoanalytic, as the development of the theory was largely spurred on by Freud's work on dreams, and from the outset Freud saw the book as his theory's true introduction to the world, writing in the original preface:

In the following pages, I shall demonstrate that there is a psychological technique which makes it possible to interpret dreams, and that on the application of this technique, every dream will reveal itself as a psychological structure, full of significance, and one which may be assigned to a specific place in the psychic activities of the waking state. Further, I shall endeavor to elucidate the processes which underlie the strangeness and obscurity of dreams, and to deduce from these processes the nature of the psychic forces whose conflict or co-operation is responsible for our dreams. (Freud, 1953, p. 1)

Contained within those two sentences is much of the subject matter of psychoanalysis, and with them an intellectual revolution had officially begun.

Further Reading

Freud, S. (1900/1953). *The Interpretation of Dreams.* Standard ed., vol. 4. London: Hogarth.

James, William (1842–1910)

Born into a wealthy family of intellectual giants (the novelist Henry James was his brother) and educated both in Europe and at Harvard, William James is regarded as the founding father of American psychology. He introduced experimental psychology to America in a laboratory founded at about the same time as Wilhelm Wundt's Leipzig facility, which usually gets credit for being the first, and was the first professor of psychology in the United States. He began teaching the subject in 1875, having no educational background in psychology himself, since no such courses were available in America until he started teaching them. He famously joked, "The first lecture in psychology that I ever heard was the first I ever gave."

From these humble beginnings, the field grew rapidly, and by 1895, more than 20 American universities were teaching psychology, the American Psychological Association had been founded, and at least three academic journals were being published. A large measure of the credit for this rapid growth belongs to William James. Because the field barely existed before his work, his influence has been profound. He published dozens of articles, and the first crop of American psychologists studied under him; but his greatest and most influential achievement was undoubtedly the publication of *Principles of Psychology* (1890), a 1,400-page, two-volume compendium of the sum total of psychological knowledge of the time, infused throughout with wit, humor, and intellectual rigor. The book has been widely credited with transforming the dry, sterile, esoteric laboratory discipline of psychology into a vibrant, widely discussed, practical subject that is highly regarded outside the narrow hallways of academia. The book was originally intended as a textbook, a use that its length rendered impractical, so James went to work on an abridged textbook version, which appeared within two years. In U.S. academic circles, the unabridged version was usually referred to as "James," while the shorter edition went by "Jimmy."

Like Wundt, Titchener, and other structuralists, James used introspection to study consciousness, but he disagreed with their theoretical approach. Rather than attempting to break down the conscious experience into its component parts, James emphasized the unitary, unbroken flow of conscious thought, likening it to a stream and pointing out that it is a continuous process rather than a thing to be measured. James also emphasized the function of consciousness rather than its structure; adopting a Darwinian perspective, arguing that consciousness, like all other human

William James, the most influential figure among the early American psychologists, about 1900. (National Library of Medicine)

traits, must have evolved to serve a particular function. The mind's complex processes, in other words, exist because of their adaptive value in ensuring survival, both of the individual and of the species. For this reason, the label usually applied to Jamesian psychology is functionalism.

James's influence may have been largely responsible for the growth of American academic psychology as a primarily laboratory-based, scientific discipline, which was in many ways hostile to Freud's entirely clinic-based theorizing, an attitude that persisted for decades. In 1923, for example, at the convention of the American Psychological Association, James McKeen Cattell famously responded to the mention of Freud's name by a conference attendee by rising and, "after expressing astonishment and painful surprise that a member of the Association should be so wanting in wisdom as to introduce Freud's name at a scientific meeting, castigated him for his folly" (Dallenbach, 1955, p. 523). What is less often recognized is James's role in helping to introduce Freud to the American audience. Prior to 1900, Freud's name was virtually unknown in America, and although his name had appeared from time to time in medical journals, his work had only merited mention once in an American psychological publication. In 1894, *Psychological Review* carried a short abstract in English of Freud and Breuer's "Preliminary Communication on the Psychical Mechanism of Hysterical Phenomena," by William James. James described it as an important paper by "distinguished Viennese neurologists." As the paper described was in German, this abstract was the only notice taken of Freud by the American psychological community at that time, and it should be noted that James's approach was not entirely positive—he described the article as primarily a replication of work already published by Pierre Janet (who, unlike Freud, was familiar to the American audience). James would make up for this faint praise toward the end of his life, however: when Freud visited America for the 20th-anniversary celebration at Clark University (see **United States, Freud's Visit to**), William James traveled out to Worcester from Boston, in very poor health, just to meet him. James and Freud took a walk together, and James told him, "The future of psychology belongs to your work."

Given their profound differences on philosophical issues as well as scientific ones, this was a remarkable compliment for James to pay him. Both men wrote at great length on issues of religion, for example, and both sought psychological explanations for religious experiences and belief. In *The Varieties of Religious Experience,* James produced a classic work, widely regarded as the founding text for the study of religious psychology. James's perspective on the experiences about which he is writing is clearly that of an insider, however. He saw religious experience as an important part of the human experience and was in part inspired by his own experiences. Freud's voluminous writings on religion, on the other hand, bring an outsider's perspective to bear—an avowed atheist, he sought to explain the origins of major religions, including his own Judaism, in terms of the same psychological mechanisms he applied to other human phenomena, and frequently portrayed religion as a harmful illusion. Despite these fairly fundamental differences, however, the two men had a great deal of respect for each other, and James was arguably the first major American psychologist to recognize the importance of what Freud was doing in Vienna.

Further Reading

Dallenbach, K. M. (1955). Phrenology vs. Psychoanalysis. *American Journal of Psychology* 68(4): 511 525.

James, W. (1890). *Principles of Psychology.* New York: Henry Holt.

James, W. (1894). Abstract of Breuer and Freud. *Psychological Review* 1: 199.

James, W. (1985, originally published 1901). *The Varieties of Religious Experience.* Cambridge, MA: Harvard University Press.

Jokes

Although far less well-known than his work concerning the meaning of dreams, Freud's work on the function of humor can serve as an excellent, simple introduction to some of the same ideas covered at great length in *The Interpretation of Dreams*. Freud wrote about the ways in which unconscious impulses intrude into conscious life in a number of different contexts (see, for example, **parapraxes**), but only one of his books deals directly and exclusively with the psychodynamic function of humor: *Jokes and Their Relation to the Unconscious,* published in 1905, a mere five years after *The Interpretation of Dreams.*

In the book, Freud presents jokes as serving a very similar function to dreams, in that they provide pleasure by releasing us from the bonds of our inhibitions and allowing the expression of sexual, aggressive, and playful impulses that would otherwise remain repressed and unexpressed. These impulses are ordinarily censored, both by external and internal forces, and jokes allow us not just to release them, but even to enjoy and derive pleasure from them, without causing any harm. Freud does not limit his analysis of the function of jokes to their role in releasing libidinal energy, however, also acknowledging other sources of pleasure, including relief from tension, recognition of one's own thoughts in those expressed by others, and especially the simple pleasure of play and just plain silliness.

Having recognized the other functions of jokes, however, Freud focuses much of his analysis where the book's title suggests he should, examining the ways in which jokes share their function with dreams. In attempting to understand how jokes serve the function of releasing instinctual energy, Freud identifies two key mechanisms via which jokes acquire this power: *condensation* and *displacement*. These are of course the same mechanisms by which the latent, repressed content of dreams becomes safely expressed in the superficial, manifest content of the dream.

In dream analysis, *condensation* is the process by which one object in the dream may actually symbolically represent several different underlying ideas or impulses, and thus a short, brief dream can contain great depths. In the same way, Freud argues that what distinguishes jokes is their great economy of words, in which a joke is often funny not because of what is said but because of the many different additional thoughts and ideas it can implicitly convey or allude to without actually expressing them. A lot of verbal humor involving double entendres depends heavily on condensation, as the joke is only funny (and therefore effective) if the listener is already aware of content not being provided, such as the various other meanings the chosen words can also convey. The personal experience of the listener will often determine whether the joke is gotten, and so pleasure is also derived from recognition and recollection here. Just as one symbol in a dream can simultaneously represent several different impulses or thoughts, one element of a joke can often make multiple simultaneous references as well, and the joke's effectiveness depends on them all being meaningful to the listener, just as the dream's effectiveness in wish fulfillment depends on the symbolized items all being known, at least unconsciously, to the dreamer.

In dream analysis, *displacement* refers to the extent to which the emotional significance of a dream element is detached from its real object or content and attached to an entirely different one, which makes it more likely to be allowed by the internal censor to remain. An adult professional who is nervous about his job performance and fears that he is unworthy of his career, for example, may have a dream in which he is still a student and arrives in a classroom unprepared on a test day, and then notices that he's also forgotten to wear pants. The individual has here allowed the anxiety to be expressed by rendering as anxiety over something completely different that is no longer a part of his life at all. In the same way, Freud argues that in jokes, very real hostility can be expressed through unpleasant but funny events that befall people other than the ones we feel the hostility toward, and inappropriate sexual impulses can be drained of their power by being expressed openly but in a humorous, clearly-I'm-not-serious fashion. Freud's argument is that jokes are, like dreams, a universal part of human life, and for very similar reasons.

Further Reading

Freud, S. (1905/1990). *Jokes and Their Relation to the Unconscious.* New York: W. W. Norton.

Jones, Ernest (1879–1958)

Welsh physician Ernest Jones first met Sigmund Freud in 1908, and beat the odds by remaining a close friend and a part of Freud's inner circle until Freud's death 30 years later. Perhaps Jones's longevity as Freud's confidant is due in part to the fact that he made no original contributions to psychoanalytic theory, and so the intellectual conflicts that tore apart Freud's professional relationships with so many others were simply not present in his friendship with Jones. This is not to say that Jones was not an important figure in psychoanalysis, but rather that his major contributions were due to his tireless work as an advocate and an unparalleled organizer and administrator rather than as a theorist.

Jones's role in the establishment of psychoanalysis in the English-speaking world was quite remarkable, so much so that a recent book about him is titled *Freud's Wizard: Ernest Jones and the Transformation of Psychoanalysis* (Maddox, 2007). As the first to practice as a psychoanalyst in English, Jones would already have assured his own place in history, but it is in his role as an organizer of the movement that he really shone. In 1910, while living in Canada, he cofounded the American Psychopathological Association, following it with the American Psychoanalytic Association in 1911. Jones served as the latter organization's first secretary until 1913. Meanwhile, in 1912, Jones, having become a part of Freud's inner circle, formed the Secret Committee of loyalists who eventually isolated and drove out Jung and Adler. In 1913, having returned to London, Jones started a psychoanalytic practice and founded the London Psychoanalytic Society. In 1919, Jones founded the British Psychoanalytical Society, which he served as president until 1944, during which time he was instrumental in attempting to resolve the rift within the society between the followers of Melanie **Klein** and Anna **Freud.** Jones also served as president of the International Psychoanalytical Association from 1920 to 1924 and again from 1932 to 1949. In 1920, he also founded the *International Journal of Psychoanalysis,* which he edited until 1939.

Jones also had a lot to do with the international dissemination of important books in psychoanalysis, as the founder of the International Psychoanalytic Library in 1921, for which he would edit and oversee the publication of at least 50 books. The library's most important contribution came when Jones negotiated the rights to the English translations of Freud's work, subsequently producing in 1924 the first two volumes of Freud's collected papers in English. Eventually Jones would work with translator James Strachey to begin the publication of the *Standard Edition* of Freud's collected works, a 24-volume set published between 1953 and 1973. In addition to his tireless advocacy of psychoanalysis in the English-speaking world and his important role in steering the international movement as well, Jones is perhaps best known as the author of a massive, three-volume biography of Freud, published between 1953 and 1957, which drew heavily on Freud's unpublished correspondence and which remains a standard reference work.

Born in the Welsh village of Gowerton, near Swansea, Jones stayed in Wales to attend Llandovery College and University College Cardiff, later moving on to medical school in London, where he received degrees in medicine and obstetrics, joining the Royal College of Physicians in 1903. Like Freud, Jones went on to specialize in neurology, and he began experimenting with hypnosis in his clinical work in hopes of improving on the remarkably poor treatment options available for the mentally ill. Early on in this work, Jones ran across Freud's work for the first time

Freud's great English champion and biographer, Ernest Jones, with Sigmund and Anna Freud upon their arrival in London in 1938. (Keystone/Getty Images)

in the form of the case study of **Dora**. Jones recorded his initial impression of Freud in his posthumously published autobiography as follows:

> A man in Vienna who actually listened with attention to every word his patients said to him . . . a revolutionary difference from the attitude of previous physicians. (Jones, 1959, p. 159)

Jones became immediately enthusiastic about trying Freud's techniques with his patients, but the London medical establishment of the Edwardian period was fairly hostile to Freudian ideas, and Jones's early attempts to apply them resulted quickly in serious legal trouble. In 1906, Jones was put on trial over allegations that he had behaved improperly with pupils in a London school, though he was acquitted of the charges. In 1908, however, Jones discovered just how unprepared the medical world was for the idea of infantile sexuality, when he was forced to resign his hospital post after curing a young girl's hysterical paralysis by helping her to uncover a repressed sexual memory (although part of the reason for the allegations of malpractice by the child's parents may have been Jones's suggestion that it was a real memory rather than an Oedipal fantasy).

As his job prospects dimmed considerably in England, Jones headed to Canada for a while in 1908, eventually taking a position in the Department of Psychiatry at Toronto University. During this same period, he also set up a private psychoanalytic practice and directed the outpatient clinic of the Toronto Asylum.

Meanwhile, Jones had met Jung in 1907 at a conference in Amsterdam, which led to his introduction to Freud at the first Psychoanalytical Congress in Salzburg in 1908. When Freud traveled to Clark University in 1909 (see **United States, Freud's Visit to**), Jones traveled down from Canada for further discussions, after which Jones set about helping to spread psychoanalytic ideas in America, delivering 20 papers and addresses to American professional societies in venues ranging from Boston to Chicago, followed by his cofounding of the American Psychoanalytic Association.

While doing all of this, Jones also maintained an intensive writing and research schedule, which culminated in his publication in 1912 of the very first collection of psychoanalytic pieces published in English, *Papers on Psycho-Analysis*. Jones's brief emigration to Canada, and the years he spent establishing psychoanalysis in America, might never have happened if Freud's ideas had not been so unpalatable to Jones's London bosses. It can be argued, however, that those years were crucial to the eventual popularity of Freud in America, which far eclipsed his influence in Europe, and also led directly to Jones's subsequent influence on the direction of international psychoanalysis more generally. Given the ubiquitous presence of Ernest Jones in international psychoanalytic circles throughout the first half of the

20th century, it seems clear that the history of Freud's influence on the world might have been far different without him.

Further Reading

Jones, E. (1912/1948). *Papers on Psycho-Analysis.* 5th ed. London: Balliere, Tindall & Cox.

Jones, E. (1959). *Free Associations: Memories of a Psycho-Analyst.* London: Hogarth.

Maddox, B. (2007). *Freud's Wizard: Ernest Jones and the Transformation of Psycho-analysis.* Cambridge, MA: Da Capo Press.

Jung, Carl Gustav (1875–1961)

C. G. Jung is a rather paradoxical figure in the history of psychology: Many of his ideas have become part of the general vocabulary, both of psychology and of the culture at large, yet most current psychologists are barely familiar with his work at all. The man who introduced the concepts of extraversion and introversion, type theories of personality, archetypes and the collective unconscious, personality with both a masculine and a feminine side, and the idea that a human needs to search for meaning in life (which he wrote about before better-known existentialists like Viktor **Frankl** and Alfred **Adler**) remains largely unread by scientific psychologists. Part of the blame for this rests with his very broad interests: although his early work was empirically based and demonstrated a quite competent familiarity with scientific method, most of his later work is focused on questions that are more of a philosophical or theological nature than a scientific one. Because his intellectual interests and appetites ranged so widely, it can be quite difficult, and may in fact be impossible, to sum up his body of work in a concise yet comprehensible fashion. Beyond his basic writings on analytical psychology, he was also interested in philosophy, both Eastern and Western, as well as the study of mythology, world religions, astrology, alchemy, anthropology, literature, and the arts. Late in life, he even became interested in whether or not unidentified flying objects (UFOs) were actually alien spacecraft. His best-known work in America today is probably his speculations on the role of archetypes in world mythology, as made famous by their application in the works of Joseph Campbell. The scope and breadth of his ideas is really quite remarkable. As a result, many psychologists are more familiar with his social relationships, especially his friendship/rivalry with Sigmund Freud, than with his actual writings.

Biography and Early Career

Among the early members of the Vienna Psychoanalytical Society whose professional and personal affiliations with Freud later ended acrimoniously, Carl Jung was surely the most important to Freud, and represented the most painful loss. Once seen by Freud himself as the heir apparent to the world of international psychoanalysis, Jung accompanied Freud on his only visit to America, in 1909, and the following year was appointed chairman for life of the International Psychoanalytical

Society. His chairmanship actually lasted only until 1914, when he resigned it, and he would never speak to Freud again. During the more than six years of their friendship, however, their relationship was very close, and indeed their collected correspondence has long been an important source of insight into both men.

Carl Jung, born in the Swiss town of Kesswil, in the canton of Thurgau, was originally christened Karl Gustav II Jung, in honor of his paternal grandfather, Carl Gustav Jung I. His father, Paul Achilles Jung, was a pastor of the Swiss Reformed Church, and came from a poor, rural background. His mother, the former Emilie Preiswerk, on the other hand, was a professor's daughter and came from a wealthy family—Paul met her while he was a student in her father's Hebrew class. While Jung was still a baby, his father received an appointment to a parish in Laufen, a more prosperous community. Although the pay and living conditions were better in Laufen, Emilie Jung was unhappy there, and spent most of her time in her own bedroom, which was separate from her husband's. Depressed and eccentric, Emilie was unpredictable and sometimes frightening, and so Carl had a much better relationship with his father. Eventually, Emilie was hospitalized for several months at a sanitarium near Basel, where Carl's father took him to live with an unmarried aunt. In later years, Jung would attribute his attitude toward women to his early experiences with his mother and her sister; he felt that he was handicapped by a firm belief that women are innately unreliable and recognized that his own views of women were often rather patriarchal as a result. After three years in Laufen, Paul Jung succeeded in getting transferred to Kleinhüningen, which was much closer to his wife's family and which resulted in a great improvement in her depression.

As a child, Jung spent a lot of his time alone and was rather shy and withdrawn. As an adult, he traced many of the ideas that later became central to his analytical psychology back to this period, including the idea of multiple sides to a personality, the importance of ritual, and the collective unconscious. He writes, for example, that in childhood he was convinced that he had two distinct personalities: one was a modern Swiss schoolboy living in the late 19th century, but the other was a gentleman of the previous century, dignified and influential. The idea of integrating the different sides of one's personality would later be an important part of his theory.

The ideas of archetypes and the collective unconscious would also involve insights from his childhood. As a boy, he carved a small human figure into the end of a ruler, which he hid in a pencil case in the attic, along with a painted stone, and he would later return to the case periodically, often bringing along notes he had written in a secret language. He had no clear reason for doing this, but he later recalled feeling a sense of inner peace and security when he did it. Many years later, he would find out about totemic rituals involving native peoples in various parts of the world and recognize that as a boy he had carried out a ritual very much like those carried out by people about whom he had no way of consciously knowing, and this would influence his thinking about archetypes and the collective unconscious.

Jung came from a family in which he was constantly exposed to religious practice, along with discussion of it—in addition to his father being a pastor, there were six other ministers in his mother's family. In his autobiography, however, Jung reports that in childhood he experienced religious visions and dreams that did not fit in with conventional church teachings, and he found his father unwilling to discuss them with him. He therefore grew up devoted to his religion while also maintaining within himself a personal, unorthodox vision that created feelings of guilt and alienation. Also, it is important to note that both Jung and his mother experienced vivid visions, which may have contributed to his later interest in schizophrenia.

Having spent most of his childhood in or near the city of Basel, where he attended school from the age of 11, Jung stayed close to home for his university education as well, attending the University of Basel beginning in 1895. In 1900, having completed his degree, Jung became an assistant physician to Eugen **Bleuler** at the Burghölzli psychiatric hospital in Zurich. His MD degree involved a dissertation, and he published his in 1903, titled *On the Psychology and Pathology of So-Called Occult Phenomena,* a subject about which Freud had written around the same time. As a young psychiatrist, he read and was strongly influenced by Freud, and carried out a large amount of work to experimentally demonstrate Freud's idea that individuals are influenced in their choices by mental contents of which they are completely unaware. The experiments used a technique that Jung pioneered the use of in mental testing: word association.

In a word association task, the experimenter presents a series of words, and the participant is to say the first thing that comes into his or her mind. In Jung's hands, word association became a tool by which to examine the contents of the unconscious mind, and he was able to demonstrate experimentally that his subjects, many of them

Carl Jung, Freud's early heir apparent and later the first prominent member of his inner circle to be cut off due to theoretical differences. (Library of Congress)

schizophrenic patients, were unaware that certain concepts were linked in their minds until they said the words out loud. Jung believed that we carry around sets of such unconsciously linked ideas in our minds, which he called *complexes,* a term that would later catch on with the psychoanalytic community.

Following the 1907 publication of *Studies in Word Association,* Jung sent a copy of the book to Freud in recognition of his debt to Freud's ideas. This eventually led to the two men meeting, and their first conversation is said to have lasted for 13 hours.

Six months later, Freud, then 50 years old, responded in kind by sending Jung a set of his latest essays. This marked the start of six years of frequent and intense correspondence, and a collaboration that would end when Jung resigned as chairman of the International Psychoanalytical Association in May 1914.

Jung always acknowledged his debt to Freud, but he was never the uncritical disciple that Freud seemed to want and to sometimes deceive himself that he had found in Jung. To the contrary, Jung disagreed often and openly with Freud, while accepting the fundamental premise that people are driven by unconscious motives and mental content. From the beginning, he felt that Freud overemphasized the role of the sexual drive, and attributed their differences in part to the different samples of patients they served. Freud, working in a private practice with wealthy Viennese patients, had little to no experience of psychosis, whereas Jung's area of expertise in the Bürgholzli was the care of patients with schizophrenia. Unsurprisingly, the two men developed rather different models of the mind, as their theories were based on rather different kinds of data.

The final split may have been triggered by the publication of Jung's *Symbols of Transformation*; Jung recalled in his autobiography that while he was working on it, he realized that its appearance would cost him Freud's friendship. Tension due to Freud's insistence on his own authority had been present in the relationship for a long time, and Jung later traced the beginning of their split all the way back to an incident that occurred when he and Ferenczi were shipboard with Freud, on the way to America. The men had taken to passing the time by discussing and analyzing each other's dreams, and Jung had interpreted one of Freud's dreams, though his analysis was incomplete as a proper understanding of the dream required Freud to divulge a few details from his private life. Freud refused to answer Jung's questions, on the grounds that allowing himself to be analyzed would risk undermining his authority. In Jung's recollection, this was the beginning of the end, as Freud, who insisted on absolute candor from everyone else in the interest of science, was valuing his personal authority above truth. In a slightly different version published elsewhere, however, the incident is a bit more scandalous: Jung had personal knowledge of an affair between Freud and his sister-in-law, and Freud's refusal to have the dream analyzed had the purpose of avoiding an admission of the affair.

In fact, differences in their fundamental ideas were present all along, but both men labored at minimizing those differences for several years. In their correspondence, for example, a running theme over a period of years is what Jung referred to some-times as his own "inability to define" libido. Actually, he is referring to his inabil-ity to accept Freud's definition of libido, and Freud's steadfast refusal to expand the concept in the way that Jung wished to. Jung fought a steady, but remarkably low-key, battle to expand the notion of libido to encompass a more general mental energy, rather than just the sexual drives. Jung's reservations about Freud's ideas are present throughout their correspondence, but Freud, who had introduced Jung as his crown prince in America, was so caught up in the idea that he had identified an intellect worthy of taking over his legacy that he was slow to notice how little of that legacy the prince actually accepted.

Tensions slowly increased between the two men, however, especially when the correspondence concerned disputes over the sexual drive, and the breaking point for Jung may well have been what he later referred to as the *Kreuzlingen ges-ture.* Another young follower of Freud, Ludwig Binswanger, had recently been appointed director of the sanatorium in Kreuzlingen, on the shore of Lake Con-stance in Switzerland. In April 1912, Binswanger was found to have a malignant tumor and underwent emergency surgery. Upon hearing of his illness, Freud wrote Binswanger an anguished letter in which he expressed his fear that one of his fol-lowers who was to continue his work after he was gone might himself be about to die. Freud then hurried to Kreuzlingen to visit the patient, who was recovering well. Since Binswanger had asked Freud to keep the reason for his visit confidential, he told no one about it. Kreuzlingen was only about 40 miles from Jung's home in Küsnacht, however, and it came to his attention that Freud had been in the area but had not stopped in for even a brief visit. Jung was offended, and wrote Freud a let-ter expressing his offense and suggesting that Freud had deliberately slighted him as a response to his independent thinking. In his turn, Freud reacted to Jung's letter by taking offense as well, feeling his character had been called into question, and later expressed his belief that the letter had constituted a formal disavowal of their prior relationship. Still smarting over the loss of Alfred Adler, Freud's inner circle, including Otto **Rank** and Sándor **Ferenczi,** implemented Ernest **Jones**'s sugges-tion that they form a small, clandestine committee of Freud loyalists to meet se-cretly to discuss any ideas that might depart from the core of psychoanalytic theory. This group, made up solely of those who still had Freud's complete trust, of course served to further alienate other psychoanalysts, including Jung, who were no longer to be included in vital discussions.

Post-Freud Ideas and Concepts

After his falling-out with Freud, Jung went through a difficult period of crisis and transformation, which he later said was the time when he truly laid the foundations of his own particular point of view. He was 38 years old at the time of his separation from Freud, and that experience was probably the origin of his later insistence that the mid-life period was an important turning point in psychological development. One of the important ways in which Jung's analytical psychology came to differ from Freud's approach is in this emphasis on continued development in adulthood. Freud's stages of psychosexual development end with adolescence, leaving the influential impression that nothing of real developmental significance occurs in adulthood. Jung saw this as a useful therapeutic model for a certain type of patient: where the client is a young adult whose main problem is insufficient emancipation from the influence of the parents, Jung advised traditional psychoanalysis. The cases that came to interest him far more, however, were people in the mid-life period who found themselves feeling stuck and felt their lives had become pointless. Jung's interpretation of these cases was that their natural process of development had been interrupted. Neurotic symptoms were actually a good sign, a valuable indicator that they had strayed from their true developmental path. Such symptoms were a positive sign, a way for the patients to realize that a reexamination of their way of life or their values was desperately needed.

One way in which people would stray from their proper path was by adopting too one-sided an approach to life, perhaps by focusing too much of their attention on themselves rather than on others, or conversely by being too outer-directed. Neurosis may result from excessive emphasis on one or the other end of the continuum from introversion to extraversion, which Jung saw as a key dimension of personality. He first identified the two personality types, introvert and extrovert, while trying to understand and explain the conflict between Adler and Freud. One reason for the acrimonious nature of Freud's split with Adler, and later with Jung, was Freud's apparent insistence that in a conflict between theories, one must be absolutely right and the other absolutely wrong. Jung saw the conflict differently, recognizing that the conflict was between two completely different points of view. Adler saw the origins of neurosis in the patient's search to ensure his own security and supremacy, in contrast to his feelings of inferiority. To Adler, the neurotic symptoms actually serve a specific purpose, as they are the patient's way of trying to gain something. In Freud's view, on the other hand, neurotic symptoms are a direct result of how the child handled the Oedipus complex. Obviously, each theory would recommend a different approach to therapy, based on its initial assumptions. Jung decided to study the difference between the two theories by examining how each could be applied to understanding the symptoms of an actual neurotic patient, and he concluded that both theories did a good job of explaining the case, and therefore that each type of therapist will see different aspects of the neurosis and ignore others, and will be sure that only his interpretation is correct. He concluded that the differences between Freud and Adler represented fundamentally different temperaments or personalities, "one of them more interested in the object, the other more interested in himself. . . . I have, finally, on the basis of numerous observations and experiences, come to postulate two fundamental attitudes, namely introversion and extroversion" (in Bennet, 1983, p. 50).

Freud, who placed tremendous emphasis on the role in the individual's development of influences external to himself, was in Jung's view an extravert. Adler, on the other hand, was an introvert, and thus his emphasis was on the subjective response of the individual to his circumstances. More generally, Jung saw introverts as people who are very reflective and thoughtful, whereas extraverts focus more on other people's reactions and behave more impulsively. Note that Jung was not asserting that all of humanity could be neatly divided into one type or the other; instead he asserted that "every individual possesses both mechanisms—extraversion as well as introversion, and only the relative predominance of the one or the other determines the type" (in Bennet, 1983, p. 53). In extraversion, the prevalent flow of mental energy is outward, and the conscious contents of the mind refer to external objects, whereas in the introvert, the conscious contents of the mind tend to be far more self-referential. Too much inner focus can be unhealthy, but so can be its absence. Jung saw one of the goals of therapy as simply helping clients to bring these opposing forces into balance within themselves, as a certain degree of extraversion and a certain degree of contrasting introversion are both good traits to possess.

Another key feature of Jungian analytical psychology, which marked a fundamental departure from other psychoanalysts, is Jung's view of the unconscious mind. It is important to note that Jung did *not* reject Freud's basic view of the unconscious—he agreed that mental illness is often the result of mental contents of which the individual is unaware, often because of repression. Where Jung differs from Freud, however, is in dividing the unconscious into two separate entities, which he called the personal unconscious and the *collective unconscious.* As the name implies, the personal unconscious is made up of personal ideas and experiences that have been hidden away. The collective unconscious, however, goes beyond personal experience. Unlike the personal unconscious, the contents of the collective unconscious are not acquired personally by the individual. In Jung's own words,

> While the personal unconscious is made up essentially of contents which have at one time been conscious but which have disappeared from consciousness through having been forgotten or repressed, the contents of the collective unconscious have never been in consciousness, and therefore have never been individually acquired, but owe their existence exclusively to heredity. (1971, pp. 59–60)

The collective unconscious, as an inherited set of unconscious mental influences on behavior, is a fairly radical departure from Freud, proposing as it does a whole additional set of influences on behavior beyond those that he and other psychologists had recognized so far.

The contents of the collective unconscious are *archetypes,* which Jung defined as "definite forms in the psyche which seem to be present always and everywhere" (1971, p. 60). He also indicates that a useful way of thinking of archetypes is as unconscious images of our instincts, or as actual patterns of instinctive behavior themselves. To Jung, these archetypes are the explanation for the various motifs that occur over and over across cultures and throughout history. All world religions, for example, place the mother in a special place of reverence. This is the mother archetype, and we project it out onto someone or something in the real world, usually our own mother. For those who lack a good relationship with their mother, however, the archetype will drive them to seek a replacement, perhaps in a dedication to a church, or nationalism (a strong affection for the mother country), or even a particular devotion to Mary, mother of us all in Christianity. Jung found one of the most compelling reasons to believe in a collective unconscious in the kinds of creative experiences in which thoughts and ideas, which have never before been consciously experienced, suddenly spring forth. He notes that "many artists, philosophers, and even scientists owe some of their best ideas to inspirations that appear suddenly from the unconscious" (in Bennet, 1983, p. 75). Experiences of this kind are common and to Jung demonstrate that unconscious is not just a place where past experiences are put aside by repression or forgetting. Clearly the unconscious mind must contain other experiences as well.

Another application of the idea of archetypes is Jung's notion of the shadow, which Jung proposed as a possible replacement for the personal unconscious. The shadow is the exact opposite of the conscious self, containing everything that it does not wish to acknowledge about itself. A person who sees himself as kind, for example, has a shadow that is unkind. The cruel person, on the other hand, has a kind shadow. The person who believes himself or herself to be ugly has a shadow that is beautiful, and the beautiful woman has an unattractive shadow. Failure to recognize the shadow will result in the unconscious projection of its attributes onto other people. As with introversion or extraversion, people's personality traits tend to be one-sided, and acknowledgment of the shadow will help to balance the personality. To Jung, an important goal of therapy was to help make the patient aware of the shadow and incorporate it into one's conscious awareness. Like other archetypes, the shadow makes its presence known in dreams, in which dark or dangerous figures of the same gender as the dreamer may appear, such as gangsters, murderers, prostitutes, or beggars. The specific figures will depend on what the individual would see as opposite to himself or herself.

Another key part of the unconscious mind, sometimes referred to as an archetype but also represented in the personal unconscious, is the *anima.* A large portion of 20th-century psychology seemed to focus on the idea that the psychology of men and women is essentially the same, an assumption that Jung viewed as fundamentally flawed. Examination of the unconscious minds of men and women makes the basic differences far clearer than the study of conscious psychology. One of Jung's most influential contributions to normal psychology, and therefore also to abnormal psychology, comes in the form of his assertion that in the unconscious of every man there is a feminine element. This element asserts itself in dreams as a female figure or image, and Jung called it the *anima,* derived from the Latin word for soul or animating force—the name captures the importance Jung attributed to it. In women, its counterpart is the animus, personified in dreams by a man or men.

As the mother is a boy's prototype of all women, her image remains important to him as he grows up, whether he is conscious of it or not. It is a natural part of growing up that a boy will, with growing masculinity, try to put aside what he sees as feminine qualities, and thus the influence of his mother, as she forms part of his anima. Jung's version of what Freud described as the Oedipus complex is the mother complex, in which the mother becomes of intense importance to the boy at a time when he should be forging his own identity independent of her. Such a boy has an overdeveloped anima, and his heterosexual drives are associated too strongly with the image of his mother. In a very different approach from Freud, however, Jung brings the idea of archetypes to bear on the situation as well. The mother is not the only source of the image of the anima; there is also a racial idea of woman, derived from the experiences of humanity's past. A man comes into the world already adapted to the idea of woman, and direct experience of the mother builds on the archetype and expands it, but is not its source.

Jung saw repression of the anima as a potent source of neurosis, as in Western culture we encourage boys to abandon their feminine nature entirely while overemphasizing the masculine. The feminine side remains, however, though repressed by stereotypical masculinity, with the result that the anima may only appear in bad moods, peevishness, irrationality, and often in sexual deviation, along with immature emotional development. A frequent criticism of Jung has been that his listing these things as functions of the anima is rather sexist, as it treats these negative traits as though they are natural expressions of the feminine. This is not an entirely fair criticism, as Jung is very clear that these traits are not a natural part of the operation of the feminine side of a man, but rather the result of repression of a natural part of himself. Jung saw a proper goal of therapy, especially in the second half of life, as helping men to better accept and express his anima, as he saw many of the ways that men bungle their own lives as ultimately symptomatic of repression of the anima. This has unfortunately become a pop culture cliché in modern America, where parodies of therapists often involve the advice that a man needs to get in touch with his feminine side.

A more general, overarching concept in Jungian psychology is illustrated in the example above of the boy who identifies too strongly with his mother: the idea of *individuation.* Individuation, the process by which a person becomes an individual, a separate, indivisible entity, developed over time to become what Jung saw as the ultimate goal of life, and therefore assisting with it became the ultimate goal of analytical therapy. Individuation represents the complete integration of the conscious and unconscious minds into a whole person. In the foregoing example, the boy's process of individuation is incomplete, as the image of his mother is too dominant a part of his image of himself. Ultimately, everyone is driven by a striving for fulfillment, which cannot be accomplished by the conscious ego by itself—it requires a joint effort of the conscious and unconscious minds. Individuation is very similar conceptually to the idea of self-actualization at the center of the work of such humanistic psychologists as Carl Rogers and Abraham Maslow. In their theories and therapeutic approaches, they and Jung are advocating helping people to recognize who they really are, and helping them to become the best version of that person that they can be. Also like Jung, the humanistic psychologists disdained broad data-based generalizations about humanity in favor of treating each person as an individual, different from all others.

Another area in which Jung had an influence, where that influence is not often recognized, is in the underlying assumptions of Alcoholics Anonymous (A.A.), and by extension other 12-step substance abuse programs. Jung was once approached by an American chronic alcoholic, whose condition seemed nearly hopeless. After failing for some time to achieve any real progress, Jung is said to have told the man that, barring some sort of spiritual experience, he was going to die of his condition, but that sort of experience had actually been known to help. The patient took Jung at his word, and joined an Evangelical Christian church upon returning to America, in hopes of having some sort of conversion experience. One of the people he shared his experience with was a close friend of Bill Wilson (usually referred to as Bill W. in A.A. circles, in keeping with their policy of anonymity), who told him about Jung's suggestion. Wilson sought out his own religious experience, and such a search found its way into the official A.A. program. Though Jung had no direct involvement in A.A., and it is not in any sense a Jungian program, he appears to have had a profound influence on it.

One additional Jungian concept that turns up in unexpected places deserves mention here. *Synchronicity* is one of Jung's ideas that has captured the imagination of his followers in the humanities, while not garnering much respect in scientific and psychological circles, partly because of its vagueness and partly because of its lack of falsifiability or scientific testability. Synchronicity is defined by Jung as *an acausal connecting principle,* or a recognition of the existence of *meaningful coincidences.* To the scientific thinker, this last term has more than a whiff of the oxymoron about it—coincidences are generally, by definition, meaningless. It is a guiding principle of scientific psychology that mere simultaneity, or co-occurrence in time, does not indicate that two things are connected. What Jung is proposing is that sometimes coincidences involve things that seem so unlikely to co-occur that some meaning can be derived from them, and that the connection between them may be real yet not involve causation.

In the original essay that introduced the concept, Jung gave the following example:

> On April 1, 1949, I made a note in the morning of an inscription containing a figure that was half man and half fish. There was fish for lunch. Somebody mentioned the custom of making an "April fish" [archaic term for "April Fool"—note the date] of someone. In the afternoon, a former patient of mine, whom I had not seen for months, showed me some impressive pictures of fish. In the evening, I was shown a piece of embroidery with sea monsters and fishes in it. The next morning, I saw a former patient, who was visiting me for the first time in ten years. She had dreamed of a large fish the night before. A few months later . . . when I had just finished writing [this series] down, I walked over to a spot by the lake in front of the house . . . a fish a foot long lay on the sea-wall. . . . I have no idea how the fish could have got there. (1971, p. 507)

Essentially, Jung's argument is that the more individual items are involved, the more highly improbable the series of coincidences becomes. The most highly improbable ones are so unlikely that they must represent some sort of connection among the items. Since the connection is, by Jung's definition, not causal, it is not actually clear what sort of connection it might actually be. Assuming that a coincidence is meaningful simply because it seems highly unlikely is of course antithetical to scientific reasoning, and so although synchronicity has become a rather popular concept among the more mystically minded (it provided the title and overall theme for the largest-selling album by rock band The Police, for example), it has made no real impact in the world of psychology.

Controversy over Jung's Actions during the Nazi Era

As the sole non-Jewish member of the early Vienna Psychoanalytical Society, Jung's prominence in medical and psychological circles rose in the 1930s at a time when many others, including Freud himself, were no longer able to work and were actively fleeing the Nazis. As a result of this, Jung spent his career dodging charges that he was anti-Semitic and a Nazi sympathizer, along with whispers that he was a Nazi collaborator. In recent decades, new biographies of Jung have resurrected these charges and expanded on them, often now including the allegation that he was an active member of the Nazi Party.

During his lifetime, Jung defended himself quite ably from such charges, as did his supporters. The charges have often been based on purely circumstantial evidence, such as the observation that although Jung maintained ties throughout the

1930s with his many Jewish friends and colleagues, he also maintained professional relations during this same period with German psychotherapists who had declared their support for the Nazis, rather than repudiating them and distancing himself from them. Accusations of Nazi collaboration have also risen out of his cooperation with the Nazi government in restructuring the General Medical Society for Psychotherapy, actions that are just as easily described (as Jung did) as having been done for the *benefit* of his Jewish colleagues. The society was a professional body based in Germany, but which had a large international membership. Under the Nazis, a new, strictly German, body was formed, the *German* General Medical Society for Psychotherapy, led by Matthias Heinrich Göring, a psychotherapist who followed Adler's ideas and who was also unfortunately the cousin of Hermann Göring, commander in chief of the Luftwaffe and Hitler's right-hand man. This organization, which over time became closed to Jews, became widely known as the Göring Institute, and was in the early 1930s the only professional organization for psychotherapists in Germany and in other occupied lands. The unfortunate name of the institute has led to occasional claims of Nazi collaboration against other prominent psychologists of the time, including the quite Jewish Viktor Frankl, who was employed by the institute before being taken away to the concentration camps.

Jung's involvement in the restructuring consisted of forming a new, separate, non-German organization for all the international members. The new organization, the International General Medical Society for Psychotherapy, became a new umbrella organization, with various national societies, including the new German group, organized underneath it. Jung was the head of the new international organization, and its constitution allowed individual doctors to join it directly, without belonging to any of the national affiliate groups, a rule to which Jung was careful to draw attention in a 1934 circular announcing the changes. This of course allowed the many German Jewish members of the old society, who would not have been allowed in the new German version under the Nazis, to maintain their active professional status by simply becoming members of the international organization instead. In easing this transition, Jung provided a great service for many of his colleagues, especially those who were Jewish, but in the postwar years he was occasionally described derisively in print as an organizer of the Göring Institute, which sounds quite slanderous when taken out of context. This, along with other innuendoes, was a source of great frustration to Jung: in his writings on the subject, he was rather clear that his sympathies lay not with the National Socialists but rather with their enemies.

In his early works, as early as World War I, he predicted the rise of such a movement, based on his theory of archetypes, and once they had risen, he warned readers of the danger they posed. In his essay "Civilization in Transition," for example, Jung describes "the Aryan bird of prey with his insatiable lust to lord it in every land, even those that concern him not at all" (1964, p. 89). In 1936, he published an essay on the influence of old Germanic and Norse mythology on the Nazis, titled "Wotan," in which he described Germany as "infected" by Hitler, who he called "obviously possessed" and "rolling towards perdition." These are clearly not the words of an admirer, nor was his description of Hitler as seeming

> like the "double" of a real person, as if Hitler the man might be hiding inside like an appendix, and deliberately so concealed in order not to disturb the mechanism. . . . You know you could never talk to this man; because there is nobody there. . . . It is not an individual; it is an entire nation. (McGuire and Hull, 1978, pp. 91–93, 115–135, 136–140)

Recognizing that his feelings and his role had been misrepresented by others, Jung defended himself further a few years after the war, saying in a 1948 interview:

> It must be clear to anyone who has read any of my books that I have never been a Nazi sympathizer and I never have been anti-Semitic, and no amount of misquotation, mistranslation, or rearrangement of what I have written can alter the record of my true point of view. Nearly every one of these passages has been tampered with, either by malice or by ignorance. Furthermore, my friendly relations with a large group of Jewish colleagues and patients over a period of many years in itself disproves the charge of anti-Semitism. (Baumann, 1949)

At the time, Jung was barred by secrecy agreements and security classifications from revealing the information that would have truly absolved him of charges of supporting the Nazis, information that only became widely known decades after his death, with the publication of a new biography by Deirdre Bair: after the United States entered the war, Carl Jung worked as an agent for the Office of Strategic Services (OSS), the organization that would later evolve into the Central Intelligence Agency (CIA).

Jung's work for the OSS consisted primarily of passing along psychological assessments and opinions of the Nazi leadership, and in return Jung was privy to top-secret Allied intelligence. Jung first made contact with the OSS through a patient, Mary Bancroft, who worked for Allen Dulles. Under diplomatic cover, Dulles, who would later be the first director of CIA, entered Switzerland in November of 1942 as the OSS agent in charge. Jung was recruited to serve as a senior advisor, consulted on at least a weekly and sometimes a daily basis. In 1943, Jung went a step further and became an actual employee of the OSS, listed in reports by Dulles as Agent 488. Agent 488's work for the Allies was quite extensive: he prepared extensive analyses of German culture and Nazi propaganda that were shared with Churchill and Eisenhower, and he even recruited additional secret operatives from among both his friends and his clients. According to Bair (2003), Dulles said that Jung understood

> the characteristics of the sinister leaders of Nazi Germany and Fascist Italy. His judgment on these leaders and on their likely reactions to passing events was of real help to me in gauging the political situation. His deep antipathy to what Nazism and Fascism stood for was clearly evidenced in these conversations. (pp. 492–493)

Much like what Henry **Murray** was doing for the same agency at the same time, Jung was constructing in-depth political profiles of Hitler and others in the hope of providing clues as to the best strategy by which to defeat them. In 1945, prior to implementing the ultimately successful Allied strategy, the Supreme Allied Commander, General Eisenhower, had in his hands Jung's recommendations on how to most effectively get the German civilian population to accept defeat, based on his analysis of Nazi propaganda.

Despite all this, however, Carl Jung, who in the postwar years sometimes described himself as having saved psychoanalysis from the Nazis, is still regularly accused of having supported them. As recently as 2008, for example, the following statement appeared in a book on anti-Semitism by Avner Falk: "In fact, during the 1930's and 1940's, Jung was an anti-Semitic Nazi collaborator" (p. 109). One piece of evidence that is frequently introduced in this regard actually appears quite damning on the surface. In 1933, the journal published by Jung's new international body, the *Zentralblatt für Psychotherapie* (Central Page for Psychotherapy), ran a statement endorsing Nazi positions in general, and Hitler's *Mein Kampf* specifically as required reading for all psychoanalysts. It should be noted that Jung's philosophical distance from Nazi Germany, where the journal's editorial offices were located, was matched by a physical distance as well, and the German national organization, with Hermann Göring's brother at its head, frequently inserted pro-Nazi propaganda without Jung's consent. In this instance, Jung wrote a response in a Zurich-based journal, the *Neue Zürcher Zeitung,* that he was surprised and disappointed that the *Zentralblatt* had caused his name to be associated with the pro-Nazi statement. He defended his continued association with the journal, however, as part of his effort to shelter and protect analytical psychology, getting "a young and insecure science into a place of safety during an earthquake" (1970, p. 538). He also saw to the appointment of Carl Meier as the new managing editor of the *Zentralblatt,* and the journal under Meier continued for several more years to defy the Nazis by continuing to acknowledge the contributions of Jewish doctors to psychotherapy, a daring approach given that the Nazis had burned Freud's books and banned the reading of them in 1933, the same year that Jung shepherded the international organization into existence. By 1939, Jung's resistance to the Nazis had become unsustainable, and he resigned the presidency of the international body and continued to work solely in Switzerland.

The charge of collaboration with the Nazis seems unlikely given Jung's work with the OSS, of which Jung's many critics were, for obvious reasons, unaware for many decades. The charge of anti-Semitism may deserve further scrutiny, however: The man who went out of his way to maintain the international status of German Jewish philosophers was simultaneously publishing statements like the following, from 1934's "The State of Psychotherapy Today":

> The Aryan unconscious has a greater potential than the Jewish uncon-scious. . . . In my opinion, current psychology has made an error by applying categories, not even applicable to all Jews, to German Christians as well as to slaves. . . . Medical psychology has claimed that the greatest secret of the Germans, the creative and fantastic depths of their soul, is only an infantile and banal swamp. I have spoken out against this, and have been suspected as an antisemite. The source of this suspicion is Sigmund Freud. He knows nothing of the German soul, nor do his followers. (Jung, 1934/1970)

In the same essay, the following observations also appear:

> The Jew, who is something of a nomad, has never yet created a cultural form of his own and as far as we can see never will, since all his instincts and tal-ents require a more or less civilized nation to act as host for their develop-ment. . . . In my opinion, it has been a grave error in medical psychology up to now to apply Jewish categories . . . to German and Slavic Christendom. (Jung, 1934/1970, pp. 165–166)

On the surface and without context, these statements appear to modern eyes to rep-resent fairly straightforward racism and anti-Semitism, but they can also be seen as statements of a particular scientific point of view. Central to Jung's notion of the collective unconscious, but rarely mentioned in popular treatments of the idea, is the notion that each distinguishable ethnic group has had different experiences, and so will have a collective unconscious that differs from that of other groups as well. The long-term historical experience of the Jewish people has been dramati-cally different from that of the Germanic tribes, and so conclusions based on one group might not generalize well to the other. This inability to generalize findings based on one idiosyncratic sample to a dissimilar group is a fundamental principle of psychological research, and one frequently articulated by Jung, in other state-ments that are also sometimes taken as evidence of a deep-seated anti-Semitism.

A frequent criticism of Freud is that he built his theory by extrapolating from his observations of a handful of idiosyncratic, neurotic Viennese patients to all of humanity. In Jung's view, it was just as egregious an error to generalize those findings, mostly based on people without serious mental disease, to the genuinely mentally ill. Unlike Freud, Jung spent the early part of his career working with schizophrenic patients in a hospital setting. Freud also generated ideas about the underlying causes of mental illness, but he did so without actually working directly with institutionalized patients. It is in the spirit of recognizing these flaws in psychoanalytic research that Jung made observations such as this one, from a footnote in *Two Essays on Analytical Psychology:* "It is a quite unpardonable mistake to accept the conclusions of a Jewish psychology as generally valid" (1958, p. 152). This is a criticism not of Judaism but of Freud's narrow vision, and appears less inflammatory when considered in the context of another observation that he made frequently, often in the same paragraph as observations like the one in the preceding text, that there are significant psychological differences to be found between all nations and races. It is unsurprising that Jung felt that a psychology based strictly on the study of German Jews could not be validly extended beyond that population, as he would have felt the same about any psychology based on a single race or nationality.

Further Reading

Bair, D. (2003). *Jung: A Biography*. New York: Little, Brown and Company.

Baumann, C. (1949). Interview with C. G. Jung. *Bulletin of the Analytical Psychology Club of New York*, December 1949.

Bennet, E. A. (1983). *What Jung Really Said*. New York: Schocken Books.

Falk, A. (2008). *Anti-Semitism: A History and Psychoanalysis of Contemporary Hatred*. Westport, CT: Praeger.

Jung, C. G. (1934/1970). The State of Psychotherapy Today. In *The Collected Works of C. G. Jung, Volume 10*. 2nd ed. Princeton, NJ: Princeton University Press.

Jung, C. G. (1958). *Two Essays on Analytical Psychology: The Collected Works of C. G. Jung, Volume 7*. Princeton, NJ: Princeton University Press.

Jung, C. G. (1964). *Civilization in Transition: The Collected Works of C. G. Jung, Volume 10*. Princeton, NJ: Princeton University Press.

Jung, C. G. (1971). *The Portable Jung* (Translated by R.F.C. Hull). New York: Viking Portable Library.

McGuire, W., and Hull, R.F.C., eds. (1978). *C. G. Jung Speaking: Interviews and Encounters*. London: Thames and Hudson.

Klein, Melanie (1882–1960)

Melanie Klein was an Austrian-born psychoanalyst who eventually spent much of her professional career in England and is known primarily for her contributions to two areas of post-Freudian thought: object relations theory and the application of psychoanalytic techniques to children. Although Freud was certainly very interested in the impact of early childhood experience on later psychological development, he based his ideas about the child psyche primarily on the reminiscences of adults or on colleagues' accounts of their own children, as in the **Little Hans** case. Klein was among the first psychoanalysts to work directly with children, providing direct experiences that led her to some intriguing differences of opinion with Freud, particularly regarding the development of female children. Object relations theory, which focuses on the central importance of the child's relationship with his or her mother (important people in the child's life are referred to as "objects" in Klein's theory), was a direct outgrowth of this work with children and was a great source of controversy. Her original ideas were so radical and transformative, in fact, that her work was largely rejected by orthodox Freudians and led to a long-standing split between two groups of child psychoanalysts: the London school, led by Klein, and the Viennese school, led by Anna Freud. Early on, psychoanalysts began to refer to Klein's ideas as *Kleinianism,* to better distinguish her approach from *Freudianism.*

Melanie Klein was born in Vienna, Austria, on March 30, 1882, to Moritz Reizes, a physician and Jewish scholar, and the former Libusa Deutsch, a Hungarian-born seller of exotic plants. Of Melanie's three siblings, two, Sidonie and Emmanuel, died in childhood, and her father died when she was just 18. She was well educated at the Vienna *gymnasium* (high school) and planned to follow in her father's footsteps and become a physician, a most unusual choice for a girl in her time and place. With her father's death, however, that plan changed along with her financial situation, and she would eventually stand out in the front ranks of psychoanalysts as the only one who lacked a university education. Following an early marriage to a second cousin, Arthur Stephan Klein, she moved to Budapest, Hungary, where her life would change its course dramatically.

Around 1914, Melanie Klein read Freud's *In Dreams,* an abridged version of *The Interpretation of Dreams,* and decided she wanted to learn more about psychoanalysis. This led her, in Budapest, to Sándor **Ferenczi,** with whom she had her first direct experience of psychoanalysis, an experience that quickly became psychoanalytic training as well, training that later continued in Berlin with Karl Abraham, who recognized and encouraged her affinity for working with children.

Very little psychoanalytic attention had been paid to children at the time, much less children under the age of five, who are presumably undergoing those early developmental conflicts that were so important to Freud's model of the psyche. One of Klein's early innovations was to develop a method for trying to understand very young children who could not yet talk, by observing and analyzing the way they played with toys. She felt she could tell a lot about a child by associations the child appeared to make between objects during free play. This approach had a lasting impact—today play therapy is a discipline unto itself, with its own professional associations and journals.

The play approach began with Klein's recognition that children could not be expected to benefit from the adult psychoanalytic setting, centered on free association on the couch, an idea that was taken further by such other psychoanalysts as Anna Freud, who argued that children under the age of seven could not be helped directly, as before that age they simply could not possibly cooperate with the adult technique. Klein disagreed, and began to see patients at the Berliner Psychoanalytische Poliklinic, where her first child patient was a young boy named Felix, starting on February 1, 1921. Klein reports that she decided, intuitively, to get some toys belonging to her own children and lend them to Felix. He immediately began to play with the toys, and Klein found that she could understand his patterns of play in the same way as the free associations produced by her adult patients. This marked the beginning of play therapy as well as the start of child psychoanalysis in general. Klein wanted, so far as possible, to be able to analyze children in the same way that adults were analyzed, by paying attention to the meaning of the play in terms of the transference and the unconscious phantasies being expressed. Instead of free-associating while lying on a couch, the child was provided with a box of his or her own small toys, chosen carefully so as to be easily manipulated and to not be particularly representative, so that the child's own imagination has the maximum opportunity to be expressed. The analyst and the actual room itself were also available to be incorporated into the child's play, so that some of the play would take the form of role-playing, just as might happen outside the clinical setting.

Melanie Klein presented her first psychoanalytic paper on the development of children in 1921 and became a member of the Hungarian Psychoanalytical Society. Shortly thereafter she moved to Berlin and began to develop her approach further, which stirred up considerable controversy among the orthodox Freudians in Berlin and elsewhere. Freud's work was mostly based on adults' retrospective accounts of early childhood rather than work with actual children, and many Freudian thinkers thought she was attributing entirely too much capability to infants and toddlers in her work, expecting them to reveal what they were simply not capable of revealing about themselves. Karl **Abraham,** director of the Berlin Psychoanalytic Institute, was of course accustomed to such internecine controversy, given his role in the split between Freud and Jung, and so was a valuable ally, mentor, and champion, encouraging her to continue her work of expanding on Freud's ideas. After Abraham's death in 1924, however, remaining in Berlin became far more difficult for Klein. Fortunately, she had already found allies in Freud's English translators, Alix and James Strachey, who invited her in 1925 to present a series of lectures on child analysis at the British Psychoanalytic Institute. Klein was received very positively by the British audience, and she was asked to join the institute, which she did in 1926, at which time she moved to London, where she remained for the rest of her professional career.

Klein was nowhere near as prolific as most of the other major figures in psychoanalysis, but her writings contain several groundbreaking, influential ideas worthy of mention, in part because of their influence on later child analysts, and in part because they help to clarify the vehemence with which the more orthodox Freudians objected to her work. Unlike some others, such as Alfred **Adler** and Carl **Jung,** Klein did not reject Freud's central ideas so much as simply develop them further. Where Freud focused on the Oedipal conflict as the ultimate source of all neurosis, for example, Klein emphasized an even earlier period of childhood. The Oedipal conflict is the central drama of the three- to five-year-old child; Klein focused her work on the first year of life, the period when development proceeds at the most rapid pace and during which the infant is at his or her most impressionable. In Klein's view, the foundation for the phallic stage, with its development of the Oedipal drama, is laid down in this earlier period of development, and the later conflict cannot be properly understood without this foundation. Like Otto **Rank,** Klein emphasizes the crucial role of anxiety based on the relationship to the mother, *prior* to the development of phallic-stage anxiety. This pre-Oedipal period, which was left as a fairly broad and empty outline by Freud, was augmented in great detail by Klein's clinical work with very young children.

While Klein considered herself a respectful follower of Freud rather than a rebel, her work with these young children led directly to new formulations of Freudian ideas that generated tremendous conflict with other psychoanalysts. While her observations of troubled children led her to agree with Freud's emphasis on the significant role of parents in the child's phantasy (which she consistently spelled with a *ph* to emphasize its primitive, inborn nature, as distinct from daydreams and imaginings) life, she stirred up controversy by arguing that the superego, rather than resulting from the child's negotiation of Oedipal-period anxiety, is actually present from birth. She also argued that Freud got the timing of the Oedipal conflict wrong, and that the infant is driven by both positive and negative instinctive impulses, an idea that eventually became part of Freud's own theory in the form of *life instincts* and *death instincts,* but which was new to the psychoanalytic model of early childhood.

In proposing that the infant is driven by both a life instinct and a death instinct, Klein was simply echoing an idea that was inherent in Freud's view of humanity, but which Freud himself would not make explicit until the 1930 publication of ***Civilization and Its Discontents,*** and so her description of the instinctive drives of early childhood was a divisive one. She assumed that the infant is born with both a life instinct and a death instinct, which at the level of psychological impulses become transformed into love and hate, respectively. She further conjectures, again following Freud's ideas closely, that due to differences of temperament and constitution, the disposition toward expressing love and hate varies widely from infant to infant. It is in her description of the infant's expression of this disposition in the act of breastfeeding that Klein strikes off into truly original territory.

While attached to the breast, the infant may have a positive experience in which his or her needs are gratified, or the experience may be frustrating. The infant will then feel either love or hate toward the breast, both the external breast and the internal mental representation or phantasy of the breast. In psychoanalysis, the concept of the *imago,* an unconscious, idealized mental image of an important person in one's life, is so central as to have provided the title for the main international psychoanalytic journal. Here, Melanie Klein provides a new notion of imago in which the image can be of a particular object or body part rather than of the entire parent: the infant creates an imago of either a highly loving and nurturing good breast or a cruel, non-nurturing bad breast, which become installed in the child's mind and affect how the child relates with the breast, and by extension, with his or her mother. Klein called this process of projecting these good or bad images into others *projective identification.* Given the repeated occurrence of feeding, the infant will produce numerous good imago versions of the breast as well as bad ones, and is therefore provided with the job of protecting the good imagos from the bad ones. The infant achieves this via splitting, a sort of primitive version of repression, in which the child produces both an internal and external worldview split into regions of all good, idealized objects and all bad objects, a state of mind that Klein called the *paranoid-schizoid position.* Here Klein is not describing a radical departure from Freud's ideas, but she is revising the timetable for some of the child's accomplishments quite a bit. *Splitting* sounds very much like the mechanism of repression, for example, which Freud described as resulting from the Oedipal conflict. In Klein's formulation, the child is dealing with anxiety by setting aside negative images at a *much* earlier point in development.

According to Klein, this tendency toward splitting is countered by an opposite tendency toward integration, with one tendency functioning to divide and hide portions of the psyche, and the other functioning to bring it together and make it whole. These tendencies occur not just in infancy but throughout life and are the basis for the underlying conflict or dialectic that defines psychic life. The difference between a child, and subsequently an adult, whose psychic development is healthy and one who is heading toward neurosis is largely a function of which of the two tendencies comes to dominate, and this important dynamic can take shape in very early infancy. According to Klein, by the age of about four months, in children whose caretaking environment is adequate and who have not split their world too violently, the tendency toward integration will begin to prevail, producing an infant who experiences the world, internal and external, as whole rather than as divided into good and bad parts. The child who experiences the world as divided rather than whole has moved on from the paranoid-schizoid position to what Klein called the *depressive position.* In proposing this process, Klein is granting the infant a much more complex internal life than Freud had conceived of, placing some of the most crucial intrapsychic conflict in the pre-Oedipal period of development.

In the paranoid-schizoid position, the infant is concerned about protecting *himself* or *herself* from damage; the child who has moved on into the depressive position is now concerned for the object, which the infant believes it has damaged or destroyed, perhaps through phantasized attacks on it. Whereas in the paranoid-schizoid position, the child's feelings may have focused on persecutory anxiety and fear of personal destruction, the child's feelings in the depressive position instead focus on remorse, sadness, and guilt over the destroyed or damaged object. The child may react in two distinct ways to this depression-inducing guilt and remorse: simple denial that any damage has occurred or attempting to repair said damage.

The result of denial is mania, in which the infant regresses to the earlier defenses of the paranoid-schizoid phase, employing splitting, projection, and introjection. This produces devaluation of, and therefore triumph over, the object. This defense may produce an endless cycle in which destructiveness is followed by remorse and guilt, which lead directly to further destructiveness, which produces more remorse and guilt, and so on ad infinitum. According to Klein's object relations theory, this cycle, once established, can prevent the child (and later, the adult) from ever internalizing a good whole object, and therefore eventually preclude ever being able to establish a loving, mature relationship with anyone. The long-term effects of this may include bipolar affective disorder or major depression.

Klein does point out another, possibly healthier response to depressive anxiety, however: reparation. The infant's acknowledgement of the phantasized damage, along with the attempt to repair it, is the basis of all future loving and healthy relationships. Denial represents the unsuccessful navigation of the depressive position—successful negotiation demands that the child accept the reality of separation, or what Margaret **Mahler** would call separation individuation. Separation is simply the recognition that the mother and the child are separate, independent entities, whose lives, though interdependent, are separate. To this Klein adds that as part of the separation process, the child must recognize that the mother is neither an avatar of evil nor the personification of perfection. Upon recognizing this, which depends on the quality of the mother's caretaking, the infant will form an *introject,* or mental representation of the mother's ideals and attitudes, of a whole, good object instead of a split and deeply flawed one. This process provides the basis for future self-efficacy and self-esteem.

The foregoing discussion of the infant's approach to coping with depressive anxiety may sound familiar to readers acquainted with Freud's developmental theory. This is because Klein saw the advent of depressive anxiety as a sign of the onset of the Oedipus complex. Freud placed this conflict and its resolution at the base of all later neuroses, calling it the *nuclear complex* of neurosis, including childhood neuroses, and placed its occurrence during the phallic stage, no earlier than age three or four. Klein agreed with Freud about the child's experience of love-hate conflict regarding the parent of the opposite sex, the resolution of which explains the development of childhood neuroses. To Freud, as described in the case of Little Hans, this resolution involves the repression of both sexual and aggressive impulses and brings along the development of the superego in its wake. Klein did not disagree with Freud regarding the basic outline of the Oedipus complex, or even with his emphasis on castration anxiety as the fundamental cause of the conflict, but rather differed as to timing and specific details. This disagreement occurs in part because of the initial data that informed the theory: In Freud's case, the theory was based on a combination of second-hand child analyses conducted by others (as was the case with Little Hans) and the retrospective recollections of adults attempting to reconstruct early childhood. Klein, on the other hand, based her revisions of Freud's ideas on direct observation and analysis of actual infants and young children.

The most obvious difference between Klein's view of the Oedipus conflict and Freud's concerns timing, as Klein places it early in the first year of life along with the development of depressive anxiety, which began as a result of good and bad imagos of the breast. According to Klein, this focus on gratification or disappointment at the breast leads to a turning toward the father's penis, which of course assumes that the infant has a primitive mental representation of the organ. Loving, positive feelings toward the breast are simply transferred onto another potential source of oral gratification; frustrated feelings about the bad breast also result in the infant's turning to the penis, however, as a substitute for the disappointing breast. As a part of this process, the child also develops a bad penis imago as a sort of generalization of the bad breast. According to Klein, the child's imagination at this early stage of development therefore contains intensely positive and negative imagos of both breast and penis, highly charged with feelings of love and hate, which form the foundation of the early Oedipus complex. These internal objects, both idealized and hateful, form the initial components of the early superego. While Klein has substantially shifted the timing of the process, therefore, she is still essentially in agreement with Freud regarding the genesis of the superego as a result of the Oedipal conflict.

Armed with these internal representations, the Oedipal development of both boys and girls proceeds along similar lines. Already somehow aware of the father's penis, and having created internal good and bad versions of the object, both boy and girl come to want the good penis. For the boy, this desire is the feminine position, which allows him to turn toward the mother with an internalized image of the penis that is loving and reparative, an image that will prevail over the destructive one in the course of normal development. This outcome will equip him to be able to have good, positive relationships with women in later life. A similar process occurs in the girl, but Klein marks a major difference with Freud in positing that, rather than turning away from the mother as a result of desiring the father, the normally developing girl will be able to maintain a loving relationship with her.

The later, phallic-stage Oedipus complex arises out of the infant's attempt to cope with depressive anxiety toward both the mother and the father, as the same sort of anxiety that the child feels regarding the breast is also felt toward the penis. Klein actually maintains a close connection to Freud's approach, including the central importance of castration anxiety, though her description of how castration anxiety is reflected in the development of girls, who after all lack a penis, is widely viewed by feminist scholars as a more realistic description of the girl's anxiety than Freud's idea of penis envy, as seen in this description of a girl named Ruth:

> Now what is the meaning of this empty space within Ruth, or rather, to put it more exactly, of the feeling that there was something lacking in her body? Here there has come into consciousness one of the ideas connected with that anxiety which, in the paper I read at the last Congress (1927) I described as the most profound anxiety experienced by girls. It is the equivalent of the castration anxiety in boys. The little girl has a sadistic desire, originating in the early stages of the Oedipus conflict, to rob the mother's body of its contents, namely, the father's penis, faeces, children, and to destroy the mother herself. This desire gives rise to anxiety lest the mother should in her turn rob the little girl herself of the contents of her body (especially of children) and lest her body should be destroyed or mutilated. (From *The Selected Melanie Klein,* 1986, p. 92)

In Klein's view, this anxiety about mutilation represents the little girl's earliest experience of feelings of danger. Whereas Freud described the dread of being alone and of loss of love as the basic infantile source of anxiety in girls and women, Klein argues that this dread is simply a modification of the mutilation fear. A little girl who fears this assault will experience intensified anxiety when she cannot see her mother, whereas the presence of the real, loving mother diminishes this dread. Just as Freud marks the resolution of the Oedipal conflict as involving the transition from fear of the same-sex parent to identification with the same, Klein argues that at a later stage of development, the girl's dread changes from fear of an attacking mother to dread that the real, loving mother may be lost, and the girl left alone and forsaken.

Despite a far more female-centered take on castration anxiety, however, Klein did not abandon the notion of penis envy, but this concept also undergoes something of a transformation in her hands. Klein makes it clear that penis envy is actually far more a reflection of concern over female body functions than with actual desire for a penis:

> One way in which the little girl's development is greatly handicapped is the following. Whilst the boy does in reality possess the penis, in respect of which he enters into rivalry with the father, the little girl has only the unsatisfied desire for motherhood, and of this, too, she has but a dim and uncertain, though a very intense, awareness. (1986, p. 70)

Klein saw bisexuality as inherent in everyone, and the girl's desire to possess a penis, and indeed to be a boy, as a natural expression of that bisexuality, just as she saw the desire to be a woman as a natural outgrowth of this same bisexual tendency in boys. She notes, however, that the girl's desire to have a penis of her own is secondary to her desire to receive the penis, in this case the idealized, internalized, admired introjection of her father's penis. Her penis envy serves to cover up her frustrated desire to take her mother's place with the father and receive children from him. Like numerous other post-Freudian psychoanalysts, notably Karen **Horney** and Alfred **Adler,** Klein also notes that penis envy is not just about the penis, but that the anxiety is greatly enhanced by the frustrations inherent in being a female in a male-dominated society, in which having a penis entails power and privilege that are otherwise unavailable. According to Klein, a girl's main identification with her father is based on the internalized penis of the father, and the relationship is based on both the feminine and masculine approaches to the penis: as a female, she is driven by sexual desire and longing for a child, to internalize her father's penis, while her masculine side wishes to emulate him in her masculine aspirations.

Like Freud, Klein saw the Oedipus complex as the underlying root of all later neurosis and mental illness, and she saw the resolution of the complex both as a source of female vanity and as a particularly potent source of the psychiatric disorders that primarily affected women:

> Because of the destructive tendencies once directed by her against the mother's body (or certain organs in it) and against the children in the womb, the girl anticipates retribution in the form of destruction of her own capacity for motherhood or of the organs connected with this function and of her own

children. Here we have also one root of the constant concern of women for their personal beauty, for they dread that this too will be destroyed by the mother. At the bottom of the impulse to deck and beautify themselves there is always the motive of restoring damaged comeliness, and this has its origin in anxiety and sense of guilt. *It is probable that this deep dread of the destruction of internal organs may be the psychic cause of the greater susceptibility of women, as compared with men, to conversion hysteria and organic diseases.* (1986, p. 78)

Here Klein provides a purely psychoanalytic explanation for the development of hysteria in women in far greater numbers than in men that entirely abandons historical notions of organic cause by the female reproductive apparatus, while still finding an explanation based in part on physiological gender differences. Klein then goes further, also finding a role for penis envy in women's complicity in their own oppression:

It is this anxiety and sense of guilt which is the chief cause of the repression of feelings of pride and joy in the feminine role, which are originally very strong. This repression results in the depreciation of the capacity for motherhood, at the outset so highly prized. Thus the girl lacks the powerful support which the boy derives from his possession of the penis, and which she herself might find in the anticipation of motherhood. (2002a, pp. 78–79)

Again, penis envy in Klein's formulation has more to do with confidence and support, and pride in one's own role, than it necessarily has to do with actually having a penis.

Penis envy was not the earliest developmentally important manifestation of envy in Klein's theory, however. Klein argued that envy plays an important role in psychic development far earlier, when primitive envy is felt by the infant relative to the bountiful and productive breast. The breast, with its ability to provide food and comfort, induces feelings of inferiority and insignificance, along with feelings of deprivation when it is unavailable. This envy then becomes connected with the child's natural aggression, and the child experiences conflicting feelings of envy and gratitude toward the breast. The nurturing breast therefore becomes both an object of love and the target of hate, and the child's subsequent development of the capacity for gratitude depends on how this conflict is resolved. Prior to Klein's writings on the subject, the topic of the development of gratitude had been largely ignored, both within the psychoanalytic community and without.

Klein argues that gratitude first emerges in very early infancy, but only if envy, which she saw as an inborn instinctive force, as much a drive as the libido, does not overpower it. If the mother deprives the child either of physical nourishment (from the breast) or of emotional nourishment (in the form of love and care), the result may be the development of excessive envy, which can deprive the child of the opportunity to experience joy. The infant can only experience absolute enjoyment if the capacity for love is adequately developed, a process that can be disrupted by the development of envy, and this enjoyment is the foundation for gratitude. A child whose envy is allowed to develop therefore becomes unable to experience gratitude, which is, according to Klein, the only available defense against the destructive nature of envy and greed. Gratitude is also crucial for the infant to develop a strong relationship with the mother, or good object, and also fosters an appreciation of oneself and others, along with the capacity for hope, trust, and goodness. The capacity for gratitude, along with the ability to defy envy, in other words, "constitute[s] not only the basis of sexual gratification but all later happiness and makes possible the feeling of unity with another person; such unity means being fully understood, which is essential for every happy love relation or friendship" (2002a, p. 18).

Klein goes on to describe gratitude as a natural byproduct of maternal love, such that the more an infant experiences maternal love, the more the infant will also experience gratitude. Klein also argues that this gratitude includes the wish to return goodness received and is thus the basis of generosity as well. In Klein's own words, "There is always a close connection between being able to accept and to give, and both are part of the relation to the good object" (2002a, p. 310).

Though she continued to see herself as a follower of Freud, Klein's innovations in child psychoanalytic treatment and theory were far from well-received in certain quarters of the psychoanalytic community. A particular source of conflict came from Anna Freud, who was widely regarded in the psychoanalytic community as the guardian of her father's legacy, and whose own endeavors in child psychoanalysis were largely incompatible with the approach being taken by Klein. Upon the death of Karl Abraham on Christmas day in 1925, the one member of Freud's inner circle who supported and encouraged Klein's work in Berlin was no longer available to mentor and defend her, and so her move to England in 1926 was not a surprise, especially given the reception she had received there the previous year when invited to speak by Alix Strachey, Freud's English translator. She joined the British Psychoanalytical Society, which was at the time only a year old, at the invitation of Ernest **Jones,** Freud's close confidante and biographer, despite being out of favor with Sigmund and Anna Freud. By all accounts, she was a welcome breath of fresh air to the British psychoanalysts and served to stir things up creatively. Alix Strachey described the impression she made by saying that she looked like a whore run mad and a dotty woman, but one whose head was filled with things of thrilling interest.

While her methods and her interpretations of what she observed caused some controversy and conflict in the field of psychoanalysis, many of her British colleagues embraced her approach. Although she was approaching things in a radically different way from Anna Freud, who saw herself as the keeper of the Freud flame, no serious conflict arose within the British Psychoanalytical Society until after the Freuds escaped from Nazi-occupied Vienna, and indeed well after Sigmund Freud's death. Once Anna Freud had settled in to practice in England as well, some sort of showdown was inevitable, as they really had very different ideas about the psyche of the child. Where the Freuds focused on the structures and forms of unconscious functioning, Klein focused her attention on the content of very primitive, psychotic anxieties. Where Freud's psychosexual stages consist of a series of maturational milestones that, once achieved, influence subsequent development from that point forward, Klein did not believe that we ever fully transcend the primitive or that any developmental achievement is ever permanently acquired. Instead, in Klein's view, new challenges to our composure and mental balance can arise internally or externally at any time, requiring that the mental balance (between id and ego, for example) be fought for all over again. The superego is not a developmental achievement in Klein's world, because it is present from birth, and so conflicts involving it begin in infancy, not at five or six years of age. The parent-centered anxieties of the Oedipal conflict are also present in infancy, and envy and destructiveness are much larger influences in Klein's theory than in Anna Freud's, though her father came around to a similar view late in life, as presented most memorably in *Beyond the Pleasure Principle* and **Civilization and Its Discontents.** In Klein's view, the inner psychic life of the child is messier, more chaotic, more hostile, and less happy than what Anna Freud was proposing. For her part, Anna Freud thought that play therapy was a waste of time, because very young children were not capable of providing any clinically useful information in that way.

To Anna Freud, Klein was a rival and a traitor or apostate, and constant bickering between the two women's supporters threatened to tear apart the British Psychoanalytical Society, until the society, in the desperate hope of working things out, staged a set of Controversial Discussions (their official title) over a period of several years in the 1940s.

Lasting from 1941 to 1946, the discussions had a deceptively simple aim: to determine whether the new views on child development and treatment advocated by Melanie Klein and her supporters were compatible with the more traditional approach taken by Anna Freud and her followers in Berlin and Vienna. If it was determined that the two sets of views were *not* compatible, the ultimate expectation was that Klein would be expelled from the international psychoanalytic community.

The discussions centered around Klein and Freud, but really represented the culmination of a broader conflict that had simmered for more than a decade, between the indigenous British approach to psychoanalysis, heavily but not exclusively influenced by Klein, and the more traditional Continental approach, often characterized by a slavish adherence to the works of Sigmund Freud. The tensions and differences between the two groups only boiled over in the wake of the Nazi occupations on the continent, which led to the emigration to England and America of most of the largely Jewish leading figures of psychoanalysis. As a medical degree was required to practice psychoanalysis in America, Anna Freud, who like Klein had no university education, remained in England after escaping Vienna with her father.

Unlike most scholarly debates lasting for years, the Controversial Discussions followed a clear-cut organizational structure. An ad hoc committee was appointed to judge the scholarly papers to be presented by each side. The committee consisted of Edward Glover, Marjorie Brierley, and James Strachey, and was chaired by Ernest Jones. The Kleinians were then required to present this committee with four papers. The first, by Susan Isaacs, was titled "On the Nature and Function of Unconscious Phantasy," and was presented on January 27, 1943. On June 23, Paula Heimann followed with "Some Aspects of the Role of Introjection and Projection in Early Development." On December 17, 1943, Isaacs and Heimann presented a paper together, titled "On Regression." Having had the groundwork laid by her supporters, Klein read a paper of her own on March 1, 1944: "The Emotional Life and Ego Development of the Infant with Special Reference to the Depressive Position." In addition to these papers laying out the theoretical approach of the Kleinians, there were also important papers on psychoanalytical therapy techniques written by Anna Freud, Klein, Sylvia Payne, Ella Sharpe, and Marjorie Brierley, which illustrated the very different approaches of the two sides to treatment. All of the papers were collected as a book which remains in print today (King and Steiner, 1992) and which is considered among the more important historical documents on the development of psychoanalysis.

The ultimate result of the Controversial Discussions was a compromise that utterly failed to resolve the differences between the two camps, but rather reminds this writer of the Caucus Race sequence in Lewis Carroll's *Alice's Adventures in Wonderland,* in which the competition, following massive cheating by all parties, is judged a tie in which "All have won, and all shall have prizes." The compromise agreement officially recognized the existence and value of the differences between the groups and left the society with an unusual structure, now divided into three distinct groups: the Kleinians, the Freudians, and the Independents. Although only two groups were actually in conflict in the discussions, the third group initially consisted of the members who were loyal to neither side, defined at first as the analysts to whom neither Anna Freud nor Melanie Klein was willing to refer training cases. This odd structure has persisted for more than half a century, with the presidency of the organization rotating among the three constituencies, and members of all three serving on the main committees, though the organization has been largely dominated by the Kleinians ever since. Following the compromise, Anna Freud became less involved with the affairs of the society, concentrating her efforts instead on the Hampstead Clinic, across the street from the house where her father had died and where she lived until her own death in 1982—although she outlived Klein by 22 years, Anna Freud and her followers never became the dominant force in British psychoanalysis that they had been on the prewar continent.

During her time in England, Klein did face some resistance to her ideas that originated closer to home, in the form of her own daughter, Melitta Schmideberg, a psychoanalyst herself. Klein and Schmideberg had a very troubled relationship, filled with tensions that may have dated back to Klein's controversial choice to base some of her early conclusions about infant and child development on the psycho-analysis of her own children. These tensions erupted into the professional realm, as Schmideberg openly argued with and histrionically lashed out at her mother at professional meetings. During the Controversial Discussions, Schmideberg stood firmly in Anna Freud's camp, and later immigrated to America. No reconciliation between the two was ever achieved, but upon her mother's death, Melitta Schmide-berg did briefly return to London. Rather than attend her mother's funeral, however, she instead gave a lecture on the day of the ceremony, to which she wore a specially purchased pair of red boots.

Her daughter's reaction notwithstanding, Klein's work has cast a long shadow on the field of child psychoanalysis, as well as on child psychology more gener-ally. Modern psychoanalysts, for example, are far likelier to follow some version of Klein's object relations theory than they are to adhere strictly to Freudian guide-lines. The Association for Play Therapy is an international organization with more than 5,000 members, offering training and other resources, as well a monthly peer-reviewed journal. The organization today downplays their historical association with psychoanalysis, however—their comprehensive, visually attractive website makes no explicit mention of either psychoanalysis or of Melanie Klein, except for a single sentence in a description of a course on the history of play therapy, which rather inaccurately describes Klein and Anna Freud together as the pioneers of the use of play therapy.

The other place where Klein's influence is both profound and poorly recog-nized is in the area of **attachment** theory. John **Bowlby,** a fellow member of the British Psychoanalytical Society, was once supervised by Klein in a case of child psychoanalysis, and her ideas appear to have influenced him quite a bit, though the influence may have been primarily negative, as the resulting theory is notable for the many ways in which it contradicts Klein's view of infancy. Both Klein and Bowlby emphasized the primacy of the mother-child relationship in producing later character, and Bowlby accepted Klein's recognition that this influence origi-nates in early infancy rather than during the much-later period of Oedipal anxiety. This idea, which was very much Klein's, especially in the World War II milieu in which Bowlby was working, inspired Bowlby to ultimately produce a very dif-ferent theory with a very different emphasis. Where Klein stressed the role of the child's phantasies about his mother, Bowlby instead emphasized the actual history of the relationship. Rather than agreeing that children were responding primarily to unconscious fantasies, Bowlby's attachment theory stresses the importance of real-life events in the child's development. Because of this, Bowlby was ultimately shut out of the psychoanalytic community, but his theory remains hugely influential among developmental psychologists, including those who carefully avoid psychoanalytic elements in the field.

Further Reading

Grosskurth, P. (1977). *Melanie Klein: Her Life and Work.* Lanham, MD: Jason Aronson Publishers.

King, P., and R. Steiner, eds. (1992). *The Freud-Klein Controversies 1941–1945.* London: Tavistock/Routledge.

Klein, M. (1986). *The Selected Melanie Klein.* New York: Free Press.

Klein, M. (2002a). *Envy and Gratitude (1946–1963).* New York: Free Press.

Klein, M. (2002b). *Love, Guilt, and Reparation, and Other Works, 1921–1945.* New York: Free Press.

Meisel, P., and W. Kendrick, eds. (1985). *Bloomsbury/Freud: The Letters of James and Alix Strachey (1924–25).* New York: Basic Books.

Lacan, Jacques (1901–1981)

Due to the widespread rejection of Freud's ideas by the more scientifically minded elements of the academic community, today's college students majoring in psychology often encounter psychoanalytic ideas primarily as a historical curiosity rather than as part of a useful, viable approach to psychology. Outside of psychology, however, students are still often exposed to psychoanalytic ideas by professors who take psychodynamic insights very seriously, especially in the arts and humanities. This continuing popularity of the Freudian influence among American English professors is largely due to the work of the French psychoanalyst Jacques Lacan. Although he considered himself a Freudian, and even named the school he founded in 1964 L'Ecole Freudienne de Paris (The Freudian School of Paris), he is primarily known for having radically altered the Freudian approach to both theory and therapy, dropping the emphasis on biological drives and sexuality in favor of a remarkably convoluted, jargon-dense, and difficult-to-follow theory based almost entirely on linguistics, along with altering therapeutic practice to the point that he was finally expelled from both the International Psychoanalytical Association *and* the French Psychoanalytic Society.

Born in 1901, Lacan grew up as the first-born son in a Catholic middle-class family and was educated in Jesuit schools all the way through to his baccalaureate degree. As an adolescent he developed an interest in philosophy, with a special attachment to the work of Spinoza, who in his own time was regarded variously as deeply spiritual and as a complete atheist, thanks to his idea that God is a part of the universe that he created and is therefore subject to its physical laws. In such a universe, God is unable to intervene in human affairs. As a result of Lacan's interest in such philosophy, he eventually lost his faith and ceased to be a practicing Christian. Curiously, his younger brother followed a very different path, eventually entering a monastery, but the brothers would remain close, and Lacan never entirely lost his interest in things religious. In 1953, for example, during a period of extravagant self-promotion following a split in the French psychoanalytic movement that he had precipitated, Lacan wrote to his brother asking if he could possibly arrange an audience with the Pope, apparently hoping to enlist the Church's cooperation in promoting his version of psychoanalysis.

Having completed his baccalaureate degree, Lacan decided to become a physician, studying medicine at Stanislas College. His clinical residency at Sainte

Anne's Hospital proved to be a turning point in his career aspirations, as he spent the 1928–1929 academic year working with female patients in the Special Infirmary Division of the Police Prefecture, one of France's more important sanitaria for the insane. In this setting, he was supervised by the psychiatrist Gaetan Gatian de Clérambault, a remarkably eccentric clinician known for his expertise in *erotomania,* on which subject he published a definitive book in 1921. Erotomania, also known as de Clérambault's syndrome in some texts, is a type of delusion in which a patient, usually following a psychotic episode or a brain injury, becomes convinced that another person, often a celebrity or a complete stranger, has fallen in love with him or her. The patient becomes convinced that the person has conveyed these feelings via secret signals, including gestures, facial expressions, and sometimes even telepathy or messages hidden in the mass media. Any attempt by the object of the delusion to deny these feelings is seen as part of a conspiracy to conceal the truth. Clérambault was himself widely regarded as an odd character, living alone in an apartment he shared with a set of wax figurines on which he practiced Arab draping, "the art and manner of pleating and folding fabrics, knotting them, causing them to fall voluptuously alongside the body, according to ancestral custom" (Roudinesco, 1990, p. 105).

Professionally, Clérambault was a fairly strict organicist, favoring purely biological explanations for mental illness. He created his own taxonomic system of psychological disorders, in which all symptoms corresponded to hypothetical underlying neurological processes. Despite this fairly progressive attitude toward the causes of mental illness, however, his work with insane criminals led Clérambault to oppose psychiatric reforms, instead favoring the incarceration of his patients and showing little interest in their welfare. During his single year working under Clérambault, Lacan appears to have fallen under his spell and adopted many of his ideas. In a 1931 article titled "Structures des psychoses paranoïaques" (Structures of paranoiac psychoses), based on some of his dissertation research, Lacan presents a modified version of Clérambault's view of the organic basis of paranoia, complete with the recommendation of systematic internment of the insane. In a sycophantic footnote, he acknowledges "the oral teaching of our master M. G. de Clérambault to whom we are indebted for the entirety of our method and material, and to whom, to avoid plagiarism, we would be obliged to pay homage for every one of our terms" (Roudinesco, 1990, p. 102). Clérambault, unmoved by the obsequious tone of the footnote, apparently agreed with Lacan on one point: he stormed into a meeting of the Medico-Psychological Society, threw copies of the article in Lacan's face, and publicly accused him of plagiarism.

Around the time of the article's publication, Lacan first began to read the works of Freud, and a definite Freudian influence crept into his 1932 dissertation and joined the elements of Clérambault's view of paranoia. Lacan had also begun to spend time with artists and literary scholars, particularly within the new surrealist movement, who had actually shown more interest in Freud than the majority of French psychiatrists had. Lacan's dissertation attracted favorable attention from both the surrealists and the nonpsychoanalytic French psychiatric community, but went unnoticed by the French psychoanalysts. The founder of psychoanalysis was also uninterested: the only correspondence that would ever take place between Lacan and Freud occurred when Lacan sent his idol a copy of the dissertation and received as his only reply a simple postcard acknowledging receipt of the manuscript.

Freud's indifference did not extinguish Lacan's interest in psychoanalysis, however, and around the time the dissertation was published he took the next step in training, entering upon analysis with Rudolf Loewenstein, a key player in the Psychoanalytic Society of Paris. The French psychoanalysts had fought an uphill battle for many years, as France had not been especially receptive to Freud's theories. In a 1907 letter to Carl Jung, Freud complained of the difficulties in establishing any sort of psychoanalytic movement there, attributing the problem to national character and chauvinism and observing that it is difficult to import *anything* into France. The difficulties experienced by psychoanalysis as a foreign movement were of course compounded by the perception of it as a German movement, thus triggering the anti-German sentiment that was still fresh from World War I. The trouble was increased further by the perception that psychoanalysis was a distinctly Jewish movement as well, thus subjecting it to the anti-Semitism that remained a potent force in most European intellectual circles. Such feelings were widespread and openly expressed, as in the 1928 press report of this opinion, from the French minister for education:

> I am assured that German youth is being poisoned by Freud. Freudianism is a northern phenomenon. It cannot succeed in France. Beyond the Rhine Freudianism will complete the work of dissolution begun by the war. (Quoted in Webster, 2002)

The result of this degree of anti-Freudian prejudice was a French psychoanalytic movement that was quite different from those established in America and England, or indeed the International Psychoanalytical Association, all of which emphasized adherence to a certain Freudian orthodoxy. The founding of the Psychoanalytic Society of Paris was accompanied by an explicit intent to redesign psychoanalysis by adapting it to French culture, making it less Germanic and more Gallic. As the early membership of the Psychoanalytic Society of Paris overlapped considerably with the right-wing anti-Semitic organization Action Française, of which Lacan was also a member, a primary goal was also to rid psychoanalysis of its Jewish origins, a goal that was accomplished partially by replacing much of its central jargon with a new French jargon, often including concepts that Freud had opposed or rejected

Possibly the most confusing of all psycho-analysts: Jacques Lacan in Paris, 1979. (Francois Leclaire/Sygma/Corbis)

outright. As a result of this strong sense of a need for a French psychoanalysis, Lacan produced his own theoretical system based on a completely different set of initial ideas and assumptions from Freud's. Although he still saw biological drives as fundamental, Lacan borrowed his basic model, and its accompanying terminology, not from biology but rather from linguistics.

Before he could pursue his new ideas, however, Lacan had other concerns to deal with, along with the rest of France. Just as Lacan had begun to settle into his career as a psychoanalyst and had published his first studies, the Nazis marched on Paris. In occupied France, it was a bad idea to be seen as in any way affiliated with a Jewish movement such as psychoanalysis, and so the Psychoanalytic Society quietly ceased operations for the duration of the war. Like most of his colleagues, Lacan immediately halted most of his scholarly activities and spent the occupation working quietly behind the scenes at a military hospital, Val de Grace. Although his psychoanalytic practice was suspended, the occupation proved to be an important time for Lacan's professional and theoretical development, thanks to the acquaintances and friendships he made during that period among the celebrities who were also in Paris during that period. He got to know leading artists such as Salvador Dalí and Pablo Picasso, for example, and even served briefly as Picasso's personal physician. It was not until the Psychoanalytic Society reopened in 1946, after the war was over, that a now 45-year-old Jacques Lacan resumed his professional activities as a psychoanalyst.

In the postwar period, Lacan became very active, organizing seminars, presenting papers, and generally working at establishing himself as an important player in the psychoanalytic community. In establishing his own, more idiosyncratically French version of psychoanalysis, he began to incorporate new influences, particularly the linguistic ideas of Saussure, whose terminology he borrowed and redefined as a set of psychoanalytic concepts. Probably the single most widely quoted idea in Lacan's oeuvre is the notion that the unconscious is structured like a language—in saying this, he was specifically referring to Saussure's definition of language, which was actually no longer current among linguists by the time Lacan began referring to it. Understanding Lacan, then, requires first understanding Saussure.

In Saussure's view of language, each word stands for, or signifies, a meaning. In his own jargon, language consists of signifiers, each of which signifies something, known as the signified. Language is therefore made up of a set of signs, each consisting of a signifier and the thing it signifies. In less jargon-filled terms, language is a system consisting both of words and of the things to which those words refer. By the 1950s, this view of language had been superseded by the work of such linguists as Chomsky, who recognized that the individual signs or words were not the appropriate unit of analysis, since they are often ambiguous or have multiple possible meanings, and therefore the focus should be on the sentence instead, where context provides words with their real meanings. Furthermore, the meanings of individual words are continually evolving and changing, and thus the signifier-signified relationship is not a constant or consistent one.

Despite these difficulties with the underlying linguistic model, however, Lacan pressed forward with a psychoanalytic theory structured along the lines of Saussure, identifying linguistic structures with corresponding bits of Freud, resulting in a model that has had little influence in the psychoanalytic world in part because it is seen simultaneously as both too simple and very difficult to follow.

In proclaiming that the unconscious is structured like a language, Lacan identifies the signifier with the conscious mind and the signified with Freud's unconscious. Superficially, this works fairly well as an analogue to Freud's model, in that he would agree that elements in the conscious mind are often symbolic representations of the contents of the unconscious. Through repression, a barrier is placed between conscious and unconscious, and thus conscious and unconscious minds, or signifier and signified, are opposed to each other and unable to communicate directly. In Lacan's modification of Saussure's linguistic model, signifiers do not point to the signified, but rather to other signifiers.

This model translates into the psychoanalytic method of therapy in that the signified remains hidden, and so our attempts to explore the unconscious through free association are doomed to fail. Our verbal thoughts are made up of signifiers, but those signifiers actually signify other signifiers, rather than the signified that we are attempting to reach, and so no amount of speaking will bring the patient any closer to the hidden truth. Through the sort of convoluted reasoning suggested by his use of Saussure's jargon, Lacan goes on to reorient much of Freud's psychoanalytic worldview around the central role of language in all things, to such an extent that he has frequently been accused by psychoanalysts of neglecting the significance of such obvious forces as biology, emotion, and sexuality. His primary goal was to demonstrate that the structure of language is the primary influence on everything from sexual desire to psychosis. While his reduced emphasis on the role of sexuality was welcomed by some psychoanalysts, his replacement of Freud's excessive reliance on sexuality with an emphasis on the role of language was more a source of confusion than an influence on most. Unlike such early rebels as Adler and Jung, his goal was not to de-emphasize sexuality so much as to recontextualize it as a force in opposition to language. Lacan described language and sexuality as mutually antagonistic, and argued that while humans are indeed both sexual beings and speaking beings, these two elements of our being cannot coexist harmoniously, due to the traumatic nature of sexuality.

The symbolic function of language in signifying the buried signifieds in the unconscious is so important to Lacan that he defines a traumatic experience simply as an event that lacks symbolization. Recovery from trauma therefore requires symbolization, or the attachment of words and meanings to what has not been symbolized yet. In Lacan's model, however, sexuality is sui generis in this regard, as there is something essentially traumatic about it that makes it unusually resistant to symbolic representation, some way in which it is simply other. Within this interpretation of sexuality lies what is arguably Lacan's most fundamental departure from Freud: where Freud regarded a child's emerging sexuality as inherently autoerotic, focused as it is on the individual deriving pleasure from his or her own actions, Lacan instead presents the first stirrings of sexuality as a confrontation with something new and alien. Where Freud emphasized a boy's attachment to his own penis, and a girl's concomitant wish to possess one herself, Lacan once wrote that no little boy feels that his penis is really his own. By removing Freud's emphasis on the autoeroticism of infantile sexuality, Lacan was not replacing it with an idea of sexuality as involving a relationship with others, but rather suggesting that the fundamental otherness of sexuality is universally traumatic.

Since this traumatic sexuality resists symbolization in the usual way, Lacanian psychoanalysts have given it its own symbolization process, which they have named "sexuation," which resembles the process others have referred to as becoming "sexed" or "gendered." In Lacan's world, the process by which a child comes to identify with one gender or the other, a process to which the Oedipus complex is central in Freud's theory, becomes the process of sexuation by which a person finds a way to symbolize sexuality and identifies himself or herself as belonging to a structure that is either male or female, masculine or feminine. Lacan emphasizes structure because to him masculinity and femininity are structural, linguistically determined categories rather than a result of either anatomy or biology. In this view, males and females can be sexuated according to either masculine or feminine structure.

Despite the differences in preferred jargon, Lacan's view of early sexuality is more an adaptation of Freud than an outright reinvention. Where the penis, both actual and desired, is central to the early development of sexual identity in Freud's theory, for example, the child's self-definition as masculine or feminine in Lacan's theory is largely achieved in relation to a particular signifier, which Lacan called the phallus. The real difference between the two approaches is a relatively subtle one: whereas Freud is concerned with the presence or absence of an actual penis, Lacan's phallus is a signifier, or symbol, rather than an actual body part. Whereas Freud sees the penis, rather obviously, as an inevitable result of a certain degree of biological determinism, Lacan describes the phallus as a symbol of sexuality that is historically contingent rather than necessary, although it is pervasive. In other words, there is no necessary, inevitable reason for the phallus to be a universal signifier of sexuality, but that is simply how things have worked out.

In Lacan's model, children spend their early months regarding their mothers as nearly godlike in their ability to fulfill all needs, without necessarily recognizing their mothers as separate entities with needs of their own. Eventually, the children learn that their mothers do not have everything, and therefore have needs and desires of their own—this realization often first occurs when the mother requires the child to delay gratification while she attends to other demands on her time, such as her job, her husband, her social life, or her other children. According to Lacan, the recognition that the mother has desires beyond the child is very difficult for that child, who will inevitably begin to wonder to what extent he or she satisfies the mother's desires. Apart from its focus on the child's questions about the mother's hypothetical desires, this process of learning that the mother has roles beyond caring for that particular child is hardly a new idea in psychoanalysis, reflecting Margaret **Mahler**'s stage of separation individuation, for example. In Lacan's version, however, the child's degree of masculine or feminine sexuation is defined in terms of the mother's desires beyond the child.

Having become concerned about the mother's desire, the child then considers what the object of her desire might be, and here the phallus begins to play its role as signifier. In Lacan's revision of the Oedipus complex, the phallus is the unconscious signifier for the object toward which, in the child's mind, the mother's desire is directed. Like Freud before him, Lacan created a theory in which the child's early assumptions about the anatomical differences between the sexes are central: the central role of the phallus in psychic life depends on Lacan's expectation that the child has discerned that his mother does not have a penis. The mother's desire may then be perceived as being, at least in part, born of the need to obtain something physical that she lacks. The phallus is a signifier, however, rather than a real object, functioning much like a metaphor does in language, putting one signifier in place of another. The phallus acts as a metaphor for two signifiers: the mother's desire (not just sexual desire, but all things she might desire beyond the child) and the name of the father. The phallus therefore acts in the unconscious as a signifier for both the mother's desire and the object of that desire. Once the phallus has become a factor in the child's unconscious, the child may either identify with the signifier itself, resulting in feminine sexuation, or the child may see himself (or herself) as the possessor of that signifier, resulting in masculine sexuation. Whether the child identifies more closely with being the phallus or merely wielding it, the child can now see himself or herself as an object of desire.

Given the differences in their conceptions of the role of the phallus itself, as either an actual body part or a metaphoric representation of desire, it comes as no surprise that Lacan's take on penis envy and castration anxiety is also rather eccentrically different from Freud's. In Freud's version of the phallic stage of development, girls envy boys their possession of a penis and assume themselves to have been castrated, whereas boys have castration anxiety and fear the loss of the penis. Lacan, however, presents both boys and girls as experiencing the stage in the same way, seeing themselves as having been castrated, though only in a symbolic rather than a literal sense: after all, neither of them either really possesses or really is the phallus. Rather than serving as a prized possession for one gender and an object of desire and longing for the other, the phallus in Lacan's perspective is a signifier for *lack,* representing for both boys and girls what they are not, along with what they do not possess.

Another central concept in Lacan's radical reconceptualization of Freud's treatment of developing sexuality is *jouissance.* He used the term to refer to sexual and sensual satisfaction, central concepts in Freud's theory, but Lacan gives the term an additional layer of meaning as a reference to enjoyment that goes well beyond what we might normally associate with sexual sensations and orgasm. To Lacan, jouissance is a special category in which pleasure and pain appear as intermingled parts of a single sensation. Rather than present positive and destructive behaviors as the result of separate instinctive impulses, as Freud and other psychoanalysts often did, Lacan sees them as part of the same impulse. In this way, an addiction makes sense as a fundamental way in which an addict seeks a particular type of satisfaction, a jouissance that is both pleasurable *and* self-destructive. Understanding this approach requires an acknowledgment that Lacan always drew a sharp distinction between instincts and drives. An instinct is satisfied in a straightforward manner, by obtaining whatever the instinct's object is. Jouissance is not the satisfaction of an instinct, however, but rather it is the satisfaction of a drive. Drives are not satisfied by simply obtaining their objects; although drives have objects, Lacan believed these objects are actually only temporary solutions, as the drive's more basic tendency is to turn back on the self. This turning back is an important part of the jouissance mechanism. According to Lacan, drives are centered on the borders of the body, the zones of the body that open up to the outside world, including the mouth, anus, and genitals, as well as the gaze and the voice. A drive starts out from these body zones, with a clear object, but it then loops around the object and turns back to its source. The jouissance provided by this return movement is completely unrelated to the fulfillment of instinctual or biological needs. Hunger is instinctual, for example, and the need to eat is satisfied by food, but eating does not satisfy the oral drive, which will continue to seek fulfillment even after the hunger has been satisfied. Whereas instinctive needs rise and decline, come and go as needed, Lacan's description of jouissance emphasizes the excessive, insistent, and repetitive nature of drives.

Lacan uses the term *jouissance* to refer to a drivelike sexual satisfaction, which appears in two varieties, a phallic jouissance and an other jouissance. Both varieties of sexuation, masculine and feminine, have access to the phallic jouissance, which is explicitly associated with the sexual anatomy (Lacan sometimes called it a "jouissance of the organ"). Feminine subjects also have access to the other jouissance, however, to which masculine subjects rarely have access. The other jouissance, which Lacan refers to as a "jouissance beyond the phallus," is not obtained primarily in genital sexual activity, but rather emerges in other areas of life, especially in religious ecstasy, meditation, art, and other practices and behaviors that bear a special relationship to language and symbolic representation.

Like Freud, Lacan regarded the satisfaction obtained in these other areas of life as still sexual, but as the satisfaction is neither phallic nor produced by the erogenous zones, this form of jouissance is closely related to the Freudian ego defense mechanism of sublimation, in which a drive is satisfied despite being diverted from its original object.

The other jouissance serves different functions in masculine and feminine sexuation. To the masculine individual, the whole person is subject to, and driven by, the phallic function. This individual recognizes the existence of the other jouissance, however, and intuits that there is another type of satisfaction that is both unavailable to him *and* superior to what is available in the genital satisfaction that he is familiar with. In the structure of masculine sexuality, therefore, the phallic jouissance and the other jouissance are in an antagonistic relationship. To the masculine subject, the other jouissance is essentially ruled out as long as the phallic jouissance is present, yet the masculine subject also believes adamantly (though unconsciously) that the other jouissance exists somewhere, and sees it as desirable, impossible, or worthy of hatred. The feminine subject, however, though subject to the phallic function as well, does not see the entire person as subject to that function, as the other jouissance, though unknowable and unrepresentable, is also present, making the phallic jouissance less than whole. Like masculine subjects, the female subjects therefore also see both types of jouissance as distinct from each other, but as less antagonistic than the way they are regarded by masculine subjects.

Since the phallic type of jouissance is the only source of satisfaction for masculine subjects and only feminine subjects are capable of experiencing the other jouissance, Lacan saw the two as incapable of complementing each other, going so far as to claim that there is no such thing as a sexual relationship. He did not, of course, deny that men and women have sex with each other, but he regarded the sexual act as entailing a fundamental miscommunication, in which what men and women experience is not what they are expecting. Since the sex act requires participants to take on specific masculine and feminine roles regarding the phallus, men and women actually do not encounter each other as masculine and feminine subjects in the context of the act, since only phallic jouissance is involved. In the sex act, the individuals identify themselves as masculine and feminine through relating themselves to the (metaphorical) phallus as a third-party mediator, rather than actually relating to each other. Feminine sexuation is, on a very fundamental level, more complex than male sexuation: while both have access in the sex act to the phallic signifier as a signifier, the female also has access to something beyond the phallus, but that which is beyond lacks a signifier, and so it cannot be expressed, and remains hidden and silent.

A frequent criticism of Lacan's writings on sexuality will come as no surprise to the astute reader: he has been widely accused of an overreliance on the male sex organ for understanding both sexuality and gender, a phallocentrism that may reflect an inability to conceive of female sexuality on its own terms. In his own defense, Lacan often claimed that the phallus is a metaphorical signifier and is not to be understood as a penis, but his critics respond that the phallus is nonetheless rather obviously derived from the penis and closely related to it, whether Lacan wishes to admit it or not. Because of this, it may be inappropriate as a neutral term for consideration of the behavior of both sexes. Lacan's defenders are quick to point out, however, that a certain degree of phallocentrism, understood as male-favoring sexism, has been endemic to human culture, which is hardly Lacan's fault, and that he is simply describing the way that this history has structured our psyches, without implying that it is ideal or even good. This is by no means a new criticism for the practitioners of psychoanalysis, since in being accused of attempting to understand all of human sexuality in terms of the male anatomy, he is simply repeating the earlier experience of Freud, who encountered (and continues to encounter) the same criticism.

Not all of Lacan's ideas about child development have been as controversial, and one piece of Lacanian psychoanalysis has made its way into some mainstream developmental psychology textbooks, even if often as a historical curiosity rather than a currently relevant idea: the mirror stage. Given his attachment to the idea of the unconscious mind functioning like a language, the mirror stage is another use of metaphor to describe psychic development. Considering the fragmented nature of modern human society, Lacan begins with the assumption that the individual is equally fractured, and furthermore saw the efforts of humanistic psychologists to help people to reassemble the shattered pieces of the self as a waste of time. After all, the self is merely a reflection of language, and language is noncohesive and constantly changing, therefore wholeness of self may be an impossible objective to achieve. Lacan recognizes a deep, internal craving for wholeness, however, along with a drive for oneness with the universe, which he explains as a desire to recapture what was once ours. At the beginning of life, all infants live in an undifferentiated world without clear categories, boundaries, or divisions, a state of bliss that Lacan calls *l'imaginaire*. Eventually, as we grow older, this world comes apart as we come to recognize the independent existence of objects and people beyond the limited bounds of our own bodies. At first, our reaction to this newfound individuation is to temporarily believe ourselves to be whole, unified selves, clearly separated from others, until we become the fragmented individuals that we all are. According to Lacan, this delusion that we are still whole arises during the mirror stage, a pre-Oedipal stage during which the infant, somewhere between the ages of 6 and 18 months, first recognizes his or her image in a mirror.

Having recognized the mirror image, the child is filled with happiness at the understanding that he or she is a unified, integrated self, separate from the rest of the world and all the people and objects in it. A parent assures the child that the image in the mirror is of the two of them, separate from each other, representing both the self and the other. Lacan refers to this process as a sort of indoctrination into a narcissistic delusion, in which the child imagines himself or herself as a fixed self that will be able to function in a capitalistic society (a remarkable level of political thought for an infant to engage in, though it is of course unconscious).

In Lacan's model, it is important to note that the mirror stage occurs at about the same time that children develop the use of language, as language is the main source of alienation and separation among people. Since the psyche is modeled on language, its introduction brings the early, unified, idyllic existence to an end. Once the child begins to name and categorize things, he or she becomes separated from an ever-increasing number of them, as it is in the act of naming objects that we recognize their independent existence. The use of language forces us to give up our sense of oneness with the universe and forever remove ourselves from the bliss of infancy. This sense of oneness is then relegated to the place without language: the unconscious. Lacan even links this language-based individuation to the Oedipus complex: rather than castration by the father, the dominant anxiety is separation by the name of the father. The child's desire for a sexual relationship with his mother is actually a desire to return to the womb, or more specifically to a place where he was still one with the universe. What prevents this is a word from the father: no.

Similarly, socialization is accomplished not by internalization of the superego, but rather by internalization of language. Language alienates us forever from both the universe and the self, and according to Lacan, this alienation is the root of all neurosis, just as the Oedipus complex is for Freud. The alienation results in an emptiness, a lack, which we cannot name or describe in language, since it resides in the part of us where language does not operate. All we can do is attempt to approximate it with language, since the signifiers we use are never up to the task of properly representing what needs to be signified.

Lacan's profound revisions to Freud's theory were not especially popular at first. Although he had been presenting and publishing papers since before World War II, it was not until the publication of his collected writings in English in the early 1970s that he became well-known internationally. This may have been in part because of the chilly reception his changes in psychoanalysis received in his own country. In addition to his writings, he developed a certain notoriety in postwar France for not adhering to standard psychoanalytic practices with his clients. He became known in Paris for his unusually brief clinical sessions, for example: rather than adhering to the standard 50-minute hour, he would sometimes meet with clients for 5 minutes or less, leaving both his colleagues and his clients feeling that he was mocking the whole enterprise. Condemnation of this practice among his colleagues was sufficiently universal that he was forced to resign from the presidency of Le Societe Psychoanalytique de Paris in 1953. Later that same year, however, he began his own organization with the help of some loyal colleagues, Le Societe Française de Psychoanalyse, effectively setting up an alternative, parallel French psychoanalytic establishment. The Societe published its own journal, which became the primary outlet for promoting Lacan's ideas, as the other psychoanalytic journals wanted nothing to do with him. The lecture series he sponsored became quite popular, however, and he developed a large following of his own, eventually establishing his own institute and training his own corps of Lacanian psychoanalysts. Despite his continuing rejection by most psychoanalysts, Lacan became a figure of international acclaim by the early 1970s, giving lectures around the world and influencing generations of literary and art critics, among others.

Further Reading

Roudinesco, E. (1990). *Jacques Lacan & Co.: A History of Psychoanalysis in France, 1925–1985*. London: Free Press Association Books.

Webster, R. (2002). The Cult of Lacan: Freud, Lacan and the Mirror-Stage. Available at http://www.richardwebster.net/thecultoflacan.html.

Lanzer, Ernst. See The Rat Man

"Little Hans" (Herbert Graf) (1904–1973)

In 1909, four years after revealing his ideas about infant sexuality to the world in *Three Essays on the Theory of Sexuality,* Freud published a case study in which he revealed what he believed to be solid evidence of several elements of that theory. The paper, *Analysis of a Phobia in a Five-Year-Old Boy,* was one of only a handful of case studies that Freud would publish in his lifetime, and the only one involving a child's current experiences rather than the reminiscences of an adult.

For several years, Freud had encouraged his friends and colleagues to keep an eye out for developments in their own children that might be helpful in confirming his conjectures about childhood sexuality, and Max Graf (1873–1958), a participant in Freud's Wednesday meetings (whose wife was in analysis with Freud), was happy to oblige. Graf's son, Herbert, who Freud would refer to as "little Hans" in his publication, had recently developed a fear of horses, and Graf believed he saw signs of various elements of the Oedipal conflict in this fear.

Graf had been reporting back to Freud on his son's interest in sexual matters and his curiosity about his body and the bodies of others, an interest that focused especially on the anatomical differences between the sexes, when little Hans suddenly developed a debilitating fear that a horse would bite him or fall on him, and he was so frightened that he refused to leave the house. Although Freud focused, obviously, on the symbolic significance of the horse and its possible actions, it should be noted that the case study includes the actual circumstances that probably led to the fear. It seems that at the age of four, Hans was on an outing in a local park, accompanied by the family's maid. At the park, he saw an exhausted horse collapse while pulling an overloaded cart, certainly a frightening sight for a small boy. He subsequently became anxious about going into the street, especially when horses and heavily burdened vehicles were about. Hans explicitly stated that his fear was that the horses and/or vehicles would fall over onto him, but his father, a budding psychoanalyst, wrote to Freud that his fear was a neurosis (which he called *equinophobia*) that resulted from a combination of sexual overexcitement as a consequence of his mother's touch, as well as fear caused by the very large penises of horses.

As the case of Little Hans is often cited as Freud's first actual child analysis, it is important to note that Freud only met the boy once—Max Graf actually conducted the analysis, under the supervision of Freud, which occurred almost entirely by way of correspondence. Graf sent his extensive notes to Freud, who condensed them and interspersed his own comments and interpretations throughout when they were published. While not rejecting Max's explanations, Freud eventually arrived at a less rigidly Oedipal explanation of the fear, though like Max, he does not treat the actual encounter with a falling horse as particularly important.

Freud describes Hans's analysis as occurring in two distinct phases: in the first stage, Hans's fear of the horses themselves is dealt with, and in the second, the subject is his fear of the boxes and containers they transported around Vienna on their carts. Early on, Hans had a very specific fear: that a white horse would bite him or collapse, and that the horse would enter his room at home prior to doing so. Freud interpreted this fear as an example of castration anxiety, in which Hans fears that his father will punish him for his attraction to his mother and for his desire to act aggressively toward his father. In addition to the clear Oedipal elements, Freud also wrote that the birth of Hans's little sister increased the conflict, as it introduced a rival for his mother's attention and affection. This last element required no symbolic analysis—Hans had openly expressed a wish that his sister would die, a fairly common sentiment expressed by young children with new siblings. In order to handle his castration anxiety while maintaining his positive feelings toward his father (while repressing the hostile impulses), Hans created an external phobic object to fear instead. The object of fear was one that could be avoided by staying indoors, as horses do not generally enter houses, thus helping him to fight off the far greater trepidation regarding castration.

Since Hans's own father, the ultimate source of the fear, was acting as the analyst in this case, Freud suggested that fear of his own father might be delaying the progress of the boy's treatment. He resolved this by inviting Hans to visit him (the only time they actually met) and explaining his fear to him. According to Freud's account, he helped the boy to see that the specific features of the horses that frightened him were actually reminiscent of his own father's moustache and spectacles, and so it was really his father he was afraid of. Far from being frightened further by these bizarre revelations, the five-year-old asked his father if Freud knew so much about him because he talked directly to God. He subsequently also asked his father to convey several dreams and bits of fantasy to Freud, confident that he would know what they really meant.

As for the second phase of treatment, dealing with his fear of the horses' cargo, as well as a newly acquired fear of excrement, Freud suggested that this fear stemmed partly from the young child's rudimentary understanding of childbirth. Hans had seen illustrations in a book indicating that babies were delivered by storks, and the boxes and containers on the horses' carts were similar to packages that the babies arrived in. The boxes therefore represented the arrival of many more anxiety-provoking babies. As for the fear of excrement, it may have been related to the same lack of reproductive understanding—he had heard that babies actually come out of their mothers, and he knew what came out of himself, so feces also came to represent the anxiety caused by his sister. Since he saw the fear as partly the result of an inadequate understanding of the source of babies, Freud encouraged Graf to speak more openly with his son about sexual matters. He reports that Hans's behavior and emotional state did improve after his father provided him with more information, and the fear of horses had begun to weaken. Freud encountered the boy again briefly 12 years later and reported that the fear was completely gone, with no new anxieties having arisen to take its place. Herbert Graf went on to a long and successful career as an opera producer, spending most of his professional life (from 1936 to 1960) at the Metropolitan Opera in New York after fleeing the Nazis.

The case of Little Hans is significant because it was the first time that Freud used clinical material, obtained directly from the treatment of a *child,* to support his ideas about infantile sexuality. Prior to this paper, everything Freud had written about the sexual life of children, including his discovery of the Oedipus complex and castration anxiety, as well as *penis envy* in girls, had been inferred from the reminiscences of adults. This case was therefore particularly important for Freud, as it seemed to confirm the presence of those phenomena in an actual child, as they were happening, rather than relying only on the reconstructed memories of neurotic adults.

Further Reading

Freud, S. (1909/2002). *The "Wolfman" and Other Cases* (Translated by Louise Adey Huish). New York: Penguin.

Graf, M. (1942). Reminiscences of Professor Sigmund Freud. *Psychoanalytic Quarterly* 11: 465–476.

Mahler, Margaret (1897–1985)

Margaret Mahler, a Hungarian-born psychoanalyst who received her training in Vienna, was a leading proponent of the use of analytic techniques with mentally ill children, but is best remembered today for her introduction of the concept of separation-individuation. Unlike many other psychoanalytical ideas whose influence has been limited to the work of other psychologists and psychiatrists operating within a Freudian perspective, the separation-individuation process remains a subject of serious discussion and research within the mainstream of developmental psychology.

The Theory

In Mahler's theory, the separation-individuation process is the source of the infant's emerging self-awareness, or the recognition that the individual child is a separate being from other people and objects. Where other psychoanalytic theorists have emphasized the importance of the child's birth experience in forming his or her later self-concept, Mahler emphasizes the significance of the development of self-awareness as a psychological birth of the infant. The separation-individuation process occupies the child over the first three years of life, with toddlers slowly becoming more aware of their own individuality over time. In early infancy, the child is not capable of exploring the environment alone, instead remaining physically attached to the mother much of the time, and receiving nourishment as a direct result of the blurring of physical boundaries between the two individuals, literally taking a part of the mother, the breast, into his or her own mouth. It is only as the child becomes more mobile that physical *separation* begins to take place more frequently and to a greater degree, contributing to the child's growing awareness (*individuation*) of his or her uniqueness as separate individual and of the existence of real physical boundaries between the self and others.

In classic psychoanalytic fashion, Mahler saw the separation-individuation process, as well as the degree of the child's success in navigating through it, as an important influence on personality development. The process consists of several phases, beginning with the first three to five months of life, during which the infant is in what Mahler referred to as the *normal symbiotic phase* (in the original formulation, the first few weeks of life were spent in the *normal autistic phase,* during which the child spends most of the time asleep, but Mahler later abandoned this phase), during which the child is in a *symbiotic relationship* with the mother or caregiver. During this period, the child is aware of the mother but lacks self-awareness and is therefore incapable of seeing himself or herself as separate from the parent. Furthermore, the child lacks awareness of even being separate from objects in the environment. This changes in the fourth or fifth month, as awareness of the existence of the self as a separate entity from the parent and environment begins to set in, a process Mahler called *hatching.* Key to the start of this hatching process, the first subphase in the *separation-individuation phase,* is the development of crawling: as infants become mobile, they gain the ability to physically move away from their caregivers. According to Mahler, this produces not only a physical separation but a psychological one as well. This post-hatching phase of the separation-individuation process, during which the child tries out different actions and experiences conflicting desires, is known as the practicing period. Though still experiencing himself or herself as one with the mother, the child begins to explore the environment more thoroughly and thus to become more distant physically from the mother.

Once the child has become more reliably mobile, the period of toddlerhood is marked by conflicting desires that emerge during the practicing subphase, as the child simultaneously wishes both to be autonomous from the parent or caregiver and to be one with that person as in earlier infancy. Since the child's task in this period is to learn to reconcile the two sets of conflicting desires, Mahler called it the *rapprochement* subphase. Once the child has been able to reconcile the conflicting desires, the *constancy* subphase begins. The ideal outcome of the phases of the separation-individuation process is for the young child to recognize the self as unique and different from everyone else, which enables the child to successfully cope with separation from the parent caregiver. According to Mahler, constancy is achieved when the child has formed an internalized representation of the mother as a truly separate individual with a separate identity. Attaining constancy prepares the child to be able to handle separation, but perhaps more crucially to be able to cope with disappointment. When a younger sibling comes along, the child who has achieved constancy is more capable of understanding that even though his mother cannot hold him while attending to the needs of his sibling, she still loves him. Where the infant and toddler regard people and events in a very black-and-white way, as either purely good or purely bad, the child who has attained constancy takes a far more nuanced view of the world.

As might be expected of any psychoanalytic theory of early childhood development, the consequences for the child of failure to achieve rapprochement between the conflicting desires for autonomy and symbiosis can lead to serious mental health consequences; indeed, Mahler's development of separation-individuation theory was inspired in part by her work in Vienna with psychotic children whose symptoms resembled those of schizophrenia. Mahler created a new diagnosis for these children, based on her own theoretical notions: the *symbiotic psychotic syndrome*. Also known as the Mahler syndrome, it occurs in children between the ages of two and four who have achieved a level of development at which they are able to differentiate between themselves and their mothers, and have a sense of being separate individuals, but are unable to fully separate, panicking whenever a separation is attempted. Symptoms include catatonia-like temper tantrums and states of complete panic. This anxiety achieves the level of psychosis because delusion is involved as well: according to Mahler, the goal of the child with this syndrome is to restore the symbiotic-parasitic delusion of oneness with the mother.

In the nonpsychotic segment of the population, problems can result from deficiencies in the internal representation of the parent that is formed when constancy is achieved. Since the child has achieved a complete sense of separation from the mother, the internalization of the mother, sounding very much like Freud's superego, is the source of guidance, support, and comfort from the mother on an unconscious level. If the image of the mother that has been internalized is not supportive or a reliable source of comfort, however, the result may be a sense of insecurity and lowered self-esteem in adulthood.

The Theorist

Although she began her career in Vienna, Margaret Mahler did her most important work in America, where she published her best-known work on the mother-child relationship and the separation-individuation process, *The Psychological Birth of the Human Infant: Symbiosis and Individuation* (2000). Like so many other Viennese scholars of Jewish descent or with ties to the Jewish community, she fled in the late 1930s in the face of the advancing Nazis, and eventually settled in the United States.

She was born Margaret Schönberger on May 10, 1897, in Sopron, Hungary, to a German mother and a Hungarian father, Eugenia (née Wiener) and Guzstav Schönberger (originally Fertoszentmiklos), and grew up speaking both languages fluently. At 16, she left for Budapest, determined to follow in her physician father's footsteps, and she began her medical studies in 1917. For a young woman to attend medical school was rare in those days, and even more so for a young Jewish woman, and the path to her degree was not an easy one. As a result of her encounters with anti-Semitism and sexism, Mahler attended schools in Budapest, Munich, Jena, and Heidelberg, finally receiving her medical degree from the University of Jena in 1922.

Having completed medical school, Mahler moved to Vienna, obtained her medical license and opened a private pediatric practice. Having been introduced to psychoanalytic ideas by Sándor **Ferenczi** while she was in Budapest, Mahler soon decided to join the Vienna Psychoanalytical Society and to undergo training in psychoanalysis, beginning the analytic process with Helene Deutsch and continuing the process with August Aichhorn, after her initial analysis was labeled a failure by Deutsch. Her professional relationship with Aichhorn was far more positive than her abortive work with Deutsch, and Mahler went on to conduct research on juvenile delinquents in Aichhorn's child guidance centers, while also working with psychotic children in several pediatric clinics and hospitals. During this period, she became a very active participant in the activities of the Vienna Psychoanalytical Society, attending seminars and publishing numerous papers in the *Journal of Psychoanalytic Pedagogy,* thus also making her mark on the training of subsequent psychoanalysts. In 1936, she married Paul Mahler, a Jewish businessman with a doctorate in chemistry, and in 1938, after the *Anschluss,* the couple followed Freud's example and left Vienna for London. Following a fairly brief stay there, they immigrated to the United States. Not everyone in Mahler's family was so fortunate, however: although she begged her parents to leave Hungary prior to its invasion, her father died a month before the Nazis entered Hungary, and her mother died after being taken to the concentration camp at Auschwitz.

In 1939, Margaret Mahler passed her state medical board examinations and became a member of the New York Psychoanalytic Society, setting up a private practice in her basement. This achievement was all the more remarkable given that neither she nor Paul spoke English, an obstacle that would ultimately prove greater for him. While Margaret thrived, he struggled to find work, which put great strain on their relationship, and the couple eventually divorced in 1953. No sooner had Margaret Mahler settled in to her new circumstances, however, than she began to expand on and spread her own theoretical ideas, providing assistance through the 1940s as an unpaid consultant to the New York State Psychiatric Institute and Mount Sinai Hospital. Eventually she also began to teach psychiatry at Columbia University, eventually joining the faculty of the Albert Einstein College of Medicine full-time in 1950. While training others, she also continued to innovate in the world of private clinical practice, along with commuting from New York to Philadelphia on weekends to serve as the director of a child psychoanalysis training program at the Philadelphia Psychoanalytic Institute.

Her impact on the field of child psychiatry in America was quite large, both through her training of others and through the innovative treatment programs she started. In 1956, for example, she started a therapeutic nursery program for psychotic children at Albert Einstein College of Medicine, and in 1957 she and Manuel Furer set up the Masters Child Center in Manhattan, a treatment center and laboratory intended to study the interactions between children under three years of age and their mothers. In both settings, she developed what she came to call the Tripartite Treatment Model, in the mother was an active participant in the child's therapy right from the initial sessions. This was an idea that was actually rather controversial at the time, given the popularity of the theory that the autism and other psychosis-like disorders were caused by poor or inappropriate interactions with the mother, an idea spread most effectively in America by *pseudo*-psychoanalyst Bruno Bettelheim. Mahler rejected that idea out of hand, based on her own observations of mothers with their autistic children, and instead popularized the idea that family members, especially mothers, should be actively involved in the child's therapy, since they controlled so many of the environmental factors that contributed to their children's condition.

In working with disturbed children in New York, Mahler had another insight regarding the study of child development that went against psychoanalytic tradition: she came to recognize that the study of disturbed children could not reveal everything about the process of normal development. The Masters Children's Center thus embarked on a program of research in which interactions between normally developing children and their caregivers provided the data, and Mahler's subsequent theoretical work on the course of normal child development was based on the observation of large numbers of children without any psychiatric diagnosis. Ever since Freud had set the example, many psychoanalytic theories, like his, were based on limited contact with small samples of disturbed individuals, whose experiences were then extrapolated, often inappropriately, to provide an account of humanity in general. Mahler's methods, in which she studied normally developing children and recognized the importance of observing the quality of interactions between mother and child instead of just retrospectively speculating on it, may therefore have actually been far more important, and ultimately had a far greater impact on the field of developmental psychology, than her particular ideas.

Further Reading

Mahler, M. (1976). *The Psychological Birth of the Human Infant: Symbiosis and Individuation.* New York: Basic Books.

Moses and Monotheism (1939)

"I venture to say this: it was one man, the man Moses, who created the Jews."

The preceding quotation is the central thesis of Sigmund Freud's final published work, a book that his own impending death after a long illness may well have prompted him to finally write. Throughout his career, and for a long time after, Freud's Jewish identity and the anti-Semitism he had to face as a man of science in Austria were both important influences on his thought and the subject of frequent speculation by others. Freud has been accused of everything from being the founder of a uniquely Jewish science to being a self-hating Jew who did everything he could to bury the influence of his cultural background on his work. The truth, as is usually the case with such trite oversimplifications, turns out to be more complicated, but some evidence of how Freud reconciled his Jewishness with both his atheism and his theories can be found in this last book of his long career, in which he addressed Jewish history, along with the history of religion, with a directness only hinted at in such earlier works as *Totem and Taboo.* It was also the only time in his career that he directly confronted, and attempted a historical and psychoanalytic exploration of, anti-Semitism.

Certainly Freud had very directly addressed his own atheism, and his feeling that it was the only reasonable intellectual position, in previous works. In *The Future of an Illusion,* for example, his central thesis was the blunt assertion that belief in God is a collective neurosis, representing a universal human longing for a father who we all rejected during the Oedipal conflict in early childhood. A similar theme runs through *Totem and Taboo.* In *Moses and Monotheism,* however, something new is in evidence: without abandoning his atheism, Freud for the first time describes the Jewish faith and culture into which he was born as a source of both cultural advancement in the past and personal inspiration in the present. Various writers have speculated that, in his 80s and highly aware of his own impending death, Freud began to recognize the beauty and utility of religion. Given the strong atheist perspective of his earlier work, this suggestion comes as something of a surprise. Ever since *The Future of an Illusion,* atheist writers have considered Freud an inspiration and a hero, from his own time up to the modern wave of antireligious polemic from such writers as Christopher Hitchens, author of *God is Not Great,* and Richard Dawkins, author of *The God Delusion.* It is therefore important to remember that, in recognizing the important role of Judaism in the development of modern civilization, including the positive role in intellectual life of the introspection inspired by religious faith, Freud does not go so far as to embrace or endorse belief in God (or gods), and indeed builds the book around a thesis sure to upset a broad range of readers raised in the Judeo-Christian tradition.

That central thesis, quoted at the start of this essay, is that Moses was indeed the patriarch of the Jewish people, but not in the way that this has been generally understood. According to Freud, Moses was not himself a Jew, but rather was actually born into ancient Egyptian nobility and a follower of the god Aten, himself constructed on the model of a living prince, the Pharaoh Akhenaten. The Jewish people are, consequently, an invention of the man Moses, who did not exist prior to his creation of them. Freud understood well the kind of reaction this hypothesis was sure to engender, opening the book with an acknowledgment both of the impending controversy and of his conviction that he is presenting the truth, and must therefore not be swayed by that controversy:

> To deny a people the man whom it praises as the greatest of its sons is not a deed to be undertaken light-heartedly, especially by one belonging to that people. No consideration, however, will move me to set aside truth in favour of supposed national interests. Moreover, the elucidation of the mere facts of the problem may be expected to deepen our insight into the situation with which they are concerned. (Freud, 1939, p. 11)

He seems here to anticipate the self-loathing Jew charge that did in fact follow him around in the wake of this posthumous work, and yet starts the book off with the suggestion that a direct confrontation with his hypothesis will lead to a deeper understanding of Jewish history.

Freud begins with the simplest facts known about Moses, pointing out that we know of him only from the religious texts of the Jews and acknowledging that such books are not considered especially reliable sources by modern scientists, especially when no other corroborating texts exist. Nevertheless, Freud argues, most modern scholars agree that the man known as Moses did exist, and that the exodus from Egypt did in fact take place. Beyond that, however, Freud suggests that not much of the rest of his story makes logical sense, beginning with the etymology of his name as described in the Bible. The Hebrew form of the name Moses is Mosche. Freud asks the following:

> Where does it come from? What does it mean? As is well known, the story in Exodus, Chapter 11, already answers this question. There we learn that the Egyptian princess who saved the babe from the waters of the Nile gave him his name, adding the etymological explanation: because I drew him out of the water. (1939, p. 12)

Freud points out that Jewish lexicographers have referred to this explanation as folk etymology, as the actual Hebrew word Mosche can mean "the drawer out," but the rest is not contained in the word. Freud adds to this analysis a simple observation: An Egyptian princess would surely not possess a broad knowledge of Hebrew etymology, as she would not know the language in the first place, and so she would be very unlikely to give him a name of particular significance in that language. Furthermore, Freud adds that scholars believe that the water out of which the child was drawn was probably not the Nile.

Assuming that Moses was not a Hebrew name, Freud then quotes other Biblical scholars on a more likely etymology for the name, based on the Egyptian language. In the ancient Egyptian language, "mose" is a word meaning "child" and was a short form of a common form of address for children. The child of Amon, for example, would be referred to as Amen-mose; "Moses" was therefore probably an abridgement of a longer name that would have included the name of his Egyptian father. Further evidence for this comes from the fact that the final *s* in the name is an addition that appeared in the Greek translation of the Old Testament: it is absent in the Hebrew version. Having pointed this out, Freud expresses amazement that, even though many scholars have made this connection and agreed that Moses was a name derived from Egyptian rather than Hebrew, nobody has previously taken the next logical step and determined that perhaps Moses was himself Egyptian. Freud speculates on why this has been the case:

> What hindered them from doing so can only be guessed at. Perhaps the awe of Biblical tradition was insuperable. Perhaps it seemed monstrous to imagine that the man Moses could have been anything other than a Hebrew. In any event, what happened was that the recognition of the name being Egyptian was not a factor in judging the origin of the man Moses, and nothing further was deduced from it. If the question of the nationality of this great man is considered important, then any new material for answering it must be welcome. This is what my little essay attempts. (1939, pp. 14–15)

Having set himself up in this way as taking a groundbreaking approach that nobody else has yet attempted, Freud then humbly acknowledges the earlier work of Otto **Rank,** whose *Myth of the Birth of the Hero* (1909) had actually set the groundwork for a psychoanalytic approach to the story of Moses. Rank begins by treating it as just a single example of a very widespread archetypal myth that appears across many human cultures.

In his book, Rank points out that there seems to be a universal tendency among human societies to endow their great heroes with mysterious origins, and that a single origin story appears, with many variations, in many different religious traditions and mythologies. In the Babylonian story of Sargon the First, for example, the infant Sargon is placed by his mother in a vessel made of reeds that she then places in a river, which carries the infant downriver to be discovered by the father who will raise him as his own. The startling correspondences between story and the Biblical account of Moses should be obvious to anyone raised in, or even slightly familiar with, the Judeo-Christian tradition. Rank acknowledges that the story of Moses and the tale of Sargon are very similar, possessing

> even an almost literal correspondence of individual traits. Already the first chapter relates that Pharaoh commanded his people to throw into the water all sons that were born to Hebrews. . . . The second chapter continues as follows . . . "and the woman conceived, and bare a son. . . . And when she could no longer hide him, she took for him an ark of bulrushes, and daubed it with slime and with pitch, and put the child therein, and she laid it in the flags by the river's brink." (Rank, 1959, p. 17).

Rank then proceeds to describe a similar tale from the ancient Hindu epic *Mahabharata,* concerning the birth of the hero Karna. His mother, the princess Pritha, was a virgin (another recurrent motif, both in Christianity and in the legend of Sargon), who after his birth hid him in a large basket made from rushes, in which he was set adrift down a river. Rank further documents similar elements in the Greek legend of Ion, as well as in the legends of Paris, Telephus, Perseus, Cyrus, Gilgamesh, Romulus and Remus, Hercules, Siegfried, Lohengrin, and Jesus.

Beginning with Rank's establishment of the relatively common nature of the details of Moses's biography, Freud then adds a detail that Rank had not included in his analysis, but which is important for Freud's initial etymological argument. The legend of Sargon, told in the first person, includes the following detail:

> The stream did not drown me, but carried me to Akki, the drawer of water. Akki, the drawer of water, in the goodness of his heart lifted me out of the water. *Akki, the drawer of water, as his own son he brought me up* [italics in original]. Akki, the drawer of water, made me his gardener. (Freud, 1939, p. 17)

With each mention of his rescuer's name, Sargon includes the explanation that the name means "drawer of water." Having demonstrated that the biblical etymology of the name of Moses is probably not correct, here Freud stresses further that the etymology is itself borrowed from another legendary hero's tale.

There are several ways, however, in which the tale of Moses does not fit the usual pattern identified by Rank. In the typical heroic origin story, the hero is the child of high-ranking parents, often the son of a king. During the pregnancy, some sort of prophecy occurs that cautions against his birth and predicts danger to the father, and he is therefore cast off, usually in some sort of box set adrift on water, rather than simply being killed. He is then rescued by humble, poor people, who raise him without knowledge of his royal identity. Eventually, in adulthood, he finds his parents and takes revenge on his father in some way.

The story of Moses follows the bare bones of this myth in some ways, but also violates them in some important ways. Rather than being born of royalty and raised by a mother in humble circumstances, Moses is actually rescued and raised by the royal family, in a major reversal of the usual pattern. His original family, enslaved Jewish Levites, is the family by which as a rule the hero would be brought up. This divergence from the usual pattern has been noticed by previous researchers, Freud points out, and some of those researchers have attempted to explain it by suggesting that the myth originally took a different form. In this original, pre-Biblical version, Pharaoh had been warned by a prophetic dream that his daughter's son would become a danger to him and his kingdom. This is why he has the child delivered to the waters of the Nile shortly after his birth. But the child is saved by Jewish people and brought up as their own. "National motives," in Rank's terminology, had transformed the myth into the form now known by us (Freud, 1939, p. 20).

Freud argues that such an earlier Moses myth, which adhered to the pattern of the other birth myths, could not have possibly existed, for the simple reason that the legend must be of either Egyptian or Jewish origin. Logically, it could not have been Egyptian, for the simple reason that Moses was not a hero to the Egyptians, and they would have had no reason to glorify him. The story therefore originates among the Jews, but the usual legendary pattern is entirely unsuitable to the story:

> If Moses is not of royal lineage our legend cannot make him a hero; if he remains a Jew it has done nothing to raise his status. Only one small feature of the whole myth remains effective: the assurance that the babe survived in spite of strong outside forces to the contrary. . . . So we really have a right to assume that in a later and rather clumsy treatment of the legendary material the adapter saw fit to equip his hero Moses with certain features appertaining to the classical exposure myths characteristic of a hero, and yet unsuited to Moses by reason of the special circumstances. (Freud, 1939, p. 21)

Freud uses this apparent clumsy accommodation of the story of Moses to the traditional heroic narrative to argue for something unexpected: this is clear evidence that Moses actually existed. On a mythical level, the two families are necessary in order to distinguish the noble from the humble family. When the myth has become attached to a historical person, however, one of the great families is the real one into which he was really born and in which he was brought up, and the other one is a fiction created by the myth. Given the probability that the legend is of Jewish rather than Egyptian origin, and it would therefore be beneficial to the legend for

Moses to have been born in humble Jewish circumstances, Freud sees the explanation here as quite straightforward: Moses is an Egyptian, probably of noble origin, who the myth transforms into a Jew. The myth has simply changed a few important specifics, like the intention of the exposure in the water. Rather than being a means of getting rid of a child, it became a means of the child's salvation.

Freud recognized that his idea that Moses was actually Egyptian and yet became the leader of the Jewish people would be seen by many observers as simply wild speculation, with no real evidence, but he proceeded to follow up that idea with further speculations that follow logically from that initial idea. Freud recognizes two difficulties in following up on the initial idea, the first of which is a straightforward riddle:

> But what could have induced a distinguished Egyptian—perhaps a prince, priest, or high official—to place himself at the head of a throng of culturally inferior immigrants, and to leave the country with them, is not easy to conjecture. The well-known contempt of the Egyptians for foreigners makes such a proceeding especially unlikely. (1939, p. 31)

Freud speculates that the difficulty of answering this question is the reason why the historians who have long recognized the name of Moses as Egyptian have failed to even consider the possibility that Moses actually *was* Egyptian. The second obstacle that Freud identifies as standing in his way has to do with Moses's role not just as liberator, but as lawgiver and originator of the Jewish religion:

> But can a single person create a new religion so easily? And when someone wishes to influence the religion of another would not the most natural thing be to convert him to his own? The Jewish people in Egypt were certainly not without some kind of religion, and if Moses, who gave them a new religion, was an Egyptian, then the surmise cannot be rejected that this other new religion was an Egyptian one. (1939, p. 31)

It seems far more likely that Moses would try to convert people to his own religion than that he would create an entirely new one, which inspires the simple objection that the Jewish religion is very different from the Egyptian religion of the time.

In the Jewish religion, there is only one God, unique and omnipotent, the sight of whose countenance cannot be endured and of whom one may neither make an image nor say his name. In the Egyptian pantheism, on the other hand, there are a bewildering variety of deities, some of whom are far more powerful and important than the others, and some of whom are remarkably trivial. Some of the Egyptian gods are personifications of celestial bodies such as the Sun and the Moon, while others represent abstractions like Justice or Truth. There are also many local gods, worshipped only in particular provincial areas, who are not presumed to have power beyond those areas. Furthermore, images of the gods are an important and ubiquitous part of ancient Egyptian culture, and many of these images have the appearance of animals. With so many gods, names and specific features are regularly mixed and matched to produce new, combination gods. Freud gives as an example of this the main god of the city of Thebes, known as Amon-Re, a compound god made up of both the ram-headed city god Amon and the hawk-headed sun god.

There are other striking contrasts between Egyptian pantheism and the monotheistic Jewish religion as well. Freud points out a basic difference in intellectual level, with one religion nearer to primitive totemism, with its animal imagery, while the other "has soared to the heights of sublime abstraction" (1939, p. 33). The Jewish religion severely condemns and punishes any kind of magic or sorcery, while such practices flourished abundantly in Egypt. Also, while one religion bluntly forbids the hubris of pretending to know enough about God to present an image of him, the other is marked by "the insatiable zest of the Egyptian for making images of his gods in clay, stone, and metal, to which our museums owe so much" (Freud, 1939, p. 33). Despite these major distinctions between the two religions, however, Freud presents as the greatest and most significant difference their contrasting attitudes toward immortality. The most popular and indisputable of the Egyptian gods, whose importance was embraced by virtually all Egyptians, was Osiris, the death god. According to Freud, "No other people of antiquity has done so much to deny death, has made such careful provision for an after-life" (1939, p. 33). The incredibly elaborate tombs of the pharaohs, with their many gruesome preparations for life after death, often including large groups of murdered servants so that the king would have his staff with him on the other side, certainly suggest an enormous preoccupation with what comes next after death. By contrast, the early Jewish religion, as represented in the books of Moses, is noteworthy among the world's religions for failing to even mention the possibility of any existence after death. We know, of course, from more recent history that an afterlife is quite readily reconciled with monotheistic religion, but the early Jews appear to have relinquished immortality entirely.

Anticipating the obvious objection that one religion could not have logically grown out of the other, Freud has conceived of a way in which it was plausible, arguing that "It is still possible that the religion Moses gave to his Jewish people was yet his own, *an* Egyptian religion though not *the* Egyptian one" (1939, p. 34). Freud has arrived at this conclusion by considering fairly recent discoveries in the religious history of Egypt, particularly the brief reign of a pharaoh who actually attempted to impose from above a monotheistic religion that was very different from the mainstream of Egyptian observance. The pharaoh in question, who ascended to the throne in 1375BC, was at first known as Amenhotep IV, as he was the successor to his father, Amenhotep III. During his 17-year reign, this king attempted to force on his subjects a new monotheistic religion that ran contrary to all their ancient traditions and all their familiar habits. According to Freud, this religion represented the very first attempt at strict monotheism in human history, and consequently also marked the birth of religious intolerance, which according to Freud was unknown in antiquity, a dubious assertion at best. His reign was long forgotten and lost to history for the simple reason that after his 17 years on the throne, a mere moment in the long recorded history of Egypt, the new religion was promptly swept away and most records were expunged of the deeds of this heretic king.

It is only through the discovery of some ruins of the new capital that Amenhotep IV had built and dedicated to his God, and the inscriptions contained therein, that archaeologists have been able to reconstruct some of what happened during his reign. The young pharaoh did not create his new religion out of nothing; the priests of the Sun God at On (known to the Greeks as Heliopolis) had already been working on the notion of a universal God who particularly cared about ethics. Under Amenhotep III, the worship of the Sun God was already on the rise, and the God became known by the name Aton, or Atum. Amenhotep IV became a worshipper of Aton, worshipping the sun not merely as a material object but as a symbol of a divine being, above all others. Freud points out that his activity was far more radical than this description suggests, however:

> We do scant justice to the king if we see in him only the adherent and protector of an Aton religion which had already existed before him. His activity was much more energetic. He added the something new that turned monotheism into the doctrine of an universal god: the quality of exclusiveness. (1939, p. 37)

Before Amenhotep IV, no religion had joined its emphasis on a particular god to the notion that other gods do not exist. According to Freud, the young pharaoh wrote hymns to his god, two of which survive, which strongly resemble the much later Psalms of the Jewish religion, particularly in expressing a familiar sentiment: "There is no other God than Thou" (1939, p. 38). During his reign, the pharaoh gradually strengthened this idea, against the strong opposition of the priest of Amon, the god who previously held the loyalty of his people, until in the sixth year of his reign he changed his name. His given royal name, Amenhotep, included the name of the now prohibited god among its syllables, so he changed his name to Akhenaton, and also went about eliminating the name of Amon wherever he could from inscriptions, and even from mentions of his own father's name. He also left Thebes, the city of Amon, to establish a new capital, which he called Akhetaton. Now both king and city were named for the new supreme god.

Very little is actually known about Egypt under Akhenaten, as his rule was quite brief and was followed by a period of anarchy that lasted for at least eight years. At the end of this interregnum period, a new dynasty was established, and all evidence of the last pharaoh of the 18th dynasty was allowed to fall into ruin and decay, and the religion of Aton vanished again from Egypt. Freud's novel historical argument about the origins of the Jews and their religion therefore starts with a simple premise: Moses was an Egyptian of high rank, close to the pharaoh, and he lived during Akhenaten's reign. This premise is supported by Biblical accounts, which do place Moses in close contact with the pharaoh, even in his household, but fail to indicate *which* pharaoh. Freud describes this important initial assumption thus:

> Let us assume that Moses was a noble and distinguished man; perhaps indeed a member of the royal house, as the myth has it. He must have been conscious of his great abilities, ambitious and energetic; perhaps he saw himself in a dim future as the leader of his people, the governor of the Empire . . . he was a convinced adherent of the new religion, whose basic principles he fully understood and had made his own. (1939, p. 46)

Upon the king's death, this ambitious man found himself without prospects in a land where he could only remain by recanting his dearly held religious convictions. Recognizing that there was no place in Egypt for him any longer, Moses conceived the plan of finding a new people to whom he could give his now-unwelcome, alien religion and founding a new empire. Freud further speculates, by his own admission without any evidence, that Moses might have been at the time the governor of the border province of Goshen, where Semitic people had already settled, and therefore chose the Semites as his people via a simple historical accident. In defense of some of the more unlikely elements of this account, Freud quotes historical sources beyond the Bible to suggest that the idea that Moses may have been both a prince and a priest is not all that unlikely, given what other historians had to say about him. The Roman historian Flavius Josephus, for example, describes the infancy of Moses as depicted in the Bible, but also presents him in later life as an Egyptian military field marshal, fighting in Ethiopia.

Beginning with the idea of Moses as an Egyptian leader of a province inhabited by Semitic people, rather than as the rescuer of his own enslaved people, Freud then makes a suggestion which follows quite logically from that premise, but which sounds quite foreign to any reader who has grown up with the Bible's version of this piece of history:

> In full contradistinction to the Biblical tradition we may suppose this Exodus to have passed off peacefully and without pursuit. The authority of Moses made it possible, and there was then no central power that could have prevented it. (1939, pp. 47–48)

According to Freud, the people most closely related to the Semitic tribes in Egypt had already settled in Canaan, thus making that place the logical destination for Moses and his people. That region had also recently been overrun by a people known as the Arameans, about whom little was known until some letters were found in 1887 in the ruined city of Amarna. In those letters, the Arameans are referred to as the Habiru, a name that was later passed on through unknown means to the new arrivals, who became known as the Hebrews.

As for the religion imparted to the travelers by their leader, Freud points out several reasons to consider the possibility that the Jewish religion began as the cult of Aton, the Sun God. In the banishment of sorcery and magic, the absence of any known personal representations of the Sun God, and the complete silence about Osiris and the afterlife, it is clear that _if_ Moses was an Egyptian, and _if_ he passed along his religion to the Jews, then that religion was surely the religion of Aton. Freud points out that direct comparison between the Mosaic religion and that of Aton is difficult, because the Egyptians so thoroughly eradicated the evidence of Aton, and therefore any similarities that can nonetheless be established between the two are especially significant. To establish this correspondence, Freud starts with the basic Jewish creed, which in Hebrew reads as "Shema Yisroel Adonai Elohenu Adonai Echod," and is generally transcribed in English as "Hear Israel, the Lord our God, the Lord is One," or "Hear Israel, Our God is the Only God." Freud points out the similarity between the Egyptian name Aton and the Hebrew word Adonai, as well as the Syrian divine name Adonis, and suggests that this "is not a mere accident, but is the result of a primeval unity in language and meaning" (1939, p. 42), which would allow the alternative translation of _Adonai_ as "Our god Aton." Freud realizes the weakness of this argument, however, and immediately reminds the reader that he is unqualified to answer the questions thus raised, moving on to the next point of his argument.

Freud points out that the complete absence of Sun worship from the Jewish religion, despite its presence in the religion of Aton, is actually an argument in favor of the roots of one in the other, since the religion of Aton arose in quite deliberate antagonism of the popular religion. To Freud, it makes sense therefore that the new religion would eliminate major elements of its predecessor, as a result of retaining that element of rebellion against what was already established. It is because of this same element that both religions, that of Aton and that of Moses, leave out discussion of an afterlife, since the emphasis on death was the most important part of the Egyptian pantheist religion. In addition to the new religion, Freud argues that it is quite certain that Moses introduced another custom: circumcision. Freud acknowledges that this is an argument that contradicts the Biblical account, in which the custom is presented as dating back only to Abraham, as a sign of the covenant with God. The Bible is nothing if not internally contradictory, however, and Freud makes use of another, more obscure passage (Exodus 4:18–31) in which, _before the_

Exodus, God threatens Moses with death for not following the rule on circumcision himself; Moses only escapes death by quickly being circumcised by his wife. Although this passage indicates an earlier origin of circumcision, however, Freud dismisses the Biblical argument as irrelevant in the face of a simple historical fact: according to Herodotus, circumcision was a long-standing practice in Egypt by the time of Moses, and yet no other people in that part of the world followed the custom at the time. Even in Biblical accounts it is made clear that circumcision was not yet the practice in Canaan at the time of the arrival of Moses's people. Clearly, since circumcision was customary in Egypt but not among the Semites, the custom must have been introduced by Moses, who by the same logic was plainly Egyptian.

In addition to the foregoing arguments, one last piece of Freud's case for an Egyptian Moses comes directly from the traits attributed to Moses in the Bible. Moses is described as being "slow of speech," suggestive of some sort of speech impediment, to such a degree that he required the assistance of Aaron in his discussions with the pharaoh. After suggesting that such a description may represent simple historical truth, Freud then proposes an alternative interpretation:

> The report may, in a slightly distorted way, recall the fact that Moses spoke another language and was not able to communicate with his Semitic Neo-Egyptians without the help of an interpreter—at least not at the beginning of their intercourse. Thus a fresh confirmation of the thesis: Moses was an Egyptian. (1939, p. 54)

Having made his arguments for the Egyptian origins of both Moses and the Jewish religion, Freud then spends many additional pages on his interpretation of the rest of the early history of the Jewish people, in which one particular new interpretation was quite controversial: the peaceful death of Moses in the Bible is replaced by Freud's conjecture that his people, tired of all the laws and restrictions imposed on them, actually rose up and killed him.

Keeping in mind the general structure of the history of religion presented by Freud in the much earlier *Totem and Taboo: Some Points of Agreement between the Mental Lives of Savages and Neurotics,* this development is unsurprising, as it is a necessary stage in the religion's development. Freud saw religions and cultures developing out of the same basic mechanisms that drive child development during the period of the Oedipus complex. The child during that stage loves and identifies with his father, but also hates and wishes to eliminate him. A key force in driving later development is the guilt and shame that arise from those feelings, and Freud argued in *Totem and Taboo* that civilization, and religion, began with rebellious sons rising up and killing their father. The guilt they felt over their actions then caused them to revere and venerate him, and ultimately led to the social structure that made civilization possible. In *Moses and Monotheism,* Freud simply imposes that basic blueprint on the early Jews: it is because of guilt over killing Moses that they later venerated him and transformed his actual life history into the account provided in the Old Testament.

Freud's suggestion that Moses was murdered is not simply his invention, in order to support his own theory, but rather comes from respected scholarship, especially the work of the Biblical scholar Sellin, who explored hints in the book of Hosea of a traditional teaching that Moses was killed by his people and his religion temporarily abandoned. Sellin further argues that references to this tradition appear in the books of most of the later prophets and was the basis of all later teachings regarding the expectation of a Messiah:

> Towards the end of the Babylonian exile the hope arose among the Jewish people that the man they had so callously murdered would return from the realm of the dead and lead his contrite people—and perhaps not only his people—into the land of eternal bliss. (Freud, 1939, p. 59)

According to Sellin, in other words, the Messianic hope among the Jews originated as a wish that Moses himself would rise from the dead and again lead his people, who were quite ashamed of their role in his death.

When other Jewish scholars caught wind of what Freud was working on in the waning months of his life, he encountered immediate resistance to the publication of his arguments, for fairly simple reasons. At a time when the old anti-Semitic currents in European society had led to the rise of the Nazis, it seemed like a bad idea to publish a book arguing that Moses not only was not Jewish, but that he had been murdered by his own people, the same people who had just spent nearly two millenia being blamed by Christians for the death of the founder of *their* religion. Indeed, when the book was published, it received many negative reviews, and it has often been accused of contributing to precisely that anti-Semitism that it sought to explain and understand. Freud's response to the negative reviews was to largely ignore them, enjoy the strong sales, and praise his own work as "a worthy exit," which it certainly was, with some very profound things to say about the role of monotheism, and of the Jews, in the advancement of world civilization.

After all of the historical speculation and alternate biography of Moses, which are necessary to make the point he ultimately wishes to make, Freud arrives at the true centerpiece of his argument, which is that the Jews, *because of* their religion, have been of great consequence in world history. The truly distinctive thing about the Jewish religion is not just its monotheism, but the fact that its one true god is invisible to his followers, which Freud saw as a direct consequence of its probable origins in the Egyptian cult of Aton. Prior to Aton, Egyptian worship, along with religion in other regions, focused on gods made visible by many statues, carvings, and other representations, who consequently took on the earthly, and distinctly nonomnipotent, physical, and personality traits of the animals, people, and objects in whose image they were cast. Judaism's true distinction as a faith arises from its commitment to belief in an invisible god, from which many important consequences follow.

Taking an invisible God into the mind marked a real evolutionary leap in human intellect, as the ability to believe in an invisible, internalized God requires the capacity for abstraction, and so doing that improved that human capacity quite dramatically. Freud describes the prohibition against making an image of God as also meaning a compulsion to worship an invisible God, and presents it as the most significant precept of the early Mosaic religion:

> If this prohibition was accepted, however, it was bound to exercise a profound influence. For it signified subordinating sense perception to an abstract idea; it was a triumph of spirituality over the senses; more precisely an instinctual renunciation accompanied by its psychologically necessary consequences. (1939, pp. 178–179)

Despite being an atheist, Freud sees the acceptance of spiritual forces that cannot be seen as a key moment in human history, because it made the life of the mind, the intellectual pursuits, just as important as pursuits with more obvious physical consequences in the world. Very simply, if people can worship what is not physically present, they can also *reflect* on things that are not present, or on things that must be represented in purely symbolic terms. This mental labor required by monotheism prepared the Jews, and eventually others in the West as well, for the development of mathematics, law, ethics, science, and literature, along with all other activities that require an abstract or nonrepresentational model of human experience.

Freud is arguing nothing less than that the Jewish people, because of their religion, laid much of the foundation for the rise of Western civilization, an argument that is strengthened further by Freud's analysis of the roots of anti-Semitism. Although much anti-Semitism has its roots in treating Jews as outsiders and nomads who are interfering with a dominant culture, Freud points out that in many of the places where they have been treated that way, the Jews have actually been present longer than the people who treat them as intruders. In Cologne, for example, archaeologists find evidence of Jewish settlers, which predates by a substantial margin the evidence of occupation by Germanic tribes. In fact, according to Freud,

> We know that of all the peoples who lived in antiquity in the basin of the Mediterranean the Jewish people is perhaps the only one that still exists in name and probably also in nature. With an unexampled power of resistance it has defied misfortune and ill-treatment, developed special character traits, and, incidentally, earned the hearty dislike of all other peoples. (1939, p. 166)

The sentence that follows this praise of the Jewish people's resilience is a prime example, however, of the ways in which Freud's observations in *Moses and Monotheism* have been able to be quite readily taken out of context as moments where Freud blames the Jews for their own troubles. "Whence comes this resistance of the Jew, and *how his character is connected with his fate* [italics mine]," writes Freud, "are things one would like to understand better" (1939, p. 166). Freud follows this statement with a quick enumeration of character traits possessed by the Jews, which influence their relationship with other people:

> There is no doubt that they have a very good opinion of themselves, think themselves nobler, on a higher level, superior to the others from whom they are also separated by many of their customs. With this they are animated by a special trust in life, such as is bestowed by the secret possession of a precious gift; it is a kind of optimism. Religious people would call it trust in God. (1939, p. 167)

Freud follows this up by reminding the reader that the secret gift alluded to here is the strong belief that they are God's chosen people, which of course leads them to be proud and confident. This passage, given the time in which it was published, has unfortunately been widely regarded as an instance of blaming the Jews for their own present-day troubles, when in fact Freud's objective was very different—it was to find in his praise of the Jews the reasons why such prejudice has persisted for so very long.

Anti-Semitism, according to Freud, is a very old force in Western society: even in the Hellenistic period, Jews living among the Greeks behaved in the same way as they do in the modern era, and the Greeks reacted in much the same way as the dominant peoples in various countries react today. Drawing on psychoanalytic theory, Freud proposes that the anti-Semitic reaction has its roots not in the fact that the Jews have different beliefs, but rather in jealousy and in the same ambivalent feelings toward one's father that characterize the Oedipal conflict in children:

> They reacted, so one might think, as if they too believed in the preference which the Israelites claimed for themselves. When one is the declared favourite of the dreaded father one need not be surprised that the other brothers and sisters are jealous (1939, p. 167).

A lot of anti-Semitism is therefore the indirect, but psychoanalytically predictable, product of the sense of exceptionality that Moses imposed on his people. He gave them great self-confidence by telling them that they were the chosen people of the only God, and he further gave them the duty of keeping apart from others. All nations and peoples think themselves special or even superior to all others, but with the Jewish people this feeling gained the additional anchor of religion, making it that much stronger, and also making their superiority an article of faith for any others who accept the teachings of their religion.

Freud notes the irony surrounding this last idea, particularly regarding the rise of Christianity:

> When later on God consented to send mankind a Messiah and Redeemer He again chose him from among the Jewish people. The other peoples would then have had reason to say: "Indeed, they were right; they are God's chosen people." Instead of which it happened that the salvation through Jesus Christ brought on the Jews nothing but a stronger hatred, while the Jews themselves derived no advantage from this second proof of being favoured, because they did not recognize the Redeemer. (1939, p. 168)

Far from providing support for the anti-Semites, Freud's analysis is firmly based not in criticizing the Jews but rather in attempting to elucidate how they, secure in what he appears to be honestly describing as their superiority, might be seen by others. His choice of language is often deliberately provocative, however, as in his description of Jewish characteristics that are "quite unpardonable": the first of these traits is that they are simply different from the majorities in the various countries in which they live. The differences are often small, and quite difficult to detect, but as Freud astutely observes, "racial intolerance finds stronger expression, strange to say, in regard to small differences than to fundamental ones" (1939, p. 146). Beyond being different, their second and more important peculiarity is simply their resilience in the face of adversity:

> It is that they defy oppression, that even the most cruel persecutions have not succeeded in exterminating them. On the contrary, they show a capacity for holding their own in practical life and, where they are admitted, they make valuable contributions to the surrounding civilization. (Freud, 1939, p. 146)

It is clear to the careful reader that in calling these characteristics "unpardonable," Freud is mocking the point of view of the anti-Semites, not supporting them, yet his final book is still sometimes employed to support, through selective quotation, the notion that Freud disavowed his Jewish identity or was in some way a self-loathing Jew. The truth is quite different, obviously: in the final statement of a career marked from the beginning by the struggle against anti-Semitism, Freud attempted to explain the degree to which all of Western civilization owes a great debt not just to Jews, but to their religion in particular, while attempting to explain the anti-Semitism along the way.

Further Reading

Freud, S. (1939). *Moses and Monotheism.* London: Hogarth Press.

Rank, O. (1959). *The Myth of the Birth of the Hero and Other Writings* (Philip Freund, ed.). New York: Vintage.

Murray, Henry (1893–1988)

Henry Murray was an American psychologist and psychoanalyst who is perhaps best known as the originator of the Thematic Apperception Test (TAT), one of the most popular and widely administered **projective tests of personality**. Given his circuitous educational and professional path, however, that he eventually found himself recognized as a psychiatrist and leading personality theorist at all is fairly remarkable. He was the first to admit that he had almost nothing in common with most of his professional colleagues, a majority of whom actually had psychology or psychiatry in mind when they began their educations. Murray, on the other hand, only signed up for a single psychology course while he was a Harvard undergraduate. It was an introductory psychology class taught by Hugo Munsterberg, and he dropped out of the class after only two lectures.

Partly as an act of rebellion against his aristocratic family's holdings in the insurance business, Murray followed his time at Harvard by entering medical school at Columbia in 1915, graduating with his MD in 1919. His plans of becoming a surgeon were destroyed by his poor eyesight, however, and so he went into medical research instead. He undertook the study of human physiology with George Draper, who would prove quite influential via his conviction that many physical ailments were actually psychological in origin, and that the psychological factors responsible for illness had physical manifestations, thus insights into personality could be gained by examining physical characteristics.

His work on calcium metabolism under Draper led to a master's degree in biology from Columbia (earned *after* the MD), after which Murray returned to Harvard to study for yet another degree, this one in biochemistry. Following this work, Murray accepted a two-year medical internship in a hospital, while continuing his active involvement in biochemistry research, including some influential work on early embryonic development of chickens. Although his educational background seems atypical for a psychiatrist, much less a psychoanalyst, it was actually his continuing participation in the Rockefeller Institute for Medical Research (again, primarily in biochemistry) that led to his interest in personality psychology. Specifically, he became fascinated by the ongoing debates between two other researchers over how to interpret their data. One felt that all functions of living organisms were best seen as the result of rigid, mechanistic, deterministic biochemical processes, whereas his colleague felt that this approach to science ignored the equally important spiritual

Henry Murray, whose Thematic Apperception Test (TAT) became one of the most
frequently administered projective tests of
personality, 1962. (AP Photo)

and psychological sides of life. Murray was fascinated and confused by this argument, given that both men were discussing the same basic data, and decided that the explanation for this difference must be psychological.

While puzzling over this dilemma, Murray happened upon a copy of Jung's *Psychological Types* (1923) in a bookstore, and immediately took it home and spent the next two days reading and absorbing it. In the book, Jung describes eight distinct types of people, each with his own characteristic way of coping with the demands of his environment. In this, Murray thought he may have found some insight into the conflict between his colleagues. Murray's fascination with this idea altered the course of his life—he started by reading all of Jung's works that were available in translation, followed by Freud's, and he began attending classes on psychology and psychoanalysis in New York when he wasn't busy with his other activities. In 1924, he went so far as to contact Jung and ask if he could come to Switzerland and discuss psychology with him—Jung affirmed the invitation. As Murray was still also heavily involved in biochemistry research, he decided to take a leave from his position with the Rockefeller Institute to go earn a PhD in biochemistry at Trinity College, Cambridge. While there, he reasoned, he could also travel over to Zurich and meet with Jung. On a three-week break from his PhD research on cell metabolism in embryos, he met with Jung and heard about his recent work on the *anima,* or feminine side of personality. Armed with new insight into his own psyche, Murray resolved to abandon biochemistry and devote his career to psychology, but only after first completing the Cambridge degree and publishing three more articles on biochemistry.

Upon his return to America, Murray was quickly appointed as research assistant to the director of the newly founded Harvard Psychological Clinic, and in 1928 he took over as its director, an appointment that also carried with it a position as assistant professor of psychology. His time there was often controversial, at least from the point of view of the academics in Harvard's psychology department, because of his open advocacy of psychoanalysis as the only approach to psychology that promised a thorough understanding of human nature. He promoted this position in a hostile environment focused on far more empirical approaches—during his first several years there, for example, one of Harvard's star hires in psychology was Karl Lashley. Lashley is today best known for his efforts to demonstrate, through systematic removal of tissue from animal brains, that memories are distributed evenly across the cortex rather than localized. Lashley's approach is fairly typical of the mechanistic determinism that was popular at the time. While Murray advocated a holistic, psychodynamically oriented approach to explaining behavior, the other psychological researchers at Harvard emphasized rigorous empirical methods in which the action of a single variable should be examined at a time. Because of this, the department was divided in 1936 when Murray's case for tenure was under consideration, and the decision to retain him was ultimately made by the college president, as the department could reach no consensus.

In 1938, Murray published *Explorations in Personality,* in which he finally presented his own psychoanalytically influenced theory of personality, along with an introduction to the Thematic Apperception Test. In Murray's theory, influenced by his involvement with both Draper and Jung, personality results from the interaction between people's needs and the influences of their environment, which he called *press.* He divided needs into primary and secondary needs. Primary needs resemble Freud's basic instinctual drives—the need for air, food, water, and avoidance of pain. Secondary, or psychogenic, needs are psychological in nature; though unnecessary for survival, they drive human behavior and interact with environmental press. Murray listed a total of 27 psychogenic needs, which he later reduced to the following 20:

- Abasement: Surrender and submission to others, acceptance of punishment.
- Achievement: To overcome obstacles and succeed.
- Affiliation: To be close to others; to make associations and friendships.
- Aggression: To forcefully overcome and defeat others; to injure others.
- Autonomy: To resist others, to break free of constraints; to be independent.
- Counteraction: To make up for failure, to try again, to defend honor.
- Defendance: To justify actions; to defend oneself against blame, to hide failure.
- Deference: To follow, yield to, or serve a superior.
- Dominance: To control and lead others, through persuasion or command.
- Exhibition: To attract attention.
- Harm avoidance: To avoid or escape pain, injury, death.
- Infavoidance: To avoid failure, shame, humiliation, or to conceal a weakness.
- Nurturance: To protect the helpless from danger.

- Order: To arrange, organize, and be precise, neat, and tidy.
- Play: To relieve tension, have fun, or relax and enjoy oneself.
- Rejection: To exclude, reject, or separate from someone seen as inferior.
- Sentience: To seek and enjoy sensuous impressions and experiences.
- Sex: To form and enjoy a sexual relationship.
- Succorance: To seek satisfaction of one's needs. To be loved, forgiven, consoled.
- Understanding: To be curious; to analyze and experience, to seek knowledge.

Murray distinguished between manifest needs, which are made apparent by people's actions, and latent needs, which are not openly displayed. The pattern of interaction between needs and environmental press, which determines personality and therefore behavior, he called the *thema*.

As a psychoanalytic theorist, Murray predictably focused on the importance of the latent needs, which are neither openly displayed nor necessarily accessible to a person's conscious awareness. Evaluating these needs therefore required a new kind of assessment, which Murray developed with Christina Morgan in the mid-1930s. The Thematic Apperception Test was the resulting attempt to measure the *thema. Apperception* refers here to the process of projecting unconscious and/or fantasy imagery onto an objective, neutral stimulus. The test consists of a series of pictures, including pen-and-ink drawings, charcoal art, and photographs, printed on large cards. For each image, the person being tested is asked to tell a story describing what is going on in the picture, including what went before and what will happen next, with special attention paid to what the characters in the pictures are saying. As with all **projective tests of personality**, the underlying hypothesis is that people's interpretations of neutral or abstract stimuli will provide insight into unconscious motivations.

In his research, Murray was particularly concerned with the needs for dominance, aggression, and achievement, perhaps due in part to his work for the U.S. government during World War II. When the United States joined the conflict in 1941, he left Harvard to serve in the Army Medical Corps, but was quickly recruited into the nascent Office of Strategic Services (OSS), the precursor to the modern Central Intelligence Agency (CIA), as a lieutenant colonel. In his work for the OSS, he pioneered the use of personality testing in job candidate selection, helping both the U.S. and British governments refine their process of selecting agents for espionage assignments. In 1943, Murray was asked by OSS founder "Wild Bill" Donovan to write a report titled *Analysis of the Personality of Adolph Hitler: With Predictions of His Future Behavior and Suggestions for Dealing with Him Now and After Germany's Surrender.* The report was based on information from a wide variety of sources, including biographies of Hitler, Hitler's own writings, print and film records of Hitler's speeches, and OSS assets, and the resulting profile was remarkable in its prescience: in it, Murray correctly predicted that Hitler would commit suicide if Germany's defeat became inevitable. Less clear is the accuracy of another speculation in the same report—that Hitler was probably impotent in heterosexual relations, and may have engaged in at least one homosexual relationship. With this document, along with his earlier work, Murray was instrumental both in establishing personality testing as a scientific part of psychology and in starting the field of offender profiling. Murray was the first psychologist to profile criminals for the government's intelligence agencies, but they have been employed there ever since.

Further Reading

Murray, H. A. (1938). *Explorations in Personality.* New York: Oxford University Press.

Murray, H. A. (1943). *Analysis of the Personality of Adolph Hitler: With Predictions of His Future Behavior and Suggestions for Dealing with Him Now and After Germany's Surrender.* Online resource of the Cornell University Law Library. http://library.lawschool.cornell.edu/WhatWeHave/SpecialCollections/Donovan/Hitler/Hitler-TOC.cfm.

Triplet, R. G. (1992). Henry A. Murray: The Making of a Psychologist? *American Psychologist* 47(2): 299–307.

National Socialist German Workers' Party (Nazis)

One of the factors that contributed greatly to the spread of psychoanalytic ideas to areas of the world beyond the immediate environs of Germany and Austria was, ironically, the rise of the Nazi Party to power in Germany in the late 1920s and early 1930s. Because of the party's explicit embrace of anti-Semitism in its proposed policies, it soon became clear to Jewish scholars, a group that included many of the leading lights of psychoanalysis, that they were unwelcome and eventually in grave danger in their own homeland. Especially following Hitler's rise to power, many psychoanalysts fled to various other countries, including the United States. One of the last of the big names to actually leave was Freud himself, who was finally convinced to leave Vienna for London when the Nazis occupied the city in 1938. His escape was only made possible at that time by the political and financial intervention of his friend Princess Marie **Bonaparte**.

Anti-Semitism had long been a potent force in the culture of Germany and Austria, but since the end of World War I, the German people had been deeply unhappy, and the Jews made an excellent scapegoat for their problems. The war ended in November 1918, and the acceptance of an armistice infuriated many Germans who had been involved in the war effort. Kaiser Wilhelm's war effort had overreached rather dramatically, especially once American resources were joined to those of Germany's opponents. Germany ended the war with massive human, material, and territorial losses. More than two million of Germany's young adult men had been killed and millions more injured. The war had lasted far longer than the government had anticipated, and the war effort had nearly depleted the nation's resources and destroyed its financial system, leading to extremely high inflation. The dissatisfaction of the German people with how things had turned out grew tremendously, however, with the Treaty of Versailles, signed in June 1919. The armistice occurred at a time when it had become clear to all involved that Germany could not possibly win the war, but the German soldiers had not actually been defeated on the battlefield. In signing the treaty, the German delegation agreed to be treated as a vanquished power and accepted full and solitary responsibility for the war, accepted significant territorial losses, and agreed to pay reparations to the victorious nations for their wartime economic losses. This was a source of great resentment among Germans across the political spectrum. The reparation costs were massive, placing a tremendous fiscal burden on the German people—except for the period of the Nazi ascendancy, the German government continued to pay until the debt was paid off, which finally happened in the fall of 2010. The reasons for which the Jews were somehow held responsible for the nation's troubles are complicated and often confusing and may stem from the general confusion and frustration of the time.

This was a time of great flux in German government: in November 1918, only two days before the armistice brought the war to an end, Kaiser Wilhelm II abdicated the throne, bringing the Second Empire (Reich) to an end. Germany became a republic, with a temporary caretaker government installed under the Socialist Friedrich Ebert. On December 30, the German Communist Party, known as the KPD, was founded, as part of a larger movement across Europe of the ideas of Karl Marx, most notably in their application in Moscow. Following the example of the Bolsheviks in Russia, in January 1919, an unsuccessful Communist uprising occurred in Berlin, and in April a short-lived Munich Soviet Republic was briefly established. In the midst of all of this, the Treaty of Versailles was signed, but it wasn't until August 1919 that the German central government had a clear structure to follow again, with the adoption of the constitution of the Weimar Republic. The great hope of the war's victors was that by replacing the Kaiser's monarchy with a parliamentary democracy in which the various German states retained some autonomy the political upheavals in Germany could quickly settle back down to some semblance of stable, normal life. Despite the establishment of the Weimar government, however, the unrest continued, with a coup attempt, known as the Kapp-Lüttwitz putsch, occurring in March 1920 in Berlin, followed by multiple additional Communist insurrections in March and April. Additional, sporadic Communist coup attempts continued into 1923. Many rank-and-file Germans were frightened by these ongoing developments, as they hoped that the Weimar republican government would return some peace and financial stability to their lives. Because many of the prime movers in the Russian revolution were Jewish, as were some of the leaders of the German Communists, many people began to think of Communism as a Jewish idea, and thus began to blame the Jews for the continuing unrest and chaos. The German nation was ready for the rise of a political party that still sought to represent the common German working man, but without any affiliation with the Communists, and the anti-Semitism, which had long been a part of the culture, was strengthened in many by the perceived Communist-Jewish connection.

Origins of the Party

The Nazi Party came into being in February 1919, as the Deutsche Arbeiterpartei (German Workers' Party), founded not by Adolf Hitler, its most famous leader, but rather by the nearly forgotten Munich toolmaker Anton Drexler. Hitler did not join the party until September 1919, but within two years he had been made chairman and given authoritarian, nearly dictatorial power over the party. In 1920, the party became the *N*ationalso*z*ialistische Deutsche Arbeiterpartei, or National Socialist German Workers' Party, modeled on Benito Mussolini's Fascist Party in several key ways. Like the Italian organization, the Nazi Party had both a political and a paramilitary wing. Like Mussolini, Hitler intended to overthrow the democratic government by means of an armed coup d'état, and so in the party's early years, the paramilitary wing, known as the Sturmabteilung, or Storm Troopers (frequently abbreviated as the SA), was the more important of the two. The Nazis had no difficulty attracting recruits to the organization, largely because of how long World War I had gone on. The surviving soldiers made up a lost generation, a group of war veterans accustomed to violence and mayhem in their everyday lives, who had a very difficult time adjusting to life in peacetime. Joining paramilitary groups like the Stormtroopers offered them the discipline, adventure, and camaraderie they had lost with the end of the war. These men tended to be deeply nationalistic, and as a group they also tended, like Hitler himself, to feel that their efforts on behalf of their country had been betrayed by the signing of the Treaty of Versailles. The other branch of the party was important as well; Early on, Hitler also used the political wing, along with his considerable oratorical abilities, quite effectively to attract new members to both the party and the SA, so it was not long before the party began to grow beyond its roots as a primarily Bavarian organization.

By 1923, Hitler's charismatic speeches had already swollen the party's ranks to 55,000 members, while the SA was 15,000 strong. In addition to the Nazi Party's own SA, Hitler found himself appointed head of the *Kampfbund,* or Combat League, an umbrella organization for the various right-wing paramilitary groups that had arisen, including the Stormtroopers. The first attempt to use these forces to pursue the coup strategy against the Weimar Republic occurred in November 1923, with the action known as the Hitler Putsch, or the Beer Hall Putsch. The Bavarian government, unhappy with actions taken by the Weimar government in its dealings with France, declared a state of emergency and gave its own leader dictatorial power. In response, the Weimar government also declared a state of emergency and gave full executive powers to the head of the *Reichswehr* (army), who tried to force the Bavarian government to ban the Nazi Party newspaper. In the ensuing power struggle, Hitler enlisted the head of the Bavarian government and some of its military leaders to join him, after the Stormtroopers surrounded a beer hall in Munich and Hitler proclaimed to the gathered crowd that the revolution had begun. The coup was stopped quite efficiently, ending almost before it had begun, when the local army units refused to join with Hitler's forces and the Bavarian leaders reneged on their promise to support him. Hitler and several of his associates were arrested and tried on charges of high treason, a charge that under most governments, under most circumstances throughout human history, would result in a death sentence. Hitler's judges sympathized with the Nazi cause, however, and gave him the remarkably lenient sentence of five years in prison instead. Imprisoned under relatively comfortable conditions at the fortress of Landsberg, Hitler was paroled after a mere nine months in jail, during which he wrote the book that brought many more sympathizers to the Nazi cause, *Mein Kampf (My Struggle)*.

Hitler was unable to continue running the Nazi Party from jail, however, and so during his imprisonment they broke apart into warring factions. Upon Hitler's release, he dealt with the divisions in a very straightforward manner: refusing to identify with *any* of the feuding splinter groups, he instead set about reorganizing the entire party from the bottom up. As with any reorganization of a political body, there was much that remained the same. Along with the swastika emblem and the name of the party, many of Hitler's close associates who had held positions of power in the old organization were also at his side in the new one. The most important change was in the emphasis placed on different party goals, with a clear shift from a paramilitary strategy to a political strategy. Hitler now understood, for example, that overthrowing the Weimar Republic by force was not going to work, and so emphasis was shifted from the SA to the party's political machine. Rather than forming a formidable military force, Hitler was determined to turn the party into a national organization that would embrace democracy, at least at first, and get more votes than anyone else. This shift of focus only resulted in a small reduction in the importance of the SA, however: they merely changed their emphasis from overthrowing the government to guarding Nazi Party rallies and engaging in political violence against the party's political enemies. The Nazi Party's apparent embrace of democracy was half-hearted at best, given their continuing willingness to use violence to improve their odds at the ballot box.

The Twenty-Five Points

In the wake of the failed coup, and as the Nazi Party set out to win hearts and minds nationwide, or at least to intimidate them, there came a renewed emphasis on clarifying their political policy goals, which they had actually laid out quite explicitly years earlier. In 1920, the German Workers Party adopted what would become the Nazi Party program, generally known in later years as the Twenty-Five Points. This document laid out the guidelines by which the Nazis proposed to restore Germany to its former greatness, and in 1925, after the failed coup led the party to redouble its political efforts, Hitler responded to demands to produce a more detailed document by proclaiming the 1920 document to be "unalterable," a promise he kept except for an April 1928 reinterpretation of the 17th item: where the party had originally demanded the government takeover of all landed estates, the 1928 version of this measure applied only to estates owned by Jews.

The program was not merely Hitler's plan, but rather the result of work by Hitler and three other party members, each with his own points that he was particularly interested in including. Where the other authors, particularly Gottfried Feder and Alfred Rosenberg, saw the plan as a serious set of guidelines for future legislation, some scholars now believe that Hitler was interested in the program primarily for its propaganda value. Many of the platform's individual planks were clearly designed to reflect and respond to the wishes and resentments of the German Workers' Party's primary target audience at its inception: skilled workers, civil servants, and lower middle-class artisans. The actual contents of the plan clearly reflect the overall Nazi message, and the concerns of the everyday citizen of Post-Treaty of Versailles Germany, divided into three categories: nationalist demands, *Völkisch* (populist) and anti-Semitic sentiments, and social and economic proposals. Some histories of the Nazi movement have suggested that the anti-Semitic attitudes that became the defining feature of so much of what they later did were added later for their scapegoating and propaganda value, but as a quick reading of the 25 points makes quite clear, those ideas were integral to the Nazi message right from the start.

The first of the 25 points insists on the inclusion of all ethnic Germans in a Great German Reich, or Empire, and focuses on the need for more living space (lebensraum), which can presumably be regained in part by taking it from people other than ethnic Germans. This point is echoed in point number two, essentially a diatribe against the Treaty of Versailles, which took away lands occupied by Germany. The treaty is described as invalid on the basis of the equal rights of the German people to the citizens of other nations, which were abrogated by the treaty. The third point is a straightforward demand for the return of Germany's colonies. In the guise of a *Völkisch* agenda, a populist movement in support of the proletarian German folk, multiple points adopted a specifically anti-Semitic tone, seeking to return the *völk* to their rightful place by stripping German Jews, who though German belonged to a different ethnic group than the pure Germans, of their political rights and what was seen by the Nazis as their excessive power in German public life. The fourth proposal in the program calls for removing Jews' German citizenship, as they are not members of the race, while point five requires that they be treated as resident aliens, "under legislation for foreigners." The sixth point reserves the right of holding public office for citizens, thus rendering it impossible for a Jew to hold such an office. According to point seven, if the Reich is unable to provide a good living for everyone, then all noncitizens, who would of course include all Jews according to the rules already listed, should be expelled. The eighth point takes the seventh a small step further, demanding that all foreigner citizens, including Jews, who have emigrated to Germany since the start of World War I, should be expelled immediately. Responding to the long-standing anti-Semitic myth that Jews controlled the international press, the program further demanded that all editors of newspapers published in Germany had to be members of the German race. In the 24th piece of the platform, the party demands freedom of religion for all denominations so long as their teachings do not endanger the state or offend the moral sensibilities of the German race, a clause that again excludes the Jews effectively from participation in German life. More explicitly, this proposal advocates a "positive Christianity," without favoring any particular denomination, as a counterbalance to the "Jewish materialistic spirit," which threatened the state and upon the elimination of which a lasting recovery of the nation depended.

The suggestion is sometimes made that anti-Semitism became a part of the Nazi agenda as the party gained power, because the Jews made a convenient scapegoat and villain: examination of the program makes it very clear that from the very beginning, anti-Semitism was at the core of the Nazi agenda and formed a crucial part of the party's ultimate goals for the nation.

Beyond the various nationalistic and anti-Semitic clauses, the Nazi Program also laid out a set of social and economic policies intended to repair Germany's ruinous post–World War I economy. Despite their frequent attacks on Marxism, which they viewed as a Jewish idea, a quick examination of the economic policies proposed by the Nazis reveals that the National Socialist Party took the Socialist in their name quite seriously, and the policies are therefore not all that different from what the Communists were elsewhere proposing. The National Socialist economic proposals consist primarily of a combination of state takeovers and the promise of extra government benefits to the lower middle class. Some proposals are fairly extreme, as in the demand made in point 18 that all usurers and profiteers be put to death—this proposal should also be considered among the anti-Semitic platform planks, given the common slur that Jews, in addition to the newspapers, also control international banking. In response to the great toll on the German economy taken by the war, point 12 defines personal enrichment through war as a crime against the people, and demands confiscation of all war profits. Point 13 goes on to demand the nationalization of all trusts, and point 14 insists on profit-sharing with the people by all heavy industries. To reward German citizens for spending their lives doing useful work for the nation, point 15 demands a large-scale expansion of old-age welfare. Other specifics include an abolition of interest charges, abolition of land speculation, and communalization of warehouses, along with far less specific calls for the creation of a healthy middle class and suitable land reform. In point 20, often attributed to Hitler, the demand is made to fundamentally restructure the German educational system so that every gifted child will have access to all levels of education.

Once the Nazis actually came to power, they implemented only some of this plan. The ambitious socialist-leaning social and economic reforms were largely ignored. Interest charges remained intact, as did large industries and banks, and government policies continued to favor large enterprises over small businesses. The Nazis did fulfill many of the nationalist and anti-Semitic portions of the plan, however, and with the Holocaust even went well beyond the discriminatory policies described in the 1920 Plan.

The Rise of Hitler

Adolf Hitler (1889–1945) was originally born in Austria-Hungary, not Germany, though his family moved to Germany when he was only three years old. He was the fourth of six children born to Alois Hitler and Klara Pölzl. When his younger brother Edmund died of measles in 1900, Hitler is said to have undergone a major personality change, transformed from a confident, outgoing boy who excelled in school to a sullen, angry, detached boy who fought constantly with his father and his teachers. As he grew older, one major battleground between Adolf and his father concerned his choice of profession: Adolf wanted to be an artist, and his father wanted him to follow in his footsteps and become an Austrian customs official. These two career paths required very different education paths under the German system at the time. To become an artist, Hitler wished to enroll in a classical high school, but his father insisted he go to the nearby technical school instead. Hitler rebelled against this choice, and in *Mein Kampf* he confessed that he deliberately failed all his classes in the first year, in the hope that his father would see his poor performance and send him to the other school instead. Alois never changed his mind, however, which made Adolf even more rebellious.

Living along the German-Austrian border with a father who had proudly served the Austrian monarchy, Hitler began to embrace German Nationalism as a form of rebellion. Where his father considered himself German-Austrian, Adolf expressed strict loyalty to Germany. When his father would sing the Austrian Imperial Anthem, Hitler and his friends would break into "Deutschland Über Alles." This German nationalism was no mere phase; following his father's death, the then-15-year-old Hitler moved to Vienna and lived a bohemian life for several years, but never stopped thinking of himself as a German.

While in Vienna, Hitler was rejected twice by the Academy of Fine Arts and was encouraged to pursue a career in architecture instead. He came to agree that he should become an architect, but this ambition, like his desire to become a painter, was not to be: in *Mein Kampf* he recalls coming to the realization that the classes he had deliberately failed in technical school, in order to torment his father, had covered precisely the material he would need to have mastered in order to succeed in an architecture program. Because of his own neglect of his education, he was unfit for the further education that would be necessary. Hitler was homeless for a time, living on the streets of Vienna and selling paintings that he modeled on postcards of Viennese attractions. Among his associates at the time were a number of Jews, including the man who sold the paintings for him, and he seems to have gotten along with them well at the time.

Hitler's own recollection, however, was that he first really became an anti-Semite during his time in Vienna, which was the first time in his life during which he was exposed to large numbers of Jews, many of them Orthodox refugees from pogroms in Russia. Unlike the Jews he had encountered as a schoolboy in Linz, these Jews stood out from the people around them, distinct in appearance in ways that the liberalized German Jews he had previously encountered had not been. Vienna at that time, the same era in which Freud was making his reputation, was in many ways a hotbed of 19th-century religious prejudice and racism, and it was while surrounded by those attitudes that Hitler first encountered Jews who were clearly and easily identified as different from himself. This was certainly not his first encounter with strong anti-Semitic prejudices; for centuries such attitudes had been a major part of German culture. His time in Vienna may have simply reinforced ideas that the young Hitler had long since absorbed, but had not had occasion to contemplate in any depth.

In 1913, Hitler received the remainder of his father's estate and moved to Munich, a move that he recollects in *Mein Kampf* as the fulfillment of a dream. Now that he was living in a proper Germany city, with German buildings, his interest in architecture was reawakened. Another possible reason for the move to Germany, however, is that it helped him to escape mandatory military service in Austria, at least for a while. Eventually, the Austrian authorities, with the cooperation of the Munich police, arrested him and returned him to Vienna. Following a physical exam, he was deemed unfit for military service and allowed to go back to Munich. His desire to avoid military service proved weaker than his German nationalism, however: when World War I began in 1914, the erstwhile Austrian draftee requested permission from the King of Bavaria, Ludwig III, to join a Bavarian army regiment, a request that was granted.

Assigned to the Sixteenth Bavarian Reserve Infantry Regiment, Hitler served on the Western front, where he seems to have acquired some of his sense of destiny as a result of an incident in which he stood up from eating dinner with his comrades and walked 20 yards along a trench before sitting down again with his food, feeling as though a voice was telling him to go over there. When he sat back down, a shell exploded over the spot that he had left, killing every other member of his group that had been eating together. A few weeks later, he told some of his fellow soldiers that they would one day hear more about him, when his time came. His feeling of having been spared for some purpose only grew stronger as the war progressed, and he continued to survive unharmed while so many others fell. Toward the end of the war, he was finally injured, and so as the war ended he was recuperating in a military hospital, having survived a poison gas attack. He was awarded the Iron Cross, a medal he would wear as part of his Nazi uniform in his later life as the head of the Nazi Party, and later as chancellor of Germany. Despite serving throughout the war and earning that decoration, however, Hitler was never promoted beyond the rank of private first class, for reasons that remain unclear.

At the war's end, Hitler's unit, like many others, was deep inside enemy territory, and the news of the armistice came as a deadly blow to many soldiers. From their perspective, combat had been going well, and the leadership's acknowledgment of defeat would become a central element in Hitler's thinking, as it would in the minds of many of his party's supporters: Germany had not been defeated, so much as it had been stabbed in the back. Rather than trying to salvage their country in the face of impending total defeat, the nation's military and political leaders were the perpetrators of the loss. Furthermore, since one of the consequences that followed quickly upon the defeat was the lifting of the remaining legal restrictions on Jews in the German states, it was obvious to Hitler that they were the responsible parties. His anti-Semitism was thus strengthened dramatically by Germany's loss in the war, along with that of many other Germans. In the immediate postwar period, Hitler, still working for the army, was assigned to help keep order by making pro-government indoctrination speeches and spying on local political movements, in hopes of preventing at least some portion of the then-current wave of coup attempts. This work proved invaluable for Hitler's future—he gained valuable experience as a public speaker, rapidly improving his oratorical skills, and it was while monitoring political groups that he came into contact with the German Workers Party. With his newfound oratorical powers, he became the group's new leader in rather fast order.

After Prison: The Party's Rapid Ascent

During his time in prison, Hitler used the pages of *Mein Kampf* to expand on some of the ideas in the party's 25 points by presenting his idiosyncratic view of world history as a constant struggle among the different races of humanity for living space. In this struggle, the naturally superior German race, the master race, would eventually dominate the entire planet. Upon Hitler's return to the party, this idea was joined to the others already contained in the party platform, and so Nazi political speeches from that point on usually joined anti-Weimar and anti-Semitic themes with calls for recognition of German superiority, and eventually demands for more wars in order to regain lost territory.

This platform was a tough sell at first. In the 1928 election for the Reichstag

Adolf Hitler, seen here at a Nazi Party rally in Nuremberg in 1928, expertly manipulated the fear and anger of the German people in the wake of the economic collapse that began for them with the concessions demanded by the rest of Europe following World War I. (National Archives)

(parliament), the National Socialist party only received 2.8 percent of the total vote. This did translate into earning 12 seats, however, so the Nazis were on their way up. The party's fortunes were helped dramatically by the events across the Atlantic on October 24, 1929, the day of the stock market crash in the United States. Germany was severely affected by the American Great Depression, because of the large scale of American investment in, and loans to, German businesses and the German government. With the onset of the Depression, most of that American money was suddenly gone, resulting in unemployment on a massive scale never before seen in Germany. At the Depression's peak in the winter of 1932–1933, there were at least seven million unemployed German workers.

The impact of the economic troubles on the political fortunes of the Nazi Party was dramatic: The Great Depression was their big chance. At the start of the Depression, the Nazis were just one of many small, radical, right-wing parties. That changed dramatically in the 1930 Reichstag election, in which the party received 6.4 million votes and gained 107 seats, making the once-fringe group the second largest party in the German parliament. In the same year, the incumbent, Field Marshal Paul von Hindenburg, held on to the presidency, but his closest challenger was Hitler.

While it is difficult to judge why people vote they way they do, people's frustrations with the actions of the parties in power were clearly a factor. Some people were attracted by the Nazi Party's activist and sometimes violent campaigns against the parties of the left, especially the German Communist Party, which many saw as a specifically Jewish organization. Others welcomed the party's aggressively nationalistic stance and its opposition to the accommodations that had been reached with the war's winners. The Nazi message about World War I was that the liberal democracy of the Weimar Republic was doomed to fail because it was the product of the November Criminals who had signed away Germany's pride and territory in the Treaty of Versailles, and that this had been accomplished through the inspiration and conniving of the Jews, whose ultimate goal was subversion of the nation and the poisoning of German blood. The Nazis promised to replace the current crisis with full employment and restored national pride, along with the suppression of the Jews and Marxists, as true national unity was not possible under the Marxists' emphasis on class divisions. Certainly many were swayed by the nationalist message and the promise of economic renewal, just as some were undoubtedly attracted by the mystical racist ideology, but many voters were simply drawn to the party by a fascination with its charismatic leader, whose oratorical flights of fancy and staged rituals presented a far more intriguing, and entertaining, spectacle than other parties' leaders were capable of mustering. The economic crisis provided the Nazis with an endless supply of ammunition against the more ordinary, conventional politicians, who had clearly failed the German people—Nazi propaganda incessantly assured the public of this.

Hitler and other Nazi candidates at local and regional levels offered radical solutions that would not have occurred to more typical politicians, often making promises that were mutually incompatible to different constituencies in different locations. The message mattered less than its lack of resemblance to the message being sent by others. Beyond the oratorical histrionics, the Nazi Party also used the crisis to demonstrate a different, compassionate approach to the victims of the crisis, with Nazi activists prominently running soup kitchens, clothing collections, and shelters, providing practical welfare for the desperately poor and unemployed in addition to mere campaign promises. Many voters came to accept, wholeheartedly, the central message of the relentless Nazi propaganda machine: in this crisis, Adolf Hitler was their only hope. Once the party had built momentum, there was no slowing down: In the July 1932 Reichstag elections, the party received 13.75 million votes and 230 seats, making them the largest caucus in the parliament. At this point, Nazis occupied posts at all levels of government and had laid the groundwork for the next phase of Hitler's revolution. By 1933, the Nazis were clearly the most powerful political party in Germany, and in January Adolf Hitler was appointed chancellor by then-president Hindenberg. In the German government, the president is a largely ceremonial position, with much of the day-to-day power, including the role of military commander in chief in times of war, residing in the position of chancellor instead, a division of labor that remains intact today. Hitler arrived in office armed with an array of radical promises, including a one-party state, a reversal of the emancipation of the Jews, and of greatest concern to the rest of Europe, his pledge to wage wars to gain back the lebensraum (living space) lost in the Treaty of Versailles.

The Third Reich and Eugenics

Taking inspiration from **eugenics** activists in America, Hitler quickly moved to implement his ideas regarding the racial purification of Germany. In 1933, a law was passed allowing the involuntary, compulsory sterilization of anyone deemed unfit to reproduce. The law was actually based quite directly on the statutes that were eventually passed in 30 U.S. states, intended to battle the perceived menace of the feeble-minded, allowing courts to determine who was unfit to reproduce due to mental deficiency. The first sterilization law was passed in Indiana in 1907, but the first Supreme Court challenge to the constitutionality of such laws, against the Virginia law, took a full 20 years to materialize. In 1927, in the case of *Buck v. Bell,* the court emboldened eugenicists on both sides of the Atlantic with its chilling decision, written by Oliver Wendell Holmes:

We have seen more than once that the public welfare may call upon the best citizens for their lives. It would be strange if it could not call upon those who already sap the strength of the state for these lesser sacrifices. . . . The principle that sustains compulsory vaccination is broad enough to cover cutting the Fallopian tubes. (Quoted in Gould, 1996)

In America, the principle of leaving up to a judge the decision as to who was unfit led quickly to a broadening of the target population from the mentally deficient to also include people who were homeless, promiscuous, criminals, vagrants, and various other categories, a model that Hitler followed quite closely in the implementation of his own eugenics program.

The Law for the Prevention of Hereditarily Diseased Offspring (in German, *Gesetz zur Verhütung erbkranken Nachwuchses*), passed on July 14, 1933, and put into action the following January, established Genetic Health Courts to determine who should undergo compulsory sterilization as a result of any of a number of alleged genetic disorders. The law declared that "Any person suffering from a hereditary disease may be rendered incapable of procreation . . . if the experience of medical science shows that it is highly probable that his descendants would suffer from some serious physical or mental hereditary defect." The law then proceeded to a list of specific diseases for which sterilization was an appropriate solution: congenital mental deficiency, schizophrenia, manic-depressive insanity (what would today be called bipolar affective disorder), hereditary epilepsy, Huntington's chorea, hereditary blindness, hereditary deafness, *any* severe hereditary deformity, and severe alcoholism. Unlike the American sterilization laws, which were mainly enforced on people who were in some sort of state custody like jails or psychiatric institutions and training schools for the mentally retarded, the German law applied to the entire population. The Genetic Health Courts each consisted of a judge, a medical officer, and a medical practitioner, who held hearings on each case to decide whether a person should be sterilized. Appeals were possible, with a Higher Genetic Health Court established for that purpose, though an amendment to the law later gave the higher court the ability to withdraw an individual's right to appeal. One unusual feature of the law that distinguishes it from similar laws in other parts of the world is its requirement that the courts also approve any voluntary sterilizations: along with the desire to eliminate reproduction among those considered genetically inferior, the Nazis wanted to *increase* Aryan procreation, so no pure German could choose sterilization without government approval.

When the law was enacted, the German government publicized it via posters that emphasized that Germany was not alone in passing such laws, but merely part of a progressive international fraternity of forward-thinking societies. These posters included the flags of other nations with similar laws, and featured the U.S. flag in the upper left corner, along with praise for the work of American eugenicists.

For their part, eugenics advocates in other parts of the world praised the German law for its clarity and broad scope, and American writers expressed their admiration for a law that was clearer and better written than the U.S. state laws it took as its model, up to and including newspaper editorials praising the moral courage and commitment to science of the new German government. Indeed, the German government was nothing if not committed to its eugenics program. In the very first year of the law's implementation, more than 62,000 forced sterilizations were performed in Germany, whereas in America, a relatively paltry 27,000 compulsory operations were performed between 1907 and 1938. As for the appeals process the Nazis had put into place, more than 3,500 of the nearly 4,000 appeals in that first year failed. By the end of the Nazi era, more than 400,000 compulsory sterilizations were performed under the authority of the Genetic Health Courts. Amid the foreign praise heaped on the German authorities for the sterilization program, it did not escape the notice of some international commentators that the people sterilized under the courts' authority, especially the women, were disproportionately Jewish.

Over the next several years, additional laws further strengthened the Nazi racial hygiene program. The Marital Health Law, also known as a piece of the *Nuremberg Laws,* passed in October 1935, banned marriages between the hereditarily healthy, which generally meant people of pure German, Aryan heritage, and people who were determined to be genetically unfit. In practice, this became primarily a prohibition on any marriages between Jews and non-Jews, though it also prohibited any other race-mixing that might occur. Meanwhile, Hitler proclaimed that getting married and having children was a sacred patriotic duty for the racially fit, declaring in a 1934 speech that the most important citizens of Nazi Germany were mothers. In 1936, the Reich Central Office for Combating Homosexuality and Abortion was established, targeting acts that by their nature obstructed reproduction. Homosexuality was increasingly a target of Nazi ire, with national police chief Heinrich Himmler explicitly linking homosexuality to the falling German birthrate, thereby making homosexuality a crime against the Nazi agenda. While regarding abortion as a serious crime when performed on pure Germans, however, Hitler relaxed the restrictions on abortion for everyone else, as this would also help to increase the proportion of German Aryans in the population.

In 1937, an additional group was targeted by the Genetic Health Courts, a very small population known derisively among the Nazis as the "Rhineland bastards." The term originated during the 1919 occupation of the Rhineland by French soldiers, in the immediate aftermath of World War I. As often happens under such circumstances, some German women married the occupying soldiers, and others became pregnant by them without benefit of marriage, the source of the disparaging bastards in the name given the children by the Nazis. The problem for the Nazis was not French inferiority, so much as it was the color of these children's skin. The French army included men from France's various African colonies, many of whom had assimilated into French culture and were welcomed as citizens. The German women's choice to procreate with these men, representatives both of a humiliating defeat and a race regarded as inferior, was seen as a sort of treason. In *Mein Kampf,* Hitler derisively described their children as a contamination of the white race by Negro blood and referred to the women as whores and prostitutes. He further suggested that these marriages were part of a plot by the French to dilute white racial purity.

The Nazis loathed black culture, as they viewed black people as inferior, and this led to prohibitions on art forms considered traditionally black, such as jazz. Since most of the tiny African German population (estimated at between 500 and 800 at the time, out of a total population of approximately 65 million) were actually members of the racially mixed families of missionaries and settlers who returned from the colonial outposts of the crumbling German empire at the end of World War I, no official laws were enacted against the black population. The children were the result of unions that predated the 1935 prohibitions on miscegenation and race mixing, after all, so they were largely left alone. The Rhineland bastards were considered a special case, however, and a commission was appointed to work out how to prevent them from procreating further. In a program that was kept secret from Germany at large, in 1937 local officials in the Rhineland were ordered to report on all mixed-race children within their jurisdictions. Approximately 400 people were rounded up, arrested, and forcibly sterilized.

The Nazis began to keep their promises regarding the Jews in earnest in 1935 with the passage of the Nuremberg laws, a set of anti-Semitic statutes introduced at the Nazis' annual Nuremberg rally. Although the Nazis were already emphatically anti-Semitic upon taking power, and had already put numerous forms of official discrimination against Jews in place, there remained a problem: there was no clear legal definition of who was and who was not Jewish. The Nuremberg laws aimed to change that, by instituting clear legal definitions of both Jews and Germans. The new laws classified anyone with four German grandparents as German, thus rendering anyone with fewer German grandparents as impure. Jews, on the other hand, were considered pure Jews even with only three Jewish grandparents out of four. With only one or two Jewish grandparents, a person was classified as a *Mischling,* or person of mixed blood. Under these new laws, only pure Germans were allowed German citizenship, thus the laws had the effect of instantly turning all German Jews into resident aliens, and of instantly cutting out all Jewish participation in German civic affairs. As noted earlier, the new laws also prohibited intermarriage between Jews and non-Jewish Germans, as well as any sexual intercourse between the two groups.

Consolidating Political and Military Might

In the first months of the new regime, Hitler wasted no time in implementing his vision of a Third Reich (empire) to replace the failed Weimar Republic.

He persuaded the president to suspend all constitutional liberties and transferred legislative duties from parliament to his cabinet, as well as abolishing all other political parties. A massive rearmament program was also begun to more quickly pursue his goal of reinvading neighboring countries and increasing Germany's territory. Most of World War I had been fought outside of German territory, so postwar investment in Germany had gone toward modernization rather than the reconstruction that occupied the governments of much of the rest of Europe. This, along with the conviction among those other nations that another great war was something to be avoided, gave Germany a head start over the rest of Europe in reconstructing their military machine. Given the devastated condition of the German economy, along with the far larger size of the other nations' economies, Germany had reason to want to make use of their military advantage while it lasted. In 1938, Hitler went so far as to proclaim that he preferred the idea of war at age 49 to the notion of waiting until he was older.

Before he could proceed with plans for war, however, Hitler needed to consolidate his power and make sure that he was free of threats to his supremacy from among the other Nazi leaders, particularly from Ernst Röhm, head of the SA (Stormtroopers). Upon assuming power, Hitler was friendly with the major industrialists, military leaders, and aristocrats, whose influence was still of strategic importance to the Nazi regime. This was a problem for the men of the SA, mostly rough men from the lower social classes who saw their social superiors as the targets of the Nazi revolution, rather than comrades in arms. In June 1934, Röhm, at the time commander of a paramilitary force of about two million men, committed the ultimately fatal error of publicly proclaiming his displeasure with Hitler:

> One victory on the road of German revolution has been won. . . . The S.A. and S.S., who bear the great responsibility of having set the German revolution rolling, will not allow it to be betrayed at the halfway mark. . . . If the Philistines believe that the national revolution has lasted too long . . . it is indeed high time that the national revolution should end and become a National Socialist one. . . . We shall continue our fight—with them or without them. And, if necessary, against them. . . . We are the incorruptible guarantors of the fulfillment of the German revolution. (Shirer, 1990, p. 205)

This position, that the Nazi revolution was a workers' movement and could not end until the powers on the Right had also been vanquished, was a popular one with other Nazi leaders as well, including Goebbels, the propaganda genius who had emphasized the *socialist* part of National Socialist in recruiting the masses to the cause. For Hitler, however, the socialist sloganeering had been mere propaganda, and now that power had been gained he was uninterested in pursuing that cause further, especially as he recognized that bringing down the big businesses and banks would simply serve to bankrupt Germany, exactly the thing he had come into office on the promise of preventing. He made his own position very plain in a July speech to the SA and SS leaders, proclaiming: "I will suppress every attempt to disturb the existing order as ruthlessly as I will deal the so-called second revolution, which would lead only to chaos" (Shirer, 1990, p. 205). Five days later he reiterated his position, with further explanation, to a gathering of Nazi state governors:

> The revolution is not a permanent state of affairs, and it must not be allowed to develop into such a state. The stream of revolution released must be guided into the safe channel of evolution. . . . We must therefore not dismiss a businessman if he is a good businessman, even if he is not yet a National Socialist, and especially not if the National Socialist who is to take his place knows nothing about business. . . . In the long run our political power will be all the more secure, the more we succeed in underpinning it economically. (Shirer, 1990, pp. 205–206)

This sort of argument was very troublesome to Röhm and some of the other more revolutionary-minded Nazi leaders, who had believed the revolution to be an anticapitalist movement that would result in wealth and positions of leadership for themselves, not the retention of the old guard in the important positions.

Hitler and Röhm had another point of disagreement, however, regarding the role of the Stormtroopers in the new regime. From the very beginning of the Nazi movement, Hitler had regarded the SA as a political force, to be used to intimidate the opposition, rather than as a military force. To Röhm, however, his men had been both the force that helped the Nazis bludgeon their way into office as well as the core of a future revolutionary army. He went so far as to present the cabinet with a memo, in February 1934, in which he proposed that the SA should be renamed the "People's Army," replacing the existing German military, and that he should be made minister of defense to preside over them. The leaders of the German military looked down on the SA as an untrained mob, as did Hitler, who recognized that it was only with the Army's cooperation that he was able to remain in power, and that their loyalty would make his war plans possible. Röhm and the men loyal to him were therefore a problem to be dealt with, and it soon became clear that they also represented a different sort of threat to the Nazi agenda, as representatives of one of the groups that stood in the way of Nazi eugenic goals: homosexuals.

Heinrich Himmler, chief of the SS (*schutz staffel*—literally, protection detachment, an elite offshoot of the SA that reported directly to Hitler) and later the Gestapo, or secret police, had discovered that Röhm was a homosexual, and he made sure that the army generals found out that most of the top SA officials were also gay. In addition to this being a problem for Nazi ideology, the top brass of the military were opposed to the participation of such men in the important task of rearmament.

Hitler's close advisors, Goebbels and Göring, meanwhile saw an opportunity to help Hitler consolidate the Nazi influence in the military while also ridding themselves of enemies who were still believed to be plotting a second, Bolshevik-influenced revolution. Although no documentation exists to support the allegation, they convinced Hitler that Röhm was a mastermind behind the planned coup. On the night of Friday, June 29, 1934, Röhm and most of the other SA leaders were to gather at a hotel at the lakeside resort of Wiessee near Munich. Röhm invited Hitler to meet with the SA leadership on Saturday, June 30. Hitler, convinced that a conspiracy against him was afoot, kept the appointment, but not in the way that Röhm expected. At around 4 a.m. on Saturday, Hitler and group of loyal Nazis arrived without warning at the establishment, where they found Edward Heines, the SA *obergruppenfuehrer* of Silesia, in bed with another man. The two were immediately escorted outside to a courtyard and shot. Hitler ordered Röhm arrested and imprisoned, and asked that a revolver be left in his cell, so that he would be spared actually being killed by others, but Röhm refused to make use of it. He was then shot at point-blank range by two SS officers.

Meanwhile, in Berlin, Göring and Himmler had gathered up an additional 150 SA leaders and had them executed by firing squads. Also murdered on that day were numerous military and political leaders who had expressed objections to the Nazi regime, as well as some of their spouses and family members who simply happened to be present at the time, as well as anti-Nazi civilians such as Erich Klausener, the leader of a group called Catholic Action (at the time the Nazis remained unpopular in Catholic areas of Germany), while some of their staff members were taken away to Dachau, the recently established concentration camp.

Overall, hundreds of people were killed in the purge of the SA, though exact numbers are difficult to confirm. The purge was kept secret from the general public until Hitler himself announced it in a speech at the Reichstag on July 13, at which time he gave the action the name by which it has been known ever since: the Night of the Long Knives. In the speech, Hitler gave his own figures, announcing that 61 people had been shot, among them 19 upper-level SA leaders; 13 more had died while resisting arrest, and 3 had committed suicide, for a total of 77. When some of the killers were finally put on trial in Munich in 1957, the number of victims given in the indictments was greater than 1,000. The true figure may never be known, but surely lies somewhere in between the two extremes. With this action Hitler had sent a very clear message to Germany, and to the larger world: he was in charge of Germany, and he would do whatever he wanted, whenever he wanted, to get his way. A similar message was read loud and clear by the German military—do not oppose Hitler's will, or indeed go so far as to be suspected of doing so.

The Holocaust

Clearly anti-Semitism was a centerpiece of Nazi ideology, but its central importance to Hitler has been a subject of some debate among historians. To Hitler, ideology was often simply a tool to be used in the pursuit of political power and then discarded once it had achieved its goal. Indeed, many of the economic goals in the original Nazi 25-point plan, the ideas that put the Socialist in National Socialist, were discarded and ignored the moment the Nazis had succeeded in taking over Germany, leading to some of the difficulties between Hitler and the SA leadership. What such an argument ignores, of course, is the simple fact that Hitler not only did not discard the anti-Semitic portions of the platform, but instead wasted no time in beginning to implement them as soon as possible. Even before the sterilization law was passed, one of the first laws handed down by the Third Reich was the explicitly anti-Jewish Law for the Restoration of the Professional Civil Service, passed on April 7, 1933. The law mandated the retirement from governmental posts of all non-Aryan officials. With this law, the war against the Jews had begun, with the initial goal of simply turning back the clock on reforms that had improved the lot of Jews since the Napoleonic wars.

Prior to the early 19th century, the Jews of the Germanic territories had been treated much as they were in many other European cities, confined to ghettoes and prevented from exercising the rights of full citizenship. With the arrival of Napoleon's armies in German lands came also the arrival of the ideals of the French Revolution, captured in the revolutionary slogan *Liberté, Egalité, Fraternité* (Liberty, Equality, Fraternity). This resulted in the liberation of the Jews, which was of course a very good thing for them, but it had the result of making the Jews even more hated than they had previously been, as they were seen by the rest of Germany as beneficiaries of the French occupation, and therefore as enemies of German nationalism.

As the 19th century progressed, German public opinion became generally more liberal, and Jews were able to participate much more freely in the economy of the various Germanic states. In any successful economic expansion, however, some participants will benefit far less than others, and many farmers, craftsmen, skilled workers, and small businessmen felt left behind by the new prosperity of the bankers and financiers who they saw as controlling the new economy. Some of these financiers were Jewish, though a majority were Gentiles, but non-Jewish Germans began to blame the Jewish bankers for their troubles. In a Germany that was primarily Christian, Jews played the role of foreign devils, the usual target of blame under such circumstances. Under Bismarck, the laws no longer prohibited Jews from owning property and participating in their society, but anti-Semitic feelings intensified, and as the 20th century dawned, the bookstores were full of paranoid anti-Semitic works such as *The Protocols of the Elders of Zion.*

One major force in the German anti-Semitism of the second half of the 19th century, and a major influence on the Nazis and their supporters, was the emergence in Germany and Austria-Hungary of the *Völkisch* movement, a populist political movement that blamed the nation's problems on the Jews and presented a pseudoscientific world view in which Jews are a biologically distinct race engaged in a massive conspiracy to achieve world domination, with only the pure German, Aryan race standing in their way. In 1895, one of the movement's leaders, Hermann Ahlwardt, gave a speech before the Reichstag in which he compared the Jews to infectious bacteria who should be exterminated. Prior to World War I, similar pronouncements continued from the *Völkisch* politicians, with a best-selling 1912 book calling for all German Jews to be stripped of their citizenship and forbidden to own land, hold public office, or participate in banking.

When World War I began to go badly, and it was becoming clear that many young men were losing their lives without any apparent benefit to the nation, the German nationalists had the choice of blaming Kaiser Wilhelm II and his generals, the soldiers who were valiantly going forth and dying for their nation, or the Jews, regarded by many as foreign devils, who seemed to be everywhere. The choice was obvious to many, and by the end of the war anti-Semitism was again everywhere, and the stage was set for the Nazis, the party that would come to power on a platform that promised to rid Germany of Jewish influence.

In addition to the passage of laws restricting the rights of Jews, another early development under the Nazi regime, largely unheralded at the time, would come to play a large part in Hitler's war on the Jews. In February 1933, within mere *days* of the Nazi takeover of power in Germany, Hermann Göring, whom Hitler had appointed minister of the interior for Prussia, announced plans for the first Nazi concentration camps, the purpose of which was initially to deprive enemies of the state of their civil liberties. Such an exercise of brutal suppression was seen by the Nazi leadership as vital to the consolidation of their power, given their perceived need to crush opposition before it could get started. Göring described this need:

> We had to deal ruthlessly with these enemies of the State. It must not be forgotten that at the moment of our seizure of power over 6 million people officially voted for Communism and about 8 million for Marxism in the Reichstag elections in March. Thus the concentration camps were created, to which we had to send first thousands of functionaries of the Communist and Social Democratic parties. (Göring, 1934, p. 89, quoted by the Avalon Project, 2008b)

It was Himmler who actually put the idea into practice, announcing the opening of an experimental camp at Dachau on March 21, 1933. The Dachau camp was intended to hold 5,000 prisoners, and its stated objective was to protect the nation from "racial traitors and Bolshevik agitators," as well as to place those offenders into "protective custody."

Unlike the situation in most Western democracies, however, the establishment of guilt was not a prerequisite for indefinite detention. Himmler decreed that individuals could be arrested and brought to Dachau simply based on the *suspicion* of involvement in activities "inimical to the state." In an SS order issued in April 1933, Himmler further indicated that mere imprisonment without trial was not sufficient to battle threats against the state, and authorized the use of torture to obtain information:

> A great deal of potentially useful information can be extracted from suspects. Even if suspicion of treasonable activities proves to be unfounded they can often be persuaded to give information that will lead to other suspects. Such information is usually readily given under duress, threat, or promise of release. (Quoted in Thompson, 2003, p. 151)

The men tasked at Dachau with fulfilling Himmler's wishes were free to interpret this instruction however they wished, and flogging quickly became a popular way of obtaining information. The effectiveness of the concentration camps in deterring resistance to the Nazi regime depended on the maintenance of an aura of terror and mystery regarding what went on inside them, and the policy of the administration of Dachau, right from the beginning, was to make sure that any information regarding the camp that managed to leak out to the rest of Germany would maintain that aura. An order issued in October 1933 by the camp commander, for example, prescribes penalties including flogging, solitary confinement, and executions for various infractions of the rules. Hanging was the promised punishment for anyone who, with the goal of agitating, did any of the following, anywhere in the camp:

> politicizes, holds inciting speeches and meetings, forms cliques, loiters around with others; who for the purpose of supplying the propaganda of the opposition with atrocity stories, collects *true or false information* [italics mine] about the concentration camp and its institution; receives such information, buries it, talks about it to others, smuggles it out of the camp into the hands of foreign visitors or others by means of clandestine or other methods, passes it on in writing or orally to released prisoners or prisoners who are placed above them, conceals it in clothing or other articles, throws stones and other objects over the camp wall containing such information. (Avalon Project, 2008a, 778-PS)

The camps were initially intended, therefore, to crush all political opposition to Nazi policies and to intimidate potential resisters out of making any attempt to resist. Early on, by imprisoning the leaders of the Social Democratic party, for example, the Nazis destroyed the labor unions, since most of the union leadership elonged to that party. In a similar vein, the camps were also used to halt the spread of any religious sentiment that might stand in the way of the planned Nazi war of expansion. In one instance, the leaders of a religious pacifist group called the *Bibel Forscher* (Bible Research Workers), which was made up primarily of Jehovah's Witnesses, were arrested for their activities, and arrangements were made to transfer them to concentration camps after their regular sentences had been served, since their pacifism would still pose a threat to the state.

Since the concentration camps were established with the purpose of confining enemies of the state, and the Nazi platform had from the start proclaimed Jews to be the enemies of Germany, it was of course only a matter of time before Jews began to be placed in the camps for no reason other than for being Jews, as part of the larger Nazi effort at extermination that eventually became known as the Holocaust. The word "Holocaust" is derived from the Greek word *holokauston,* which

Slave laborers in the Buchenwald barracks, photographed five days after the U.S. Army assumed control of the camp. (National Archives)

traditionally referred to the sacrifice of an animal to the gods by means of burning the animal completely. Although "Holocaust" has become the standard term for the Nazi slaughter of millions of Jews, it is important to note that the preferred term among many Jews, especially in Europe and Israel, is the Hebrew word *Shoah,* meaning calamity, perhaps in part because of the apparent demeaning tone of using a word associated with pagan animal sacrifices to refer to a great loss of human life.

The real start of the Holocaust, the systematically organized effort to eliminate the Jews rather than merely restricting their rights, may be traced, at least linguistically, to a speech Hitler gave in 1935 upon the introduction of the Nuremberg Laws, in which he noted that if these laws did not succeed in resolving the Jewish problem, then the Nazi Party could be counted on to provide the *final solution.* From that point onward, "final solution" became the standard Nazi euphemism for the eradication of the Jews. By 1938, many Jews who possessed the means to do so had already departed from Germany, but the worst was still to come for those who remained. In November 1938, Nazi policy toward Jews changed over from official repression and disenfranchisement to large-scale outright violence and killing with the events of a single night, which became known as *Kristallnacht,* or the Night of Broken Glass.

On that night, in response to the killing of a Nazi diplomat by a Jewish assassin, mass pogroms were carried out throughout Nazi Germany and Austria, organized by the Nazi Party and the SA but represented to the world as spontaneous public outrage against the Jews, in which Jews were attacked and their property vandalized. More than 7,000 Jewish shops and more than 1600 synagogues, which amounts to nearly every synagogue in Nazi Germany, were damaged or destroyed. The official death toll among Jews was only 91, but historians have generally assumed it to be much higher. More than 30,000 Jews were sent to concentration camps, where they were kept until they transferred all their property to the Nazis or proved that they were about to emigrate. The same week, on November 11, 1938, a law was passed making it illegal for Jews to possess firearms or other weapons, thus removing from them any ability to defend themselves against further attacks. Adding insult to injury, the Nazis made the German Jews responsible for restitution for the public property damage committed during the pogrom, along with a new atonement tax, totaling more than a billion Reichsmark. It was in the wake of *Kristallnacht* that Freud was finally convinced to leave Austria for London, with the help and goading of his friend Princess Marie Bonaparte.

Prior to the start of World War II, the Nazi considered plans to simply export all Jews out of German territory, and eventually out of all of Europe. They considered various destinations, including a seriously debated plan to use Madagascar as a territorial final solution. Madagascar was considered ideal because of its remoteness, but also because its harsh tropical climate was expected to result in a quick death for many of the Jews. In 1938, this plan actually got as far as receiving approval by Hitler, and the idea of resettlement was only abandoned once the mass killing of Jews had begun instead, around 1941.

The need to develop a clearer plan became more urgent after the Nazis invaded Western Poland in September 1939, a land with about two million Jewish residents. This invasion led Britain, Australia, South Africa, Canada, New Zealand, and France to declare war on Germany, and thus marked the start of World War II. The Nazi plan for the Polish Jews involved concentrating them in ghettos in the major cities, where they would become slave labor for the German war industries. The Germans were careful to put the ghettos near major railroad junctions, however, with the goal of making future measures that might be taken, including physical removal and even extermination, easier to plan for. At first, the Jews in the ghettos were put to work, and thousands of them were killed in various ways for a variety of infractions, under rules similar to those followed in the concentration camps, described earlier, and many more died of disease, starvation, and exhaustion, but there was no systematic program of killing in place yet. The Nazis did see forced labor as a form of extermination, however, frequently using the expression *Vernichtung durch Arbeit* (destruction through work) to refer to the practices in place in Poland. By 1941, Himmler and other members of the SS hierarchy were clearly determined to begin a policy of killing all the Jews under German control, but support for such a policy within the Nazi regime was not unanimous. Göring, who by this time was in control of the German war industry, recognized that an enormous Jewish labor force, consisting of more than a million strong, reasonably healthy workers, was still too useful to Germany alive, especially given Germany's plans to invade the Soviet Union.

In other Nazi-occupied countries, eventually including Norway, the Netherlands, France, Belgium, Luxembourg, Yugoslavia, and Greece, anti-Semitic measures were also introduced, but the speed and severity of implementation varied widely from country to country. Restrictions on Jewish participation in economic and political life were implemented in all countries, but physical deportation did not become widespread until 1942.

Once deportation became the norm, with large numbers of Jews being forcibly transported out of their homelands to destinations still vaguely designated by the Nazis as "to the East," it soon became clear that the Nazis were running low on places in which to detain them. The concentration camps, which had been a part of the Third Reich since its founding, were known to be dangerous places, with mortality rates running as high as 50 percent, but they were not designed to serve primarily as killing centers. By 1942, however, six large extermination camps had been established in occupied Poland, differing from the older concentration camps in that their sole purpose was to kill whoever was sent there. The large camps in Poland were the most notorious, but it has been estimated that the Germans established as many as 15,000 camps in the occupied countries, generally establishing them in areas with large populations of Jews, Communists, intellectuals, and Romani (Gypsies). Transportation to the camps was generally accomplished under terrible conditions using rail cars, and many died without ever reaching the camps. Once in the camps, many were eliminated by being worked to death, or at least by being worked until they could no longer perform the job they had been given, at which time they would be selected for extermination. Eventually, as the German war effort continued to struggle, camps were built with the rapid execution of large numbers of prisoners in mind, using gas chambers constructed for that sole purpose. The death camps were run by the SS, with regular German soldiers largely kept well away from the extermination effort.

The ultimate impact of the Nazi extermination program on the Jewish population of Europe is truly horrifying. In 1933, Poland had the largest Jewish population in all of Europe, numbering in excess of 3 million. By 1950, Poland's Jews were down to about 45,000. Romania's Jewish population dropped from 980,000 to about 280,000 over the same period. Germany's own Jewish population of 565,000 in 1933 was reduced to 37,000 by 1950. In Freud's homeland of Austria, the pre-Nazi occupation Jewish population of about a quarter of a million people was down to a mere 18,000 in 1950. When the Nazis came to power in 1933, the Jewish population of Europe was approximately 9.5 million. By 1950, that number was down to 3.5 million, and a startling shift had occurred in the distribution of the world's Jewish population: In 1933, 60 percent of all Jews lived in Europe, but by 1950 more than half of the world's Jews lived in North and South America, leaving only about a third of the total population in Europe. Even when the war appeared to be lost, Hitler never wavered from his racist agenda, continuing to push for the killing of Europe's Jews all the way to his final hours. Before his suicide, he even insisted in his will that the Germans continue to follow his racial policies after his death.

Further Reading

The Avalon Project (2008a). *Nazi Conspiracy and Aggression.* Vol. 1, chap. 11: *The Concentration Camps.* The Lillian Goldman Law Library, Yale Law School. Available at http://avalon.law.yale.edu/imt/chap_11.asp.

The Avalon Project (2008b). *Nazi Conspiracy and Aggression.* Vol. 4, Document No. 2324-PS. The Lillian Goldman Law Library, Yale Law School. Available at http://avalon.law.yale.edu/imt/2324-ps.asp.

Gould, S. J. (1996). *The Mismeasure of Man (Revised and Expanded).* New York: W. W. Norton.

Shirer, W. L. (1990). *The Rise and Fall of the Third Reich: A History of Nazi Germany.* New York: Simon and Shuster.

Thompson, R. S. (2003). *The Complete Idiot's Guide to Nazi Germany.* Indianapolis: Alpha Books.

Neurology in the Late 19th Century

Sigmund Freud's primary goal in the early days of his career was to explain the connections between nervous system functioning and behavior. He was heavily influenced in this by several major debates in 19th-century neurology. The first of these, which dominated most discussion of brain function, especially in the first half of the century, concerned whether or not various mental functions were a product of the functioning of specific areas of cortex (localization), as opposed to the idea that what matters is simply the sheer quantity of cortex available for use, rather than how it is arranged.

One of the most influential early advocates of the localization hypothesis, Franz Gall (1758–1828), arrived there from an unusual starting point—the idea that external physical features are linked to psychological traits. Physiognomy, the idea that mental aptitudes and strengths and weaknesses of character can be deduced from the shape and size of facial features, was not a new idea (the ancient Greeks wrote about it, for example), but attempts to formulate a *science* of physiognomy were 18th- and 19th-century phenomena, and were given a substantial boost by the publication of Charles Darwin's writings, which explicitly connected humanity to the rest of the animal kingdom. Cesare Lombroso's theory of hereditary criminality, for example, posits a set of facial features that are characteristic of the born criminal, which Lombroso explicitly connects to common ancestry with apes. The more apelike a person looks, the more likely the person will behave like an animal. Lombroso's reasoning that gorillas are more likely to behave savagely and in a criminal fashion than humans was of course based on the remarkably incomplete knowledge of ape behavior that was available at the time.

Lombroso's ideas regarding criminal features, which he called *stigmata of degeneracy,* were popular in the late 19th century, and had a heavy and continuing influence on literature. For every instance of a criminal described as having a prominent jaw, heavy-set forehead, thick eyebrows, unusually long arms, small (or even beady) deep-set eyes, or even dark skin, we may blame the popularity of Lombroso's physiognomy.

While physiognomy was largely ignored by neurologists and, eventually, psychologists, it did help set the stage for a related theory, Franz Josef Gall's *phrenology.* Like the physiognomists, Gall believed that the contours of the skull provide important clues to character traits and mental abilities, but for very different

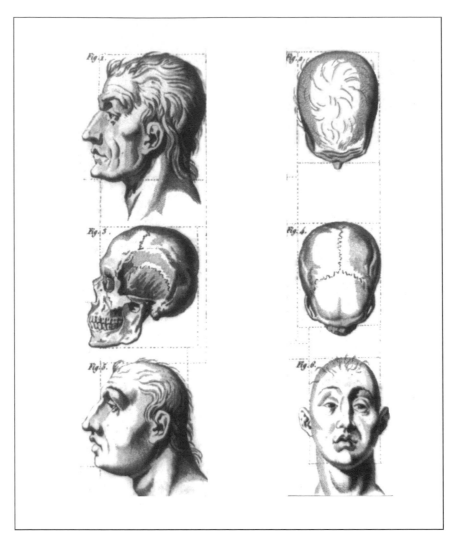

The assumption that indications of moral character and mental health could be found in facial features and the shape of the school was quite widespread in the 19th century, as seen in this illustration from an 1809 medical text by Philippe Pinel, comparing the skull shape of the sane man (figures 3 and 4) to that of an insane man. (Library of Congress)

reasons. Where the physiognomists saw the stigmata thus revealed as resulting from atavisms (evolutionary throwbacks), Gall thought the differences in skull shape occurred as a result of underlying differences in brain shape and development. Gall arrived at this theory after first contributing tremendously to our knowledge of brain structure through anatomical dissection. Franz Gall, known to modern readers primarily as the originator of phrenology, now widely regarded as fairly useless pseudoscience, is in fact responsible for the discovery of the following three fundamental pieces of anatomical knowledge that continue to be central to the study of the nervous system:

- He established that the two hemispheres of the brain are connected to each other by fibers of white matter (known as commissures), which allow communication between the two brain halves.
- He established that the fibers of the spinal cord cross over and connect contralaterally (meaning the left hemisphere controls/senses the right side of the body, and vice versa).
- He established clearly the difference in function between white matter and gray matter (cortex), and that species with a larger amount of cortex are more intelligent.

Rather than being remembered for these major contributions to science, without which the continued growth of neuroscience in the 19th century would have been impossible, Gall is instead remembered best for the much less scientific idea that larger brain structures would deform the skull over them, thus feeling the bumps on a person's skull can provide insight into his or her aptitudes. The theory possesses a certain anatomical plausibility, especially given the state of knowledge of skeletal and neurological development in the late 18th century. Gall reasoned this way: since humans have more cortex than animals and are therefore more intelligent, then differences in aptitudes between humans must also be due to measurable differences in cortical endowment. He added to this a personal observation: When he was a student, his colleagues who were really good at memorizing information all seemed to have bulging eyes. Clearly the area immediately behind the eyes must be responsible for verbal memory, as theirs is so overdeveloped that their eyes barely fit in front of it!

With his colleague, Johann Spurzheim, Gall proceeded to examine the heads of hundreds of people, including prisoners, insane asylum inmates, patients, and friends, eventually producing a map of 27 different regions of the skull, each assumed to represent an underlying cortical area in which a faculty resided, and which would be elevated in anyone in whom that trait was prominent. The trait of benevolence, for example, was localized beneath the center of the upper forehead, while combativeness was centered behind both ears. Gall and Spurzheim published these findings together at first, but by the 1820s Spurzheim had gone his own way, and was largely responsible for phrenology's huge popularity in America, where Broadway sported phrenological parlors and traveling phrenologists gave readings all over the country. He was also responsible for the name—Gall called it *cranioscopy,* not phrenology.

However, despite the huge popularity of phrenology with the public, it was almost completely ignored by the scientific community, although its central insight was not. In spreading his pseudoscience, Franz Gall also popularized the notion that particular faculties and traits were locally controlled in specific areas of the cortex, and the debate over whether this was true or not dominated 19th-century neurological research.

A French physiologist, Pierre Flourens (1794–1867), was so horrified at Gall's sloppy methodology that he set out to explore, through careful experimentation, whether specific functions are localized in particular areas of the brain. His methods are shocking by modern standards: He carefully operated on the brains of small animals, especially rabbits and dogs, making small lesions or removing small amounts of tissue, and then allowed the animals to recover completely from the surgery before examining them to see how their behavior had been affected by his ministrations. He began by targeting specific structures hypothesized by Gall, such as the *organ of amativeness* (at the base of the back of the skull). He removed steadily larger amounts of a dog's cerebellum (the structure that is actually under that part of the skull) and was able to establish that its function has nothing to do with amativeness (love), but it is crucial to coordinating deliberate movement. In other experiments, he found that removing larger and larger amounts of cortex from various animals resulted in the gradual loss of response to sensory stimuli and of their ability to initiate movement, but he concluded that small lesions produced no specific effect—what mattered was the total amount of tissue removed, not its location. Flourens concluded that high-level brain functions, including perception, judgment, motivation, and memory, were evenly distributed throughout the cortex, a position that influenced many 19th-century neuroscientists, several of whom established their own careers by proving Flourens wrong about localization of brain function.

Paul Broca, who upended the world of 19th-century brain physiology with his demonstration that language production occurred in a very specific part of the brain. (National Library of Medicine)

One of the most important discoveries of a localized high-level function was made, quite accidentally, by Paul Broca (1824–1880), a young French surgeon who happened on the right patient at exactly the right time. In 1861, he met a 51-year-old man named Leborgne, who was transferred from the Bicêtre (a famous Parisian asylum) to Broca's surgical ward for treatment of a gangrenous leg. Leborgne had been hospitalized for 21 years, since he lost the power of speech. He had not lost it entirely, however. His response to all questions was the single syllable "tan," and when he became extremely annoyed at his own inability to get words out, he could curse and blaspheme a bit (an ability that went away when he calmed down). He clearly understood the language of those around him, but he was unable to deliberately produce words of his own, a disorder known as aphasia. Leborgne passed away a mere six days after coming to Broca's attention. Curious about Leborgne's very specific language deficit, Broca performed an autopsy, during which he found that an area of tissue the size of a hen's egg had been destroyed in the left frontal lobe. He concluded that this area was responsible for the production of speech, and it has been referred to ever since as Broca's area.

In the mid-1870s, Carl Wernicke, a German physician, encountered several patients with what appeared to be a very different sort of aphasia. Wernicke's patients spoke quite fluidly, but made no sense, using many strange new words and using the recognizable ones incorrectly. They also did not appear to understand what was said to them. Like Broca, Wernicke had the opportunity to examine their brains, and discovered that these patients also had damage in the left hemisphere, this time in the temporal lobe. Where Broca's area governs the production of speech, Wernicke's area is responsible for processing word meanings (both incoming and outgoing), thus demonstrating that some areas of cortex, *contra* Flourens, are very specialized indeed.

Sigmund Freud's scientific training occurred in the midst of the debate and discoveries regarding localization of brain function—his first published physiological research (on eel glands) emerged in 1877, when he was 21. He worked for six years in Ernst Brücke's laboratory and established himself as a neuroscientist *before* his interest in psychology came to the fore. Among other contributions, Freud published a new tissue staining method involving gold chloride, which he used to study the myelination of neurons in the medulla. He eventually published more than 100 articles and monographs on neurological topics.

Freud's early training as a neurologist involved mentors who, while prominent in their field, adopted very different positions from each other on the localization of brain function and, consequently, the role of physical damage to the brain in mental illness. Theodor Hermann Meynert (1833–1892), who has a small subcortical structure named after him (the basal optic nucleus of Meynert), had his own unique way of conceiving localization. He divided the brain into a front *motoric* part and a rear *sensitive* part. However, another prominent German neuroscientist, Paul Flechsig, called Meynert's work "a true labyrinth of mistakes," and suggested that it was a mistake to try categorize mental illnesses based on specific localization of psychological functions. Flechsig went so far as to call neuroses *functional* mental illnesses—disturbances of nervous activity without anatomical damage. This idea clearly influenced Freud's later development as a theorist, as did Flechsig's idea that drives are produced by the deeper parts of the brain, and thus mature at birth, while cortex (and its associated mental functions) takes longer to develop.

The first of Freud's monographs that historians see as psychoanalytic is clearly a response to the prevailing debates of the time: published in 1891, it is called *On Aphasia (Zur Auffassung)*. In *On Aphasia,* Freud establishes some themes that will become central to his later work while joining in the physiological debate about the causes of aphasia. He comes out strongly *against* the Wernicke or Broca view of aphasia as the result of lesions in language centers of the brain, suggesting instead that cases of aphasia represent instances of *retrogression* to an earlier state of functional development. He based this notion in part on having seen patients with recurring aphasic problems in the absence of brain injury—his later interest in slips of the tongue clearly demonstrates his continuing interest in *paraphasias*—small instances of aphasia that occur in a state of fatigue or great excitement.

Further Reading

Freud, S. (1953). *On Aphasia: A Critical Study* (Translated by E. Stengel). New York: International Universities Press. (Original published in 1891.)

Keegan, E. (2003). Flechsig and Freud: Late 19th-Century Neurology and the Emergence of Psychoanalysis. *History of Psychology* 6 (1): 52–69.

Pankejeff, Sergei Konstantinovitch. *See* The Wolf Man
Pappenheim, Bertha. *See* Anna O.

Parapraxes

Parapraxes is a Greek term that refers to Sigmund Freud's concept that errors in speaking can reveal the speaker's unconscious or hidden concerns, a notion that in popular culture has come to be known as a slip of the tongue or a Freudian slip. A recent famous example comes from a 2004 press conference in which Condoleezza Rice, then national security adviser to President George W. Bush, referred to a conversation with the president by beginning, "As I was telling my husb—," catching herself before completing the word. A sure sign of the extent to which Freud continues to influence the American popular and political cultures is the inclusion of his name in virtually all press mentions of this tiny speech error, which is now easily found on the Internet by searching for *Condoleezza Rice Freudian slip*. The implication made by all who made use of that terminology is of course that this was an instance of deeply buried romantic or sexual tension rising to the surface. As the term Freudian slip has become a part of popular culture, it has come to be applied frequently to any sort of slip of the tongue in an attempt to connect an air of sexual innuendo to the mistake, as in the application of the term to Ms. Rice's mistake.

Among Freud's many influences on popular culture, this remains one of the most enduring concepts: the idea that what Freud (through his translator A. A. Brill) called *speech blunders* can reveal hidden, unconscious concerns of the speaker, in much the same way as the analysis of dreams can do. Freud's terminology can be a bit confusing, partly as a result of his work only being known to Anglophone audiences in translation. In the original German, he used the term *Fehlleistungen* (literally "faulty actions" or "faulty performances"), and the Greek term *parapraxes* (plural of *parapraxis,* meaning "another action"), often attributed to Freud, actually appears only in translations, but not in the original German. In English, discussion of slips also frequently centers on *malapropisms* (a term for slips of the tongue that predates Freud by over a century—it is based on the name of Mrs. Malaprop, a character in Richard Brinsley Sheridan's 1775 play *The Rivals*).

The extent to which the idea of slips revealing one's inner thoughts has completely joined the mainstream can be seen in its frequent use as a source of humor in film and television. A classic example appears in the John Hughes film *Uncle Buck,* in a scene in which Buck Russell confronts a school principal, who has a large, distracting mole on her face, regarding the treatment of his niece, Maisie. He introduces himself by saying "Hi, I'm Buck Melanoma, Moley Russell's wart.

[Catching himself, attempting to correct.] Not her wart. Not her wart! I'm . . . I'm the wart. She's my tumor. I'm her tumor."

Freud explored speech blunders in one of his most popular books, *The Psychopathology of Everyday Life,* in which the basic mechanisms and ideas in psychoanalysis are explained through the very common experiences of everyday people rather than through dense clinical case studies. In addition to errors in speech, chapter titles in the book include "Forgetting of Proper Names," "Forgetting of Foreign Words," and "Mistakes in Reading and Writing." The entire book is centered on the notion that the small errors we make in everyday life can be just as revealing of our inner motives and conflicts as the memories explored by patients in psychoanalysis.

Other psychologists, including Wilhelm **Wundt,** had written on the subject of errors in speech previously, but they had focused their attention on more superficial influences, such as the simple fact that many words contain similar sounds, and thus when we produce the wrong word, the resulting word is usually one which contains phonemes similar to the ones in the word we are attempting to produce. Freud recognized the importance of such factors as what he called "a fore-sound or echo," but also felt that slips of the tongue are *always* influenced by unconscious motivations as well. Regarding Wundt, for example, Freud wrote the following:

Among the examples of the mistakes collected by me I can scarcely find one in which I would be obliged to attribute the speech disturbance simply and solely to what Wundt calls "contact effect of sound." Almost invariably I discover besides this a disturbing influence something outside of the intended speech. The disturbing element is either a single unconscious thought, which comes to light through the special blunder, and can only be brought to consciousness through a searching analysis, or it is a general psychic motive, which directs against the entire speech. (2005, p. 28)

Freud agreed with other psychologists that speech blunders could be caused by other components within the same statement, including prediction of a sound appearing later in the sentence, but simply pronounced too soon, as when I recently heard someone say "It's nime!" when the intended statement was "It's not time." Outside influences (outside the statement being made by the speaker) are just as important to Freud, however, and many of them are actually unconscious motivations or attitudes.

One of Freud's favorite examples of a blunder that clearly reveals the speaker's secret wish concerns the president of the lower house of the Austrian parliament, who opened a parliamentary session by saying, "Gentlemen, I take notice that a full quorum of members is present, and herewith declare the sitting *closed.*" Freud favored this example for a simple reason: Just as "open" and "closed" share little in terms of English phonetics other than a single long *o* sound, this is actually an even better example in the original German. It is unlikely that a man who intends to say *offen* would be moved to say *geschlossen* instead due to how similar the words sound. To Freud, this error occurred because the speaker had little faith in the assembled legislators and expected them to accomplish nothing, an expectation that slipped out unbidden when he addressed them.

Freud had an unexpected influence on later generations of cognitive psychologists by drawing attention to these speech errors as an important subject area for psychology—cognitive psychologists also study them, and also see them as crucial for understanding the unconscious processes that underlie our language production, but they are interested in a fundamentally different set of processes than Freud was. Indeed, the modern cognitive psychologist's concerns sound more like Wundt than Freud, emphasizing the role of similar sounds, for example. Slips of the tongue are actually quite useful in learning more about how words and word sounds are stored in the brain. According to recent cognitive research, more than 80 percent of slips share an initial sound with the intended target word, and more than 70 percent of word endings are identical or very similar as well. This information has driven a large body of research regarding the extent to which words are stored in memory in an *echoic* store (by sound) rather than an *iconic* (visual representation) store. This sort of research on slips of the tongue also sheds light on the cognitive mechanisms involved in the tip-of-the-tongue phenomenon, in which it is often possible to remember the initial or final sounds in a word while nevertheless being unable to recall the word completely. The modern cognitive explanation is that, since words are stored in memory according to their sounds, sometimes the attempt to retrieve a word will activate traces of similar-sounding words but not the desired word, leading to either an inability to produce the word (tip-of-the-tongue phenomenon) or to production of a wrong word that sounds similar (slip of the tongue).

Freud's response to the primitive version of this argument, when it was presented by Wundt, was to point out errors where sound is an inadequate explanation, such as the example of the Austrian parliament, or Ms. Rice's almost-reference to the president as her husband. Rather than infer unconscious desires or conflicts, however, the cognitive psychologists would interpret those instances as the result of *priming*. When we say, hear or think a word (or idea) frequently, that word becomes primed to be more easily brought to mind than one which is used infrequently.

Similarly, any word we have used recently will be more primed than one we haven't encountered in a while. Ms. Rice's own explanation of her slip was quite straightforward—she was thinking of her husband right before speaking, and so the thought of him, well primed as it was, slipped into a sentence where she didn't intend to mention him. On the other hand, recent cognitive research supports at least a small portion of Freud's interpretation of slips as well: in the laboratory, a reliable technique for inducing slips of the tongue involves provoking anxiety in the research participants. As anxiety increases, so does the likelihood of producing a malapropism, so clearly involuntary internal emotional states *are* a factor in producing slips, just as Freud maintained.

Further Reading

Freud, S. (2005). *The Psychopathology of Everyday Life.* Stilwell, KS: Digireads.com Books. (Original published 1901; translation published by A. A. Brill in 1914.)

Motley, M. T. (1985). Slips of the Tongue. *Scientific American* 253(3): 116–127.

Peale, Norman Vincent (1898–1993)

Sigmund Freud's influence turns up in some unexpected places at times. In 1952, Norman Vincent Peale (1898–1993), a Protestant minister who oversaw a congregation in Manhattan that eventually grew to more than 5,000 people, published one of pop psychology's perennial bestsellers, *The Power of Positive Thinking*, a book that remains in print today and that has sold more than seven million copies over the years. What is perhaps not as widely recognized as it should be is the extent to which this extremely popular book covertly introduced many Americans to a few of Freud's ideas, especially the notion that much of what motivates us is unconscious. His best-known book was actually the culminating event of a career in which he had already devoted considerable attention to blending his ministry with psychological ideas. In 1940, for example, he had coauthored the book *Faith Is the Answer: A Psychiatrist and a Pastor Discuss Your Problems* with psychoanalyst Smiley Blanton, in which the advice offered is an unusual blend of psychoanalysis and born-again Christianity. Blanton had excellent credentials, having experienced psychoanalysis with Freud himself in Vienna before returning to the United States to practice psychiatry. In 1951, the two men founded the American Foundation of Religion and Psychiatry, a clinic that eventually employed more than 20 psychiatrists and psychologists, with Peale serving as president and Blanton as executive director.

Peale's basic technique (as presented in the book) involves repeating positive affirmations over and over again until they sink into the unconscious mind and are internally repeated automatically, without volition. The central idea is that if you say the positive things about yourself over and over again, you will come to believe them. Furthermore, negative thoughts and attitudes are not to be tolerated, but must be avoided and destroyed or repressed when they occur. His critics in the psychological and psychiatric profession have long argued that he is basically promoting self-hypnosis rather than any new technique.

Peale promises, however, that using his methods will allow people to overcome any adversity that life presents. The repetition was necessary to defeat the conscious will, which Peale presents as unreliable and troublesome. By giving up control to the unconscious, he teaches that God's power becomes available to the individual (clearly this is a different view of the contents of the unconscious mind than anything promoted by Freud, an avowed atheist). Ultimately, in other words, thinking positive things will cause positive things to happen, and negative thoughts will cause

Norman Vincent Peale, Protestant preacher who sought to reconcile psychoanalysis and Christianity, resulting in the single most influential of all pop psychology books, *The Power of Positive Thinking*. (Library of Congress)

negative things to happen. This remarkably durable idea sustained Peale through a long list of additional books, including *The Power of Positive Thinking for Young People* (1954), *The Art of Real Happiness* (1956), *The Amazing Results of Positive Thinking* (1959), *Enthusiasm Makes the Difference* (1967), *The Positive Principle Today: How to Renew and Sustain the Power of Positive Thinking* (1976), and *Sin, Sex, and Self-Control* (1965). The central idea of these books has cast a long shadow over pop psychology, with many other authors freely borrowing from Peale, including this recent cribbing of his title for Scott Ventrella's *The Power of Positive Thinking in Business: 10 Traits for Maximum Results* (2001).

Further Reading

Peale, N. V. (1952). *The Power of Positive Thinking*. New York: Prentice-Hall.

Peale, N. V., and S. Blanton. (1955). *Faith Is the Answer: A Psychiatrist and a Pastor Discuss Your Problems*. Englewood Cliffs, NJ: Prentice-Hall.

Pfister, Oskar (1873–1956)

In a career in which many of his professional relationships fell apart within a few years once serious theoretical differences arose, Freud somehow kept up a friendly and thoughtful correspondence with Oskar Pfister, a Swiss lay (nonmedical) analyst from 1909 until his own death. This is particularly unusual given Freud's well-documented atheism and hostility toward religion (see *Moses and Monotheism, Totem and Taboo, The Future of an Illusion, and Civilization and Its Discontents*), as Oskar Pfister was a practicing Protestant minister who not only saw theology and psychology as compatible fields of endeavor, but actually sought to establish a subspecialty of pastoral analysis. As a minister, Pfister advocated a return to the fundamental teachings of Jesus Christ and saw the elimination of fear from religious practice as a high priority, for which psychoanalysis might prove a particularly useful tool.

Pfister was a part of the psychoanalytical community in Zurich that was centered around Eugen **Bleuler** and Carl **Jung,** and was the founder in 1919 of the Swiss Society for Psychoanalysis. Pfister kept up a remarkable schedule; his work as a lay psychoanalyst coexisted with his full-time job as the pastor of the Predigerkirche in Zurich from 1902 to 1939, his work as a secondary school teacher during most of that period, and his work as a teacher of new teachers at the Cantonal Teaching Academy from 1908 to 1918. Jung introduced Pfister to Freud's ideas in 1908, and Pfister immediately saw the possibility of a meaningful synthesis of psychology with theology. Pfister began right away to incorporate psychoanalytical insights into his pastoral counseling and his teaching, and sent one of his first psychoanalytic papers to Freud in 1909, thus beginning their three-decade correspondence.

Once having begun, Pfister quickly authored one of the first popular treatments of Freud's ideas, along with a wide range of other works, applying psychoanalytic ideas to history, religion, art, political science, and most notably, education. In 1913, Pfister authored the first textbook on psychoanalytic therapy, *The Psychoanalytic Method,* with a preface by Freud and additional material contributed by Jung. Pfister and Jung worked closely on multiple projects, which put Pfister in a difficult position at the time of the schism between Jung and Freud, which led Bleuler and Jung to officially withdraw from the International Psychoanalytical Society. Freud confided in letters to Ernest **Jones** and Sándor **Ferenczi** that he worried that Pfister would take Jung's side against him, but Pfister wrote to Freud only five days after the Zurich contingent's withdrawal to announce that he wished to join the Vienna society. It was this split that led to Pfister's formation of the new Swiss society in 1919.

Oskar Pfister may well have been very prolific author in Freud's circle, publishing several hundred articles and books on a wide range of topics within psychoanalysis and theology. Beyond the *The Psychoanalytic Method*, probably his best-known and most important book is his 1928 reply to Freud's 1927 *The Future of an Illusion*, which bears the wonderfully cheeky title *The Illusion of a Future*. Whereas Freud severed ties with close associates who disagreed with him on fundamentals of psychoanalytic theory, he was somehow able to maintain his friendship with this Lutheran minister with whom he disagreed on the most fundamental questions of human existence, purpose, and history. This surely reflects well on Pfister's good humor and respect for Freud's ideas, though it may also provide useful insight regarding just how seriously Freud took his theory.

Pfister's influence on the field of pastoral psychology, and attempts to reconcile psychology and theology more generally, has been enormous, despite his fairly low profile among psychoanalysts. He detailed his thoughts on the use of psychoanalysis in the search for spiritual wholeness in his 1927 *Analytische Seelsorge* (*Analytic Soul-Searching*), but his most important work in this regard is probably *Das Christentum und die Angst* (*Christianity and Fear,* 1944), which breaks down the historical importance of what he saw as Christianity's great flaw, its reliance on fear of punishment. Pfister felt that Christianity could be saved, and that the grace to do so could be found in psychoanalysis. Throughout his work on these and similar projects, until Freud's death, the two men communicated regularly and kept up an animated discussion of the ways in which their ideas did or did not mutually support each other. Until recently, the best source of information on this most curious friendship was the 1963 edition of the Freud-Pfister correspondence, published as *Psychoanalysis and Faith.* The collection, gathered primarily from the official Freud archives, included only a handful of Pfister's letters, however, rendering its account of their relationship quite incomplete. This problem is in the process of being corrected, however, as a group of Swiss scholars are currently working on a new annotated edition of the complete Freud-Pfister correspondence, drawing on a more recently discovered collection of letters, which is itself longer than the entire 1963 book. Once this collection is published, a whole new understanding of the odd friendship between the Lutheran pastor and the Jewish atheist will no doubt emerge. Meanwhile, Pfister's own place in the history of psychology has been secured by the naming of an annual award given by the American Psychiatric Association, in association with the Association of Professional Chaplains. The Oskar Pfister award is given in recognition of significant contributions to the field of religion and psychiatry, and past recipients have included such luminaries as Viktor **Frankl,** theologian Hans Küng, neurologist Oliver Sacks, and Freud biographer Peter Gay.

Pfister's continuing influence can also be seen in the naming of the psychoanalytical training institute at the Pontifical University of Salamanca, in Spain: Centro Psicoanalitico Oskar Pfister.

Further Reading

Freud, S., and O. Pfister. (1963). *Psychoanalysis and Faith: The Letters of Sigmund Freud and Oskar Pfister* (Ernst Freud and Heinrich Meng, eds.). London: Chatto & Windus.

Pfister, O. (1917). *The Psychoanalytic Method* (Translated by Charles R. Payne). New York: Moffat, Yard, & Company.

Polymorphous Perversity

A central concept in Freud's stages of **psychosexual development,** polymorphous perversity simply refers to the ability of young children to derive sexual pleasure from any part of the body. Before the formation of the superego and education in the conventions of civilization, the child can derive sexual gratification from a variety of body parts, with no consideration for the rules that determine what is considered perverse in adulthood. It is important to note that Freud frequently used "perversion" as a non-judgmental term, referring to any behavior that falls outside socially acceptable norms.

Polymorphously perverse sexuality continues from birth to around age five or six, progressing through the first three psychosexual stages. Humans enter the world with an unfocused *libido,* able to derive sexual pleasure from any part of the body, and driven by this indistinct instinct to do so. This drive is directed at any object which might provide pleasure, as well. During the *oral* stage, for example, the child forms an important early bond to mother by deriving pleasure from sucking the breast. This pleasure is quickly generalized to other stimuli, however, and the child comes to derive satisfaction from putting virtually anything in his or her mouth. The *anal* and *phallic* stages proceed similarly, with the libido's focus shifting to other parts of the body.

Once the child is in school, education takes over and the developing superego quickly suppresses these polymorphous possibilities for sexual gratification in the child. Subsequent developmental stages lead up to normal adult heterosexual behavior focusing specifically on the genitals and reproduction. Freud explained some adult sexual perversions by postulating that some adults retain such polymorphous perversity, leading to arousal by inappropriate objects or people.

Freud taught that the undifferentiated libidinal impulses of infancy normally include incestuous and bisexual urges, approaches to gratification that the child will eventually learn are forbidden. Freud suggests that we then protect our adult selves from these inappropriate and uncomfortable urges by forgetting that we ever had them, via repression. People with sexual disorders and neuroses, in this view, are simply people who failed to successfully outgrow their undiscriminating infant sexuality. In this way, a man with a shoe fetish (who is sexually aroused by footwear, which most will agree is an inappropriate object of sexual desire) is simply someone who never focused his sexuality more narrowly on women not directly related to him by blood. Homosexuality is just another variation on the same phenomenon, according to Freud, but so is exhibitionism, and the once very common practice of smoking before or after sex may be as well.

As with so many of Freud's distinctive phrases, *polymorphous perversity* is a word pair that lives on in popular culture, though shorn of at least some of its original meaning. In at least two of Woody Allen's films, for example, the term or a variation on it has been used to describe characters. In *Celebrity,* the female model played by Scarlett Johansson calls herself a "polymorphic perverse," which another character finds "invigorating." In *Annie Hall,* Woody Allen's character (Alvy Singer) tells a woman he loves her because she is "polymorphic perverse." In a more recent example, a character in the biographical Harvey Pekar film *American Splendor* describes cartoonist Robert Crumb as "polymorphously perverse." In each case, the intended humorous use of the term involves the suggestion that the person thus described has unconventional sexual tastes, including bisexuality.

A more unexpected use of the concept may reflect the attitude many modern research psychologists have toward Freud: gentle mockery tempered by respect, along with a sense of absurdity. Since 1984, the *Journal of Polymorphous Perversity* has existed as the *only* satirical psychological research journal currently being published. At first glance it simply appears to be an obscure academic journal, complete with incomprehensible research reports full of esoteric jargon, theoretical manifestos with a potential interested audience that can be counted on one hand, and a standard boring, monochromatic cover. A closer look reveals that something is different, however. The articles are pitch-perfect parodies of real research, often written pseudonymously by rather famous names (they tend to use pseudonyms so that their reputation for serious scientific publication is unharmed). Some topics that have been covered in recent years include a new diagnosis for people who have to attend too many meetings (productivity-deficit hyperactivity disorder) and the development of The Scale of Mental Abilities Requiring Thinking Somewhat (SMARTS). Often the humor has a serious point to make about psychology: An article on the psychological assessment of the dead, for example, began with the (real) observation that on one of the world's most popular intelligence tests, nonresponses still receive a score, such that a person who answered *none* of the questions would still be assigned an IQ of 45. In other words, the dead would be rated as moderately mentally retarded. The journal was started by the Manhattan psychologist Glenn Ellenbogen, who published two parody articles that were represented as having been published in it. He began receiving submissions almost immediately and had to begin publishing the journal in earnest, and it now receives so many submissions that its rejection rate is higher than that of some genuine peer-reviewed research journals.

Further Reading

Doskoch, P. (1998). Exhibiting a Funny Twist of Mind (review of *More Oral Sadism and the Vegetarian Personality* by Glenn C. Ellenbogen). *Psychology Today,* March 1, 1998.

Projective Tests of Personality

One of the most enduring, if indirect, pieces of Freud's influence on psychiatric and psychological practice is surely the continuing popularity of projective tests of personality. Freud was not himself the creator of these tests, but they have their foundation in his ideas. *Projection* is of course one of Freud's ego **defense mechanisms,** in which individuals unconsciously see their own negative personality traits and impulses quite clearly in others rather than in themselves. This notion combines readily with Freud's recognition that seemingly abstract or nonsensical dream content may actually reveal hidden impulses, wishes, and motivations, to produce what has become known as the "projective hypothesis": presented with ambiguous or abstract stimuli, respondents will project information about the hidden parts of their personalities into their attempts to make sense of those stimuli.

In a projective test, the examiner presents unstructured, vague, or ambiguous stimuli (such as the inkblots of the Rorschach test), with the belief that responses to the test represent revelations about the unconscious mental processes of the respondent. These tests have been fairly popular since Freud's time, and as of the mid-1990s, 5 of the 15 most frequently used psychological tests were still projective techniques. This is somewhat surprising, given that the psychoanalytic approach in which the tests are solidly grounded has been out of favor in the mainstream of American psychology for more than 50 years, yet most projective tests demand a psychoanalytic approach in scoring and interpretation. The popularity of the tests is even more surprising given the lack of solid proof that they are even capable of providing any useful diagnostic information, along with a substantial body of evidence indicating that the tests lack reliability and validity—this is sometimes referred to as the "projective paradox." Validity is the extent to which a test is actually measuring what it claims to measure, as well as its ability to predict behavior. Reliability simply refers to the extent to which a person taking the same test more than once will obtain the same results each time, as well as the extent to which the test will yield similar results regardless of who scores it.

Certainly the best-known projective test is the Rorschach test, introduced in the 1920s by the Swiss psychiatrist Hermann Rorschach (1884–1922). The origins of his test date back to his school days, when Rorschach was an enthusiastic participant in an art game/technique known at the time as Klecksographie (also known as Blotto), in which players fold paper over ink in order to produce abstract patterns.

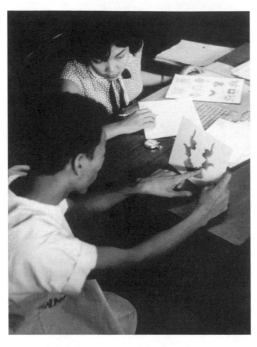

The Rorschach test, seen being administered here, remains the best known of the projective tests. (WHO/National Library of Medicine)

Rorschach, who spent his youth torn between his interests in science and in art, played so much that he was known by the nickname "Klex." Eventually he chose to study psychiatry under Eugen **Bleuler,** Jung's mentor, and became a committed psychoanalyst.

While working with adolescent patients, he began to use his Klecksographie pictures as an icebreaker with them, and he noticed that different teens with different diagnoses tended to respond differently to the same inkblots, and it occurred to him that there might be a pattern to these responses. From this observation, it is a short logical distance to the notion that particular types of mental illness might produce particular sorts of responses, and therefore inkblots might provide a potentially useful diagnostic technique. Approaching this idea from a psychoanalytic perspective, it seemed clear that responses to such completely ambiguous stimuli as inkblots might provide insight into elements that were otherwise unconscious. Rorschach published these ideas, rather tentatively, in a 1921 monograph titled *Psychodiagnostik,* which was the first appearance of his set of 10 inkblots. In the monograph, he referred to the pictures as a Form Interpretation Test, and he emphasized that his findings with his patients were preliminary, inconclusive, and required far more experimentation and testing before they could be considered validated. The original publication of the inkblots did not include a clear scoring system, and Rorschach died, at age 37, less than a year later.

In the absence of clear guidelines, multiple authors published their own instructions on how to administer, score, and interpret the test, with major points of disagreement between them. This did not prevent the test from becoming one of the most popular tools in psychiatry, and the Rorschach inkblot technique was virtually synonymous with psychiatry and clinical psychology in the 1940s and 1950s. In the test, people are shown Rorschach's series of 10 inkblots and asked to describe what they see. Five of the inkblots are monochromatic, and five introduce color (primarily shades of red and pink). Responses are generally scored in terms of actual content, which portions of the inkblot are involved, and how common (or unusual) the answer is. The actual inkblots have been a closely guarded secret among clinicians since their publication, based on the notion that the test's validity as a diagnostic instrument would be compromised if respondents had seen them before. Modern communications have recently frustrated therapists in this regard, as the entire set of inkblots, along with scoring information, have become widely available on the Internet, including complete presentation in the Wikipedia entry on Hermann Rorschach.

The Rorschach is far and away the most popular projective technique, even now given to many hundreds of thousands of people annually. It came under harsh attack as long ago as the 1950s, due to its lack of standardized procedures and norms (averaged results from a representative sample of the population, used as a reference point). Without them it is impossible to determine whether an individual's results are normal or not. Standardization of procedures is also important, because apparently minor differences in how a test is given can strongly influence a person's responses.

Since the 1970s, Rorschach users have felt protected against such criticism by John Exner's Comprehensive System, an ambitious attempt to standardize both the administration and the scoring of the test. In addition to its detailed procedures for standardized administration of the test, the comprehensive system also provides norms for both children and adults. Unfortunately, the test continues to have major problems with reliability and validity, largely because of the continuing subjective nature of many of the scoring criteria. The person scoring the test rates the subject's responses on more than 100 characteristics, including such things as whether the person described the whole blot or just parts, whether the response was typical or unusual, whether the response was based on shape or color or both, whether the person focused on the dark portions or the white spaces, and many other details. As a result, two well-trained examiners may come up with strikingly different interpretations of a single person's responses.

The result of this lack of reliability is a remarkable lack of validity: The Rorschach is quite poor as a diagnostic tool for most psychiatric conditions, with the possible exception of schizophrenia and other thought disturbances, and even then the evidence is mixed. Quite clearly false, however, are the claims by some Rorschach proponents that the method can reliably detect depression, anxiety disorders, sexual abuse in children, antisocial personality disorder, and tendencies toward violence, impulsivity, and criminal behavior. Furthermore, the norms that exist for the test are unrepresentative of the U.S. population, and their use results in substantial overestimation of maladjustment. In one California study using responses provided by a sample of blood donors, for example, one in six appeared to have schizophrenia, according to their Rorschach scores.

The test also is remarkably susceptible to faking, an important consideration for a test so frequently introduced as evidence in court. A 1980 study is typical: Rorschach responses of 24 people were submitted to a panel of experts (in this case, psychoanalytically oriented therapists convinced of the test's utility) for diagnosis. The profiles actually came from the following four groups: six actual mental patients with a diagnosis of paranoid schizophrenia, six uninformed fakers instructed to try to fake the responses of a paranoid schizophrenic, six informed fakers who listened to a detailed tape about schizophrenia first, and six normal control subjects who simply took the test under standard conditions. Each person's profile was rated by six to nine judges. The informed fakers were diagnosed as psychotic 72 percent of the time, versus only 48 percent for the actual psychotics. The uninformed fakers were also diagnosed as psychotic almost half of the time, and even the normal controls were diagnosed 24 percent of the time.

The pattern of rapid, widespread adoption without standardized procedures has characterized other projective tests as well, resulting in similar serious concerns over their reliability and validity. After the Rorschach, the most widely used projective test has been The Thematic Apperception Test (TAT), which is based on the ideas of Henry **Murray,** founder of the Boston Psychoanalytic Institute. Like the Rorschach, the TAT has neither standardized administration procedures nor an established scoring procedure. In the TAT, respondents are shown a series of ambiguous scenes presented on large cards. Some are simple pen-and-ink drawings, some are fairly elaborate charcoals, and several are photographs, but none are in color. For each picture, the respondent is asked to make up a story, including what led up to the scene depicted on the card, as well as what will happen next. One card takes the projective approach to an extreme: it is totally blank. Individual clinicians choose the number of cards to show, up to 31, as well as which particular cards are used. One frequent criticism of the TAT is that the dreary black-and-white pictures produce an overall negative mood, resulting in too many respondents appearing depressed. This has led to numerous attempts to create alternate versions of the test, but the problems with the TAT are far more basic than the issue of picture content: Although many standardized scoring systems have been created for the TAT, a survey of North American psychologists practicing in juvenile and family courts found that only 3 percent used *any* of them. Research suggests that using them would not help in any case. The systems show poor reliability and are unable to differentiate normal individuals from people who are either psychotic or depressed. Furthermore, these scoring systems provide no norms.

A third projective approach in wide use, again mostly by the courts, asks the person to draw a picture. The most widely used drawing test is the rather self-explanatory draw-a-person test. Interpretation proceeds in what has been called a "clinical-intuitive" manner, based on signs (features of the body or clothing, for example), usually guided by rather tentative psychodynamically based hypotheses. Large eyes might indicate paranoia and long ties might suggest sexual aggression, for example. A house with no windows might indicate feeling trapped. A person whose genitalia, or hands, or knees, or other features, depending on the interpretive guide used, are prominently visible might indicate a history of sexual abuse or latent homosexuality. There is no evidence, however, supporting the validity of this approach. Clinicians, in other words, have no grounds for believing any particular signs indicate any particular problem, other than their own prejudices and those of whoever trained them. Furthermore, studies suggest that clinicians will often attribute mental illness to many normal individuals who simply don't draw very well.

At present, it is clear that projective tests fail to meet even the most basic standards of reliability and validity. In fact, a recent review of projective tests commissioned by the American Psychological Society (APS) concluded that "as usually administered, the Rorschach, TAT and human figure drawings are useful *only in very limited circumstances*" (author emphasis). Given this, how shall we interpret the projective paradox? Why are they still among the most popular tests? Of the various possible explanations, two seem especially important here. As human beings, clinicians are as susceptible as anyone to confirmation bias, or the tendency to take into account evidence that supports one's own beliefs and expectations while failing to consider evidence that fails to do so. A clinician who believes large eyes indicate paranoia, for example, will place great importance on the single client who drew large eyes and actually was paranoid, while remaining unmoved by (and possibly not even having noticed) the many large-eyed pictures drawn by clients who were not paranoid.

A second, more positive possibility to consider is the fact that many clinicians who use projective methods do not use them as tests or diagnostic tools at all, but rather as auxiliary tools in clinical interviews. They help the clinician to form initial, tentative hypotheses about the client, to be tested by closer examination with better tools. This use of the tests seems more appropriate, given the apparent uselessness of projectives where diagnosis is concerned. Unfortunately, surveys suggest that many clinicians, despite the clear evidence to the contrary, continue to believe in the diagnostic efficacy of projective tests.

Further Reading

Lilienfeld, S. O., J. M. Wood, and H. N. Garb. (2000). The Scientific Status of Projective Techniques. *Psychological Science in the Public Interest* 1(2): 27–66.

Psychic Phenomena

In the early days of scientific psychological research, in the mid- to late 19th century, and on into the 20th, many of the most prominent thinkers in both Europe and America turned their attention to reports of what were then termed *psychical* or spiritual phenomena. Far from immune to such intellectual fashions, Freud joined the Society for Psychical Research in 1911, as well as its American counterpart five years later, and he presented papers on multiple occasions that addressed cases he felt were suggestive of telepathy. Due to the poor scientific and intellectual reputation of such pursuits, this portion of Freud's work has been largely ignored by the psychoanalytic community: Peter Gay's nearly 800-page biography devotes approximately 2 pages to Freud's papers and experiments on telepathy, for example. His other primary biographer, Ernest Jones, is quite blunt in his dismissal of this area of interest, writing that Freud's enthusiasm for the paranormal demonstrates "that highly developed critical powers may co-exist in the same person with an unexpected fund of credulity" (1957).

The initial burst of interest in scientific study of the paranormal was a direct result of the explosion in popularity of spiritualism (also called *spiritism*) in mid-19th-century America and Europe. In spiritualism, which eventually became an organized church based in New England, people interested in communicating with the spirits of the dead would hold *séances,* in which they would gather about a table in a darkened room, holding hands, and ask the spirits to communicate with them. The response would usually come in the form of mysterious rapping noises. Over time, the phenomena involved in séances grew to include such things as trumpets floating in the air and being mysteriously blown, the table rising briefly into the air, and the production of *ectoplasm,* or ghost substance, a mysterious shimmering product that the medium would pull from thin air, or sometimes from various body parts, and wave about.

Unlike the initial moments of most heavily studied phenomena, the birth of the Spiritualist movement can be dated quite precisely: the first séances were held in 1848, in the Hydesville, New York, home of the teenage Fox sisters (Margaret and Kate), who decided to have a bit of fun at their parents' expense. Margaret had developed the ability to produce loud rapping sounds with her toes, which seemed to be mysterious communications from beyond when performed in a dark room with everyone holding hands on the table. Very soon the Fox sisters were performing

In a classic séance, with all participants holding hands and concentrating, the medium appears to levitate, one of the more popular (but difficult) tricks among 19th-century Spiritualists. (Library of Congress)

séances with a wide range of people, and others followed their lead until people all over Europe and America were communicating with the dead, and performing ever more elaborate variations on their initial deception.

Within a few years, some eminent men of science, believing the phenomena to be real, began to investigate the conditions under which they occurred. The first attempt to describe a method of investigating these phenomena (and to provide a theory of sorts to explain them) was produced by the French author Léon-Dénizarth-Hippolyte Rivail, writing under the pseudonym Allan Kardec, primarily in two books: *Le Livre des Esprits* (1856) and *Le Livre des Mediums* (1861).

Kardec's interest in the subject seems to have begun when he met two young mediums, whose father was known to him, and they told him (or rather, the spirits whose words were coming through them told him) that he had an important spiritual mission to carry out. The resulting spiritist theory that he detailed in his books was the result of responses produced by these mediums via rapping and planchette movement (the trick best known today as the Ouija board). Indeed, the pseudonym was provided by the spirits as well: both *Allan* and *Kardec* were alleged to have been his names in prior lives. The spirits even told him what to call the book.

Le Livre des Esprits become an instant sensation, making converts to his brand of spiritualism all over Europe. Kardec founded the Parisian Society of Psychologic Studies, which met in his home on Fridays in order to receive, via automatic writing (another standard medium technique), further instructions from the spirits. One outgrowth of this organization was his editorship of *La Revue Spirite,* which he continued to produce until his death (though not thereafter; it is still published today by the World Spiritist Congress).

Kardec's impact on his world was remarkably far-reaching: Napoleon III even sent for him several times to discuss the teachings in *Le Livre des Esprits.* In the wake of the founding of Kardec's organization, other such groups were rapidly formed throughout Europe and America. As with most spiritual movements, schisms were evident early on, however, as the French version of Spiritualism differed markedly from the American in Kardec's endorsement of the idea of compulsory reincarnation—in Kardec's books, it is made clear that all are required to live multiple lifetimes. This is an odd feature of Kardec's teachings, given that he followed up his early successes with books such as *The Gospel as Explained by Spirits* (1864), *Heaven and Hell* (1865), and *Genesis* (1867), whose target audience couldn't be expected to be particularly receptive to the doctrine of reincarnation.

As the phenomena produced by mediums began to attract the attention of more scientifically minded observers as well, these men also became interested in investigating the claims of mind readers, hypnotists, and fortune tellers, whose popularity had been boosted by the explosion in mediumship. Soon the scientists had formed formal organizations, and their psychical research was a respectable and rapidly growing enterprise. The Society for Psychical Research formed in London in 1882; the American Society for Psychical Research, today the Parapsychological Association, followed in 1885. Early in their investigations, they began to document a few things about the conditions under which such phenomena seemed more likely to occur. A successful séance, for example, required darkness—the materializations would not occur in a well-lit room, and the spirits would often not communicate at all. The presence of very skeptical people, who might watch very closely, also seemed to make the spirits less likely to turn up.

Despite these inconvenient facts, several skilful superstar mediums emerged (D. D. Home and Eusapia Palladino are probably the best known) over several decades following the Fox sisters' initial breakthrough, and they were instrumental in attracting the interest of serious scientists. Sir William Crookes, the great chemist (known for, among other accomplishments, the discovery of thallium, as well as early developments in the field of chemical fertilizer), for example, became interested in spiritist phenomena following the death of his brother. After attending a séance with the Fox sisters, Crookes was instrumental in getting other scientists to take more seriously the phenomena they produced, along with validating the levitation and table-tilting of D. D. Home. Following his example, the Society for

Psychical Research counted several members of the British Royal Society among its early constituency. Alfred Russel Wallace, best-known as Charles Darwin's chief competitor for the discoverer's role in the saga of evolutionary theory, also dabbled in psychical research, attending séances and speculating on the sources of the phenomena witnessed therein.

Given its origins in the séance room, it is important to note that the *scientific* study of psychic phenomena began to abandon the notion that psychics were actually communicating with the dead over a century ago. In the late 19th century, the Society for Psychical Research had already begun to turn its attention toward paranormal phenomena beyond those manifested by the spirit mediums. In an 1886 two-volume collection of reports of ghosts and contact with the dead, titled *Phantasms of the Living*, Society members Edmund Gurney and Frederic W. H. Myers speculated that some of the apparitions they studied were actually due to *thought-transference* (a theory, incidentally, about which Alfred Russel Wallace then wrote a highly critical paper), for which they coined a new word: *telepathy*.

By the early 20th century, psychical researchers had become less interested in the spirit mediums and were concentrating their attention more fully on telepaths and clairvoyants. As their methods became more rigorous and quantitative, and psychologists began to take over a field previously dominated by physical scientists, the new science began to find a home at major universities. Pride of place for publishing the first report of an experiment on clairvoyance (card guessing, in this case) goes to John Coover, the first holder of a Fellowship in Psychical Research at Stanford University. In the monograph *Experiments in Psychical Research,* he published the results of four large studies, involving 100 research participants. Somewhat prophetically for the field of study as a whole, he concluded that he had found nothing supportive of belief in extrasensory perception (ESP). Perhaps in part because of his willingness to publicize his negative results, Coover is largely forgotten even among those who know the parapsychological literature well.

Given the pedigree of some of the supporters of psychic research, it is unsurprising that a man as interested in the mysteries of the mind as Freud would also look into these occult phenomena. Freud expressed an interest in investigating telepathy as early as 1905, and in March 1908, he made a presentation to the Vienna Psychoanalytical Society regarding three cases that might have indicated thought transference, while still excluding the possibility of telepathy. His subsequent acquaintance with Jung, who was far more open to the possibility, appears to have influenced his subsequent thought on the subject. Both in his published papers and his personal correspondence, Freud appears to have concerned himself primarily with two varieties of paranormal experience: prophetic and telepathic dream content, and telepathy while awake.

Freud used the term *thought transference* interchangeably with telepathy, which he defined as the instantaneous transmission of information between two minds.

He believed that the two individuals involved must have a strong emotional bond with each other, and that the transmitted information will generally be charged with negative emotional content. Freud was clearly uncomfortable with the idea of endorsing a phenomenon that did not make a lot of sense physically, yet which he felt could be quite useful in psychoanalysis, if it actually existed. He was very careful, consequently, to avoid taking a clear position on its existence when he spoke publicly on the matter. In 1922, for example, he presented a paper in which he warned, "From this lecture you will learn nothing about the riddle of telepathy, nor even be informed whether I believe in the existence of 'telepathy' or not" (quoted in Gay, 1988, p. 444). In the conclusion of the same paper, he described himself as having "no opinion" on the matter.

For a man with no opinion, however, he certainly seems to have devoted a lot of time and energy to describing the phenomenon anyway. His training in medicine produced a certain internal tension regarding these spiritual-sounding processes, leading him to attempt to produce as physiological and materialistic a mechanism for thought transference as possible. In *New Introductory Lectures on Psychoanalysis,* for example, he explains telepathy via analogy to the workings of both the telephone (then an exciting new invention) and the communication that occurs among large groups of insects:

> The telepathic process is supposed to consist in a mental act in one person instigating the same mental act in another person. What lies between these two mental acts may easily be a physical process into which the mental one is transformed at one end and which is transformed back once more into the same mental one at the other end. The analogy with other transformations, such as occur in speaking and hearing by telephone, would then be unmistakable. . . . It is a familiar fact that we do not know how the common purpose comes about in the great insect communities: possibly it is done by means of a direct psychical transference of this kind. One is led to a suspicion that this is the original, archaic method of communication between individuals and that in the course of phylogenetic evolution it has been replaced by the better method of giving information with the help of signals which are picked up by the sense organs. But the older method might have persisted in the background and still be able to put itself into effect under certain conditions—for instance, in passionately excited mobs. (Freud, 1933, p. 55)

In this explanation, Freud manages to suggest an evolutionary plausibility for telepathy, thus moving it further away from the world of the spirit mediums and toward the possibility of serious scientific consideration. As with his other mentions of the phenomenon, however, he stops short of definitely endorsing its existence. In his correspondence with Sándor **Ferenczi** and Jung circa 1911, he is very cautious about allowing any public association to be made between psychoanalysis and occultism, as he fears that this would undo all of his efforts to have psychoanalysis taken seriously as science. In one 1911 letter, responding to Ferenczi's description of his own efforts at conducting telepathy experiments, for example, he explicitly refuses to join his "dangerous expeditions." Nevertheless, his interest in telepathy as a possible tool for psychoanalysis persisted in his writings. He even wrote in a paper instructing physicians on psychoanalytic technique that, *if* telepathy exists, it might be useful on the psychoanalytic couch, where the analyst should "turn his unconscious like a receptive organ towards the transmitting unconscious of the patient."

Much of Freud's attention to the paranormal focused not on what happens while awake, however, but rather on the appearance of occult phenomena in dreams, especially dreams that appear to be prophetic or clairvoyant, and he published several papers on the subject. His ambivalence regarding waking telepathy is also clearly in evidence in his discussions of dreams and paranormal phenomena, in which he takes great pains to emphasize that they are distinct from each other, and that the paranormal is *not* any part of his overall theory of dreams. He is instead interested in the question of why paranormal phenomena surface so readily under dream conditions, and the slightly contradictory parallel question of whether the observed dream phenomena are actually paranormal at all.

Freud rarely considered prophetic dreams, focusing instead on telepathic dreams— he believed that the sleeping, dreaming mind was more receptive to telepathic communications than the waking mind. He suggested that telepathic messages would be used by the mind just like any other material that gets incorporated into dreams, and dreams containing such content should follow the same basic rules as all other dreams, thus requiring no alteration of his theory of dreams at all. In Freud's theory the surface, or manifest, content of a dream serves to disguise and conceal the real purpose of the dream, the symbolically obscured latent content. He suggested that a telepathic message received by a dreamer would form the latent content of the dream, and thus it would be distorted in the dream. The only way to distinguish a telepathic from a nontelepathic dream, therefore, would be via psychoanalytic examination of the dream.

In his 1922 paper, "Dreams and Telepathy," Freud describes a dream that may be indicative of telepathic communication (again, he is cautious to suggest only that it may demonstrate telepathy). The dreamer, a widower who had remarried, had a pregnant daughter from his first marriage whose baby was not due to arrive for another month. In his dream, his second wife was pregnant, and gave birth to a pair of twins. Based on the dream, the man was able to give a very vivid description of the babies, including their sex (one boy and one girl) and the color of their hair. Two days after the dream, he found out that his daughter had given birth to twins matching his dream description at approximately the time he was asleep and having the dream. In the paper, Freud offers both paranormal *and* nonparanormal explanations for the dream. In a fairly standard interpretation, Freud suggests that the dream may be an expression of the father's repressed desire to incestuously impregnate his daughter, with whom he was very close—she appears in the dream as his second wife, expressing his wish that his daughter were his wife instead. This is a rather typical Freudian interpretation of a dream as wish-fulfillment fantasy, but Freud also proposes in the paper that this does not disprove the telepathic interpretation. As the dream was reported to him in a letter, by someone he did not know personally, he argues that the possibility of telepathy could only be eliminated if he were able to examine *all* circumstances surrounding the dream, which was not possible in this case.

Another paper, "A Premonitory Dream Fulfilled," represents the only time Freud publicly analyzed an apparently prophetic dream. The dreamer, called Frau B by Freud, dreamt of meeting her old friend Dr. K at a particular location in Vienna, and the next day actually encountered him at that precise spot. This is precisely the sort of scenario that often leads people to believe in the prophetic nature of dreams, but Freud adopts a far more skeptical approach here than he did with the idea of telepathic dreams, in part because he found out early on that Frau B did not record the dream at the time she had it, and only remembered the dream *after* encountering Dr. K. Further information fueled a distinctly non-paranormal interpretation. In speaking with Frau B, Freud found that she had been married twice. The first marriage had been to a wealthy older man. Several years into the marriage, he lost his fortune and contracted tuberculosis, from which he eventually died. During his illness, Frau B had to support the family by giving music lessons. Dr. K was very supportive during this period, and helped her to find students. Meanwhile, Herr B's affairs were being managed by an attorney, also named Dr. K, with whom Frau B also carried on an extramarital affair. Although the affair did not last long, the attorney was very supportive, and she particularly remembered an occasion on which she was terribly upset and wishing he was there to comfort him, on which he walked in at the precise moment of her wishing it.

Twenty-five years later, having remarried and become a widow again, Frau B had the dream. She was left much better off financially by the second husband than when her first husband died, and the attorney Dr. K was once again handling her affairs, though their more intimate relationship was in the distant past. Based on all of this, Freud interpreted the dream as follows: Frau B had been expecting Dr. K, but he did not show up. This led to a nostalgic dream of the time when he visited right when she wanted him to. Since that was an unpleasant and difficult time in her life, however, and thinking about the inappropriate affair made her uncomfortable, she repressed the dream and didn't remember it when she awoke. Later that day, she met the *physician* Dr. K, her old friend, and consciously remembered a distorted *derivative* of the dream, in which the more emotionally neutral of the two

Dr. K's was substituted for the charged, dangerous attorney. As both had the same name, she believed she had dreamt the actual encounter, rather than recognizing the repressed content for what it was. Clearly Freud was more skeptical about the appearance of future events in dreams than he was of telepathic content: on the only occasion on which he directly examined a prophetic dream, Freud concluded with a fairly standard dream analysis, requiring no paranormal event at all.

Beyond dreams, Freud also attempted to study psychic phenomena that occurred while conscious. Early on in their acquaintance, Sándor Ferenczi, who spent much of his own career openly fascinated by the paranormal, wrote to Freud regarding his own experiments with telepathy. Far from rigorous, these early experiences consisted primarily of Ferenczi's attempts to guess the names of strangers on public transit. The evidence he thus accumulated, however, was sufficient to convince him that telepathy was real, and in their 1910–1911 correspondence Freud devotes some energy to trying to restrain Ferenczi's newborn enthusiasm for trying to read his patients' thoughts. Freud's correspondence with Jung during this same period reveals that Freud may also have originally become intrigued by psychic phenomena after seeing Jung demonstrate an ability to apparently cause objects to rattle with his mind. His friendship with Jung, along with Ferenczi's apparent successes, were enough to convince Freud to explore the subject further, however, and he conducted a series of experiments in attempted thought transference with the help of his own daughter Anna as well as Ferenczi. Still concerned for the implications for the public image of psychoanalytic science, Freud objected for years to the idea of revealing those experiments publicly, responding to Ferenczi's plans to present an account of them to a 1925 international congress as follows: "I advise you against. Don't do it. . . . By it you would be throwing a bomb into the psychoanalytical house which would be certain to explode" (Jones, 1957, pp. 393–394). Ferenczi did not present the account of the experiments, and neither he nor Anna Freud ever published a description of what exactly the experiments consisted of. Whatever the experiments comprised, however, led to Freud's rather more enthusiastic private reaction to the tests. In 1926, he wrote to Ernest Jones that "[my] own experiences through tests I made with Ferenczi and my daughter won such a convincing force for me that the diplomatic considerations on the other side had to give way" (Jones, 1957, pp. 395–396). In the same letter, however, the old ambivalence also remains in evidence, as Freud reminds his colleague "that the theme of telepathy is in essence alien to psychoanalysis" (p. 396), and suggests that his belief in the subject is a private matter, like his smoking and his Jewishness.

Freud's ambivalent embrace of the occult is also clearly illustrated by a letter he wrote in 1921 to an American psychical researcher, in which he stated that if he had it all to do over again, he would prefer to have devoted himself to psychical research rather than to psychoanalysis. By 1929, however, he was denying to Ernest Jones that he had ever made that statement. These experiments were inconclusive, and never convinced Freud absolutely of the reality of the paranormal, but his interest had an impact on the rest of the psychoanalytic community, as writers as diverse as Ferenczi, Helene Deutsch, and Istvan Hollis all published papers on the possible uses of the occult in psychoanalysis, and Jung wrote extensively about a wide range of mystical ideas after his break with Freud.

Despite Freud's plain interest in psychic phenomena, his writings on the subject have largely been overlooked, perhaps as a result of the subsequent bad reputation of psychic research in the psychological community. Even as Freud was becoming interested, it was increasingly clear that many of the best-known demonstrations of such phenomena were fraudulent, and that *all* of them were at least potentially so. Even under the legitimizing influence of Crookes, Wallace, and other prominent scientists (in America, William James was also an early enthusiast), Home and Palladino, for example, were frequently caught cheating. This was readily overlooked by clients as well as by some of the prominent scientists, who were quick to accept the idea that too-close scrutiny prevented the rather shy spirits from showing up. People who *openly* deceived others for a living (especially such magicians as Houdini), however, began to take notice of these competitors who claimed their miracles were real. Houdini, still the best known of all conjurers, made a second career of attending séances and exposing fraud therein.

Unlike most who arrived in a medium's parlor, Houdini was uniquely qualified to detect the trickery involved in spirit manifestations. Early in his career, he and his wife hosted regular séances for a Midwestern medicine show, during which he would cause tables to tip and float, while he also played musical instruments, all while tied to his chair! After his career as an escape artist took off around 1899, Houdini left the stage medium business behind and largely forgot about it.

His interest was revived in the early 1920s when he befriended Sir Arthur Conan Doyle, author of the Sherlock Holmes mysteries. Theirs was an odd friendship, balancing Houdini's professional skepticism with Doyle's extreme credulousness (among other things, he wrote a book endorsing the clearly faked photos three young girls took of fairies at Cottingley). Having become a Spiritualist leader, Doyle introduced Houdini to several prominent mediums in hopes of convincing him of the reality of the manifestations they produced. Far from being converted to Spiritualism, Houdini immediately recognized the fairly obvious tricks he had given up earlier in his career, and was offended at their deception of grieving people hoping only to reunite with their loved ones. He was especially sympathetic toward the victims, as he was still tormented by the unexpected death of his own mother a decade earlier.

He set out to show that the business of psychic readings, far from being helpful to those left behind, was in fact built on their exploitation. An early book on the subject, *Miracle Mongers and Their Methods* (1920), set the template for the far more influential *A Magician among the Spirits* (1924). Houdini made big changes in his stage act, in order to demonstrate far and wide that as a mere magician, he could not only reproduce all the effects associated with the mediums, but could actually perform them more convincingly. He went beyond reproducing their effects, however, going so far as to attend séances and expose the trickery while it was occurring. This had the added benefit, of course, of keeping his name before the public at a time when he was becoming too old to continue performing the very physically demanding stunts on which he built his career.

According to his book, Houdini frequently attended séances in disguise, with both a reporter and a police officer in tow, so that he could simultaneously have the medium arrested for fraud and have a story about the incident (prominently featuring Houdini's own role, naturally) published in the local newspaper. He would also sometimes forego the disguise, instead challenging local mediums in the cities where he performed to demonstrate their powers on stage. The most noteworthy of these challenges involved a medium who went by the name of Margery (real name: Mina Crandon), billed as "The Boston Medium." Margery had already convinced some prominent scientific investigators, a committee put together by *Scientific American,* that she was the real deal. When the committee sent Houdini to investigate, however, he found that she was just like all the other mediums he had seen, using the same fraudulent techniques (he published a separate pamphlet concerning this case, titled *"Margery" The Medium Exposed,* expanded to book length as *Houdini Exposes the Tricks Used by Boston Medium "Margery"*). Among other things, he reported catching her ringing an electric bell with her foot and levitating a table by leaning over and lifting its edge with her head. So confident was he of her methods that he offered her $10,000 to demonstrate her abilities on stage at Boston's Symphony Hall. The only condition attached to the prize was that she produce a manifestation he could not duplicate. When she refused, Houdini recreated her entire act for the audience, and subsequently went on to do so as a permanent part of his stage act.

Following his success with Margery, he went on to expose the methods used by many other famous mediums, including the Fox sisters, as well as the single most famous medium of the time, Eusapia Palladino. The impact of earlier exposures of fraud on the popularity of the mediums had been quite minimal (a common reaction: the spirits don't always respond, so of course they have to cheat sometimes—that doesn't mean it isn't real on the other occasions! This justification continues as a major part of the arsenal of certain psychic performers today), even when the originator of the movement admitted her fraud. In 1888 (40 years after getting it all started, but 36 years *before* Houdini's book), Margaret Fox, by this time a widow, told her story and gave public demonstrations of how the effects were achieved. The almost nonexistent impact of this recantation is perhaps made clear by the fact that almost 20 years *later,* Freud was just beginning to show an interest in psychic mediums.

While Freud was taking his tentative steps toward describing a physically plausible mechanism for telepathy, an American researcher was attempting to completely throw off the trappings of mysticism and occultism to create a scientific approach to the paranormal, starting with a new name for the field. *Parapsychology* is the term introduced in the 1930s by J. B. (Joseph Banks) Rhine, one of the field's pioneers, for the scientific study of scientifically paranormal claims. Rhine was the cofounder (in 1934) and director of the Parapsychology Laboratory at Duke University, located in North Carolina. Rhine and his wife, Louisa, first went to Duke to join the Psychology department and work with William McDougall, who shared their interest in paranormal phenomena, and soon this shared interest took psychical research in a new and altogether more scientific direction.

Although he agreed with Houdini after a session with Margery that the medium was guilty of fraud and trickery, Rhine was nonetheless fascinated by telepathy and similar phenomena, and he wanted to establish the study of this more scientifically observable subject matter as a subject distinct from the study of those who claimed communion with the dead. It was Rhine who shook off the phrase "psychical research" with its attendant baggage and popularized the more scientific-sounding *parapsychology* (a term used as far back as 1889 by the psychologist Max Dessoir) to replace it. He also introduced the terms *extrasensory perception* and *psychokinesis,* and was easily the most influential of all parapsychologists, both in his methods and in his ability to popularize the field in his books, articles, and lectures. The term *extrasensory perception* captures well the inherent contradictions of the field, which caused so much ambivalence for Freud, as perception is typically defined as the brain's cognitive processing of information received from the senses. Perception is therefore sensory *by definition*—ordinarily the only circumstances under which it occurs in the absence of sensory input would involve either hallucination or direct stimulation of the brain. This is one of the things that makes psychic research both fascinating and frustrating. If parapsychologists are able to establish convincingly that these phenomena occur, then much of what we know about how the human brain functions (to say nothing of the rest of the physical world, including the basic laws of physics) must be, at best, incomplete and obsolete, and at worst, just plain wrong. This tension was central to Freud's writings on the subject, as he always considered himself first and foremost a man of science, and so throughout his career he was careful to keep his private passion and his public endorsement apart.

Freud was certainly not the only intellectual giant of the early 20th century to grapple with the attractions and contradictions of telepathy. It should be noted that two years after Rhine began his studies of ESP at Duke, Pulitzer Prize winner Upton Sinclair published a book detailing a series of clairvoyance experiments he conducted with his wife. The book was a popular seller, and the extent to which the idea of clairvoyance was seen as a legitimate topic for study at the time is illustrated by the fact that Albert Einstein wrote a preface to the book. In the preface, Einstein stresses Sinclair's honesty and integrity, as well as the dubious nature of the phenomenon itself:

> It is out of the question in the case of so conscientious an observer and writer as Upton Sinclair that he is carrying on a conscious deception of the reading world; his good faith and dependability are not to be doubted. So if somehow the facts here set forth rest not upon telepathy, but upon some unconscious hypnotic influence from person to person, this also would be of high psychological interest. (Quoted in Sinclair, 1929)

This passage is sometimes presented as indicating an endorsement of paranormal abilities on Einstein's part. It does not indicate any such thing, but he was clearly open to further study of the phenomena, especially the idea that something psychological rather than paranormal is at work. Einstein's language is remarkably similar to Freud's. Given the number and position of the people who find the evidence compelling, and the potential usefulness of studying the phenomenon for increasing our understanding of human psychology, both men, though skeptical, are unwilling to simply dismiss the phenomenon out of hand.

Further Reading

Freud, S. (1933). *New Introductory Lectures on Psychoanalysis.* Reprinted 1990, *Complete Psychological Works of Sigmund Freud, The Standard Edition, Vol. 22.* New York: W. W. Norton.

Freud, S., and S. Ferenczi. (1994). *The Complete Correspondence of Sigmund Freud and Sándor Ferenczi, Volume I: 1908–1914.* (E. Brabant and E. Falzeder, eds.). Cambridge, MA: Belknap.

Gay, P. (1988). *Freud: A Life for Our Time.* New York: W. W. Norton.

Gurney, E., F. W. Myers, and F. Podmore. (1886). *Phantasms of the Living.* London: Trubner and Co.

Houdini, H. (1924). *Houdini Exposes the Tricks Used by the Boston Medium "Margery" to Win the $2500 Prize Offered by the Scientific American. Also a Complete Exposure of Argamasilla, the Famous Spaniard Who Baffled Noted Scientists of Europe and America, with His claim to X-ray Vision.* New York: Adams Press.

Houdini, H. (1972). *A Magician among the Spirits.* New York: Arno Press. (Originally published 1924.)

Houdini, H. (1981). *Miracle Mongers and Their Methods: A Complete Exposé.* Buffalo, NY: Prometheus. (Originally published 1920.)

Hyman, R. (1989). *The Elusive Quarry: A Scientific Appraisal of Psychical Research.* Buffalo, NY: Prometheus, 1989.

Jones, E. (1957). *The Life and Work of Sigmund Freud. Vol. 3: The Last Phase.* New York: Basic Books.

Jung, C. G., S. Freud, and W. McGuire, eds. (1976). *The Freud/Jung Letters.* Princeton, NJ: Princeton University Press.

Kardec, A. (1874). *Book on Mediums (Le Livre des Mediums).* Boston: Colby and Rich.

Kardec, A. (1993). *The Spirits' Book (Le Livre des Esprits).* Albuquerque, NM: Brotherhood of Life.

Rhine, J. B. (1937). *New Frontiers of the Mind: The Story of the Duke Experiments.* New York: Farrar & Rinehart.

Sinclair, U. (1962). *Mental Radio.* Springfield, IL: C. C. Thomas. (Originally published 1929.)

Psychosexual Development, Stages of

Possibly the most controversial portion of Freud's theory is his view of child development. Freud saw personality development as proceeding through an orderly, invariant set of five stages, each named for the primary focus of the *libido* for the id at the time. Freud believed that if conflicts that arise are not resolved in a satisfactory manner, it is possible to become fixated on the particular stage, resulting in an abnormal preoccupation with that stage's source of pleasure later in life. A heavy smoker or gum-chewer, for example, might be regarded as fixated at the oral stage, during which the primary focus of sensual pleasure is the mouth. The stages are as follows:

- *Oral Stage:* It occupies approximately the first two years of life, during which casual observation reveals that children do indeed use their mouths to explore new objects and enjoy putting things in their mouths. Freud explained that this occurs in part because the child's first contact with the mother in feeding is via the mouth and that the child's bond with the mother is therefore inextricably bound up with oral contact. He further speculated that oral fixation might be a result of either insufficient time or too much time spent nursing, depending on the case.

- *Anal Stage:* Between ages two and four, the child gains control over his or her bowels, making the act of defecation one of the very few things the child can control in an environment that is almost entirely determined by the whims and preferences of adults. How parents handle the task of toilet training can therefore influence subsequent development, including the creation of two different types of fixation. The *anal-retentive person* learned as a child to exercise control and get what he wants by refusing to excrete; and as an adult is excessively concerned with neatness and organization, controlling his environment by keeping everything in its place. The *anal-expulsive* type may have instead controlled his parents by excreting freely and liberally, and as an adult may attempt to control others through sloppiness.

- *Phallic Stage:* This is the period, roughly from four to six years old, during which a boy discovers his penis and derives pleasure from contact with it. Some boys also fear that they may lose theirs as a punishment; Freud called this *castration anxiety.* As with the oral stage, the evidence that boys go through something like this is easily obtained; getting little boys to understand that they mustn't sit with their hands in their pants is a major concern in preschools and day-care centers. Not to leave anyone out, Freud would point out that girls are also concerned with penises during this stage, specifically with the question of why they don't have one. Observing that boys have penises and girls do not, a little girl may wish that she did and suspect deep down that she had one at one time and that it was removed. Freud called this penis envy. This is also the stage in which Freud suggested the existence of the *Oedipal conflict* or *complex,* named after the Greek protagonist Oedipus, who inadvertently kills his father and marries his mother. During the phallic stage, boys go through a period in which they bond strongly with their mothers and show less interest in their fathers. According to Freud, the boys fantasize about growing up and marrying their mothers. Only one thing stands in the way: Dad. Recognizing his powerlessness against his father, who might take away the penis if he finds out, the boy resolves this conflict by identifying strongly with the father instead of competing with him for Mother's affection. When the same essential conflict occurs in girls (substitute Father for Mother in the preceding text), it is called the *Electra complex.* Freud, like much of the psychological community until the early 1970s, regarded **homosexuality** as a disorder and believed it had its roots in a failure to properly resolve the Oedipal conflict.

- *Latency Period:* This period follows the phallic stage with several years of concentration on schoolwork until sensual concerns blossom again with the coming of adolescence.

- *Genital Stage:* This period begins with the onset of puberty, when the id turns its attention outward in the direction of contact with others, usually of the opposite sex.

Much of the controversy over this portion of the theory may have been exacerbated by the name by which the stages have become known: stages of psychosexual development. While Freud's concern was indeed the id's quest for sensual pleasure, most of what he was suggesting about children was not particularly sexual in nature, at least not as an adult understands sexuality. It also should be noted that this was the first fairly comprehensive view of child development based on stages, an idea that Jean Piaget would later use to further revolutionize the study of child development.

Anal-Retentive Personality

From Freud's time until the 1970s, the disorder now referred to as obsessive-compulsive disorder (OCD) was widely referred to as the anal-retentive personality, or *anal character.* The basics signs of the disorder have not changed as the newer label has caught on, but basic assumptions about what causes it certainly have. The older name of course carries within it a theory as to the etiology of the problem (and usually refers to a less serious set of symptoms than OCD does). As the name suggests, people with the signs of the disorder were assumed to have developed it as a result of fixation at the anal stage of development (see **Psychosexual Development**).

The pattern of symptoms, which the early Freudians preferred to call the *anal character,* was thought to result from parent-child conflicts over toilet training in the second to third year of life. As the child develops the ability to control bowel function, a conflict must arise between the child's desire to implement that newfound ability to control his or her environment and the parents' need to set clear limits and rules on the same activity. The child has two basic ways of defying the parents during toilet training: elimination (expulsiveness) at inappropriate times or in inappropriate places, and retention (retentiveness) when elimination would be preferred by the parents. How such conflicts are resolved is thought to have a major impact on subsequent personality, and resolution can go wrong in a number of ways.

If toilet training is started too soon, this will intensify the child-caretaker conflict. Increased conflict can also arise as a result of delaying the start of training for too long, however. If toilet training is experienced as too frustrating or as excessively gratifying, this can also increase conflict, along with the possibility of fixation at the anal stage. Parents who are too strict, too punitive, or lack sufficient patience may produce a problem, but parents whose approach to toilet training is too lax and permissive may cause trouble as well. The result of such conflict may be that the child learns to control his or her environment through excessive retention or expulsiveness, which may result in the development of an obsessive-compulsive personality structure, known to the Freudians as an *anal character.*

The psychoanalysts have generally drawn a clear distinction, however, between the anal character, which is a distinct type of personality but lacks psychiatric symptoms, and obsessive-compulsive disorder. The anal-retentive personality is perhaps best thought of as a person with subclinical levels of obsessive-compulsive symptoms; the signs are not severe or maladaptive enough to rise to the level of mental illness, in other words. While obsessive-compulsive neurosis (as the psychoanalysts referred to the disorder) is fairly rare, Pollak (1979) points out that the anal character is actually a dominant, successful character type in modern capitalist societies like the United States and Japan.

According to Freud, the anal retentive personality type is characterized by obstinacy, parsimony, and orderliness. Orderliness refers to how the individual approaches both personal hygiene (exceptional cleanliness is the rule) and carrying out tasks (everything is done with a high level of conscientiousness, no matter how trivial the action). Parsimony here refers to frugality, sometimes to the point of stinginess and greediness. Orderliness is thought to develop as a result of parental demands for bowel control, which become internalized as a high need for control of all aspects of one's environment. Frugality emerges in response to both the simple erotic pleasure Freud believed infants derive from retaining feces and the need to hoard the feces rather than lose this source of pleasure. Obstinacy is simply a continuation of the child's struggle with the parents for autonomy, which in the traditional Freudian model generates aggression and sadistic impulses that cannot be directly expressed to the parents. Instead, the anal retentive person will express this unresolved aggression in a variety of obstinate ways, including passive-aggressive behavior, the adoption of very strict, reactionary attitudes, or even fairly overt attempts to control others. At the core of all of this is the belief that the obsessive-compulsive person is acting out of ambivalent feelings regarding the expression of hostile and aggressive feelings, or indeed the expression of emotions generally.

The anal-retentive character does not come up often in conversation among psychologists and psychiatrists these days, as more explanation-neutral terminology such as *obsessive* is generally preferred. But the idea has certainly penetrated deep into American pop culture. References to such a personality are still readily found, though often the term is shortened and people are simply referred to as "anal." Phil Hartman played a popular recurring character known as The Anal-Retentive Chef on *Saturday Night Live* in the 1980s and 1990s, for example. No explanation was ever offered for the title, as clearly the audience still understood the reference.

Further Reading

Freud, S. (1953). *A General Introduction to Psychoanalysis.* Garden City, NJ: Perma Books-Doubleday.

Freud, S. (1963). Character and Anal Eroticism. In P. Rieff, ed. *Collected Papers.* Vol. 10. New York: Collier. (Originally published in 1908.)

Pollak, J.M. (1979). Obsessive-Compulsive Personality: A Review. *Psychological Bulletin* 86(2): 225–241.

Rank, Otto (1884–1939)

Otto Rank held a special place in Freud's inner circle in the early days of psycho-analysis, as he was the first "lay analyst" (Freud's own phrase) in an organization otherwise made up entirely of medical doctors. In 1906, Rank caught Freud's attention with a scholarly essay in which he applied Freud's dream theory to the creativity of artists—Freud was impressed enough that he hired Rank as the secretary of the Vienna Psychoanalytical Society, with the goal of bringing a greater degree of order to the group's work. Rank served in this capacity until 1916, cofounding the journal *Imago* along the way. He made important contributions to psychoanalytic theory during those early days, and despite eventually publishing theoretical works that alienated him from Freud's affection, he lasted far longer as Freud's friend and confidante than most others, despite promoting ideas that were remarkably similar to those of Jung and Adler. Indeed, when it had become clear to Freud that Jung and Adler were no longer to be considered part of his trusted inner circle, Rank was one of the six confidantes brought together by Freud as a secret committee dedicated to defending psychoanalysis from their less orthodox ideas.

Otto Rank was actually born Otto Rosenfeld, but he changed his surname in 1901, in what he described as an act of self-creation, an ideal that he would later uphold as one of the more important principles of life. In addition to the goal of self-creation, however, his act can also be interpreted as a way of separating himself further from his father, a violent alcoholic who both Rank and his brother stopped speaking to altogether at the age of 16, despite their continued residence in his house. His difficult home life was reflected in his mental state: his diaries indicate multiple periods of depression, and as a young man he preferred not to be touched, going so far as to wear gloves to shake hands.

The family was unable to afford college, so Rank trained as a locksmith instead. He was very interested in reading philosophy and literature, however, and loved music, poetry and the arts, and he set about educating himself as thoroughly as he could without actually attending a university. Through his reading he became a big admirer of Friedrich Nietzsche and existentialism, a set of influences that was also central to the work of Adler and Frankl, but it was his discovery of Freud's work that profoundly affected his thought and his path in life. After reading *The Interpretation of Dreams,* Rank wrote an essay tying together Freud's dream analysis and his own love of the arts, which eventually became the book *Art and Artist.*

As Rank's family doctor was Alfred Adler, young Otto had the opportunity to meet Freud in 1905, an encounter to which he brought along a copy of the manuscript of *Art and Artist.* Freud was so impressed with Rank that he encouraged him to pursue a university education, even helping him financially and hiring him as the secretary of the Vienna Psychoanalytical Society. With Freud's assistance and support, Rank attended the University of Vienna, obtaining a PhD in 1912 at the age of 28. In addition to making him the first academic in the psychoanalytic group's sea of medical diplomates, his degree was awarded as a result of the very first academic dissertation on the subject of psychoanalysis. In his dissertation, *The Incest Theme in Literature and Legend* (1912), Rank explored the frequent occurrence in folklore and literature across cultures of the themes of incest, patricide, and the Oedipus complex. In that same year, the founding issue of Freud's new journal, *Imago,* appeared under the editorship of Rank and Hanns Sachs, with an opening editorial piece titled "The Significance of Psychoanalysis for the Humanities," establishing a clear interdisciplinary and theoretical identity distinct from the medical and therapeutic concerns of the other psychoanalytic journals, as well as clearly establishing Rank's influence on the concerns of the Vienna Psychoanalytical Society.

Otto Rank, the first lay analyst in a circle otherwise made up of medical doctors, photographed around 1920. (Hulton Archive/Getty Images)

To get a true sense of the impact of the young PhD student on the world of psychoanalysis, one need look no further than the preface to the 1911 edition of *The Interpretation of Dreams,* where Freud records the following: "Herr Otto Rank has afforded me valuable assistance in the selection of supplementary examples, and has revised the proofs of this edition. I have to thank him and many other colleagues for their contributions and corrections." The same preface also openly acknowledges the influence of Wilhelm **Stekel** on Freud's understanding of the importance of symbolism in dreams, but that sentence was omitted in later editions, whereas the acknowledgment of Rank's help endured. Furthermore, later editions included chapters on myth and legend actually authored by Rank, whose name appeared for many years under Freud's on the title page of the book.

Rank's influence on the development of psychoanalytic theory extended well beyond his work on dreams and myths, however. Numerous sources suggest that Freud's emphasis on the importance of the mother in a child's psychic development may have originated in his discussions with Adler, and indeed Adler's best-known contribution to the psychoanalytic literature, *The Trauma of Birth,* focuses heavily on the role of the mother-child relationship in the development of neuroses. The book contains the idea for which Rank is most famous outside of psychoanalytic circles, and which gives the book its title: The first traumatic event in a person's life, and thus the source of some of the inner conflict that must later be resolved, is birth itself. In the process of birth, we are forcibly removed from a warm, quiet place of comfort and serenity, and rudely thrust into a frightening, overwhelming world that we do not understand and with which we are poorly equipped to cope. Rank did not disagree with Freud that the sexual drive is an important underlying source of a large share of human motivation, but they did disagree on how to explain it. Whereas Freud saw the sexual drive as the natural expression of libido, the energy that underpins everything, Rank suggested that the sexual drive is primarily an expression of a fundamental desire to return to the safety of the womb. Every act of sexual intercourse therefore becomes, to some degree, an attempt to return home.

Though this view of the sex drive was a source of some contention between Freud and Rank, *The Trauma of Birth* contained the seeds of a much more fundamental breakdown in their professional relationship. According to Freud, the Oedipus complex was the origin of all neurosis, and by extension the ultimate source of all human culture and civilization, including art, myth, religion, and philosophy, and by extension the ultimate source of any and all effective courses of psychotherapy. Rank's book, however, focused on the role of separation anxiety in infancy as the source of those same things, and he explicitly referred to its importance *in the period before the development of the Oedipus complex.* This was problematic for Freud, for the simple reason that his theories did not recognize the existence of such a period, at least not in the sense of it having any real importance in later character development. The publication of *The Trauma of Birth* marked the first occasion on which any member of Freud's inner circle had ever publicly suggested that something other than the Oedipus complex might be the most important causal factor in a psychoanalytic explanation. Rank later recalled that he was also the first person to use the term "pre-Oedipal" in a public psychoanalytic forum, in 1925, and he greatly resented that Melanie **Klein** had later greatly emphasized the importance of pre-Oedipal superego development, without acknowledging his earlier work.

Having lost Adler and Jung already, Freud was reluctant to throw away 20 years of friendship over a scholarly difference of opinion, but eventually came to regard Rank's pre-Oedipal period as a sort of psychoanalytic heresy, and began to more directly oppose Rank's ideas among the other members of the inner circle. Rank soon saw that he was no longer welcome in the Vienna Psychoanalytical Society, and by 1926 had left his posts in psychoanalytic publishing and moved to Paris. Following a brief stay in France, Rank then moved on to America, where he spent the rest of his professional career, which included the creation of his own approach to therapy, which he called *will therapy,* and which differed from standard psychoanalysis in some very important ways.

The beginnings of will therapy can be seen in a short book Rank coauthored with fellow insider Sándor **Ferenczi** at around the same time as *The Trauma of Birth,* titled *The Development of Psychoanalysis* (also published under the lesser-known but more informative English title *Developmental Goals of Psychoanalysis*). In the book, Ferenczi and Rank essentially point out, in a very straightforward manner, the various ways in which psychoanalytic therapy, when conducted according to Freud's recommendations, was faulty and in need of serious change. Their suggested changes constitute an assault on some of Freud's most basic assumptions. Freud had long advised analysts, for example, to be emotionless in the therapeutic situation, a requirement that Ferenczi and Rank indicate was leading to "an unnatural elimination of all human factors in the analysis" (1925, pp. 40–41). They further suggest that, in looking for elements of early childhood crises in all patient responses, the psychoanalyst was often ignoring the role of basic emotional differences between people—instead of recording the self-evident fact that some people were happy, some sad, some angry, and so forth, the analyst was always reducing all reported emotional experiences to evidence, often heavily disguised, of the action of libido. To Freud, emotion is the cause of neurosis, and the goal of therapy is to remove it. Beginning in the collaboration with Ferenczi, and becoming much more explicit in later works, Rank presented the notion that one of Freud's greatest mistakes was to reduce all emotional experience to sex.

In the same book, Ferenczi and Rank also introduce another idea that would become a mainstay of Rank's later approach to therapy, what became known as here and now therapy. In traditional Freudian psychoanalysis, the starting assumption is that the source of all neurosis is the Oedipus complex, meaning that the ultimate goal of therapy is therefore to uncover trauma and conflict in early childhood that are contributing to present-day trouble. Just as this approach ignores the role of current emotion in causing a patient's troubles, it also omits a role for current real-life troubles, ignoring the contributions to the patient's state of mind of things that might be going on in the here and now. This was of course seen as another heresy by Freud—rather than tracing everything back to early childhood, Ferenczi and Rank are suggesting that some of the contributing factors in neurosis might be of much more recent vintage.

Presented with Freud's increasing displeasure over Rank's rebellion, Ferenczi, as one who shared some of Rank's ideas but not all of them, found himself in a difficult position. He certainly agreed with Rank regarding the idea that psychoanalytic therapy as it was generally conducted was focused on the wrong concerns and was often ineffective, while also taking far too long. Even after he lost touch with Rank, Ferenczi continued to feel strongly about these issues, as revealed in a diary entry written in 1932 but not published until 1995:

> One learned from [Freud] and from his kind of technique various things that made one's life and work more comfortable: the calm, unemotional reserve; the unruffled assurance that one knows better; and the theories, the seeking and finding of the causes of failure in the patient instead of partly in ourselves . . . and finally the pessimistic view, shared only with a few, that neurotics are a rabble, good only to support us financially and to allow us to learn from their cases; psychoanalysis as a therapy may be worthless. (Ferenczi, 1995, pp. 185–186)

This passage reveals clearly that Ferenczi's differences with Freud over therapeutic methods were just as profound as their sometimes serious theoretical differences about the sources of neurosis, as in the affair of the **seduction theory,** yet Ferenczi was not prepared to entirely alienate his mentor by openly rejecting the preeminence of the Oedipal complex in favor of pre-Oedipal separation anxiety, and so he ultimately remained at Freud's side while ending his friendship with Rank. This choice came as a painful surprise to Rank, who reported being snubbed by Ferenczi on the occasion of a chance encounter in New York City's Pennsylvania Station: "He was my best friend and he refused to speak to me," Rank wrote of the encounter (Taft, 1958, p. xvi).

After his separation from Freud's inner circle, Rank moved from Vienna to Paris in 1926, where he refined his (and Ferenczi's) objections to the standard conduct of psychoanalysis into a brand-new approach to psychotherapy, which he called *will therapy.* Between lectures at the Sorbonne and the treatment of such famous literary clients as Anaïs Nin and Henry Miller, Rank made a truly radical departure from Freud by arguing that, rather than being primarily a product of the distant past, all emotional life is grounded in the present. In *Will Therapy,* he presents the argument that Freud commits a very fundamental error by focusing therapy on childhood experiences rather than experiences of the here and now, a term Rank introduced for the first time in the psychotherapeutic literature in *Will Therapy.* According to Rank, Freud

> confuses the psychological meaning of the past as a memory problem with the real meaning of the past as historical material. Psychic causality is evidently different from natural science causality, as different as the psychic past from the historical. Freud . . . attempted to infer or, as he said, to reconstruct the actual historical past from the recollection of it as it manifests itself psychically.

It remains to be seen how far this is technically justified; yes, whether it is possible at all. (Rank, 1945, p. 36)

Here, Rank describes the most basic idea in psychoanalytic therapy, that the underlying problem in all neurosis is the patient's repressed memories, and that therapy should therefore consist of digging up those buried memories in order to better understand the past, as an error, and the use of those recovered reminiscences as evidence of the actual past as unjustified, if not actually a technical impossibility.

In addition to rejecting the central role of childhood trauma in neurosis, Rank went so far in *Will Therapy* as to describe psychoanalysis itself as a failure where it counts most: in improving our actual understanding of human character. According to Rank, in fact, the history of psychoanalytic theory is a series of failures:

Psychoanalysis in its mingling of theory and therapy has failed to detect the actually effective therapeutic agent, the psychological understanding of which alone can furnish the basis for theoretical generalization. First it was the making conscious of the unconscious (association), which we know today is not itself therapeutic. Then it was the abreaction of the affects, a kind of psychic emptying (catharsis) which at best means only a temporary relief, nothing lasting or constructively effective. Finally it was the transference relationship which forms a kind of synthesis of these two psychological factors. Transference not only contains something passive, temporary, derived, but actually represents that aspect of the relationship to the analyst. But passivity, dependence, or weakness of will in any form is just the difficulty on account of which the neurotic comes for treatment, therefore transference cannot be the therapy to which we attach the idea of something positive. (1945, p. 7)

In Rank's view, in other words, the central problem in the neurotic is a failure to express one's own will, but the psychoanalytic therapist's office is a place in which transference, which involves passivity and dependence, is often seen as a positive development in therapy. To Rank, the will is the "thing that is potent in every relationship between human beings. . . . Two wills clash, either the one overthrows the other or both struggle with and against one another for supremacy" (1945, p. 7). The psychoanalytic relationship promoted by Freud, however, has as a primary goal "freeing from, rooting out, mastering, or sublimating" the will (1945, p. 8), rather than recognizing that what the neurotic may not be doing enough is expressing or exerting it.

Rank freely acknowledged that Alfred **Adler** had at least recognized this battle of wills in analysis, which he characterized as a *striving for superiority,* but argued that Adler had failed to grasp its importance in the individual to exactly the same degree as had Freud. In Freudian psychoanalysis, the individual will is acknowledged in two different ways: when it is seen as an underlying driving force, it appears as instinct or drive, and when it appears more directly in the therapeutic situation, it is called *resistance.* Resistance to the treatment or therapist, which is seen in traditional psychoanalysis as an obstacle to successful treatment that must be overcome, represents something quite different in Rank's work:

> It is important that the neurotic above all learn to *will,* discover that he *can* will without getting guilt feeling on account of willing. . . . In this will psychology I will show how the rehabilitation of will solves many problems at one stroke; in therapy, it has always played a great role, but it has lacked its own psychology which would have made it scientifically acceptable as a therapeutic agent and therefore also therapeutically effective. (1945, pp. 9–10)

Rank sees the primary goal of therapy as teaching the neurotic to take charge of his life, to take control of his circumstances, while characterizing Freudian psychoanalysis as striving instead to deny the will and teach the patient to accept a very deterministic view of his own life, in which everything has an external, distant, and often hidden cause. Although Adler had at least recognized the role of the individual will in character formation, he followed Freud's example of treating the striving for superiority as a cause of trouble, which was to be rooted out in therapy, and was therefore described by Rank as committing exactly the same error as Freud.

Rank's will therapy was a remarkably radical revision of Freud's psychoanalysis, and so its harsh reception within the psychoanalytic community is surprising only in its vehemence. While Freud's inner circle could certainly be expected to rise to his defense, for example, it is still rather surprising that Erich **Fromm** went so far as to call will therapy a Nazi-style philosophy, a remarkably vicious attack from one Jewish scholar to another.

Such was the thoroughness of Rank's blacklisting by the international psychoanalytic community that, following his emigration to America, anyone who had been analyzed by Rank was required to undergo a second complete analysis by a more acceptable psychoanalyst before being allowed to join the American Psychoanalytic Association.

The powerful resistance to Rank's ideas among psychoanalysts, especially those loyal to Freud, is doubly surprising considering the extent to which one of Freud's major thematic evolutions during his career, from a focus on survival-oriented instincts to the recognition of the role of both life instincts and death instincts (Eros and Thanatos), is philosophically very similar to a duality present in Rank's theory as well: the dual roles of the seemingly opposite *life fear* and *death fear.* Although the idea was more fully elaborated in *Psychology and the Soul* (1930), it was present in an earlier form in *The Trauma of Birth,* in which the fear of living is a central theme. In the earlier book, Rank argues that much of the anxiety in life is driven by a fundamental fear of living, which begins with the difficult separation from the womb and the uncertainty that follows. He later elaborated on this idea, however, arguing in *Will Therapy* that the fear eventually divides into two distinct currents that run in opposite directions: we fear separation and individuation, which is thrust on us at birth, but we also fear union and collectivity, which also represent the loss of individuality and separate existence which comes with death. He proposes the following:

> The typical neurotic crisis, as has been already indicated, seems to break out at a certain age when the life fear which has restricted the ego development, meets with the death fear as it increases with growth and maturity. The individual then feels himself driven forward by regret for wasted life and the desire to retrieve it. But this forward driving fear is now death fear, the fear of dying without having lived, which, even so, is held in check by fear of life. (1945, pp. 188–189)

This passage, in addition to presenting a picture of aging as involving a conflict between opposite impulses, very much like Freud's own theory does, also predates Erik **Erikson**'s now widely disseminated idea of the so-called midlife crisis, in which men's pathological behavior is driven by the recognition of their own impending mortality and the fear it creates.

Although the early version of life fear, presented in *The Trauma of Birth,* was focused primarily on the fear of uncertainty and lack of security, by the time of *Will Therapy* the concept has become much more refined, and Rank's description of the fear is focused on our sense of connectedness in our relationships with other human beings rather than the widely caricatured fear of leaving the womb. Rank also suggests that fear of living and fear of dying may actually represent different perspectives on the same anxiety:

> The fear in birth, which we have designated as fear of life, seems to me actually the fear of having to live as an isolated individual, and not the reverse, the fear of the loss of individuality (death fear). That would mean, however, that primary fear corresponds to a fear of separation from the whole, therefore a fear of individuation, on account of which I should like to call it fear of life, although it may appear later as fear of the loss of this dearly bought individuality, as fear of death, of being dissolved again into the whole. Between these two fear possibilities, these poles of fear, the individual is thrown back and forth all his life, which accounts for the fact that we have not been able to trace fear back to a single root, or to overcome it therapeutically. (1945, p. 124)

One reason for the resistance to this idea by the psychoanalytic establishment is its implicit criticism of psychoanalytic therapy, which focuses on finding and addressing the underlying cause of the anxiety—in Rank's conception of the anxiety, it has multiple causes, and one of these is death. As the neurotic individual has not yet experienced death, resolving the fear by locating its root among the patient's memories is doomed to fail, and so traditional psychoanalysis is unprepared to help with this fear. Rank proposes instead that the goal of therapy should be to help the client achieve a constructive, healthy balance between individuation and union with other people. Starting with his early studies of artists and the artistic impulse, including 1903's *Art and Artist,* Rank saw this balance as essential in leaving the individual free to create.

Following his time in Paris, Rank in 1935 followed the example of many other Jewish scholars in the early days of the rise of the Nazis and emigrated to the United States, where he taught at the Pennsylvania School of Social Work. Upon emigrating, Rank embraced his new American identity with gusto, going so far as to adopt the nickname "Huck," in honor of his favorite character in American literature, Huckleberry Finn. Although his work was rejected by the psychoanalytic community prior to his departure from Europe, in America his work eventually found new favor among an unexpected group of psychologists—the humanistic psychotherapists of the 1970s, who rejected both psychoanalysis and the more scientifically oriented psychology that sought to reach general conclusions about human nature instead of considering each person as a unique individual. Rogers is best known for his development of what he called *client-centered* therapy, in which the therapist is non-directive and makes no a priori assumptions about the underlying sources of the client's troubles. By his own admission, however, the genesis of his approach was a personal encounter with Otto Rank in 1936, at which time he later recalled, "I became infected with Rankian ideas." In addition to the elements of will therapy, Rogers was also influenced by Rank's refusal to follow along in Freud's avowedly atheist footsteps. Toward the end of his career, Rogers began to emphasize the existence of a spiritual, transcendent realm of human existence that is beyond the reach of scientific psychology—this idea was also the centerpiece of Rank's *Psychology and the Soul,* written shortly after *Will Therapy,* in which he laments as follows:

> Today we are psychologists shaped by our denial of the soul's reality. We explain causally what the soul is and does; science substitutes knowledge for credo but in the end our knowing rests upon belief. . . . From this come many quirks and contradictions of our inner life and our psychologies. (Rank, 1996, p. 193)

After such humanist psychologists as Rogers and Rollo May expressed their admiration for his spiritual ideas, *Psychology and the Soul* was finally published in English in 1996, nearly 60 years after its author's death.

There is one other area of scholarship in which Rank's contributions have received insufficient recognition. It is possible that Rank's rejection by the inner circle in Vienna may help to explain the fact that his work on the psychoanalytical interpretation of mythology, despite predating and acting as a clear influence on Jung's work regarding the same subject, is far less well-known today than Jung's. *The Myth of the Birth of the Hero,* first published in 1909, was a groundbreaking work that argued that mythological narratives share some universal elements across cultures, and that these similarities simply reflect some universal truths about psychological reality. He starts the book with a simple, yet crucial observation:

> The prominent civilized nations—the Babylonians and Egyptians, the Hebrews and Hindus, the Persians, the Greeks and the Romans, as well as the Teutons and others—all began at an early stage to glorify their national heroes—mythical princes and kings, founders of religions, dynasties, empires, or cities—in a number of poetic tales and legends. The history of the birth and early life of these personalities came to be especially invested with fantastic features, which in different nations—even though widely separated by space and entirely independent of each other—present a baffling similarity, or, in part, a literal correspondence. (Rank, 1959, p. 3)

In the book, Rank documents the frequently startling correspondences between seemingly unrelated heroes' tales. In the Babylonian story of Sargon the First, for example, the infant Sargon is placed by his mother in a vessel made of reeds that she then places in a river, which carries the infant downriver to be discovered by the father who will raise him as his own. This is a tale quite familiar to anyone raised in the Judeo-Christian tradition, reflecting as it does the personal history of Moses, which

> presents the greatest similarity to the Sargon legend, even an almost literal correspondence of individual traits. Already the first chapter relates that Pharaoh commanded his people to throw into the water all sons that were born to Hebrews. . . . The second chapter continues as follows . . . "and the woman conceived, and bare a son. . . . And when she could no longer hide him, she took for him an ark of bulrushes, and daubed it with slime and with pitch, and put the child therein, and she laid it in the flags by the river's brink." (Rank, 1959, p. 17)

Rank then describes a similar tale from the ancient Hindu epic *Mahabharata,* concerning the birth of the hero Karna. His mother, the princess Pritha, was a virgin (another recurrent motif, both in Christianity and in the legend of Sargon), who after his birth hid him in a large basket made from rushes, in which he was set adrift down a river.

In the Greek legend of Ion, ancestor of the Ionians, the boy was born of the union of the god Apollo and a woman named Creusa, who left the child behind in a woven basket. All of these stories are united by another common element: the mother has concealed the child's birth, and in later life his parents recognize his true identity, sometimes before the secret has led to tragic results, but sometimes not. Writing in the early days of his association with Freud, Rank naturally uses these tales to lead up to the story of Oedipus, though he also points out common elements between the myths enumerated so far and the accounts of Paris, Telephus, Perseus, Cyrus, Gilgamesh, Romulus and Remus, Hercules, Siegfried, Lohengrin, and Jesus.

Rank summarizes the common elements of the hero myth as follows:

> The hero is the child of most distinguished parents, usually the son of a king. His origin is preceded by difficulties, such as continence, or prolonged barrenness, or secret intercourse of the parents due to external prohibition or obstacles. During or before the pregnancy, there is a prophecy, in the form of a dream or oracle, cautioning against his birth, and usually threatening danger to the father (or his representative). As a rule, he is surrendered to the water, in a box. He is then saved by animals, or by lowly people (shepherds), and is suckled by a female animal or by an humble woman. After he has grown up, he finds his distinguished parents, in a highly versatile fashion. He takes his revenge on his father, on the one hand, and is acknowledged, on the other. (p. 65)

This rough outline matches up well with a majority of heroic narratives, which most anthropologists and folklorists would attribute at least in part to the frequent wholesale borrowing of stories from neighboring peoples, especially following a conquest. Rank takes a different approach, however, suggesting that an underlying, common psychological reality is responsible for this standardized mythological format.

Having established the universality of the elements of the heroic myth, Rank then presents as a central hypothesis the notion that unconscious psychosexual impulses play a central role in myth formation. His analysis of the myths is conducted along the lines of a Freudian-style dream analysis, which is unsurprising given Rank's own role in the writing of *The Interpretation of Dreams*. He begins with the assumption that, like a dream, the myth represents the fulfillment of an unconscious desire, and further assumes that myths are constructed by the same processes as dreams, including displacement, condensation, and symbolization. It is of course vital that one of the myths that follows the standard narrative is that of Oedipus, since Rank ultimately argues that the heroic myth in general represents the Oedipal theme of rebellion and triumph over the father, although the parallel Oedipal motif of fulfilled desire for the mother appears less universal. Rank further argues that both myth narratives and the daydreams of prepubescent children reflect a desire to replace parents to whom we are rather indifferent with richer, nobler, more prestigious parents. The central analogy of Rank's book, in other words, is between the child's ego and the mythic hero, with the conflicts that arise in the heroic legend mirroring the conflicts that confront the developing ego.

Prefiguring ideas that would eventually be made famous by Carl **Jung,** Rank bases much of his analysis on perceived parallels between dream and myth, recognizing that many of the common elements of heroic legends are also common motifs in dreams. While he does not actually use the term *archetypes* or refer explicitly to a *collective unconscious,* Rank's ideas, published in 1909, sound remarkably similar to the ideas that Jung and Joseph Campbell would later make famous. The central notions of Rank's book are in fact quite similar to the ideas explored many years later in Campbell's far more widely read *The Hero with a Thousand Faces,* first published some 40 years after Rank's book. Campbell has become a household name over the ensuing decades, while Rank's contribution to the psychology of mythology is almost entirely forgotten (though his important role in the field is openly acknowledged by Campbell in a footnote on the first page of his book). The reason for this may be simply that Campbell had a strong professional connection with Carl Jung, as the editor of Jung's works in English. Unlike Rank, Jung parted from Freud without being completely shut out by the rest of the psychoanalytic world, and he additionally became one of the world's best-selling authors, and so Campbell had a ready audience for his own adaptations of ideas that were, justly or not, seen by the world as originating with Jung, which greatly exceeded the potential readership of Rank's very similar works.

Further Reading

Ferenczi, S. (1995). *The Clinical Diary of Sandor Ferenczi* (Judith Dupont, ed.). Cambridge, MA: Harvard University Press.

Ferenczi, S., and Rank, O. (1925). *The Development of Psychoanalysis.* New York: Nervous and Mental Disease Publishing Company.

Kramer, R. (1995). The Birth of Client-Centered Therapy: Carl Rogers, Otto Rank, and "The Beyond." *Journal of Humanistic Psychology* 35(4): 54–110.

Rank, O. (1941). *Beyond Psychology.* New York: Dover.

Rank, O. (1945). *Will Therapy* and *Truth and Reality.* New York: Knopf.

Rank, O. (1959). *The Myth of the Birth of the Hero and Other Writings.* P. Freund, ed. New York: Vintage.

Rank, O. (1992). *The Incest Theme in Literature and Legend* (Translated by G.C. Richter). Baltimore: Johns Hopkins University Press.

Rank, O. (1996). Psychology and the Soul. *Journal of Religion and Health* 35(3): 193–201.

Rank, O., and H. Sachs. (1961). The Significance of Psychoanalysis for the Humanities. *The American Imago,* 22: 6–133.

Taft, J. (1958). *Otto Rank: A Biographical Study Based on Notebooks, Letters, Collected Writings, Therapeutic Achievements, and Personal Associations.* New York: Julian Press.

The Rat Man (Ernst Lanzer) (1878–1914)

The psychoanalytic treatment of the Rat Man is one of the four early case studies (see also **The Wolf Man, Little Hans,** and **Dora**) with which Freud established the apparent reality of some of his more controversial theoretical notion, along with creating for himself a reputation for curing very challenging cases. "Rat Man" is the nickname given by Freud to Ernst Lanzer (1878–1914), a young lawyer suffering from what in Freud's time was known as an *obsessional neurosis,* though today his diagnosis would probably be obsessive-compulsive disorder. The case study, *Notes upon a Case of Obsessional Neurosis,* had its first German publication in 1909, and represented what Freud and his followers considered a remarkably speedy cure: Lanzer saw Freud for less than a year. This is especially remarkable given his disorder's reputation at the time; Freud considered obsessives far more difficult to treat than hysterical patients. This was partly because hysterical patients present with obvious conversion symptoms (physical symptoms without clear physical cause), whereas the symptoms presented by an obsessive patient are harder to see clearly, as they consist primarily of irrational, apparently illogical thought patterns.

Lanzer was a very open patient, willing to follow Freud's direction to whatever destination presented itself, and so the particular obsession that gave him his nickname, and around which Freud centered his treatment, became clear within the first two hours of treatment. In the first hour, Lanzer detailed his particular set of complaints to Freud, chief among which was that he frequently had obsessive fears that something terrible was going to happen to either his father or his fiancée. He also frequently felt criminal impulses, such as the desire to kill people, followed by the desire to punish himself for such thoughts, including an overwhelming urge to cut his own throat with a razor. These thoughts all arrived unbidden and unwelcome, and were very difficult to get out of his mind. He had apparently created a defense against them by replacing them with other obsessive thoughts, such as a preoccupation with trivial matters, like the settling of a minor debt. While he was thinking of these things, he could stop thinking the disturbing thoughts for a while.

In the second hour, the conversation turned to the obsessive thought that troubled him most of all, the one that drove him to seek help from Freud. This one he had difficulty talking about—between sentences he would stand up and pace, and refuse to say more, but sentence by sentence, Freud was able to pry it out of him. It seems that the previous summer, while on military maneuvers, Lanzer heard a captain describe a torture that he had heard was used somewhere in Asia. In this torture, the prisoner's trousers are removed and he is made to lie face down. A pot full of rats is then applied to the victim's buttocks, where they proceed to eat their way into the victim's anus. In Freud's account, Lanzer could not bring himself to finish the last sentence of his account, stuttering and verbally flailing his way around it, until Freud provided the last three words himself: "into his anus." Upon hearing the description, Lanzer began immediately to have intrusive visions of his father and his fiancée experiencing the torture, visions that he fought off by focusing his attention on such minutiae as paying back a small debt to a fellow soldier.

As analysis proceeded, it became clear that Lanzer had been having such irrational thoughts about something terrible happening to his father for a very long time. Lanzer's earliest recollection of such a fear dated back to the age of six, which Lanzer himself referred to as "the beginning of my illness." Early on in treatment, because he thought it was the sort of thing Freud would want to talk about, he also brought up his apparently quite precocious sexuality. He recalled having pretty governesses who he would watch undress, along with actually having fondled some of them, but also recalled his early sexual desires being undermined by a powerful feeling that if he kept thinking such thoughts, his father would die. These worries about his father, which continued at the time that he came to Freud's attention, were especially irrational given that his father had actually been dead for years.

In addition to the worries about his father and fiancée, Lanzer produced many other odd thoughts and rituals. To stop the torture scenario whenever it played in his head, for example, he would loudly proclaim "but whatever you are thinking of," while making a particular gesture of repudiation. In sifting through the many odd thoughts expressed by Lanzer, Freud indicated in his notes that the patient also used rats as symbols for gambling, penises, babies, money, anuses, the Rat Man himself, penetration, and his mother, among other things. Freud was concerned that the sheer volume of odd thoughts reported to him by the Rat Man would make the case history "inaccessible to anyone except those closest to us" (Gay, 1988, p. 264), and Jung later admitted to having found the report quite difficult to understand.

Freud ultimately determined that the obsessive thoughts were largely a result of unacknowledged, competing impulses, both loving and aggressive, toward the people involved. Although he loved his father, he also feared and hated him, possibly because of harsh punishment for childhood masturbation, and so he simultaneously imagined his father dying and felt fear that it would actually happen. The torture story was therefore an expression of his conflicted feelings about his father, while also expressing an otherwise repressed sadism—he continued to think about it because his horror at the cruelty was mixed with a somewhat lascivious interest in it. Indeed, at one point Lanzer told Freud that when he first experienced actual sexual intercourse, a few years after his father's death, the thought came uninvited: "For this one could murder one's father!" (Gay, 1988, p. 265). Freud also suggested that

Lanzer's fear of rats might be this precocious heterosexual's expression of disguised homosexual fantasies, considering the torture story's images of rats (which sometimes represent genitalia) entering an anus.

Once Lanzer had accepted Freud's interpretations of his obsessions and compulsions, they disappeared and Lanzer became better able to function, and the Rat Man became one of Freud's best-known cures. Unfortunately, no long-term follow-up on the extent to which he was cured was ever possible, as the Rat Man was killed in action in World War I. A closer look at the original case has been possible, however, as this is the only case for which Freud's entire set of case notes survives— usually he would destroy them after writing up the case study. Researchers who have examined those notes have found significant disparities between the notes and the published narrative, suggesting that Freud exaggerated some details and flat-out lied about others, in order to make his own powers, both deductive and curative, seem greater. In 1986, Patrick Mahony published *Freud and the Rat Man,* in which he gives numerous examples of how Freud altered specifics of the case to better support his theory, as well as to make himself seem more impressive. One example should suffice—in the published narrative, Freud says that he was able to guess the name of the patient's fiancée (*Gisela*) based on a word puzzle that Lanzer gave him (*Glejisamen*), thus impressing his patient. The case notes, however, show that the patient gave Freud her name willingly, and he later used the name to determine what the anagram meant.

Further Reading

Freud, S. (1909/1996). Notes upon a Case of Obsessional Neurosis. In *Three Case Studies*. New York: Touchstone.

Gay, P. (1988). *Freud: A Life for Our Time*. New York: W. W. Norton.

Mahony, P. (1986). *Freud and the Rat Man*. New Haven, CT: Yale University Press.

Reich, Wilhelm (1897–1957)

On November 3, 1957, Wilhelm Reich, a psychiatrist who was part of Freud's inner circle in the 1920s, at which time he was highly respected among psychoanalysts, died in a U.S. federal prison while serving a two-year sentence for contempt of court. The conviction was a result of his direct defiance of an order from the Food and Drug Administration to cease treating people with devices, and according to a theory, which the agency had determined was scientifically worthless and likely to divert people from seeking treatment that might actually help them. This sad end was merely the terminus of a long slide from scientific and medical respectability, which had begun as far back as the early 1930s, when he was first formally expelled from the International Psychoanalytical Association. Since his death, the general consensus both within and without the psychoanalytic community has been that he was, at least in the second half of his career, at best a crackpot and at worst seriously mentally ill. This has not prevented his supporters from continuing to publish works in his defense, and to train therapists in his methods.

Early in his life, there was no indication whatsoever that he would eventually become such a uniquely controversial figure. He was born in the village of Dobrzanica (not, as some sources suggest, in Vienna), a village in Galicia, at the time part of the German Ukraine, which was in turn under the control of the Austro-Hungarian Empire. His father, Leon Reich, was a prosperous farmer in possession of nearly a thousand acres of land; his mother also came from a financially comfortable farming family. Reich's father, although Jewish, was not religious and had not raised his children as Jews. To the contrary, his response to the widespread anti-Semitism of the day was to not even allow his children to play with other children who spoke Yiddish. Reich carried this influence with him for the rest of his days, and as an adult was known to correct anyone who referred to him as a Jew. His efforts to hide his Jewishness and avoid being treated as an outsider were ultimately futile as a defense against anti-Semitism, however, as he still had to flee Austria along with other prominent Jewish scholars once the Nazis came to power.

In his early years, Reich's education appears to have come primarily at the hands of private tutors, along with the education in the lives of plants and animals that naturally accompanies a farm-based upbringing. In addition to his fascination with his insect collections, he also began to develop the interest in sexuality that would

Revolutionary genius or dangerous madman? Wilhelm Reich, seen here in 1952, drew a very different response from government regulators than from his followers. (Bettmann/Corbis)

later define his career at an early age. He himself attributed this later interest primarily to having grown up in a place where reproductive functions were often going on right in front of him, recalling that by the age of four, sex had no secrets from him. His observations were not limited to the animals, either: in a memoir of his early years, *Passion of Youth: An Autobiography 1897–1922* (2005), he claimed to have had sexual intercourse for the first time, with the family maid, at the age of only 11 and a half, although in later sources he said it happened at the age of 13.

His own apparent confusion over his own age at the time of this significant incident in his life may be due in part to the other event that occurred at about the same time: when Reich was 11 or 12 (different sources cite different ages), his mother committed suicide following the discovery that she was having an affair with Reich's tutor. The suicide was an especially unpleasant one, involving poisoning with a household cleaner, which left her in tremendous pain for days before she died. In his memoir, Reich recalls that he had been aware of the affair, watching her sneak into the tutor's bedroom and listening outside the door. Torn between his sense of obligation to tell his father and his desire to protect his mother, Reich did nothing, and later blamed himself for her death, often waking up overwhelmed by the belief that he had somehow killed her.

Left without a tutor, Reich went to school for the first time at age 12, attending the all-male Czernowitz gymnasium. He was an excellent student, and he did particularly well in classical languages and natural sciences. When Reich was 17, his father died of pneumonia and tuberculosis, and so Reich also took over farm operations, without interrupting his studies. He graduated in 1915, which occasion unfortunately coincided with the start of World War I—after the family farm was destroyed by the Russian army in 1915, Reich and his brother fled to Vienna, leaving everything they owned behind. Left with nothing of his prosperous childhood, Reich joined the Austrian army and served as a lieutenant on the Italian front until the end of the war.

Upon his return in 1918, he embarked on the study of medicine at the University of Vienna, supporting himself by working as a tutor. During his time as an undergraduate, he quickly became fascinated by the work of Sigmund Freud, and while organizing a seminar on sexology, he met his hero in 1919 on a visit to obtain some literature for the class. The two men made a powerful impression on one another, and Reich quickly became one of Freud's favorite student acolytes. Following a short period of training and analysis by Paul Federn, one of the earliest members of the Vienna Psychoanalytical Society, Reich was made a member of the association and allowed to begin seeing patients in 1920, some two years before completing his medical degree.

Over the next several years, Reich became an integral part of Freud's professional circle in Vienna. In 1922, Reich completed his studies and immediately set up a private practice in psychoanalysis, while also working in internal medicine at University Hospital, Vienna, and studying neuropsychiatry for the next two years at the Neurological and Psychiatric Clinic. Meanwhile, Reich had also published several key articles on psychoanalysis, and his scholarly work combined with his skills as an analyst prompted Freud to appoint him as an assistant physician, and subsequently deputy director, when organizing his Psychoanalytic Polyclinic in 1922. Reich was also appointed to the faculty of the Psychoanalytic Institute in 1924, conducting classes and seminars both there and at the clinic—his skills in that setting led to his becoming the institute's director of training. At the time, his work focused on the social causes of neurosis, an approach that was influenced by his membership in the Socialist, and later Communist, parties.

At the institute, Reich began to work more specifically on the causes of psychoanalytic failures, seeking ways to improve the practice of psychoanalysis that would improve patient outcomes, and it was in the context of this work that some of the differences with Freud that would eventually lead to his ouster would first begin to become clear. Where Freud believed it was important that the analyst sit out of sight behind the head of the reclining patient, for example, Reich instead began to recommend moving out from behind the couch, sitting next to the patient, and making eye contact. To Reich's way of thinking, the customary approach involved treating the neurosis rather than making direct contact with the individual behind the neurosis. Among other things, he also began to question the importance of transference and claimed to have proven that the notion of the death instinct was a fallacy.

As with many other early psychoanalysts, Reich's ultimate split with Freud came about as a result of differences of opinion regarding the importance Freud placed on sexuality. Unusually, however, Reich's objection was that Freud placed *insufficient* emphasis on the importance of sex. He agreed with Freud on several basic notions, including the idea that difficulties in sexual development were the ultimate source of mental illness and neurosis. Both agreed that sexuality is present in infancy but is repressed, and that this repression has clear consequences in later life. Reich's Marxist political leanings ultimately caused him to carry the idea in a different direction, however, which places far more of a burden of responsibility on the libido than even Freud advocated. In *The Function of the Orgasm* (1942), Reich argues that the real source of sexual repression is bourgeois moral standards, along with the socioeconomic political structures that support them. Since sexual repression is the source of all neuroses, the antidote to neuroses is for everyone to enjoy an active, guiltless sex life.

Based on his studies of psychoanalytic successes and failures, Reich concluded that a consistent pattern revealed that the cured patients were those who had developed a satisfactory sex life, whereas the uncured were those who had not. Where Freud viewed sexual problems as symptoms of a neurosis, Reich took this a step further and came to regard sexual dissatisfaction as the core of all neuroses. He quickly came under scrutiny for this conclusion by other psychiatrists who insisted that many neurotics have perfectly normal sex lives, a criticism he parried by introducing the concept of *orgastic potency.* It is not enough to be sexually active; most individuals do not achieve full gratification in the sexual act, and are therefore not orgastically potent. This was a distinction that had not previously been made by other writers—even a sexual act that proceeds to full ejaculation may not achieve the desired result, since even such an experience could be unsatisfactory in some way. Orgastic potency involves the full release of excess, pent-up energy. Where Freud used libido as a psychic concept that helped to explain unconscious mental functioning, Reich came to believe that it was a genuine form of physical energy, the proper flow of which requires orgasm to regulate it. He called this energy *orgone,* and began to recommend a new approach, orgone therapy, which focused on helping people to become orgastically potent.

Reich's advocacy of orgastic potency served a political as well as a therapeutic goal, as he viewed many of society's problems as the result of there being too few orgastically potent people around. Coinciding with the rise of the Nazis, he published *The Mass Psychology of Fascism* in 1933, in which he argued that the absence of such individuals renders most political action pointless. No matter how much we change political institutions, they get taken over by the same neurotic individuals, whose sick impulses rapidly overtake good intentions and lead to the same old problems. According to Reich, this is why the Russian Revolution was ultimately a failure that left a totalitarian government in charge that was just as bad as its predecessors—until we have a society made up of orgastically potent citizens, we will be unable to establish a usable political order. In such a society, compulsory laws and moral standards will no longer be necessary. Unsurprisingly, Reich's work remains popular in anarchist and anti-government circles.

As he began to formulate these ideas and drift further away from Freud, Reich moved with his family to Berlin in 1930, where he joined the Communist Party and began to set up clinics in working-class areas with the intent of teaching sex education and helping to begin the creation of an orgastically potent proletariat. Once his book, *The Sexual Revolution,* was published in Vienna, the German communists came to see him as too outspoken even for them, and expelled him from the party. The title of the book has since come to be used to refer to the changing sexual morality of the modern era, but Reich intended it quite literally: he believed that effective political revolution could only occur if all citizens were orgastically potent, which required that they were either properly raised by their parents and their society (a rare occurrence, in Reich's estimation) or that they successfully undergo orgone therapy.

Despite the profound ways in which he was beginning to deviate from the standard psychoanalytic approach, it was actually Reich's unseemly political involvement, at a time when the mostly Jewish psychoanalysts were trying to keep a low profile so as not to arouse the enmity of the Nazis, which ultimately led to his formal removal from the ranks of the International Psychoanalytical Association in 1934. The psychoanalysts' concerns were well founded: on March 2, 1933, a mere two months into Hitler's chancellorship, the official newspaper of the National Socialist Worker's Party, *Volkischer Beobachter* (The Populist Observer, roughly translated), published an attack on Reich's work, in which he was derisively described as a womanizer, a communist, a Jew, and an advocate of free love. While all of these things were, in fact, true, the accusations were not helpful to the reputation of the psychoanalytic community, and Reich left Berlin the next day, eventually settling for a while in Scandinavia. A stop in Denmark was short-lived, however, as Reich went about his usual business and was quickly accused of corrupting Danish youth with his German sexology. By the fall of 1934, Reich was in Norway.

During a five-year stay in Oslo, Reich refined the concept of orgone energy quite a bit based on some unusual experiments. He first laid out the principles of orgone therapy, which was at first known as vegetotherapy, in a paper he presented in 1934 titled "Psychic Contact and Vegetative Current." In that paper, which the reader will note was presented in the same year that the international psychoanalytic community rejected him, he describes his attempts to measure orgastic potency by taking physiological measurements of the male orgasm. As a result of these measurements, Reich described the orgasm as consisting of four distinct phases: first, there is a buildup of energy or tension; next, the penis becomes erect, which is accompanied by a measurable electrical charge. At the moment of orgasm, Reich claims to have measured an electrical discharge, which is followed by the fourth stage, relaxation. Reich believed that the electrical discharge represented a new kind of energy, present in all life forms. He went on to argue that the primary cause of neurosis is the tension created by unreleased sexual energy, which produces actual physical blockage in the muscles and organs of the body, which he called *armor.* The most effective way to break through the armor was through achieving orgasm, and the amount of energy released, which was a function of just how good an orgasm was achieved, was directly responsible for the amount of relief experienced—a really good experience would leave insufficient orgone energy in the body to support neurotic symptoms. Without orgastic potency, the ability to experience a really good, energy-clearing orgasm, a person will remain in a constant state of tension, and will develop rigid body armor to keep it in.

It was in Norway that Reich began to move away from psychiatry and toward regarding himself as a sort of biophysicist, starting with the claim that he had actually observed orgone energy directly, a discovery he himself ranked with the discoveries of Copernicus in its importance to humanity. Far beyond his initial speculations regarding the proper release of energy in orgasm, he began to regard orgone as an energy that permeates the entire natural world. It is the life force, the vital essence on which so many philosophers had speculated. Reich explained away the failure of traditional physicists to detect the existence of this energy by describing it as a nonelectromagnetic force, which conveniently removes it from all known categories of detectable energy. Reich was convinced that he had visual evidence of the orgone, however, and even described its color: blue. In Reich's own words,

> Blue is the specific color of orgone energy within and without the organism. Classical physics tries to explain the blueness of the sky by the scattering of the blue and of the spectral color series in the gaseous atmosphere. However, it is a fact that blue is the color seen in all functions which are related to the cosmic or atmospheric or organismic orgone energy. . . . The color of luminating, decaying wood is blue; so are the luminating tails of glowworms, St. Elmo's fire, and the aurora borealis. The lumination in evacuated tubes charged with orgone energy is blue. (Cited in Gardner, 1957, p. 253)

Reich is here making the sort of statement that is historically a hallmark of the crackpot pseudoscientist: the physicists are all wrong about why the sky is blue, which in turn requires that they are all also wrong about optics and prisms, gas spectroscopy, the spectrum itself, and the causes of the aurora, among other things. Given his predilection to see the color blue where others do not, as in the decay of wood or on glowworms, which generally appear yellowish green to most observers, some writers have speculated that he may have had some sort of undiagnosed visual impairment that made neutral surfaces appear to glow blue. This seems a reasonable speculation, given the color's frequent recurrence in his writings about phenomena not generally regarded as possessing a particular color—he claimed to have experienced a deep blue-black hurricane, for example, and would no doubt reject scientific explanations for why rain clouds might look like that.

Reich attributed many other phenomena to orgone as well, rather than accepting more orthodox scientific explanations. The heat shimmer that sometimes appears above pavement, for example, has nothing to do with heat. It is produced instead by waves of orgone energy, along with most other phenomena that are attributed by scientists to static electricity and its atmospheric discharge. These would include lightning, radio interference, and electrical disruptions during solar flares, as well as clouds and storms in general. A believer in a broad range of questionable phenomena, Reich also published an article in 1951 in which he claimed to have proven that dowsing rods operate via orgone energy as well.

Within the body, the orgone is of course the basis of libido, or sexual energy. Ordinarily flowing throughout the body, during sexual intercourse, orgone becomes increasingly concentrated in the genitalia. At the moment of orgasm, the orgone energy is released to flow back through the rest of the body. It is the energy that all cells contain and require to function—during breathing, for example, red blood cells are charged with orgone energy, which they then transfer to the body as they flow back out through it. Again, regular scientists, with their understanding that what red corpuscles pick up during breathing is actually oxygen, would have to be profoundly mistaken for Reich to be right. He is confident in his conclusion, however, because he has looked at the cells under a microscope, at which time he saw a blue glimmer as they absorbed more orgone. Reich further bolstered his confidence in the existence of orgone by detecting it by other means. In 1947, for example, he claimed to have measured orgone with a Geiger counter.

Along with his observation of the orgone glow in blood cells, Reich reported another fundamental, paradigm-shattering discovery under his microscope: He found out that the simplest unit of living matter is not the cell, nor for that matter is it any of the known structures, such as organelles, found within a living cell. Rather, living things are made up of *bions*. A bion, which he described as an "energy vesicle," is a liquid-filled membrane that pulsates continually with orgone energy, and so naturally it appears blue under the microscope. This pulsation is a basic rhythm of life, which Reich saw as reaching its fullest expression in the pulsations of the four-stage orgasm. Reich discovered the bions by boiling a mix of grass, sand, iron, and animal tissue, to which he added potassium and gelatin. When he cooled the liquid and poured it into Petri dishes with growth media, bions appeared spontaneously in the dishes, and over time clumped together and organized as protozoa, bacteria, amoebas, and paramecia. Based on these observations, Reich concluded that bions are being constantly formed in the disintegration and decay of both organic and inorganic substances.

As bions are the building blocks of other life forms, it was clear to Reich that life is sometimes spontaneously generated from nonliving matter. Indeed, in 1936 he bizarrely blended this idea with Marxist dialectic to suggest that since everything in the world is arranged antithetically, there must exist two different kinds of single-celled organisms. The negative, life-destroying organisms form through organic decay, whereas positive, life-promoting organisms form spontaneously from inorganic matter. While this in itself would of course mean that all of biology was wrong, Reich was not done; he quickly came up with a medical application for this idea. In his 1948 book, *The Cancer Biopathy,* he argues that cancer is a result of spontaneously generated organisms, which he called *T-bacilli,* with the *T* coming from *Tod,* a German word for death. In the book, he describes verifying their existence by examining a culture of rotting cancerous tissue he obtained from a hospital. In a bizarre experiment, he injected the bacteria he found there into mice, in which they caused cancer. From all of this, he concluded that cancer is ultimately a result of the reduction of orgone energy in cells as a result of aging or injury, which in turn causes the cells to undergo what he called *bionous degeneration,* as the T-bacilli form from the protein of the dying cells, thus accelerating the process.

Reich further suggested that the cancer cells themselves, produced by the T-bacilli, are themselves protozoa that are produced by the breakdown of body tissues, as he has seen under the microscope that many cancer cells "have a tail and move in the manner of a fish" (cited in Gardner, 1957, p. 256). In *The Cancer Biopathy,* Reich even speculates that if the spread of these protozoa were not eventually halted by the death of the cancer patient, the patient would eventually come to be made up entirely of protozoa.

Reich appears to have been working alone at the microscope when making these observations, with no other observer present to verify his interpretations of what he was seeing. The first look most "orthodox" biologists (this was Reich's derisive term for them) got at Reich's observations came with the publication of *The Cancer Biopathy,* in which he reproduced a series of photomicrographs of various single-celled organisms in the process of formation from clumps of bions. The general consensus of actual microbiologists upon seeing the photographs was that his cultures became contaminated by airborne microbes, and that some of them were already present in a dormant state in his decaying material. At least one microbiologist who was allowed a look through his Oslo microscope was able to see the T-bacilli, but unfortunately recognized them as ordinary staphylococcus bacteria, which notoriously spread rapidly on nonsterile surfaces in hospitals. What no observer other than Reich was able to see, in any photo or through any optical instrument, was either the bions themselves or their telltale blue glow.

Reaction to Reich's work among scientists in Norway was strong and quite negative, with most regarding his conclusions as utter nonsense. In an echo of his prior experiences in Germany and Denmark, Reich found himself the target of a series of attacks in *Tidens Tegn,* a leading Oslo newspaper, in 1937, with the support of the scientific community and eventually of other newspapers. This was not a minor campaign—between fall of 1937 and fall of 1938, more than a hundred anti-Reich articles appeared in the major Oslo newspapers. Leiv Kreyberg, Norway's leading cancer specialist, was the scientist who had recognized ordinary staphylococcus bacteria in Reich's culture, and he promptly accused Reich in print of lacking even the most basic understanding of either anatomy or bacteria. Reich responded by sending samples to another prominent bacteriologist, who concurred (again in the press) that the bacteria resulted from air contamination. Reich responded by requesting that the scientists conduct a larger, controlled study to test his ideas, Kreyberg responded (again in print) that Reich knew less about bacteria than a first-year medical student, and the claim did not merit additional study.

Rather than pursue additional, better-controlled research himself, Reich responded by publishing *The Bion Experiments on the Origin of Life* (1938), which unfortunately contained a paragraph prefiguring his later writings, in which he indicated that bion theory allows a better understanding of cancer. In publishing this, Reich transformed himself, in the eyes of the Norwegian scientific establishment, from a man with crazy ideas about the origins of life to a dangerous quack who might be promoting a phony cure for cancer. When the book was published, Reich's visa had expired, and several influential scientists argued against an extension. While they did not wish to return him to Austria and the Gestapo, they did not wish to allow him to remain in Norway either. The Norwegians prided themselves on their intellectual tolerance, but also recognized that Reich was advocating positions and practices far outside the mainstream, and so he was allowed to remain only as a result of a compromise: his visa was renewed, but under a new royal decree, psychoanalysis could only be practiced by those with a license. Given his standing in the psychoanalytic community, there was no chance that Reich would get one.

Given the hostile environment he now faced in Norway, Reich eagerly accepted an invitation the following year to teach at The New School for Social Research in New York. He received his visa in August of 1939 and sailed for America on August 19, a mere two weeks before the start of World War II. Arriving in New York, he remained at the New School for two years, also setting himself up in private practice as a therapist. In New York he became known for his social isolation, becoming distant even from old friends who had also settled in the area. He quickly developed a reputation at the school for being a man with whom nobody was on a first-name basis. This may have simply been a reaction to the hostility toward his work that he had endured in Scandinavia, but rumors of possible mental illness had followed him since his days with the Vienna Psychoanalytical Society, with various writers describing him as paranoid and fanatical. His career in the United States is perhaps best regarded with this in mind.

Having established to his own satisfaction that both mental and physical illness resulted from, respectively, either insufficient orgone or an unreleased buildup of it, in America Reich altered his approach to therapy by constructing a device to fix the problem. In 1940, Reich built and tested his first Orgone Energy Accumulator. The accumulator is essentially a box, strongly resembling a small telephone booth, made of both organic and inorganic materials. In the first accumulators, the inside surface of the box was made of sheet metal, with an outer layer of wood. Later models had as many as 23 layers, alternating layers of steel wool and stone between the outer and inner walls. The theory behind the accumulator's structure is that orgone is attracted to the organic material on the outside, and is passed along from there to the metal, which radiates it inward. Reich further believed that the metal reflects orgone, so the box will quickly build up an unusually large orgone charge.

Treatment for a variety of mental and physical ills is accomplished quite simply: The patient sits in the box for a few minutes and soaks up the orgone energy. According to Reich's promotional literature, sitting in the box results in "a prickling, warm sensation, accompanied by reddening of the face and a rise in body temperature. There is a feeling that the body is 'glowing' " (Gardner, 1957, p. 255). A person should not sit in the box for too long, however, as it is possible to accumulate too much orgone. This will result in feelings of dizziness and nausea, which should be followed immediately by stepping out of the box and breathing fresh air. Reich believed firmly enough in the accumulator to provide this additional warning:

> Under no circumstances . . . should one sit in the accumulator for hours, or, as some people do, go to sleep in it. This can cause serious damage (severe vomiting, etc.). It is better, if necessary, to use the accumulator several times a day at shorter intervals than to prolong one sitting unnecessarily. At this stage of research, no accumulator over 3-layers should be used without medical supervision. (Gardner, 1957, p. 255)

Not wishing to leave out the bedridden patient who cannot make it to the box, Reich also produced an orgone accumulator blanket, a sort of rigid wood and metal tent that is placed over the bed while a matching set of flat layers goes beneath the mattress.

Although the accumulators have gotten most of the attention, a far more bizarre product is the orgone *shooter,* intended for the selective application of orgone energy to particular areas of the body. It consists of a hollow-core iron cable, attached to the orgone accumulator box at one end, which conveys the orgone to the part of the body being treated. For treatment of areas larger than the end of the cable, a funnel is attached to the end of the cable—according to the pamphlet Reich produced to accompany the device, it is vital that metal funnels be used, as plastic funnels are ineffective. Reich claimed that the wound-healing process is accelerated dramatically by using the shooter, going so far as to say the following:

> Even severe pain will be stopped soon after the accident if orgone energy is applied locally through the shooter. . . . In severe cases of burns, experience has revealed the amazing fact that no blisters appear, and that the initial redness slowly disappears. The wounds heal in a matter of a few hours; severe ones need a day or two. Only chronic, advanced degenerating processes

require weeks and months of daily irradiation. But here, too, severe lesions . . . will yield to orgone energy irradiation. (Gardner, 1957, p. 256)

Beyond these already wildly inflated claims, Reich also indicated that the shooter could sterilize wounds, and further suggested that it was dangerous to mix the use of the shooter with chemical antiseptics, as the results of such a mixture might prove quite dangerous. In actual use, this would of course result in failure to properly disinfect wounds, since the shooter is assumed to have already done so.

Reich also believed the Orgone Accumulator possessed tremendous disease-fighting power, listing the following as ailments that can benefit from the application of orgone energy: "fatigue, anemia, cancer in early stages (with the exception of tumors of the brain and the liver), acute and chronic colds, hay fever, arthritis, chronic ulcers, some types of migraine, sinusitis, and any kind of lesion, abrasion, or wound" (cited in Gardner, 1957, p. 256). In making this claim, Reich was not completely ignorant of contemporary medicine, with its recognition that many of these ailments are actually caused by bacteria and other microorganisms—he just disagreed about where those microbes came from. In Reich's view, disease-causing microbes resulted from the degeneration of body bions, which was in turn produced by neuroses. This odd variation on the idea of autoimmune disease, which he sees as underlying most illness, can be treated by simply sitting in the box, though he acknowledged that chronic ailments may require years of treatment. Much of Reich's research on the orgone accumulator took place at a laboratory he set up in rural Maine, where he constructed a room-sized orgone accumulator. The reader will at this point not be surprised to learn that Reich reported that in the dark, the entire room had a blue glow about it.

Not content to limit the applications of orgone energy to medicine, Reich also claimed to have made advances both theoretical and practical in both physics and meteorology. Reich's foray into astrophysics and cosmology, *Cosmic Superimposition,* was published in 1951, and suggests nothing less than that, although unrecognized by physicists, orgone energy actually underlies everything in the universe. Matter, for example, is a result of the movement of units of orgone energy—when two orgone units approach each other, they come together in a way very much like a sexual embrace, and the result is a particle of matter. A similar occurrence explains the birth of galaxies. Space is filled with directionless, structureless streams of orgone energy, which are attracted to each other. When they embrace—physics would no doubt use a less loving terminology, calling it a collision—the result is a new galaxy. Reich further suggests that, because physicists do not recognize that space is filled with orgone energy, they have failed to properly understand gravity:

The sun and the planets move in the same plane and revolve in the same direction due to the movements and direction of the cosmic orgone energy stream in the galaxy. Thus, the sun does not "attract" anything at all. (Cited in Gardner, 1957, p. 261)

The spiral shape of galaxies, in other words, is due to the natural spiral direction in which orgone energy is continuously moving.

Having thoroughly alienated the astrophysicists, Reich then proceeded to drive away the subatomic physicists as well, with what he considered the most important work of his career: finding a way to counteract the effects of nuclear weapons. Shortly after the first use of the atom bomb in 1945, Reich speculated that orgone energy is the original, natural form of atomic energy. Where atomic energy destroys life and matter, however, orgone energy creates matter and supports life. Borrowing from Freud's late-career emphasis on the duality of life instincts and death instincts, which were after all manifestations of libido, which he felt he had explained and expanded on with orgone energy, Reich saw the two energies as nothing less than the universe's underlying principles of love and hate, or good and evil. In his journal, he wrote the following:

The horror . . . at the "discovery" of the atom bomb has its counterpart in the quiet but glowing enthusiasm of anyone who works with orgone energy or experiences its therapeutic effects. (Cited in Gardner, 1957, p. 261)

Considering his conviction that the two energies have such contradictory natures, the logical next step for Reich was to speculate on the possible utility of orgone as a natural antidote for the effects of atomic radiation:

If, against any expectation, I should ever discover any murderous potentiality of the orgone energy . . . I would keep the process secret. We shall have to learn to counteract the murderous form of the atomic energy with the life-furthering function of the orgone energy and thus render it harmless. (Cited in Gardner, 1957, p. 261)

Reich and his laboratory staff set out to discover this anti-radiation function in January 1951, in what he called the ORANUR (Orgonomic Anti-Nuclear Radiation) project. Results were self-published in the *Orgone Energy Bulletin,* rather than in any mainstream scientific journal.

Early on in the ORANUR project, something went seriously wrong, though Reich's own interpretation of what exactly happened is quite different from what an actual nuclear physicist would say. At the time, the extent to which radium and other radioactive elements could produce serious illness and death was already fairly well understood in the scientific community (Madame Curie, widely known to have died as a result of long-term exposure to ionizing radiation, mostly from radium, passed away in 1934!), but Reich was apparently less well-informed. Without taking any of the customary precautions against radiation exposure, Reich purchased a supply of radium and cobalt-60 (a highly radioactive isotope) and brought them into the orgone accumulator room, to allow the orgone energy to neutralize the ionizing radiation that they release. What happened next, according to Reich, was that the nuclear energy of the radioactive elements, rather than being neutralized by the orgone energy, turned the good energy evil. The orgone energy somehow became transformed into DOR (Deadly Orgone Energy), and the entire laboratory staff became ill with "ORANUR sickness." In a report dated May 12, 1952, Reich writes:

> Since March 21, 1952, an acute emergency exists at Orgonon [the name of Reich's headquarters in Rangeley]. The emergency is due to severe Oranur activity. *This activity set in a few hours after the tornado developed in the Middle West on March 21.* . . . The routine work at Orgonon has collapsed. Several workers had to abandon their jobs. Most buildings at Orgonon became uninhabitable. No work could be done in these buildings up to date. (Cited in Gardner, 1957, p. 262; italics mine)

Reich's idiosyncratic interpretation of these events is far less parsimonious than the explanation proffered by scientists who heard about the incident: highly radioactive isotopes were brought into an unshielded laboratory, and handled by people inexperienced in such work, without ordinary safety precautions, and the result was that the laboratory became contaminated with radiation and several staffers experienced radiation poisoning. The problem was not that orgone energy turned evil, but simply that it was incapable of protecting against the usual effects of ionizing radiation.

Perhaps the oddest portion of Reich's account of the ORANUR crisis is his mention of a tornado in the Midwest on the same day as the accident. This apparent connection makes more sense when considered alongside Reich's conviction that the list of phenomena that are best explained by orgone energy includes the weather, and cloud formation in particular. The tornado therefore was a symptom of the same change in orgone energy observed in the lab: the dark orgone sickened lab technicians and mysteriously also caused severe weather hundreds of miles away. Based on Reich's belief that clouds result from the flow of orgone, he developed and marketed, as part of a line of CORE (Cosmic Orgone Engineering) projects, a rainmaking device that he referred to as a *cloudbuster*. A contemporary source describes the machine as follows:

> a bank of long hollow pipes tilting at the sky and sections of hollow cable, all of which are mounted on a metal box; it resembles a stylized version of an

anti-aircraft gun, and works with surpassing ease. The clouds are not sprayed with any substance; the hollow pipes merely draw orgone out of them—thus weakening their cohesive power and eventually causing them to break up. (Ross, 1954, cited in Gardner, 1957, p. 344)

The hollow cables ran from the pipes to a tank of water set in the base of the device, which was alleged to attract and store atmospheric orgone. As the preceding description notes, the device had no visible action of any sort—although the pipes were pointed at clouds, nothing emerged from them toward the clouds. Reich proposed that accumulations of DOR (deadly orgone energy) were the cause of drought and desertification, and the cloudbuster allowed him to manipulate streams of both kinds of orgone in the atmosphere, thus causing clouds to form and then break up, bringing rain where it was most needed.

His device, nonsensical though it seemed to meteorologists, quickly found customers, and subsequently testimonials as to its effectiveness. In 1953, for example, Maine's blueberry crop was threatened by drought, and a group of farmers came to Rangely, Maine, where Orgonon was located, and offered to pay Reich to break the drought. On July 6, 1953, his team set up a cloudbuster in the morning near Bangor, and the following night about a quarter of an inch of rain fell. The farmers, satisfied that the device had worked, paid Reich for his services, and soon Reich had cloudbusters operating in North Carolina in addition to Maine, with plans for further expansion.

The scientific community was not nearly as enthusiastic about Reich's ideas as the blueberry farmers, however, and the general reaction from medicine, psychiatry, physics, astronomy, and meteorology was fairly uniformly negative, when the members of those professions were not simply ignoring Reich entirely. Reich's rather paranoid and grandiose response to his negative reception by the medical community lends some credence to those who have suggested that he was mentally ill. In 1948, for example, a year after the Pure Food and Drug Administration began to investigate the orgone accumulators (as potentially fraudulent medical devices), Reich published a book aimed at his detractors with the title of *Listen Little Man!*, with illustrations by popular cartoonist and children's book author William Steig, later the creator of *Shrek*—Steig was an early adherent to orgone therapy, and was an associate board member of the Wilhelm Reich Foundation. The book, an attack on the neurotic little man who, in failing to see his own sexually based sickness, is responsible for all of the world's troubles, including the rise of fascism, is actually a strikingly vicious assault on everyone who has failed to acknowledge Reich's greatness, including established scientists. Reich addresses the oncology establishment, for example, as follows:

When the discoverer has just found out why people die of cancer . . . and . . . you, Little Man, happen to be a Professor of Cancer Pathology, with a steady salary, you say that the discoverer is a faker; or that he does not understand anything about air germs . . . or you insist that you have a right to examine him, to find out whether he is qualified to work on "your" cancer problem, the problem you cannot solve; or you prefer to see many, many cancer patients die rather than admit that *he* has found what *you* so badly need if you are to save your patients. To you, your professional dignity, or your bank account, or your connection with the radium industry means more than truth and learning. And that's why you are small and miserable, Little Man. (Cited in Gardner, 1957, p. 259)

This passage makes it clear that Reich regarded failure to embrace his ideas not as a sign of disagreement, but of fear and jealousy, with the cancer researchers motivated by the need to hold onto their status rather than seeking real answers. Reich's sense of persecution and delusions of grandeur appeared in other publications as well. In 1947, his supporters published a pamphlet containing a statement by Reich in which he compares his own suffering to that of Giordano Bruno and Galileo at the hands of the Inquisition.

Reich and his followers were also fond of claiming, falsely, that Reich had convinced Albert Einstein of the existence of orgone energy. It appears that Reich actually did visit Einstein in Princeton in 1941, at which time they spoke at some length about Reich's ideas. Einstein even consented to test an orgone accumulator, agreeing that if Reich was right and an object's temperature could rise without any outside heat source while in the box, then physics would be hit by a major bombshell. In his test of the device, Einstein noted a rise in temperature. Where Reich attributed this to the accumulation of orgone, however, Einstein and his lab assistant recognized that the temperature was slightly lower at the floor of the box than at its ceiling, and so the effect was simply due to a normal temperature gradient. Einstein wrote to Reich, explaining his experiment in detail and suggesting to Reich that he should approach his experiments with a more skeptical attitude. Reich's response was a nonsensical 25-page letter in which he attempted to explain away the new findings in terms of a wide range of concepts in physics—we know this because Reich published the exchange in 1953 as *The Einstein Affair,* probably without Einstein's permission.

The FDA may have only paid attention to Reich in 1947 because of an article by Mildred Brady in the *New Republic* of May 26, 1947—prior to the publication of her *The Strange Case of Wilhelm Reich,* he had largely been left alone by the American press. His psychoanalytic work was being taught in universities, and psychiatric and medical journals were publishing articles that cited his theories. The stranger side of orgone theory had gone largely unnoticed until 1947, but that changed with Brady's article, which mentioned both Reich's belief that insufficient orgastic potency causes cancer and his use of orgone accumulators to increase orgastic potency. Her implication (which was, after all, true) that Reich was promoting a cancer cure unsupported by science got the attention of the FDA, which is responsible, along with the Federal Trade Commission, for regulating the sale of medical devices. At the request of the FTC, the FDA assigned an investigator to look into Reich's claims about the health benefits of orgone. The investigator quickly found that more than 250 accumulators had already been built and that the accumulators were often rented to patients rather than being sold outright. Within the first few months of the investigation, the FDA had already concluded that Reich was operating a large-scale fraud, and further suspected that some sort of tawdry sexual racket was afoot as well. Reich's practice at the time of having patients strip to their underwear, and sometimes completely naked, did little to remove this suspicion.

In response, he wrote *Conspiracy: An Emotional Chain Reaction,* in which he presented himself as a victim of persecution, and the FDA as orchestrating a smear campaign against him. He further came to believe that Brady was a Stalinist sent after him by the Communist Party, though it remains unclear why he thought they would come after him.

The war of words between Reich and medical investigators came to a head in July of 1952, when a team from the FDA carried out an unannounced inspection at Orgonon. Reich attempted to chase them from the property, shouting at them that they were unqualified to examine his laboratory or to speak with him until they had read his books, then ordering them to leave. This was the start of a lengthy period of investigation by the FDA, during which they interviewed Reich's students and patients, along with other physicians, focusing on the use of the accumulator boxes.

Reich's aggressive responses continued to show evidence of paranoia and delusional thinking—he took to calling the FDA investigators *higs,* an acronym for Hoodlums in Government, when he wasn't calling them red fascists. He also came to believe that he had powerful friends, including President Dwight Eisenhower, who would protect him from prosecution, and that the U.S. Air Force was regularly flying overhead to check on his welfare.

In 1954, as a result of Reich's claims to treat physical illness, including cancer, with the orgone accumulator, the U.S. Attorney in Maine sought a permanent injunction from the FDA, under rules prohibiting interstate shipment and sale of worthless medical devices. Reich decided to defend himself, and his defense in the case consisted entirely of a long letter to the judge in which he argued that neither the court nor the FDA was qualified to judge the scientific genius of his own work, and that therefore he would refuse to appear in court, confident that the judge would see things his way. As it turned out, the judge failed to share Reich's perspective, and granted the injunction on March 19, 1954. His ruling went far beyond the original complaint, however, citing the likelihood that cancer patients relying on the accumulators for treatment would probably forego treatment that might actually help. This made the device actively likely to produce harm, rather than simply worthless, and so instead of simply banning further sale or rental of the devices, the judge ordered the destruction of all orgone energy accumulators and their parts, as well as all written material, promotional material, and printed instructions regarding orgone energy and its use.

Believing himself to be the target of a massive conspiracy designed to stop his important work, Reich's response to the injunction was to keep conducting research with the accumulators at Orgonon in Maine, while no longer selling or renting new ones. This strategy unfortunately came to the attention of the authorities when one of his students, Dr. Michael Silvert, transported some accumulators to New York, in clear violation of the original injunction against interstate transportation of accumulators. Both men were charged with contempt of court, and Reich once again refused to mount a case in his own defense, instead admitting to the violation and sending the judge copies of his books in hopes of convincing him of the injustice of the injunction. With this ineffective defense, Reich was found guilty and sentenced to two years in prison, and the Wilhelm Reich Foundation, which promoted the use of the accumulators, was fined $10,000. Contemporary observers have noted that the FDA's case was very weak, and that lawyers had advised Reich that they could easily get him off, but Reich refused to let them because he saw himself as an important historical figure fighting what would prove to be a historically important battle. He later appealed his sentence at several levels, all the way to the Supreme Court, and lost at every level, for the simple reason that he clearly intended to continue promoting the device if released.

In 1956, the FDA's actions in supervising the destruction of the accumulators and related literature had the unusual result of making Reich a martyr for civil libertarians, because of the unfortunately broad language of the injunction. In ordering the destruction of all materials concerning the use of orgone energy, the judge produced a list of publications that included several of his less-controversial books that were still widely read in the psychoanalytic community, including *The Sexual Revolution, Character Analysis,* and *The Mass Psychology of Fascism.* When they supervised the destruction of the accumulators, the FDA also burned some of the literature, which prompted a critical press release from the American Civil Liberties Union (ACLU). After the press release got little attention, Reich asked the ACLU to stay out of it, not because of their support of his books but because the press release did not also criticize the destruction of the orgone accumulators. Without any organized opposition, on August 23, 1956, a full six *tons* of Reich's books, journals, and papers were burned in a public incinerator on Manhattan's Lower East Side, marking what has been called the worst example of censorship in U.S. history. Combined with his advocacy of sexual libertinism and rejection of government power, this excessive government response to his ideas made Reich a folk hero of sorts to the youth counterculture of the late 1960s, and ensured, paradoxically, that his ideas would be kept alive by his followers. When Reich died in prison, FDA officials and scientific observers alike expected that they would hear nothing further about orgone accumulators and cloudbusters.

Instead of being dead and gone, however, Reich's ideas continue to be circulated by a new generation of orgone therapists and meteorological interventionists. Today, some 53 years after Reich's death, the American College of Orgonomy, based in Princeton, New Jersey, is alive and well, and has an actively maintained website (www.orgonomy.com). They produce a very slick, professional-looking journal, the *Journal of Orgonomy,* which covers a broad range of topics but never strays far from Reich's original concerns. As of this writing, their most recent issue opens with a story offering proof of the existence of glowing orgone energy in jellyfish, for example. The college's website includes articles repeating Reich's cosmological and biological claims, along with a wealth of material comparing Reich to Galileo and chastising mainstream science for ignoring his brilliance. More surprisingly, members of the college have in the past 20 years continued to promote cloudbusting as a way to defeat drought and desertification.

The Reich follower most responsible for continuing to promote orgonomy and cloudbusting is James DeMeo, who has for several decades traveled and lectured on Reich's ideas and claiming to break droughts. His culminating achievement, promoted on his www.orgonelab.org website, is what he has dubbed the *Saharasia* hypothesis. In addition to recognizing the obvious famine-related problems caused by drought and desertification, DeMeo claims that *all* social problems, including war, poverty, violence, injustice, mental illness, patriarchy, and environmental destruction, are caused by desertification. He draws on current biological anthropology to acknowledge that all of humanity originated in Africa, but then suggests that until about 5,000 to 7,000 years ago, humanity lived in peace and harmony, and that all changed with the growth of the Sahara desert in Northern Africa. All of humanity's problems can be fixed with the cloudbuster, in other words.

Probably the strangest intrusion of Reich's ideas into the 21st century occurred in Mozambique, in early 2009, when four people were arrested on suspicion of attempting to sabotage the Cahora Bassa dam, on the lower Zambezi River. The suspects were a German architect, a Portuguese hotelier, a pilot from Botswana, and a South African who calls himself a "prophet," and all are members of an organization calling itself *Orgonise Africa,* described in the local press in Mozambique as "a lunatic fringe group." Far from being a clandestine mission to sabotage a dam, their voyage was openly advertised on the group's website, as "Operation Paradise." Orgonise Africa is a cultlike group founded by followers of Reich, who believe, like Reich himself, that everything wrong on the planet is caused by insufficient orgone. Their way of dealing with this involves a substance they call *orgonite,* which is a mixture of metal shavings and fiberglass resin, with a large quartz crystal at the center, which somehow accumulates and stores orgone energy.

The group was engaging in a practice they call "orgone gifting," which involves dropping lumps of orgonite into bodies of water, with the idea that they will purify the water, increase life within it, and therefore improve the lives of the people along the gifted body of water. The orgonite is also alleged to reduce the negative energy flowing from places like ritual murder sites and facilities used for torture, as well as counteract the effects of entropic technologies, whatever those may be. Since the orgonite was unlikely to either pollute the water or do any damage to the dam, the initial charges of sabotage were dropped. Instead, in a move sure to cheer the hearts of metaphor-minded scientific observers everywhere, the charge against these orgone enthusiasts was reduced to dumping garbage in a lake.

Further Reading

Gardner, M. (1957). *Fads and Fallacies in the Name of Science*. New York: Dover.

Reich, W. (1953). *The Einstein Affair*. New York: Orgone Institute Press.

Reich, W. (1974a). *The Cancer Biopathy*. New York: Farrar, Straus, & Giroux.

Reich, W. (1974b). *Listen, Little Man!* New York: Farrar, Straus, & Giroux.

Reich, W. (1980). *The Mass Psychology of Fascism*. New York: Farrar, Straus, & Giroux.

Reich, W. (1986). *The Sexual Revolution: Towards a Self-Regulating Character Structure*. New York: Farrar, Straus, & Giroux.

Reich, W. (2005). *Passion of Youth: An Autobiography, 1897–1922*. New York: Farrar, Straus, & Giroux.

Seduction Theory

While it is well-known even among readers with only a passing acquaintance with Freud's ideas that he saw the sexual impulses and fantasies of early childhood as crucial to the formation of later personality and neuroses, Freud embraced a very different perspective on the causes of neuroses early in his career, the abandonment of which was of crucial importance in the development of psychoanalytic theory. In the mid-1890s, Freud proposed that all neuroses are the result of an adult's sexual abuse of a child, an idea that became, somewhat unfortunately, known as the *seduction theory*. The name is unfortunate because of the consensus implied by the use of a relatively pleasant word for the assault; in addition to *seduction*, however, other words Freud used in his writings for such contact include *rape, abuse, attack, assault, aggression*, and *trauma*.

In these early years, Freud recognized the existence of two separate categories of neurosis: the *psychoneuroses* and the *actual* neuroses. The psychoneuroses were those resulting from defensive attempts to cope with traumatic events in childhood, and included hysteria and obsessional neurosis, or what would today be called obsessive-compulsive disorder. *Actual* neuroses, including anxiety and neurasthenia, were those with adult onset, in which contemporary or present causes were considered sufficient to explain the psychopathology. Neurasthenia, also known as nervous exhaustion, was a common diagnostic category in Freud's time, and was a catch-all term for any person presenting with vague physical complaints with no clear organic cause, and was believed to result from the physical and emotional consequences of too much stress on the nervous system. By 1895, Freud was losing interest in the actual neuroses in favor of the psychoneuroses, but his perspective on nervous anxiety is unsurprising given his later writings on hysteria: he believed the causes of the actual neuroses were *always* sexual in nature, frequently involving various kinds of sexual frustration, including guilt over masturbation, impotence, coitus interruptus, and fear of pregnancy.

It is unsurprising that Freud would also be open to a sexual explanation of the psychoneuroses, and in the mid-1890s, he published a series of papers in which he argued that the various neuropsychoses of defense (treating hysteria, obsessional neurosis, and phobias separately) each follow a distinct etiological path from a particular, distinctive childhood sexual trauma. In 1895 he proposed, in a letter to Wilhelm Fliess, that a crucial difference in the development of hysteria rather than obsessional neurosis has to do with the exact nature of the early sexual experience: hysteria results from a presexual sexual scare, whereas obsessional neurosis is the product of presexual sexual pleasure. In other words, obsessional neurosis is the result of guilt arising from precocious, prepubescent sexual pleasure, an idea he would explore further in the case of *the Rat Man,* some decades later. Hysteria, however, resulted from inappropriate sexual contact from an adult. He based this notion on a simple fact: he saw numerous patients who, one after another, remembered having been sexually abused, even raped, by significant adults, including their own fathers in several cases.

In 1896, Freud committed this idea to print, in a paper titled "Further Remarks on the Neuropsychoses of Defense." In this paper, he argued on the basis of 13 separate cases that the traumas that cause hysteria "belong to early childhood (the time before puberty), and their content must consist of an actual irritation of the genitals (proceedings resembling coitus)." This sort of sexual abuse was of course unacceptable in Freud's time, as in our own, and consequently his readers may have understandably been shocked at the proposition that adults would behave in this way toward children. Freud himself was somewhat reluctant to fully expose what he had uncovered with these 13 patients—although his letters to Fliess repeatedly mention fathers as the perpetrators of the abuse, in the article he limits description of the abusers to various servants, older children, teachers, and adult strangers. He was right to expect some resistance to the idea, as he discovered in April 1896, when he lectured on the subject of "The Etiology of Hysteria" to the Vienna Society for Psychiatry and Neurology, to an audience of experts in the field of sexuality and psychopathology, which included Richard von Kraft-Ebing, author of *Psychopathia Sexualis,* essentially the inventor of the scientific study of sexuality. He spoke of 18 separate cases, all of whom had recalled being mistreated sexually in childhood, up to and including rape, in whom the sexual abuse was clearly the origin of their hysterical symptoms. The reception was decidedly chilly, with Kraft-Ebing proclaiming his theory "a scientific fairy tale," and Freud coming to feel that he was being ostracized from the local medical community. He also had difficulty attracting new patients during this period.

What happened next has been the subject of some debate. According to Freud, he came to recognize that sexual assault was unlikely to be the cause of *all* cases of hysteria, as such widespread child sexual abuse seemed highly improbable. After all, his explanation of hysteria also involved a biologically based predisposition to develop neuroses, thus sexual abuse would be a necessary but not sufficient condition for the development of hysteria. This would of course mean that sexual assault on children was happening far more frequently than even the incidence of hysteria would suggest. In addition, he would write a paper in 1899 on what he called "screen memories," focused on a basic practical problem in psychoanalysis—the impossibility of distinguishing memory from fantasy in the unconscious mind. As a result of all of this, Freud came to believe that what he was hearing from his hysterical patients was not recollection of real events, but rather recollection of fantasies they had experienced (a central notion in the case of *Dora*). This movement away from a traumatic etiology would become the foundation for subsequent psychoanalytic theory, in which the central event, the "nuclear complex" (in Freud's own words) at the root of *all* neurosis became the Oedipal conflict. Rather than being caused by actual sexual contact with an adult, in other words, hysterical symptoms resulted from incomplete resolution of the distress created by fantasies of such contact.

An alternative explanation for Freud's change of focus has long been popular among feminist writers, however. They have argued that Freud's change of mind resulted in a period of many decades in which the occurrence of child sexual abuse was largely ignored, and during which adults who mentioned incest to their therapists could expect to be assured that it had not actually happened. This criticism is almost as old as psychoanalysis—one of Freud's more famous patients, **Dora**, was very frustrated by his attempts to convince her that her memory of the inappropriate advances by her father's friend was actually a manifestation of her own secret wishes. The charge of ignoring *all* real sexual abuse has never been entirely fair—Freud never abandoned the recognition that at least some of his neurotic patients really had been assaulted by their fathers, but he did come to believe that such revelations were usually a result of childhood fantasies.

As central as this notion is to psychoanalysis, the charges of ignoring real abuse have generally been ignored by the psychoanalytic community at large. The charge became impossible to disregard, however, when it came from one of their own. In 1984, Jeffrey Moussaieff Masson, the recently appointed director of the Freud Archives in London, and thus in some ways the ultimate Freud insider, published *The Assault on Truth: Freud's Suppression of the Seduction Theory,* which presented a new perspective on Freud's change of heart, based on new discoveries he had made among Freud's papers. The book's title is unsubtle and rather self-explanatory, but the argument within is actually rather more cautious than that sensationalistic title leads the reader to anticipate. As expected, he argues that Freud altered his theory under outside pressure, despite knowing the initial version to be true. He bases the argument on Freud's own words, however, and uncovers what he has described as no less than a conspiracy by Freud's daughter and inner circle to keep some of his correspondence hidden.

Masson's story began with his examination of the correspondence between Freud and Wilhelm **Fliess**, and his discovery that some letters had been left out of the published edition, which led him to propose editing a new, complete edition of the correspondence. The editors of the original, who included Anna **Freud** and Marie **Bonaparte**, wrote that they had included all letters that were of any scientific interest. Masson approached Anna with a letter he thought provided tremendous new insight into the period during which her father was leaving the seduction theory behind. In the letter, dated December 22, 1897, some three months after Freud proposed in print that the memories of abuse were actually fantasies, Freud wrote to Fliess about a patient who had been brutally raped by her father at the age of two and had nearly bled to death as a consequence of the assault. At the end of the letter, Freud proposes a quotation from a Goethe poem as a new motto for psychoanalysis: "Poor child, what have they done to you?" He encountered resistance from Anna at first to the idea of publishing the previously unpublished letters, but eventually she acknowledged that there was quite a bit more unpublished material and consented to his examining the rest of the 1897 letters in search of more insight into the abandonment of the seduction theory.

Within the psychoanalytic community there has been dissent over the years against the idea that all such memories are fantasies, and Masson had published papers to that effect in psychoanalytic journals in the past. Here was a crucial piece of evidence regarding what Freud believed at the time, and it had not been seen previously. As Masson soon found, there was more, including another letter, also from December 1897, in which Freud wrote, "My confidence in the father-etiology has risen greatly." According to Masson, the unpublished letters included numerous case histories in which Freud returned repeatedly to a recognition of the reality of childhood sexual abuse, and in which he recognized that the incidence of fathers raping their daughters was much higher than anyone at the time was willing to admit.

Masson's book marshaled this evidence to argue that Freud had abandoned the seduction theory professionally while still believing in it personally, and furthermore that his inner circle, including Anna, must have been aware of this but had actively concealed it. The book was very well-received in most intellectual circles, and almost universally savaged by the psychoanalytic community, and both reactions occurred for the same essential reason: the book was seen as calling into question one of the central assumptions on which the entire psychoanalytic edifice was constructed. What Masson saw as an exciting new chapter in our understanding of Freud was seen by much of the psychoanalytic world as a fundamental betrayal. Indeed, shortly after he began to publicly present his findings, Masson was fired as the director of the Freud Archives. A common reaction, both by psychoanalysts and sympathetic members of the press, was to call Masson's character and motivations into question rather than address his evidence directly. According to Masson, when he attended a gathering of psychoanalysts that included Erik **Erikson**, Erikson's reaction was that "the interesting thing was not the words of Freud, but why I [Masson] had found them. This was followed by a murmur of approval" (Masson, 1984, p. 47).

In short, Freud's abandonment of the seduction theory of hysteria either represents the commission of a major scientific error, accompanied by a serious injustice toward those who have been victims of childhood sexual abuse, or the avoidance of such an error, accompanied by a recognition of the previously unacknowledged role of sexual impulses and fantasies in child development. Which point of view is seen as correct seems to depend on how personally committed to the truth of psychoanalytic theory the particular author is, and it is likely that both points of view have some merit. Indisputably, however, Freud's abandonment of the seduction theory was the turning point that made the subsequent development of psychoanalysis possible, for the entire structure depends on how those early childhood memories are interpreted.

Further Reading

Davis, D. (1994). A Theory for the 90s: Traumatic Seduction in Historical Context. *Psychoanalytic Review* 81: 627–639.

Masson, J. (1984). The Persecution and Expulsion of Jeffrey Masson as Performed by Members of the Freudian Establishment & Reported by Janet Malcolm of *The New Yorker. Mother Jones,* December, 35–47.

Masson, J. (1998). *The Assault on Truth: Freud's Suppression of the Seduction Theory.* New York: Pocket Books.

Skinner, B. F. (1904–1990)

Beyond Freud, surely the most influential psychological thinker among his contemporaries in the early 20th century was the American behaviorist B. F. Skinner. Philosophically they appear on the surface to have been polar opposites, with many textbooks on the history of psychology presenting Skinner's ideas as a reaction to Freud's, proposing the least psychoanalytical approach to psychology possible. Recent scholarship (Overskeid, 2007, for example), however, suggests that despite their fundamental differences, Freud had a clear and definite influence on Skinner.

As a behaviorist, Skinner envisioned a psychology free of mentalistic constructs and ideas, such as consciousness, will, or even thinking, which would superficially make his ideas appear to be completely incompatible with Freud's. Since mental processes cannot be directly observed, the behaviorists did not see them as a proper object for scientific study, preferring a psychology focused exclusively on overt, observable behavior. Although John B. **Watson** was the originator of behaviorism, it was through the efforts of Burrhus Frederic (B. F.) Skinner that behaviorist principles found widespread practical application, through the therapeutic approach known as behavior modification, or applied behavior analysis.

Skinner's greatest contribution is probably the distinction he drew between classical (respondent) conditioning (Pavlov's discovery and the primary explanatory mechanism favored by Watson) and operant conditioning. Classical conditioning involves the study of how behaviors, such as a dog's reflexive salivation, are elicited by environmental stimulus conditions such as the presence of food. Where classical conditioning focuses on the role of *antecedent* conditions in producing behavior, operant conditioning instead examines the role of the *consequences* of a behavior in determining the likelihood of that behavior occurring again. Two different categories of consequences determine behavior: *reinforcement* and *punishment.*

Reinforcement is the term applied to any consequence that *increases* the frequency of the behavior that precedes it, whereas punishment is any consequence that *decreases* the frequency of a behavior. Praising a child for saying a particular word (i.e., Daddy), for example, will make the child more likely to say it again, but yelling at the same child after saying a particular word will make the child *less* likely to say it again. Although people often conflate the concept of reinforcement with the idea of a reward, *any* consequence that serves to strengthen a response is a reinforcer.

There are actually two different kinds of reinforcement: positive and negative. Positive reinforcement involves presenting a positive stimulus (such as food, attention, money, or approval) after a behavior, thus making the behavior more likely to occur again. Negative reinforcement involves removal of an aversive stimulus after the behavior, and by that removal making the behavior more likely to occur again under the same circumstances. Taking pain medication serves as a somewhat counterintuitive example: if the behavior of taking a painkiller leads to the pain going away, the person becomes more likely to take one the next time similar pain occurs. In common usage, negative reinforcement is often confused with punishment, and many people use the terms interchangeably, but the difference between them is quite straightforward and easy to grasp. Punishment reduces a behavior by *applying* an aversive stimulus, whereas negative reinforcement increases a behavior by *removing* an aversive stimulus. If a parent yells at a child in response to a bad behavior, and the behavior stops, punishment of the child has occurred. If a child throws a tantrum in a store and stops fussing when the parent gives in and buys the thing the child has been screaming for, however, that child has just negatively reinforced the parent's behavior: the next time a similar situation arises, the parent will be more likely to give in again, because doing so made an unpleasant condition (the screaming child) stop.

Skinner further distinguished between primary and secondary reinforcers. Primary reinforcers, such as food, water, sex, or relief from pain, are innately reinforcing, as they satisfy a biological need. They are naturally reinforcing, with no learning required. Secondary reinforcers, also called conditioned reinforcers, are learned, as they only acquire the ability to reinforce behavior through their association with primary reinforcers. Money, for example, is a powerful reinforcer for most humans, despite the fact that it cannot be eaten, drunk, and so forth, and possesses no healing power. It does allow us to obtain primary reinforcers, however—though I cannot eat money, I can certainly use it to purchase food.

Skinner explored the principles of operant conditioning through the use of a specialized cage called an operant chamber, popularly known as a Skinner box (a name Skinner disliked). The glass-and-metal chamber is typically large enough for a rat or pigeon, Skinner's preferred experimental subjects, to walk around in comfortably, and is equipped with a bar or key that the animal can peck or press, a small chute near the bar through which edible reinforcers can be dropped, and a device that records bar-press responses.

Using the operant chamber, Skinner found that he could produce remarkably complicated behavior patterns by reinforcing simple behaviors and sequences of behaviors. Before a behavior can be reinforced, however, it must occur. To deal with the problem of getting a behavior to occur in the first place, Skinner found that he could lead a subject to engage in the desired behavior through a process he called shaping. In shaping, a behavior that is not already occurring, such as the pressing of a bar by a rat, is produced by reinforcing successive approximations of the desired behavior, until the target behavior appears on its own, at which time it becomes the only behavior that is reinforced. Upon entering the chamber, a rat will typically explore its surroundings, walking around the chamber and sniffing all of its surfaces. During this exploration, the rat will at some point come into contact with the wall into which the bar is set. The moment this contact occurs, a food pellet is dropped down the chute. If the wall is touched again, the reinforcement will immediatcly occur again. This will result in the rat, which has been kept hungry prior to entering the chamber, spending most of its time against that

Apart from Freud, B.F. Skinner has almost certainly had a greater impact on the definition and treatment of psychological disorders than any other individual. (AP/Wide World Photos)

wall. In its movements, the rat will occasionally raise its body up and touch the wall with its front paws. The first time this behavior (a closer approximation of the desired bar-press than simply being next to the wall) occurs, immediate reinforcement will occur, while reinforcement for the other behaviors stops. Soon the rat will be reaching up more frequently, allowing selective reinforcement only of reaching behavior that occurs near the bar. Eventually, this will result in the rat accidentally pressing the bar—once this happens, only bar pressing will be reinforced. Through shaping, the rat is now engaging in a behavior that was not previously in its repertoire. The shaping procedure can be remarkably powerful in producing new behaviors, as shown by a famous film shot by Skinner of two pigeons playing a lively game of table tennis.

All the preceding examples assume continuous reinforcement—reinforcement happens every single time the desired response occurs. This pattern of reinforcement has a built-in weakness, however—when reinforcement stops, extinction (the response dies out) occurs rapidly. If the experimenter stops providing food pellets, the rat stops pressing the bar, just as when a soda machine fails to provide a drink, we immediately stop putting money into it, as we have learned that we get a soda every time. Real life usually does not provide continuous reinforcement, however, and yet many of our behaviors are persistent despite this. The sales associate does not make a sale to every customer, for example, nor does the fisherman always bring home a catch. Skinner observed that, in the laboratory as in real life, intermittent reinforcement, in which some occurrences of a response are reinforced and some are not, produces behaviors that are far more resistant to extinction. How else to explain the behavior of gamblers in casinos, who despite rarely winning anything of significance, will continue to pump money into slot machines? The soda machine, which reinforces continuously, loses the customer the first time no drink comes out, but the slot machine only reinforces occasionally, so the behavior of putting in money and pushing a button is far more persistent. The most common intermittent schedules of reinforcement are ratio schedules and interval schedules.

In a fixed-ratio schedule, behavior is reinforced after a set number of responses, as in a clothing factory where a worker is paid a set amount for every 10 shirts produced. The 9th shirt will produce no reinforcement; it only occurs after the 10th. In a variable-ratio schedule, on the other hand, reinforcement arrives after an unpredictable number of responses, producing behaviors that are far more difficult to extinguish. This is the schedule followed by slot machines: because an unknown number of responses will be required before reinforcement occurs, and the unknown number itself keeps changing, this schedule produces high and persistent rates of responding, since that is the only way to increase the frequency of reinforcement.

Interval schedules are based on elapsed time rather than the number of responses. In a fixed-interval schedule, the first response after a fixed time period is reinforced, but responses that occur prior to the end of the interval are not reinforced. This leads to an increased frequency of responses as the end of the interval approaches, with very low responding at the beginning of the interval. An example would be checking more frequently for the mail as the usual delivery time approaches, but not checking at all when the usual time is still a long way off. If a consistently high rate of response is desired, this is clearly not an ideal schedule. A solution to the problem of inconsistent responding is the variable-interval schedule, in which the time interval that must pass before reinforcement is varied unpredictably. This results in slow, steady responding, which is resistant to extinction.

Skinner's ideas have been a source of much controversy, in part due to his willingness to explore the philosophical implications of his ideas, in such books as *Beyond Freedom and Dignity* and the utopian novel *Walden Two,* which proposes a society modeled on his learning principles. Since his theory ignores mental phenomena and proposes that all behavior is under the control of external contingencies, it leaves no room for such notions as free will and personal freedom. His critics see him as dehumanizing people, both by denying free will and by suggesting that our behavior can be explained by the same mechanisms as that of animals.

All controversy aside, however, Skinner's legacy is a set of principles that have found much broader, and more effective, application than the theories of any other psychologist. Behaviorist ideas are now a major influence on educational practice; childrearing, where his terminology is now as ubiquitous as Freud's used to be; and highly effective therapeutic approaches for nearly all psychological disorders.

As a theorist, Skinner is often presented as Freud's polar opposite, the *yin* to Freud's *yang,* and on the surface the contrast is apt. Given Skinner's hostility to the inclusion of mental phenomena in his explanations of human behavior, he surely would have had little use for explanations that require the existence of large areas of *unconscious* mental influence, as this is even less amenable to direct observation than mental processes that the research subject is aware of having. Westen (1997, p. 530) went so far as to call Skinner "one of the least psychoanalytic thinkers in twentieth-century psychology." Dig a little deeper, however, and the two men have more in common philosophically than is at first evident. Both Freud and Skinner were avowed determinists, for example: free will has no more place in Freud's theory, where we are all at the mercy of drives, instincts, and buried conflicts that we are not even aware of, than in Skinner's world in which we are the puppets of our own reinforcement histories. They also both regarded their theories as biologically based, despite the very different directions in which they eventually carried their ideas.

Given the overlapping time periods in which they worked, it would be extremely unlikely for Freud to have had no influence on Skinner, even if only to represent what he wanted to fight against. Although Freud left no evidence that he had ever even heard of Skinner's work, Freud was of course one of the world's best-known psychological thinkers in Skinner's youth, and his influence on the young behaviorist may have been more profound than most authors have been willing to acknowledge. At least one scholar (Richelle, 1993) has observed that in his psychological writings, Skinner actually cited Freud more often than any other writer. This is not to say that Freud directly influenced Skinner's ideas, but in arguing against Freud's, Skinner may have overlooked Freud's philosophical influence on his work. Both men proposed big, all-encompassing theories that attempted to account for all of human behavior, and both placed a strong emphasis on causes of behavior that are not directly available to the conscious mind. Where Freud proposed a distinction between the conscious and unconscious minds, Skinner proposed that human motivations could be broken down into rule-governed behavior and contingency-shaped behavior. When we deliberately follow rules of behavior, we are conscious of our motivations, but much of our behavior is the result of the consequences, or contingencies, of prior behavior, and Skinner regarded conscious awareness as irrelevant to this sort of behavior.

The two theorists also shared a fundamental biological emphasis. Freud regarded the basic unconscious drives that govern the id as inborn, instinctive forces, with the rest of the mind ultimately built on these drives as a foundation. In a similar vein, Skinner saw that people must be born with a repertoire of innate, reflexive behaviors in order for contingencies to then shape the more complex behaviors that eventually appear. He even occasionally gave explicit acknowledgment to Freud's influence on his thinking about the unconscious nature of the motivations behind behaviors, recognizing that sometimes a man may come to believe that he understands the causes of his behavior:

> He may be wrong, however; he may invent a set of variables. He is particularly likely to do so if the actual variables are grounds for punishment. This is rationalization in the Freudian sense. (Skinner, 1969, p. 165)

Here Skinner acknowledges the role in human behavior, in cognition even, of one of Freud's **defense mechanisms**. Also little-known, perhaps because it doesn't fit the modern narrative of Skinner as the antidote to all things Freudian, is Skinner's perspective on Freud's dream work, presented in his *Science and Human Behavior* (1953):

> The principal realm of the symbol is the dream which occurs when we are asleep. This is a species of private event which is extremely difficult to study and is, therefore, the subject of much conflicting discussion. In a dream the individual engages in private discriminative behavior. . . . He sees, hears, feels, and so on, in the absence of the usual stimuli. Controlling variables may sometimes be discovered in the immediate environment or in the recent history of the individual . . . for example, one may dream of driving a car if one has been driving for many hours. More often, however, the relevant variables are harder to identify. The attempt to do so is commonly called the interpretation of dreams. Freud could demonstrate certain plausible relations between dreams and variables in the life of the individual. The present analysis is in essential agreement with his interpretation. (Skinner, 1953, pp. 293–294)

In this passage, Skinner, far from the usual portrayal of him as completely hostile to discussions of consciousness, acknowledges the importance of dreams as a way to symbolically experience things that are not available to conscious awareness. Elsewhere in the same book, he also allows a role in human activity for several of Freud's defense mechanisms, suggesting, for example, that people who are fervently religious may be so as a result of reaction formation. Although he avoided the incorporation of many cognitive ideas into his psychology, Skinner was clearly open to at least some of Freud's ideas, an influence that is quite infrequently acknowledged.

Further Reading

Overskeid, G. (2007). Looking for Skinner and Finding Freud. *American Psychologist* 62(6): 590–595.

Richelle, M. N. (1993). *B. F. Skinner: A Reappraisal.* Hove, England: Erlbaum.

Skinner, B.F. (1953). *Science and Human Behavior.* New York: Macmillan.

Skinner, B.F. (1969). *Contingencies of Reinforcement: A Theoretical Analysis.* Englewood Cliffs, NJ: Prentice-Hall.

Skinner, B.F. (1976). *About Behaviorism.* New York: Vintage.

Westen, D. (1997). Towards a Clinically and Empirically Sound Theory of Motivation. *International Journal of Psycho-Analysis* 78: 521–548.

Slip of the Tongue. See Parapraxes

Stekel, Wilhelm (1868–1940)

Stekel, a founding member of the Wednesday Psychological Society (a precursor to the **Vienna Psychoanalytical Society**), was one of Freud's earliest student/ followers, having joined him in 1902. Indeed, multiple sources suggest that Stekel was the one who suggested the meetings in the first place, though in his own writings Freud refers to him generically as a "colleague who had experienced the beneficial effects of analytic therapy." Although he described himself frequently as an "apostle" of Freud, he eventually had a falling-out with Freud (around 1912) over differences of opinion both theoretical and ethical.

Early on, the relationship between the two men was mutually beneficial. Stekel began as a patient seeking help with impotence, and in turn Freud's thinking on dreams was heavily influenced by Stekel. In *The Interpretation of Dreams* (1899), Freud explicitly acknowledges his debt to Stekel's ideas, eventually also published, as *The Language of Dreams* (1911). The extent of Stekel's influence may be best seen in the translated title of the 1922 American edition of the book: *Sex and Dreams*. Like Freud's longer work, Stekel's book is heavily concerned with the examination of dreams for unconscious, symbolically coded sexual content.

In April 1911, the Vienna Psychoanalytical Society took up Stekel's book as its topic of discussion, much of which was highly critical. Much of the criticism of Stekel within the group centered on the veracity of the examples he gave—members of the society, including Freud, came to believe that he was inventing the patients that he described to them. While Freud was clearly impressed by the idea of examining hidden sexual content in dreams (his *The Interpretation of Dreams* was first published in 1899, with a revised edition appearing within the same year as Stekel's book, and the two books acknowledge each other's arguments), the actual examples given by Stekel were far less subtle, and therefore less believable, than the client dreams described by Freud. Consider the following example, the opening illustration of one of Stekel's chapters:

A woman goes to the butcher shop, to make some purchases, finds the meat stall exposed, chooses a big, hard piece of meat, shaped as a sausage (*Wurst*), shoves it in her pocket, where it hardly fits, as it melts in the warmth of the pocket; every detail of the dream is obvious when we know that it relates to *fleischliche Geliiste,* lusts of the flesh, and to purchases in the love mart. (Stekel, 1922, pp. 57–58)

One reason for the use of such unsubtle, straightforward examples is simply that Freud and Stekel differed quite fundamentally on where the important dream content lay. Freud found the surface, or *manifest,* content to be merely a hiding place for the heavily disguised, symbolic *latent* content of the dream. Stekel believed instead that for many dreams, such as the one described previously, the symbolic meaning can be gleaned entirely from a more superficial examination. Stekel alienated Freud rather thoroughly by stating in his own book, in direct response to Freud's work, that he had "endeavored to prove that the manifest dream material itself displays the most important content" (Stekel, 1922, p. 56). As in the case of many other followers who came to question or disagree with Freud, Stekel was out of the Society in 1912 (he left at around the same time as Alfred **Adler**).

Beyond his status as *the* charter member of the Vienna Psychoanalytical Society and as a follower of or the influence on Freud, Stekel's most lasting influence may well be his indirect influence via one of his students. As part of the second generation of psychoanalysts, Stekel trained some of the third wave, including Immanuel Velikovsky. Early in his career Velikovsky became a prominent ambassador of psychoanalytic thought to new areas where it had yet to take root, spending 15 years practicing in what would become modern Israel (Palestine at the time). Despite the reputation he made for himself as a psychoanalyst, Velikovsky is today known primarily for his 1950 book *Worlds in Collision,* in which he brings a psychoanalytic approach to bear on worldwide myths, legends, and religious traditions. In the book, he argues that much of modern science, including advances in physics, geography, and biology, are necessarily wrong because he finds that many of the descriptions of major catastrophic events in the Bible and elsewhere are symbolic accounts of major geophysical and astrophysical events that actually happened.

As an example of his thinking, consider his argument that the planet Venus did not exist until rather recently. Instead, it was ejected from the planet Jupiter at some unknown time in the past, passed close to earth as a comet a couple of times, and settled into its orbit about 3,500 years ago. He bases this on a range of myths, including the Greek idea that Athena sprang from the head of Zeus, which he explains as a symbolic description of a literal cosmological event (note that the ancient Greeks did *not* identify Athena with the planet Venus). He then uses this idea to explain various Biblical events, suggesting that the plagues (frogs, flies, etc.) that started the Exodus from Egypt were a result of the Venus comet heating up the atmosphere and causing these small animals to reproduce at well above normal rates.

Velikovsky continues to inspire a small cult-like following, but his arguments have never been taken seriously by a majority of scholars in any field. Unfortunately for Wilhelm Stekel, while his book on dreams was long ago eclipsed in the scholarly consciousness by Freud's work, most sources on Velikovsky continue to mention his psychoanalytic mentor by name.

Further Reading

Stekel, W. (1922). *Sex and Dreams: The Language of Dreams* (Translated by S. James van Teslaar). Boston: Richard G. Badger/Gorham Press.

Velikovsky, I. (1950/1972). *Worlds in Collision.* New York: Dell.

Superego. *See* Id, Ego, and Superego

Three Essays on the Theory of Sexuality. See Psychosexual Development, Stages of

Totem and Taboo (1913)

Between 1912 and 1913, Sigmund Freud published a series of four essays in *Imago*, which were subsequently published together in book form under the title *Totem and Taboo: Some Points of Agreement between the Mental Lives of Savages and Neurotics*. The essays, which were heavily influenced by the work of Charles Darwin and the Scottish social anthropologist Sir James G. Frazer, represent an early attempt to apply psychoanalytic ideas about individual psychic development to the development of societies and cultures. In drawing parallels between individual and cultural development, Freud proposes that preliterate societies struggling toward civilization experience a developmental sequence similar to that experienced by the individual striving toward psychological maturity; like the individual, the society must confront and overcome a series of neuroses, conflicts, and fantasies on the way to adulthood or civilization. The essays center on the now largely discredited idea that primitive peoples actually think differently, and therefore function differently as communities, from members of highly technological societies, a major theme in 19th-century and early 20th-century anthropology.

"The Horror of Incest"

The first essay, "The Horror of Incest," which is also the shortest of the four, shows how incest taboos are implemented in primitive societies, mostly using examples concerning the Australian Aborigines. As a mere dabbler in the subject rather than a full-time anthropologist, Freud did not actually study the Aborigines himself, but merely reached conclusions based on information previously collected and discussed by Frazer, thus conducting an anthropological study of sorts without ever actually leaving Vienna. Properly judging the validity of Freud's observations and interpretations here may also benefit from the knowledge that Frazer, on whose information Freud relied, also never visited Australia. The essay concerns the ways in which incest is avoided by the Australian natives through elaborate marriage rules, including laws that expressly forbid marriage to members of the same totemic clan. This elaborate set of restrictions is surprising to Freud, in light of the apparent lack of any other sexual restrictions in their culture. In the essay, Freud discusses various ways in which the totem system helps to prevent incest not only within individual families, but among extended families as well.

Freud chose the Aborigines of Australia as his subject due to a simple scientific prejudice of the 19th century by which they were thought to be the most backward, most primitive people on the planet, at least in the eyes of white European scientists who had never met them. In place of European-style religion and social institutions, they are organized by *totemism,* by which each tribe is subdivided into a set of clans, each with a different totem. Generally these totems are animals, though more rarely plants are used as well. Clans name themselves for their totem, and it serves the purpose of providing inspiration, magical extension of its own virtues, and a clear sense of identity. According to Frazer, an Aborigine's relationship with his totem forms the basis of all his social relations and obligations, to a greater degree than either tribal membership or family relationships. Among the Aborigines, it was therefore of great interest to Freud that a clear law existed against persons of the same totem having sexual relations with one another or marrying each other. The law was quite strictly enforced—the standard penalty for violating the rule was death, regardless of the circumstances or the outcome. Whether or not the two parties involved were blood relatives did not matter, nor did the matter of the union resulting or not resulting in children—all cases were treated in the same manner. According to Freud, this is reflected in the fact that the Aborigines use the terms "brother" and "sister" to refer not just to children of the same parents, but rather to all members of a particular totem clan. Freud speculates that the resulting clan exogamy (marriage allowed only outside the group) may be a relic of an earlier time in which group marriage was common, and thus it was actually likely that all members of a particular totem group were blood relatives. Under such circumstances, totemic exogamy would have been the only effective way of truly preventing incest. Freud's explanation for the severity of these laws is quite straightforward: The incestuous wishes that are repressed in the unconscious mind among civilized peoples (and which form the ultimate basis for all neurosis) are still a conscious peril to the uncivilized people described by Frazer. Since they are consequently subject to greater temptation as a result of their incestuous desires being conscious rather than unconscious, their resulting horror of incest is also greater than ours, and they require greater protection from it.

Freud's argument here is based rather explicitly on the notion that the libido represents the most primitive part of the mind, and with greater civilization comes greater repression of certain instinctual drives. Toward the end of the essay, Freud illustrates this by focusing his attention on a particular taboo that seems to be widespread among primitive societies and relatively unknown among more modern ones: the mother-in-law taboo. According to Freud, variations on this taboo can be found across a wide range of cultures:

The most widespread and strictest avoidance, which is perhaps the most interesting one for civilized races, is that which restricts the social relations between a man and his mother-in-law. It is quite general in Australia, but it is also in force among the Melanesian, Polynesian and negro races of Africa as far as the traces of totemis and group relationship reach, and probably further still. Among some of these races similar prohibitions exist against the harmless social intercourse of a wife with her father-in-law, but these are by far not so constant or so serious. (Freud, 1918, p. 19)

These restrictions on the interaction between a man and his mother-in-law are widespread and often quite strict. Freud gives several instructive examples:

On the Banks Island these prohibitions are very severe and painfully exact. A man will avoid the proximity of his mother-in-law as she avoids his. If they meet by chance on a path, the woman steps aside and turns her back until he is passed, or he does the same. In Vanna Lava (Port Patterson) a man will not even walk behind his mother-in-law along the beach until the rising tide has washed away the trace of her foot-steps. . . . It is quite out of the question that he should ever pronounce the name of his mother-in-law, or she his. On the Solomon Islands, beginning with his marriage, a man must neither see nor speak with his mother-in-law. If he meets her he acts as if he did not know her and runs away. . . . Among the Basogas, a negro tribe living in the region of the Nile sources, a man may talk to his mother-in-law only if she is in another room . . . and not visible to him. Moreover, the race abominates incest to such an extent as not to let it go unpunished even among domestic animals. (Freud, 1918, pp. 20–21)

Having established that primitive societies go to great length to keep men and their wives' mothers apart, Freud suggests, with characteristic humor, that although more modern societies no longer impose such rules, mother-in-law relationships remain a rich source of jokes for the simple reason that the tensions being avoided by the primitive rules are still present, but they are no longer consciously acknowledged. The actual tensions being dealt with by these laws, Freud is careful to note, are sometimes straightforwardly sexual, but also sometimes far more subtle. In the straightforwardly sexual camp, Freud quotes a Zulu woman who was asked about the mother-in-law taboo as carefully responding, "'It is not right that he should see the breasts which nursed his wife" (Freud, 1918, p. 23).

On the more subtle side, Freud suggests that a simple power struggle holds part of the answer:

The mother-in-law is unwilling to give up the possession of her daughter; she distrusts the stranger to whom her daughter has been delivered, and shows a tendency to maintain the dominating position, to which she became accustomed at home. On the part of the man, there is the determination not to subject himself any longer to any foreign will. (Freud, 1918, p. 24)

In this analysis, the mother-in-law taboo is not just a tool against incest, but also a simple protection from the inevitable conflict between man and mother-in-law over possession of her daughter. This is not to say that incestuous feelings are entirely absent from the mother-in-law's psyche, of course:

> Where the psychosexual needs of the woman are to be satisfied in marriage and family life, there is always the danger of dissatisfaction through the premature termination of the conjugal relation, and the monotony in the wife's emotional life. The ageing mother protects herself against this by living through the lives of her children, by identifying herself with them *and making their emotional experiences her own* [italics mine] . . . This emotional identification with the daughter may easily go so far with the mother that she also falls in love with the man her daughter loves, which leads . . . to severe forms of neurotic ailments. . . . At all events the tendency to such infatuation is very frequent with the mother-in-law. . . . Very often it is just this harsh and sadistic component of the love emotion which is turned against the son-in-law in order better to suppress the forbidden tender feelings. (Freud, 1918, pp. 25–26)

Freud is arguing here that the mother-in-law taboo exists largely to protect the son-in-law from his wife's mother's sexual feelings and potential sexual advances, rather than to protect her from his. Indeed, Freud arrives at this conclusion after dismissing the latter by observing that "It was quite incomprehensible why all these races should manifest such great fear of temptation on the part of the man for an elderly woman, old enough to be his mother" (Freud, 1918, pp. 21–22). This is not to say that the man's feelings for the woman are not important in this analysis as well—Freud argues that whatever underlying feelings the man has for his own mother, his very first love object, may be transferred onto his mother-in-law, the positive feelings as well as any underlying conflict. In modern European society, all of these feelings, incestuous and otherwise, are repressed and buried deeply in the unconscious mind, but in primitive societies they are conscious and open, and thus require rigid laws and penalties. The cultural prohibitions take the place of the self-censorship of incestuous desires in which more advanced people naturally engage.

In healthy individuals in a modern civilization, the individual has freed himself from incestuous attractions, whereas the neurotic has either been unable to liberate himself from the psychosexual conditions of early childhood, or else he has returned to them via regression, according to Freud. In his view, the Oedipus complex, the apotheosis of those incestuous desires of childhood, is "the central complex of the neurosis" (1918, p. 28), and so all neurosis really represents a step backward to a more primitive state of sociocultural development. When he wrote this essay, still fairly early in his career, Freud was already quite aware of the skepticism with which his ideas would be received:

> This discovery of the significance of incest for the neurosis naturally meets with the most general incredulity on the part of the grown-up, normal man. . . . We are forced to believe that such a rejection is above all the product of man's deep aversion to his former incest wishes which have since succumbed to repression. It is therefore of importance to us to be able to show that man's incest wishes, which later are destined to become unconscious, are still felt to be dangerous by savage races who consider them worthy of the most severe defensive measures. (Freud, 1918, pp. 28–29)

Here Freud recognizes that his ideas will be ridiculed, but he is able to use that ridicule as evidence that he must be correct: if you object to his claim that you harbor deep-seated incestuous desires, it is not because you don't have them, but because you are ashamed by them. This is demonstrated clearly by comparing the repression of those desires by Europeans to the open acknowledgement of those same desires among more primitive peoples.

"Taboo and Emotional Ambivalence"

The second essay, "Taboo and Emotional Ambivalence," draws a connection between ritual taboos observed among the Polynesian people and the personal prohibitions of obsessional neurosis. Freud begins with several pages devoted to an attempted definition of *taboo,* a word of Polynesian origin, "the translation of which provides difficulties for us because we no longer possess the idea which it connotes" (Freud, 1918, p. 30). By this Freud appears to mean that as a civilization, we no longer accept the idea of preexisting prohibitions, absent any logical justification, which are simply handed down to us. In making this argument, Freud is not simply arguing, as he often did, that religion is an outdated approach to life that we should have already moved beyond. To the contrary, he is suggesting that taboos represent something even older, that predates even the development of religions:

> The taboo restrictions are different from religious or moral prohibitions. They are not traced to a commandment of a god but really they themselves impose their own prohibitions; they are differentiatied from moral prohibitions by failing to be included in a system which declares abstinences in general to be necessary and gives reasons for this necessity. *The taboo prohibitions lack all justification and are of unknown origin.* Though incomprehensible to us they are taken as a matter of course by those who are under their dominance. (Freud, 1918, p. 31).

Religious commandments, in other words, are followed because of a clear justification: Our God or gods told us to behave, or to avoid behaving, in a particular way. Taboos are more basic, lacking that clear origin, and are simply followed because they must be.

Taboos tend to follow a particular pattern and to concern particular sorts of behavior; they

> mostly concern matters which are capable of enjoyment such as freedom of movement and unrestrained intercourse; in some cases they appear very ingenious, evidently representing abstinences and renunciations; in other cases their content is quite incomprehensible, they seem to concern themselves with trifles and give the impression of ceremonials. Something like a theory seems to underlie all these prohibitions, it seems as if these prohibitions are necessary because some persons and objects possess a dangerous power which is transmitted by contact with the object so charged, almost like a contagion. (Freud, 1918, pp. 36–37)

Freud here defines taboos as prohibitions against particular behaviors, which seem to begin with the underlying assumption that violating the taboos would result in something dangerous being passed along to the violator, rather like a disease. Following this definition, he reiterates his claim that "this word and the system corresponding to it express a fragment of psychic life which really is not comprehensible to us" (Freud, 1918, p. 37), suggesting that we cannot even understand it without also studying the belief in spirits and demons "which is so characteristic of these low grades of culture" (Freud, 1918, p. 37).

Freud then argues that traditional explanations of taboo like Wilhelm Wundt's, which trace the origin of taboos to primitive fear of demonic powers, are disappointing in that they do not really reach deep enough to the real source of taboo. Once again invoking his own atheism as part of his explanation, Freud argues that "It would be different if demons really existed; but we know that, like gods, they are only the product of the psychic powers of man; they have been created from and out of something" (Freud, 1918, p. 41).

In the absence of real demonic forces in the world, the psychoanalyst's task becomes the identification of the actual psychic forces from which taboos originate, in the service of which Freud finds the symptoms of obsessional neurosis, or what modern readers might recognize as obsessive-compulsive disorder, quite helpful. Freud notes that things against which a taboo exists are often things that may not be touched. In many cultures, for example, certain animals may not be eaten, certain people, such as menstruating women, may not be touched. Under such taboos, the prohibited object is in some way holy or awe-inspiring but simultaneously dangerous, forbidden, or unclean. This is exactly the sort of ambivalence that often appears in obsessional neurosis: an affectionate relationship is combined with, and undermined by, an underlying hostility toward, and fear of, the object of desire, and this ambivalence is manifested in an aversion to, and avoidance of, touching.

According to Freud, the basic description of the sacred/unclean ambivalence inherent in primitive taboos is quite familiar to someone like himself; the psychoanalyst "needs but a moment's reflection to realize that these phenomena are by no means foreign to him" (1918, p. 43). To Freud, the parallel is extremely obvious, in fact,

> [the psychoanalyst] knows people who have individually created such taboo prohibitions for themselves, which they follow as strictly as savages observe the taboos common to their tribe or society. If he were not accustomed to call these individuals "compulsion neurotics" he would find the term "taboo disease" quite appropriate for their malady. (1918, pp. 43–44)

Freud acknowledges that the resemblance between primitive taboos and obsessive-compulsive symptoms may be superficial, without shedding any light on the underlying sources of either condition, even drawing on evolutionary theory to point out that similar adaptive structures often evolve under radically different circumstances and for radically different reasons, as with the structural similarities between the stems of terrestrial plants and some corals. Having given this warning, he then proceeds to examine the similarities.

The first important correspondence between the compulsive prohibitions of neurotics and adherents to taboos is that the origin of both appears, to the believer, to be equally unmotivated and enigmatic. In Freud's words,

> They have appeared at some time or other and must now be retained on account of an unconquerable anxiety. An external threat of punishment is superfluous, because an inner certainty (a conscience) exists that violation will be followed by unbearable disaster. (1918, p. 45)

The compulsive patient will generally only report a vague premonition that someone or something will suffer harm if he or she violates the compulsion or prohibition. The exact nature of the harm to come is generally unspecified. This is very similar to the nature of a taboo—it must not be violated, because bad things will result, but no clear logical relationship is evident between the act and the vaguely specified consequences. Freud observes further that in both the taboo and the neurotic prohibition, the nucleus is often the act of touching something or someone, and the prohibition extends from direct contact to even thinking about the object of prohibition; mental contact is just as much off-limits as physical contact.

Another common feature of both taboos and obsessive prohibitions is that some prohibitions have a clear purpose or logic underlying them, while others do not.

When a neurotic fears contact with doorknobs and requires hand sanitizer immediately after touching one, his reaction, though disproportionate, is at least understandable: microorganisms that are invisible to the naked eye are in fact a common source of disease. By the same token, a taboo against the eating of pork or shellfish in a pre-refrigeration era may well have saved many lives. What are we to make, however, of the man who will not step on a crack in the sidewalk without feeling great anxiety? Freud designated these seemingly purposeless rituals as "ceremonials" and argued that similarly pointless taboo-related customs also occur.

An additional commonality between taboos and obsessive prohibitions, according to Freud, can be seen in a typical feature of obsessions and compulsions:

> Obsessive prohibitions possess an extraordinary capacity for displacement; they make use of almost any form of connection to extend from one object to another and then in turn make this new object "impossible," as one of my patients aptly puts it. . . . The compulsion neurotics act as if the "impossible" persons and things were the carriers of a dangerous contagion which is ready to displace itself through contact to all neighboring things. (1918, p. 45)

If an object is not allowed to be touched, such as the previously mentioned doorknob, then anyone or anything that has been in contact with it also becomes an embargoed object that may not be touched without consequence. This is very similar to what is often seen in taboos, under which any person who has come in contact with an unclean person, animal, or object also becomes unclean and forbidden as a result of that contact. Freud demonstrates this kind of displacement in taboo and obsession by directly comparing an observation by Frazer of the ritual behavior of a Maori chief with the behavior of one of his own patients, a woman suffering from a compulsion neurosis:

> A Maori chief would not blow on a fire with his mouth; for his sacred breath would communicate its sanctity to the fire, which would pass it on to the meat in the pot, which would pass it on to the man who ate the meat, which was in the pot, which stood on the fire, which was breathed on by the chief; so that the eater, infected by the chief's breath conveyed through these intermediaries, would surely die. (1918, pp. 46–47)

Clearly, to the Maori, the deadly nature of the chief's breath can be transferred to whatever it comes in contact with, thus posing a clear and present danger to anyone unfortunate enough to come into contact with it. Freud then contrasts this example with the equally primitive reasoning of a modern woman in Vienna:

> My patient demanded that a utensil which her husband had purchased and brought home should be removed lest it make the place where she lives

impossible. For she has heard that this object was bought in a store which is situated, let us say, in Stag Street. But as the word stag is the name of a friend now in a distant city, whom she has known in her youth under her maiden name and whom she now finds "impossible," that is taboo, the object bought in Vienna is just as taboo as this friend with whom she does not want to come into contact. (1918, p. 47)

Freud's point here is a simple but important one: the behavior of the Viennese lady is just as irrational and primitive as that of the Maori and is based on the same idea of transference of contagion.

One last similarity between the observance of primitive taboos and the behavior of the civilized neurotic may be the most obvious point of commonality between the two. Like taboo prohibitions, compulsion prohibitions, or what modern psychiatrists would call obsessions, "entail the most extraordinary renunciations and restrictions of life, but a part of these can be removed by carrying out certain acts which now also must be done because they have acquired a compulsive character" (1918, p. 47). The person with obsessive-compulsive disorder will concoct rituals that must be undergone whenever a prohibition is violated, the most common of which is washing hands after touching something that is prohibited. This is remarkably similar to the cleansing and purification rituals that often accompany taboos and serves a similar purpose: when the taboo has been violated, there is often a ritual which, if performed immediately, can ceremonially erase the violation.

Freud has thus identified several ways in which adherence to taboos resembles the behavior of people with obsessions and compulsions, and he then proceeds to suggest some similarities in the genesis of the two phenomena. As an example of how such behaviors develop in the modern, civilized European, Freud turns to the example of masturbation:

In the very beginning, during the early period of childhood, the person manifested a strong pleasure in touching himself. . . . Presently the carrying out of this very pleasurable act of touching was opposed by a prohibition from without. (1918, pp. 47–48)

Because of the development of the superego, the prohibition was internalized and supported from within, and thus proved stronger than the self-touching impulse. The child's primitive mind did not succeed in actually abolishing the impulse, however, but was merely able to repress the impulse, concealing it deep within the unconscious. As a result, both the impulse and the prohibition remain in the child's mind—without the prohibition, the impulse would become conscious and would be carried out. Freud called this unsolved situation, this conflict between the impulse and the prohibition, a *psychic fixation*.

This psychic fixation results in ambivalent behavior of the individual toward the object of the fixation, in this case his own genitalia, as well as toward the desired action, in this case touching himself for pleasure. The individual constantly wants to carry out the action, which is quite pleasurable, but also feels strongly that he may not, and may even see the action as an abomination. According to Freud, these two streams of psychic life are so localized that they cannot meet—the prohibition therefore becomes fully conscious, while the pleasure of touching remains completely unconscious. Because of this repression, the prohibition remains, but any knowledge of its motivation has been lost, and any attempt on the part of the individual to figure it out will fail, because it is buried deep in the unconscious. The prohibition and its compulsive character owe their strength to their association with this unknown, unknowable counterpart. Compulsions develop in response to an inner need into which the individual has no conscious insight. The transferability of the compulsion is facilitated by the unconscious mind's own self-protective mechanisms, as the pleasure of the impulse undergoes displacement in order to find surrogates for the forbidden by substituting other objects or actions. As the impulse wanders, however, so does the prohibition:

> Every new advance of the repressed libido is answered by the prohibition with a new severity. The mutual inhibition of these two contending forces creates a need for discharge and for lessening the existing tension. . . . In the neurosis there are distinctly acts of compromise which on the one hand may be regarded as proofs of remorse and efforts to expiate and similar actions, but on the other hand they are at the same time substitutive actions which recompense the impulse for what has been forbidden. (Freud, 1918, p. 51)

The individual, in other words, will develop other behaviors, not necessarily directly related to the originally prohibited one, which will require new rituals (acts of compromise) of expiation and purification, none of which can be traced back by the individual to the initial scolding for masturbation, at least not without the help of a psychoanalyst.

Freud then goes on to propose that a similar mechanism to that described previously may underlie the development of cultural taboos in primitive societies, while recognizing that, like the prohibitions observed by the neurotic patient, the taboos currently being observed in such a culture are probably not the original ones that they began with. Taboos started as very ancient prohibitions that must have been forced on a generation of primitive people from outside, probably by an earlier generation, and these prohibitions, like the prohibition against masturbation, concerned actions for which there existed a strong desire. These prohibitions were maintained across generations, at first by paternal and social authority, but they eventually become psychic baggage of the culture, simply accepted by everyone, almost like innate ideas that everyone is born with. According to Freud, however, the taboos persist because the original impulse to do the forbidden thing also persists. The people therefore adopt an ambivalent attitude toward the prohibitions—unconsciously, they would like to transgress, but consciously they fear doing so, and the fear is stronger than the desire for pleasure. According to Freud, the actual desire is unconscious in every member of the race, just as it is in the neurotic. Taboos, in other words, emerge through a very similar process to the obsessions and compulsions of neurotics. The most universal, and therefore likely the most ancient and important, taboo prohibitions in totemistic societies are not to kill the totem animal and not to have sexual intercourse with members of the same totem clan of the opposite sex. According to Freud, these must therefore be the most important and oldest of human desires. He then proceeds through a lengthy dissection of customs throughout the world concerning the killing of enemies and the treatment of kings, customs which usually appear to be based, like the actions of the neurotic, on deeply ambivalent feelings and the internal conflict between a desire and a prohibition against that desire. Ultimately, the behavior of primitive peoples worldwide in their construction of and response to taboos confirms Freud's psychoanalytic worldview.

"Animism, Magic, and the Omnipotence of Thought"

In the third essay, "Animism, Magic, and the Omnipotence of Thought," Freud continues to elaborate the comparison between the savage and the obsessional neurotic. Freud's basic claim in this piece is that both groups share a fundamental piece of magical thinking, a belief in the omnipotence of thoughts. By this term, he refers to the belief that a mere wish or desire for something to happen is enough to bring it about, and consequently negative wishes deserve to be punished as thought they were actual bad deeds. Before approaching the omnipotence of thought directly, however, and once again drawing heavily on the work of Sir James Frazer, Wilhelm Wundt and Herbert Spencer, Freud examines *animism* as a notion that may drive neurotics as well as savages, defining animism as follows:

> These [primitive] races populate the world with a multitude of spiritual beings which are benevolent or malevolent to them, and attribute the causation of natural processes to these spirits and demons; they also consider that not only animals and plants, but inanimate things as well are animated by them. (1918, p. 127)

Freud suggests that the belief in so many different kinds of souls has its origin in a notion that he was personally surprised hadn't disappeared from modern Europe yet, the idea that the human soul is somehow independent of the body. The spirits in other things correspond to souls that have become independent, and so he felt that animism was a later cultural development than the idea of human souls. Freud goes further to speculate that the basic body-soul dualism that was required in order for animism to take hold may have developed as a result of attempts to explain sleep (with its accompanying dreams) and death, which after all resembles sleep. He goes on as follows:

> To primitive man the continuation of life—immortality—would be self-evident. The conception of death is something accepted later, and only with hesitation, for even to us it is still devoid of content and unrealizable. (1918, p. 126)

Freud's atheism again comes to the fore here, as he suggests that the idea of an immortal human soul is a primitive conception that we have not yet shaken off.

In animistic societies, all objects, including the inanimate, have a life and a soul, which makes it possible to manipulate them via magic. Because of this, Freud, describing the three great systems of thought that have dominated the world, calls animism the most consistent and exhaustive, above religion and science in its ability to explain the nature of the world in its entirety. In describing the animistic societies' methods of manipulating the world, Freud points out that anthropologists have called the strategy of animism "sorcery and magic" but then draws a crucial distinction between the two:

> Sorcery is essentially the art of influencing spirits by treating them like people under the same circumstances, that is to say by appeasing them, reconciling them, making them more favorably disposed to one, by intimidating them, by depriving them of their power and by making them subject to one's will; all that is accomplished through the same methods that have been found effective with living people. Magic, however, is something else; it does not essentially concern itself with spirits, and uses special means, not the ordinary psychological method. (1918, pp. 129–130)

This distinction is crucial for Freud, as he is far more interested in magic than in sorcery, especially where his analogy to the behavior of the neurotic is concerned. Quoting E. B. Taylor, Freud describes the basic principle of magical thinking as "mistaking an ideal connection for a real one" (p. 130), a characteristic he then goes on to explain in terms of two different kinds of magical acts.

The first kind, which Frazer labeled *homeopathic* magic, and which is also sometimes called imitative or sympathetic magic, is based on the conviction that similar things affect one another, and is the basis for one of the primitive world's most widely implemented procedures for harming an enemy: making an effigy of him.

The particular material used seems to matter little, and the object does not need to particularly look like the enemy either, as long as the effigy has been clearly named for the enemy. Whatever is subsequently done to the effigy is expected to be directly reflected on the actual person. Sticking pins in the wax figure of an enemy, for example, is expected to be accompanied by disease or injury in the corresponding area of the actual enemy's body. The technique is more versatile than is usually recognized, however, as Freud points out that the same sort of magic can be employed for pious purposes as well as for revenge and was thus actually be used by ancient Egyptian priests to help the gods in their struggles against demons, by destroying figures of the demons involved in the battles.

Homeopathic magic has also been used very widely throughout the world to produce rain, through a variety of procedures that have in common the goal of imitating either the rain itself or the clouds and storm conditions that produce it. In Japan, for example, Freud reports that the Aino attract rain to their crops by pouring water through a large sieve while other participants in the ceremony equip a large bowl with sails and oars and drag it around the village and gardens. In many other cultures, dances that involve reproducing the sound of thunder via drums and other percussive means have also long been used to attract rain in times of drought. More striking, perhaps, are the world's various attempts to magically ensure the fertility of soil by, in Freud's words,

> showing it the spectacle of human sexual intercourse. To cite one out of many examples; in some part of Java, the peasants used to go out into the fields at night for sexual intercourse when the rice was about to blossom in order to stimulate the rice to fruitfulness through their example. At the same time it was feared that proscribed incestuous relationships would stimulate the soil to grow weeds and render it unfruitful. (1918, p. 133)

These practices are based on the simple assumption that human fecundity is sufficiently like the fertility of the earth for one to magically affect the other. As with the other examples, the effective force is assumed to be the similarity between the performed action and the expected outcome.

The second category of magic identified by Freud, again borrowing Sir James Frazer's terminology, is *contagious* magic, in which the principle of similarity is not involved. Contagious magic is instead founded on the idea that once two things have been in close contact, that contact cannot be severed, even if they are separated by a great distance. If you come into possession of something belonging to an enemy, such as hair, fingernail clippings, or even clothing, you have the means with which to harm that enemy, simply by damaging or destroying the object. Anything that happens to the things that belong to him must happen to him as well. This can be done with less tangible possessions as well, hence the many myths in which

TOTEM UND TABU

EINIGE ÜBEREINSTIMMUNGEN
IM SEELENLEBEN DER WILDEN
UND DER NEUROTIKER

VON

PROF. DR. SIGM. FREUD

ZWEITE, UNVERÄNDERTE AUFLAGE

1 9 2 0

INTERNATIONALER PSYCHOANALYTISCHER VERLAG
LEIPZIG   WIEN   ZÜRICH

The title page from the 1920 German edition of *Totem and Taboo* in which Freud proposed a view of history in which the development of the human race closely parallels the development of the individual, complete with Oedipal conflict. (Sigmund Freud, *Totem und Tabu,* Vienna: Internationaler Psychoanalytischer Verlag, 1920)

obtaining the name of an enemy or a spirit conveys power over the name's bearer. According to Freud, in this type of magic, similarity is simply replaced by relationship. This sort of magic has its most extreme manifestation in cannibalism, which has been motivated in some cultures by the belief that by consuming parts of a person we may come to possess the properties, abilities, skills, and virtues that belonged to that person. Contagious magic may also explain the taboos in certain cultures that restrict the diet of women who are pregnant or nursing, for example, prohibiting the meat of an animal believed to be especially cowardly, lest that trait be passed along to the newborn. This sort of magic has influenced many different sorts of customs, including battlefield medicine. In Melanesia, for example, Freud reports that if a warrior gains possession of the bow by which he was wounded, he will put it in a cool place in hopes of reducing the inflammation of the wound. Conversely, his enemy, if he has held onto the bow, will place it near a fire, in order to maximize the wound's inflammation. To prevent the reader from simply dismissing such customs as the realm of primitive minds only, Freud points out a belief still held at that time by English peasants, that if they injure themselves with a scythe or other sharp tool, they should proceed to keep the instrument very clean from that moment on, to avoid infection.

In Freud's analysis, the neurotic has a desire to exert control which is very similar to that which must have driven the first humans, and his frustrations with conventional means of achieving satisfaction induce him to relieve his tension through obsessive acts, which are remarkably similar to magical rituals. The reason the neurotic engages in these acts, and the underlying principle of animism as well, is what Freud calls the "Omnipotence of Thought," a term he borrowed from one of his patients, a man with compulsion neurosis. The patient used the term to refer to the various superstitious modes of thought that he found himself engaging in all the time, as a way of understanding the uncanny and peculiar things that seemed to happen. If he thought of a person, for example, he might then encounter that person, as though he had somehow conjured him up. If he inquired about the health of an acquaintance he had not seen in a while, he would surely hear that the person had died; if he muttered a halfhearted curse against a stranger, that person might die soon. In Freud's words, "All compulsion neurotics are superstitious in this manner and often against their better judgment" (1918, p. 143). He then cautions the reader against seeing this as a distinguishing characteristic of this particular neurosis, however, emphasizing that the same mechanism can be seen in the other neuroses as well:

> Neurotics live in a special world in which, as I have elsewhere expressed it, only the "neurotic standard of currency" counts, that is to say, only things intensively thought of or affectively conceived are effective with them, regardless of whether these things are in harmony with outer reality. . . . Thus the omnipotence of thought, the over-estimation of psychic processes as opposed to reality, proves to be of unlimited effect in the neurotic's affective life and in all that emanates from it. (Freud, 1918, pp. 143–144)

Like the savage, the neurotic believes that his unconscious, dark wishes, including murderous thoughts, may come to fruition merely because he has thought of them, and he hopes, by engaging in the correct rituals, to avoid disaster.

"The Infantile Recurrence of Totemism"

In the final essay, Freud closely examines the relationship between totemism and exogamy (the practice of only marrying someone outside one's own clan), and arrives at the unexpected position of equating the institution of the incest taboo with the start of human culture, as well as the start of religion. The essay begins with Freud explicitly stating that his goal is to provide an explanation of the origin of religion, while carefully dissembling and allowing that any explanation he provides will be only a portion of the whole truth, apparently in hopes of easing the anxiety of the reader:

> The reader need not fear that psychoanalysis . . . will be tempted to derive anything so complicated as religion from a single source. If it necessarily seeks, as it is duty bound, to gain recognition for one of the sources of this institution, it by no means claims exclusiveness for this source or even first rank among the concurring factors. Only a synthesis from various fields of research can decide what relative importance in the genesis of religion is to be assigned to

the mechanism which we are to discuss; but such a task exceeds the means as well as the intentions of the psychoanalyst. (Freud, 1918, p. 165)

This passage reveals an unusually cautious and humble Sigmund Freud, perhaps highly wary of the hostile reception the essay might engender, given its emphasis on an idea that is controversial even by Freudian standards.

Early in the essay, Freud reintroduces the idea of totemism as a form of cultural organization, examining the various theories that have emerged regarding the origins of totemism, attempts to answer the question that Freud formulates as "How did primitive people come to select the names of animals, plants, and inanimate objects for themselves and their tribes?" (1918, p. 180).

Freud divides answers to this question into three categories: nominalistic theories, sociological theories, and psychological theories. Nominalistic theories, into which category he places the ideas of Max Müller and Herbert Spencer, center on the primitive and prosaic need of human communities to have something to call themselves, a way of representing themselves and distinguishing themselves from other clans and families. Freud compares this use of animal symbols with the use of heraldic badges among European nobility. In the earliest days of humanity, our existence was symbiotically tied to that of the animals among whom we lived, and so they were the obvious choice as community symbols, in addition to being fairly easy to represent pictorially in a prelinguistic time. Freud highlights Lang's observation that the borrowing of animal names is hardly surprising, given the modern continuation of this tradition in the naming of football teams. For a different take on the issue, Spencer suggests that in the early days of humanity, the attributes of certain individuals led to their being given the names of animals with whom they shared those attributes—later generations may have taken these nicknames as proof of their descent from the animals themselves. Totemism, in other words, is in Spencer's view simply a misunderstood form of ancestor worship. Eventually this misunderstanding led to respect, and finally veneration, for the animal itself.

Sociological theories place less importance on the importance of naming, and far more on the actual social organization of totemistic groups. Emile Durkheim, for example, famously called the totem "the visible representative of the social religion of these races. It embodies the community, which is the real object of veneration" (in Freud, 1918, p. 186). Freud also reports A. C. Haddon's theory that every primitive tribe originally lived on a particular plant or animal species and traded with this food, thus becoming known to other tribes by the name of the species that played such an important role in its daily life and livelihood. The tribe would develop their special familiarity and identification with the particular totem based on the most pressing and primitive of needs, hunger. Freud dispatches this theory with a simple but elegant bit of logic—totemistic groups usually abstain totally from eating the species which serves as their totem. It is unclear how such a relationship, in which eating the animal is absolutely forbidden, could emerge in a group in which that same animal has historically been the favorite and most important food.

In one rather extreme sociological theory, Frazer came to believe that a group of Australian tribes that he referred to as the Arunta nation represented the most primitive people currently living on the earth, and thus their totemistic organization was surely the original form, as it was the most primitive. He arrived at the insight that they were the most primitive people on the planet because of their views on death and conception. They apparently believed that the spirits of dead tribe members wait around particular locations for young women to pass by, at which point they penetrate the womb and are eventually born again. Surely, Frazer reasoned, the most primitive people on the planet would be the ones who have not yet drawn a connection between the sexual act and the conception of children! Freud examines the Arunta nation for evidence of the other theories cited thus far, but he then undercuts their usefulness as an example by bringing up some (at that time) recent controversial findings. Rather than serving as the best, earliest representation of totemism, as Frazer believed them to be, the Arunta may instead have been the most developed of Australia's indigenous people; rather than representing the beginning stages of totemism, they best represented the late stages of its dissolution.

Unsurprisingly, Freud aligns himself with psychological theories as the preferred explanation, though he dismisses other psychological theories before presenting his own. Frazer, for example, proposed a psychological theory based on belief in an external soul, though he later abandoned the theory in favor of his more sociological theories, as described previously, looking for a simpler, more primitive superstition behind the totem structures, as in his speculations regarding the Arunta failure to recognize the connection between sexuality and conception. Freud dismisses Frazer's psychological ideas as he did Frazer's sociological speculation—by reminding the reader that the Arunta are actually well removed from the beginnings of totemism, and can therefore shed little light on the subject. Freud then moves from Frazer to Wilken, who in 1884 proposed the idea that totemism is connected to, and preceded by, belief in the transmigration of souls, or the passage of souls from dead bodies into new ones, potentially including inanimate objects. Freud echoes critical anthropologists who have argued that it is far more likely that totemism precedes belief in transmigration, which then develops out of the core ideas of totemism.

Having dismissed other psychological speculations, Freud then presents his own theory regarding the origin of totemism, which starts with speculation from the world of biology and ends in a very psychoanalytical place, explaining the origin of religion along the way. Here the incest taboo once again plays an important role, but Freud makes a new argument: The incest taboo is not based on any instinctive aversion to incest, nor is it due to humanity's conscious awareness of the dangers of inbreeding. The argument against an instinctive opposition to incest is based on an older passage, again from Frazer, which Freud quotes at some length:

> The law only forbids men to do what their instincts incline them to do; what nature itself prohibits and punishes it would be superfluous for the law to prohibit and punish. Accordingly we may always safely assume that crimes forbidden by law are crimes which many men have a natural propensity to commit. If there were no such propensity there would be no such crimes, and if no such crimes were committed, what need to forbid them? *Instead of assuming therefore, from the legal prohibition of incest, that there is a natural aversion to incest we ought rather to assume that there is a natural instinct in favor of it, and that if the law represses it, it does so because civilized men have come to the conclusion that the satisfaction of these natural instincts is detrimental to the general interests of society* [italics mine]. (1918, p. 204)

Drawing on his own theory of human development, Freud of course agrees wholeheartedly with Frazer's logic, arguing that his own experience as a psychoanalyst shows him that clearly the earliest sexual feelings are entirely incestuous, and so any instinctive aversion to such feelings is clearly not present.

Having presented the interpretation of incest dread as an innate instinct as a theory that must be abandoned, Freud then proceeds to argue for abandoning another widely held explanation of the incest prohibition, the assumption that primitive races observed the dangers of inbreeding to their survival and therefore instituted the prohibition for a deliberate purpose. This explanation appears to be the one favored by Frazer as an alternative to the instinct-based exegesis, but Freud's agreement with his opposition to instinct stops short of supporting the alternative, as the "objections to this attempted explanation crowd upon each other" (Freud, 1918, 205). His first objection is simply that the prohibition must be older than the breeding of domestic animals, the most obvious source of information about the harmful effects of inbreeding, since the earliest totemistic societies, in which exogamy was already established, predate organized animal agriculture. He adds that the harmful consequences of inbreeding are in any case not universal or entirely established beyond all doubt, as under some circumstances inbreeding can actually be helpful to a species. Freud then proceeds to a simple logical objection:

> Besides, everything that we know about contemporaneous savages makes it very improbable that the thoughts of their far-removed ancestors should already have been occupied with preventing injury to their later descendants. It sounds almost ridiculous to attribute hygienic and eugenic motives such as have hardly yet found consideration in our culture, to these children of the race who lived without thought of the morrow. (1918, pp. 206–207)

Given that in Freud's time the effects of a restricted gene pool were still poorly understood, it indeed made little sense to assume that totemistic societies were particularly concerned with it. As a final blow to this explanation of the incest prohibition, Freud simply points out that an inverse relationship actually seems to exist between a culture's level of understanding of heredity and the strength of its incest taboo. Although our own society feels a deep abhorrence against incest, this dread seems to be even more active and stronger among the primitive races still living than among the civilized.

To present his own theory, Freud introduces an idea originally proposed by Darwin based on the habits of gorillas and chimpanzees: that humans originally lived in small groups consisting of a single adult male with his multiple mates and children. In such a grouping, at maturity, the young males were probably driven off in order to prevent the dangers of inbreeding, and would then have to defeat the leader of a different group in order to mate. These conditions would of course in practice lead to exogamy for the young males, which would over time bring about the rule that has since become law: no sexual intercourse with the members of the harem group. With the advent of totemism, this rule is slightly transformed: no sexual intercourse within the totem clan. Freud notes that this interpretation was becoming widely accepted, but often by writers who simultaneously embraced Durkheim's idea that exogamy is a result of the rise of totemism, rather than an antecedent condition. Freud's response to this controversy is simple and elegant: "Into this darkness psychoanalytic experience throws one ray of light" (1918, p. 209).

The particular enlightenment to which Freud refers once again takes on the form of a comparison between the development of a culture and the developmental experience of a small child:

> The relation of the child to animals has much in common with that of primitive man. The child does not yet show any trace of the pride which afterwards moves the adult civilized man to set a sharp dividing line between his own nature and that of all other animals. The child . . . probably feels himself more closely related to the animal than to the undoubtedly mysterious adult, in the freedom with which he acknowledges his needs. (1918, p. 209)

In their great comfort and familiarity with animals, children will sometimes suddenly develop an irrational fear of an animal toward which they were previously quite positively disposed, or with which they have had little or no experience, either positive or negative. Such animal phobias are, according to Freud, the most commonly encountered neurotic symptoms in young children. In some cases, it is possible in psychoanalysis to uncover a particular experience or moment at which the fear began, but phobias directed at larger animals all seem after psychoanalysis to reveal a common underlying cause: if the children examined are boys, the fear is actually of the father, and merely displaced onto the animal. Freud supports this argument by returning to a description of one of his most famous cases, that of **Little Hans**. In that case, the boy had a fear of horses, which Freud decided was a displacement of a fear of castration by his father, resulting from the boy's wish for his father to be dead or absent.

In his paper about the case, Freud described Hans as displaying the typical attitude of a child in the midst of the Oedipus complex, but here he focuses on the lessons of the case for our understanding of totemism, especially the idea that under these conditions the child displaces part of his feelings from the father onto an animal. Little Hans eventually came to identify with and respect the horse, while at the same time retaining some fear of it, a set of ambivalent feelings that he eventually applied to his father as well. As in most instances, the resolution of Little Hans's Oedipus complex involved forming a strong identification with his father. Freud sees this case as quite significant for our understanding of totemism, observing that

> at present we will only point out two traits that show a valuable correspondence with totemism: the complete identification with the totem animal, and the ambivalent affective attitude towards it. In view of these observations we consider ourselves justified in substituting the father for the totem animal in the male's formula of totemism. (1918, p. 217)

Freud notes that his choice to equate the father with the totem animal is not the new or daring logical step that it appears to be, as members of totemic societies themselves refer to the totem as their ancestor or primal father. Where ethnologists have taken this way of expressing the relationship and treated it as a minor detail of the totemic society, the psychoanalyst recognizes its importance and chooses to emphasize it as a way to fully explain totemism, by taking the expression quite literally. Freud goes on:

> The first result of our substitution is very remarkable. If the totem animal is the father, then the two main commandments of totemism, the two taboo rules which constitute its nucleus,—not to kill the totem animal and not to use a woman belonging to the same totem for sexual purposes,—agree in content with the two crimes of Oedipus, who slew his father and took his mother to wife, and also with the child's two primal wishes whose insufficient repression or whose re-awakening forms the nucleus of perhaps all neuroses. (1918, p. 218)

In this analysis, Freud is expanding the importance in human development of the Oedipus conflict, which at the time he has already presented in numerous places as the source of all neurosis, and is giving the same conflict a place of honor at the birth of human civilization.

Freud's analysis of the origin of civilization and religion is a puzzle requiring one more piece, however, which he provides in the form of an anthropological study by Robertson Smith, who argues that from the very beginning, a centerpiece of totemic societies was a ceremony he calls the *totemic feast,* which typically involves a sacrifice at some sort of altar. The sacrifice is the single, essential unifying component of all old religions. As it appears to play the same role in all religions, it must have originated in a single set of general causes that were universal for primitive man. Although the usual meaning of such a sacrifice has generally been understood as an offering to a deity in order to reconcile him or to gain his favor, Freud argues that it originally meant something different. According to Freud, Smith demonstrated that the first sacrifice was nothing more than an "act of social fellowship between the deity and his worshippers" (1918, p. 220). In this social gathering, food and drink were offered to the deity, or totem, and man offered his good the same things on which himself lived. Into this analysis, Freud adds a further detail of the sacrificial custom: the sacrifice was always a feast in which the entire clan participated, whereas no individual could perform a sacrifice alone. The sacrifice is a community activity that strengthens the bonds within the community while helping to distinguish the totem clan from others. Freud further observes that in both primitive and modern societies, execution of a member found guilty of a crime is also a community activity, performed by the entire clan. The sacrificial animal, in other words, was treated like a member of the clan, along with the members of the sacrificing community *and* their god.

This bond between community and sacrifice was strengthened further when difficult times occasionally required sacrifice of the totem animal, or of animals considered holy, in order to ensure clan survival. This has led to the custom, still common in various modern societies and religions, of seeing the common consumption of the same flesh by an entire community as establishing a bond between the people and their god, as the life of the sacrificed animal lives on in the flesh and blood of the participants in the feast. With this description, Freud's explanation of the birth of civilization is nearly complete. According to Freud,

> the totem animal is really a substitute for the father, and this really explains the contradiction that it is usually forbidden to kill the totem animal, that the killing of it results in a holiday and that the animal is killed and yet mourned. The ambivalent emotional attitude which today still marks the father complex in our children and so often continues into adult life also extended to the father substitute of the totem animal. (1918, pp. 232–233)

Armed with this explanation of the deeper significance of blood sacrifices, Freud then returns to Darwin's description of the earliest human societies, acknowledging that nowhere on earth do we see such a grouping today, but rather that our most primitive societies are more advanced than that.

This leaves the question of how human society went from that most primitive form to the less primitive forms that eventually developed into modern society. Based on his understanding of totemic societies, Freud has an answer. He proposes that at one point, the expelled sons of a father at the head of Darwin's primitive horde joined together, rebelled, and killed their father, who they then ate. This violent, primal father had been envied and feared by the brothers, who nonetheless also took him as their model for how they should aspire to behave. By devouring him and each acquiring a part of his strength and character, the sons identified with their father. In Freud's view, the totem feast, mankind's earliest traditional celebration, "would be the repetition and commemoration of this memorable, criminal act with which so many things began, social organization, moral restrictions, and religion" (1918, p. 234). For this analysis to be acceptable, according to Freud, requires only the assumption that the brothers were dominated by the same contradictory feelings toward their father as are evident in the ambivalent feelings toward the father seen in all children and neurotics. These brothers hated the father, because he stood in the way of both their sexual demands and their desire for power, but they also loved and admired him.

Having killed their father, who they did love as well as hate, the brothers were overcome with guilt over their action. They dealt with this guilt by undoing their deed, by declaring that the killing of the totem, the clan's father substitute was not allowed, as well as by renouncing the other fruit of their crime, the women who had thus been liberated. This was the origin of both the taboo against the killing of the totem animal and the prohibition against incest. The two fundamental taboos of totemism were thus created out the sense of guilt of the sons, and so, according to Freud, had to correspond with the two repressed wishes of the Oedipus complex. The beginning of the development of human culture, in other words, is enacted again by every child in the earliest stages of individual development.

In the inauguration of the totem, acting as a kind of father-substitute, Freud also saw the beginning of religious worship, as he identified the totem with God. He argues that the father-surrogate, or totem, was used to assuage the sense of guilt and bring about a kind of reconciliation with the father:

> The totemic system was a kind of agreement with the father in which the latter granted everything that the child's phantasy would expect from him, protection, care, and forbearance, in return for which the pledge was given to honor his life, that is to say, not to repeat the act against the totem through which the real father had perished. (Freud, 1918, p. 238)

In addition to reconciliation, however, totemism also contains an attempt at self-justification, suggesting that if the father had treated his people like the totem does, they never would have had to kill him. Like many human ex post facto explanations of a phenomenon, Freud argues that this one helped to cover up the real state of affairs and allowed the people to forget the event to which totemism owed its origin.

Freud's connection of this event to the start of human religion is guaranteed to raise the hackles of the genuinely religious everywhere:

> In this connection some features were formed which henceforth determined the character of every religion. The totem religion had issued from the sense of guilt of the sons as an attempt to palliate this feeling and to conciliate the injured father through subsequent obedience. *All later religions prove to be attempts to solve the same problem . . . they are all . . . reactions aiming at the same great event with which culture began and which ever since has not let mankind come to rest.* (1918, p. 239)

Freud adds another element that characterizes all religions: the ambivalence of feelings toward the deity, resulting in sacrifices that, even when they involve a sacrificial animal, make it a religious duty to repeat the crime of patricide periodically as necessary to ensure the continuation of the benefits of the deed, including possession of the father's property and power. Freud focuses some of his commentary on the later emphasis in Christianity on repetition, at least weekly, of the central sacrifice of the religion, reflects this pattern, in part because of the specific emphasis in Christianity on the relationship between father and son, as well as the earlier Jewish focus on the origin of sin in Man's disobedience of his heavenly father.

A constant, pervasive influence underlying all four essays is of course Freud's theory of the Oedipus complex: all the essays require the initial assumption that a child unconsciously desires, and wants to marry, his mother and is jealous and fearful of his father, toward whom his feelings are ambivalent. He wishes for his father's death but also loves him, and these feelings make him feel guilty and fear harsh retribution, including the possibility of castration. The healthy adult is one who has learned to overcome these incestuous and murderous inclinations, just as the healthy, civilized human society has overcome them by establishing universal rules forbidding incest and the killing of the totem, which began as a representation of the father. The obsessional neurotic, on the other hand, is still engaged in the struggle with these inclinations, resulting in additional self-imposed taboos and rules to follow, which he or she has unconsciously created for self-protection from the imagined consequences of the forbidden desires. Human society has followed the same general course of development as is followed by individual human children, and modern civilization takes the role of the healthy, well-adjusted adult in this analogy, whereas more primitive societies, which would be defined by a scientist of Freud's time as societies that have not developed in the same way as modern

Europe and America, fill the role of the obsessive compulsive neurotic, who still struggles to master these urges and desires.

It would be negligent to fail to point out that few, if any, cultural anthropologists or archaeologists, or indeed any scientists engaged in the study of human origins, would today take Freud's theories of the origins of human society at all seriously. His speculations on the birth of human culture suffer from the same scientific weakness as much of the rest of his *oeuvre,* in that his speculations have a powerful internal logic and are quite intellectually engaging, but are not based on any actual empirical evidence. For the same reason, the parallels he draws between the development of the individual and the overall development of humanity, which in Freud's defense represent a very popular and widely held nineteenth century conceit, are not taken seriously by developmental psychologists today. Freud's view of the development of civilization is not completely without its modern adherents, however. René Girard, the French philosopher and historian of science, for example, has presented a very similar argument, in which both religion and culture have their foundation in the collective murderous impulses of humanity and the need to control them, which was accomplished initially through the use of animal sacrifice. This argument has been echoed by others, including Walter Burkert and Jonathan S. Smith, though they tend not to acknowledge Freud as a major influence. Along with Freud, however, Girard and the others sit comfortably beyond the boundaries of the mainstream of anthropological thought.

Further Reading

Frazer, J. G. (1922). *The Golden Bough: A Study in Magic and Religion.* New York: Dover.

Freud, S. (1918). *Totem and Taboo: Resemblances between the Psychic Lives of Savages and Neurotics* (Translated by A. A. Brill). New York: Moffat, Yard, and Company.

Hamerton-Kelly, R., ed. (1988). *Violent Origins: Walter Burkert, René Girard, and Jonathan S. Smith on Ritual Killing and Cultural Formation.* Palo Alto, CA: Stanford University Press.

United States, Freud's Visit to (1909)

It is curious to note that, although the United States ultimately embraced Freud's ideas and brought them into the mainstream far more enthusiastically than the rest of the world, Freud visited America only once and came away with very mixed feelings about the experience.

In 1909, the 10th anniversary year of *The Interpretation of Dreams,* 53-year-old Freud was invited to visit the United States, deliver a series of lectures, and receive an honorary degree as part of the 20th anniversary celebration of Clark University in Worcester, Massachusetts. The invitation was a surprise to Freud, as his influence remained minor in Europe. The Vienna Psychoanalytical Society had a very small circle of followers, along with a few supporters in other cities, but psychoanalysts were still a tiny minority in the psychiatric profession, and Freud's ideas were still more a source of scandal than academic respect. In America, however, some leading psychological thinkers were intrigued.

The invitation came from G. Stanley Hall, first president of Clark University and also first president of the American Psychological Association, and thus a very influential member of the psychological profession. Hall is widely regarded as the father of the study of adolescent psychology, and in his 1904 work on the subject, *Adolescence,* he had referred multiple times to Freud's ideas about sexuality, exposing those ideas to the larger American audience for the first time. Apart from Hall's advocacy, Freud was virtually unknown in America, and the New World could boast only two practicing psychoanalysts at the time: Abraham A. Brill and Ernest **Jones**.

Despite the surprising accolade and opportunity to reach a wider audience, Freud almost turned down the invitation for financial reasons. The lectures were originally scheduled for June, and Freud felt that this would cut into his calendar of patients far too deeply and reduce his income. He had other concerns as well—he worried that he and his colleagues would receive a hostile reception once audiences realized that so much of his psychology was built on sexuality. As remains true today, a common European prejudice against Americans in Freud's time was that Americans are far more prudish and sexually repressed than Europeans, and so he naturally expected his words to be quite unwelcome. He wasn't entirely wrong about that—E.L. Thorndike, the prominent educational psychologist and early

On his only visit to America, Freud (*lower left*) posed with (*clockwise from Freud*) Abraham Brill, Ernest Jones, Sándor Ferenczi, Carl Jung, and G. Stanley Hall at Clark University, where Hall was president. (Imagno/Getty Images)

behaviorist, commented privately on Hall's use of Freud's sexual ideas, calling him a "mad man."

Hall dealt with Freud's financial and scheduling concerns in a very straightforward way: he rescheduled the festivities for September and guaranteed substantially more money for travel expenses than had previously been set aside. Freud agreed to the invitation and invited Sándor **Ferenczi** to accompany him, along with Carl Jung, who had been invited separately by Hall. The three psychoanalysts spent the eight-day sea voyage in classic psychoanalyst style, entertaining themselves via the interpretation of one another's dreams. Freud had obtained books about America to prepare for the trip but ultimately read none of them, saying that he preferred to be surprised.

Freud had booked the trip carefully, allowing for a week of sightseeing in New York City before traveling up to Worcester. In New York, the travelers were met and escorted around by Jones and Brill, the two American psychoanalysts: Brill lived and practiced in New York, and Jones traveled down from Toronto for the occasion. A few reporters also met them as they disembarked, but Freud was not yet famous enough to merit much attention—the only newspaper that covered his arrival got his name wrong, announcing that "Professor Freund" was in town.

After exploring New York fairly thoroughly, the travelers headed to Massachusetts, where Freud was a guest in Hall's rather fancy presidential home. His approach to the lectures themselves was remarkable, given that they remain in print today as a highly readable and accessible introduction to his ideas: he improvised them, working without notes. He spoke in German, with simultaneous translation. Furthermore, he chose to change his topic from what Hall had originally requested. Although Hall had asked him to speak about dream interpretation, Freud felt that dreams were too narrow and esoteric a topic for his introductory American lectures, opting instead to discuss the history and a general overview of psychoanalysis. His only preparation for the lectures consisted of a walk each morning with Ferenczi, during which he planned out and rehearsed what he intended to say.

His lectures, to a room full of most of the prominent American psychologists of the day, were well-received throughout, even the fourth lecture, which worried him the most. It was in the fourth lecture that he presented his ideas on sexuality, including infantile sexuality, along with the assertion that the Oedipus complex "with its ramifications presents the *nuclear complex* of every neurosis" (Freud, 2007, p. 38). In other words, there can be no explanation of psychopathology without acknowledging infantile sexual impulses. A skillful speaker if ever there was one, he pulled it off handily, presenting his ideas to a mostly warm reception. There were exceptions, naturally—Ernest Jones later reported hearing a dean at the University of Toronto react by saying, "[A]n ordinary reader would gather that Freud advocates free love, removal of all restraints, and a relapse into savagery."

On his last day at Clark, Freud was awarded an honorary degree, which he accepted with the words, "This is the first official recognition of our endeavors." He was visibly moved by the honor, which would turn out to be the only formal academic recognition he would receive in his lifetime. He later reminisced about his lectures in America as the first time he felt that psychoanalysis was being seen as a valuable contribution to the world. There were other honors as well—William James, the most renowned and influential psychologist and philosopher in America, who was quite ill and would be dead within a year, made the trip out from Boston to meet him. They took a walk together, discussing (in fluent German) the lectures, and at the end of the stroll, James said to Freud, "The future of psychology belongs to your work" (Taylor, 1999, p. 466). Freud, for his part, expressed great personal respect for James as a result of their time together. While they were walking, James experienced an attack of chest pain (a symptom of his illness), and simply handed Freud his briefcase and asked him to walk ahead, as he would catch up when the angina passed. Freud later expressed his admiration for James's stoicism by observing, "I have always wished that I might be as fearless as he was in the face of approaching death" (Freud, 1989, p. 32).

Given the friendly reception and professional accolades he received, and the importance of his visit in establishing him as an intellectual force in the United States, Freud's subsequent grumbling about America in general, and his visit in particular, remains a bit of a mystery. Some of his complaints are at least understandable—as most Europeans learn multiple languages growing up, Freud was distressed that so few Americans understood him when he spoke in German. The lack of old-world manners and decorum bothered him as well, and he especially tired of being addressed as "Sigmund" by people who back in Europe would surely have called him Herr Professor Freud or something equally formal, but certainly would not presume to use his first name. Oddly, however, his dislike of American informality and excessive friendliness was accompanied by the continuing impression that Americans are overcome by inhibitions and prudery.

Other complaints were less rational: He blamed his ongoing digestive difficulties (which, along with a prostate problem, had already been troubling him in Europe, and which would continue to do so upon his return there) on the excessively rich American food, as well as the odd American habit of serving water with ice in it. He also complained bitterly about the shortage of public urinals in New York City (again, probably more of a problem for a man with prostate trouble). His most bizarre complaint, however, was that his visit to America had caused his handwriting to deteriorate. His close friends, such as Ernest Jones, tended to conclude that his hostility toward America had little to do with America itself, as he rarely ever again had anything kind to say about the country. Indeed, he told Jones, "America is a mistake; a gigantic mistake, it is true, but none the less a mistake." Although psychoanalysis soon became a major force in American academic and therapeutic circles, Freud never returned to the site of one of his greatest personal vindications.

Further Reading

Jones, E. (1910). Letter from Ernest Jones to Sigmund Freud, April 20, 1910. In R. A. Paskauskas, ed. (1993). *The Complete Correspondence of Sigmund Freud and Ernest Jones, 1908–1939*. Cambridge, MA: Belknap.

Freud, S. (1989). *The Freud Reader* (Peter Gay, ed.). New York: W. W. Norton.

Freud, S. (2007). *The Origins and Development of Psychoanalysis*. Sioux Falls, SD: NuVision Publications.

Taylor, E. (1999). William James and Sigmund Freud: "The Future of Psychology Belongs to Your Work." *Psychological Science* 10(6): 465–469.

Vienna Psychoanalytical Society

In November 1902, Sigmund Freud sent out invitations to four other men proposing that they begin meeting at his home once a week to discuss psychoanalysis. The four were Alfred **Adler,** Max Kahane, Wilhelm **Stekel,** and Rudolf Reitler. Kahane directed an outpatient psychotherapy clinic, and Stekel ran a thermal therapy center. In Freud's simple, elegant language, the postcard received by Adler read as follows:

> A small circle of colleagues and supporters afford me the great pleasure of coming to my house in the evening (8:30 P.M. after dinner) to discuss interesting topics in psychology and neuropathology. I know Reitler, Stekel, and Max Kahane will come. Would you be so kind as to join us? (Schwartz, 1999, p. 100)

The first meeting was held on a Thursday, but subsequently their regular gatherings occurred on Wednesdays, so they began to refer to themselves early on as the Wednesday Psychological Society. In each meeting, a case history or formal paper would be presented, to be followed by discussion. Freud kept tight control over the group at first: new members were added only at his invitation, and his way of ensuring that all present contributed to the discussion was to choose a topic and then draw names, asking each to add to the discussion as his name was called. By 1906, the group had grown to 17, and Otto **Rank** had been hired as the group's secretary, to collect dues and to keep minutes, so that a record of the increasingly complicated discussions would be maintained. These minutes would eventually be published, and they have proven an excellent source of insight into the formative years of psychoanalytic thought.

By 1908, the group had 14 full members and had officially become the Vienna Psychoanalytical Society, with Alfred Adler presiding as the group's president. The name change was a result of Freud's official dissolution of the original, informal group, which had become less civil in its discussions, and the formation of a new, more democratic group. At Adler's suggestion, the membership-by-invitation policy was replaced by the use of secret ballots to elect new members. At this time, the membership had grown to include, in addition to those already named, Carl **Jung,** Sándor **Ferenczi,** Karl Abraham (later a president of the International Psychoanalytical Association), and Carl Alfred Meier, who would later be named the first president of the C. G. Jung Institute in Zurich. Also attending meetings was Ernest Jones, who would later write a lengthy, influential biography of Freud in which he described the early days of the society in great detail.

In 1908, the society arranged an international meeting in Salzburg, the First Congress for Freudian Psychology. This led directly to the formation of the International Psychoanalytical Association (IPA), which was established at the second congress, which came together in Nuremberg in 1910. Even as the international influence of psychoanalysis grew, Freud and his inner circle retained fairly tight control over it—the IPA's first five presidents (Jung, Abraham, Ferenczi, Jones, and Abraham) were all Wednesday Psychological Society members.

Further Reading

Schwartz, J. (1999). *Cassandra's Daughter: A History of Psychoanalysis.* London: Penguin UK.

Vygotsky, Lev Semenovich (1896–1934)

Lev Vygotsky was a short-lived but very influential Russian psychologist whose entire life span coincided roughly with Freud's adult career, as well as the early stages of Jean Piaget's work, and who thus, perhaps inevitably, was influenced to some degree by both theorists, and who was known to both of them. Understanding Vygotsky, however, requires first understanding something of Russian history. It is important to first note that Vygotsky began his professional career just after the Bolshevik Revolution. Like all successful Soviet scholars of the time, his survival depended on his being a committed Marxist, and his theory of child development provides an excellent example of the influence of politics and society on scientific progress. In Western Europe and the United States, Jean Piaget, whose theory emphasizes the role of the child's own independent action on his environment, has long been the dominant voice in child development. When Vygotsky first became well known among American psychologists in the late 1970s, it was largely because his approach, which emphasizes the interaction between the child and other people as the source of cognitive development, was seen as an alternative to Piaget.

Because of his goal of creating a psychology consistent with Marxism's emphasis on collective action over individualism, Vygotsky inevitably produced a very different theory than Piaget. In *The Communist Manifesto,* for example, Marx argues that the development of language made cooperation among people, and therefore the development of civilization, possible. In his two best-known works, *Thinking and Speech* and *Mind in Society,* Vygotsky lays out the basics of his theoretical approach, in which the development of language precedes the development of most higher mental functions, and the role of interaction between adults and children is emphasized far more than the role of the individual child.

According to Vygotsky, all cognitive functions originate in social interaction and are eventually internalized as the child becomes more competent. This includes language, which begins as a means of communicating with others before it evolves into what Vygotsky calls private speech (Piaget's term for the same thing was egocentric speech), easily seen in young children talking to themselves as they play. Where Piaget saw private speech as something that eventually stops as children outgrow it, Vygotsky instead argued that it never goes away—it simply goes underground, continuing silently rather than out loud. Through this mechanism, the child goes from requiring external instructions to self-regulating via internal ones.

As has occurred often in the history of psychology, the two theorists agree on the existence of the phenomenon, but disagree as to its function.

Much has been written about how Vygotsky's ideas differ from Piaget's, but surprisingly little attention has been given to his responses to Freud, which also inform his theory a great deal, and indeed form a crucial part of his quarrel with Piaget as well. Vygotsky's criticism of Piaget is actually based at least in part on his sense that Piaget is too heavily influenced by Freud in his thinking, in at least two areas: the idea of conflict between biology and cognition, and the idea of biologically determined stages.

It should come as no surprise that, despite the Soviet Union's lack of communication with scientists in Western Europe, Vygotsky should have been aware of, and influenced by, Freud, due to a biographical detail that has gone nearly unnoticed in most work on Vygotsky: one of his mentors, Sabina Spielrein, had been a patient of Carl Jung at the Bughölzli, as well as his sexual partner, according to some sources. She later became a psychoanalyst herself, with Freud as one of her teachers, and continued corresponding with him for years afterward. She became a prominent theorist in her own right, and her ideas on schizophrenia and the death drive were acknowledged as influences in their later work by both Freud and Jung. Spielrein's role with Freud and Jung has been reasonably well-known; somewhat less remarked-on has been her return to Russia in 1923, shortly before the government there outlawed the practice of psychoanalysis. She joined the Russian Psychoanalytic Society upon her arrival, and as a student and colleague of Freud, was treated with great respect by the younger members, including Vygotsky. It also bears mentioning that before heading back to Russia, she was Jean Piaget's psychoanalyst for a time. At least one author has speculated that Spielrein could be a sort of missing link between Piaget and Vygotsky, as she may have influenced both in their thinking about language development.

In his writings, Vygotsky specifically addressed Freud as part of a critical analysis of Piaget, whom he regarded as intrinsically Freudian in the assumptions he made. In *Thought and Language,* Vygotsky describes Piaget's view of a two-year-old child in explicitly Freudian terms, objecting to the idea of two separate mental realms, governed by the pleasure principle and the reality principle. To Vygotsky, it was clear that Piaget fundamentally accepted this view, as he proposed "a very peculiar theory of socialization indeed. . . . Socialization is a force that is alien to the child's nature. . . . To say such a thing means to claim that the external reality plays no substantial role in the development of a child's thought" (Vygotsky, 1986, pp. 47–48). Just as Freud had the imposition of external reality arise in conflict with the child's internal nature, Piaget did as well, whereas Vygotsky was proposing a very different model, in which the external reality comes first in social contact, and its internalization is what ultimately produces the contents of the child's internal mental life. According to Vygotsky, social interaction is ultimately the source of consciousness and all things mental, and thus there is no need to "divorce realistic thinking from all needs, interests, and desires" (Vygotsky, 1986, p. 46). Vygotsky therefore explicitly rejects Freud's placement of instinct as a core explanatory mechanism, along with the whole idea of the unconscious mind as fundamentally antagonistic toward the social functioning that Vygotsky places at the center of development. As a result of this rejection of the central role of unconscious biological forces, Vygotsky also rejected another idea that was central to both Freud and Piaget: the idea that acquiring more sophisticated mental activity and learning requires progress through a sequence of invariant, biologically programmed stages. Though the Soviet political system is widely acknowledged as a source of Vygotsky's ideas, Marxism and Freud may therefore have been equally central influences on the course of Vygotsky's thought.

In addition to developmental psychology, Vygotsky has had an outsized influence on educational psychology. Vygotsky's greatest impact on American psychologists came with the concept of the Zone of Proximal Development (ZPD). Vygotsky felt that the way we test students, focusing on what they already know rather than what they are capable of learning, an approach now known among educational psychologists as static testing, should be replaced by a more dynamic approach, in which we measure how much more the children are capable of doing when provided with supportive help. The gap between what the children can do on their own and what they can accomplish with help is the ZPD, and Vygotsky believed that measuring it would yield far more useful information than the static tests currently in use. These ideas have become very popular among educational psychologists in America today, some 70 years after Vygotsky's death, in part because it is viewed as both a radical departure from Piaget, which is not entirely true (since as with most dichotomies, there is actually much about which they agree), and as a more realistic description of what actually occurs in child development.

Vygotsky's work was unknown in the West until 1958, largely due to the Cold War between the United States and the Soviet Union, and didn't really become popular until several decades later. What many of Vygotsky's followers today fail to realize, however, is that his work was also largely unknown within the Soviet Union as well, as his version of Marxist psychology was, ironically, too Western European, and showed too much of Freud's influence, for Stalin, and so his works were suppressed for many years.

Further Reading

Aldridge, J. (2009). Another Woman Gets Robbed? What Jung, Freud, Piaget, and Vygotsky Took from Sabina Spielrein. *Childhood Education 85*(5): 318.

Vygotsky, L. S. (1930). *Mind in Society.* Cambridge, MA: Harvard University Press.

Vygotsky, L. S. (1986; originally published 1934). *Thought and Language* (Translated and edited by Alex Kozulin). Cambridge, MA: MIT Press.

Watson, John B. (1878–1958)

Born in Greenville, South Carolina, in 1878, John Broadus Watson was one of the most influential figures in American psychology, despite a relatively short academic career and very little significant research. His influence comes as a result of an idea, most fully expressed in his 1913 paper, "Psychology as the Behaviorist Views It."

In this paper, Watson argued that the proper subject matter of psychology is overt, observable behavior, whereas mental and emotional phenomena, which cannot be directly and objectively observed, should form no part of the new science. Indeed, he suggested that psychologists' preoccupation with consciousness might prevent psychology from truly becoming a science. Instead, the behaviorist should concern himself only with stimulus-response connections. Watson believed that human behavior was entirely predictable, given sufficient knowledge of the individual's history of stimuli and responses. He famously expressed this by claiming that, given full charge of a dozen healthy infants, he could provide the learning experiences necessary to produce any sort of person desired—doctor, lawyer, even criminal.

Watson was in part reacting to the work of Wundt and other psychologists who were advocating the use of introspection as a way to understand the human mind. As Freud's concepts took things a step further and proposed *unconscious* mental influences, which are of course not directly observable, Watson (and those who were influenced by his ideas) came to view much of his theory as untestable, and therefore unscientific. Many histories of psychology present Watson's behaviorism as the major critic of, and competitor to, Freud in the United States in the early 20th century. While this analysis is essentially accurate, it leaves out an essential dimension of the competition of ideas: Watson was driven in part by the desire to experimentally test some of Freud's ideas, and in suggesting alternatives to them he was a major force in popularizing them in America. Consider his best-known attempt at providing a non-Freudian explanation of a phenomenon that was already beginning to be widely described in psychoanalytic terms: phobias.

Watson's most famous experiment was his demonstration that emotional experiences could be produced through classical conditioning (the learning mechanism discovered by Pavlov). This demonstration involved a baby (forever known in the

American psychologist Dr. John B. Watson, founder of behaviorism, about 1935. (Hulton Archive/Getty Images)

psychological literature as Little Albert, or Albert B), a loud noise, and a white rat. Albert enjoyed playing with the laboratory rat, looking at it and touching it with obvious pleasure, which made it the ideal object for Watson to turn into a source of fear. A series of trials was conducted in which, as Albert reached for the rat, a large metal bar behind him was struck with a hammer, producing a loud noise, which startled and frightened him. Soon, he began to show a fear response at the sight of the rat, demonstrating that emotional states could be produced as conditioned responses. Watson further claimed that the fear response transferred to other similar objects, including a stuffed toy rabbit, a dog, and even a Santa Claus mask. One of the more controversial details of this experiment is the fact that Albert B's mother, who may not have been aware of the experiment at all, removed him from the premises before the experimenters could conduct further trials to get rid of the new fear response. Watson, in speculating on how this may affect Albert in later life, adopts a distinctly mocking tone toward psychoanalysis, as seen in the following excerpt:

The Freudians twenty years from now, unless their hypotheses change, when they come to analyze Albert's fear of a seal skin coat—assuming that he comes to analysis at that age—will probably tease from him the recital of a dream which upon their analysis will show that Albert at three years of age attempted to play with the pubic hair of the mother and was scolded violently for it. (We are by no means denying that this might in some other case condition it). (Watson and Rayner, 1920/2000, p. 317)

Despite the irreverent description of a possible psychoanalytic explanation, the parenthetical clause at the end displays an acceptance nevertheless that in some cases that sort of explanation may be the correct one. Another sign of Watson's acceptance of some basic psychoanalytic ideas comes in the following description of how he and his assistant might, given the opportunity, have attempted to remove the fear response:

> Had the opportunity been at hand we should have tried out several methods, some of which we may mention. . . . (2) By trying to "recondition" by showing objects calling out fear responses (visual) and simultaneously stimulating the erogenous zones (tactual). We should try first the lips, then the nipples and as a final resort the sex organs. (3) By trying to "recondition" by feeding the subject candy or other food just as the animal is shown. (Watson and Rayner, 1920/2000, p. 317)

Here Watson suggests pairing the feared object with a positive stimulus, with the goal of replacing the conditioned fear reaction with a new, positive conditioned response. What is striking about this passage to a modern reader, keeping in mind that its subject is a baby, is that the suggestion to try stimulation of the erogenous zones, including the sex organs, appears *before* the suggestion to try giving him candy. Clearly Freud's ideas involving infantile sexuality have lost some of the aura of scandal they previously possessed, and more importantly form a part of the worldview of the man history often presents as one of his great enemies.

Watson's academic career ended shortly after the Albert B experiment, which oddly may have led to his having a major impact on the spread of Freud's ideas. Watson's career at Johns Hopkins University, where he edited the *Psychological Review* and founded the *Journal of Experimental Psychology,* lasted only from 1908 to 1920. The reason for this was an ill-advised affair with Rosalie Rayner, his graduate assistant on the Little Albert study, which resulted in a highly publicized, scandalous divorce (after which he married Rayner), followed by an administration request for his resignation. Watson went on to great success in the advertising world, where he has been credited with, among other things, inventing the concept of the coffee break in a series of magazine ads.

He also continued to write books and articles for popular magazines, but he never taught or published in academic journals again. His popular writings were vastly more widely read than his academic pieces in any case, making him America's first highly successful pop psychologist. In his popular writings, he promoted a behaviorist perspective on a variety of topics, including a book on childrearing, and this often required contrasting his ideas with those of Freud. This gave Freud's ideas a great deal of exposure with readers who might not otherwise have encountered them. He also freely promoted the psychoanalytic ideas that he felt could be demonstrated empirically—he saw the unconscious mind as a scientific dead end, as it couldn't be directly observed, yet he clearly accepted the notion that early experiences would affect later emotional responses, for example.

Watson's primary objection to psychoanalysis was actually to its focus on treatment and independence from the laboratory, as he saw the psychoanalysts' refusal to provide scientific evidence as a barrier to psychology becoming a science. In the following quotation, he went so far as to call them a "cult":

> Probably the too ready attempt to make a complete and independent system of psychoanalysis and the failure on the part of the devotees of this new cult to maintain an intellectual freedom in their system have hindered a widespread and scientific study of the methods of Freud and Jung. (Watson, 1912, p. 916)

While he did object to some of their ideas, his major objection to psychoanalysis concerned their inclination to stand apart from the scrutiny of the scientific psychology that was just emerging in the United States and Europe.

As regards the portions of Freud and Jung's theories that he felt involved observable behavior, Watson's hostility toward them has been greatly exaggerated and oversimplified— indeed, Watson's research on fear with Albert B came about precisely because of his *acceptance* of Freud's idea that psychopathology in adults can be traced back to experiences in early childhood. Where he differed from Freud was in how this could be demonstrated. Where Freud based his ideas on the content of retrospective interviews with adults, whose memories might or might not accurately represent what went on so many years ago, Watson wanted to directly observe the formation of traumatic memories in the lab, thus giving the study of early childhood a far more solid scientific foundation. Furthermore, his proposed mechanism for the creation of fears represents an attempt to provide a more empirically sound description of Freud's ideas of *transference* and displacement of affect—just as the patient may displace onto the therapist emotions that are actually felt about a parent, the person with a phobia is displacing the affective response of fear onto an inappropriate object. Pavlov's concept of classical conditioning gave Watson a mechanism via which that transfer could occur, providing an explanation that didn't require resort to an unobservable unconscious mind. The experiment was also a part of Watson's attempt to demonstrate that, although the sexual instinct played a distinct role in the development of neuroses (again, he did not disagree with Freud about this), Freud was focusing on too narrow a scope of instinctive responses, and researchers should consider fear and rage as well. In doing this sort of research and writing about it, he actually was an effective popularizer of Freudian ideas, by putting them into a simpler vocabulary that many more people would understand. In addition to fear, he also wrote a paper in which he provided a behaviorally based description of the illogical nature of dreams, and another in which he provided evidence (based on interviews with small children rather than retrospective interviews with adults) for the existence of the Oedipus complex!

Further Reading

Rilling, M. (2000). Watson's Paradoxical Attempt to Explain Freud. *American Psychologist* 55(3): 301–312.

Watson, J. B. (1912). Content of a Course in Psychology for Medical Students. *Journal of the American Medical Association* 58: 916–918.

Watson, J. B. (1913). Psychology as the Behaviorist Sees It. *Psychological Review* 20: 158–177.

Watson, J. B., and R. Rayner (1920/2000). Conditioned Emotional Reactions. *American Psychologist* 55(3): 313–317. (Originally published in the *Journal of Experimental Psychology* in 1920.)

The Wolf Man (Sergei Konstantinovitch Pankejeff) (1886–1979)

Sergei Konstantinovitch Pankejeff (Pankejeff is how Freud transliterated the name from the cyrillic alphabet—today it would be rendered as Pankeyev) was an aristocratic Russian, from Odessa, who became the subject of one of Sigmund Freud's best-known case studies. To protect his identity when writing about him, Freud referred to him as *der Wolfsmann,* basing the nickname on a childhood dream about wolves that became a subject of analysis.

Pankejeff's primary complaint was depression, a condition that had previously affected multiple family members. In 1906, for example, his sister committed suicide while on vacation, on a visit to the site of the duel in which the great Russian poet Lermontov died. The following year, Sergei's father, who had suffered from depression for years, also committed suicide, by taking an overdose of sleeping pills. Sergei himself began to show signs of serious depression a few months before his father's suicide and travelled to Munich in search of treatment. He spent years in Germany, seeing a variety of doctors and spending time in various psychiatric hospitals catering to the rich, though he always returned to Russia for the summer.

Eventually he was brought to Freud for consultation, and the two met many times over the course of four years, from 1910 to 1914, with a brief return for further psychoanalysis in 1919. In addition to his overwhelming depression, Sergei presented with some nervous problems of the sort that might be called hysterical if he had been female, including an inability to produce a bowel movement without the use of an enema. Freud's treatment proceeded in the usual way, with careful exploration of relationships both at present and in childhood, but eventually focused on a dream that Sergei remembered having as a very young child. In the dream, it was night and Sergei was lying in bed, a bed with a window at its foot, beyond which stood a row of old walnut trees. In the dream, the window opened on its own, revealing six or seven white wolves sitting in one of the trees. The wolves had big bushy tails, like foxes, and their ears were pricked up like those of attentive dogs. Sergei awoke screaming, and took a while to realize that he had only been dreaming, so vivid was the image of the window and the wolves.

Freud published his account of the Wolf Man, *From the History of an Infantile Neurosis,* in 1918, though he appears to have had the manuscript written by the end of 1914. In it, Freud finally had a complete case study that appeared to confirm the disparate elements of his theory, tying together infantile sexuality, dream interpretation, and the development and treatment of hysterical symptoms in a tidy package. His interpretation of the wolf dream was that it had resulted from what he would in later writings refer to as the *primal scene:* That Pankejeff had, at a very young age, witnessed his parents engaging in sexual intercourse. This had of course frightened him and stirred up uncomfortable Oedipal feelings, along with castration anxiety. All of this became, symbolically, wolves who were going to eat him. In an odd bit of (possibly unconscious) diagnostic punning, Freud explained Pankejeff's unconscious choice of wolves to represent these fears by suggesting that he had seen his father taking his mother from behind, sometimes referred to as doggy-style.

This case was very important to Freud, as it seemed to him to establish quite plainly the role of Oedipal conflict and castration anxiety in the formation of neurosis. This is crucial evidence, since Freud regarded those factors as the core of *all* neurosis, and even argued that they are the fundamental source of the formation of each individual's superego. As the superego is responsible for suppressing and controlling our primitive impulses, the Oedipus complex is ultimately responsible for nothing less than making civilization possible, and thus demonstrating its role in the formation of neurosis was critical. In addition to supporting his theory, the case also showed promise in establishing Freud's reputation for effective treatment—one of the doctors that Pankejeff had already seen, and not been cured by, was Emil Krapelin, the most famous psychiatrist in Europe. In the Wolf Man, Freud felt that he had a case that proved both the core of his theory and his therapy's effectiveness, and so in the 1918 paper he claimed to have cured Pankejeff and freed him from his fears and his depression.

This claim has been a source of some controversy, not least from the Wolf Man himself, who, despite having allegedly been cured, continued to show various unusual symptoms and to experience depression, and remained in psychoanalysis off and on until his death at age 92. During this time, he was variously diagnosed as depressed, obsessional, paranoid, anxious, and even psychotic. Within a few years of his treatment by Freud, for example, Sergei developed a psychotic delusion: he was convinced that a doctor had drilled a hole in his nose, and walked the streets looking for the hole in a mirror. Ruth Brunswick, another psychoanalyst who was asked by Freud to review Pankejeff's case, explained his delusion bizarrely as an instance of displaced castration anxiety.

In his old age, the most famous of Freud's case studies weighed in on Freud's analysis of his dream when a journalist, Karin Obholzer, located him in Vienna for an interview. Pankejeff, many decades removed from his encounters with Freud, described Freud's interpretation of the white wolves as "terribly far-fetched." More importantly, he disputed the claim that he had been cured, and indicated some resentment over having been used as propaganda for psychoanalysis. In his own words, shortly before his death, "I am in the same state as when I came to Freud, and Freud is no more."

Posthumously, a new detail has emerged that makes the case of the Wolf Man, and Freud's analysis of it, look rather different. Jeffrey Moussaieff Masson, in his capacity as the official archivist at the Freud Archives, uncovered Ruth Brunswick's notes for an unpublished paper about the Wolf Man. In these notes, she indicated that she had uncovered evidence that Pankejeff had been sexually abused by a family member during his childhood. Given his conviction that such accounts represented fantasies (see **seduction theory**), Freud would probably not have taken Pankejeff at his word if he brought up the subject, which may also explain Pankejeff's initial resistance to opening up fully to Freud, a resistance Freud devotes some pages to in the case study.

Further Reading

Freud, S. (1918/1995). From the History of an Infantile Neurosis. In Peter Gay, ed. *The Freud Reader*. London: Vintage.

Masson, J.M. (1984). *The Assault On Truth: Freud's Suppression of The Seduction Theory*. New York: Pocket Books.

Obholzer, K. (1982). *The Wolf-Man: 60 Years Later. Conversations with Freud's Controversial Patient*. New York: Continuum.

Wundt, Wilhelm (1832–1920)

By the time Freud began to make his mark on the world of psychology, the German-speaking nations had taken the lead in the development of psychology as a science, thanks in no small part to the efforts of Wilhelm Wundt. Indeed, Wundt is widely acknowledged by textbook authors as the father of modern, scientific psychology. This is due to his establishment at Leipzig, Germany, of the world's first psychological laboratory. Certainly other scientists had begun to study the mind and the nervous system prior to this, but Wundt's program, begun in 1879, was the first degree-granting laboratory science program devoted exclusively to psychology.

Prior to the establishment of Wundt's Psychological Institute (as the sign over the door proclaimed it), psychological researchers were physiologists, physicists, physicians, and philosophers. Wundt's own history reflected this: after graduating from medical school, he worked for a time in the lab of physiologist Johannes Müller, followed by an appointment in the laboratory of noted physicist Hermann von Helmholtz. Müller is known in psychological history books for having described the inner workings of the eye and ear in great detail, as well as establishing the notion that the nerves of particular senses carry only one kind of sensory data. The optic nerve, in other words, carries only visual information to the brain, just as the auditory nerve carries only sound—he called this the doctrine of specific nerve energies. Helmholtz, meanwhile, remains an important name in the history of both psychology and physics and was known for his demonstrations that the neurological processes underlying mental activity are potentially measurable. Helmholtz is also known for his explanation of how color vision works. Wundt, trained as a medical doctor, physiologist, philosopher, took from his experiences with these eminent scientists a recognition that psychology was becoming a worthy academic discipline unto itself, and in 1879 submitted a budget request to the University of Leipzig to fund a new laboratory. After Wundt, therefore, the first generation of researchers emerged who were actually educated as *psychologists*.

Some textbook authors, mostly American, make a case for William **James** (1842–1910) as the real founder of psychology, due to a remarkable coincidence of timing: James *also* established a psychology laboratory in 1879, at Harvard University. Unlike the training facility being developed by Wundt, however, James's laboratory was used primarily for classroom demonstrations rather than as part of a degree program in psychological research, so Wundt generally gets the credit.

In the early days of his institute, Wundt devoted himself to the study of conscious experience, through the use of introspection. Introspection was approached very formally at Leipzig, with extensive training in self-observation and self-report required before a subject participated in Wundt's experiments. In a typical early experiment, the participant would be presented with a stimulus, perhaps a visual image, and would then describe the immediate conscious experience, including feelings, emotions, volitions, and ideas, according to a complex, predetermined rubric. The early psychologists were inspired by 19th-century progress in chemistry and the physical sciences, and so Wundt hoped to train his subjects to analyze their own conscious experiences into more basic elements, much as chemists do with compounds. Wundt believed that once these elements were identified and the processes by which they were related and integrated became understood, the structure of conscious experience would no longer be a mystery. Wundt's first important work to make use of this perspective was 1874's *Principles of Physiological Psychology,* which focused on the self-examination of conscious experience by objective observation of one's consciousness.

Because of this philosophical underpinning, Wundt's approach to psychology became known eventually as structuralism, or at least that is how it is usually presented by textbooks. In fact, Wundt did not use that term to refer to his ideas—*structuralism* was the word used by one of his students who returned to America to popularize the introspective approach in the laboratory: Edward Titchener. Wundt's own word for his approach at the time was *voluntarism,* but Wundt's actual theoretical perspective can be very difficult to pin down, as he did not adhere consistently to either a single set of interests or a single coherent explanatory framework. In those early days, although most accounts focus on the introspective study of sensation and perception, he also

Wilhelm Wundt, widely credited with the founding of psychology as a separate scientific and scholarly enterprise independent of physics, philosophy, and physiology. (Edmund König, *W. Wundt: Seine Philosophie und Psychologie,* Stuttgart: Fr. Frommanns Verlag, 1901)

devoted attention to understanding different forms of mental illness and mapping damaged areas of the brain, for instance. Much has been made of his division of psychology into experimental psychology and *volkerpsychologie* (people's, or folk, psychology), for example. *Volkerpsychologie* consists of the social psychological phenomena which were becoming a popular subject of study at the time, and which Wundt is said to have believed could not be studied scientifically. Some recent sources (Greenwood, 2003, for example) argue, however, that an examination of Wundt's writings does not support such an account at all.

Perhaps part of the problem is the sheer volume of writing that Wundt produced over the course of a 65-year career, ranging over a very wide field of interests, including physics, physiology, philosophy, and medicine, in addition to psychology. In 1960, American psychological historian Edwin G. Boring estimated the total volume of Wundt's work at 490 publications, with an average length of 110 pages. Boring suggests that this makes Wundt the most productive scientist of all time, and one estimate is that he wrote more than 53,000 pages in total! The sheer difficulty of pinning Wundt down to a single perspective or subject area is perhaps reflected in the name his students gave to his approach following his death: *Ganzheit* psychology. The word is often translated as "holistic," but a better translation might be *entireness*. He was far more interested in documenting the whole of psychological knowledge, regardless of perspective, than he was in advocating a single theoretical perspective.

Because of the polymath nature of his work, Wundt's actual ideas have had little enduring influence on the field of psychology, yet he is widely regarded as the most influential psychologist of all time. This is primarily because of the influence he wielded through his students. Prior to the establishment of Wundt's laboratory, there were no degreed psychology professors and no psychology programs at the world's universities. That changed dramatically, and quite rapidly, as students began to graduate from Wundt's program. James McKeen Cattell, the first professor of psychology in the United States, was working in Wundt's laboratory in 1879; G. Stanley Hall, first president of the American Psychological Association and also first president of Clark University, as well as the man often credited with starting child developmental psychology as a specialization, also studied with Wundt. It was also Hall who later invited Freud to America for his one and only visit to these shores. The aforementioned Edward Titchener returned to America and established the psychology program at Cornell University, also establishing structuralism as a major perspective in psychology. Oswald Külpe, who went on to establish a program at the University of Würzburg, was also a Wundt student, as was Hugo Münsterberg, known as the founder of industrial-organizational psychology. Charles Hubbard Judd studied under Wundt and then returned to the American Midwest as the director of the School of Education at the University of Chicago. Lightner Witmer, who established the first psychological clinic in the United States, was also a Wundt student, as was Charles Spearman, inventor of several statistical techniques that became essential tools for psychological researchers, as well as an important intelligence theorist. Wundt's own theories have never been central to psychological science, but most of the first generation of great psychologists were directly or indirectly influenced by his choices regarding appropriate subject matter and research methodology.

Wundt also made an important contribution to psychology through the ideas and research he inspired in those who disagreed with him. When his methods came to America with his student, E. B. Titchener, they immediately came under fire from William James, who insisted that to break down conscious experience into its component parts was to remove the continuous, flowing nature that is a defining feature of consciousness. This notion of the stream of consciousness became one of James's most enduring ideas, and its clearest expression came as a criticism of structuralism. Meanwhile, back in Germany, a group of psychologists who became known as the **Gestalt** school made a similar argument, pointing out that the whole conscious experience was more than just the sum of its component parts, and so breaking it down into those components was a scientific dead end. In Vienna, meanwhile, Freud went in a different direction as well. Believing that much of what goes on in the human mind and motivates us to action is below the level of consciousness, Freud was also critical of the method of introspection as incapable of truly illuminating the human mind, as it assumes that the subject is aware of his or her own thoughts and feelings and is able to articulate them.

Wundt's ideas and methods have long since faded from psychology, but his status in the history of the discipline remains secure, thanks to his major contribution toward establishing psychology as a legitimate scientific discipline.

Further Reading

Greenwood, J. D. (2003). Wundt, Völkerpsychologie, and Experimental Social Psychology. *History of Psychology* 6(1): 70–88.

Rieber, R. W., and D. K. Robinson, eds. (2001). *Wilhelm Wundt in History: The Making of a Scientific Psychology.* New York: Kluwer.

ANNOTATED BIBLIOGRAPHY

The resources listed below will help readers delve more deeply into the topics covered in this book. This is a listing of books and other sources that were especially useful in putting this book together, and which are therefore particularly rich sources for the reader interested in becoming better informed about Freud and the history of psychoanalytic ideas, as well as the history of psychology more generally.

Freud's Writings

Freud, S. (1900/1953). *The Interpretation of Dreams (Standard Edition, Volume IV)*. London: Hogarth.

Freud's most widely read and influential work. Most of the fundamentals of the psychoanalytic view of the mind are contained in this book, and it is required reading for anyone who wants to understand Freud.

Freud, S. (1910). The Origin and Development of Psychoanalysis. *American Journal of Psychology* 21: 181–218.

Who is more qualified to write about the early history of the movement than Freud himself?

Freud, S. (1918). *Totem and Taboo: Resemblances between the Psychic Lives of Savages and Neurotics* (Translated by A. A. Brill). New York: Moffat, Yard, and Company.

Freud, S. (1930/1989). *Civilization and Its Discontents*. New York: W. W. Norton.

Freud, S. (1939). *Moses and Monotheism*. London: Hogarth Press.

Freud, S. (1989). *The Standard Edition of the Complete Psychological Works of Sigmund Freud. Volume 21: The Future of an Illusion* (1927) (Translated by James Strachey). New York: W. W. Norton.

These four books, taken together, represent Freud's attempt to extend his account of individual development, Oedipus complex and all, to the development of human civilization itself. Arguments presented initially in *Totem and Taboo* are expanded on steadily in the subsequent volumes, culminating in Freud's rewriting of Jewish history as psychodrama in *Moses and Monotheism*. Essential reading.

Writings by Freud's Colleagues, Disciples, and Heirs

Ferenczi, S. (1949). Confusion of Tongues between the Adult and the Child. *The International Journal of Psychoanalysis* 30: 225–230.

Although Freud abandoned the seduction theory in the late 19th century, his friend Ferenczi never did, and a half-century later published this defense of the idea that many neurotics had been sexually abused as children.

Frankl, V. E. (1959). *Man's Search for Meaning: An Introduction to Logotherapy*. Boston: Beacon.

The book for which Frankl is best remembered, this is an introduction to the ideas about psychology and human nature that he developed during his time in Nazi concentration camps.

Freud, A. (1977). *The Ego and the Mechanisms of Defense [Writings of Anna Freud, Vol. II: 1936].* London: International Universities Press.

Anna Freud's most important work—when later psychoanalysts refer to the defense mechanisms, it is often to her presentation of them, rather than her father's.

Horney, K. (1939/1966). *New Ways in Psychoanalysis.* New York: W. W. Norton.

This is an excellent collection of Horney's essays, detailing the various ways in which she, as a woman, felt a need to make fundamental changes in psychoanalysis while accepting Freud's basic premises.

Jung, C. G. (1971). *The Portable Jung* (Translated by R.F.C. Hull). New York: Viking Portable Library.

This collection of essays and book excerpts is a good introduction to Jung's wide range of interests and ideas.

King, P., and R. Steiner, eds. (1991). *The Freud-Klein Controversies 1941–1945.* London: Tavistock/Routledge.

An excellent snapshot of the state of British psychoanalysis during World War II, this book collects the essays that made up the Controversial Discussions between Melanie Klein and Anna Freud and their respective cadres of supporters.

Masson, J. M. (1984). *The Assault on Truth: Freud's Suppression of The Seduction Theory.* New York: Pocket Books.

This is the controversial book that led to Masson's exit from the position of director of the Freud Archives. Citing letters between Freud and Ferenczi, among others, which had been previously suppressed by Anna Freud, Masson argues that the abandonment of the seduction theory (and its consequent replacement by the Oedipus complex) occurred more out of political expediency and the need to salvage a career than because of any fundamental change of mind.

Rank, O. (1959). *The Myth of the Birth of the Hero and Other Writings* (P. Freund, ed.). New York: Vintage.

This is the book in which Rank expands on the ideas he and Freud generated in writing *The Interpretation of Dreams,* producing a view of world mythology that would profoundly influence both Jung and Joseph Campbell.

Books about Freud

Gay, P. (1988). *Freud: A Life for Our Time.* New York: W. W. Norton.

Widely regarded as the best, most objective biography of Freud published so far.

Jones, E. (1953). *The Life and Work of Sigmund Freud.* New York: Basic Books.

The classic biography of Freud by a man who knew him well, and therefore less objective than the later work by Peter Gay, who included unflattering episodes left out by the more loyal, subservient Jones.

Maddox, B. (2007). *Freud's Wizard: Ernest Jones and the Transformation of Psychoanalysis.* Cambridge, MA: Da Capo Press.

An intriguing recent book arguing for Jones's central role in bringing Freud's odd ideas to a wider audience.

Other Topics of Interest

Black, E. (2003). *War against the Weak: Eugenics and America's Campaign to Create a Master Race.* New York: Four Walls Eight Windows.

It is probably impossible to understand some of the intellectual currents against which Freud swam without understanding the huge popularity of eugenics in Europe and America prior to World War II. This is a very thorough history of that movement.

Shirer, W.L. (1990). *The Rise and Fall of the Third Reich: A History of Nazi Germany.* New York: Simon and Shuster.

Like the eugenics movement, the rise of the Nazis is a vital current in the formation of Freud's ideas, especially his late works.

INDEX

Page numbers in **bold** refer to the main entries.

About the Author

LUIS A. CORDÓN is a professor of psychology at Eastern Connecticut State University in Willimantic, Connecticut. He was educated at Louisiana State University and the University of Notre Dame and taught at Skidmore College prior to his current post. In addition to the present volume, he is the author of *Popular Psychology: An Encyclopedia*, also from this publisher. He has published research papers in such journals as the *Journal of Educational Psychology* and the *Journal of Research and Development in Education*, along with multiple book chapters, and has made numerous presentations at psychology conferences.